AA

Money-saving motoring

AA Money-

Money-saving motoring

was edited and designed by
The Reader's Digest Association Limited
for Drive Publications Limited
Berkeley Square House, London W1X 5PD

First Edition Copyright © 1974
Drive Publications Limited

Printed in Great Britain

saving motoring

Published by Drive Publications Limited for the Automobile Association
Fanum House, Basingstoke, Hampshire RG21 2EA

Contents

Repairing your car

Buying and selling

Insuring your car

Consultant editor
Marcus Jacobson Dip A M (Sheff), C Eng, F I Mech E,
M S A E (USA), M I Prod E, F I M I, F Inst Pet
Chief engineer of the Automobile Association

Contributors
Stuart Bladon
Michael Butcher
Jack M Hay
Harry Heywood
Joss Joselyn
Harry Loftus
John Miles
Douglas Mitchell
P B H Moore M I S T C
Graham Robson M A (Oxon)
Michael F Saunders F C I I
Chris Webb

Art and photography
Allard Graphic Arts
Maria Bartha
Bill Bennett M S I A
Brian Delf
Design Practitioners Limited
Bill Easter
Eurograf Limited
Hayward and Martin Limited
Jackson Day Designs
Eric Jewell Associates Limited
Launcelot Jones M S I A
David Kennard

Cecil Misstear Associates
Nigel Osborne
Malcolm Russell
Kim Sayer
Sherwood Designs Limited
Leslie Smith
S A Thornton Limited
Venner Artists Limited
David Warner
Peter Warner
Michael J Woods Dip A D
Sidney W Woods A R C A

The publishers are indebted to the following people and organisations for providing information and
helping to check the accuracy of the advice in this book

AC-Delco Division of General
   Motors Limited
Adwest Engineering Limited
A E Auto Parts Limited
Air Jet International
Armstrong Patents Company
   Limited
Audi NSU (GB) Limited
Automotive Products Limited
   (A P Lockheed and A P Borg
   & Beck)
Aviatrics Limited
Avon Rubber Company Limited

Bergen Line
D F Blake
BMW Concessionaires GB
   Limited
J H Boddy B Sc (Eng), C Eng,
   M I Mech E, F Inst Pet
The Boots Company Limited
Borg-Warner Limited—
   Transmission Division
Bosch Limited
Britax Limited
British Insurance Association
British Leyland Motor Corporation
   Limited
British Railways Board
British Standards Institution
British Vehicle Rental and
   Leasing Association
Burmah-Castrol Company

Cam Gears Limited
Car Preservation Limited
Champion Sparking Plug
   Company Limited
Chrysler United Kingdom Limited
Citroën Cars Limited
Jacqueline da Costa

DAF Motors (GB) Limited
Datsun UK Limited
Godfrey Davis (Car Hire) Limited
Peter Denayer
Desmo Limited
DFDS Seaways
Dial Contracts Limited
D J Sports Cars Limited

Ducellier Limited
Duron Friction Materials Brake
   Linings Limited

European Ferries Limited

Ferodo Limited
Fiat (England) Limited
Force Three, of Cambridge
Ford Motor Company Limited
Ford Motorcraft
Fram Europe Limited
Barry Francis
Fry's Motor Works Limited,
   London SE13

General Motors Limited
   (Adam Opel AG)
Girling Limited Sales and Service

Holt Products Limited
John Hood
Hovercraft Seaspeed
Hoverlloyd Limited

Peter Ing

Jaguar Cars (British Leyland UK
   Limited)

Kangol Magnet Limited
Kenlowe Accessories and
   Company Limited

G S Lasts Limited, Chelmsford
Lex Vehicle Leasing
R D Loder
Logikontrol Limited
Joseph Lucas (Sales and
   Service) Limited

Victor McDonough
Marelli Limited
Mazda Car Imports (GB) Limited
Michelin Tyre Company Limited
Mobil Oil Company Limited
H A G Morgan T Eng (C E I),
   A M I M I
The Motor Agents' Association
   Limited

Fred Olsen Line Limited

Petro Steam Limited
Peugeot Automobiles UK Limited
Prinz Ferries

Redex Limited
Renault Limited
Rist's Wires & Cables Limited
Romford Motor Company Limited
Rover-Triumph British Leyland
   (UK) Limited

F W E Saunders R Tech Eng,
   A M I R T E
Shell Marketing Limited
Smiths Industries Limited
Society of Motor Manufacturers
   and Traders Limited
Southern and North Sea Ferries
   Limited
Spartan Autocare (UK) Limited
SPQR Engineering Limited
SU Carburettors
Charles Surridge R Tech Eng,
   A M I R T E, A M A E T

Thatcham Motor Insurance Repair
   Research Centre
Tor Line Limited
Toyota (GB) Ltd
Transport and Road Research
   Laboratory
Trico-Folberth Limited
Mike Twite

Uniroyal Limited

Vauxhall Motors Limited
Volkswagen Limited
Volvo Concessionaires Limited

Warwick Wright Motors Limited
Weber Limited
Peter Williams
Wilmot Breeden

Zenith Carburetter Company
   Limited
Ziebart (GB) Limited

FOREWORD

by
A. C. Durie C.B.E.
Director-General
of the
Automobile Association

The cost of running a car is constantly rising. Since the Association published its first Schedule of Estimated Running Costs in 1934, the weekly cost of an average family saloon has risen from £1.60 to just over £11.50. It has often been said that the motor car is the second most expensive item in our lives: this is no longer necessarily so. Statistics show that the car now costs many families more per week than their mortgage or their food bill.

It is in everyone's interest — the motorist's, his family's and the country's — to reduce the amount we all have to spend on our motor cars.

The Association has produced *Money-saving motoring* as a pointer to the ways you can help yourself: driving to save vital and expensive petrol, maintaining your car regularly for economy and safety, repairing it yourself when possible, choosing wisely when you come to change your car and getting the best from your insurance.

There is no one complete answer to a complex problem, but I commend *Money-saving motoring* as a first step towards checking the ever-rising graph of motoring costs.

A. C. Durie

How the costs

The cost of running a car rises by about £50 every year—even without abnormal fluctuations in the price of fuel or labour charges at garages.

Between 1960 and 1969, increases in the cost of motoring were lower than increases in other living costs. Indeed in the very early 1960s, the cost actually fell. But it has risen steeply since 1970 and seems likely to continue to do so.

Motoring costs are usually considered in two distinct parts—standing costs and running costs. Standing costs, which include depreciation, insurance, driving licence and so on, are difficult to reduce. They are the costs you have to pay whether you use the car, or keep it standing in a garage or at the pavement. In fact, the less you use the car, the greater is the proportion of your standing costs to your total spending.

The biggest element in the costs shown opposite is usually depreciation—whatever the size or type car. The cost of buying a car, new or secondhand, has risen steadily and is likely to continue increasing for as long as there is a growing demand for greater safety, comfort and space.

Government and international regulations to eliminate noise and air pollution call for more complex engineering, and rapidly changing fashions demand frequent restyling of models. Although they increase the car's price, they do little to maintain its value, for by the time the car is sold a new development or fashion has made it out-of-date.

Running costs—for example, petrol, repairs and servicing—are greatly influenced by how often and how hard you use the car. The most important single factor is undoubtedly maintenance. There is no long-term saving in skimping on proper and adequate servicing: economy motoring is not cut-price motoring. A car must be in as near perfect condition as possible if it is to give its best performance and fuel consumption and maintain its value.

Money-saving motoring sets out in five sections how costs can be reduced. How by altering your driving techniques you can get many more miles for every gallon of petrol. How by proper and regular servicing you can maintain your car in peak condition. How by undertaking some repairs yourself you can save on garage charges. How by careful selection when you buy a car you can avoid later losses. And how by proper planning you can make sure that you are getting the best possible insurance deal.

# of running a car have risen

1973
1972
1971
1970
1969
1968
1967

Depreciation The cost of depreciation—the difference between what you pay for a car and how much you get when you sell it—is usually the highest single factor in any motorist's annual costs. An average family saloon loses just under £2.50 a week in value: in the high-price, luxury-car market, depreciation may account for as much as £30 a week.

Petrol Petrol prices increased 15 times in the ten years between 1963 and 1973. The average weekly cost of petrol for a family saloon (based on 50p a gallon and an annual mileage of 10,000 miles) is £3.14. For a 2 litre car, it is just under £4.50 a week. Every 1p increase on the price of a gallon of petrol is estimated to cost the average motorist about £5 a year.

Insurance Premiums have risen by an average of 20 per cent a year since 1967. The AA's 1973 *Schedule of Estimated Running Costs* showed that the cost for a medium-size car, comprehensively insured in a city area, was just under £2 a week (without a no-claim discount).

Repairs and replacements The AA estimates the average cost for a family saloon at £1.50 a week. This assumes that the owner is maintaining his vehicle in first-class condition, and selling it before repair costs start to rise.

Garaging and parking The estimate for a garage at home and parking elsewhere is £1 a week.

Interest on capital The money you spend on your car could cost you at least £1.30 a week—assuming that, if you had not bought a car, you would have invested in something that would earn at least 5 per cent a year.

Servicing The average cost is just under 50p a week for an average family saloon.

Vehicle excise licence The licence costs 37p a week— provided that you buy it for a year at a time.

Tyres The estimated weekly cost of maintaining tyres in a safe, roadworthy and legal condition is 25p.

Engine oil Lubrication, vital to the engine's efficiency, costs about £7.60 a year for an average car.

Motoring organisations Membership of a motoring organisation—a kind of insurance—costs less than 10p a week.

Driving licence The driving licence accounts for 6p expenditure in the motorist's weekly budget.

Depreciation

The amount of depreciation—which is the difference between the price you pay for your car and the price you get when you sell it—depends on the type of car, how long you keep it, how much mileage it has covered, its condition and the state of the market when you sell.

The AA writes off a car after eight years or 80,000 miles. This means that you can estimate that its value depreciates by one-eighth each year—after that it probably has no resale value.

In practice, however, the biggest

drop in value is from when the car is new to two years old. As the car gets older, depreciation steadies.

The longer you keep the car, the less the weekly cost of depreciation. For example, the Austin Maxi might depreciate after two years by £472, which amounts to £4.50 a week over that period. At the end of the third year, depreciation may have risen to £543, but that would reduce the weekly average to £3.40.

How you can save

Your choice of car must be influenced by the length of time you intend to keep it. If you are looking for long-term ownership, choose a car with an established reputation for durability. If you intend to keep it for only a couple of years, look for something that will have resale value.

From time to time, certain types of

cars depreciate more quickly—in 1974, for example, the market for secondhand Japanese cars slumped because of repair costs.

When you have bought the car, preserve its value as much as possible with regular cleaning and maintenance (see pp. 32-136).

Choose the right time to sell so that you get the best possible price (see p. 272). It is best to sell the car before you reach a 'milestone' figure by which secondhand values could be assessed—when the car has done just under 20,000 miles, for example, rather than just over.

When buying a secondhand car, you may be able to cut the cost of depreciation altogether, if you look for one that has reached an age where depreciation has dropped to a negligible figure. You may even be able to make improvements, and sell for more than you paid.

Tyres

Most modern cars are fitted with tubeless tyres, which are less likely to fail than tubed ones.

There are two main types—cross-plies or radial-plies. Radial-ply tyres, because of their construction —which reduces wear when cornering—last longer and give better grip. But they may give a harder ride at low speeds.

If your car is fitted with cross-ply tyres as standard, radials may be available as an alternative. But before changing, find out how they will affect the car's handling.

Radial-ply tyres—more expensive but with a longer life—are likely to be more economical if you do a high annual mileage. They run for between 50 and 100 per cent more miles than cross-plies—saving £6-£7 a year. On twisting roads they may also save a little fuel.

Most tyres are designed to be used all the year round in varying weather conditions. Winter tyres, with chunkier treads designed for use on snow, slush and mud, are available; but they affect the car's handling, and wear out rapidly if used on dry surfaces. They can be fitted with studs to improve grip on ice or snow; but they cut the maximum speed by 10 mph.

Remould or retread tyres are cheaper than new tyres. On a re-

mould, the rubber throughout the carcass is completely renewed, and on a retread, only the tread is renewed. They may be satisfactory under some operating conditions, but they are not suitable for prolonged high-speed driving.

The best kind are those marked 'remould quality', which are new tyres that are slightly sub-standard.

When you buy new tyres, make sure that they match those already fitted or that they are a suitable alternative. Tyres of different types and sizes must never be fitted to the same axle on the car.

Cross-ply tyres can be fitted to the front wheels with radial-ply at the rear, but it is dangerous to fit cross-ply at the rear with radial-ply at the front, because of the difference in cornering ability of the two types.

Never fit steel-braced radials at the front and textile-braced radials at the rear.

How you can save

Always buy a reputable make of tyre that carries a guarantee, and make sure the supplier provides free fitting and balancing.

Check that the tyres are still in their wrappers. Tyres deteriorate whether they are on the car or stored unwrapped in a warehouse. Wrappers delay deterioration.

Run in new tyres carefully. Do not travel faster than 50 mph for the first 50-100 miles, and increase speeds gradually during the next

250 miles. Have the wheel balance checked after 500 miles.

Always maintain the tyres at the correct pressure. Over-inflation can affect the handling of the car and cause an accident. Under-inflation increases wear and fuel consumption because of the extra power needed to push the car along.

Avoid high-speed cornering, fierce braking and harsh acceleration. Taking a corner at speed can increase tread wear by 50 per cent. High-speed driving also accelerates wear, though on motorways, where little cornering or braking is necessary, the rate of wear is not so high.

Make sure that defects in the car's steering geometry are not causing irregular tread wear (see pp. 95, 133).

As front tyres usually wear out more quickly, it is more economical to replace them first and fit new rear ones later.

If you change the position of the wheels on the car, have them rebalanced. (The cost of doing this can more than outweigh any saving that may be made in tyre life by changing the positions.) Always find out whether the car manufacturer recommends changing.

Do not use tyres after the tread depth has worn down to 2 mm. Never try to economise by running the tyres down to the minimum tread depth (1 mm.). You are increasing the risk of a puncture as well as an accident, and the extra mileage you might get—perhaps 10 per cent— would not be worthwhile.

Petrol

There is little or no difference in quality among the many brands of petrol available in Britain. But the quality does vary from one time of the year to another. The oil companies change their blending formula according to season—twice or maybe four times a year—to ensure trouble-free motoring during a cold winter or hot summer.

This system, however, does not affect the grading of petrol—which is a measurement of its ability to resist 'knocking' or 'pinking'—a light hammering noise sometimes heard when the engine is labouring.

British Standards classifications for petrol range from 90 to 100 octane: the higher the rating, the higher its resistance to knocking. For convenience, these gradings have been given a star rating:

2 star minimum 90 octane
3 star 94·96 octane
4 star 97·99 octane
5 star minimum of 100 octane

In general, the higher the compression ratio (see p. 250) of an engine, the higher its octane requirement. Suitable grades are:

2 star 7·5:1 ratio
3 star 8·2:1
4 star up to 9:1
5 star over 9:1

But the car's mechanical condition, its ignition timing, and the way it is driven may affect its octane requirement. Even cars with the same compression ratio or the same model may need different grades of petrol—due to small differences in casting in mass production, which result in an octane requirement one or two points higher than normal.

How you can save

Before buying a car, study the road test reports of all the models that are likely to fit your needs—to find out which one is most likely to give you the best economy in the conditions that you generally drive in.

Look for a petrol station that does not offer gifts or stamps, but may be selling petrol 1p or 2p cheaper—even 1p less on every gallon saves the average motorist about £5 a year.

It is false economy to buy petrol with too low an octane rating, because it can cause engine damage. But there is nothing to be gained by using petrol of a higher grade than your engine needs—you are merely wasting money.

You may in fact be able to run your car safely on petrol of a lower star rating than the manufacturer has specified. It is therefore worth trying a mixture of your recommended grade with a gallon or two of a lower grade.

If there is no 'knocking', and provided that the engine does not continue running for a time after it is switched off, it is safe to use the lower-grade mixture.

Petrol deteriorates during long storage. If you go to a country filling station where the turnover is limited, the petrol may already be a point or two lower than when it was first delivered to the pump.

For maximum economy, the car must be running at its best. Make sure that spark-plugs are clean, ignition timing and carburation properly adjusted, and that the engine temperature is not too high or too low. Do not be tempted, however, to remove the car's cooling fan. In some circumstances it can cause overheating and expensive damage.

Even incorrect tyre pressures make a difference (see p. 37).

If the pressure of the tyres is too high, you may get better fuel consumption, but the handling will be poorer. When the pressure is too low it takes more power and therefore more fuel to keep the car going. Loading of the car adds to petrol consumption also. Towing increases it considerably and so does a roof-rack.

When driving, do not use too much choke, harsh acceleration, or travel at high speeds (see pp. 14-17).

If you park, do not leave the car in direct sunlight—especially with a full tank—since petrol expands and evaporates in heat.

Choose your route to avoid bad traffic conditions. The ideal for fuel economy is an uninterrupted run at a steady cruising speed. Heavy traffic, where the average speed that can be maintained is 8-10 mph, can increase consumption by 100 per cent. Light traffic, with an average speed of 18-21 mph, can increase it by 34 per cent. A gradient of only 1 in 25 can cause a 50-100 per cent increase in petrol consumption.

Economy devices do not normally make much difference to petrol consumption. AA tests show that they cannot equal or improve on good maintenance and careful driving.

Insurance

Insurance companies' costs depend on the cost of repairs and the number of claims made.

As cars get more complex they are more expensive to repair, and costs are also affected by increasing labour rates. More vehicles on the road mean more accidents, and therefore more claims. Court awards for compensation arising out of claims after accidents are also tend-ing to rise; for example, they increased by about 15 per cent in 1972.

Even if insurance were not compulsory, you might not save anything by cutting out the cost of your annual premium. If you were involved in an accident, you could be faced with a bill of thousands of pounds for compensation that would take you a lifetime to pay. Even worse, anyone injured would have to wait years for compensation.

How you can save

Shop around for the most favourable premium you can get, but make sure you are getting adequate cover (see pp. 276-81). It is unwise to skimp on insurance. The cheapest could turn out to be the most expensive in the long run, since the cover provided might be extremely limited. Avoid cut-price insurance companies: it is an expensive risk to take.

Make sure that the type of insurance you have is realistic. There is no point in paying for comprehensive cover if the car is not worth it.

Keep your premium as low as possible by maintaining a claim-free record (see p. 292).

Take advantage of any worthwhile discounts that you may be able to get, but make sure they are not likely to involve you in unnecessary extra expense under certain circumstances (see pp. 287-9).

Servicing

Costs of servicing vary according to the car. Some need only 10 hours'

Engine oil

Oil is needed to provide a film between the moving parts of the engine to reduce friction and heat.

If the oil is too thin it does not provide enough lubrication, and engine wear is rapid. If it is too thick it will impede movement, and therefore affect efficiency and petrol consumption. If it is of inferior quality, it may leave deposits on moving parts and so increase wear.

Oil is graded according to its resistance to flow—called viscosity. The higher an oil's viscosity, the thicker it is. Oil gets thinner when heated, so it must have a suitable viscosity to remain effective at the engine's working temperature.

The scale mostly used is that

work a year, others 100 or more. The more complex the car, the less likely you are to be able to do the work yourself.

Manufacturers give a schedule of the time estimated for servicing operations, but the actual time taken will depend on the condition of the car. If parts are seized or

developed by the American Society of Automotive Engineers. The grades for summer use are SAE 20, 30, 40 and 50—20 being the lowest and 50 the highest viscosity. For winter use, they are 5W (lowest) 10W and 20W (highest).

Multigrade oils have a wider viscosity range than conventional oils and are less affected by temperature, although they are not suitable for all engines. The usual range recommended for use in Great Britain is SAE 10W/50.

How you can save

You cannot economise on oil, as you can on petrol, by using the cheapest possible. If repair and maintenance costs are to be kept as low as possible, the engine must be efficiently lubricated. Always use a reputable brand of the recommended grade.

corroded, or if the car has been hard used, operations take longer.

How you can save

Choose a car that needs the minimum amount of servicing work, and try to do as much of it as you can safely undertake yourself.

Do not buy old oil that has been cleaned after already being used.

You can, however, save on cost by buying in bulk at discount prices in an accessory shop or supermarket.

Make sure that the oil in the engine is as clean as possible. Be particularly careful not to let dirt in when you top up or fill the sump.

Never leave an oil change longer than the maker's recommended interval. If you use the car mostly on short journeys or in stop-start traffic, change more frequently.

Do not over-use the choke, or forget to return it. Over-rich fuel mixture dissolves and weakens the oil in the upper cylinder, which increases wear. The oil in the sump may also be contaminated.

Do not let the oil level in the sump fall below minimum, but do not overfill it. Never drive if the oil-pressure warning light is on.

Repairs and replacements

The pattern of repair costs is not the same throughout a car's life. The greatest expense is likely to be between 40,000-60,000 miles. If you buy a new car and keep it for only two years, therefore, your weekly repair bill will be as high as the AA average (see p. 9).

Repair costs vary according to the type of car, its usage, and the labour rates charged by the repairers.

The cost of a repair depends not only on the cost of the part—which can vary considerably according to the model, but also on the time estimated to do the job. This also varies; on some cars, because of their construction, the time taken can be twice as long as on another car. Parts for imported cars may be 10 to 20 per cent more expensive than for British-built cars of the same size and type. Remember that the cost of repairs especially in later years

will affect the car's value when you come to sell it.

How you can save

Do repairs yourself whenever possible. Otherwise, use a garage that deals in your make of car. It should be able to do the job at the most economical rate.

When you buy a car, try to find out the particular weaknesses of the model and how much the replacements and repairs cost.

Avoid repairs by regular maintenance and careful driving.

Other costs

Some motoring costs cannot be avoided.

DoE test The only way you can save on the annual compulsory vehicle test for cars more than three years old is by taking the car back to the same examiner if you have to have it re-tested after a failure.

Road fund licence The cheapest way to buy your road fund licence is

to tax the car for a year—which costs £25. If you buy a licence every four months, it costs £27.45 a year.

Driving licence There is no way in which you can save money on the cost of a driving licence.

Motoring organisations Belonging to a motoring organisation can save you many pounds on breakdown assistance, legal help, technical

advice and other valuable services.

Interest on capital If you had not bought a car you could have invested the money where it would have brought a return.

Garaging and parking A garage may be part of a house and therefore be a charge on the rates whether you have a car or not. Parking charges are usually unavoidable.

Driving your car

More miles per gallon/1

How to cut the cost of driving a car

Money-saving motoring depends on maintaining and driving your vehicle correctly. Driving economy is achieved by concentration and timing, and by skilful and unhurried use of the controls. Its essence is control of the accelerator and gears.

Acceleration should be smooth and gentle. Never drive in such a way that if you are not accelerating you are braking. Control your speed by acceleration and deceleration. Make sure it is in the correct gear according to the road speed of the car, and use the brakes as little as possible.

Think ahead all the time—making allowances for the movement of other traffic, and never hurrying when progress is restricted—so that the car flows along with as few interruptions as possible. This will give you the minimum wear on brakes, gears, clutch and engine.

For petrol economy, always aim for the lowest possible pressure on the accelerator pedal, and travel in the highest possible gear.

Starting the car in the most economical way

Ignition, starter motor and battery
Do not use the starter in short bursts; it will damage the flywheel. Do not keep it engaged so long that it runs the battery flat. If the engine will not start after 10 seconds, stop and wait 20 seconds before trying again. If it will not start after three attempts, find out what is wrong (see p. 138). After a normal start it takes 3 miles to recharge a battery, 7-10 miles in cold weather. Prolonged attempts to start waste petrol and wash off the cylinder oil film.

Using the choke when starting from cold
Pull a manual choke fully out to start the engine. Return it progressively as the engine warms up. A prolonged over-rich mixture wastes petrol.

Move off immediately the engine starts. It is more economical to warm up the engine on the move. If you feel reluctant to start before the engine has warmed up, stay in the car and reduce the choke as the engine warms up. Do not leave the car while it is warming up. It is uneconomical and illegal. Never rev the engine when first started.

Automatic chokes may take some time to disengage. If you feel that the engine is warm enough and the choke is still engaged, blip the accelerator pedal to free it.

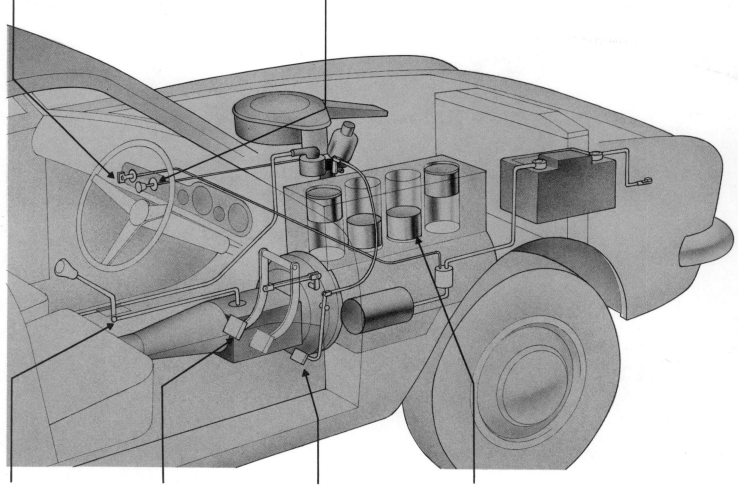

Moving away—the gears
Avoid fast starts and high revving in each gear before changing up to the next one. This technique can use up to 50 per cent more petrol than a smooth start with steady progression through the gears. Constant hard use also wears out the clutch and transmission – especially the axle.

Do not move off in second gear, you will have to slip the clutch, causing wear.

Moving away—the clutch
Depress the clutch pedal firmly, as far as it will go. Release it gradually to take up the drive. Avoid letting the clutch out quickly. If the wheels spin, the tyres wear; if the clutch slips, the lining is worn. Do not rest your foot on the clutch pedal. Even the slightest pressure will put the race or carbon thrust in contact with moving parts, which will promote wear.

Using the accelerator
On fixed-jet carburettors, with an accelerator pump, gently press the accelerator pedal as the engine is started. On constant-depression carburettors—SU and Stromberg CD—press the pedal down only halfway.

If the engine fails to start it is probably flooded. Press the accelerator fully down. As the engine fires, slowly release the pedal: never use choke on a warm engine.

What can happen inside an engine
If care is not taken, a considerable amount of damage can be caused to either a cold or warm engine.

Cold starting If the choke is kept out for too long, unvaporised petrol is allowed into the cylinders and washes the oil film from the cylinder bores. This causes the pistons to run in dry bores, and accelerates the amount of piston ring and cylinder bore wear.

Avoid revving the engine as soon as it fires. The oil will be cold and thick, and will not circulate freely. Some part of the engine may suffer oil starvation and fail earlier than need be.

Warm starting If the accelerator pedal is pumped up and down, petrol will wash the cylinder bores. These will already be short of lubricant because of the engine heat.

How speed affects fuel consumption

Fast driving and economy are not compatible. At a steady speed of 80 mph in top gear, fuel consumption may be twice as heavy as at 30 mph. The diagram on the right shows the results obtained when driving a 2 litre saloon at steady speeds between 20 and 90 mph.

Think of the accelerator as a fuel tap: the more you press it, the more fuel is consumed by the engine. Never push the pedal sharply to the floor unless you need the extra speed quickly—for example, for safety when overtaking.

It is more economical to press the pedal gently, even if it takes a little longer to reach the speed you want.

Remember that a car gives its best performance, combined with economy, at the speed at which the engine develops maximum torque (see p. 250)—usually between 2000 and 3000 rpm at a road speed of 50 mph.

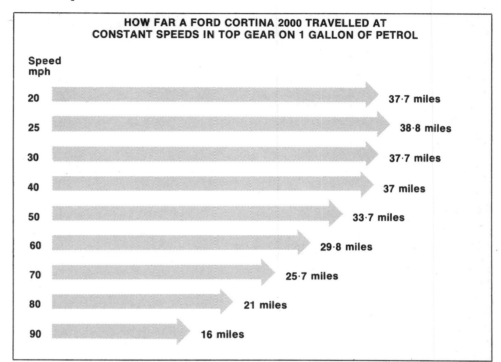

HOW FAR A FORD CORTINA 2000 TRAVELLED AT CONSTANT SPEEDS IN TOP GEAR ON 1 GALLON OF PETROL

Speed mph	Distance
20	37·7 miles
25	38·8 miles
30	37·7 miles
40	37 miles
50	33·7 miles
60	29·8 miles
70	25·7 miles
80	21 miles
90	16 miles

Braking correctly for economy and safety

Never brake unless it is really necessary. Look at the road ahead, and drive in such a way that you can anticipate the need to stop, in time to allow you to slow the car by deceleration—that is by simply taking your foot off the accelerator pedal.

Harsh braking increases the wear on both the brakes and the tyres unnecessarily. Your first pressure on the brake pedal should be light, but continue with increasing firmness so that the car slows gradually.

Negotiating a corner
The diagram on the right shows two methods of approaching a bend or roundabout, but the lessons could apply equally to any situation where you have to slow and then continue. The bottom example shows how to use least fuel, with anticipation, gradual braking and minimum use of the gears. Note that only one change is made (from top gear directly into second) when the car has reached a suitable road speed (see p. 16).

The top example indicates harsh braking and unnecessary gear changing, wasting petrol and increasing wear. Note, however, that in some situations it may be necessary to change gear in order to get better control of the car—for example on a series of bends or on a corner that is unusually acute. Try to judge the road ahead from the behaviour of any vehicles in front.

For safety, do not brake, change

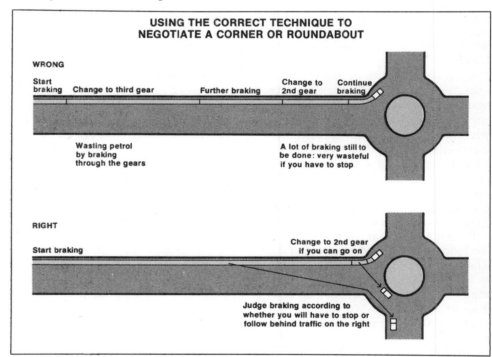

USING THE CORRECT TECHNIQUE TO NEGOTIATE A CORNER OR ROUNDABOUT

WRONG
Start braking | Change to third gear | Further braking | Change to 2nd gear | Continue braking

Wasting petrol by braking through the gears

A lot of braking still to be done: very wasteful if you have to stop

RIGHT
Start braking

Change to 2nd gear if you can go on

Judge braking according to whether you will have to stop or follow behind traffic on the right

gear or over-accelerate while you are still in a bend: wait until you see the road straight ahead. With a front-wheel-drive car, too much acceleration takes the car on a wider course than you want (called understeer), and you have to cause more tyre wear by applying harder steering. With rear-engine rear-wheel-drive cars, the same fault results in oversteer, which is also wasteful.

Driving downhill safely
Never try to save petrol by coasting downhill with the car out of gear or the engine switched off. The saving is negligible, and the car could become uncontrollable. On steep hills, do not rely entirely on the brakes. Make sure that you change down to the gear that best suits the slower speed you have reached (see p. 16).

Using the handbrake
When you apply the handbrake, use the release button to avoid wear on the ratchet, and make sure the brake is firmly on. Do not try to stop the car with the handbrake, except in an emergency: you are likely to lock the rear wheels and cause a skid.

More miles per gallon/2

Using the gears economically

Different gears are provided to use the power of the engine to suit the work it has to do. In a low gear, the engine revs faster, and so uses more fuel than it normally would at the same road speed in a higher gear.

The diagram on the right shows that it pays to change up through the gears to top as soon as possible—but not before the road speed is adequate. Do not labour the engine; the car will use more fuel.

Deciding when to change gear

For maximum economy, gear changes must be made at the right moment—that is, when the speed you have reached in a lower gear can be maintained without increased acceleration in the next highest gear, or when you can change down without causing a noisy, racing surge in the engine speed.

If your car has a rev-counter (see p. 18) you can decide the time to change gears precisely. For best economy, do not allow the engine speed to rise above or fall below the 2000-3000 rpm range, the speed at which most cars develop maximum torque (see p. 250).

Even without a rev-counter, however, you can devise an adequate system to follow. Find out, from the car handbook or car specifications, what maximum speeds the manufacturer recommends for each gear. Change gear when the car's road speed is half these figures. For example, if 50 mph is given as the maximum for third gear, change up from and down to second at 25 mph.

Do not try to stay in a high gear too long when you are driving uphill. The best way to save petrol is to try to build up speed beforehand and to maintain it, without acceleration in a lower gear. Never accelerate hard.

Above all avoid peak revs in each gear. Remember that over-revving the engine can cause damage.

When the car has an overdrive

Some cars have an overdrive or fifth gear which gives greater fuel economy when cruising at high speeds. Fifth gear is engaged in the normal way, but overdrive is often operated by a separate switch, without using the clutch.

Overdrive may give an additional gear ratio in third as well as top gear—when it is engaged, the engine revolutions are slower than in the direct gears. But consult the car handbook for the recommended speeds to switch on. Changing too soon can waste fuel.

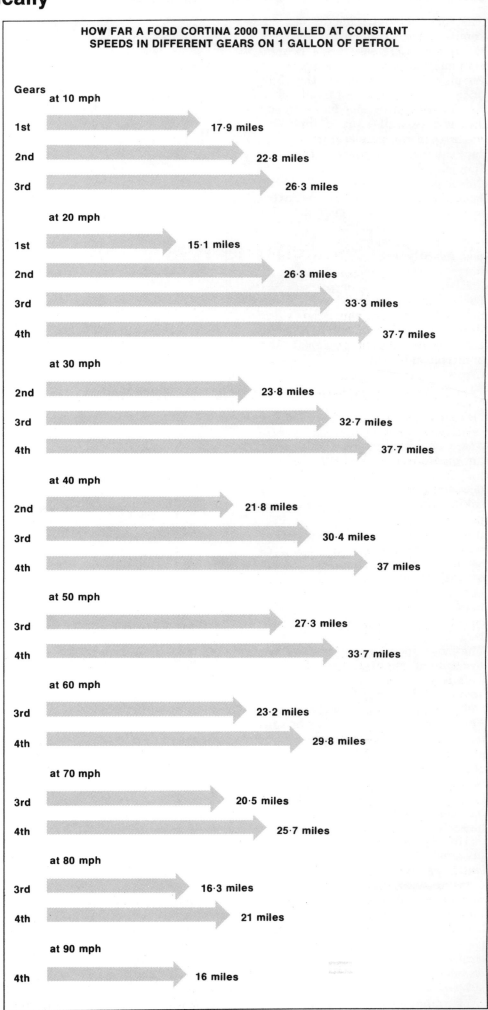

HOW FAR A FORD CORTINA 2000 TRAVELLED AT CONSTANT SPEEDS IN DIFFERENT GEARS ON 1 GALLON OF PETROL

Gears

at 10 mph
1st — 17·9 miles
2nd — 22·8 miles
3rd — 26·3 miles

at 20 mph
1st — 15·1 miles
2nd — 26·3 miles
3rd — 33·3 miles
4th — 37·7 miles

at 30 mph
2nd — 23·8 miles
3rd — 32·7 miles
4th — 37·7 miles

at 40 mph
2nd — 21·8 miles
3rd — 30·4 miles
4th — 37 miles

at 50 mph
3rd — 27·3 miles
4th — 33·7 miles

at 60 mph
3rd — 23·2 miles
4th — 29·8 miles

at 70 mph
3rd — 20·5 miles
4th — 25·7 miles

at 80 mph
3rd — 16·3 miles
4th — 21 miles

at 90 mph
4th — 16 miles

When the car has an automatic gearbox

Most cars with automatic gearboxes —usually less economical than the equivalent manual model—have a lever with six positions: Low or Drive 1, Intermediate or Drive 2, Drive, Neutral, Reverse and Park.

The most convenient way to operate—and in many cases the most economical—is always to use the Drive position, where all gear changes are automatic. Most automatics of recent design sense for themselves when a change down will give the best economy, as well as the best acceleration. But some three-speed automatics, fitted on smaller cars, will give better response and economy if the manual override is used to select a lower gear.

With the lever in the low position, the gearbox will not change out of the selected gear. With the lever on Drive, all changes up and down are automatic—the less you press on the accelerator, the lower the speed at which the gear changes. For economy, do not push hard on the accelerator, especially from start.

A 'kick-down' is incorporated in the drive gear. If you push the accelerator to the floor suddenly, the next lowest gear is engaged, provided that it is within the speed range. When you release the pedal, the gearbox changes up again.

Using the 'kick-down' increases petrol consumption. Use it only when you need maximum acceleration. It is more economic to override the gearbox manually to select a lower gear, so that you press the accelerator no more than you need.

How traffic conditions affect fuel consumption

The importance of good route-planning and of choosing a quiet time to travel (see pp. 20-21) is illustrated in the diagram on the right. City rush-hour traffic can increase your fuel bills by 100 per cent over the conditions on main roads. On the other hand, the higher speeds allowed on motorways may increase costs by more than one-third.

Worst hit is the driver who regularly uses his car only to travel short journeys. Even with relatively uncongested roads, you can expect the car's fuel consumption to be twice as much as normal in the first 3 miles of driving from cold. Even the next 3 miles improves fuel consumption only slightly. On a 2 litre car that averages 37 miles per gallon at 30 mph, you could expect to get only 17 mpg in the first 3 miles and 29 mpg overall in 6 miles.

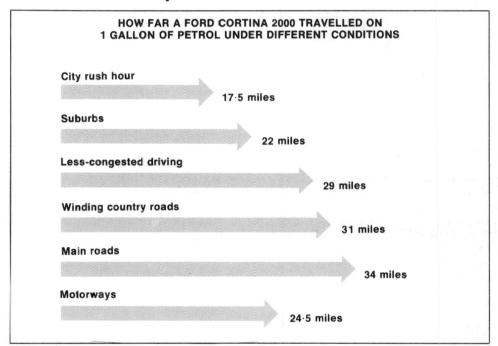

HOW FAR A FORD CORTINA 2000 TRAVELLED ON 1 GALLON OF PETROL UNDER DIFFERENT CONDITIONS

City rush hour — 17·5 miles
Suburbs — 22 miles
Less-congested driving — 29 miles
Winding country roads — 31 miles
Main roads — 34 miles
Motorways — 24·5 miles

How your driving technique affects fuel consumption

Whatever type of car you have and in whatever conditions you have to drive, one of the most important factors is the way in which you drive.

The diagram on the right shows the differences in fuel consumption when the same car is driven normally, when it is driven deliberately roughly—with gear changes made too late and too much braking (see pp. 15-16)—and when it is driven extremely quietly, producing probably the best possible fuel figures obtainable with that car.

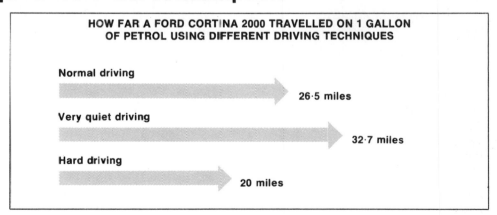

HOW FAR A FORD CORTINA 2000 TRAVELLED ON 1 GALLON OF PETROL USING DIFFERENT DRIVING TECHNIQUES

Normal driving — 26·5 miles
Very quiet driving — 32·7 miles
Hard driving — 20 miles

Flat-out acceleration

It takes much more petrol to get the car moving from standing than to maintain a constant speed.

A car, for example, that will average more than 37 miles per gallon at a steady 30 mph, will give you less than 9 miles per gallon if you accelerate flat out from standstill to maximum speed.

As a general rule, it takes as much petrol to move a car for the first 20 yds from stop as it does to cover half a mile at 30 mph. That is why, with flat-out acceleration, you will get only 9 miles per gallon over the first quarter mile, but get slightly better consumption—say 11 mpg— over half a mile.

In town, particularly, when you approach traffic lights, try to control the car so that it is still moving as the lights change from red and amber to green. Racing up to a red light and braking hard causes tyre wear and wastes petrol. Anticipation saves fuel. Look out for pedestrian crossings and other hazards, and adjust your speed in good time.

Instruments

Getting the best from warning instruments

Most cars are fitted with only a speedometer and fuel gauge and a system of warning lights indicating oil pressure and ignition.

But warning lights signal danger only when trouble has occurred. Instruments can warn of technical trouble in time to prevent serious damage and costly repairs. For that reason, it may save money to fit at least some of the more useful instruments. In some cases, you can remove them without damage when you sell the car.

Fitting instruments

Position new instruments so that they can be clearly seen without diverting the eyes very far from the road ahead. Ideally, they should be mounted in line with existing instruments. If this is not possible, buy an instrument pod—a plastic or glass-fibre moulding.

Do not mount the instruments where they may be hidden by the steering wheel or the driver's arms.

Ammeter

The main job of an ammeter is to show the rate of charge or discharge to or from the battery. But it can also give information about the rest of the circuits and components.

Checking the charging system

If the charging system is working properly and the battery in reasonable condition, when the engine is run at almost 30 mph, the ammeter should show a charge rate of between 20 and 30 amps (if the electrical equipment is not in use). After a few minutes the rate should drop and after several miles it should settle between 0 and 5 amps.

When the engine is running at 30 mph, the ammeter should not show a discharge even when the headlamps, wiper and heater motors are turned on. If it does, check the fanbelt tension. If this is correct, check the generator or voltage control unit (see pp. 184-7).

A continuous low rate of charge could be caused by a slipping generator belt. Tighten it (see p. 119).

Testing electrical circuits

Individual circuits on the car can also be checked with the ammeter.

Flashing indicators Switch on the ignition, but do not start the engine. Operate the flasher switch. Each side should register the same amount of discharge. If one shows more than the other, the bulb, cable connections or earth may be faulty (see pp. 188-192).

Windscreen wipers Thoroughly wet the windscreen and switch on the wipers. The ammeter reading should be steady, except for a slight increase as the blades change direction at the end of their stroke. If the needle fluctuates as the blades cross the screen, or if the discharge rate gradually increases, the wiper drive mechanism is faulty (see p. 226).

Battery condition indicator

The ammeter indicates how rapidly electrical energy is flowing into or out of the battery, and whether electrical equipment is consuming more or less electricity than is being generated, but it gives no direct guidance as to how well charged the battery already is.

A constant check on how much energy is stored inside the battery is given by a battery condition indicator or voltmeter. The indicator dial is usually marked from just under 11 volts to just over 15 volts, with the section below 13 volts marked 'off charge'. If the needle moves into this section when the ignition is switched on, the battery is not producing its proper output. If the dial shows more than 15 volts while the car is being driven, the battery is being overcharged.

Oil-pressure gauge

Most cars have only an oil-pressure warning light designed to come on when pressure drops below a certain level—normally 5-10 lb. per sq. in., but higher on some cars. By the time the pressure has dropped to that level, serious damage might already have occurred. The normal running pressure for an average car is between 45 and 60 lb. per sq. in., and the idling pressure for a warm engine between 20 and 25 lb. per sq. in.

An oil-pressure gauge gives an immediate indication of pressure loss. If this occurs while you are driving, stop and investigate.

When the engine is cold, the gauge will probably read higher than the normal figure. Do not drive hard until it reaches normal. (If the normal figure is not given in your handbook, ask a dealer.) The needle should remain at about this pressure while you are driving.

Cars suffer some small pressure loss when driven hard, since oil gets thinner as it gets hotter.

Water temperature gauge

A water temperature gauge gives an early warning if the engine is running too hot or too cool. After a cold start the needle should reach the normal setting after about 3 miles. Do not drive hard before it does. In town or stop-start driving in hot weather, the water temperature in the cooling system may rise above normal—80-85°C—but should not reach the hot mark.

If the needle rises abnormally on the open road, stop and investigate at once. Unless the thermostat has stuck (see p. 181), the cause will probably be a broken fan belt, a leaking radiator or a broken hose.

Let the engine cool before removing the radiator cap (see p. 180). Top up with clean water (hot, if possible) —use water from the windscreen washer in an emergency.

Rev-counter (tachometer)

A rev-counter (tachometer) shows the number of revolutions of the engine crankshaft per minute. It is often far more accurate than a speedometer, and can be used for economy in top gear by keeping the engine speed between 2000 and 3000 rpm. This is about the speed at which most cars develop maximum torque (see p. 250) and are running most efficiently. It will also enable you to change gear at the right moment for maximum economy.

Some rev-counters are marked

with figures only, with a red line to show the danger point. Others are marked in coloured sectors. Some have a cautionary sector (sometimes yellow or orange), usually starting 500 rpm before the safe maximum. Do not let the indicator needle enter this sector unless you need a reserve of power such as for overtaking—otherwise you will waste petrol and accelerate engine wear.

Never allow the needle to enter the red sector. If it does the engine will be over-revving dangerously.

Vacuum gauge

Vacuum or performance gauges give information about the condition of the engine. They are calibrated in mercury inches (in. Hg), usually from 0 to 30, and record the difference in pressure between the outside atmosphere and the inlet manifold. Performance gauges also have coloured sectors to mark different engine conditions.

When an engine is in good condition, at idling speed the indicator needle should be steady in the 17-21

in. Hg range (a green sector). At driving speed the needle should be in the 10-18 in. Hg range—the higher the better (a blue sector).

Steady, but low, vacuum readings can indicate retarded ignition (see p. 164) or weak compression on all cylinders (see p. 135). Fluctuating vacuum readings indicate an ignition fault or lack of compression on one or more (but not all) cylinders. A very low vacuum reading usually indicates a leaking inlet manifold.

UNDERSTANDING VACUUM GAUGE READINGS

Steady reading below 5 in. Hg shows leaking manifold or carburettor gasket (see p. 166).

Between 8 and 14 in. Hg is an indication of incorrect valve timing (see p. 176).

A fast, vibrating reading between 14 and 19 points to worn valve guides (see p. 172).

If reading drops to zero and returns to 22 while revving, piston rings are worn (see pp. 167-175).

Weak valve springs (see p. 172) cause the needle to swing back and forth erratically when you press the accelerator.

A reading dropping 3-5 in. Hg from normal indicates a sticking valve (see p. 172) or worn contact breaker (see p. 160).

When the needle drifts between 5 and 19 in. Hg the cause may be a compression leak between two or more cylinders.

A reading that is consistently higher than normal (17 to 21 in. Hg) indicates a choked carburettor air cleaner (see pp. 122-3).

Route planning

Maps and how to choose them

When you choose a map, remember that a lot of detail is not much of an advantage unless it is clear and relevant. Clearly marked road numbers and place names are most important, and a good key is essential.

Make sure the map is as up to date as possible. Maps are not always marked with publication dates, but one way to check is to see if they include a stretch of motorway that you know has been opened fairly recently.

For Great Britain, route-planning maps on a scale of 10 miles to 1 in. are normally available in two sheets, showing main towns and cities, motorways, primary routes (marked in green), main A roads and some lesser roads. For greater detail, you need a larger scale: a touring map of 4 miles to 1 in. is usually adequate. But for the motorist whose destination is really off the beaten track, the Ordnance Survey 1 mile to 1 in. or 1:50,000 maps are readily available. It takes 189 of the 1 in. maps to cover Great Britain.

Maps of recommended through-routes from various centres are available to AA members.

For continental routes Kümmerly and Frey provide a two-sheet route-planning map on a scale 1:2,750,000 (about 43 miles to 1 in.). The AA *Map of Western Europe* in one sheet is on a scale of 32 miles to 1 in. with Greece, Scandinavia and Yugoslavia included on a scale of about 80 miles to 1 in.

The AA *Continental Route Books* provide a key map of selected routes with an accompanying description. There are books of continental through-routes for overall planning, which can be linked with more detailed maps for various countries.

If you are planning to visit any towns you do not know well, a town plan will stop you getting lost. The Reader's Digest/AA *Book of the Road* contains town plans, and the AA can supply plans of many places in the UK and on the Continent.

How to understand maps and choose a route

The scale on British maps is given either as miles to the inch or as a representative fraction: for example, 1:625,000 or about 10 miles to 1 in.

On continental maps the scale is always shown by a representative fraction: for example 1:1,000,000, 1 centimetre to 1 kilometre ($1\frac{1}{2}$ miles to 1 in.).

The cheapest way to measure distances is by placing a piece of thread along the route, then measuring it against the scale of the map. You can do the same thing with a map measure (they cost about £1), which has a dial on which you read off the distance in inches and convert according to the scale.

Mark your starting and finishing points on the route-planning map— or maps. Decide whether you want the quickest route, the quietest route or the prettiest route, and plan accordingly.

The quickest route is not always the shortest. You have to take into account where there are likely to be hold-ups. Look out for ferries, tunnels, toll bridges, steep hills and routes through towns.

Gradients on classified roads are shown on touring maps by means of an arrow on the line of a road. The arrow points downhill. Sometimes there is a number (for example, 10) alongside the arrow, which means the gradient is 1 in 10—for every 10 ft of horizontal distance travelled, there is a vertical rise or fall of 1 ft. A 1-in-7 hill is fairly steep; a 1-in-3 hill is very steep.

In France and Italy, tolls are charged on various stretches, and these can add several pounds to the cost of your journey. In France there is usually a toll-free parallel route that is nearly as fast, but in Italy the alternative is usually slower.

Choosing the time to travel

You may have to adjust your route according to the time at which you intend to travel. Avoid towns during rush hours or Saturday mornings if possible. Motorways are usually crowded on Friday nights and Sunday evenings. Do not drive through a capital city on a Sunday evening.

Sometimes a road is slow because of a temporary hold-up due to bad weather, roadworks or special functions. Local radio stations broadcast regular traffic bulletins, or you can ring the nearest Post Office Motoring Information Service, whose number is given at the front of the telephone directory.

When planning continental routes, apply for information about potential hold-ups from national tourist offices in London. Maps showing major closures are sometimes displayed at main AA Service Centres at Channel ports.

Time your border crossings carefully. Most main border posts are open at night, but minor ones may close. If you need Customs clearance for a caravan or trailer, make sure that you cross during the day.

To work out approximately the time a journey will take, first calculate what your average speed is likely to be on the types of road to be covered, then allow extra time for heavy traffic or hold-ups.

Average speed varies according to the driver and the car, but it could be something like this: motorways 60 mph (unless special speed restrictions are in force), dual carriageways 50 mph, good A roads 40 mph, and minor roads 30 mph. If you are towing a caravan or trailer, you will have to reduce these figures.

Navigating by being prepared

Before you start, make a summary of the route on a piece of card, listing road numbers and main towns and noting whether changes of route are left or right turns.

Either ask a passenger to read this summary to you, or place it where you can glance at it quickly and safely when the car stops.

In Britain, navigate mainly by road numbers, but make sure you know whether you turn left or right into a road. Never rely entirely on place names, because the same place may be signposted on two different routes—only one of which leads directly to the next road you want.

On the Continent it is not always practicable to navigate by road numbers—place names are often more prominent on road signs. There is a European International road network. The signs have white E numbers on a green background. National road numbers are displayed as well. In some countries, roads are identified by numbers only. Most motorway systems are clearly signposted, but make sure you are familiar with the signs before you go.

Preparing for Europe /1

Planning a European journey

Any trip to Europe consists of three main stages — getting from your starting point to a port, crossing to Europe and crossing Europe to your destination. When you are planning such a journey, start from the destination and work backwards. Because driving in Europe is generally more expensive than in Britain, keep your European mileage low.

European routes

Some possible routes are given on these pages, but remember that the distances shown for routes in Europe do change from year to year as new motorways open.

When you are trying to assess how long it will take to drive from the port to your destination, do not be over-optimistic. It is estimated that

Destination	Some possible routes	Continental ports	Journey time	Distance in miles	Approximate cost		UK ports	Ferry (p. 25)
Austria								
Central	By road via Cologne, Nürnberg, Munich, to Salzburg	Ostend	13 hrs	660	£11.00		Dover Folkestone	15 14
	By road via Strasbourg, Stuttgart to Salzburg	Boulogne	15 hrs	705	£11.50		Dover Folkestone	11 9
Eastern	By road via Cologne, Nürnberg, Salzburg to Vienna	Ostend	17 hrs	850	£14.00		Dover Folkestone	15 14
	By road via Strasbourg, Stuttgart, Salzburg to Vienna	Boulogne	19 hrs	890	£15.00		Dover Folkestone	11 9
	By road to Cologne, then car-sleeper Cologne-Vienna	Ostend	4 hrs road 12½ hrs train	215	£3.50 £75.00 £110.00	petrol single return	Dover Folkestone	15 14
Southern	By road via Cologne, Limburg Stuttgart, Ulm to Innsbruck	Ostend	13 hrs	640	£10.50		Dover Folkestone	15 14
Belgium								
North	By road from Boulogne to Ostend	Boulogne	2 hrs	75	£1.25		Dover Folkestone	11 9
	By road from Calais to Ostend	Calais	1 hr	55	£1.00		Dover Folkestone Ramsgate	12 10 13
Central	By road from Ostend to Brussels	Ostend	1½ hrs	70	£1.25		Dover Folkestone	15 14
Denmark								
East	By road from Esbjerg via Knudshoved-Halsskov ferry (50 min.) to Copenhagen	Esbjerg	4½ hrs road 1 hr sea	175	£10.00		Newcastle Harwich	27 21
	By road from Hamburg (see Germany) and Puttgarden-Rødbyhavn ferry to Copenhagen	Hamburg Bremerhaven	4 hrs 5½ hrs road 1 hr sea	190 270	£15.00 £16.50		Harwich Harwich	20 19
	By road from Copenhagen to Helsingør	Esbjerg	5 hrs	205	£10.50		Harwich Newcastle	27 21
		Hamburg	4½ hrs	220	£15.50		Harwich	20
	By road from Hamburg to Ålborg	Hamburg	6 hrs	270	£4.50		Harwich	20
North	By road from Esbjerg to Ålborg	Esbjerg	4 hrs	155	£2.50		Newcastle Harwich	27 21
France								
North-west (Brittany)	By road from Cherbourg to St Nazaire	Cherbourg	5 hrs	205	£3.50		Southampton	5
	By road via Rouen, Alençon to St Nazaire	Dieppe	6½ hrs	280	£4.50		Newhaven	8
North	By road via Abbeville to Paris	Boulogne	4 hrs	150	£2.50		Dover Folkestone	11 9
	By road via Arras to Paris	Calais	4 hrs	180	£4.00		Dover Folkestone Ramsgate	12 10 13
	By road via Nantes to Paris	Dieppe	3 hrs	120	£2.50		Newhaven	8
Central	By road via Rouen, Chartres to Tours	Dieppe	4½ hrs	205	£3.50		Newhaven	8
	By road via Rouen, Chartres to Tours	Boulogne	6½ hrs	280	£4.50		Dover Folkestone	11 9
South-west	By road via Tours to Bordeaux	Dieppe	9½ hrs	410	£7.00		Newhaven	8
	By road via Fougères, Nantes to Bordeaux	Cherbourg	9½ hrs	400	£7.00		Southampton	5
	By road via Bordeaux to Biarritz	Dieppe	12 hrs	525	£8.50		Newhaven	8
	By car-sleeper from Dieppe to Biarritz	Dieppe	12 hrs train	—	£60.00 £90.00	single return	Newhaven	8
South-east	By road via Paris, Chalon-sur-Saône, Lyon to Avignon	Boulogne	12 hrs motorway 15 hrs main roads	580 595	£16.50 £10.00		Dover Folkestone	11 9
		Dieppe	11 hrs motorway 14 hrs main roads	540 560	£16.00 £9.50		Newhaven	8
		Le Havre	11 hrs motorway 14½ hrs main roads	555 580	£16.25 £9.75		Southampton	6
	By car-sleeper from Boulogne to Avignon	Boulogne	13 hrs train	—	£65.00 £90.00	single return	Dover Folkestone	11 9
South	By road via Avignon to Narbonne	Boulogne	15 hrs	700	£19.50		Dover Folkestone	11 9
	By road via Rouen, Orléans, Limoges, Toulouse to Narbonne	Boulogne	17 hrs	690	£11.50		Dover Folkestone	11 9
	By road via Angers, Limoges, Toulouse to Narbonne	Cherbourg	16 hrs	625	£10.50		Southampton	5
	By car-sleeper from Dieppe to Narbonne	Dieppe	14 hrs train	—	£65.00 £90.00	single return	Newhaven	8

Preparing for Europe/2

Planning a European journey/continued

half the 5000 British cars that break down, or are involved in accidents in France every year, do so within 150 miles of the Channel—usually because an inadequate car has been over-stressed, or because the driver has not been physically or mentally attuned to driving conditions in Europe. The average attainable daily mileage is about 300 miles.

Choosing the ferry
When you have decided on the European route that is most convenient, consider the different ferries available (see pp. 24-25), not only from the point of view of where you live in Britain, but also bearing in mind the actual journey time and likely total cost. On long voyages, you may need berths or extra meals.

Destination	Some possible routes	Continental ports	Journey time	Distance in miles	Approximate cost		UK ports	Ferry (p. 25)
West Germany								
North-west	By road via Antwerp, Aachen to Cologne	Ostend	4½ hrs	215	£3.50		Dover Folkestone	15 14
	By road via Arnhem, Oberhausen to Cologne	Hook of Holland	4½ hrs	190	£3.00		Harwich	17
Central	By road via Cologne, Limburg, Karlsruhe to Stuttgart	Hook of Holland	8½ hrs	410	£6.75		Harwich	17
		Calais	10 hrs	500	£8.50		Dover Folkestone Ramsgate	12 10 13
	By road via Reims, Nancy, Strasbourg to Stuttgart	Boulogne	11½ hrs	490	£8.50		Dover Folkestone	11 9
South-east	By road via Strasbourg, Stuttgart to Munich	Boulogne	13 hrs	615	£12.00		Dover Folkestone	11 9
	By road via Cologne, Limburg, Stuttgart to Munich	Hook of Holland	12 hrs	550	£9.00		Harwich	17
South-west	By road via Reims, Strasbourg to Freiburg	Boulogne	10 hrs	440	£7.00		Dover Folkestone	11 9
Greece								
North	By road via Belgrade (see Yugoslavia), Niš, Skopje to Thessaloniki (Salonika)	Ostend	35 hrs	1620	£27.00		Dover Folkestone	15 14
West	By ferry from Brindisi (see Italy) via Corfu to Igoumenitsa	Calais	28 hrs road 8½ hrs sea	1280	£24.00 £65.00	petrol fares	Dover Folkestone Ramsgate	12 10 13
South-west	By ferry direct from Brindisi to Patrai (see Italy)	Calais	28 hrs road 20 hrs sea	1280	£24.00 £65.00	petrol fares	Dover Folkestone Ramsgate	12 10 13
South-east	By road via Belgrade (see Yugoslavia), Thessaloníki, Larisa to Athens	Ostend	44 hrs	1970	£34.00		Dover Folkestone	15 14
	By Brindisi-Patrai ferry then by road via Korinthos to Athens	Calais	38 hrs road 20 hrs sea	1416	£26.00 £65.00	petrol fares	Dover Folkestone Ramsgate	12 10 13
Italy								
North	By road via Reims, Lausanne, Aosta and Grand St Bernard Pass to Milan	Calais	15½ hrs	655	£12.00		Dover Folkestone Ramsgate	12 10 13
	By road via Reims, Lausanne, Brig and Simplon Pass to Milan	Calais	15½ hrs	660	£12.50		Dover Folkestone Ramsgate	12 10 13
	By car-sleeper from Boulogne to Milan	Boulogne	16 hrs train	—	£70.00 £110.00	single return	Dover Folkestone	11 9
	By road via Cologne, Stuttgart, Innsbruck (Brenner Pass), Cortina to Venice	Ostend	18 hrs	845	£15.50		Dover Folkestone	15 14
North-west	By road via Cologne, Innsbruck, Cortina to Trieste	Calais	21 hrs	940	£16.00		Dover Folkestone Ramsgate	12 10 13
West	By road via Genoa, Pisa to Rome	Calais	24 hrs	1010	£17.00		Dover Folkestone Ramsgate	12 10 13
	By road via Milan, Bologna, Florence to Rome	Calais	22 hrs	1020	£21.00		Dover Folkestone Ramsgate	12 10 13
South-east	By road via Milan, Rimini, Foggia to Brindisi	Calais	28 hrs	1280	£24.00		Dover Folkestone Ramsgate	12 10 13
	By car-sleeper from Milan to Brindisi	Boulogne	15 hrs road 12 hrs train	655	£12.00 £70.00 £110.00	petrol single return	Dover Folkestone	11 9
Netherlands								
West	By car ferry direct to Amsterdam	Amsterdam	12 hrs sea	—	—		Immingham	22
	By road via The Hague to Amsterdam	Hook of Holland	1 hr	45	£0.75		Harwich	17
Norway								
South-east	By road from Stavanger via Kristiansand to Oslo	Stavanger	9 hrs	390	£6.50		Newcastle	30
	By road from Bergen via Geilo (summer) or Brunkeberg (winter)	Bergen	8 hrs summer 9 hrs winter	310 355	£7.00 £8.00		Newcastle	31
	(Kvanndal-Kinsarvik ferry, both routes, about 40 min. to Oslo)							
	By road via Ålborg (see Denmark) and Frederikshavn-Larvik ferry to Oslo	Hamburg Esbjerg	9 hrs 7½ hrs road 7 hrs sea	400 280	£26.00 £24.00		Harwich Newcastle Harwich	20 27 21
	By road via Ålborg (see Denmark) and Hirtshals-Arendal ferry to Oslo	Hamburg Esbjerg	11½ hrs 10 hrs road 4 hrs sea	490 370	£28.50 £26.50		Harwich Newcastle Harwich	20 27 21

Destination	Some possible routes	Continental ports	Journey time	Distance in miles	Approximate cost		UK ports	Ferry (p. 25)
Portugal								
North	By road from Bilbao or San Sebastian (see Spain) via Burgos, Salamanca, Guarda to Oporto	Bilbao Cherbourg	13 hrs 26 hrs	505 1080	£8.50 £18.00		Southampton Southampton	3 5
	By road from Lisbon via Coimbra to Oporto	Lisbon	4½ hrs	195	£3.75		Southampton	1
Central	By road from Bilbao or San Sebastian (see Spain) via Burgos, Salamanca, Guarda, Coimbra to Lisbon	Bilbao Dieppe	12 hrs 25 hrs	475 1055	£8.75 £18.25		Southampton Newhaven	3 8
South	By road from Lisbon to Faro	Lisbon	4½ hrs	190	£4.00		Southampton	1
	By road from Bilbao or San Sebastian (see Spain) via Burgos, Salamanca, Badajoz, Evora, Aljustrel to Faro	Bilbao Dieppe	16½ hrs 32 hrs	660 1245	£11.00 £22.00		Southampton Newhaven	2 8
Spain								
North	By road via Biarritz (see France), St-Jean-de-Luz to San Sebastian	Dieppe	13 hrs	555	£9.50		Newhaven	8
North-east	By road via Narbonne (see France), Perpignan, Gerona to Barcelona	Boulogne	19 hrs	860	£22.00		Dover Folkestone	11 9
	By road from Bilbao to Barcelona	Bilbao	11 hrs	395	£7.50		Southampton	2
East	By road via San Sebastian, Zaragoza, Teruel to Valencia	Dieppe	23 hrs	920	£16.00		Newhaven	8
	By road from Bilbao to Valencia	Bilbao	11 hrs	410	£7.00		Southampton	2
Sweden								
South	By car-ferry from Helsingør (see Denmark) to Hälsingborg	Esbjerg	5 hrs road ½ hr sea	205	£13.50		Harwich Newcastle	27 21
	By car-ferry from Copenhagen (see Denmark) to Malmö	Esbjerg	4½ hrs road 1½ hrs sea	175	£13.50		Harwich Newcastle	27 21
	By road from Hälsingborg to Malmö	Esbjerg	6 hrs	245	£14.50		Harwich Newcastle	27 21
South-west (Gothenburg)	By road via Åborg (see Denmark) then car-ferry from Frederikshavn to Gothenburg	Esbjerg	5½ hrs road 3½ hrs sea	195	£12.00		Harwich Newcastle	27 21
	By road from Gothenburg to Stockholm	Gothenburg	7 hrs	320	£5.50		Tilbury Immingham	24 26
South-east	By road via Hamburg, Travemunde-Trelleborg ferry then road via Malmö, Hälsingborg, Jonköping to Stockholm	Hamburg	10 hrs road 6-8 hrs sea	480	£34.50		Harwich	20
	By road via Copenhagen (see Denmark), Helsingø-Hälsingborg ferry and road via Jonköping to Stockholm	Esbjerg	12½ hrs road ½ hr sea	580	£20.00		Harwich Newcastle	27 21
Switzerland								
North-east	By road via Calais, Reims, Langres, Belfort to Basle	Calais	10½ hrs	440	£7.50		Dover Folkestone Ramsgate	12 10 13
	By car-sleeper Calais-Lyss then by road via Berne to Basle	Calais	1½ hrs road 12 hrs train	75	£1.25 £60.00 £95.00	petrol single return	Dover Folkestone Ramsgate	12 10 13
Central	By road via Basle, Berne to Interlaken	Calais	12½ hrs	535	£9.00		Dover Folkestone Ramsgate	12 10 13
	By road via Reims, Langres, Pontarlier to Interlaken	Calais	12 hrs	505	£8.50		Dover Folkestone Ramsgate	12 10 13
Yugoslavia								
North	By road via Cologne, Munich, Lienz to Ljubljana	Calais	19 hrs	905	£15.00		Dover Folkestone Ramsgate	12 10 13
	By car-sleeper Boulogne-Milan, then by road to Ljubljana	Boulogne	7½ hrs road 16 hrs train	340	£7.50 £70.00 £110.00	petrol single return	Dover Folkestone	11 9
	By car-sleeper Ostend-Ljubljana	Ostend	21 hrs train	—	£80.00 £150.00	single return	Dover Folkestone	15 14
South-east	By road via Cologne, Munich, Salzburg, Graz to Belgrade	Ostend	26 hrs	1195	£20.00		Dover Folkestone	15 14
	By road via Strasbourg, Stuttgart, Munich, Graz to Belgrade	Boulogne	26 hrs	1235	£20.50		Dover Folkestone	11 9
South-west	By road via Cologne, Stuttgart, Innsbruck, Cortina, Trieste to Dubrovnik	Calais	31 hrs	1375	£24.50		Dover Folkestone Ramsgate	12 10 13

Preparing for Europe/3

Choosing how to travel

When you have chosen your destination, and the most convenient European motoring route to it (see pp. 20-21), there are still a number of choices open to you. You could decide to leave your car at home and use a hired vehicle in Europe; you could ship your car across to Europe by ferry or by air; you could choose a hotel or a camping holiday — either in a caravan, hired in Europe, or at a continental camping site.

Hiring a car or caravan

The best way to hire a car is to arrange with a British firm to pick the car up at a European depot. Hire charges vary according to the country. The cost of hiring a car in the Renault 12—Cortina 1600 range for seven days' unlimited mileage might vary from £66 in Spain to £88 in West Germany.

Hiring abroad is most worth while if you have a car that is too small for comfort on holiday (see pp. 244-5), or if your car is old enough to be a potential problem on Europe's high-speed roads.

Touring caravan hire arranged in Britain, for use on the Continent, is usually part of a package holiday. You can hire caravans from some ferry operators at British ports. If you travel both ways on the firm's ferry service, you get a rebate.

Motor caravans hired for use on the Continent usually have to be collected in Britain. To hire a four-berth caravan for a continental holiday might cost about £80 a week.

If you plan to hire a touring caravan when you get to Europe, make sure you have the right coupling equipment. Some cars still use 2 in. balls and five-pin plugs, which will not fit the standard 50 mm. balls and sockets and seven-pin plugs standard on the Continent and now becoming common in Britain. It is cheaper to get the conversion done before you go.

Taking the car by train

Car-sleeper trains are more expensive than going by road, but save time and strain. The extra cost should be considered against the cost of food and accommodation for a longer journey by road.

Some services in Europe operate only during the summer, and may run only once or twice a week. They usually have reduced return rates, depending on the number of people travelling with the car. You can also usually book a connecting cross-Channel ferry and car-sleeper at the same time.

If you live in Scotland or the north of England, you may find it convenient to save the strain of driving to a Channel port by using a British Rail Motorail service.

You can also get package holidays in which you make your own way to booked accommodation — villa, fixed caravan site, ready-pitched tent — and cross-Channel bookings are included. Some British firms arrange for fully equipped touring caravans to be hired at various depots, with insurance and Channel crossings included in the cost.

Flying with your car

Fly-drive holidays include the cost of the return flight, and the use of a hired car that you collect at the European airport. Some operators also arrange accommodation.

Fly-drive is more expensive than taking your own car, but, because the travelling time is reduced, you have a wider choice of areas within a limited holiday period. You can reach southern France refreshed after two hours, rather than tired after two days' drive. The cars provided tend to be rather small.

Taking a package holiday

Package motor tours have fixed routes for you to drive to various destinations, but most formalities — ferry bookings and accommodation — are arranged by the tour operator. They usually include one-night stops at inward and outward centres about 100-250 miles apart, and several nights' stay at one or two centres.

One disadvantage is that you have little freedom to wander off route, since you have to cover a certain mileage each day to reach booked accommodation. But operators usually allow a fair amount of flexibility in choosing overnight stops.

Choosing your route in Britain

There are 11 seaports in Britain from which you can go with your car to Europe. In many cases, ferry services from more than one port will serve the part of the Continent to which you want to travel. The choices are then between the cost of the ferries, and the time taken both on the boat and on getting to the port in this country.

The distances of the ports from the main towns in Britain (opposite) are based on the AA's Throughroute map service. They assume that you are making your way to the port in the most direct way possible. But remember that if the distance from your home to the port you have chosen is more than, say, 300 miles, you will probably have to allow for an overnight stop. Do not forget the cost of meals along the route.

Remember always to allow considerably more time if your chosen route takes you through major towns. Do not drive through such areas during the peak hours or on Sunday evenings.

On very long distances it may be worth while — both to save money and to ensure that you do not have to arrive at your holiday destination exhausted after days of driving — to take your car to the port in this country by a British Rail Motorail service.

APPROXIMATE DISTANCES OF PORTS FROM BRITISH TOWNS										
	B'm'gh'm	Bristol	Carlisle	Edinb'gh	Exeter	Glasgow	Leeds	London	Norwich	Nottingham
Dover	200	200	390	490	240	485	275	70	165	210
Felixstowe	170	210	320	405	265	415	210	85	55	150
Folkestone	195	190	385	485	240	480	270	70	165	205
Harwich	185	205	325	405	255	420	215	75	65	150
Hull	145	235	150	235	315	245	55	200	190	190
Immingham	125	220	190	265	295	280	75	175	145	75
Newcastle	210	300	55	105	375	145	90	275	255	155
Newhaven	185	165	375	475	175	465	260	60	195	195
Plymouth	205	115	395	500	42	490	335	210	330	255
Ramsgate	200	200	395	490	245	490	275	75	185	215
Southampton	130	75	330	435	105	430	230	75	190	170
Tilbury	150	160	340	400	210	430	225	30	110	150
Weymouth	165	70	350	455	60	445	275	130	250	215

Choosing the cheapest and most convenient ferry

Your choice of ferry is influenced both by where you are going (see pp. 22-23), and where you live in Britain (see p. 24). But, whatever you choose, it is advisable to make sure of your ferry booking before you try to make any accommodation booking in Europe. Most hotels and camping sites will charge a penalty if you later have to cancel.

If you travel in the high season — generally July and August, but in some cases earlier and later than these months — you will have to pay more than the ordinary fare. Most operators charge more for very high or very long vehicles. The high-season family fares shown below are based on two adults and two children travelling at half-price.

On long sea journeys, you will normally also have to pay for meals and possibly berths, in addition to the standard fare in operation.

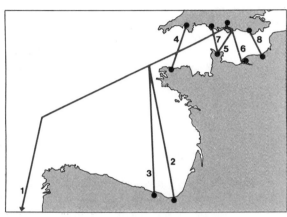

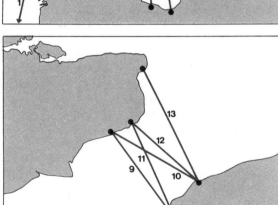

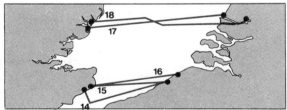

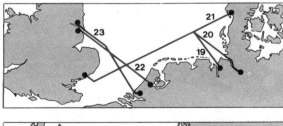

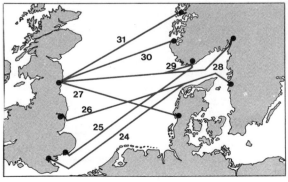

Service	Operator	Approx. distance in miles	Duration	Frequency of sailings in July and August	Approx. family fare: high season
1 Southampton-Lisbon	Southern Ferries	865	42 hrs	5-7 a month	£130
2 Southampton-San Sebastian	Southern Ferries	540	29 hrs	8-9 a month	£64
3 Southampton-Bilbao	Swedish Lloyd	540	37 hrs	7-8 a month	£68
4 Plymouth-Roscoff	Brittany Ferries	100	7-8 hrs	1 a day	£38
5 Southampton-Cherbourg	Townsend Thoresen	85	5 hrs	3-4 a day	£28
6 Southampton-Le Havre	Townsend Thoresen	115	6 hrs 30 min day 8 hrs night	2 a day	£28
	Normandy Car Ferries	115	7 hrs day 8 hrs 30 min night	2-4 a day	£28
7 Weymouth-Cherbourg	Sealink	70	4 hrs	1-2 a day	£27
8 Newhaven-Dieppe	Sealink	65	3 hrs 45 min	6 a day	£25
9 Folkestone-Boulogne	Sealink	25	1 hr 40 min	3 a day	£19
10 Folkestone-Calais	Sealink	25	1 hr 40 min	4 a day	£19
11 Dover-Boulogne	Sealink	25	1 hr 30 min	8-10 a day	£19
	Seaspeed (Hovercraft)	25	35 min	15-17 a day	£19
	Townsend Thoresen	25	1 hr 30 min	3 each weekend	£19
12 Dover-Calais	Sealink	20	1 hr 30 min	9-12 a day	£19
	Seaspeed (Hovercraft)	20	30 min	15-17 a day	£19
	Townsend Thoresen	20	1 hr 30 min	12-13 a day	£19
13 Ramsgate-Calais	Hoverlloyd (Hovercraft)	30	40 min	20 a day	£18
14 Folkestone-Ostend	Sealink	75	3 hrs 45 min-4 hrs	2-3 a day	£19
15 Dover-Ostend	Sealink	70	3 hrs 45 min-4 hrs	8-9 a day	£19
16 Dover-Zeebrugge	Townsend Thoresen	80	4 hrs	4-6 a day	£19
17 Harwich-Hook of Holland	Sealink	120	6 hrs 15 min day 8 hrs 15 min night	2 a day	£28
18 Felixstowe-Rotterdam	Transport Ferry Service	115	7 hrs	2 a day	£29
19 Harwich-Bremerhaven	Prins Ferries	310	18 hrs	Alternate days	£55
20 Harwich-Hamburg	Prins Ferries	360	20 hrs	Alternate days	£60
21 Harwich-Esbjerg	DFDS	340	19 hrs 30 min	3 a week	£58 weekdays £64 weekends
22 Immingham-Amsterdam	Tor Line	210	12 hrs	1 a week	£48
23 Hull-Rotterdam	North Sea Ferries	215	14 hrs	1 a day	£50
24 Tilbury-Gothenburg	Swedish Lloyd	580	36 hrs	7 a month	£64
25 Harwich-Kristiansand	Fred Olsen Lines	670	22 hrs	7 a month	£67
26 Immingham-Gothenburg	Tor Line	505	25 hrs	6 a week	£72
27 Newcastle-Esbjerg	DFDS	340	19 hrs 30 min	6-7 a month	£65
28 Newcastle-Oslo	Fred Olsen Lines	350	38 hrs 30 min	4-6 a month	£94
29 Newcastle-Kristiansand	Fred Olsen Lines	350	24-26 hrs	4-6 a month	£70
30 Newcastle-Stavanger	Bergen Line	340	19 hrs	4-6 a month	£76 weekdays £85 weekends
31 Newcastle-Bergen	Bergen Line	410	19-24 hrs	5 a week	£76 weekdays £85 weekends

Preparing for Europe /4

The basic insurance you need to drive in Europe

Third-party motor insurance cover is compulsory in nearly all European countries. Portugal and Greece are exceptions, and in Yugoslavia such insurance is not compulsory for foreign visitors.

Nearly all British motor insurance policies now automatically include cover for the eight other countries in the European Economic Community, and similar arrangements are also being made with Austria, Finland, Norway, Sweden and Switzerland.

But the automatic cover provided is less than that given under a third-party policy for this country. It covers only the minimum requirements of the law in the country concerned, and is similar to a British Road Traffic Act Only policy (see p. 287). It is not therefore adequate, and a motorist who relies on it entirely could be in difficulties.

In some countries, the minimum compulsory cover for personal injury is low, and court awards are likely to be much higher. This means that a motorist relying on automatic cover would have to pay the difference himself.

If you do decide to risk travelling abroad with only the minimum EEC cover, you must still notify your insurance company. If you do not, you will have the legally required cover for third-party claims, but the insurance company will try to recover the money from you. You may also have difficulty at non-EEC frontiers, since Green Cards (see below) are still inspected; the practice of checking them at EEC frontiers has been discontinued.

Remember that for some European countries outside the EEC, notably Spain, automatic cover is not provided at all.

How you can extend your own policy

The usual method of obtaining adequate insurance cover for a European journey is to ask your insurance company for a Green Card (an International Motor Insurance Certificate). You will have to pay extra for this, but it is recognised internationally (except in East Germany) as evidence of minimum legal insurance. It is also valuable in countries where insurance is not compulsory, because it provides evidence that money is available to meet claims, and may thus help the holder out of difficulties.

The cover you buy is usually an extension of your cover in the United Kingdom. If you have only third-party cover, you will have only third-party cover on the Continent. But if you have comprehensive cover, you will also have it on the Continent. Sometimes, however, such things as cover for personal effects are not included in the extension. Check with your own insurance company.

Because the cost of repairs abroad is high, insurance companies generally prefer to get the car home for repair. The cost of this may be covered in the policy, or it may be covered only as far as the frontier of the country where the accident occurred.

Most policy extensions include cover during transit for a sea voyage of not more than 65 hours' duration, and many include the cost of import duty that you would have to pay abroad if the car is stolen or a write-off, and cannot be exported back to Britain.

What you have to pay
The charge for the Green Card depends on the age and driving record of the vehicle owner, the type of car and the period covered. You can arrange cover for any period longer than eight days. Always allow a few extra days for delays.

The minimum charge for 21 days' cover for a driver of 25 years or more, with a minimum no-claim discount, would be about £3. A younger driver could pay up to £10, depending on his car and discount.

Informing the company
Give yourself plenty of time when you apply for a Green Card and make quite clear the countries you are visiting. If you are going to an EEC country, the card has to be valid for all EEC countries. If you are going to Scandinavia, the card has to be valid for all Scandinavian countries.

Let the insurance company know if you are towing a caravan or trailer. If it is not mentioned on the card, there will be delays.

A Green Card is not effective until you have signed it. When you do so, you are authorising the Motor Insurers' Bureau of the country concerned to handle claims for you.

Without a Green Card
Unless you can produce a Green Card on demand at the frontier or port of entry, most countries outside the EEC require you to buy short-term insurance cover on the spot. This gives only the minimum cover legally required and does not give you any personal insurance cover. Not only does it cause delay, but it is usually more expensive. For example, on a 21-day holiday to Italy, journeying through France and Switzerland, short-term insurance costs might be:

France: 21-day cover | £6
Switzerland: 29p for each frontier crossing | 58p
Italy: 15-day cover | £5

This means £11.58 for minimum cover, against a Green Card cost of between £3 and £10 for fuller cover.

If you are driving in Spain
Motorists visiting Spain or any Spanish territory are advised to obtain a Bail Bond, which will be supplied by the insurance company for about £1.50. It should be applied for at the same time as a Green Card. A Bail Bond is a written guarantee that a cash deposit, of up to £500, will be paid by the insurance company to any Spanish court as a surety for bail, and as security against any fine that might later be imposed by the court.

Accidents or major traffic infringements in Spain can have serious consequences, including the imprisonment of the driver and the impounding of his car until a trial can be held.

The possession of a Bail Bond usually means that the driver and his car are freed at once on bail, until the date of any court hearing. Remember, however, that any money paid out by the insurance company must be reimbursed, later, by the holder of the Bail Bond.

Using European Accident forms
Printed in the language of the driver carrying it, the European Accident Statement (Constat Européen d'accident) is used by most motorists in the EEC countries, Austria, Switzerland, Norway and Sweden.

If you are asked, in the event of an accident, to help complete one of these forms, you are merely being asked to agree various facts. Completion of the form is voluntary, but it does save enquiries and disputes later, and drivers can exchange copies to avoid subsequent misunderstandings.

How you can obtain extra insurance cover

If your vehicle breaks down while you are travelling on the Continent, or if injury or sickness affects the driver, you will have no insurance cover unless an accident is involved, and even then you may not be eligible for compensation under the terms of the policy.

Additional insurance, for the car and people in it, is advisable.

The 5-star scheme

The AA 5-star Travel Scheme is valid for any number of journeys within Europe, Algeria, Morocco, Tunisia, Turkey and all Mediterranean islands in any calendar year, provided that no previous claims have been made. The total cost for two people would be £13.25.

The benefits include: free recovery of the vehicle to the UK if, as a result of fire, accident or breakdown, it becomes unusable and cannot be repaired economically abroad; a chauffeur service if the only driver in the party becomes medically unfit to drive; credit vouchers for the payment of emergency expenses. These are generally acceptable instead of cash in most countries to pay medical fees, fees for legal assistance, and fares for the return home.

Without the protection of this type of insurance, the motorist running into trouble overseas must not only arrange for the repatriation of his vehicle, but must meet costs which are unlikely to be below £75 and are more likely to be about £200.

If you fall ill

There are reciprocal agreements with Denmark, Norway, Sweden, Yugoslavia, Bulgaria and Poland, under which British visitors can obtain emergency medical treatment, without the full cost.

In all other European countries (pending changes arising from Britain's membership of the European Economic Community) any hospital and medical expenses are the personal responsibility of British travellers. They can be heavy.

The average charge for accommodation in a European hospital is likely to be about £100 a week, without treatment, drugs and consultants' fees. Charges for examination by a general practitioner will be at least £5, and any drugs prescribed by him will certainly cost more than in the UK.

A simple injury or a minor illness requiring medical care and hospital treatment abroad, could result in expenses totalling more than £25.

A major accident involving lengthy treatment in hospital for a party of four persons could involve costs exceeding £1000.

A number of insurance companies offer holiday insurance to cover the cost of medical and hospital expenses, and the loss of any deposits, money and luggage.

A typical holiday insurance policy will cost up to £1.50 for each person, for 31 days' cover, but the first £2.50 of any claim may be excluded.

The benefits are likely to include: reimbursement of any medical, surgical, hospital and nursing-home expenses up to a maximum of £250; personal accident cover for death, loss of a limb or an eye, or permanent disablement to a maximum amount of £1000; loss of any money (for example, hotel deposits) due to death, sickness or certain other causes up to £500; loss of cash or luggage up to £250.

Claims must be submitted to your own insurance company when you return to Britain, and you must have receipts.

In the case of the claims for loss, or theft of money or luggage, it is particularly important to produce evidence that the loss was reported to the local police within 24 hours.

THE GRADES AND PRICES OF PETROLS AVAILABLE IN EUROPE

Only two grades of petrol, regular and premium, are generally available in Europe, and their octane ratings differ from the four grades of fuel normally sold in Britain (see p. 11).

Minimum octane ratings

	Premium	Regular
Austria	97-98	87-88
Belgium	98-100	90-94
Bulgaria	98	78
	(intermediate:86)	
Czechoslovakia	96	80
	(intermediate:90)	
Denmark	100	93-94
East Germany	92-96	79-88
Finland	98-100	91-93
France	98-99	89-92
Gibraltar	96-98	
Greece	96-98	84-90
Italy	98-99	85-87
Luxembourg	98-100	90-94
Netherlands	98-100	90-93
Norway	99-101	94-95
Poland	98	78
	(intermediate:92)	
Portugal	95-98	85-86
Rumania	98	88-92
Spain	95-97	85-86
	(super:97-99)	
Sweden	99-101	94-95
Switzerland	98-100	89-94
Turkey	94-95	80-85
USSR	93-95	
West Germany	97-99	90-92
Yugoslavia	98-100	86-89

Regular-grade petrol sold in Austria, Belgium, France, Greece, Italy, the Netherlands, Luxembourg, Portugal, Spain, Switzerland, West Germany and Yugoslavia, have octane ratings below the British 2-star petrol, and are unsuitable for most British cars.

In Austria, Greece, Portugal, Spain and West Germany, the octane ratings of even the premium grades are lower than the rating of British 4-star fuel, and in these countries it may be necessary to retard the ignition slightly on a high-compression engine, to avoid loss of power and possible damage.

If you are going to a country that has only low-octane fuel, take a test bulb (see p. 189) with you. When you fill up with the low-octane petrol, connect the bulb between the distributor low-tension terminal and earth. Remove the distributor cap and switch on the ignition. Slowly turn the engine crankshaft until the test bulb just lights. Loosen the distributor-clamp bolt and turn the distributor body, in the same direction as the rotation of the rotor-arm, until the bulb goes out. Tighten the distributor-clamp bolt and refit the cap.

If the engine still 'pinks' under load, retard the ignition further.

When petrol coupons are available

There is a wide variation in fuel and oil prices from country to country, with prices usually higher than the British average in Belgium, France, Greece, Italy, the Netherlands, Norway, Portugal, Spain, Sweden and West Germany.

In Austria, Luxembourg, Switzerland and Yugoslavia, however, they are lower.

Tourist petrol coupons or special tourist rates of exchange are available in a number of European countries.

Bulgaria A 5 per cent reduction on normal petrol prices can be obtained by purchasing tourist coupons from Balkan Holidays Ltd, 44 South Moulton Street, London W1Y 2DA. Coupons are also sold at frontier posts.

Czechoslovakia Tourist petrol coupons can be obtained from Zivnostenska Banka, 48 Bishopsgate, London EC2N 4AJ; Cedok (London) Ltd, 45 Oxford Street, London W1R 1RD; S. F. T. Gondrand Frères, 32-38 Leman Street, London E1 8EW.

Hungary Petrol coupons from Danube Travel, 6 Conduit Street, London W1R 9TG.

Italy It is usually possible to reduce the cost of petrol by about one-third with the purchase of tourist coupons and a carta carburante (fuel card). Coupons can be obtained in advance from the motoring organisations, at offices of the Automobile Club de Italia (ACI), and at frontier posts.

Poland Coupons giving a 30 per cent reduction can be purchased from American Shipping Line (London) Ltd, 40 Margaret Street, London W1N 7FB; Fregata Travel Ltd, 100 Dean Street, London W1V 5RA.

Rumania Coupons allowing a 15 per cent discount are obtainable from the Rumanian tourist agencies.

Yugoslavia Coupons from Yugotours Ltd, Chesham House, 150 Regent Street, London W1R 5FA, give a 5 per cent discount.

The economies that can be made from using tourist petrol coupons are marginal except, possibly, if you cover a very high mileage in Italy.

Preparing for Europe/5

Inspecting and servicing the car before going abroad

One car out of every 100 taken abroad from the UK has a major breakdown, and cannot be driven back home under its own power. In addition, one car out of every 100 is able to continue its journey only after spare parts have been sent from Britain.

Unless the owner of the car is insured under the AA 5-star Travel Scheme, or under one of a number of similar services (see p. 26), he risks considerable expense. The cost of having an immobile car transported to Britain can range from £75 (if the car is abandoned near a French or Belgian Channel port) to £200 (if it has to be brought back from Southern Spain, Southern Italy or from Yugoslavia).

Even minor breakdowns can be expensive. Replacement parts frequently cost more than the UK price, and can be 200 per cent higher in West Germany and in Spain. Garage labour charges, too, can be higher, and additional hotel expenses may have to be met.

The most frequent breakdowns are caused by faults in electrical systems, followed by faults in fuel systems, engine and transmission units and defective tyres.

All these can be avoided or minimised by a thorough inspection and servicing. A comprehensive inspection by a qualified engineer can be arranged through the AA for about £7.50. But it is possible for any car owner to tackle a pre-holiday inspection and service, without specialist knowledge or special tools.

If you are going to drive at sustained high speeds in Europe, it is advisable to test-drive the car on a British motorway some weeks before you leave. A car that is used only for town driving may show faults after a hard, fast trip.

Adapting your lights

Motorists are not generally obliged to alter headlights to dip to the right side of the road on the Continent (except in Denmark, Sweden and Germany), but it is good manners and safer to do so.

The easiest way to do this is to buy lens converters, which only require clipping on to the headlamp unit. They cost about £1.60. But converters are not allowed in the UK, so put them on and take them off while abroad.

In France your headlights should produce an amber light. Use either a lens converter or paint the headlights with a yellow plastic paint.

ITEMS THAT MUST BE CHECKED

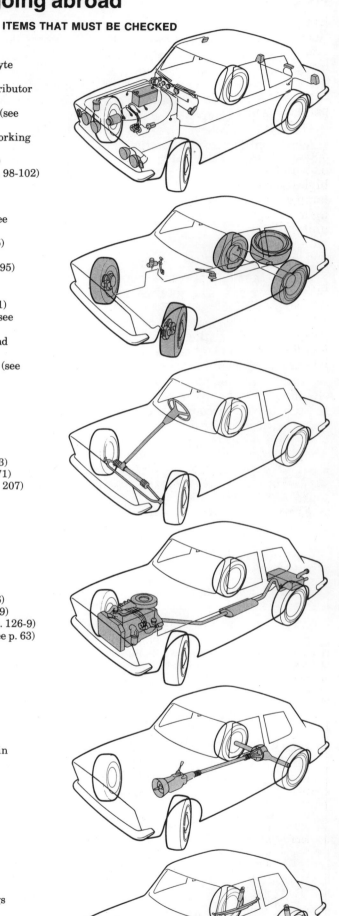

Electrics
Battery terminals and electrolyte level (see p. 37)
Wiring and connections to distributor and plugs (see p. 105)
Fan belt condition and tension (see p. 119)
Generator and starter motor working properly (see pp. 184 and 138)
Spark-plug gaps (see pp. 106-7)
Contact-breaker points (see pp. 98-102)
Lead to coil (see p. 160)

Tyres and wheels
Tread wear, including spare (see p. 37)
Inner and outer walls (see p. 95)
Wheel rims (see p. 95)
Tightness of wheel nuts (see p. 95)

Brakes
Handbrake travel (see pp. 90-91)
Fluid level in master cylinder (see p. 202)
Condition of hydraulic hoses and wheel cylinders (see pp. 196-8)
Linings or pads, drums or discs (see pp. 84-89)

Steering
Steering-box oil level (see p. 133)
Swivel pins and bushes (see p. 71)
Steering wheel free-play (see p. 207)

Engine
Oil level (see pp. 96-97)
Joints and gaskets (see p. 166)
Radiator coolant level (see p. 36)
Water hoses and clips (see p. 179)
Carburettor adjustment (see pp. 126-9)
Condition of exhaust system (see p. 63)

Gearbox
Oil level (see p. 79)
No excessive noise or difficulty in engaging gears

Clutch
Pedal travel (see p. 76)
No unusual noise or judder

Suspension
No broken leaves in road springs (see pp. 64-67)
Condition of spring shackles and U-bolts (see pp. 64-67)
Rubber bushes (see pp. 64-69)
Condition of hydraulic dampers (see p. 69)
Greasing points clean and filled with grease (see pp. 64-69)

Being prepared for a breakdown abroad

Even the most intensive preparation cannot always ensure that a breakdown will not happen away from home in the middle of a holiday. For that reason it is vital to carry a comprehensive kit of spare parts for your own car.

A typical kit might contain: spark-plugs, contact-breaker points, condenser, rotor arm and cap for the distributor, an ignition coil and high-tension lead, fuses, a head-lamp bulb or sealed-beam unit, stop-light or tail-light bulb, a flasher-unit bulb, a fuel pump or a fuel pump replacement kit, a fan belt and hoses.

Most of these spare parts can be hired by AA members for about £1 a week for each complete week, plus 15p a day for any part of the week. Any spares that you have to use will be charged for later at the manufacturers' recommended price in the UK. Contact your nearest AA regional office for details of the spares kits available.

Note that if you have a European car – for example a Volkswagen or a Fiat – you might find it more expensive to use spares that you had to buy in this country. Ask your local dealer whether you should be able to get cheaper spares abroad.

Buying spares

For the motorist who regularly makes more than one trip abroad with the car each year, it may be more economical to buy spares.

To the basic kit illustrated below, you should add: windscreen wiper blades, an inner tube (if you do not have tubeless tyres), insulated wire to suit the car's electric system, insulating tape, sealing compounds for radiator and gaskets, a torch, and a tow-rope strong enough for the car.

Remember also that most countries demand that British cars should carry the internationally recognised GB plate.

Preparing for an emergency

Most continental countries require motorists to carry with them a red warning triangle to display after an accident. A first-aid kit (required by law in Austria) is also advisable. It should have: bandages, absorbent lint, gauze and waterproof plasters; anti-histamine cream; antiseptic cream; insect-repellent cream; intestinal-infection tablets; water-purifying tablets and aspirin.

Find out when you are planning your holiday whether the countries to which you are going have any special regulations. For example, Switzerland and Italy require wheel chains in winter, and mudflaps are advisable for Yugoslavia.

A BASIC SPARES KIT FOR OVERSEAS TOURING

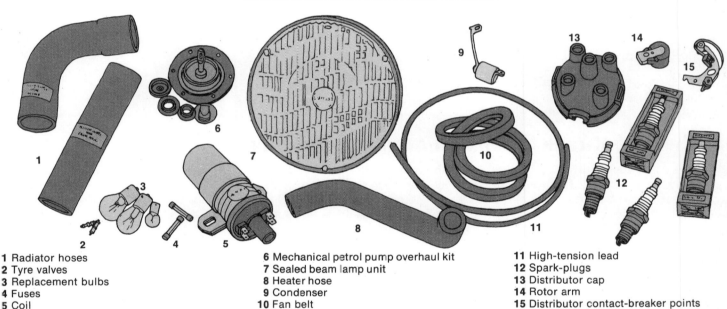

1 Radiator hoses	**6** Mechanical petrol pump overhaul kit	**11** High-tension lead
2 Tyre valves	**7** Sealed beam lamp unit	**12** Spark-plugs
3 Replacement bulbs	**8** Heater hose	**13** Distributor cap
4 Fuses	**9** Condenser	**14** Rotor arm
5 Coil	**10** Fan belt	**15** Distributor contact-breaker points

---

MANAGING YOUR MONEY ON A FOREIGN HOLIDAY

The government introduces regulations from time to time limiting the amount of money British subjects can take abroad, and for that reason it is important to pay for as much of your holiday as possible in Britain, leaving the money you can take to cover only day-to-day shopping and food.

The safest way to carry money is by travellers' cheques, obtainable from banks and travel agents. Because of fluctuation in currency rates, get your travellers' cheques in the currency of the country to which you are going, especially if its currency is stable.

This safeguards the value of your holiday money, and means that you do not have to pay commission or other charges when you change the cheques abroad.

It is also possible to cash them in more places than sterling cheques.

Duty-free goods

All ferry companies have duty-free shops at ports and on board ferries. Facilities are also available at airports and on aircraft. On cigarettes the saving is usually about £1 for 200, and on spirits just under £1 per bottle. You may find that it is cheaper to buy enough for your holiday needs on the outward journey. But remember that wine is invariably cheaper in most continental countries than at the duty-free shops.

Customs duty

Remember, too, to have enough cash available in sterling, to pay any Customs duty when you return from abroad.

There are two scales of duty-free allowances, depending on whether you have bought the goods inside or outside the seven European countries of the Common Market – France, Belgium, West Germany, Luxembourg, Italy, the Netherlands and Denmark. If you have bought the goods at a duty-free shop or in a non-Common Market country, you may bring back duty-free:
200 cigarettes or
100 cigarillos (up to 3 gm. each) or
50 cigars or
250 gm. tobacco.
1 litre of spirits exceeding 38·8° proof, or
2 litres of other spirits and 2 litres of wine.
50 gm. (2 fl. oz.) of perfume
0·25 litre (8¼ fl. oz.) of toilet water
Other articles worth £10.

If you have bought the goods and paid duty on them within the Common Market, you may bring:
300 cigarettes or
150 cigarillos or
75 cigars or
400 gm. tobacco.
1·5 litres of spirits exceeding 38·8° proof or
3 litres of other spirits and 3 litres of wine.
75 gm. (3 fl. oz.) of perfume
0·375 litre (12½ fl. oz.) of toilet water
Other articles worth £50.

Using a roof-rack

How a roof-rack affects petrol consumption and speed

For the most economical motoring, always try to stow suitcases and other items of luggage in the boot or inside the car.

If you do use a roof-rack, carefully select the luggage going on to it, and make sure it is properly stowed (see below). On an average family saloon, a badly packed roof-rack can reduce maximum speed by as much as 15 mph, and significantly increase petrol consumption.

The size of the increase will depend upon the speed of the car. Petrol consumption can increase from between 12 and 13½ per cent at 20 mph, to as much as 25-27½ per cent at 70 mph. This will mean a considerable increase in petrol bills on a long journey where high average speeds can be maintained.

On the other hand, a well-packed roof-rack will increase consumption by only 8-9½ per cent at 20 mph, or between 14 and 15 per cent at 70 mph. Maximum speed will be cut by only 8 or 9 mph, so make sure that the roof-rack is properly packed.

When a roof-rack is not being used, take it off the car. An empty roof-rack reduces maximum speed by 2-3 mph, and can increase petrol consumption by at least 5 per cent at 20 mph and 6½ per cent at 70 mph.

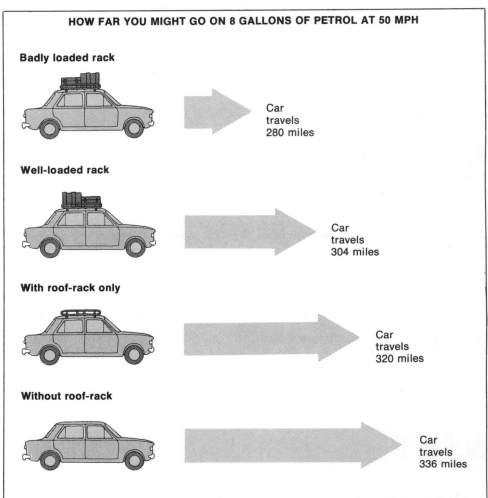

HOW FAR YOU MIGHT GO ON 8 GALLONS OF PETROL AT 50 MPH

Badly loaded rack
Car travels 280 miles

Well-loaded rack
Car travels 304 miles

With roof-rack only
Car travels 320 miles

Without roof-rack
Car travels 336 miles

Loading a roof-rack for minimum wind resistance

Select the cases most suited to the shape and size of the roof-rack. Arrange the largest at the bottom and pile the smaller cases, in order

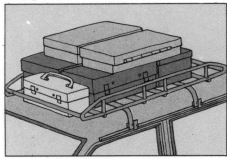

of size, on top in 'step' fashion towards the back of the car. This provides the smallest frontal area and is the most aerodynamic.

Do not stand cases upright or on edge facing the direction of travel. This presents a solid wall against the air stream, slows the car and causes it to use more fuel.

Having found the most suitable pieces of luggage to use on the roof-rack, there will be even less wind resistance if you shroud them in a cover. Use a piece of tarpaulin or leather cloth wide enough to cover the sides of the stacked cases, and

long enough to cover the bottom of the rack and be folded back over the cases on the roof.

Lay the cover over the bottom of the roof-rack, and hang the surplus over the front edge. Place the larger cases on top of the cover on the roof-rack. This will hold the cover firmly

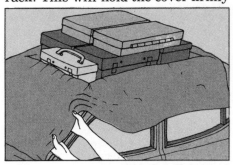

in position and prevent the wind from getting underneath it and causing too much drag. Position the other cases on top, angled towards the back.

Draw the front of the cover over the cases and tuck it in at the back to secure it. Fold down the sides of the cover and tuck them in. Fold the front edge round the sides to prevent the wind getting under the cover. Secure the cover either with

rope or a good-quality 'spider', a braided elastic grip with eight arms. Make sure that the cover and lug-

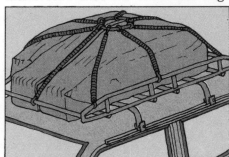

gage are held firmly in position on the roof-rack.

Never exceed the manufacturer's recommended weight for roof loading, given in the owner's handbook. After travelling for about 20 miles, stop and check the tightness of the roof-rack securing clamps. The roof-rack will usually have settled under its laden weight and can be tightened down slightly. An unstable roof-rack is a potential danger.

Note: Do not pack clothes needed on the journey in the cases going on the roof-rack. This eliminates the need to unload and re-pack the roof-rack during the journey.

Servicing your car

Tools and equipment/1

Equipping yourself for routine and major servicing

You do not need a fully equipped, expensive workshop to service your own car, but certain basic tools are essential. Extra tools can be bought if you decide to do more difficult work.

The quality of tools varies—cheap ones are mostly a waste of money. Buy the best you can afford—British and German makes are the most reliable. Those marked 'foreign' may be made from inferior metals. Cheap spanners are likely to distort and cause damage; mild-steel screwdrivers are likely to bend and chip. Buy only those marked chrome-vanadium.

Worn tools, like cheap equipment, can be dangerous and cause damage. Hammers with split shafts or loose heads should be thrown away. Burred drifts should be filed or cut to present a clean striking head.

Be careful not to over-tighten nuts, especially when using a ring spanner, or sockets and extension bar.

Spanners

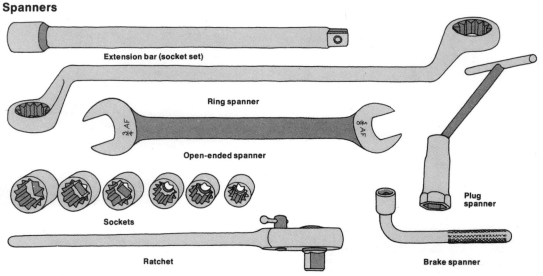

Extension bar (socket set)

Ring spanner

Open-ended spanner

Sockets

Ratchet

Plug spanner

Brake spanner

Torque wrench

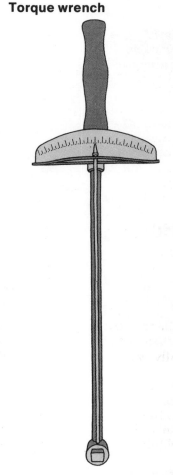

Open-ended spanners
These may be needed for tightening unions or other nuts and bolts that cannot be reached over the top. They grip on the flat side of the nut or bolt. Make sure good-quality spanners are used and that they fit the nut or bolt properly, or they may slip.

Ring spanners
These completely surround a nut or bolt and grip it at six points. They cannot slip, are safer and enable more pressure to be exerted.

Spanner sizes for cars made after 1956 are AF or metric. Sizes most used are AF $\frac{3}{8}$-$\frac{11}{16}$ in., or 9-17 mm. Car handbooks do not usually specify nut and bolt sizes, so check with your dealer before buying spanners. Sizes are often repeated in a set of spanners —for example, $\frac{3}{8}$ and $\frac{7}{16}$ in. and $\frac{7}{16}$ and $\frac{1}{2}$ in.—because two spanners of the same size may be needed at once. Combined ring and open-ended spanners have the same sizes at each end.

If you need only two or three sizes of spanner for your car, it is cheaper to buy them separately; if you need five or six, it may be cheaper to buy a set.

Socket spanners
These are heads of various sizes that are turned with a ratchet or common handle and bar. They grip in the same way as ring spanners, and can be used to reach all parts of the car. A socket with a universal joint may be needed for reaching nuts in awkward parts of the car.

Sockets can be bought in sets or separately. Sets vary in price according to the number of pieces included; longer extensions or universal joints are likely to be in the medium or high-price sets only. Socket sizes usually range from $\frac{3}{8}$ to $1\frac{1}{8}$ in. or 10-24 mm. Drive sizes (the part where the operating handle is inserted) are usually $\frac{1}{4}$, $\frac{1}{2}$ or $\frac{3}{8}$ in. The depth of sockets limits their use; some deeper sockets are available for recessed nuts or bolts.

Plug spanner
This is the only spanner that should be used on a spark-plug. It is a deep socket-type spanner with a rubber insert. The insert is designed to grip and protect the ceramic insulator of the spark-plug. If a normal box spanner is used, there is a danger of breaking the plug. The usual size is 14 mm.

Strap spanner
This tool may be needed for removing a cartridge oil filter. The strap is placed round the filter unit and passed through a slot in the handle. As leverage is applied to the handle, so the strap is tightened, gripping the filter body to enable it to be turned.

Brake-adjusting spanner
This is specially designed for reaching the brake-shoe adjusting screw on the brake back-plate. Some have socket-shaped heads on a swivel end, which enables awkward adjuster screws to be reached. Others have a fixed square head the size of the square adjuster screw.

Valve-adjusting spanner
Some engines need a specially shaped tool for adjusting the valve clearances.
Fiat A special tool is needed only on the overhead-camshaft engines. This is placed under the camshaft and is designed to compress the valve spring, to enable the clearance shims on top of the cam follower to be removed and replaced. On some of the Fiat push-rod engines, a special socket-key is needed to turn the adjusting screw.
Ford and Datsun On the indirect overhead-camshaft engines, it may be necessary to use an angled spanner to loosen the adjusting screw lock-nut.
Daf On earlier Daf engines the valve clearance adjuster was an Allen screw. An Allen key is needed to adjust the valve clearances on these engines.

This is used in combination with a socket for tightening nuts or bolts, for which a specific torque setting is given. Some have a scale, attached to the handle, and a pointer. As pressure is applied to the handle it moves, taking the scale with it. The pointer remains in its original position. Apply pressure on the handle until the required torque is indicated by the position of the pointer on the scale.

The more expensive type of torque wrench can be preset to the torque required, by a scale on the handle. Unscrew the handle until the correct torque is registered on the scale.

When the correct torque is applied to the nut, the handle will jump, indicating that no more pressure is necessary. Whatever type of torque wrench is used, make sure it has a scale up to 150 lb./ft.

Combination drain-plug wrenches — male/female

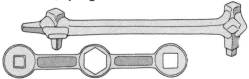

These have been designed to remove the oil drain-plugs on the engine, gearbox and rear axle. They are specially shaped spanners with six or eight heads of different sizes, designed to fit both internal and external drain-plugs.

Screwdrivers

You will need a selection of both bladed and cross-headed screwdrivers. Start with a short-handled screwdriver (about 3 in. long), a medium screwdriver (about 6 in. long) and an engineers' screwdriver (about 8-10 in. long). An insulated electrical screwdriver, is also useful.

Allen keys

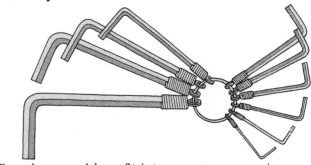

These hexagonal keys fit into the heads of certain types of bolts and screws, often used on more expensive cars. Sizes range from $\frac{1}{16}$ to $\frac{3}{4}$ in. and from 1·27 to 10 mm.

Feeler gauge

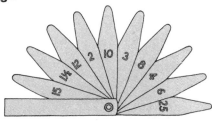

The blades of a feeler gauge are used for measuring valve clearances, the gap between the spark-plug electrodes and contact-breaker points. They can also be used for measuring close tolerances on other components. A set comprises a number of blades from ·001 to ·025 in.

Spark-plug gapping tool

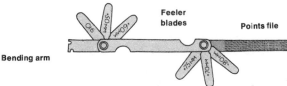

Bending arm • Feeler blades • Points file

This is a special tool used for adjusting the gap between the two electrodes of a spark-plug. It has a bending arm, designed to fit the earth electrode and enable it to be moved without damage, a range of feeler blades for checking the clearance between the two electrodes, and a points file for cleaning and levelling the contact faces.

Wire brush

Useful for cleaning dirty and rusted surfaces, especially if a component is to be examined for possible damage.

Circuit tester

This is used for tracing circuits and faults in 6 and 12 volt electrical systems. It consists of a pointed probe with an insulated handle containing a test bulb. From the end of the handle is a length of cable with a crocodile clip. The clip is fixed to a good earth point, and the probe is used to touch the live lead of a circuit. The pointed probe can also be used for piercing insulation to make contact with the internal wiring when testing for breaks.

Pliers and side-cutters

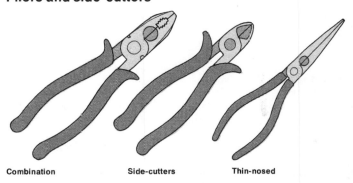

Combination • Side-cutters • Thin-nosed

The most useful gripping tools are a pair of combination engineers' pliers, with a circular and flat gripping face and insulated handle. Use a pair of thin-nosed pliers to reach awkward or small components, and a pair of side-cutters to cut and strip the covering of electrical cables.

Hammers and mallets

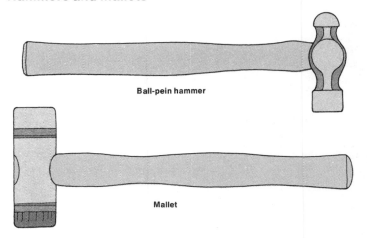

Ball-pein hammer

Mallet

Have available a $\frac{3}{4}$ and 2 lb. engineers' ball-pein hammer.
A hide or wooden mallet can be used on soft metals or specially shaped parts like the hub grease caps. Mallets are also available with copper, plastic and rubber heads. On some it is possible to change the heads.

Hydrometer

An instrument for checking the state of charge of the battery. It is used to draw off a quantity of the electrolyte from a battery cell. A float in the centre of the hydrometer indicates the specific gravity, which tells you the state of charge of that cell. Check each cell individually.

Tools and equipment/2

Equipping yourself for routine and major servicing/continued

Drifts and punches

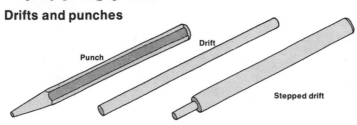

Punch

Drift

Stepped drift

A drift is usually steel, alloy, copper or brass, and is the same diameter along its whole length – with the exception of a stepped drift used for removing and replacing valve guides. Use an alloy drift on soft metals, such as bronze or brass bushes, and a steel drift on harder metals, such as wheel bearing races.

Always keep the head of a drift in good condition. If the end splays out with hammering, splinters may fly off.

Punches are made of steel and have a tapered end. Use a punch for tapping out steel pins and for bending over tab locking-washers. A pointed centre-punch is needed to mark holes before drilling.

Micrometer

A micrometer is used for measuring parts, like the valve clearance shims, to within a thousandth of an inch. The thimble, the part which is turned to set the micrometer, moves up and down a graduated sleeve. The sleeve is marked in fortieths of an inch. Each fourth graduation – which is numbered – is equal to 100 thou. (·1 in.). There are 25 calibrations round the periphery of the thimble, so one full turn of

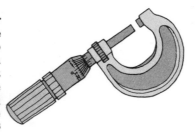

the thimble is equal to 25 thou. (·025 in.). This is achieved because there are 40 threads to the inch on the setting screw; 25×40=1000.

Axle stands

These are tripod stands, with a centre pillar which can be adjusted to the height required. The height range varies according to the size of the stand – between 10 and 24 in. – as does the weight

that the stand is capable of taking. Make sure that the type used will support your car. These can be bought from an accessory shop, or sometimes may be hired from a tool hire company.

Hub puller

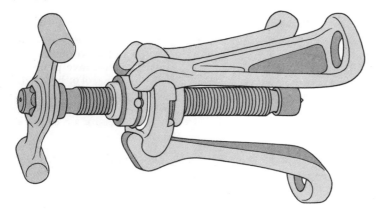

There are two basic types of hub puller. One is a flat bar or disc, and the other is a universal puller that has adjustable legs. Both types bolt to the wheel studs. When the centre bolt is turned in,

it presses against the stub axle and draws the hub assembly off the axle. The flat bar or disc is fairly cheap, but the universal puller is more expensive. These can be hired from a tool hire company.

Grease gun

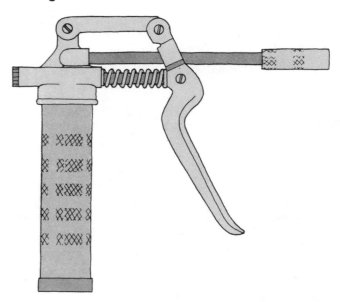

Capacities usually vary from 1½ oz. to 6 oz. There are two main types, side-lever guns, in which the grease or oil is loaded into a container, and a lever at the side is pumped up and down to eject it, and a trigger type which may be filled with grease or designed to take a grease cartridge. By pressing the trigger the grease is ejected.

The same type of grease cannot be used for all purposes – you may prefer to have two guns rather than have to change the contents.

Wipe the grease nipple clean. Push the nozzle of the grease gun on to the nipple. It will snap firmly into place, so that it grips and seals itself against the head of the nipple.

If a nipple is blocked, unscrew it, connect the grease gun to it, and pump grease through to clear it. If it cannot be cleared, buy a new nipple of the correct type and size. Check that the new one is clear, and clean out the hole that the nipple fits into. Screw the new nipple into position and apply the amount of grease needed.

Battery charger

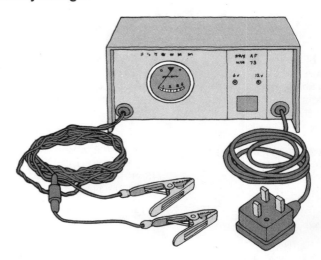

A charger plugs into the mains and has a conversion plug so that it can be used to charge 6 or 12 volt batteries. Chargers are fitted with leads for

connecting to the battery – red for positive and black for negative. The charge rate is shown on a meter. The output is usually from 2 to 6 amps.

Battery filler

Use a filler with a special filler nozzle that cuts off the

flow of distilled water when the level in a cell is correct.

Tyre tread-depth and pressure gauges

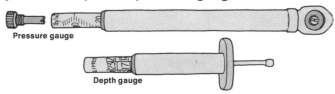

Pressure gauge

Depth gauge

Used to check the depth of the tyre tread, it measures the depth in millimetres.

A tyre pressure gauge and valve remover is usually more accurate than the kind of equipment found in a garage forecourt. The top can be unscrewed and used to remove and replace tyre valves.

Strobe light

Used for checking the ignition timing while the engine is running. The lamp is connected in series with a spark-plug lead, and lights up when the spark occurs. Pointed at the timing marks, it illuminates them as the plug fires.

Oil syringe

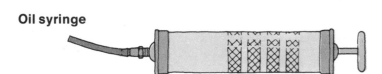

A syringe may be necessary for topping up fluid reservoirs with side filler holes. Some fluids are in dispensers.

Compression tester

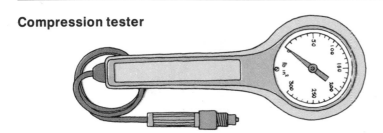

Use a tester to measure the pressure in each cylinder. The gauge fits into the cylinder spark-plug hole and is usually calibrated from zero to 300 lb./in². (lb.psi).

Brake-bleeding equipment

Brake-bleeding kits contain a dispenser for topping up the master cylinder, and a valve to fit on the bleed nipple so that fluid can be drained without air entering. You should have available a container to catch the brake fluid in.

Tyre pump

A pump is useful not only for inflating tyres but also for blowing dust from some components, such as a paper element filter. A pump with a pressure gauge costs more.

Car vacuum cleaner

A small vacuum cleaner, used for cleaning the interior, that can be run for a short time off the car battery.

Garden hose

For car washing and for flushing out the cooling system, a hose with an adjustable nozzle is most suitable.

Wash brush and cleaning brushes

A hollow-handled brush can be fixed to a hose and used to wash the car. Better than a sponge, it dislodges grit and will not scratch the paintwork. Buy one 2 in. and one 1 in. brush for cleaning various components in petrol.

Cleaning fluids

Most components can be cleaned in petrol or paraffin. Some of the more delicate parts, like the distributor contact points, should be cleaned in methylated spirit. A special removing fluid can be used to eliminate tar, petrol and road grime from the bodywork. A wide range of upholstery cleaners is available, according to the type of material. Very difficult stains on upholstery can be removed with c.t.c. (carbon tetrachloride), available from chemist shops. Make sure all the doors of the car are kept open until the vapour has cleared. Carbon tetrachloride can be harmful to health.

Use proprietary flushing oil when cleaning inside the engine. Wash all hydraulic brake parts in only clean hydraulic brake fluid.

Containers

These are necessary for draining off engine, gearbox and transmission oils. Some old basins are ideal, but they must be big enough to hold the contents of the sump (see p. 96). If the cooling system is to be drained into a container, to retain the antifreeze, ensure the container is clean.

Rags, cloths and leathers

Any rags used for cleaning components should be lint-free material. If particles of a rag peel off they could block vital oil passages.

Use clean dry dusters to polish the bodywork after it has been cleaned.

A good-quality chamois leather is the best equipment to use to dry a car body after it has been washed and rinsed off. If a new chamois leather is bought, soak it in warm water to remove any surplus oil from the skin. Never use a leather in water containing a detergent.

Marking tools

Use a ball-point pen to mark labels; it is less likely to be erased by petrol or solvents than a pencil mark. Have a pad for noting the order in which components are removed, or for marking shim sizes when adjusting valve clearances. Use white paint to mark the timing marks when adjusting the ignition timing with a strobe light.

Miscellaneous equipment

An old chisel or screwdriver; a piece of stiff wire to use as a probe; a thin sharp spike for prising out oil element housing seals; a hardwood block, about 2×2 in.; a piece of wood cut to fit between the disc-brake caliper pistons; a selection of thin rods $\frac{1}{16}$, $\frac{1}{8}$, $\frac{3}{16}$ and $\frac{1}{4}$ in. diameter, about 6 in. long. The rods are useful as probes and for adjusting the roller on BMW overhead-camshaft engines. Have plugs for blocking off petrol or hydraulic pipes and a brake-pipe clamp; a steel bar, about 2 ft long and about 1 in. diameter, to use as a lever for checking suspension wear points; a trigger-type oil can; and small plastic funnel.

Greases and oils

In most cases a good-quality high-melting-point grease can be used. There are a few jobs, for instance some brake linkages, where it is advisable to use a graphite-based grease. Always use engine lubricating oil recommended by the manufacturers. This oil can also be used to lubricate moving pivots. Occasionally, on some distributors, it is advisable to use a light machine oil for lubrication. Use petroleum jelly to protect the battery terminals from corrosion.

Routine checks/1

Saving money by simple, weekly maintenance checks

The best insurance against expensive repair bills or an inconvenient breakdown is regular preventive car maintenance—thoroughly servicing the car at the intervals recommended by the manufacturer (see p. 40).

But there are simpler, yet essential checks on fluid and oil levels, air pressures and important components that should be carried out more frequently, depending largely on how much and how hard the car is used. Whatever the use or the mileage, there are some checks that should ideally be made daily: on lights, petrol level, seat belts, windscreen wipers and washers.

The other checks in this section—hydraulic fluid levels, radiator coolant and battery electrolyte level, the amount of oil in the engine and the condition of the tyres—should normally be carried out once a week. But if your mileage is high—say, 150-200 miles a day—check these points before starting every morning. If your mileage is low, but comprised mainly of short journeys in heavy traffic, the amount of wear and tear increases. This is because the engine is never able to reach a suitable operating temperature—the hotter the engine the more efficient it is. Check all the items at least every two or three days.

Windscreen wipers

Check that these are working. Examine the wiper blades to see if they are worn. The rubber on both blades should be springy and have a sharp wiping edge. It is usual to buy complete blades, but you can renew rubbers only (see p. 225).

Some blades are attached to the arm by a bayonet clip. If you have to remove a blade, disengage the locking pin, press down the spring and slide the blade off.

Some blades have a slot containing a spring that holds the hooked end of the arm. Press the blade and arm together to disengage the locking post. To free the blade, turn it upwards.

If there is a squeak from the wiper mechanism, put a little lubricating oil along the shafts of the wiper arms. Use

Oil wiper shaft

a water-repellent lubricant. If the noise persists, check the wiper motor (see pp. 226-7).

Brake and clutch fluids

The fluid in the brake and clutch reservoirs should be kept at the recommended level. Sometimes the reservoirs are transparent, with a level mark.

Before you remove a reservoir cap, clean the surrounding area to make sure that no dirt gets in. If the reservoir needs topping up, use only clean fluid of the type recommended by the manufacturer. Never use lubricating oil or petrol.

Keep the topping-up fluid in a moisture-proof container. If you leave it in an open or half-filled can, it will absorb moisture from the atmosphere, which will lower its boiling point and make it useless. Make sure you do not spill any fluid on the paintwork. Keep the reservoir

cap air vents free from dirt. If the fluid level needs topping up continually, check for leaks (see p. 62).

Radiator

Check the level of coolant only when the engine is cold. It is dangerous to remove the radiator cap when the engine is hot. If the level is low, top up with either water or a mixture of water and anti-freeze.

Make sure the radiator cap is properly replaced, because it regulates the operating pressure of the cooling system. If the radiator needs constant topping up, check the system for leaks (see p. 118).

Some cars have semi-sealed cooling systems, which can be checked by looking at the level in the transparent overflow tank.

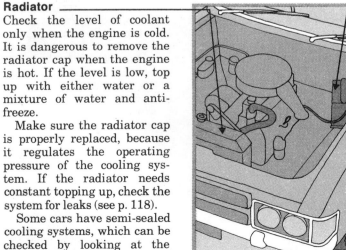

Battery level

The level of electrolyte in the battery is usually visible just below the filling hole. It should

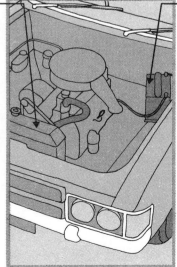
Battery plates

be kept at about $\frac{1}{4}$ in. above the plates. Do not use a naked light to check the level—the acid fumes from the battery are highly inflammable.

Top up only those cell holes that are in need of fluid. Use distilled or de-ionised water.

Seat-belt condition

The webbing of the belts should not be worn or frayed. If it is, fit a new belt. Check that the mounting bolts are tight and that the anchor points pivot freely. If they do not, remove and clean them.

Screenwasher

Make sure the spray nozzles are not blocked. Soak out any dirt, removing the nozzles if necessary. Check that they spray to the correct height—three-quarters up the windscreen. Keep the washer bottle filled with water and a cleaning fluid that also prevents freezing.

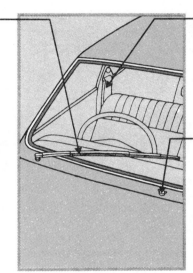

Engine oil

Check the oil level with the car parked on level ground, or you will get a false reading.

Remove the dipstick, wipe it with a clean rag, and replace it. Take it out again and note the oil level. It should be on the maximum line. If it is below, top up.

Use only the type of engine oil recommended by the car manufacturer.

The filler cap is usually on top of the rocker cover. Do not over-fill.

Generally it takes 2 pints to raise the engine oil level from the minimum to maximum mark.

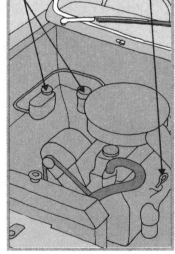

Do not over-fill, as this weakens the electrolyte.

You can use a special dispenser that controls the amount of water used. Some batteries have a trough into which you pour the water, and this controls the amount supplied to each cell. After filling, use a rag to wipe the top of the battery thoroughly clean and dry.

If the battery continually needs topping up, it could be over-charging (see p. 37). If the battery is in the engine compartment it will need topping up more often in hot weather, as distilled water will evaporate faster.

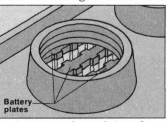

Petrol

Checking that the fuel gauge is not reading low may seem obvious, but a good many motorists become stranded through lack of petrol. This is particularly frustrating if it happens on a motorway.

Driving with the petrol tank almost empty can result in deposits in the tank causing a blockage. Keep the fuel tank at least quarter full.

Lights and indicators

Check that all the lights and flashers are working properly. If you have no one to help you, check the stop lights by backing the car close to a wall and looking for a reflection against the wall when you press the brake pedal.

Always carry a stock of spare bulbs. If a light does not work when fitted with a new bulb, there may be a blown fuse or loose connection (see p. 192). Make sure the panel lights are working so that the instruments can be seen at all times.

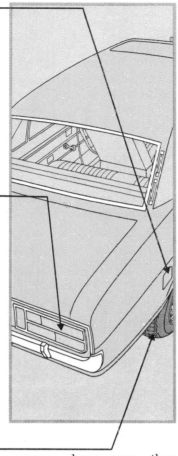

Tyres and tyre condition

It is a legal requirement that the tyres are in good condition. There is a minimum tread depth (see below), which must be maintained, and the tyres must be kept inflated within the pressure range stipulated by the makers.

Make sure that the spare also complies with these regulations. If it does not, and you fit it to the car, you are breaking the law.

Tyre pressures

Note the manufacturer's recommended pressure for your car and the type of tyre — pressures for radial-plies and cross-plies are different. Note also if different pressures are advised for front and rear tyres, for loads or high-speed motoring.

Pressures quoted are for cold tyres, so check them before you start a journey — not when the car has been running for some time and the tyres are hot, because the air will expand and the pressures will have increased. Always replace the valve caps finger tight. Check the pressure in the spare wheel at the same time.

Not all garage pressure gauges are accurate, so if possible always use the same gauge to ensure consistency, or use a hand gauge. If the

pressure drops more than 2-3 lb. per sq. in. during a week, the tyre or valve may be faulty. Have it checked by a specialist tyre dealer.

Tyre condition

When checking pressures, look

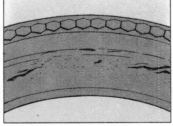

at the tyres to see if there are any cracks or bulges. If there are, get the tyre replaced.

Tread depth

Check tread depths from time to time. Measure both the

centre and outside grooves in the tread pattern. The legal requirement is only 1 mm., but it is unsafe to drive with less than 2 mm. of tread. Discard tyres with less than 2 mm.

Additional checks on the battery

The battery is one of the most important parts of a car. The following checks should be carried out every time the car is serviced, but also at least once a month.

Battery case

If the electrolyte level falls quickly, check the battery casing for leaks. They leave white, powdery deposits. If you find such deposits, remove the two battery leads, and carefully pour a kettle of hot water over the battery case to wash away the deposits. Check any parts of the case where there was a build up of deposits, to see if there are any cracks.

If there are cracks above the line of the electrolyte level, it may be possible to seal them with melted sealing wax. If the cracks are below the line

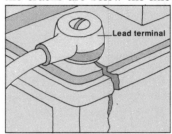

of the electrolyte level, fit a new battery.

Battery connections

The battery leads may be clamped to the terminals by a pinch bolt or a cup-shaped

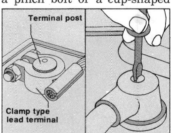

cap secured by a screw. Remove the battery leads. Clean the posts and connections. Rub the two mating surfaces lightly with fine emery cloth

until they are bright, then smear them with petroleum

jelly. Refit them. If your car is fitted with an alternator, never undo the battery leads while the engine is running, or the alternator will be damaged beyond repair.

Battery earth strap

One of the battery terminals is connected to the body of the car by a braided strap.

Check that the connection to the car body is clean and making a good return contact.

The state of charge of the battery

Cars fitted with dynamos may suffer from undercharging if the car is used mostly for short journeys, especially if these involve a lot of stopping.

You can check the state of charge by measuring the strength of the electrolyte with a hydrometer (see p. 33). Place the tip into one of the battery cells and squeeze the rubber bulb to suck in enough fluid to raise the float. Note the reading on the hydrometer scale at the point where the float breaks the surface, then

return the fluid to the same cell. For a fully charged bat-

tery, the reading should be between 1·270 and 1·290. If it is below 1·120, the battery is flat and needs charging.

Trickle-charging the battery

If your battery is not being fully charged by the generator, supplement the charge every two weeks by connecting it to a trickle-charger overnight.

Remove the battery filler plugs or lid and connect the leads of the charger to the battery terminals — black lead

to the negative post and red lead to the positive. Plug the charger into the electricity supply and switch on the power. Make sure that the correct voltage is set.

Switch off the charger before removing the leads. Replace the filler plugs.

Routine checks /2

Cleaning and polishing the car regularly

It costs far more to leave your car dirty than to clean it. Dirt paves the way for rust and general deterioration of the bodywork. The car's appearance, moreover, makes a difference to the price you get when you sell it. Unless you clean it regularly, even a thorough spring-clean just before selling will have little effect.

Cleaning inside
Take out the front seats if possible and remove the carpets and underfelt. Carpet round the wheel arches and transmission tunnel may be stuck down. If so, leave it in place and clean the rest of the floor pan with a portable vacuum cleaner.

Beat the dust out of the carpets and clean them with a carpet cleaner. Strengthen worn parts by sticking patches of rubber sheeting on the top surface. You can buy rubber mats, shaped for many makes of car, to cover areas most liable to wear. Tears in the carpet can be mended with adhesive webbing. Be sure to mend any tears round the driver's footwell, where they are dangerous.

While the carpets are out, wash and dry the floor and examine it for rust. Treat any rusted areas (see pp. 232-4) and give them a coat of primer and finishing paint (see pp. 239-41).

Cleaning outside
Never wash the car in direct sunlight or while the bonnet is still warm, as you will cause unsightly smears.

A dirty car has tiny particles of grit sticking to the paintwork. These must be sluiced off—never rubbed

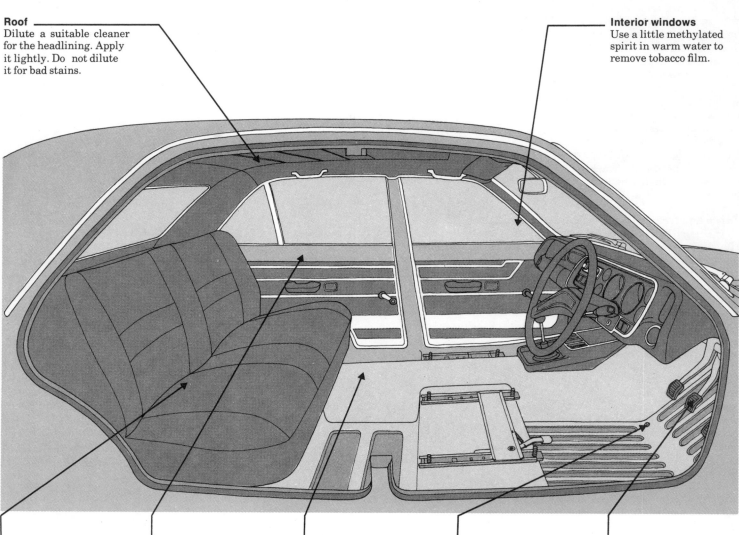

Roof
Dilute a suitable cleaner for the headlining. Apply it lightly. Do not dilute it for bad stains.

Interior windows
Use a little methylated spirit in warm water to remove tobacco film.

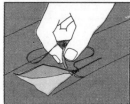

Vinyl seat covers
Use a special cleaner, for some household detergents may discolour the material. Avoid using too much water. Dry thoroughly. If there is a split, cut a piece from under the seat and glue it under the tear to repair it.

Interior paintwork
Wash, rinse and dry with a leather. Do not use too much water, especially round trim panels or the dashboard. Check the mountings of the seat runners and seat-belt anchor points for security and signs of rust.

Carpets
Grit or stones left in the carpet will quickly wear holes. Clean carpets with a vacuum cleaner if possible. Treat stains with a carpet cleaner. From time to time, take out the parts that can be removed and brush them.

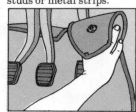

Floor studs
Most carpets are held by studs or metal strips. Secure fitting is important, otherwise the carpet might slide forward and obstruct the pedals. Studs may break if you remove the carpet for cleaning. Replace them.

Pedals
Wash and dry the rubbers. If they are split, worn or oil-contaminated, replace them. Oil leaks from the master cylinder can run down the pedal and foul the rubbers, making them slippery and dangerous.

off dry. Dirt and insects rubbed into the paintwork will accelerate rust.

You therefore need plenty of water—the more the better. Make sure that all the windows are closed and use a hose or throw buckets of clean water over the car, starting at the top. If you use a hose, do not turn the pressure jet on the body panels or windows. Be sure to hose underneath the car where mud and de-icing salt become lodged and encourage corrosion.

After sluicing, wash the car from the top down with a car brush, ideal-ly one attached to a hose. If you have to use a sponge or cloth, make sure it is perfectly clean and has no grit particles that will scratch the paint. Use tepid water. A few drops of washing-up liquid will help to loosen grit. Add a drop of vinegar if the road haze is particularly bad.

After washing, rinse thoroughly with cold, clean water and dry with a chamois leather—make sure the leather is clean and will not scratch.

Polishing is usually necessary only about once every six months. If the paintwork is dull you can use a cutting compound, but remember that it is mildly abrasive; use it carefully. Its purpose is to cut through the road grime and tarn-ished paintwork to expose the fresh, bright colour underneath. If you use it too much or too often, it will cut through all the paint, making a complete respray necessary.

Wash chrome, stainless steel, plastic or anodised alloy trim in the same way as paintwork. Use a chrome cleaner only if the chrome is marked. If anodised aluminium tarnishes, use an alloy cleaner.

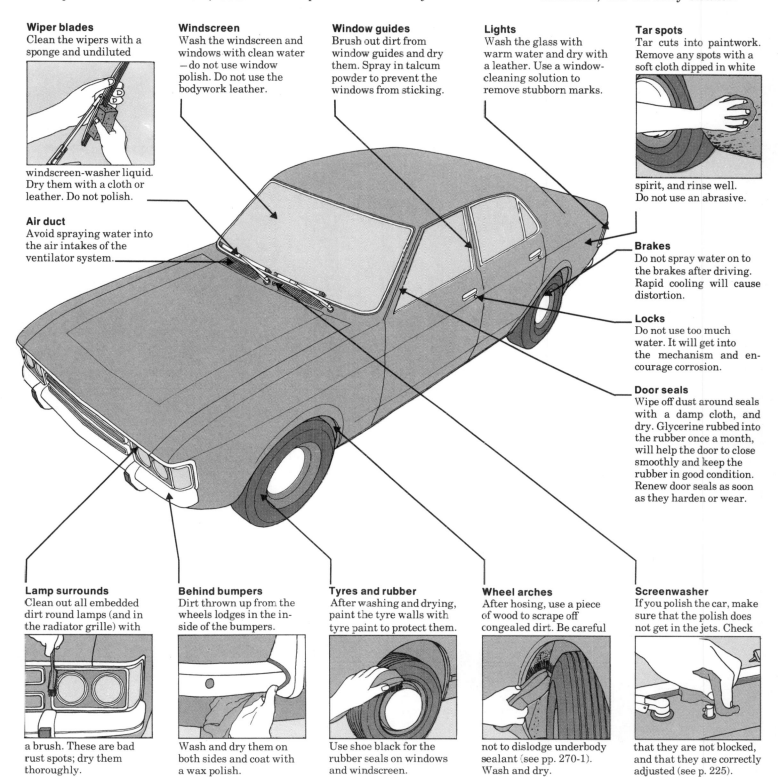

Wiper blades
Clean the wipers with a sponge and undiluted windscreen-washer liquid. Dry them with a cloth or leather. Do not polish.

Air duct
Avoid spraying water into the air intakes of the ventilator system.

Windscreen
Wash the windscreen and windows with clean water —do not use window polish. Do not use the bodywork leather.

Window guides
Brush out dirt from window guides and dry them. Spray in talcum powder to prevent the windows from sticking.

Lights
Wash the glass with warm water and dry with a leather. Use a window-cleaning solution to remove stubborn marks.

Tar spots
Tar cuts into paintwork. Remove any spots with a soft cloth dipped in white spirit, and rinse well. Do not use an abrasive.

Brakes
Do not spray water on to the brakes after driving. Rapid cooling will cause distortion.

Locks
Do not use too much water. It will get into the mechanism and en-courage corrosion.

Door seals
Wipe off dust around seals with a damp cloth, and dry. Glycerine rubbed into the rubber once a month, will help the door to close smoothly and keep the rubber in good condition. Renew door seals as soon as they harden or wear.

Lamp surrounds
Clean out all embedded dirt round lamps (and in the radiator grille) with a brush. These are bad rust spots; dry them thoroughly.

Behind bumpers
Dirt thrown up from the wheels lodges in the in-side of the bumpers. Wash and dry them on both sides and coat with a wax polish.

Tyres and rubber
After washing and drying, paint the tyre walls with tyre paint to protect them. Use shoe black for the rubber seals on windows and windscreen.

Wheel arches
After hosing, use a piece of wood to scrape off congealed dirt. Be careful not to dislodge underbody sealant (see pp. 270-1). Wash and dry.

Screenwasher
If you polish the car, make sure that the polish does not get in the jets. Check that they are not blocked, and that they are correctly adjusted (see p. 225).

39

Manufacturers' recommendations

How to get the best from the servicing section

The servicing instructions on pp. 62-136 have been compiled in close association with the principal British and foreign car manufacturers. The section is a complete summary of all the instructions given by the manufacturers for small, medium and major servicing on 193 makes and models.

Using the charts

The key to the servicing information is contained in the charts on pp. 41-60. Each servicing job has been allocated a number, and the list of jobs to be carried out at any particular service is compiled by using the charts. First have available a pencil or pen and paper.

Find your car in the extreme top left-hand corner of each chart section and then check which of the 1000 mile stages shown alongside it is the nearest above your own car's mileage figure.

If you regularly complete only a very low mileage—say less than 1000 miles in every three months—use the line of figures showing the age of the car in months. Take the figure nearest above the age of your car. Note that some manufacturers do not give time intervals.

From the mileage or month figure read down to find the service code.

Next, consult the chart below these figures and letters. Write down all the job numbers that are shown opposite the code you found.

The list of numbers you now have is your job list. Go through the servicing section on pp. 62-136 and complete the instructions.

If your car is not on the list

Each job in the servicing section is also given a title. If your car is not on the list, ask your dealer to give you a copy of the manufacturer's servicing recommendations.

It may then be possible for you to carry out most of the servicing yourself by using the appropriate job descriptions on pp. 62-136.

HOW TO READ THE SERVICING CHARTS

1 Make and model
Check that the make and model given match your car exactly.

2 Mileage done
Check the mileage shown on your car.
Find the nearest figure above it in this line.
(Note that 8=8000, 24=24,000 and so on).

3 Age of car
If you regularly do a low mileage, find the age of your car (in months) on this line.

4 Service code
When you have established the mileage or age of your car, read off the service code letter on this line—your key to what you should do to your car at this time.

Chrysler Minx V VI Hillman Singer Gazelle V VI		15	20	25	30	35	40	45	50	55	60	65	70	75	80	85	90
	miles in thousands	15	20	25	30	35	40	45	50	55	60	65	70	75	80	85	90
	age of car in months	18	24	30	36	42	48	54	60	66	72	78	84	90	96	102	108
	look for service code letter	D	B	A	C	A	B	D	B	A	C	A	B	D	B	A	C

Code	Job	Code	Job	Code	Job	Code	Job	Code	Job	Code	Job	Code	Job	Code	Job	Code	Job
ABCD	1	ABCD	29	BC	40	ABCD	67	BC	80	A D	86	ABCD	95	ABCD	113	ABCD	127
C	5	ABCD	30	ABCD	43	ABCD	69	ABCD	81	ABCD	87	ABCD	96	ABCD	115	ABCD	128
C	7	ABCD	31	ABCD	50	ABCD	70	ABCD	82	ABCD	89	ABCD	97	ABCD	117	CD	129
ABCD	10	ABCD	34	ABCD	58	ABCD	73	ABCD	83	ABCD	90	ABCD	101	ABCD	124		
ABCD	17	ABCD	35	BC	61	ABCD	74	ABCD	84	BC	91	ABCD	107	ABCD	125		
ABCD	27	BC	36	ABCD	62	ABCD	76	BC	85	BC	92	BC	108	ABCD	126		

5 Job list
Look down the left-hand columns for the service code letter that you have established. Write down the job numbers you find listed against that letter. Ignore all other job numbers.

6 Using the servicing section
When you have written down all the jobs that have to be done, go through the section (pp. 62-136) and follow the instructions for each job. Do only the jobs on your list.

Audi – BMW

Jobs to be done

Read page 40 before using these charts

Audi 100 GL / Audi 100 LS

miles in thousands	6	12	18	24	30	36	42	48	54	60	66	72
look for service code letter	A	B	C	E	A	D	A	E	C	B	A	F

Code	Job	Code	Job	Code	Job	Code	Job	Code	Job	Code	Job	Code	Job	Code	Job
ABCDEF	1	ABCDEF	21	AB E	37	BCDEF	79	ABCDEF	104*	ABCDEF	133	ABCDEF	159	ABCDEF	203
ABCDEF	2	ABCDEF	22	ABCDEF	42	BCDEF	82	ABCDEF	105	ABCDEF	134	ABCDEF	162	ABCDEF	213
ABCDEF	4	ABCDEF	23	ABCDEF	43	BCDEF	83	ABCDEF	106	ABCDEF	136	ABCDEF	173	ABCDEF	220
ABCDEF	6	ABCDEF	25	ABCDEF	51	ABCDEF	85	BCDEF	108	ABCDEF	138	BCDEF	176	ABCDEF	221
ABCDEF	8	ABCDEF	28	ABCDEF	52	ABCDEF	86	BCDEF	115	ABCDEF	148	ABCDEF	181	ABCDEF	222
ABCDEF	9	ABCDEF	29	ABCDEF	54	ABCDEF	87	ABCDEF	118	ABCDEF	151	ABCDEF	184	ABCDEF	223
ABCDEF	11	ABCDEF	32	ABCDEF	59	EF	88	ABCDEF	120	ABCDEF	153	ABCDEF	188	ABCDEF	224
ABCDEF	12	ABCDEF	34	ABCDEF	60	ABCDEF	91	ABCDEF	122	ABCDEF	154	ABCDEF	193	ABCDEF	226
ABCDEF	18	CD F	35	ABCDEF	61	ABCDEF	94	ABCDEF	130	CD F	155	ABCDEF	200		
ABCDEF	19	CD F	36	BCDEF	78	ABCDEF	103*	ABCDEF	132	ABCDEF	156	ABCDEF	202	*Adjust only	

Audi 100 GL automatic / Audi 100 LS automatic

miles in thousands	6	12	18	24	30	36	42	48	54	60	66	72
look for service code letter	A	B	C	E	A	D	A	E	C	B	A	F

Code	Job	Code	Job	Code	Job	Code	Job	Code	Job	Code	Job	Code	Job	Code	Job
ABCDEF	1	ABCDEF	21	ABCDEF	54	ABCDEF	87	ABCDEF	118	ABCDEF	151	ABCDEF	184	ABCDEF	222
ABCDEF	2	ABCDEF	22	ABCDEF	59	EF	88	ABCDEF	120	ABCDEF	153	ABCDEF	188	ABCDEF	223
ABCDEF	4	ABCDEF	23	ABCDEF	60	ABCDEF	91	ABCDEF	122	ABCDEF	154	ABC E	193	ABCDEF	224
ABCDEF	6	ABCDEF	25	ABCDEF	61	ABCDEF	94	ABCDEF	130	CD F	155	ABCDEF	200	ABCDEF	226
ABCDEF	8	ABCDEF	28	BCDEF	78	ABCDEF	103	ABCDEF	132	ABCDEF	156	ABCDEF	202		
ABCDEF	9	ABCDEF	29	BCDEF	79	ABCDEF	104	ABCDEF	133	ABCDEF	159	ABCDEF	203		
ABCDEF	11	ABCDEF	32	BCDEF	82	ABCDEF	105	ABCDEF	134	ABCDEF	162	ABCDEF	213		
ABCDEF	12	ABCDEF	34	BCDEF	83	ABCDEF	106	ABCDEF	136	ABCDEF	173	ABCDEF	219		
ABCDEF	18	ABCDEF	51	ABCDEF	85	BCDEF	108	ABCDEF	138	ABCDEF	176	ABCDEF	220		
ABCDEF	19	ABCDEF	52	ABCDEF	86	BCDEF	115	ABCDEF	148	ABCDEF	181	ABCDEF	221		

BMW 1800 / BMW 2000/2002

miles in thousands	4	8	12	16	20	24	28	32	36	40	44	48	52	56	60	64	68	72	76	80
look for service code letter	A	B	H	C	A	J	A	C	H	E	A	F	A	B	H	C	A	J	A	G

Code	Job	Code	Job	Code	Job	Code	Job	Code	Job	Code	Job	Code	Job
ABCDEFGHJ	1	ABCDEFGHJ	28	ABCDEFGHJ	61	ABCDEFGHJ	87	A H	131	ABCDEFGHJ	159	BCDEFG J	211
ABCDEFGHJ	4	ABCDEFGHJ	29	ABCDEFGHJ	62	F HJ	88	BCDEFG J	132	ABCDEFGHJ	162	BCDEFG J	212
ABCDEFGHJ	6	ABCDEFGHJ	31	ABCDEFGHJ	63	ABCDEFGHJ	90	BCDEFG J	133	ABCDEFGHJ	171	ABCDEFGHJ	213
ABCDEFGHJ	8	ABCDEFGHJ	34	ABCDEFGHJ	64	BCDEFG J	94	BCDEFG J	135	A H	175	ABCDEFGHJ	220
ABCDEFGHJ	9	D F J	35	ABCDEFGHJ	65	E G	95	BCDEFG J	136	BCDEFG J	176	ABCDEFGHJ	221
ABCDEFGHJ	10	D F J	36	ABCDEFGHJ	66	ABCDEFGHJ	105	BCDEFG J	141	ABCDEFGHJ	181	ABCDEFGHJ	223
ABCDEFGHJ	12	ABCDEFGHJ	51	BCDEFG J	78	ABCDEFGHJ	106	BCDEFG J	145	ABCDEFGHJ	184	BCDEFG J	224
ABCDEFGHJ	18	ABCDEFGHJ	52	BCDEFG J	79	ABCDEFGHJ	108	BCDEFG J	149	ABCDEFGHJ	187	ABCDEFGHJ	225
ABCDEFGHJ	19	ABCDEFGHJ	53	BCDEFG J	80	ABCDEFGHJ	115	BCDEFG J	152	ABCDEFGHJ	189	BCDEFG J	226
ABCDEFGHJ	23	ABCDEFGHJ	54	BCDEFG J	81	ABCDEFGHJ	118	ABCDEFGHJ	153	ABCDEFGHJ	190		
ABCDEFGHJ	24	ABCDEFGHJ	58	BCDEFG J	83	ABCDEFGHJ	120	ABCDEFGHJ	154	ABCDEFGHJ	199		
ABCDEFGHJ	25	ABCDEFGHJ	59	BCDEFG J	85	ABCDEFGHJ	122	D F J	155	ABCDEFGHJ	202		
ABCDEFGHJ	26	ABCDEFGHJ	60	ABCDEFGHJ	86	ABCDEFGHJ	130	ABCDEFGHJ	156	ABCDEFGHJ	203		

BMW 1800 automatic / BMW 2000 automatic / BMW 2002 automatic

miles in thousands	4	8	12	16	20	24	28	32	36	40	44	48	52	56	60	64	68	72	76	80
look for service code letter	A	B	H	C	A	J	A	C	H	E	A	F	A	B	H	C	A	J	A	G

Code	Job	Code	Job	Code	Job	Code	Job	Code	Job	Code	Job	Code	Job
ABCDEFGHJ	1	ABCDEFGHJ	28	ABCDEFGHJ	64	BCDEFG J	94	BCDEFG J	135	A H	175	ABCDEFGHJ	214
ABCDEFGHJ	4	ABCDEFGHJ	29	ABCDEFGHJ	65	E G	95	BCDEFG J	136	BCDEFG J	176	ABCDEFGHJ	220
ABCDEFGHJ	6	ABCDEFGHJ	31	ABCDEFGHJ	66	ABCDEFGHJ	105	BCDEFG J	141	ABCDEFGHJ	181	ABCDEFGHJ	221
ABCDEFGHJ	8	ABCDEFGHJ	34	BCDEFG J	78	ABCDEFGHJ	106	BCDEFG J	145	ABCDEFGHJ	184	ABCDEFGHJ	223
ABCDEFGHJ	9	ABCDEFGHJ	51	BCDEFG J	79	ABCDEFGHJ	108	BCDEFG J	149	ABCDEFGHJ	187	BCDEFG J	224
ABCDEFGHJ	10	ABCDEFGHJ	52	BCDEFG J	80	ABCDEFGHJ	115	BCDEFG J	152	ABCDEFGHJ	189	ABCDEFGHJ	225
ABCDEFGHJ	12	ABCDEFGHJ	54	BCDEFG J	81	ABCDEFGHJ	118	ABCDEFGHJ	153	ABCDEFGHJ	190	BCDEFG J	226
ABCDEFGHJ	18	ABCDEFGHJ	58	BCDEFG J	83	ABCDEFGHJ	120	ABCDEFGHJ	154	ABCDEFGHJ	199		
ABCDEFGHJ	19	ABCDEFGHJ	59	BCDEFG J	85	ABCDEFGHJ	122	D F J	155	ABCDEFGHJ	202		
ABCDEFGHJ	23	ABCDEFGHJ	60	ABCDEFGHJ	86	ABCDEFGHJ	130	ABCDEFGHJ	156	ABCDEFGHJ	203		
ABCDEFGHJ	24	ABCDEFGHJ	61	ABCDEFGHJ	87	A H	131	ABCDEFGHJ	159	BCDEFG J	211		
ABCDEFGHJ	25	ABCDEFGHJ	62	F HJ	88	BCDEFG J	132	ABCDEFGHJ	162	BCDEFG J	212		
ABCDEFGHJ	26	ABCDEFGHJ	63	ABCDEFGHJ	90	BCDEFG J	133	ABCDEFGHJ	171	ABCDEFGHJ	213		

BMW 2500 / BMW 2800

miles in thousands	4	8	12	16	20	24	28	32	36	40	44	48	52	56	60	64	68	72	76	80
look for service code letter	A	B	H	C	A	J	A	C	H	E	A	F	A	B	H	C	A	J	A	G

Code	Job	Code	Job	Code	Job	Code	Job	Code	Job	Code	Job	Code	Job
ABCDEFGHJ	1	ABCDEFGHJ	28	ABCDEFGHJ	61	ABCDEFGHJ	87	A H	131	ABCDEFGHJ	159	BCDEFG J	213
ABCDEFGHJ	4	ABCDEFGHJ	29	ABCDEFGHJ	62	F HJ	88	BCDEFG J	132	ABCDEFGHJ	162	ABCDEFGHJ	220
ABCDEFGHJ	6	ABCDEFGHJ	31	ABCDEFGHJ	63	ABCDEFGHJ	90	BCDEFG J	133	ABCDEFGHJ	171	ABCDEFGHJ	221
ABCDEFGHJ	8	ABCDEFGHJ	34	ABCDEFGHJ	64	BCDEFG J	94	BCDEFG J	135	A H	175	ABCDEFGHJ	223
ABCDEFGHJ	9	D F J	35	ABCDEFGHJ	65	E G	95	BCDEFG J	136	BCDEFG J	176	BCDEFG J	224
ABCDEFGHJ	10	D F J	36	ABCDEFGHJ	66	ABCDEFGHJ	105	BCDEFG J	141	ABCDEFGHJ	181	ABCDEFGHJ	225
ABCDEFGHJ	12	ABCDEFGHJ	51	BCDEFG J	78	ABCDEFGHJ	106	BCDEFG J	145	ABCDEFGHJ	184	BCDEFG J	226
ABCDEFGHJ	18	ABCDEFGHJ	52	BCDEFG J	79	ABCDEFGHJ	108	BCDEFG J	149	ABCDEFGHJ	187		
ABCDEFGHJ	19	ABCDEFGHJ	53	BCDEFG J	80	ABCDEFGHJ	115	BCDEFG J	152	ABCDEFGHJ	189		
ABCDEFGHJ	23	ABCDEFGHJ	54	BCDEFG J	81	ABCDEFGHJ	118	ABCDEFGHJ	153	ABCDEFGHJ	193		
ABCDEFGHJ	24	ABCDEFGHJ	58	BCDEFG J	83	ABCDEFGHJ	120	ABCDEFGHJ	154	ABCDEFGHJ	200		
ABCDEFGHJ	25	ABCDEFGHJ	59	BCDEFG J	85	ABCDEFGHJ	122	D F J	155	ABCDEFGHJ	202		
ABCDEFGHJ	26	ABCDEFGHJ	60	ABCDEFGHJ	86	ABCDEFGHJ	130	ABCDEFGHJ	156	ABCDEFGHJ	203		

BMW – British Leyland

Read page 40 before using these charts

Jobs to be done

BMW 2500 automatic
BMW 2800 automatic

miles in thousands	4	8	12	16	20	24	28	32	36	40	44	48	52	56	60	64	68	72	76	80
look for service code letter	A	B	H	C	A	J	A	C	H	E	A	F	A	B	H	C	A	J	A	G

Code	Job	Code	Job	Code	Job	Code	Job	Code	Job	Code	Job	Code	Job
ABCDEFGHJ	1	ABCDEFGHJ	28	ABCDEFGHJ	64	BCDEFG J	94	BCDEFG J	135	A H	175	ABCDEFGHJ	214
ABCDEFGHJ	4	ABCDEFGHJ	29	ABCDEFGHJ	65	E G	95	BCDEFG J	136	BCDEFG J	176	ABCDEFGHJ	220
ABCDEFGHJ	6	ABCDEFGHJ	31	ABCDEFGHJ	66	ABCDEFGHJ	105	BCDEFG J	141	ABCDEFGHJ	181	ABCDEFGHJ	221
ABCDEFGHJ	8	ABCDEFGHJ	34	BCDEFG J	78	ABCDEFGHJ	106	BCDEFG J	145	ABCDEFGHJ	184	ABCDEFGHJ	223
ABCDEFGHJ	9	ABCDEFGHJ	51	BCDEFG J	79	ABCDEFGHJ	108	BCDEFG J	149	ABCDEFGHJ	187	BCDEFG J	224
ABCDEFGHJ	10	ABCDEFGHJ	52	BCDEFG J	80	ABCDEFGHJ	115	BCDEFG J	152	ABCDEFGHJ	189	ABCDEFGHJ	225
ABCDEFGHJ	12	ABCDEFGHJ	54	BCDEFG J	81	ABCDEFGHJ	118	ABCDEFGHJ	153	ABCDEFGHJ	190	BCDEFG J	226
ABCDEFGHJ	18	ABCDEFGHJ	58	BCDEFG J	83	ABCDEFGHJ	120	ABCDEFGHJ	154	ABCDEFGHJ	200		
ABCDEFGHJ	19	ABCDEFGHJ	59	ABCDEFGHJ	86	ABCDEFGHJ	122	C FG	155	ABCDEFGHJ	202		
ABCDEFGHJ	23	ABCDEFGHJ	60	ABCDEFGHJ	87	ABCDEFGHJ	130	D F J	156	ABCDEFGHJ	203		
ABCDEFGHJ	24	ABCDEFGHJ	61	F HJ	88	A H	131	ABCDEFGHJ	159	BCDEFG J	211		
ABCDEFGHJ	25	ABCDEFGHJ	62	ABCDEFGHJ	90	BCDEFG J	132	ABCDEFGHJ	162	BCDEFG J	212		
ABCDEFGHJ	26	ABCDEFGHJ	63			BCDEFG J	133	ABCDEFGHJ	171	ABCDEFGHJ	213		

Austin A40
Austin A60

miles in thousands	3	6	9	12	15	18	21	24	27	30	33	36	39	42	45	48	51	54	57	60
look for service code letter	A	B	A	C	A	D	A	C	A	B	A	E	A	B	A	C	A	D	A	C

Code	Job	Code	Job	Code	Job	Code	Job	Code	Job	Code	Job	Code	Job	Code	Job	Code	Job
ABCDE	1	ABCDE	23	C E	47	C E	78	ABCDE	105	B D	131	ABCDE	153	C E	176	ABCDE	211
ABCDE	4	ABCDE	26	ABCDE	49	ABCDE	79	BCDE	106	C E	132	ABCDE	154	ABCDE	181	ABCDE	212
ABCDE	6	ABCDE	27	ABCDE	51	C E	81	A	107	BCDE	133	C E	155	ABCDE	182	BCDE	213
ABCDE	8	BCDE	28	ABCDE	52	C E	83	ABCDE	108	BCDE	134	ABCDE	156	ABCDE	186	ABCDE	220
ABCDE	9	ABCDE	29	ABCDE	53	ABCDE	85	C E	109	BCDE	136	C E	157	ABCDE	187	ABCDE	221
BCDE	12	BCDE	31	BCDE	58	DE	88	BCDE	118	BCDE	137	ABCDE	158	BCDE	189	C E	222
ABCDE	13	ABCDE	34	ABCDE	61	ABCDE	90	BCDE	120	BCDE	140	BCDE	161	BCDE	191	ABCDE	223
ABCDE	18	BCDE	37	ABCDE	63	ABCDE	94	BCDE	128	BCDE	148	ABCDE	162	ABCDE	197	C E	224
ABCDE	19	BCDE	39	BCDE	65	ABCDE	95	BCDE	130	BCDE	151	ABCDE	168	ABCDE	202	C E	226

Austin A110

miles in thousands	3	6	9	12	15	18	21	24	27	30	33	36	39	42	45	48	51	54	57	60
look for service code letter	A	B	A	C	A	D	A	C	A	B	A	E	A	B	A	C	A	D	A	C

Code	Job	Code	Job	Code	Job	Code	Job	Code	Job	Code	Job	Code	Job	Code	Job	Code	Job	Code	Job
ABCDE	1	ABCDE	19	BCDE	39	C E	78	ABCDE	94	BCDE	128	BCDE	148	ABCDE	168	ABCDE	201	C E	222
ABCDE	4	C E	20	C E	47	ABCDE	79	C E	95	ABCDE	130	BCDE	151	AB D	175	ABCDE	202	BCDE	223
ABCDE	5	ABCDE	23	ABCDE	51	C E	81	ABCDE	105	B D	131	ABCDE	153	C E	176	ABCDE	203	BCDE	224
ABCDE	6	ABCDE	26	ABCDE	52	C E	83	BCDE	106	C E	132	ABCDE	154	ABCDE	181	C E	204	BCDE	226
ABCDE	8	ABCDE	27	ABCDE	53	ABCDE	85	A	107	BCDE	133	C E	155	ABCDE	182	ABCDE	211		
ABCDE	9	BCDE	28	BCDE	58	ABCDE	86	ABCDE	108	BCDE	134	ABCDE	156	ABCDE	186	ABCDE	212		
ABCDE	11	ABCDE	29	ABCDE	61	ABCDE	87	C E	109	BCDE	136	ABCDE	158	ABCDE	187	BCDE	213		
ABCDE	13	BCDE	31	ABCDE	63	DE	88	BCDE	118	BCDE	137	BCDE	161	ABCDE	189	ABCDE	220		
ABCDE	18	BCDE	37	BCDE	65	ABCDE	90	BCDE	120	BCDE	140	ABCDE	164	ABCDE	191	ABCDE	221		

Austin Maxi 1500
Austin Maxi 1750

miles in thousands	3	6	9	12	15	18	21	24	27	30	33	36	39	42	45	48	51	54	57	60
look for service code letter	A	B	A	C	A	B	A	C	A	B	A	C	A	B	A	C	A	B	A	C

Code	Job	Code	Job	Code	Job	Code	Job	Code	Job	Code	Job	Code	Job	Code	Job	Code	Job	Code	Job
ABC	1	ABC	21	ABC	51	B	82	C	103	BC	120	C	141	ABC	158	ABC	186	AB	213
ABC	2	ABC	22	ABC	52	B	83	C	104	BC	128	C	142	ABC	159	ABC	187	ABC	218
ABC	4	ABC	23	ABC	53	ABC	85	ABC	105	ABC	130	C	149	B	161	BC	189	ABC	220
ABC	6	ABC	25	ABC	59	A	86	BC	106	A	131	C	152	ABC	163	ABC	191	ABC	221
ABC	7	BC	28	ABC	60	B	87	A	107	B	132	ABC	153	B	172	ABC	197	ABC	223
ABC	8	BC	29	ABC	61	C	88	ABC	108	ABC	133	ABC	154	BC	176	ABC	202	BC	224
ABC	9	BC	31	B	78	ABC	90	AB	109	C	135	C	155	ABC	181	ABC	203	ABC	225
ABC	17	ABC	48	ABC	79	ABC	94	ABC	118	C	136	ABC	156	BC	182	B	204	B	226

Austin/Morris
1100; 1300

miles in thousands	3	6	9	12	15	18	21	24	27	30	33	36	39	42	45	48	51	54	57	60
look for service code letter	A	B	A	C	A	D	A	C	A	B	A	E	A	B	A	C	A	D	A	C

Code	Job	Code	Job	Code	Job	Code	Job	Code	Job	Code	Job	Code	Job	Code	Job	Code	Job	Code	Job
ABCDE	1	ABCDE	21	ABCDE	52	ABCDE	85	ABCDE	105	AB D	131	ABCDE	153	AB D	175	ABCDE	202	ABCDE	225
ABCDE	2	ABCDE	22	ABCDE	53	BCDE	86	BCDE	106	C E	132	ABCDE	154	C E	176	ABCDE	203	BCDE	226
ABCDE	4	ABCDE	23	ABCDE	59	BCDE	87	A	107	BCDE	133	C E	155	ABCDE	181	E	206		
ABCDE	6	ABCDE	25	ABCDE	60	DE	88	BCDE	108	C E	134	ABCDE	156	BCDE	182	BCDE	213		
ABCDE	7	BCDE	28	ABCDE	61	ABCDE	90	BCDE	109	C E	136	ABCDE	158	BCDE	186	ABCDE	220		
ABCDE	8	BCDE	29	C E	78	ABCDE	94	BCDE	118	C E	137	BCDE	161	BCDE	187	ABCDE	221		
ABCDE	9	BCDE	31	ABCDE	79	E	100	C E	120	C E	140	BCDE	164	BCDE	189	C E	222		
ABCDE	17	ABCDE	48	C E	82	E	103	BCDE	128	C E	148	C E	168	BCDE	191	ABCDE	223		
ABCDE	18	ABCDE	51	C E	83	C E	104	ABCDE	130	C E	151	C E	173	ABCDE	197	BCDE	224		

Austin/Morris
1000 and 1300 automatic

miles in thousands	3	6	9	12	15	18	21	24	27	30	33	36	39	42	45	48	51	54	57	60
look for service code letter	A	B	A	C	A	D	A	C	A	B	A	E	A	B	A	C	A	D	A	C

Code	Job	Code	Job	Code	Job	Code	Job	Code	Job	Code	Job	Code	Job	Code	Job	Code	Job	Code	Job
ABCDE	1	ABCDE	21	ABCDE	59	BCDE	87	A	107	BCDE	133	C E	155	ABCDE	181	E	206	BCDE	226
ABCDE	2	ABCDE	22	ABCDE	60	DE	88	BCDE	108	C E	134	ABCDE	156	BCDE	182	BCDE	213		
ABCDE	4	ABCDE	23	ABCDE	61	ABCDE	90	BCDE	109	C E	136	ABCDE	158	BCDE	186	ABCDE	218		
ABCDE	6	ABCDE	25	C E	78	ABCDE	94	BCDE	118	C E	137	BCDE	161	BCDE	187	ABCDE	220		
ABCDE	7	BCDE	28	ABCDE	79	E	100	C E	120	C E	140	BCDE	164	BCDE	189	ABCDE	221		
ABCDE	8	BCDE	29	C E	82	E	103	BCDE	128	C E	148	C E	168	BCDE	191	C E	222		
ABCDE	9	BCDE	31	C E	83	C E	104	ABCDE	130	C E	151	C E	173	ABCDE	197	ABCDE	223		
ABCDE	17	ABCDE	51	ABCDE	85	ABCDE	105	AB D	131	ABCDE	153	AB D	175	ABCDE	202	BCDE	224		
ABCDE	18	ABCDE	52	BCDE	86	BCDE	106	C E	132	ABCDE	154	C E	176	ABCDE	203	ABCDE	225		

British Leyland

Jobs to be done

Read page 40 before using these charts

Austin/Morris 1300 GT / MG 1100; 1300 / Riley Kestrel

miles in thousands	3	6	9	12	15	18	21	24	27	30	33	36	39	42	45	48	51	54	57	60
age of car in months	3	6	9	12	15	18	21	24	27	30	33	36	39	42	45	48	51	54	57	60
look for service code letter	A	B	A	C	A	D	A	C	A	B	A	E	A	B	A	C	A	D	A	C

Code	Job	Code	Job	Code	Job	Code	Job	Code	Job	Code	Job	Code	Job	Code	Job	Code	Job	Code	Job
ABCDE	1	ABCDE	21	ABCDE	52	ABCDE	85	BCDE	106	C E	132	ABCDE	154	AB D	175	ABCDE	202	ABCDE	225
ABCDE	2	ABCDE	22	ABCDE	53	BCDE	86	A	107	BCDE	133	C E	155	C E	176	ABCDE	203	BCDE	226
ABCDE	4	ABCDE	23	ABCDE	59	BCDE	87	BCDE	108	C E	134	ABCDE	156	ABCDE	181	E	206		
ABCDE	6	ABCDE	25	ABCDE	60	DE	88	BCDE	109	C E	136	C E	157	BCDE	182	BCDE	213		
ABCDE	7	BCDE	28	ABCDE	61	ABCDE	94	BCDE	118	C E	137	ABCDE	158	BCDE	186	ABCDE	220		
ABCDE	8	BCDE	29	C E	78	E	100	C E	120	C E	140	BCDE	161	BCDE	189	ABCDE	221		
ABCDE	9	BCDE	31	C E	79	E	103	BCDE	128	C E	148	BCDE	164	BCDE	191	C E	222		
ABCDE	17	ABCDE	48	C E	82	C E	104	ABCDE	130	C E	151	C E	168	ABCDE	201	ABCDE	223		
ABCDE	18	ABCDE	51	C E	83	ABCDE	105	AB D	131	ABCDE	153	C E	173			BCDE	224		

Austin/Morris 1800 Mk II

miles in thousands	3	6	9	12	15	18	21	24	27	30	33	36	39	42	45	48	51	54	57	60
age of car in months	3	6	9	12	15	18	21	24	27	30	33	36	39	42	45	48	51	54	57	60
look for service code letter	A	B	A	C	A	D	A	C	A	B	A	E	A	B	A	C	A	D	A	C

Code	Job	Code	Job	Code	Job	Code	Job	Code	Job	Code	Job	Code	Job	Code	Job	Code	Job	Code	Job
ABCDE	1	ABCDE	18	ABCDE	48	ABCDE	79	ABCDE	94	BCDE	120	C E	137	ABCDE	159	ABCDE	187	ABCDE	220
ABCDE	2	ABCDE	21	ABCDE	51	C E	81	C E	103	BCDE	128	C E	140	BCDE	163	BCDE	189	ABCDE	221
ABCDE	4	ABCDE	22	ABCDE	52	C E	83	ABCDE	105	BCDE	130	C E	151	C E	173	BCDE	191	C E	222
ABCDE	6	ABCDE	23	ABCDE	53	ABCDE	85	BCDE	106	B D	131	ABCDE	153	AB D	175	BCDE	197	ABCDE	223
ABCDE	7	ABCDE	25	BCDE	59	BCDE	86	A	107	C E	132	ABCDE	154	C E	176	ABCDE	202	BCDE	224
ABCDE	8	ABCDE	28	BCDE	60	BCDE	87	BCDE	108	BCDE	133	C E	155	ABCDE	181	ABCDE	203	ABCDE	225
ABCDE	9	ABCDE	29	ABCDE	61	DE	88	BCDE	109	C E	134	ABCDE	156	BCDE	182	E	204	BCDE	226
ABCDE	17	BCDE	31	C E	78	ABCDE	90	BCDE	118	C E	136	C E	157	ABCDE	186	BCDE	213		

Austin/Morris 1800 Mk II automatic

miles in thousands	3	6	9	12	15	18	21	24	27	30	33	36	39	42	45	48	51	54	57	60
age of car in months	3	6	9	12	15	18	21	24	27	30	33	36	39	42	45	48	51	54	57	60
look for service code letter	A	B	A	C	A	D	A	C	A	B	A	E	A	B	A	C	A	D	A	C

Code	Job	Code	Job	Code	Job	Code	Job	Code	Job	Code	Job	Code	Job	Code	Job	Code	Job	Code	Job
ABCDE	1	ABCDE	18	ABCDE	51	C E	83	ABCDE	105	BCDE	130	C E	151	C E	173	BCDE	191	ABCDE	221
ABCDE	2	ABCDE	21	ABCDE	52	ABCDE	85	BCDE	106	B D	131	ABCDE	153	AB D	175	BCDE	197	C E	222
ABCDE	4	ABCDE	22	BCDE	59	BCDE	86	A	107	C E	132	ABCDE	154	C E	176	ABCDE	202	ABCDE	223
ABCDE	6	ABCDE	23	ABCDE	60	BCDE	87	BCDE	108	BCDE	133	C E	155	ABCDE	181	ABCDE	203	BCDE	224
ABCDE	7	ABCDE	25	ABCDE	61	DE	88	BCDE	109	C E	134	ABCDE	156	BCDE	182	E	204	ABCDE	225
ABCDE	8	ABCDE	28	C E	78	ABCDE	90	BCDE	118	C E	136	C E	157	ABCDE	186	BCDE	213	BCDE	226
ABCDE	9	ABCDE	29	ABCDE	79	ABCDE	94	BCDE	120	C E	137	ABCDE	159	ABCDE	187	A	218		
ABCDE	17	BCDE	31	C E	81	C E	103	BCDE	128	C E	140	BCDE	163	BCDE	189	ABCDE	220		

Austin/Morris 1800 'S'

miles in thousands	3	6	9	12	15	18	21	24	27	30	33	36	39	42	45	48	51	54	57	60
age of car in months	3	6	9	12	15	18	21	24	27	30	33	36	39	42	45	48	51	54	57	60
look for service code letter	A	B	A	C	A	D	A	C	A	B	A	E	A	B	A	C	A	D	A	C

Code	Job	Code	Job	Code	Job	Code	Job	Code	Job	Code	Job	Code	Job	Code	Job	Code	Job	Code	Job
ABCDE	1	ABCDE	18	ABCDE	48	C E	78	ABCDE	90	BCDE	118	C E	136	C E	157	ABCDE	186	BCDE	213
ABCDE	2	ABCDE	21	ABCDE	51	ABCDE	79	ABCDE	94	BCDE	120	C E	137	ABCDE	159	ABCDE	187	ABCDE	220
ABCDE	4	ABCDE	22	ABCDE	52	C E	81	C E	103	BCDE	128	C E	140	BCDE	163	BCDE	189	ABCDE	221
ABCDE	6	ABCDE	23	ABCDE	53	C E	83	ABCDE	105	BCDE	130	C E	151	C E	173	BCDE	191	C E	222
ABCDE	7	ABCDE	25	BCDE	59	ABCDE	85	BCDE	106	B D	131	ABCDE	153	AB D	175	BCDE	201	ABCDE	223
ABCDE	8	ABCDE	28	ABCDE	60	BCDE	86	A	107	C E	132	ABCDE	154	C E	176	ABCDE	202	BCDE	224
ABCDE	9	ABCDE	29	ABCDE	61	BCDE	87	BCDE	108	BCDE	133	C E	155	ABCDE	181	ABCDE	203	ABCDE	225
ABCDE	17	BCDE	31	BCDE	62	DE	88	BCDE	109	C E	134	ABCDE	156	BCDE	182	E	204	BCDE	226

Austin/Morris 2200

look for service code letter	A	B	A	C	A	D	A	C	A	B	A	E	A	B	A	C	A	D	A	C

Code	Job	Code	Job	Code	Job	Code	Job	Code	Job	Code	Job	Code	Job	Code	Job	Code	Job	Code	Job
ABCDE	1	ABCDE	21	ABCDE	52	ABCDE	85	A	107	BCDE	133	C E	155	BCDE	182	ABCDE	209	BCDE	226
ABCDE	2	ABCDE	22	ABCDE	53	BCDE	86	BCDE	108	C E	135	ABCDE	156	ABCDE	186	ABCDE	210		
ABCDE	4	ABCDE	23	BCDE	59	BCDE	87	BCDE	109	C E	136	C E	157	ABCDE	187	BCDE	213		
ABCDE	6	ABCDE	25	ABCDE	60	DE	88	BCDE	118	C E	141	ABCDE	159	BCDE	189	ABCDE	220		
ABCDE	7	ABCDE	28	ABCDE	61	ABCDE	90	BCDE	120	C E	142	BCDE	163	BCDE	191	ABCDE	221		
ABCDE	8	ABCDE	29	C E	78	ABCDE	94	BCDE	128	C E	149	C E	173	BCDE	201	C E	222		
ABCDE	9	BCDE	31	ABCDE	79	C E	103	BCDE	130	C E	152	AB D	175	ABCDE	202	ABCDE	223		
ABCDE	17	ABCDE	48	CDE	81	ABCDE	105	B D	131	ABCDE	153	C E	176	ABCDE	203	BCDE	224		
ABCDE	18	ABCDE	51	C E	83	BCDE	106	C E	132	ABCDE	154	ABCDE	181	E	204	ABCDE	225		

Austin/Morris Midget / Sprite

miles in thousands	3	6	9	12	15	18	21	24	27	30	33	36	39	42	45	48	51	54	57	60
age of car in months	3	6	9	12	15	18	21	24	27	30	33	36	39	42	45	48	51	54	57	60
look for service code letter	A	B	A	C	A	B	A	C	A	B	A	D	A	B	A	C	A	B	A	C

Code	Job	Code	Job	Code	Job	Code	Job	Code	Job	Code	Job	Code	Job	Code	Job	Code	Job	Code	Job
ABCD	1	ABCD	19	BCD	31	BCD	61	BCD	87	BCD	109	CD	134	CD	155	BCD	182	ABCD	220
ABCD	4	CD	20	BCD	32	BCD	63	D	88	BCD	118	CD	136	ABCD	156	ABCD	186	ABCD	221
ABCD	6	ABCD	21	ABCD	34	CD	78	ABCD	89	BCD	120	CD	137	CD	157	ABCD	187	CD	222
ABCD	8	ABCD	22	BCD	37	ABCD	79	ABCD	94	BCD	128	CD	140	ABCD	158	BCD	189	ABCD	223
ABCD	9	BCD	23	ABCD	51	CD	81	ABCD	105	ABCD	130	CD	148	BCD	161	BCD	191	BCD	224
ABCD	13	BCD	27	ABCD	52	CD	83	BCD	106	B	131	CD	151	BCD	164	BCD	201	ABCD	225
ABCD	18	BCD	28	ABCD	53	ABCD	85	A	107	CD	132	ABCD	153	CD	173	ABCD	202	BCD	226
		BCD	29	BCD	58	BCD	86	BCD	108	BCD	133	ABCD	154	BCD	178	BCD	213		

British Leyland

Read page 40 before using these charts

Jobs to be done

Austin/Morris
Mini 850
Mini 1000
Riley Elf
Wolseley
Hornet

miles in thousands	3	6	9	12	15	18	21	24	27	30	33	36	39	42	45	48	51	54	57	60
age of car in months	3	6	9	12	15	18	21	24	27	30	33	36	39	42	45	48	51	54	57	60
look for service code letter	A	B	A	C	A	D	A	C	A	B	A	E	A	B	A	C	A	D	A	C

Code	Job	Code	Job	Code	Job	Code	Job	Code	Job	Code	Job	Code	Job	Code	Job	Code	Job	Code	Job
ABCDE	1	ABCDE	21	ABCDE	52	ABCDE	85	ABCDE	105	AB D	131	ABCDE	153	AB D	175	ABCDE	202	ABCDE	225
ABCDE	2	ABCDE	22	ABCDE	53	BCDE	86	BCDE	106	C E	132	ABCDE	154	C E	176	ABCDE	203	BCDE	226
ABCDE	4	ABCDE	23	ABCDE	59	BCDE	87	A	107	BCDE	133	C E	155	ABCDE	181	E	206		
ABCDE	6	ABCDE	25	ABCDE	60	DE	88	BCDE	108	C E	134	ABCDE	156	BCDE	182	BCDE	213		
ABCDE	7	BCDE	28	ABCDE	61	ABCDE	90	BCDE	109	C E	136	BCDE	161	BCDE	186	ABCDE	220		
ABCDE	8	BCDE	29	C E	78	ABCDE	94	BCDE	118	C E	137	BCDE	164	BCDE	187	ABCDE	221		
ABCDE	9	BCDE	31	ABCDE	79	E	100	C E	120	C E	140	BCDE	164	BCDE	189	C E	222		
ABCDE	17	ABCDE	48	C E	82	E	103	BCDE	128	C E	148	C E	168	BCDE	191	ABCDE	223		
ABCDE	18	ABCDE	51	C E	83	C E	104	ABCDE	130	C E	151	C E	173	ABCDE	197	BCDE	224		

Austin/Morris
Mini Cooper
Mini Cooper S
Mini Clubman

miles in thousands	3	6	9	12	15	18	21	24	27	30	33	36	39	42	45	48	51	54	57	60
age of car in months	3	6	9	12	15	18	21	24	27	30	33	36	39	42	45	48	51	54	57	60
look for service code letter	A	B	A	C	A	D	A	C	A	B	A	E	A	B	A	C	A	D	A	C

Code	Job	Code	Job	Code	Job	Code	Job	Code	Job	Code	Job	Code	Job	Code	Job	Code	Job	Code	Job
ABCDE	1	ABCDE	21	ABCDE	52	ABCDE	85	ABCDE	105	AB D	131	ABCDE	153	C E	173	ABCDE	201	BCDE	224
ABCDE	2	ABCDE	22	ABCDE	53	BCDE	86	BCDE	106	C E	132	ABCDE	154	AB D	175	ABCDE	202	ABCDE	225
ABCDE	4	ABCDE	23	ABCDE	59	BCDE	87	A	107	BCDE	133	C E	155	C E	176	ABCDE	203	BCDE	226
ABCDE	6	ABCDE	25	ABCDE	60	DE	88	BCDE	108	C E	134	ABCDE	156	ABCDE	181	E	206		
ABCDE	7	BCDE	28	ABCDE	61	ABCDE	90	BCDE	109	C E	136	C E	157	BCDE	182	BCDE	213		
ABCDE	8	BCDE	29	C E	78	ABCDE	94	BCDE	118	C E	137	ABCDE	158	BCDE	186	ABCDE	220		
ABCDE	9	BCDE	31	ABCDE	79	E	100	C E	120	C E	140	BCDE	161	BCDE	187	ABCDE	221		
ABCDE	17	ABCDE	48	C E	82	E	103	BCDE	128	C E	148	BCDE	164	BCDE	189	C E	222		
ABCDE	18	ABCDE	51	C E	83	C E	104	ABCDE	130	C E	151	C E	168	BCDE	191	ABCDE	223		

Jaguar
3·4 & 3·8

miles in thousands	3	6	9	12	15	18	21	24	27	30	33	36	39	42	45	48	51	54	57	60
look for service code letter	A	B	A	C	A	E	A	D	A	B	A	F	A	B	A	D	A	E	A	C

Code	Job	Code	Job	Code	Job	Code	Job	Code	Job	Code	Job	Code	Job	Code	Job
ABCDEF	1	BCDEF	26	CD F	49	BCDEF	87	ABCDEF	128	ABCDEF	153	BCDEF	186	CD F	222
ABCDEF	5	ABCDEF	28	ABCDEF	51	EF	88	ABCDEF	130	ABCDEF	154	ABCDEF	188	BC E	223
ABCDEF	6	ABCDEF	29	ABCDEF	52	BCDEF	93	AB E	131	CD F	155	BCDEF	194	BC E	224
ABCDEF	8	CD F	30	ABCDEF	53	BCDEF	94	CD F	132	ABCDEF	156	BCDEF	196	BC E	225
BCDEF	9	BCDEF	31	CD F	55	CD F	96	ABCDEF	133	BCDEF	158	BCDEF	201	BC E	226
ABCDEF	11	BCDEF	34	AB E	58	ABCDEF	105	D F	135	BCDEF	161	ABCDEF	202		
BCDEF	13	CD F	35	ABCDEF	61	ABCDEF	106	D F	136	BCDEF	164	ABCDEF	203		
ABCDEF	18	CD F	36	ABCDEF	63	ABCDEF	108	D F	141	A	175	BCDEF	207		
ABCDEF	19	AB E	37	BCDEF	64	ABCDEF	109	D F	142	BCDEF	176	ABCDEF	213		
BCDEF	23	CD F	38	BCDEF	65	ABCDEF	118	D F	149	ABCDEF	177	ABCDEF	220		
BCDEF	25	CD F	41	BCDEF	86	ABCDEF	120	D F	152	ABCDEF	182	ABCDEF	221		

Jaguar
3·8 S type

miles in thousands	3	6	9	12	15	18	21	24	27	30	33	36	39	42	45	48	51	54	57	60
look for service code letter	A	B	A	C	A	E	A	D	A	B	A	F	A	B	A	D	A	E	A	C

Code	Job	Code	Job	Code	Job	Code	Job	Code	Job	Code	Job	Code	Job	Code	Job
ABCDEF	1	ABCDEF	28	ABCDEF	51	ABCDEF	66	ABCDEF	118	D F	149	ABCDEF	177	ABCDEF	220
ABCDEF	5	ABCDEF	29	ABCDEF	52	BCDEF	86	ABCDEF	120	D F	152	BCDEF	182	ABCDEF	221
ABCDEF	6	CD F	30	ABCDEF	53	BCDEF	87	ABCDEF	128	ABCDEF	153	BCDEF	186	CD F	222
ABCDEF	8	BCDEF	31	CD F	55	EF	88	ABCDEF	130	ABCDEF	154	ABCDEF	188	BC E	223
BCDEF	9	BCDEF	34	AB E	58	BCDEF	89	AB E	131	CD F	155	BCDEF	194	BC E	224
ABCDEF	11	CD F	35	BCDEF	59	BCDEF	94	CD F	132	ABCDEF	156	BCDEF	196	BC E	225
ABCDEF	18	CD F	36	ABCDEF	61	CD F	96	ABCDEF	133	BCDEF	158	BCDEF	201	BC E	226
ABCDEF	19	AB E	37	BCDEF	62	ABCDEF	105	D F	135	BCDEF	161	ABCDEF	202		
BCDEF	23	CD F	38	BCDEF	63	ABCDEF	106	D F	136	BCDEF	164	ABCDEF	203		
BCDEF	25	CD F	41	BCDEF	64	ABCDEF	108	D F	141	A	175	BCDEF	207		
BCDEF	26	CD F	49	BCDEF	65	ABCDEF	109	D F	142	BCDEF	176	ABCDEF	213		

Morris
Marina 1·3
Marina 1·8

miles in thousands	3	6	9	12	15	18	21	24	27	30	33	36	39	42	45	48	51	54	57	60
age of car in months	3	6	9	12	15	18	21	24	27	30	33	36	39	42	45	48	51	54	57	60
look for service code letter	A	B	A	C	A	D	A	C	A	B	A	E	A	B	A	C	A	D	A	C

Code	Job	Code	Job	Code	Job	Code	Job	Code	Job	Code	Job	Code	Job	Code	Job	Code	Job	Code	Job
ABCDE	1	ABCDE	21	ABCDE	51	ABCDE	80	C E	95	BCDE	128	C E	148	A	175	ABCDE	202	ABCDE	225
ABCDE	4	ABCDE	22	ABCDE	52	C E	81	C E	101	ABCDE	130	C E	151	BCDE	176	ABCDE	203	BCDE	226
ABCDE	6	BCDE	23	ABCDE	53	C E	83	ABCDE	105	B D	131	ABCDE	153	ABCDE	181	E	204		
ABCDE	8	BCDE	25	BCDE	58	ABCDE	85	BCDE	106	C E	132	ABCDE	154	BCDE	182	BCDE	213		
ABCDE	9	BCDE	28	ABCDE	61	BCDE	86	A	107	BCDE	133	C E	155	ABCDE	186	ABCDE	220		
ABCDE	13	BCDE	29	ABCDE	63	BCDE	87	BCDE	108	C E	134	ABCDE	156	ABCDE	187	ABCDE	221		
ABCDE	15	BCDE	32	ABCDE	66	DE	88	BCDE	109	C E	136	ABCDE	158	BCDE	189	C E	222		
ABCDE	19	ABCDE	34	C E	78	ABCDE	90	BCDE	118	C E	137	BCDE	161	BCDE	191	ABCDE	223		
C E	20	BCDE	37	ABCDE	79	ABCDE	94	BCDE	120	C E	140	BCDE	163	ABCDE	197	BCDE	224		

British Leyland

Jobs to be done

Read page 40 before using these charts

Morris Marina 1·8 TC

	3	6	9	12	15	18	21	24	27	30	33	36	39	42	45	48	51	54	57	60
miles in thousands	3	6	9	12	15	18	21	24	27	30	33	36	39	42	45	48	51	54	57	60
age of car in months	3	6	9	12	15	18	21	24	27	30	33	36	39	42	45	48	51	54	57	60
look for service code letter	A	B	A	C	A	D	A	C	A	B	A	E	A	B	A	C	A	D	A	C

Code	Job	Code	Job	Code	Job	Code	Job	Code	Job	Code	Job	Code	Job	Code	Job	Code	Job	Code	Job
ABCDE	1	ABCDE	21	ABCDE	51	ABCDE	80	C E	95	BCDE	128	C E	148	BCDE	176	ABCDE	203	BCDE	226
ABCDE	4	ABCDE	22	ABCDE	52	C E	81	C E	101	ABCDE	130	C E	151	ABCDE	181	E	204		
ABCDE	6	BCDE	23	ABCDE	53	C E	83	ABCDE	105	B D	131	ABCDE	153	BCDE	182	BCDE	213		
ABCDE	8	BCDE	25	BCDE	58	ABCDE	85	BCDE	106	C E	132	ABCDE	154	BCDE	186	ABCDE	220		
ABCDE	9	BCDE	28	ABCDE	61	BCDE	86	A	107	BCDE	133	C E	155	ABCDE	187	ABCDE	221		
ABCDE	13	BCDE	29	ABCDE	63	BCDE	87	BCDE	108	C E	134	ABCDE	156	BCDE	189	C E	222		
ABCDE	15	BCDE	31	ABCDE	66	DE	88	BCDE	109	C E	136	ABCDE	159	BCDE	191	ABCDE	223		
ABCDE	19	ABCDE	34	C E	78	ABCDE	90	BCDE	118	C E	137	BCDE	163	ABCDE	201	BCDE	224		
C E	20	BCDE	37	ABCDE	79	ABCDE	94	BCDE	120	A	140	A	175	ABCDE	202	ABCDE	225		

Morris Minor 1000

	3	6	9	12	15	18	21	24	27	30	33	36	39	42	45	48	51	54	57	60
miles in thousands	3	6	9	12	15	18	21	24	27	30	33	36	39	42	45	48	51	54	57	60
age of car in months	3	6	9	12	15	18	21	24	27	30	33	36	39	42	45	48	51	54	57	60
look for service code letter	A	B	A	C	A	D	A	C	A	B	A	E	A	B	A	C	A	D	A	C

Code	Job	Code	Job	Code	Job	Code	Job	Code	Job	Code	Job	Code	Job	Code	Job	Code	Job	Code	Job
ABCDE	1	ABCDE	21	BCDE	42	ABCDE	79	ABCDE	105	B D	131	ABCDE	153	A	175	BCDE	197	BCDE	226
ABCDE	4	ABCDE	22	BCDE	43	C E	81	BCDE	106	C E	132	ABCDE	154	BCDE	176	ABCDE	202		
ABCDE	6	ABCDE	23	ABCDE	51	C E	83	A	107	BCDE	133	C E	155	ABCDE	181	BCDE	213		
ABCDE	8	ABCDE	27	ABCDE	52	ABCDE	85	ABCDE	108	C E	134	ABCDE	156	BCDE	182	ABCDE	220		
ABCDE	9	BCDE	28	BCDE	58	DE	88	BCDE	109	C E	136	C E	157	BCDE	186	ABCDE	221		
ABCDE	13	BCDE	29	BCDE	61	ABCDE	90	BCDE	118	C E	137	ABCDE	158	ABCDE	187	C E	222		
ABCDE	15	BCDE	31	BCDE	63	ABCDE	94	BCDE	120	C E	140	BCDE	161	BCDE	189	ABCDE	223		
ABCDE	19	ABCDE	34	BCDE	65	C E	97	BCDE	128	C E	148	BCDE	164	BCDE	191	BCDE	224		
C E	20	BCDE	37	C E	78	C E	101	ABCDE	130	C E	151	ABCDE	168	BCDE	194	ABCDE	225		

Morris MGB

	3	6	9	12	15	18	21	24	27	30	33	36	39	42	45	48	51	54	57	60
miles in thousands	3	6	9	12	15	18	21	24	27	30	33	36	39	42	45	48	51	54	57	60
age of car in months	3	6	9	12	15	18	21	24	27	30	33	36	39	42	45	48	51	54	57	60
look for service code letter	A	B	A	C	A	D	A	C	A	B	A	E	A	B	A	C	A	D	A	C

Code	Job	Code	Job	Code	Job	Code	Job	Code	Job	Code	Job	Code	Job	Code	Job	Code	Job	Code	Job
ABCDE	1	C E	20	BCDE	37	ABCDE	79	C E	95	BCDE	128	C E	148	A	175	ABCDE	203	BC E	226
ABCDE	4	ABCDE	21	ABCDE	51	C E	81	C E	101	ABCDE	130	C E	151	BCDE	176	E	204		
ABCDE	6	ABCDE	22	ABCDE	52	C E	83	ABCDE	105	B D	131	ABCDE	153	BCDE	182	BCDE	213		
ABCDE	8	BC E	23	ABCDE	53	ABCDE	85	BCDE	106	C E	132	ABCDE	154	ABCDE	186	ABCDE	220		
ABCDE	9	ABCDE	27	BCDE	58	BCDE	86	A	107	BCDE	133	C E	155	ABCDE	187	ABCDE	221		
ABCDE	11	BCDE	28	ABCDE	61	BCDE	87	BCDE	108	C E	134	ABCDE	156	BCDE	189	C E	222		
ABCDE	13	BCDE	29	ABCDE	63	DE	88	BCDE	109	C E	136	ABCDE	159	BCDE	191	ABC E	223		
ABCDE	18	BCDE	31	ABCDE	66	ABCDE	90	BCDE	118	C E	137	BCDE	164	ABCDE	201	BC E	224		
ABCDE	19	ABCDE	34	C E	78	ABCDE	94	BCDE	120	C E	140	BCDE	173	ABCDE	202	ABC E	225		

Morris MGC

	3	6	9	12	15	18	21	24	27	30	33	36	39	42	45	48	51	54	57	60
miles in thousands	3	6	9	12	15	18	21	24	27	30	33	36	39	42	45	48	51	54	57	60
age of car in months	3	6	9	12	15	18	21	24	27	30	33	36	39	42	45	48	51	54	57	60
look for service code letter	A	B	A	C	A	D	A	C	A	B	A	E	A	B	A	C	A	D	A	C

Code	Job	Code	Job	Code	Job	Code	Job	Code	Job	Code	Job	Code	Job	Code	Job	Code	Job	Code	Job
ABCDE	1	ABCDE	19	BCDE	31	BCDE	86	BCDE	106	B D	131	C E	151	A	175	ABCDE	202	ABCDE	223
ABCDE	4	C E	20	ABCDE	34	BCDE	87	A	107	C E	132	ABCDE	153	BCDE	176	ABCDE	203	BCDE	224
ABCDE	6	ABCDE	21	ABCDE	51	DE	88	BCDE	108	BCD	133	ABCDE	154	BCDE	182	E	204	ABCDE	225
ABCDE	8	ABCDE	22	ABCDE	52	ABCDE	90	BCDE	109	C E	134	C E	155	ABCDE	186	BCDE	213	BCDE	226
ABCDE	9	ABCDE	23	BCDE	58	ABCDE	94	BCDE	118	C E	136	ABCDE	156	ABCDE	187	ABCDE	214		
ABCDE	11	ABCDE	27	ABCDE	61	C E	95	BCDE	120	C E	137	ABCDE	159	BCDE	189	ABCDE	220		
ABCDE	13	BCDE	28	ABCDE	63	C E	101	BCDE	128	C E	140	BCDE	164	BCDE	191	ABCDE	221		
ABCDE	18	BCDE	29	ABCDE	66	ABCDE	105	ABCDE	130	C E	148	BCDE	173	ABCDE	201	C E	222		

Rover 2000 SC

	3	6	9	12	15	18	21	24	27	30	33	36	39	42	45	48	51	54	57	60
miles in thousands	3	6	9	12	15	18	21	24	27	30	33	36	39	42	45	48	51	54	57	60
age of car in months	3	6	9	12	15	18	21	24	27	30	33	36	39	42	45	48	51	54	57	60
look for service code letter	A	B	A	C	A	D	A	C	A	B	A	D	A	B	A	C	A	D	A	C

Code	Job	Code	Job	Code	Job	Code	Job	Code	Job	Code	Job	Code	Job	Code	Job	Code	Job	Code	Job
ABCD	1	ABCD	19	ABCD	51	BCD	64	BCD	106	BCD	130	ABCD	156	BCD	182	CD	211	ABCD	225
ABCD	4	BCD	26	ABCD	52	ABCD	86	A	107	B D	131	ABCD	158	BCD	186	BCD	213	BCD	226
ABCD	6	BCD	28	ABCD	53	ABCD	87	BCD	108	CD	132	CD	161	ABCD	188	ABCD	220		
ABCD	8	BCD	29	BCD	58	D	88	BCD	109	BCD	133	CD	162	BCD	191	ABCD	221		
ABCD	12	BCD	32	ABCD	59	ABCD	89	BCD	118	ABCD	153	CD	173	BCD	197	CD	222		
CD	16	ABCD	34	ABCD	61	ABCD	94	BCD	120	ABCD	154	A	175	ABCD	202	ABCD	223		
ABCD	18	BCD	37	ABCD	63	ABCD	105	BCD	128	CD	155	BCD	176	ABCD	203	BCD	224		

Rover 2000 SC automatic

	3	6	9	12	15	18	21	24	27	30	33	36	39	42	45	48	51	54	57	60
miles in thousands	3	6	9	12	15	18	21	24	27	30	33	36	39	42	45	48	51	54	57	60
age of car in months	3	6	9	12	15	18	21	24	27	30	33	36	39	42	45	48	51	54	57	60
look for service code letter	A	B	A	C	A	D	A	C	A	B	A	D	A	B	A	C	A	D	A	C

Code	Job	Code	Job	Code	Job	Code	Job	Code	Job	Code	Job	Code	Job	Code	Job	Code	Job	Code	Job
ABCD	1	ABCD	19	ABCD	52	ABCD	87	BCD	108	CD	132	CD	161	ABCD	188	BCD	214	BCD	226
ABCD	4	BCD	26	BCD	58	D	88	BCD	109	BCD	133	CD	162	BCD	191	ABCD	220		
ABCD	6	BCD	28	ABCD	59	ABCD	89	BCD	118	ABCD	153	CD	173	BCD	197	ABCD	221		
ABCD	8	BCD	29	ABCD	61	ABCD	94	BCD	120	ABCD	154	A	175	ABCD	202	CD	222		
ABCD	12	BCD	32	ABCD	63	ABCD	105	BCD	128	CD	155	BCD	176	ABCD	203	ABCD	223		
CD	16	ABCD	34	BCD	64	BCD	106	BCD	130	ABCD	156	BCD	182	CD	211	BCD	224		
ABCD	18	ABCD	51	ABCD	86	A	107	B D	131	ABCD	158	BCD	186	BCD	213	ABCD	225		

British Leyland

Read page 40 before using these charts

Jobs to be done

Rover 2000 TC

miles in thousands	3	6	9	12	15	18	21	24	27	30	33	36	39	42	45	48	51	54	57	60
age of car in months	3	6	9	12	15	18	21	24	27	30	33	36	39	42	45	48	51	54	57	60
look for service code letter	A	B	A	C	A	D	A	C	A	B	A	D	A	B	A	C	A	D	A	C

Code	Job	Code	Job	Code	Job	Code	Job	Code	Job	Code	Job	Code	Job	Code	Job	Code	Job	Code	Job
ABCD	1	ABCD	19	ABCD	51	BCD	64	BCD	106	BCD	130	ABCD	156	BCD	182	CD	211	ABCD	225
ABCD	4	BCD	26	ABCD	52	ABCD	86	A	107	B D	131	ABCD	158	BCD	186	BCD	213	BCD	226
ABCD	6	BCD	28	ABCD	53	ABCD	87	BCD	108	CD	132	CD	161	ABCD	188	ABCD	220		
ABCD	8	BCD	29	BCD	58	D	88	BCD	109	CD	133	CD	162	BCD	191	ABCD	221		
ABCD	12	BCD	32	ABCD	59	ABCD	89	BCD	118	ABCD	153	CD	173	BCD	201		222		
CD	16	ABCD	34	ABCD	61	ABCD	94	BCD	120	ABCD	154	A	175	ABCD	202	ABCD	223		
ABCD	18	BCD	37	ABCD	63	ABCD	105	BCD	128	CD	155	BCD	176	ABCD	203	BCD	224		

Triumph 1300

miles in thousands	3	6	9	12	15	18	21	24	27	30	33	36	39	42	45	48	51	54	57	60
age of car in months	3	6	9	12	15	18	21	24	27	30	33	36	39	42	45	48	51	54	57	60
look for service code letter	A	B	A	C	A	D	A	C	A	B	A	D	A	B	A	C	A	D	A	C

Code	Job	Code	Job	Code	Job	Code	Job	Code	Job	Code	Job	Code	Job	Code	Job	Code	Job	Code	Job
ABCD	1	ABCD	19	CD	31	ABCD	61	ABCD	85	A	107	CD	132	ABCD	153	B D	175	ABCD	202
ABCD	2	ABCD	21	BCD	37	BCD	63	ABCD	86	BCD	108	BCD	133	ABCD	154	CD	176	BCD	213
ABCD	6	ABCD	22	ABCD	51	BCD	65	ABCD	87	BCD	109	CD	134	CD	155	CD	183	ABCD	220
ABCD	7	BCD	23	ABCD	52	BCD	66	D	88	BCD	118	CD	136	ABCD	156	BCD	186	ABCD	221
ABCD	8	ABCD	24	ABCD	53	CD	78	ABCD	89	BCD	120	CD	137	CD	157	ABCD	187	CD	222
ABCD	9	BCD	25	BCD	58	ABCD	79	BCD	94	BCD	128	CD	140	ABCD	158	BCD	189	ABCD	223
ABCD	11	BCD	28	ABCD	59	CD	81	ABCD	105	BCD	130	CD	148	CD	161	BCD	192	BCD	224
ABCD	18	BCD	29	ABCD	60	CD	83	BCD	106	B D	131	CD	151	CD	162	BCD	198	BCD	226

Triumph 1500

miles in thousands	3	6	9	12	15	18	21	24	27	30	33	36	39	42	45	48	51	54	57	60
age of car in months	3	6	9	12	15	18	21	24	27	30	33	36	39	42	45	48	51	54	57	60
look for service code letter	A	B	A	C	A	D	A	C	A	B	A	E	A	B	A	C	A	D	A	C

Code	Job	Code	Job	Code	Job	Code	Job	Code	Job	Code	Job	Code	Job	Code	Job	Code	Job
ABCDE	1	ABCDE	21	ABCDE	51	BCDE	66	ABCDE	89	BCDE	128	C E	148	B D	175	ABCDE	203
ABCDE	2	ABCDE	22	ABCDE	52	C E	78	BCDE	94	BCDE	130	C E	151	C E	176	E	204
ABCDE	6	BCDE	23	ABCDE	53	ABCDE	79	ABCDE	105	B D	131	ABCDE	153	C E	182	BCDE	213
ABCDE	7	ABCDE	24	BCDE	58	C E	81	BCDE	106	C E	132	ABCDE	154	BCDE	186	ABCDE	220
ABCDE	8	BCDE	25	ABCDE	59	C E	83	A	107	BCDE	133	C E	155	ABCDE	187	ABCDE	221
ABCDE	9	BCDE	28	ABCDE	60	ABCDE	85	BCDE	108	C E	134	ABCDE	156	BCDE	189	C E	222
ABCDE	11	BCDE	29	ABCDE	61	ABCDE	86	BCDE	109	C E	136	C E	157	BCDE	191	ABCDE	223
ABCDE	18	C E	31	BCDE	63	ABCDE	87	BCDE	118	C E	137	ABCDE	159	BCDE	197	BCDE	224
ABCDE	19	BCDE	37	BCDE	65	DE	88	BCDE	120	C E	140	C E	162	ABCDE	202	BCDE	226

Triumph 2000

miles in thousands	3	6	9	12	15	18	21	24	27	30	33	36	39	42	45	48	51	54	57	60
age of car in months	3	6	9	12	15	18	21	24	27	30	33	36	39	42	45	48	51	54	57	60
look for service code letter	A	B	A	C	A	D	A	C	A	B	A	E	A	B	A	C	A	D	A	C

Code	Job	Code	Job	Code	Job	Code	Job	Code	Job	Code	Job	Code	Job	Code	Job	Code	Job	Code	Job
ABCDE	1	ABCDE	22	ABCDE	51	C E	78	ABCDE	94	BCDE	120	C E	140	C E	162	BCDE	192	ABCDE	223
ABCDE	4	BCDE	23	ABCDE	52	ABCDE	79	C E	98	BCDE	128	C E	148	C E	166	BCDE	198	BCDE	224
ABCDE	6	BCDE	24	ABCDE	53	C E	81	C E	101	BCDE	130	C E	151	C E	173	ABCDE	202	ABCDE	225
ABCDE	8	BCDE	25	BCDE	58	C E	83	ABCDE	105	B D	131	ABCDE	153	AB D	175	ABCDE	203	BCDE	226
ABCDE	9	BCDE	28	BCDE	59	ABCDE	85	BCDE	106	C E	132	ABCDE	154	C E	176	E	206		
ABCDE	10	BCDE	29	ABCDE	60	ABCDE	86	A	107	BCDE	133	C E	155	C E	183	BCDE	213		
ABCDE	18	C E	31	ABCDE	61	ABCDE	87	BCDE	108	C E	134	ABCDE	156	BCDE	186	ABCDE	220		
ABCDE	19	ABCDE	34	BCDE	62	DE	88	BCDE	109	C E	136	ABCDE	158	ABCDE	187	ABCDE	221		
ABCDE	21	BCDE	37	ABCDE	63	ABCDE	91	BCDE	118	C E	137	BCDE	161	BCDE	189	C E	222		

Triumph 2000 automatic

miles in thousands	3	6	9	12	15	18	21	24	27	30	33	36	39	42	45	48	51	54	57	60
age of car in months	3	6	9	12	15	18	21	24	27	30	33	36	39	42	45	48	51	54	57	60
look for service code letter	A	B	A	C	A	D	A	C	A	B	A	E	A	B	A	C	A	D	A	C

Code	Job	Code	Job	Code	Job	Code	Job	Code	Job	Code	Job	Code	Job	Code	Job	Code	Job	Code	Job
ABCDE	1	ABCDE	22	ABCDE	52	CDE	81	CDE	101	BCDE	130	CDE	151	CDE	173	ABCDE	202	BCDE	224
ABCDE	4	BCDE	23	BCDE	58	CDE	83	ABCDE	105	B D	131	ABCDE	153	AB D	175	ABCDE	203	ABCDE	225
ABCDE	6	BCDE	24	ABCDE	59	ABCDE	85	BCDE	106	CDE	132	ABCDE	154	CDE	176	E	206	BCDE	226
ABCDE	8	BCDE	25	ABCDE	60	ABCDE	86	A	107	BCDE	133	CDE	155	CDE	183	BCDE	213		
ABCDE	9	BCDE	28	ABCDE	61	ABCDE	87	BCDE	108	CDE	134	ABCDE	156	BCDE	186	BCDE	214		
ABCDE	10	BCDE	29	BCDE	62	DE	88	BCDE	109	CDE	136	ABCDE	158	ABCDE	187	ABCDE	220		
ABCDE	18	CDE	31	ABCDE	63	ABCDE	91	BCDE	118	CDE	137	BCDE	161	BCDE	189	ABCDE	221		
ABCDE	19	ABCDE	34	CDE	78	ABCDE	94	BCDE	120	CDE	140	CDE	162	BCDE	192	CDE	222		
ABCDE	21	ABCDE	51	CDE	79	CDE	98	BCDE	128	CDE	148	CDE	166	BCDE	198	ABCDE	223		

Triumph Dolomite

miles in thousands	3	6	9	12	15	18	21	24	27	30	33	36	39	42	45	48	51	54	57	60
age of car in months	3	6	9	12	15	18	21	24	27	30	33	36	39	42	45	48	51	54	57	60
look for service code letter	A	B	A	C	A	D	A	C	A	B	A	E	A	B	A	C	A	D	A	C

Code	Job	Code	Job	Code	Job	Code	Job	Code	Job	Code	Job	Code	Job	Code	Job	Code	Job	Code	Job
ABCDE	1	ABCDE	21	ABCDE	37	BCDE	66	DE	88	BCDE	118	C E	135	C E	155	ABCDE	187	ABCDE	220
ABCDE	4	ABCDE	22	ABCDE	51	C E	78	ABCDE	89	BCDE	119	C E	136	ABCDE	156	BCDE	189	ABCDE	221
ABCDE	6	ABCDE	23	ABCDE	52	ABCDE	79	BCDE	94	BCDE	120	C E	141	ABCDE	159	BCDE	192	C E	222
ABCDE	8	ABCDE	25	ABCDE	53	C E	81	ABCDE	105	BCDE	129	C E	142	C E	162	BCDE	198	ABCDE	223
ABCDE	9	BCDE	28	BCDE	58	C E	83	BCDE	106	ABCDE	130	C E	149	AB D	175	ABCDE	202	BCDE	224
ABCDE	12	BCDE	29	BCDE	61	ABCDE	85	A	107	B D	131	C E	152	C E	176	ABCDE	203	ABCDE	226
ABCDE	18	C E	31	BCDE	63	ABCDE	86	BCDE	108	C E	132	ABCDE	153	C E	183	E	204		
ABCDE	19	ABCDE	34	BCDE	65	ABCDE	87	BCDE	110	BCDE	133	ABCDE	154	BCDE	186	BCDE	213		

British Leyland

Jobs to be done

Read page 40 before using these charts

Triumph GT-6

	miles in thousands	6	12	18	24	30	36	42	48	54	60	66	72
	age of car in months	6	12	18	24	30	36	42	48	54	60	66	72
	look for service code letter	A	B	C	B	A	C	A	B	C	B	A	C

Code	Job	Code	Job	Code	Job	Code	Job	Code	Job	Code	Job	Code	Job	Code	Job	Code	Job	Code	Job
ABC	1	ABC	18	BC	32	BC	59	ABC	86	ABC	106	BC	132	ABC	153	A C	175	ABC	202
ABC	4	ABC	19	ABC	34	BC	61	ABC	87	ABC	108	ABC	133	ABC	154	BC	176	ABC	213
ABC	5	ABC	21	ABC	37	BC	63	C	88	BC	110	BC	134	BC	155	BC	183	ABC	220
ABC	6	ABC	22	BC	39	BC	78	BC	91	ABC	119	BC	136	ABC	156	ABC	186	ABC	221
ABC	8	ABC	23	ABC	51	ABC	79	ABC	94	BC	120	BC	137	BC	157	ABC	187	ABC	223
ABC	9	ABC	25	ABC	52	BC	81	BC	98	ABC	129	BC	140	ABC	159	ABC	189	ABC	224
ABC	11	ABC	28	ABC	53	BC	83	BC	101	ABC	130	BC	148	BC	162	ABC	192	ABC	226
ABC	14	ABC	29	ABC	58	ABC	85	ABC	105	A C	131	BC	151	BC	173	ABC	198		

Triumph Herald

	miles in thousands	6	12	18	24	30	36	42	48	54	60	66	72
	age of car in months	6	12	18	24	30	36	42	48	54	60	66	72
	look for service code letter	A	B	C	B	A	C	A	B	C	B	A	C

Code	Job	Code	Job	Code	Job	Code	Job	Code	Job	Code	Job	Code	Job	Code	Job	Code	Job	Code	Job
ABC	1	ABC	19	ABC	34	ABC	61	BC	92	ABC	109	BC	134	BC	155	BC	176	ABC	220
ABC	4	ABC	21	ABC	37	BC	63	ABC	94	BC	118	BC	136	ABC	156	BC	184	ABC	221
ABC	6	ABC	22	BC	39	BC	78	BC	97	BC	120	BC	137	BC	157	ABC	187	ABC	223
ABC	8	ABC	23	ABC	51	ABC	79	BC	101	ABC	128	BC	140	ABC	158	BC	189	ABC	224
ABC	9	ABC	25	ABC	52	BC	81	BC	104	ABC	130	BC	151	BC	162	ABC	199	ABC	226
ABC	11	ABC	28	ABC	53	BC	83	ABC	105	A C	131	BC	151	BC	173	ABC	202		
ABC	14	ABC	29	ABC	58	ABC	85	ABC	106	BC	132	ABC	153	ABC	190	ABC	213		
ABC	18	ABC	32	BC	59	C	88	BC	108	ABC	133	ABC	154	A C	175				

Triumph Spitfire Mks I, II & III

	miles in thousands	3	6	9	12	15	18	21	24	27	30	33	36	39	42	45	48	51	54	57	60
	age of car in months	3	6	9	12	15	18	21	24	27	30	33	36	39	42	45	48	51	54	57	60
	look for service code letter	A	B	A	C	A	D	A	C	A	B	A	D	A	B	A	C	A	D	A	C

Code	Job	Code	Job	Code	Job	Code	Job	Code	Job	Code	Job	Code	Job	Code	Job	Code	Job	Code	Job
ABCD	1	ABCD	21	CD	39	ABCD	79	CD	98	BCD	129	CD	148	CD	162	CD	191	BCD	226
ABCD	4	ABCD	22	ABCD	51	CD	81	CD	101	BCD	130	CD	151	CD	173	CD	201		
ABCD	6	BCD	23	ABCD	52	CD	83	ABCD	105	B D	131	ABCD	153	AB D	175	ABCD	202		
ABCD	8	BCD	25	ABCD	53	ABCD	85	BCD	106	CD	132	ABCD	154	CD	176	BCD	213		
ABCD	9	BCD	28	BCD	58	ABCD	86	A	107	BCD	133	CD	155	ABCD	177	ABCD	220		
ABCD	11	BCD	29	CD	59	ABCD	87	BCD	108	CD	134	ABCD	156	CD	182	ABCD	221		
ABCD	14	CD	32	BCD	61	D	88	ABCD	110	CD	136	CD	157	ABCD	186	CD	222		
ABCD	18	ABCD	34	CD	63	BCD	91	BCD	119	CD	137	ABCD	158	ABCD	187	ABCD	223		
ABCD	19	BCD	37	CD	78	ABCD	94	BCD	120	CD	140	BCD	161	CD	189	BCD	224		

Triumph Stag

	miles in thousands	3	6	9	12	15	18	21	24	27	30	33	36	39	42	45	48	51	54	57	60
	age of car in months	3	6	9	12	15	18	21	24	27	30	33	36	39	42	45	48	51	54	57	60
	look for service code letter	A	B	A	C	A	D	A	C	A	B	A	E	A	B	A	C	A	D	A	C

Code	Job	Code	Job	Code	Job	Code	Job	Code	Job	Code	Job	Code	Job	Code	Job	Code	Job	Code	Job
ABCDE	1	ABCDE	19	BCDE	37	C E	78	ABCDE	90	BCDE	118	C E	141	C E	164	ABCDE	196	ABCDE	221
ABCDE	4	ABCDE	21	ABCDE	51	C E	79	ABCDE	94	BCDE	120	C E	142	C E	166	BCDE	198	BCDE	223
ABCDE	5	ABCDE	22	ABCDE	52	C E	80	C E	98	BCDE	128	C E	149	AB D	175	ABCDE	202	BCDE	224
ABCDE	6	ABCDE	23	ABCDE	53	C E	81	C E	101	BCDE	130	C E	152	C E	176	ABCDE	203	BCDE	226
ABCDE	8	ABCDE	24	ABCDE	54	C E	83	ABCDE	105	B D	131	ABCDE	153	C E	183	E	204		
ABCDE	9	BCDE	28	BCDE	58	ABCDE	85	BCDE	106	C E	132	ABCDE	154	BCDE	186	ABCDE	209		
ABCDE	10	BCDE	29	C E	59	ABCDE	86	A	107	BCDE	133	C E	155	ABCDE	187	ABCDE	210		
ABCDE	12	C E	31	BCDE	61	ABCDE	87	BCDE	108	C E	135	ABCDE	156	C E	189	BCDE	213		
ABCDE	18	ABCDE	34	C E	63	DE	88	BCDE	109	C E	136	ABCDE	159	C E	192	ABCDE	220		

Triumph Toledo

	miles in thousands	3	6	9	12	15	18	21	24	27	30	33	36	39	42	45	48	51	54	57	60
	age of car in months	3	6	9	12	15	18	21	24	27	30	33	36	39	42	45	48	51	54	57	60
	look for service code letter	A	B	A	C	A	D	A	C	A	B	A	E	A	B	A	C	A	D	A	C

Code	Job	Code	Job	Code	Job	Code	Job	Code	Job	Code	Job	Code	Job	Code	Job	Code	Job	Code	Job
ABCDE	1	ABCDE	21	BCDE	37	BCDE	66	DE	88	BCDE	118	C E	134	C E	155	ABCDE	187	ABCDE	220
ABCDE	4	ABCDE	22	ABCDE	51	C E	78	ABCDE	89	BCDE	120	C E	136	ABCDE	156	BCDE	189	ABCDE	221
ABCDE	6	ABCDE	23	ABCDE	52	ABCDE	79	BCDE	94	BCDE	128	C E	137	ABCDE	159	BCDE	191	C E	222
ABCDE	8	ABCDE	25	ABCDE	53	C E	81	ABCDE	105	ABCDE	129	C E	140	ABCDE	162	ABCDE	197	ABCDE	223
ABCDE	9	BCDE	28	BCDE	58	C E	83	BCDE	106	ABCDE	130	C E	148	AB D	175	ABCDE	202	BCDE	224
ABCDE	12	BCDE	29	BCDE	61	ABCDE	85	A	107	B D	131	C E	151	C E	176	ABCDE	203	BCDE	226
ABCDE	18	C E	32	BCDE	63	ABCDE	86	BCDE	108	C E	132	ABCDE	153	C E	182	E	204		
ABCDE	19	ABCDE	34	BCDE	65	ABCDE	87	BCDE	109	BCDE	133	ABCDE	154	BCDE	186	BCDE	213		

Triumph TR4

	miles in thousands	3	6	9	12	15	18	21	24	27	30	33	36	39	42	45	48	51	54	57	60
	age of car in months	3	6	9	12	15	18	21	24	27	30	33	36	39	42	45	48	51	54	57	60
	look for service code letter	A	B	A	C	A	D	A	E	A	B	A	D	A	B	A	E	A	D	A	C

Code	Job	Code	Job	Code	Job	Code	Job	Code	Job	Code	Job	Code	Job	Code	Job	Code	Job	Code	Job
ABCDE	1	ABCDE	21	BCDE	37	ABCDE	65	D	88	BCDE	108	BC E	133	ABCDE	154	BCDE	183	ABCDE	220
ABCDE	4	ABCDE	22	ABCDE	51	C E	78	ABCDE	89	BCDE	109	C E	134	C E	155	BCDE	186	ABCDE	221
ABCDE	6	ABCDE	23	ABCDE	52	ABCDE	79	ABCDE	94	BCDE	118	C E	136	ABCDE	156	BCDE	187	C E	222
ABCDE	8	ABCDE	25	ABCDE	53	C E	81	E	98	BCDE	120	C E	137	C E	157	BCDE	189	ABCDE	223
ABCDE	9	BCDE	28	BCDE	58	C E	83	E	101	BCDE	128	C E	140	ABCDE	158	BCDE	192	BCDE	224
ABCDE	11	BCDE	29	BCDE	61	ABCDE	85	ABCDE	105	B D	131	C E	151	C E	161	BCDE	198	BCDE	226
ABCDE	13	BCDE	31	ABCDE	63	ABCDE	86	BCDE	106	C E	132	ABCDE	153	BCDE	162	ABCDE	202		
ABCDE	19	ABCDE	34	ABCDE	64	ABCDE	87	A	107					BCDE	178	BCDE	213		

British Leyland — Chrysler

Read page 40 before using these charts

Jobs to be done

Triumph TR4A / TR5

miles in thousands	3	6	9	12	15	18	21	24	27	30	33	36	39	42	45	48	51	54	57	60
age of car in months	3	6	9	12	15	18	21	24	27	30	33	36	39	42	45	48	51	54	57	60
look for service code letter	A	B	A	C	A	D	A	C	A	B	A	D	A	B	A	C	A	D	A	C

Code Job	Code Job	Code Job	Code Job	Code Job	Code Job	Code Job	Code Job	Code Job	Code Job
ABCD 1	ABCD 22	ABCD 51	BCD 63	D 88	BCD 109	CD 136	CD 157	ABCD 192	BCD 226
ABCD 6	ABCD 23	ABCD 52	BCD 65	BCD 90	BCD 118	CD 137	ABCD 158	BCD 198	
ABCD 8	ABCD 24	ABCD 53	CD 78	ABCD 94	BCD 120	CD 140	CD 161	ABCD 202	
ABCD 9	ABCD 25	ABCD 54	ABCD 79	CD 98	BCD 128	CD 148	CD 162	ABCD 203	
ABCD 11	BCD 28	BCD 58	CD 81	CD 101	BCD 130	CD 151	BCD 178	BCD 213	
ABCD 19	BCD 29	CD 59	CD 83	ABCD 105	B D 131	ABCD 153	BCD 183	ABCD 220	
BCD 20	CD 32	BCD 60	ABCD 85	BCD 106	CD 132	ABCD 154	BCD 186	ABCD 221	
ABCD 21	ABCD 34	BCD 61	ABCD 86	A 107	BCD 133	CD 155	ABCD 187	ABCD 223	
	BCD 37	BCD 62	ABCD 87	BCD 108	CD 134	ABCD 156	BCD 189	BCD 224	

Triumph TR6

miles in thousands	3	6	9	12	15	18	21	24	27	30	33	36	39	42	45	48	51	54	57	60
age of car in months	3	6	9	12	15	18	21	24	27	30	33	36	39	42	45	48	51	54	57	60
look for service code letter	A	B	A	C	A	D	A	C	A	B	A	D	A	B	A	C	A	D	A	C

Code Job	Code Job	Code Job	Code Job	Code Job	Code Job	Code Job	Code Job	Code Job	Code Job
ABCD 1	ABCD 21	ABCD 34	BCD 60	CD 83	CD 101	BCD 128	CD 140	ABCD 159	ABCD 221
ABCD 4	ABCD 22	BCD 37	BCD 61	ABCD 85	ABCD 105	BCD 130	CD 148	B D 175	ABCD 223
ABCD 6	ABCD 23	ABCD 51	BCD 62	ABCD 86	BCD 106	B D 131	CD 151	CD 176	BCD 224
ABCD 8	ABCD 24	ABCD 52	CD 63	ABCD 87	A 107	CD 132	ABCD 153	BCD 198	BCD 226
ABCD 9	ABCD 25	ABCD 53	BCD 65	D 88	BCD 108	BCD 133	ABCD 154	ABCD 202	
ABCD 11	BCD 28	ABCD 54	CD 78	BCD 90	BCD 109	CD 134	CD 155	ABCD 203	
ABCD 19	BCD 29	BCD 58	ABCD 79	ABCD 94	BCD 118	CD 136	ABCD 156	BCD 213	
BCD 20	CD 32	CD 59	CD 81	CD 98	BCD 120	CD 137	CD 157	ABCD 220	

Triumph Vitesse

miles in thousands	6	12	18	24	30	36	42	48	54	60	66	72
age of car in months	6	12	18	24	30	36	42	48	54	60	66	72
look for service code letter	A	B	C	B	A	C	A	B	C	B	A	C

Code Job	Code Job	Code Job	Code Job	Code Job	Code Job	Code Job	Code Job	Code Job	Code Job
ABC 1	ABC 18	BC 31	BC 59	ABC 86	ABC 106	BC 132	ABC 153	BC 173	ABC 198
ABC 4	ABC 19	ABC 34	BC 61	ABC 87	ABC 108	ABC 133	ABC 154	A C 175	ABC 202
ABC 5	ABC 21	ABC 37	BC 63	C 88	BC 109	BC 134	BC 155	BC 176	ABC 213
ABC 6	ABC 22	BC 39	BC 78	BC 91	BC 118	BC 136	BC 156	BC 183	ABC 220
ABC 8	ABC 23	ABC 51	ABC 79	ABC 94	BC 120	BC 137	BC 157	ABC 186	ABC 221
ABC 9	ABC 25	ABC 52	BC 81	BC 98	ABC 128	BC 140	ABC 158	ABC 187	ABC 223
ABC 11	ABC 28	ABC 53	BC 83	BC 101	ABC 130	BC 148	BC 161	ABC 189	ABC 224
ABC 14	ABC 29	ABC 58	ABC 85	ABC 105	A C 131	BC 151	BC 162	ABC 192	ABC 226

Chrysler Rootes Avenger

miles in thousands	5	10	15	20	25	30	35	40	45	50	55	60	65	70	75	80	85	90
age of car in months	5	10	15	20	25	30	35	40	45	50	55	60	65	70	75	80	85	90
look for service code letter	A	B	C	B	A	D	A	B	C	B	A	D	A	B	C	B	A	D

Code Job	Code Job	Code Job	Code Job	Code Job	Code Job	Code Job	Code Job	Code Job	Code Job
ABCD 1	ABCD 22	ABCD 42	ABCD 79	B D 98	ABCD 128	CD 148	B D 162	ABCD 198	ABCD 225
ABCD 4	ABCD 23	ABCD 43	B D 81	B D 101	ABCD 130	CD 151	ABCD 169	ABCD 202	ABCD 226
ABCD 6	ABCD 25	ABCD 51	B D 83	ABCD 105	A C 131	ABCD 153	B D 176	ABCD 213	
ABCD 8	ABCD 28	ABCD 52	ABCD 85	ABCD 106	B D 132	ABCD 154	ABCD 181	ABCD 220	
ABCD 9	ABCD 29	ABCD 58	ABCD 86	ABCD 108	ABCD 133	CD 155	ABCD 183	ABCD 221	
ABCD 10	ABCD 32	ABCD 61	ABCD 87	ABCD 109	CD 134	ABCD 156	ABCD 186	CD 222	
ABCD 19	ABCD 34	B D 63	B D 89	ABCD 118	CD 136	ABCD 158	ABCD 187	ABCD 223	
ABCD 21	ABCD 37	B D 78	B D 94	ABCD 120	CD 137	ABCD 161	ABCD 192	ABCD 224	

Chrysler Rootes Avenger GT

miles in thousands	5	10	15	20	25	30	35	40	45	50	55	60	65	70	75	80	85	90
age of car in months	5	10	15	20	25	30	35	40	45	50	55	60	65	70	75	80	85	90
look for service code letter	A	B	C	B	A	D	A	B	C	B	A	D	A	B	C	B	A	D

Code Job	Code Job	Code Job	Code Job	Code Job	Code Job	Code Job	Code Job	Code Job	Code Job
ABCD 1	ABCD 22	ABCD 42	ABCD 79	B D 98	ABCD 128	CD 148	B D 162	ABCD 198	ABCD 223
ABCD 4	ABCD 23	ABCD 43	B D 81	B D 101	ABCD 130	CD 151	ABCD 169	ABCD 202	ABCD 224
ABCD 6	ABCD 25	ABCD 51	B D 83	ABCD 105	A C 131	ABCD 153	B D 176	ABCD 203	ABCD 225
ABCD 8	ABCD 28	ABCD 52	ABCD 85	ABCD 106	B D 132	ABCD 154	ABCD 181	D 204	ABCD 226
ABCD 9	ABCD 29	ABCD 58	ABCD 86	ABCD 108	ABCD 133	CD 155	ABCD 183	ABCD 213	
ABCD 10	ABCD 32	ABCD 61	ABCD 87	ABCD 109	CD 134	ABCD 156	ABCD 186	ABCD 220	
ABCD 19	ABCD 34	B D 63	B D 89	ABCD 118	CD 136	ABCD 158	ABCD 187	ABCD 221	
ABCD 21	ABCD 37	B D 78	B D 94	ABCD 120	CD 137	ABCD 161	ABCD 192	CD 222	

Chrysler Rootes Chamois Imp

miles in thousands	5	10	15	20	25	30	35	40	45	50	55	60	65	70	75	80	85	90
age of car in months	5	10	15	20	25	30	35	40	45	50	55	60	65	70	75	80	85	90
look for service code letter	A	B	C	B	A	D	E	B	A	B	A	D	A	E	C	B	A	D

Code Job	Code Job	Code Job	Code Job	Code Job	Code Job	Code Job	Code Job	Code Job	Code Job
ABCDE 1	ABCDE 21	ABCDE 51	ABCDE 79	D 101	ABCDE 130	CD 149	ABCDE 162	ABCDE 199	ABCDE 225
ABCDE 3	ABCDE 22	ABCDE 52	B DE 81	ABCDE 105	A C E 131	CD 152	ABCDE 169	ABCDE 202	ABCDE 226
ABCDE 4	ABCDE 23	ABCDE 53	B DE 83	ABCDE 106	B DE 132	ABCDE 153	AB E 175	ABCDE 213	
ABCDE 6	ABCDE 25	AB E 56	ABCDE 85	ABCDE 108	ABCDE 133	ABCDE 154	CD 176	ABCDE 220	
ABCDE 8	ABCDE 27	CD 57	E 88	ABCDE 109	ABCDE 135	CD 155	ABCDE 184	ABCDE 221	
ABCDE 9	ABCDE 28	B DE 59	ABCDE 89	ABCDE 118	ABCDE 136	ABCDE 158	ABCDE 187	CD 222	
ABCDE 11	ABCDE 29	ABCDE 61	ABCDE 94	ABCDE 120	CD 141	ABCDE 161	ABCDE 189	ABCDE 223	
ABCDE 19	ABCDE 31	B DE 78	D 97	ABCDE 128	CD 142		ABCDE 193	ABCDE 224	

Chrysler

Read page 40 before using these charts

Jobs to be done

Chrysler Rootes 180

miles in thousands	5	10	15	20	25	30	35	40	45	50	55	60	65	70	75	80	85	90
age of car in months	5	10	15	20	25	30	35	40	45	50	55	60	65	70	75	80	85	90
look for service code letter	A	B	C	B	A	D	A	B	C	B	A	D	A	B	C	B	A	D

Code	Job	Code	Job	Code	Job	Code	Job	Code	Job	Code	Job	Code	Job	Code	Job	Code	Job	Code	Job
ABCD	1	ABCD	19	ABCD	32	ABCD	54	ABCD	87	ABCD	108	ABCD	133	ABCD	154	ABCD	187	ABCD	221
ABCD	4	ABCD	21	ABCD	34	B D	55	CD	88	ABCD	113	ABCD	135	CD	155	ABCD	189	ABCD	223
ABCD	6	ABCD	22	B D	35	A C	58	ABCD	91	ABCD	118	ABCD	136	ABCD	159	ABCD	193	ABCD	224
ABCD	8	ABCD	23	B D	36	ABCD	61	ABCD	94	ABCD	120	ABCD	141	ABCD	162	ABCD	195	ABCD	225
ABCD	9	ABCD	24	A C	37	ABCD	63	CD	98	ABCD	125	ABCD	147	AB	175	ABCD	200	ABCD	226
ABCD	10	ABCD	25	ABCD	51	B D	64	CD	101	ABCD	130	ABCD	149	CD	176	ABCD	202		
ABCD	12	ABCD	28	ABCD	52	ABCD	66	ABCD	105	A C	131	ABCD	152	ABCD	184	ABCD	213		
ABCD	18	ABCD	29	ABCD	53	ABCD	86	ABCD	106	B D	132	ABCD	153			ABCD	220		

Chrysler Rootes Hillman Minx 1500 Hunter 1500/1725

miles in thousands	5	10	15	20	25	30	35	40	45	50	55	60	65	70	75	80	85	90
age of car in months	6	12	18	24	30	36	42	48	54	60	66	72	78	84	90	96	102	108
look for service code letter	A	B	C	B	A	D	A	B	C	B	A	D	A	B	C	B	A	D

Code	Job	Code	Job	Code	Job	Code	Job	Code	Job	Code	Job	Code	Job	Code	Job	Code	Job	Code	Job
ABCD	1	ABCD	23	ABCD	51	B D	80	ABCD	94	ABCD	120	ABCD	137	ABCD	158	ABCD	186	ABCD	221
ABCD	4	ABCD	25	ABCD	52	B D	81	CD	98	ABCD	128	ABCD	140	ABCD	159	ABCD	187	ABCD	223
ABCD	6	ABCD	26	ABCD	53	B D	83	CD	101	ABCD	130	ABCD	148	ABCD	161	ABCD	189	ABCD	224
ABCD	8	ABCD	28	ABCD	58	ABCD	85	ABCD	105	A C	131	ABCD	151	ABCD	162	ABCD	192	ABCD	225
ABCD	9	ABCD	29	ABCD	61	ABCD	86	ABCD	106	B D	132	ABCD	153	ABCD	169	ABCD	198	ABCD	226
ABCD	10	ABCD	32	ABCD	63	ABCD	87	ABCD	108	ABCD	133	ABCD	154	A C	175	ABCD	202		
ABCD	13	ABCD	34	B D	78	B	88	ABCD	109	ABCD	134	CD	155	B D	176	ABCD	213		
ABCD	19	ABCD	37	ABCD	79	ABCD	89	ABCD	118	ABCD	136	ABCD	156	ABCD	183	ABCD	220		

Chrysler Rootes Humber Sceptre

miles in thousands	5	10	15	20	25	30	35	40	45	50	55	60	65	70	75	80	85	90
age of car in months	6	12	18	24	30	36	42	48	54	60	66	72	78	84	90	96	102	108
look for service code letter	A	B	C	B	A	D	A	B	C	B	A	D	A	B	C	B	A	D

Code	Job	Code	Job	Code	Job	Code	Job	Code	Job	Code	Job	Code	Job	Code	Job	Code	Job	Code	Job
ABCD	1	ABCD	23	D	38	B D	78	B	88	ABCD	109	ABCD	134	CD	155	B D	176	ABCD	213
ABCD	4	ABCD	25	D	41	ABCD	79	ABCD	89	ABCD	118	ABCD	136	ABCD	156	ABCD	183	ABCD	220
ABCD	6	ABCD	26	ABCD	51	B D	80	ABCD	94	ABCD	120	ABCD	137	ABCD	158	ABCD	186	ABCD	221
ABCD	8	ABCD	28	ABCD	52	B D	81	CD	98	ABCD	128	ABCD	140	ABCD	159	ABCD	187	ABCD	223
ABCD	9	ABCD	29	ABCD	53	B D	83	CD	101	ABCD	130	ABCD	148	ABCD	161	ABCD	189	ABCD	224
ABCD	10	ABCD	32	ABCD	58	ABCD	85	ABCD	105	A C	131	ABCD	151	ABCD	162	ABCD	192	ABCD	225
ABCD	13	ABCD	34	ABCD	61	ABCD	86	ABCD	106	B D	132	ABCD	153	ABCD	169	ABCD	198	ABCD	226
ABCD	19	D	36	ABCD	63	ABCD	87	ABCD	108	ABCD	133	ABCD	154	A C	175	ABCD	202		

Chrysler Rootes Stiletto

miles in thousands	5	10	15	20	25	30	35	40	45	50	55	60	65	70	75	80	85	90
age of car in months	5	10	15	20	25	30	35	40	45	50	55	60	65	70	75	80	85	90
look for service code letter	A	B	C	B	A	D	E	B	A	B	A	D	A	E	C	B	A	D

Code	Job	Code	Job	Code	Job	Code	Job	Code	Job	Code	Job	Code	Job	Code	Job	Code	Job	Code	Job
ABCDE	1	ABCDE	21	ABCDE	51	ABCDE	79	D	101	ABCDE	130	CD	149	ABCDE	162	ABCDE	192	ABCDE	223
ABCDE	3	ABCDE	22	ABCDE	52	B DE	81	ABCDE	105	A C E	131	CD	152	ABCDE	169	ABCDE	198	ABCDE	224
ABCDE	4	ABCDE	23	ABCDE	53	B DE	83	ABCDE	106	B DE	132	ABCDE	153	AB	175	ABCDE	202	ABCDE	225
ABCDE	6	ABCDE	25	AB E	56	ABCDE	85	ABCDE	108	ABCDE	133	ABCDE	154	CD	176	ABCDE	203	ABCDE	226
ABCDE	8	ABCDE	27	CD	57	E	88	ABCDE	109	ABCDE	135	CD	155	ABCDE	183	ABCDE	213		
ABCDE	9	ABCDE	28	B DE	59	ABCDE	89	ABCDE	118	ABCDE	136	ABCDE	156	ABCDE	186	ABCDE	220		
ABCDE	11	ABCDE	29	ABCDE	61	ABCDE	94	ABCDE	120	CD	141	ABCDE	158	ABCDE	187	ABCDE	221		
ABCDE	19	ABCDE	31	B DE	78	D	97	ABCDE	128	CD	142	ABCDE	161	ABCDE	189	CD	222		

Chrysler Rootes Singer Gazelle/Vogue

miles in thousands	5	10	15	20	25	30	35	40	45	50	55	60	65	70	75	80	85	90
age of car in months	6	12	18	24	30	36	42	48	54	60	66	72	78	84	90	96	102	108
look for service code letter	A	B	C	B	A	D	A	B	C	B	A	D	A	B	C	B	A	D

Code	Job	Code	Job	Code	Job	Code	Job	Code	Job	Code	Job	Code	Job	Code	Job	Code	Job	Code	Job
ABCD	1	ABCD	23	ABCD	51	B D	80	ABCD	94	ABCD	120	ABCD	137	ABCD	158	ABCD	186	ABCD	221
ABCD	4	ABCD	25	ABCD	52	B D	81	CD	98	ABCD	128	ABCD	140	ABCD	159	ABCD	187	ABCD	223
ABCD	6	ABCD	26	ABCD	53	B D	83	CD	101	ABCD	130	ABCD	148	ABCD	161	ABCD	189	ABCD	224
ABCD	8	ABCD	28	ABCD	58	ABCD	85	ABCD	105	A C	131	ABCD	151	ABCD	162	ABCD	192	ABCD	225
ABCD	9	ABCD	29	ABCD	61	ABCD	86	ABCD	106	B D	132	ABCD	153	ABCD	169	ABCD	198	ABCD	226
ABCD	10	ABCD	32	ABCD	63	ABCD	87	ABCD	108	ABCD	133	ABCD	154	A C	175	ABCD	202		
ABCD	13	ABCD	34	B D	78	B	88	ABCD	109	ABCD	134	CD	155	B D	176	ABCD	213		
ABCD	19	ABCD	37	ABCD	79	ABCD	89	ABCD	118	ABCD	136	ABCD	156	ABCD	183	ABCD	220		

Chrysler Rootes Sunbeam Alpine

miles in thousands	5	10	15	20	25	30	35	40	45	50	55	60	65	70	75	80	85	90
age of car in months	6	12	18	24	30	36	42	48	54	60	66	72	78	84	90	96	102	108
look for service code letter	A	B	C	B	A	D	A	B	C	B	A	D	A	B	C	B	A	D

Code	Job	Code	Job	Code	Job	Code	Job	Code	Job	Code	Job	Code	Job	Code	Job	Code	Job	Code	Job
ABCD	1	ABCD	23	D	38	B D	78	B	88	ABCD	109	ABCD	134	CD	155	B D	176	ABCD	213
ABCD	4	ABCD	25	D	41	ABCD	79	ABCD	89	ABCD	118	ABCD	136	ABCD	156	ABCD	183	ABCD	220
ABCD	6	ABCD	26	ABCD	51	B D	80	ABCD	94	ABCD	120	ABCD	137	ABCD	158	ABCD	186	ABCD	221
ABCD	8	ABCD	28	ABCD	52	B D	81	CD	98	ABCD	128	ABCD	140	ABCD	159	ABCD	187	ABCD	223
ABCD	9	ABCD	29	ABCD	53	B D	83	CD	101	ABCD	130	ABCD	148	ABCD	161	ABCD	189	ABCD	224
ABCD	10	ABCD	32	ABCD	58	ABCD	85	ABCD	105	A C	131	ABCD	151	ABCD	162	ABCD	192	ABCD	225
ABCD	13	ABCD	34	ABCD	61	ABCD	86	ABCD	106	B D	132	ABCD	153	ABCD	169	ABCD	198	ABCD	226
ABCD	19	D	36	ABCD	63	ABCD	87	ABCD	108	ABCD	133	ABCD	154	A C	175	ABCD	202		

Chrysler – Citroën

Read page 40 before using these charts

Jobs to be done

Chrysler Rootes Sunbeam Rapier

miles in thousands	5	10	15	20	25	30	35	40	45	50	55	60	65	70	75	80	85	90
age of car in months	6	12	18	24	30	36	42	48	54	60	66	72	78	84	90	96	102	108
look for service code letter	A	B	C	B	A	D	A	B	C	B	A	D	A	B	C	B	A	D

Code	Job	Code	Job	Code	Job	Code	Job	Code	Job	Code	Job	Code	Job	Code	Job	Code	Job	Code	Job
ABCD	1	ABCD	23	D	38	B D	78	B	88	ABCD	109	ABCD	134	CD	155	B D	176	ABCD	213
ABCD	4	ABCD	25	D	41	ABCD	79	ABCD	89	ABCD	118	ABCD	136	ABCD	156	ABCD	183	ABCD	220
ABCD	6	ABCD	26	ABCD	51	B D	80	ABCD	94	ABCD	120	ABCD	137	ABCD	158	ABCD	186	ABCD	221
ABCD	8	ABCD	28	ABCD	52	B D	81	CD	98	ABCD	128	ABCD	140	ABCD	159	ABCD	187	ABCD	223
ABCD	9	ABCD	29	ABCD	53	B D	83	CD	101	ABCD	130	ABCD	148	ABCD	161	ABCD	189	ABCD	224
ABCD	10	ABCD	32	ABCD	58	ABCD	85	ABCD	105	A C	131	ABCD	151	ABCD	162	ABCD	192	ABCD	225
ABCD	13	ABCD	34	ABCD	61	ABCD	86	ABCD	106	B D	132	ABCD	153	ABCD	169	ABCD	198	ABCD	226
ABCD	19	D	36	ABCD	63	ABCD	87	ABCD	108	ABCD	133	ABCD	154	A C	175	ABCD	202		

Chrysler Simca 1000

miles in thousands	3	6	9	12	15	18	21	24	27	30	33	36	39	42	45	48	51	54	57	60
look for service code letter	A	B	A	C	A	B	A	C	A	B	A	C	A	B	A	C	A	B	A	C

Code	Job	Code	Job	Code	Job	Code	Job	Code	Job	Code	Job	Code	Job	Code	Job	Code	Job	Code	Job
ABC	1	ABC	19	C	39	ABC	60	BC	87	C	108	BC	133	ABC	156	ABC	184	ABC	221
ABC	3	ABC	21	ABC	49	ABC	61	C	88	C	113	BC	134	ABC	158	ABC	187	ABC	223
ABC	4	ABC	22	ABC	51	C	78	BC	92	C	118	BC	136	BC	161	BC	189	ABC	224
ABC	6	ABC	23	ABC	52	ABC	79	ABC	94	C	120	BC	137	BC	162	BC	190	ABC	226
ABC	8	ABC	25	ABC	53	C	81	C	98	ABC	125	BC	151	BC	173	ABC	199		
ABC	9	ABC	28	A	56	C	83	C	101	ABC	130	ABC	153	AB	175	ABC	202		
ABC	12	ABC	29	BC	57	ABC	85	ABC	105	AB	131	ABC	154	C	176	BC	213		
ABC	14	BC	32	C	59	BC	86	ABC	106	C	132	C	155	ABC	181	ABC	220		

Chrysler Simca 1100 'S' automatic

miles in thousands	3	6	9	12	15	18	21	24	27	30	33	36	39	42	45	48	51	54	57	60
look for service code letter	A	B	A	C	A	B	A	C	A	B	A	C	A	B	A	C	A	B	A	C

Code	Job	Code	Job	Code	Job	Code	Job	Code	Job	Code	Job	Code	Job	Code	Job	Code	Job	Code	Job
ABC	1	ABC	18	BC	32	BC	62	C	88	C	118	C	136	ABC	159	BC	190	ABC	224
ABC	2	ABC	19	ABC	34	C	78	ABC	92	C	120	C	137	C	162	ABC	199	ABC	225
ABC	4	ABC	21	ABC	51	ABC	79	ABC	94	ABC	125	C	148	BC	173	ABC	202	ABC	226
ABC	6	ABC	22	ABC	52	C	81	C	104	ABC	130	C	151	AB	175	BC	213		
ABC	7	ABC	23	BC	55	C	83	ABC	105	AB	131	ABC	153	C	176	ABC	219		
ABC	8	ABC	25	ABC	59	ABC	85	ABC	106	C	132	ABC	154	ABC	184	ABC	220		
ABC	9	ABC	28	ABC	60	BC	86	C	108	BC	133	C	155	ABC	187	ABC	221		
ABC	15	ABC	29	ABC	61	BC	87	C	113	C	134	ABC	156	BC	189	ABC	223		

Chrysler Simca 1301; 1501

miles in thousands	3	6	9	12	15	18	21	24	27	30	33	36	39	42	45	48	51	54	57	60	63	66	69	72
look for service code letter	A	B	A	C	A	B	A	D	A	D	A	B	A	C	A	B	A	D	A	B	A	C	A	B	A	D

Code	Job	Code	Job	Code	Job	Code	Job	Code	Job	Code	Job	Code	Job	Code	Job	Code	Job	Code	Job
ABCD	1	ABCD	25	ABCD	49	ABCD	66	CD	88	CD	113	CD	134	ABCD	156	BCD	189	ABCD	220
ABCD	4	ABCD	26	ABCD	51	CD	78	BCD	92	BCD	118	CD	136	BCD	157	BCD	190	ABCD	221
ABCD	6	ABCD	28	ABCD	52	BCD	79	ABCD	94	BCD	120	CD	137	ABCD	159	BCD	195	ABCD	223
ABCD	8	ABCD	29	ABCD	53	CD	81	CD	98	ABCD	125	CD	148	CD	162	BCD	200	ABCD	224
ABCD	9	CD	33	BCD	55	CD	83	CD	101	ABCD	130	CD	151	BCD	173	ABCD	202	ABCD	225
ABCD	12	ABCD	34	ABCD	61	BCD	85	ABCD	105	AB	131	ABCD	153	BCD	176	CD	211	ABCD	226
ABCD	19	BCD	35	CD	63	BCD	86	ABCD	106	CD	132	ABCD	154	ABCD	181	CD	212		
ABCD	23	BCD	36	BCD	64	BCD	87	CD	108	BCD	133	CD	155	ABCD	187	CD	213		

Chrysler Simca 1301 automatic / 1501 automatic

miles in thousands	3	6	9	12	15	18	21	24	27	30	33	36	39	42	45	48	51	54	57	60	63	66	69	72
look for service code letter	A	B	A	C	A	B	A	D	A	D	A	B	A	C	A	B	A	D	A	B	A	C	A	B	A	D

Code	Job	Code	Job	Code	Job	Code	Job	Code	Job	Code	Job	Code	Job	Code	Job	Code	Job	Code	Job
ABCD	1	ABCD	25	ABCD	53	CD	81	CD	98	ABCD	125	CD	148	CD	162	BCD	200	ABCD	223
ABCD	4	ABCD	26	BCD	55	CD	83	CD	101	ABCD	130	CD	151	BCD	173	ABCD	202	ABCD	224
ABCD	6	ABCD	28	ABCD	61	BCD	85	ABCD	105	AB	131	ABCD	153	BCD	176	CD	211	ABCD	225
ABCD	8	ABCD	29	CD	63	BCD	86	ABCD	106	CD	132	ABCD	154	ABCD	181	CD	212	ABCD	226
ABCD	9	CD	33	BCD	64	BCD	87	CD	108	BCD	133	CD	155	ABCD	187	CD	213		
ABCD	12	ABCD	34	ABCD	66	CD	88	CD	113	CD	134	ABCD	156	BCD	189	ABCD	219		
ABCD	19	ABCD	51	CD	78	BCD	92	BCD	118	CD	136	BCD	157	BCD	190	ABCD	220		
ABCD	23	ABCD	52	BCD	79	ABCD	94	BCD	120	CD	137	ABCD	159	BCD	195	ABCD	221		

Citroën Ami 8

miles in thousands	3	6	9	12	15	18	21	24	27	30	33	36	39	42	45	48	51	54
look for service code letter	A	B	A	C	A	D	A	E	A	B	A	D	A	B	A	E	A	D

Code	Job	Code	Job	Code	Job	Code	Job	Code	Job	Code	Job	Code	Job	Code	Job	Code	Job
ABCDE	1	ABCDE	18	BCDE	31	C E	57	E	81	ABCDE	105	D	133	CDE	162	ABCDE	202
ABCDE	2	ABCDE	21	ABCDE	34	ABCDE	59	E	83	ABCDE	106	BCDE	134	CDE	177	CDE	213
ABCDE	4	ABCDE	22	ABCDE	42	ABCDE	60	ABCDE	85	D	108	BCDE	136	CDE	184	BCDE	220
ABCDE	6	ABCDE	23	ABCDE	43	ABCDE	61	ABCDE	86	D	117	BCDE	137	BCDE	187	BCDE	221
ABCDE	8	ABCDE	25	ABCDE	51	ABCDE	62	ABCDE	87	D	127	BCDE	148	CDE	189	CDE	223
ABCDE	9	ABCDE	28	ABCDE	52	E	78	ABCDE	89	ABCDE	131	BCDE	151	BCDE	190	CDE	224
ABCDE	12	ABCDE	29	AB D	56	E	79	ABCDE	94	ABCDE	132	ABCDE	158	ABCDE	200	CDE	226

Citroën – Datsun

Jobs to be done

Read page 40 before using these charts

Citroën Ami 6 & Dyane

miles in thousands	3	6	9	12	15	18	21	24	27	30	33	36	39	42	45	48	51	54
look for service code letter	A	B	A	C	A	D	A	E	A	B	A	D	A	D	A	B	A	E A D

Code	Job	Code	Job	Code	Job	Code	Job	Code	Job	Code	Job	Code	Job	Code	Job	Code	Job
ABCDE	1	ABCDE	18	BCDE	31	C E	57	E	81	D	108	BCDE	136	CDE	184	BCDE	220
ABCDE	2	ABCDE	21	ABCDE	34	ABCDE	59	E	83	D	117	BCDE	137	BCDE	187	BCDE	221
ABCDE	4	ABCDE	22	ABCDE	42	ABCDE	60	ABCDE	85	D	127	BCDE	148	CDE	189	CDE	223
ABCDE	6	ABCDE	23	ABCDE	43	ABCDE	61	ABCDE	89	ABCDE	131	BCDE	151	BCDE	190	CDE	224
ABCDE	8	ABCDE	25	ABCDE	51	ABCDE	62	ABCDE	94	ABCDE	132	ABCDE	158	ABCDE	200	CDE	226
ABCDE	9	ABCDE	28	ABCDE	52	E	78	ABCDE	105	D	133	CDE	162	ABCDE	202		
ABCDE	12	ABCDE	29	AB D	56	E	79	ABCDE	106	BCDE	134	BCDE	177	CDE	213		

Daf 33 44

miles in thousands	3·3	6·6	10	13·3	16·6	20	23·3	26·6	30	33·3	36·6	40	43·3	46·6	50	53·3	56·6	60	63·3	66·6
look for service code letter	A	B	A	C	A	B	A	C	A	D	A	C	A	B	A	C	A	B	A	E E

Code	Job	Code	Job	Code	Job	Code	Job	Code	Job	Code	Job	Code	Job	Code	Job	Code	Job
ABCDE	1	ABCDE	18	CDE	30	ABCDE	74	DE	88	BC E	113	BCDE	134	BCDE	173	ABCDE	202
ABCDE	4	ABCDE	19	BCDE	51	BCDE	76	BC E	90	BC E	118	BCDE	136	A C	175	BCDE	213
ABCDE	6	ABCDE	21	ABCDE	52	ABCDE	77	ABCDE	94	BC E	120	BCDE	137	B DE	176	BCDE	220
ABCDE	8	ABCDE	22	ABCDE	67	C E	78	DE	97	BC E	125	BCDE	148	BCDE	184	BCDE	221
ABCD	9	ABCDE	23	C E	68	BCD	79	DE	101	BC E	130	BCDE	151	ABCDE	187	BCDE	223
ABCD	10	ABCDE	25	C E	69	ABCDE	81	ABCDE	105	AB D	131	BCDE	158	BCDE	189	BCDE	224
ABCDE	12	ABCDE	28	AB D	71	C E	83	ABCDE	106	C E	132	BCDE	161	BCDE	190	BCDE	225
ABCDE	14	ABCDE	29	AB D	72	BCDE	84	BC E	108	BCDE	133	BCDE	162	ABCDE	199	BCDE	226

Daf 55

miles in thousands	3·3	6·6	10	13·3	16·6	20	23·3	26·6	30	33·3	36·6	40	43·3	46·6	50	53·3	56·6	60	63·3	66·6
look for service code letter	A	B	A	C	A	B	A	C	A	D	A	C	A	B	A	C	A	B	A	E E

Code	Job	Code	Job	Code	Job	Code	Job	Code	Job	Code	Job	Code	Job	Code	Job	Code	Job	Code	Job
ABCDE	1	ABCDE	18	CDE	30	ABCDE	74	DE	88	BC E	113	BCDE	134	ABCDE	156	ABCDE	187	BCDE	223
ABCDE	4	ABCDE	19	ABCDE	51	BCDE	76	BCDE	90	BC E	118	BCDE	136	BCDE	158	BCDE	189	BCDE	224
ABCDE	6	ABCDE	21	ABCDE	52	ABCDE	77	ABCDE	94	BC E	120	BCDE	137	BCDE	161	BCDE	190	BCDE	225
ABCDE	8	ABCDE	22	ABCDE	67	C E	78	DE	97	BC E	125	BCDE	148	BCDE	162	ABCDE	199	BCDE	226
ABCD	9	ABCDE	23	C E	68	BCD	79	DE	101	BC E	130	BCDE	151	BCDE	173	ABCDE	202		
ABCD	10	ABCDE	25	C E	69	ABCDE	81	ABCDE	105	AB D	131	ABCDE	153	A C	175	BCDE	213		
ABCDE	12	ABCDE	28	AB D	71	C E	83	ABCDE	106	C E	132	ABCDE	154	B DE	176	BCDE	220		
ABCDE	14	ABCDE	29	AB D	72	BCDE	84	BC E	108	BCDE	133	CDE	155	BCDE	184	BCDE	221		

Daf 66

miles in thousands	3·3	6·6	10	13·3	16·6	20	23·3	26·6	30	33·3	36·6	40	43·3	46·6	50	53·3	56·6	60	63·3	66·6
look for service code letter	A	B	A	C	A	B	A	C	A	D	A	C	A	B	A	C	A	B	A	E E

Code	Job	Code	Job	Code	Job	Code	Job	Code	Job	Code	Job	Code	Job	Code	Job	Code	Job	Code	Job
ABCDE	1	ABCDE	18	CDE	30	C E	69	ABCDE	81	DE	97	BC E	125	BCDE	148	BCDE	173	ABCDE	202
ABCDE	4	ABCDE	19	CDE	32	AB D	71	C E	83	DE	101	BC E	130	BCDE	151	A C	175	BCDE	213
ABCDE	6	ABCDE	21	ABCDE	51	AB D	72	BCDE	84	ABCDE	105	AB D	131	ABCDE	153	B DE	176	BCDE	220
ABCDE	8	ABCDE	22	ABCDE	52	ABCDE	74	ABCDE	86	ABCDE	106	C E	132	BCDE	154	BCDE	184	BCDE	221
ABCD	9	ABCDE	23	ABCDE	53	BCDE	76	ABCDE	87	BC E	108	BCDE	133	CDE	155	ABCDE	187	BCDE	223
ABCD	10	ABCDE	25	ABCDE	54	ABCDE	77	DE	88	BC E	113	BCDE	134	ABCDE	156	BCDE	189	BCDE	224
ABCDE	12	ABCDE	28	ABCDE	67	C E	78	BCDE	90	BC E	118	BCDE	136	ABCDE	159	BCDE	190	BCDE	225
ABCDE	14	ABCDE	29	C E	68	BCD	79	ABCDE	94	BC E	120	BCDE	137	BCDE	162	ABCDE	199	BCDE	226

Datsun 240Z

miles in thousands	3	6	9	12	15	18	21	24	27	30	33	36	39	42	45	48	51	54	57	60
look for service code letter	A	B	A	C	A	B	A	C	A	D	A	C	A	B	A	C	A	B	A	D

Code	Job	Code	Job	Code	Job	Code	Job	Code	Job	Code	Job	Code	Job	Code	Job	Code	Job	Code	Job
ABCD	1	ABCD	28	ABCD	59	CD	81	D	98	BCD	126	BCD	146	CD	162	BCD	191	ABCD	223
ABCD	4	ABCD	29	ABCD	60	CD	83	D	101	ABCD	129	BCD	149	CD	166	BCD	201	BCD	224
BCD	6	BCD	32	ABCD	61	ABCD	85	ABCD	105	B D	131	BCD	152	AB D	175	ABCD	202	ABCD	225
ABCD	8	ABCD	34	D	62	ABCD	86	ABCD	106	CD	132	ABCD	153	CD	176	CD	203	BCD	226
ABCD	9	ABCD	51	ABCD	63	ABCD	87	ABCD	108	BCD	133	ABCD	154	BCD	182	CD	213		
ABCD	10	ABCD	52	BCD	65	CD	88	ABCD	116	BCD	135	CD	155	ABCD	186	ABCD	217		
ABCD	18	ABCD	54	CD	78	ABCD	91	CD	118	BCD	136	ABCD	156	ABCD	187	ABCD	220		
ABCD	19	ABCD	58	ABCD	79	CD	94	CD	120	BCD	141	ABCD	159	BCD	189	ABCD	221		

Datsun 2600 Custom de luxe

miles in thousands	3	6	9	12	15	18	21	24	27	30	33	36	39	42	45	48	51	54	57	60
look for service code letter	A	B	A	C	A	B	A	C	A	D	A	C	A	B	A	C	A	B	A	D

Code	Job	Code	Job	Code	Job	Code	Job	Code	Job	Code	Job	Code	Job	Code	Job	Code	Job	Code	Job
ABCD	1	ABCD	28	ABCD	52	ABCD	63	ABCD	87	ABCD	108	BCD	133	ABCD	154	BCD	182	CD	213
ABCD	4	ABCD	29	ABCD	53	ABCD	65	CD	88	ABCD	116	BCD	135	CD	155	ABCD	186	ABCD	220
ABCD	6	BCD	32	ABCD	54	CD	78	ABCD	91	CD	118	BCD	136	ABCD	156	ABCD	187	ABCD	221
ABCD	8	ABCD	34	ABCD	58	ABCD	79	CD	94	CD	120	BCD	141	ABCD	159	BCD	189	ABCD	223
ABCD	9	D	35	ABCD	59	CD	81	D	98	BCD	126	BCD	146	CD	162	BCD	191	BCD	224
ABCD	10	D	36	ABCD	60	CD	83	D	101	ABCD	130	BCD	149	CD	166	BCD	201	ABCD	225
ABCD	18	ABCD	37	ABCD	61	ABCD	85	ABCD	105	B D	131	BCD	152	AB D	175	ABCD	202	BCD	226
ABCD	19	ABCD	51	D	62	ABCD	86	ABCD	106	CD	132	ABCD	153	CD	176	CD	203		

Datsun

Read page 40 before using these charts

Jobs to be done

Datsun 260C Custom de luxe auto.

miles in thousands	3	6	9	12	15	18	21	24	27	30	33	36	39	42	45	48	51	54	57	60
look for service code letter	A	B	A	C	A	B	A	C	A	D	A	C	A	B	A	C	A	B	A	D

Code	Job	Code	Job	Code	Job	Code	Job	Code	Job	Code	Job	Code	Job	Code	Job	Code	Job	Code	Job
ABCD	1	ABCD	28	ABCD	59	CD	81	D	98	BCD	126	BCD	146	CD	162	BCD	191	ABCD	223
ABCD	4	ABCD	29	ABCD	60	CD	83	D	101	ABCD	130	BCD	149	CD	166	BCD	201	BCD	224
ABCD	6	BCD	32	ABCD	61	ABCD	85	ABCD	105	B D	131	BCD	152	AB D	175	ABCD	202	ABCD	225
ABCD	8	ABCD	34	D	62	ABCD	86	ABCD	106	CD	132	ABCD	153	CD	176	CD	203	BCD	226
ABCD	9	ABCD	51	ABCD	63	ABCD	87	ABCD	108	BCD	133	ABCD	154	BCD	182	CD	213		
ABCD	10	ABCD	52	BCD	65	CD	88	ABCD	116	BCD	135	CD	155	ABCD	186	ABCD	217		
ABCD	18	ABCD	54	CD	78	ABCD	91	CD	118	BCD	136	ABCD	156	ABCD	187	ABCD	220		
ABCD	19	ABCD	58	ABCD	79	CD	94	CD	120	BCD	141	ABCD	159	BCD	189	ABCD	221		

Datsun Bluebird 160B; 180B

miles in thousands	3	6	9	12	15	18	21	24	27	30	33	36	39	42	45	48	51	54	57	60
look for service code letter	A	B	A	C	A	B	A	C	A	D	A	C	A	B	A	C	A	B	A	D

Code	Job	Code	Job	Code	Job	Code	Job	Code	Job	Code	Job	Code	Job	Code	Job	Code	Job	Code	Job
ABCD	1	ABCD	28	ABCD	52	ABCD	63	ABCD	87	ABCD	108	BCD	133	ABCD	154	BCD	182	CD	213
ABCD	4	ABCD	29	ABCD	53	ABCD	65	CD	88	ABCD	116	BCD	135	CD	155	ABCD	186	ABCD	220
ABCD	6	BCD	32	ABCD	54	CD	78	CD	91	CD	118	BCD	136	ABCD	156	ABCD	187	ABCD	221
ABCD	8	ABCD	34	ABCD	58	ABCD	79	CD	94	CD	120	BCD	141	ABCD	159	BCD	189	ABCD	223
ABCD	9	D	35	ABCD	59	CD	81	D	98	BCD	126	BCD	146	CD	162	BCD	191	BCD	224
ABCD	10	D	36	ABCD	60	CD	83	D	101	ABCD	130	BCD	149	CD	166	BCD	197	ABCD	225
ABCD	18	ABCD	37	ABCD	61	ABCD	85	ABCD	105	B D	131	BCD	152	AB D	175	ABCD	202	BCD	226
ABCD	19	ABCD	51	D	62	ABCD	86	ABCD	106	CD	132	ABCD	153	CD	176	CD	203		

Datsun Bluebird 160B; 180B automatic

miles in thousands	3	6	9	12	15	18	21	24	27	30	33	36	39	42	45	48	51	54	57	60
look for service code letter	A	B	A	C	A	B	A	C	A	D	A	C	A	B	A	C	A	B	A	D

Code	Job	Code	Job	Code	Job	Code	Job	Code	Job	Code	Job	Code	Job	Code	Job	Code	Job	Code	Job
ABCD	1	ABCD	28	ABCD	59	CD	81	D	98	BCD	126	BCD	146	CD	162	BCD	191	ABCD	223
ABCD	4	ABCD	29	ABCD	60	CD	83	D	101	ABCD	130	BCD	149	CD	166	BCD	197	BCD	224
ABCD	6	BCD	32	ABCD	61	ABCD	85	ABCD	105	B D	131	BCD	152	AB D	175	ABCD	202	ABCD	225
ABCD	8	ABCD	34	D	62	ABCD	86	ABCD	106	CD	132	ABCD	153	CD	176	CD	203	BCD	226
ABCD	9	ABCD	51	ABCD	63	ABCD	87	ABCD	108	BCD	133	ABCD	154	BCD	182	CD	213		
ABCD	10	ABCD	52	BCD	65	CD	88	ABCD	116	BCD	135	CD	155	ABCD	186	ABCD	217		
ABCD	18	ABCD	54	CD	78	ABCD	91	CD	118	BCD	136	ABCD	156	ABCD	187	ABCD	220		
ABCD	19	ABCD	58	ABCD	79	CD	94	CD	120	BCD	141	ABCD	159	BCD	189	ABCD	221		

Datsun Bluebird 180SSS

miles in thousands	3	6	9	12	15	18	21	24	27	30	33	36	39	42	45	48	51	54	57	60
look for service code letter	A	B	A	C	A	B	A	C	A	D	A	C	A	B	A	C	A	B	A	D

Code	Job	Code	Job	Code	Job	Code	Job	Code	Job	Code	Job	Code	Job	Code	Job	Code	Job	Code	Job
ABCD	1	ABCD	28	ABCD	52	ABCD	63	ABCD	87	ABCD	108	BCD	133	ABCD	154	BCD	182	CD	213
ABCD	4	ABCD	29	ABCD	53	ABCD	65	CD	88	ABCD	116	BCD	135	CD	155	ABCD	186	ABCD	220
ABCD	6	BCD	32	ABCD	54	CD	78	CD	91	CD	118	BCD	136	ABCD	156	ABCD	187	ABCD	221
ABCD	8	ABCD	34	ABCD	58	ABCD	79	CD	94	CD	120	BCD	141	ABCD	159	BCD	189	ABCD	223
ABCD	9	D	35	ABCD	59	CD	81	D	98	BCD	126	BCD	146	CD	162	BCD	191	BCD	224
ABCD	10	D	36	ABCD	60	CD	83	D	101	ABCD	130	BCD	149	CD	166	BCD	201	ABCD	225
ABCD	18	ABCD	37	ABCD	61	ABCD	85	ABCD	105	B D	131	BCD	152	AB D	175	ABCD	202	BCD	226
ABCD	19	ABCD	51	D	62	ABCD	86	ABCD	106	CD	132	ABCD	153	CD	176	CD	203		

Datsun Cherry 100A range / 120 range

miles in thousands	3	6	9	12	15	18	21	24	27	30	33	36	39	42	45	48	51	54	57	60
look for service code letter	A	B	A	C	A	B	A	C	A	D	A	C	A	B	A	C	A	B	A	D

Code	Job	Code	Job	Code	Job	Code	Job	Code	Job	Code	Job	Code	Job	Code	Job	Code	Job	Code	Job
ABCD	1	ABCD	28	ABCD	52	ABCD	63	ABCD	87	ABCD	108	BCD	133	ABCD	154	BCD	184	ABCD	223
ABCD	4	ABCD	29	ABCD	53	ABCD	65	CD	88	ABCD	116	BCD	134	CD	155	BCD	189	BCD	224
ABCD	6	BCD	32	ABCD	54	CD	78	ABCD	91	CD	118	BCD	136	ABCD	156	BCD	190	ABCD	225
ABCD	8	ABCD	34	ABCD	58	ABCD	79	CD	94	CD	120	BCD	137	ABCD	159	BCD	200	BCD	226
ABCD	9	D	35	ABCD	59	CD	81	D	98	BCD	126	BCD	138	CD	162	ABCD	202		
ABCD	10	D	36	ABCD	60	CD	83	D	101	ABCD	130	BCD	148	CD	166	CD	213		
ABCD	18	ABCD	37	ABCD	61	ABCD	85	ABCD	105	B D	131	BCD	151	AB D	175	ABCD	220		
ABCD	19	ABCD	51	D	62	ABCD	86	ABCD	106	CD	132	ABCD	153	CD	176	ABCD	221		

Datsun Sunny 1200

miles in thousands	3	6	9	12	15	18	21	24	27	30	33	36	39	42	45	48	51	54	57	60
look for service code letter	A	B	A	C	A	B	A	C	A	D	A	C	A	B	A	C	A	B	A	D

Code	Job	Code	Job	Code	Job	Code	Job	Code	Job	Code	Job	Code	Job	Code	Job	Code	Job	Code	Job
ABCD	1	ABCD	19	ABCD	37	ABCD	61	ABCD	85	ABCD	105	B D	131	BCD	151	AB D	175	ABCD	220
ABCD	4	ABCD	26	ABCD	51	D	62	ABCD	86	ABCD	106	CD	132	ABCD	153	CD	176	ABCD	221
ABCD	6	ABCD	28	ABCD	52	ABCD	63	ABCD	87	ABCD	108	BCD	133	ABCD	154	BCD	184	ABCD	223
ABCD	8	ABCD	29	ABCD	53	ABCD	65	CD	88	ABCD	116	BCD	134	CD	155	BCD	189	BCD	224
ABCD	10	BCD	32	ABCD	54	CD	78	ABCD	91	CD	118	BCD	136	ABCD	156	BCD	190	ABCD	225
ABCD	13	ABCD	34	ABCD	58	ABCD	79	CD	94	CD	120	BCD	137	ABCD	159	BCD	200	BCD	226
ABCD	18	D	35	ABCD	59	CD	81	D	98	BCD	126	BCD	138	CD	162	ABCD	202		
		D	36	ABCD	60	CD	83	D	101	ABCD	130	BCD	148	CD	166	CD	213		

Fiat

Read page 40 before using these charts

Jobs to be done

Fiat 124

miles in thousands	6	12	18	24	30	36	42	48	54	60	66	72
look for service code letter	A	B	C	B	A	D	A	B	C	B	A	D

Code	Job	Code	Job	Code	Job	Code	Job	Code	Job	Code	Job	Code	Job	Code	Job	Code	Job	Code	Job
ABCD	1	ABCD	19	ABCD	32	ABCD	51	ABCD	86	ABCD	108	ABCD	133	ABCD	154	ABCD	176	ABCD	220
ABCD	4	ABCD	23	ABCD	34	ABCD	52	ABCD	87	ABCD	114	ABCD	134	CD	155	ABCD	184	ABCD	221
ABCD	6	ABCD	24	CD	35	CD	55	D	88	ABCD	120	ABCD	136	ABCD	156	ABCD	188	ABCD	223
ABCD	8	ABCD	25	CD	36	AB	58	ABCD	89	ABCD	123	ABCD	137	ABCD	158	ABCD	190	ABCD	224
ABCD	9	ABCD	26	AB	37	ABCD	61	ABCD	94	ABCD	130	ABCD	148	ABCD	161	ABCD	200	ABCD	225
ABCD	11	ABCD	28	ABCD	42	ABCD	63	ABCD	105	A C	131	ABCD	151	ABCD	162	ABCD	202	ABCD	226
ABCD	18	ABCD	29	ABCD	43	CD	65	ABCD	106	B D	132	ABCD	153	B D	168	ABCD	213		

Fiat 124S

miles in thousands	6	12	18	24	30	36	42	48	54	60	66	72
look for service code letter	A	B	C	B	A	D	A	B	C	B	A	D

Code	Job	Code	Job	Code	Job	Code	Job	Code	Job	Code	Job	Code	Job	Code	Job	Code	Job	Code	Job
ABCD	1	ABCD	19	ABCD	32	ABCD	51	ABCD	86	ABCD	108	ABCD	133	ABCD	154	ABCD	176	ABCD	220
ABCD	4	ABCD	23	ABCD	34	ABCD	52	ABCD	87	ABCD	114	ABCD	134	CD	155	ABCD	184	ABCD	221
ABCD	6	ABCD	24	CD	35	CD	55	D	88	ABCD	120	ABCD	136	ABCD	156	ABCD	188	ABCD	223
ABCD	8	ABCD	25	CD	36	AB	58	ABCD	89	ABCD	123	ABCD	137	ABCD	158	ABCD	190	ABCD	224
ABCD	9	ABCD	26	AB	37	ABCD	61	ABCD	94	ABCD	130	ABCD	148	ABCD	161	ABCD	200	ABCD	225
ABCD	11	ABCD	28	ABCD	42	ABCD	63	ABCD	105	A C	131	ABCD	151	ABCD	162	ABCD	202	ABCD	226
ABCD	18	ABCD	29	ABCD	43	CD	65	ABCD	106	B D	132	ABCD	153	B D	168	ABCD	213		

Fiat 125

miles in thousands	6	12	18	24	30	36	42	48	54	60	66	72
look for service code letter	A	B	C	B	A	D	A	B	C	B	A	D

Code	Job	Code	Job	Code	Job	Code	Job	Code	Job	Code	Job	Code	Job	Code	Job	Code	Job	Code	Job
ABCD	1	ABCD	19	ABCD	32	ABCD	51	ABCD	86	ABCD	108	ABCD	133	ABCD	153	ABCD	176	ABCD	220
ABCD	4	ABCD	23	ABCD	34	ABCD	52	ABCD	87	ABCD	114	B D	135	ABCD	154	ABCD	184	ABCD	221
ABCD	6	ABCD	24	CD	35	CD	55	D	88	ABCD	120	B D	136	CD	155	ABCD	188	ABCD	223
ABCD	8	ABCD	25	CD	36	AB	58	ABCD	89	ABCD	123	B D	141	ABCD	156	ABCD	190	ABCD	224
ABCD	9	ABCD	26	AB	37	ABCD	61	ABCD	94	ABCD	130	B D	143	ABCD	159	ABCD	200	ABCD	225
ABCD	11	ABCD	28	ABCD	42	ABCD	63	ABCD	105	A C	131	B D	150	ABCD	162	ABCD	202	ABCD	226
ABCD	18	ABCD	29	BCD	43	CD	65	ABCD	106	B D	132	B D	152	B D	168	ABCD	213		

Fiat 127

miles in thousands	6	12	18	24	30	36	42	48	54	60	66	72
look for service code letter	A	B	C	B	A	D	A	B	C	B	A	D

Code	Job	Code	Job	Code	Job	Code	Job	Code	Job	Code	Job	Code	Job	Code	Job	Code	Job	Code	Job
ABCD	1	ABCD	14	ABCD	28	ABCD	51	ABCD	85	ABCD	108	ABCD	134	ABCD	156	B D	184	ABCD	220
ABCD	2	ABCD	18	ABCD	29	ABCD	52	ABCD	86	ABCD	114	ABCD	136	ABCD	158	B D	185	ABCD	221
ABCD	4	ABCD	19	ABCD	32	ABCD	53	ABCD	87	ABCD	120	ABCD	137	CD	161	ABCD	187	ABCD	223
ABCD	6	ABCD	21	ABCD	34	CD	78	D	88	ABCD	123	ABCD	148	ABCD	162	ABCD	189	ABCD	224
ABCD	7	ABCD	22	CD	35	CD	79	ABCD	92	ABCD	130	ABCD	151	ABCD	166	ABCD	190	ABCD	225
ABCD	8	ABCD	23	CD	36	CD	80	ABCD	94	A C	131	ABCD	153	B D	169	ABCD	199	ABCD	226
ABCD	9	ABCD	24	AB	37	ABCD	82	ABCD	105	B D	132	ABCD	154	ABCD	176	ABCD	202		
ABCD	10	ABCD	25	ABCD	49	ABCD	83	ABCD	106	ABCD	133	CD	155	ABCD	181	ABCD	213		

Fiat 128

miles in thousands	6	12	18	24	30	36	42	48	54	60	66	72
look for service code letter	A	B	C	B	A	D	A	B	C	B	A	D

Code	Job	Code	Job	Code	Job	Code	Job	Code	Job	Code	Job	Code	Job	Code	Job	Code	Job	Code	Job
ABCD	1	ABCD	14	ABCD	28	ABCD	51	ABCD	85	ABCD	108	B D	135	ABCD	156	B D	185	ABCD	221
ABCD	2	ABCD	18	ABCD	29	ABCD	52	ABCD	86	ABCD	114	B D	136	ABCD	159	ABCD	187	ABCD	223
ABCD	4	ABCD	19	ABCD	32	ABCD	53	ABCD	87	ABCD	120	B D	141	ABCD	162	ABCD	189	ABCD	224
ABCD	6	ABCD	21	ABCD	34	CD	78	D	88	ABCD	123	B D	150	ABCD	166	ABCD	190	ABCD	225
ABCD	7	ABCD	22	CD	35	CD	79	ABCD	92	ABCD	130	B D	152	B D	169	ABCD	199	ABCD	226
ABCD	8	ABCD	23	CD	36	CD	80	ABCD	94	A C	131	ABCD	153	ABCD	176	ABCD	202		
ABCD	9	ABCD	24	AB	37	ABCD	82	ABCD	105	B D	132	ABCD	154	ABCD	181	ABCD	213		
ABCD	10	ABCD	25	ABCD	49	ABCD	83	ABCD	106	ABCD	133	CD	155	B D	184	ABCD	220		

Fiat 500

miles in thousands	6	12	18	24	30	36	42	48	54	60	66	72
look for service code letter	A	B	C	B	A	D	A	B	C	B	A	D

Code	Job	Code	Job	Code	Job	Code	Job	Code	Job	Code	Job	Code	Job	Code	Job	Code	Job	Code	Job
ABCD	1	ABCD	19	ABCD	34	ABCD	60	D	88	ABCD	120	ABCD	136	ABCD	166	ABCD	199	ABCD	226
ABCD	3	ABCD	23	ABCD	42	ABCD	61	ABCD	94	ABCD	123	ABCD	137	ABCD	176	ABCD	202		
ABCD	4	B D	26	ABCD	43	ABCD	78	CD	104	ABCD	130	ABCD	148	ABCD	181	ABCD	213		
ABCD	6	B D	27	ABCD	51	ABCD	79	ABCD	105	A C	131	ABCD	151	ABCD	184	ABCD	220		
ABCD	8	ABCD	28	ABCD	52	ABCD	81	ABCD	106	B D	132	ABCD	158	ABCD	187	ABCD	221		
ABCD	9	ABCD	29	AB	56	ABCD	83	ABCD	108	ABCD	133	ABCD	161	ABCD	189	ABCD	223		
ABCD	14	B D	33	CD	57	ABCD	85	ABCD	114	ABCD	134	ABCD	162	ABCD	190	ABCD	224		

Fiat 600D

miles in thousands	6	12	18	24	30	36	42	48	54	60	66	72
look for service code letter	A	B	C	B	E	D	A	B	C	E	A	D

Code	Job	Code	Job	Code	Job	Code	Job	Code	Job	Code	Job	Code	Job	Code	Job	Code	Job	Code	Job
ABCDE	1	ABCDE	23	ABCDE	42	ABCDE	78	ABCDE	94	ABCDE	130	ABCDE	151	ABCDE	166	ABCDE	190	ABCDE	226
ABCDE	3	ABCDE	26	ABCDE	43	ABCDE	79	CD	104	A C E	131	ABCDE	153	B DE	169	ABCDE	199		
ABCDE	4	ABCDE	27	ABCDE	51	ABCDE	81	ABCDE	105	B DE	132	ABCDE	154	ABCDE	176	ABCDE	202		
ABCDE	6	ABCDE	28	ABCDE	52	ABCDE	82	ABCDE	106	ABCDE	133	ABCDE	155 CD		ABCDE	181	ABCDE	213		
ABCDE	8	ABCDE	29	AB E	56	ABCDE	83	ABCDE	108	ABCDE	134	ABCDE	156	ABCDE	184	ABCDE	220		
ABCDE	9	ABCDE	31	CD	57	ABCDE	85	ABCDE	114	ABCDE	136	ABCDE	158	ABCDE	185	ABCDE	221		
ABCDE	11	E	33	ABCDE	60	D	88	ABCDE	120	ABCDE	137	ABCDE	161	ABCDE	187	ABCDE	223		
ABCDE	19	ABCDE	34	ABCDE	61	ABCDE	89	ABCDE	123	ABCDE	148	ABCDE	162	ABCDE	189	ABCDE	224		

Fiat – Ford

Read page 40 before using these charts

Jobs to be done

Fiat 850

miles in thousands	6	12	18	24	30	36	42	48	54	60	66	72
look for service code letter	A	B	C	B	A	D	A	B	C	B	A	D

Code	Job	Code	Job	Code	Job	Code	Job	Code	Job	Code	Job	Code	Job	Code	Job	Code	Job	Code	Job
ABCD	1	ABCD	23	ABCD	43	ABCD	79	ABCD	94	ABCD	120	ABCD	137	ABCD	161	ABCD	189	ABCD	224
ABCD	3	ABCD	26	ABCD	51	ABCD	81	B D	98	ABCD	123	ABCD	148	ABCD	162	ABCD	190	ABCD	226
ABCD	4	ABCD	27	ABCD	52	ABCD	83	B D	101	ABCD	130	ABCD	151	ABCD	166	ABCD	199		
ABCD	6	ABCD	28	AB	56	ABCD	85	CD	104	A C	131	ABCD	153	ABCD	176	ABCD	202		
ABCD	8	ABCD	29	CD	57	ABCD	86	ABCD	105	B D	132	ABCD	154	ABCD	181	ABCD	213		
ABCD	9	B D	33	ABCD	60	ABCD	87	ABCD	106	ABCD	133	CD	155	ABCD	184	ABCD	220		
ABCD	14	ABCD	34	ABCD	61	D	88	ABCD	108	ABCD	134	ABCD	156	ABCD	185	ABCD	221		
ABCD	19	ABCD	42	ABCD	78	ABCD	89	ABCD	114	ABCD	136	ABCD	158	ABCD	187	ABCD	223		

Ford Anglia 105E 123E

miles in thousands	2·5	5	7·5	10	12·5	15	17·5	20	22·5	25	27·5	30	32·5	35	37·5	40	42·5	45	47·5	50	52·5	55	57·5	60
look for service code letter	A	B	A	B	C	B	A	B	A	C	A	B	A	B	C	D	A	B	A	C	A	B	A	B

Code	Job	Code	Job	Code	Job	Code	Job	Code	Job	Code	Job	Code	Job	Code	Job	Code	Job	Code	Job
ABCD	1	ABCD	18	BCD	32	ABCD	58	ABCD	85	A CD	107	BCD	132	ABCD	153	A CD	175	BCD	213
ABCD	3	ABCD	19	ABCD	34	ABCD	61	BCD	88	BCD	108	BCD	133	ABCD	154	BCD	176	ABCD	220
ABCD	4	BCD	20	ABCD	37	ABCD	63	BCD	91	BCD	111	BCD	134	CD	155	BCD	181	ABCD	221
ABCD	6	BCD	23	ABCD	43	ABCD	65	ABCD	94	BCD	118	BCD	136	ABCD	156	BCD	184	ABCD	223
ABCD	8	BCD	25	ABCD	49	BCD	78	BCD	97	BCD	120	BCD	137	ABCD	158	BCD	188	BCD	224
ABCD	9	BCD	26	ABCD	51	ABCD	79	BCD	101	BCD	121	BCD	140	BCD	161	BCD	190	BCD	226
ABCD	10	BCD	28	ABCD	52	BCD	81	ABCD	105	ABCD	130	BCD	148	BCD	162	ABCD	199		
BCD	13	BCD	29	ABCD	53	BCD	83	BCD	106	ABCD	131	BCD	151	ABCD	171	ABCD	202		

Ford Classic; Capri 109E

miles in thousands	3	9	15	21	27	33	39	45	51	57	63	69	75	81	87
look for service code letter	A	A	B	A	C	E	A	A	B	C	A	E	A	A	D

Code	Job	Code	Job	Code	Job	Code	Job	Code	Job	Code	Job	Code	Job	Code	Job	Code	Job	Code	Job
ABCDE	1	ABCDE	18	ABCDE	34	ABCDE	58	ABCDE	87	ABCDE	108	ABCDE	133	ABCDE	155	ABCDE	188	ABCDE	226
ABCDE	3	ABCDE	19	A	35	ABCDE	63	E	88	ABCDE	109	ABCDE	134	ABCDE	156	ABCDE	190		
ABCDE	4	ABCDE	23	A	36	ABCDE	78	ABCDE	91	ABCDE	118	ABCDE	136	ABCDE	158	ABCDE	199		
ABCDE	6	ABCDE	25	BCDE	37	ABCDE	79	ABCDE	94	ABCDE	120	ABCDE	137	ABCDE	161	ABCDE	202		
ABCDE	8	ABCDE	26	ABCDE	42	ABCDE	81	CD	98	ABCDE	128	ABCDE	148	ABCDE	162	ABCDE	220		
ABCDE	9	ABCDE	28	ABCDE	43	ABCDE	83	CD	101	ABCDE	130	ABCDE	151	A C	175	ABCDE	221		
ABCDE	10	ABCDE	29	ABCDE	51	ABCDE	85	ABCDE	105	ABCDE	131	ABCDE	153	B DE	176	ABCDE	223		
ABCDE	13	ABCDE	32	ABCDE	52	ABCDE	86	ABCDE	106	ABCDE	132	ABCDE	154	B DE	184	ABCDE	224		

Ford Corsair 120E

miles in thousands	5	10	15	20	25	30	35	40	45	50	55	60	65	70	75
look for service code letter	A	A	B	A	A	B	A	C	B	A	A	B	A	A	B

Code	Job	Code	Job	Code	Job	Code	Job	Code	Job	Code	Job	Code	Job	Code	Job	Code	Job	Code	Job
ABC	1	ABC	19	ABC	37	ABC	65	ABC	87	ABC	108	ABC	133	ABC	156	ABC	188	ABC	221
ABC	4	ABC	23	ABC	49	ABC	78	C	88	ABC	109	ABC	134	ABC	158	ABC	190	ABC	223
ABC	6	ABC	25	ABC	51	ABC	79	ABC	91	ABC	118	ABC	136	ABC	161	ABC	199	ABC	224
ABC	8	ABC	26	ABC	52	ABC	80	ABC	94	ABC	120	ABC	137	ABC	162	ABC	202	ABC	225
ABC	9	ABC	28	ABC	53	ABC	81	B	98	ABC	128	ABC	151	ABC	171	B	211	ABC	226
ABC	10	ABC	29	ABC	58	ABC	83	B	101	ABC	130	ABC	153	A C	175	B	212		
ABC	13	ABC	31	ABC	61	ABC	85	ABC	105	A C	131	ABC	154	B	176	B	213		
ABC	18	ABC	34	ABC	63	ABC	86	ABC	106	B	132	B	155	ABC	184	ABC	220		

Ford Corsair V4 1700

miles in thousands	3	9	15	21	27	33	39	45	51	57	63	69	75	81	87
age of car in months	3	9	15	21	27	33	39	45	51	57	63	69	75	81	87
look for service code letter	A	A	B	A	C	E	A	A	B	C	A	E	A	A	D

Code	Job	Code	Job	Code	Job	Code	Job	Code	Job	Code	Job	Code	Job	Code	Job	Code	Job	Code	Job
ABCDE	1	ABCDE	19	ABCDE	37	ABCDE	79	ABCDE	89	ABCDE	118	ABCDE	134	ABCDE	158	ABCDE	190	ABCDE	220
ABCDE	4	ABCDE	23	ABCDE	51	ABCDE	80	ABCDE	94	ABCDE	119	ABCDE	136	ABCDE	161	ABCDE	199	ABCDE	221
ABCDE	6	ABCDE	25	ABCDE	52	ABCDE	81	ABCDE	98	ABCDE	120	ABCDE	137	ABCDE	162	ABCDE	202	ABCDE	223
ABCDE	8	ABCDE	26	ABCDE	53	ABCDE	83	ABCDE	101	ABCDE	121	ABCDE	148	ABCDE	174	ABCDE	203	ABCDE	224
ABCDE	9	ABCDE	28	ABCDE	58	ABCDE	85	ABCDE	105	ABCDE	130	ABCDE	151	A C	175	B DE	205	ABCDE	225
CD	10	ABCDE	29	ABCDE	61	ABCDE	86	ABCDE	106	ABCDE	131	ABCDE	153	B DE	176	B DE	211	ABCDE	226
ABCDE	13	ABCDE	32	ABCDE	63	ABCDE	87	ABCDE	108	ABCDE	132	ABCDE	154	ABCDE	184	B DE	212		
ABCDE	18	ABCDE	34	ABCDE	78	E	88	ABCDE	111	ABCDE	133	ABCDE	156	ABCDE	188	ABCDE	213		

Ford Cortina Mk I 1200; 1500

miles in thousands	5	10	15	20	25	30	35	40	45	50	55	60	65	70	75
look for service code letter	A	A	B	A	A	B	A	C	B	A	A	B	A	A	B

Code	Job	Code	Job	Code	Job	Code	Job	Code	Job	Code	Job	Code	Job	Code	Job	Code	Job	Code	Job
ABC	1	ABC	19	ABC	37	ABC	65	ABC	87	ABC	108	ABC	133	ABC	156	ABC	188	ABC	221
ABC	4	ABC	23	ABC	49	ABC	78	C	88	ABC	109	ABC	134	ABC	158	ABC	190	ABC	223
ABC	6	ABC	25	ABC	51	ABC	79	ABC	91	ABC	118	ABC	136	ABC	161	ABC	199	ABC	224
ABC	8	ABC	26	ABC	52	ABC	80	ABC	94	ABC	120	ABC	137	ABC	162	ABC	202	ABC	225
ABC	9	ABC	28	ABC	53	ABC	81	B	98	ABC	128	ABC	151	ABC	171	B	211	ABC	226
ABC	10	ABC	29	ABC	58	ABC	83	B	101	ABC	130	ABC	153	A C	175	B	212		
ABC	13	ABC	31	ABC	61	ABC	85	ABC	105	A C	131	ABC	154	B	176	B	213		
ABC	18	ABC	34	ABC	63	ABC	86	ABC	106	B	132	B	155	ABC	184	ABC	220		

Ford

Jobs to be done

Read page 40 before using these charts

Ford Cortina Mk I GT

miles in thousands	5	10	15	20	25	30	35	40	45	50	55	60	65	70	75
look for service code letter	A	A	B	A	A	B	A	C	B	A	A	B	A	A	B

Code	Job	Code	Job	Code	Job	Code	Job	Code	Job	Code	Job	Code	Job	Code	Job	Code	Job	Code	Job
ABC	1	ABC	19	ABC	37	ABC	65	ABC	87	ABC	108	ABC	133	ABC	156	ABC	188	ABC	220
ABC	4	ABC	23	ABC	49	ABC	78	C	88	ABC	109	ABC	134	ABC	158	ABC	190	ABC	221
ABC	6	ABC	25	ABC	51	ABC	79	ABC	91	ABC	118	ABC	136	ABC	161	ABC	195	ABC	223
ABC	8	ABC	26	ABC	52	ABC	80	ABC	94	ABC	120	ABC	137	ABC	162	ABC	200	ABC	224
ABC	9	ABC	28	ABC	53	ABC	81	B	98	ABC	128	ABC	151	ABC	171	ABC	202	ABC	225
ABC	10	ABC	29	ABC	58	ABC	83	B	101	ABC	130	ABC	153	A C	175	B	211	ABC	226
ABC	13	ABC	31	ABC	61	ABC	85	ABC	105	A C	131	ABC	154	B	176	B	212		
ABC	18	ABC	34	ABC	63	ABC	86	ABC	106	B	132	B	155			B	213		

Ford Cortina Mk II

miles in thousands	3	9	15	21	27	33	39	45	51	57	63	69	75	81	87
age of car in months	3	9	15	21	27	33	39	45	51	57	63	69	75	81	87
look for service code letter	A	A	B	A	C	E	A	A	B	C	A	E	A	A	D

Code	Job	Code	Job	Code	Job	Code	Job	Code	Job	Code	Job	Code	Job	Code	Job	Code	Job	Code	Job
ABCDE	1	ABCDE	19	ABCDE	37	ABCDE	79	ABCDE	91	ABCDE	118	ABCDE	134	ABCDE	158	ABCDE	190	ABCDE	220
ABCDE	4	ABCDE	23	ABCDE	51	ABCDE	80	ABCDE	94	ABCDE	119	ABCDE	136	ABCDE	161	ABCDE	199	ABCDE	221
ABCDE	6	ABCDE	25	ABCDE	52	ABCDE	81	CD	98	ABCDE	120	ABCDE	137	ABCDE	162	ABCDE	202	ABCDE	223
ABCDE	8	ABCDE	26	ABCDE	53	ABCDE	83	CD	101	ABCDE	121	ABCDE	148	ABCDE	174	ABCDE	203	ABCDE	224
ABCDE	9	ABCDE	28	ABCDE	58	ABCDE	85	ABCDE	105	ABCDE	130	ABCDE	151	A C	175	B DE	205	ABCDE	225
CD	10	ABCDE	29	ABCDE	61	ABCDE	86	ABCDE	106	ABCDE	131	ABCDE	153	B DE	176	B DE	211	ABCDE	226
ABCDE	13	ABCDE	31	ABCDE	63	ABCDE	87	ABCDE	108	ABCDE	132	ABCDE	154	ABCDE	184	B DE	212		
ABCDE	18	ABCDE	34	ABCDE	78	E	88	ABCDE	111	ABCDE	133	ABCDE	156	ABCDE	188	ABCDE	213		

Ford Corsair V4 2000

miles in thousands	3	9	15	21	27	33	39	45	51	57	63	69	75	81	87
age of car in months	3	9	15	21	27	33	39	45	51	57	63	69	75	81	87
look for service code letter	A	A	B	A	C	E	A	A	B	C	A	E	A	A	D

Code	Job	Code	Job	Code	Job	Code	Job	Code	Job	Code	Job	Code	Job	Code	Job	Code	Job	Code	Job
ABCDE	1	ABCDE	19	ABCDE	37	ABCDE	79	ABCDE	89	ABCDE	118	ABCDE	134	ABCDE	158	ABCDE	193	ABCDE	213
ABCDE	4	ABCDE	23	ABCDE	51	ABCDE	80	ABCDE	94	ABCDE	119	ABCDE	136	ABCDE	161	ABCDE	195	ABCDE	220
ABCDE	6	ABCDE	25	ABCDE	52	ABCDE	81	ABCDE	98	ABCDE	120	ABCDE	137	ABCDE	162	ABCDE	200	ABCDE	221
ABCDE	8	ABCDE	26	ABCDE	53	ABCDE	83	ABCDE	101	ABCDE	121	ABCDE	148	ABCDE	174	ABCDE	202	ABCDE	223
ABCDE	9	ABCDE	28	ABCDE	58	ABCDE	85	ABCDE	105	ABCDE	130	ABCDE	151	A CD	175	ABCDE	203	ABCDE	224
CD	10	ABCDE	29	ABCDE	61	ABCDE	86	ABCDE	106	ABCDE	131	ABCDE	153	B DE	176	B DE	205	ABCDE	225
ABCDE	13	ABCDE	32	ABCDE	63	ABCDE	87	ABCDE	108	ABCDE	132	ABCDE	154	ABCDE	184	B DE	211	ABCDE	226
ABCDE	18	ABCDE	34	ABCDE	78	E	88	ABCDE	111	ABCDE	133	ABCDE	156	ABCDE	188	B DE	212		

Ford Cortina Mk II GT

miles in thousands	3	9	15	21	27	33	39	45	51	57	63	69	75	81	87
age of car in months	3	9	15	21	27	33	39	45	51	57	63	69	75	81	87
look for service code letter	A	A	B	A	C	E	A	A	B	C	A	E	A	A	D

Code	Job	Code	Job	Code	Job	Code	Job	Code	Job	Code	Job	Code	Job	Code	Job	Code	Job	Code	Job
ABCDE	1	ABCDE	19	ABCDE	37	ABCDE	79	ABCDE	91	ABCDE	118	ABCDE	134	ABCDE	158	ABCDE	190	ABCDE	213
ABCDE	4	ABCDE	23	ABCDE	51	ABCDE	80	ABCDE	94	ABCDE	119	ABCDE	136	ABCDE	161	ABCDE	195	ABCDE	220
ABCDE	6	ABCDE	25	ABCDE	52	ABCDE	81	CD	98	ABCDE	120	ABCDE	137	ABCDE	162	ABCDE	200	ABCDE	221
ABCDE	8	ABCDE	26	ABCDE	53	ABCDE	83	CD	101	ABCDE	121	ABCDE	148	ABCDE	174	ABCDE	202	ABCDE	223
ABCDE	9	ABCDE	28	ABCDE	58	ABCDE	85	ABCDE	105	ABCDE	130	ABCDE	151	A CD	175	ABCDE	203	ABCDE	224
CD	10	ABCDE	29	ABCDE	61	ABCDE	86	ABCDE	106	ABCDE	131	ABCDE	153	B DE	176	B DE	205	ABCDE	225
ABCDE	13	ABCDE	31	ABCDE	63	ABCDE	87	ABCDE	108	ABCDE	132	ABCDE	154	ABCDE	184	B DE	211	ABCDE	226
ABCDE	18	ABCDE	34	ABCDE	78	E	88	ABCDE	111	ABCDE	133	ABCDE	156	ABCDE	188	B DE	212		

Ford Cortina Mk III 2000

miles in thousands	3	9	15	21	27	33	39	45	51	57	63	69	75	81	87
age of car in months	3	9	15	21	27	33	39	45	51	57	63	69	75	81	87
look for service code letter	A	A	B	A	C	E	A	A	B	C	A	E	A	A	D

Code	Job	Code	Job	Code	Job	Code	Job	Code	Job	Code	Job	Code	Job	Code	Job	Code	Job	Code	Job
ABCDE	1	ABCDE	21	ABCDE	37	ABCDE	66	E	88	ABCDE	118	ABCDE	136	ABCDE	165	ABCDE	202	ABCDE	226
ABCDE	4	ABCDE	22	ABCDE	44	ABCDE	78	ABCDE	89	ABCDE	119	ABCDE	141	ABCDE	174	ABCDE	203		
ABCDE	6	ABCDE	23	ABCDE	51	ABCDE	79	ABCDE	94	ABCDE	120	ABCDE	146	A C	175	B DE	204		
ABCDE	8	ABCDE	24	ABCDE	52	ABCDE	80	CD	98	ABCDE	121	ABCDE	150	B DE	176	ABCDE	213		
ABCDE	9	ABCDE	25	ABCDE	53	ABCDE	81	CD	101	ABCDE	130	ABCDE	152	ABCDE	184	ABCDE	220		
ABCDE	11	ABCDE	28	ABCDE	54	ABCDE	83	ABCDE	105	ABCDE	131	ABCDE	153	ABCDE	188	ABCDE	221		
ABCDE	12	ABCDE	29	ABCDE	58	ABCDE	85	ABCDE	106	ABCDE	132	ABCDE	154	ABCDE	190	ABCDE	223		
ABCDE	18	ABCDE	31	ABCDE	61	ABCDE	86	ABCDE	108	ABCDE	133	ABCDE	156	ABCDE	195	ABCDE	224		
ABCDE	19	ABCDE	34	ABCDE	63	ABCDE	87	ABCDE	111	ABCDE	135	ABCDE	159	ABCDE	200	ABCDE	225		

Ford Escort

miles in thousands	3	9	15	21	27	33	39	45	51	57	63	69	75	81	87
age of car in months	3	9	15	21	27	33	39	45	51	57	63	69	75	81	87
look for service code letter	A	A	B	A	C	E	A	A	B	C	A	E	A	A	D

Code	Job	Code	Job	Code	Job	Code	Job	Code	Job	Code	Job	Code	Job	Code	Job	Code	Job	Code	Job
ABCDE	1	ABCDE	21	ABCDE	37	ABCDE	63	ABCDE	87	ABCDE	111	ABCDE	134	ABCDE	161	ABCDE	202	ABCDE	226
ABCDE	4	ABCDE	22	ABCDE	42	ABCDE	66	E	88	ABCDE	118	ABCDE	136	ABCDE	162	ABCDE	203		
ABCDE	6	ABCDE	23	ABCDE	45	ABCDE	78	ABCDE	89	ABCDE	119	ABCDE	137	ABCDE	174	B DE	205		
ABCDE	8	ABCDE	24	ABCDE	51	ABCDE	79	ABCDE	94	ABCDE	120	ABCDE	148	A C	175	ABCDE	213		
ABCDE	9	ABCDE	25	ABCDE	52	ABCDE	80	CD	98	ABCDE	121	ABCDE	151	B DE	176	ABCDE	220		
ABCDE	11	ABCDE	28	ABCDE	53	ABCDE	81	CD	101	ABCDE	130	ABCDE	153	ABCDE	184	ABCDE	221		
ABCDE	12	ABCDE	29	ABCDE	54	ABCDE	83	ABCDE	105	ABCDE	131	ABCDE	154	ABCDE	188	ABCDE	223		
ABCDE	18	ABCDE	31	ABCDE	58	ABCDE	85	ABCDE	106	ABCDE	132	ABCDE	156	ABCDE	190	ABCDE	224		
ABCDE	19	ABCDE	34	ABCDE	61	ABCDE	86	ABCDE	108	ABCDE	133	ABCDE	158	ABCDE	199	ABCDE	225		

Ford – Renault

Read page 40 before using these charts

Jobs to be done

Ford Zephyr & Zodiac Mk III

miles in thousands	3	9	15	21	27	33	39	45	51	57	63	69	75	81	87
age of car in months	3	9	15	21	27	33	39	45	51	57	63	69	75	81	87
look for service code letter	A	A	B	A	C	E	A	A	B	C	A	E	A	A	D

Code	Job	Code	Job	Code	Job	Code	Job	Code	Job	Code	Job	Code	Job	Code	Job	Code	Job	Code	Job
ABCDE	1	ABCDE	18	ABCDE	34	ABCDE	54	E	88	ABCDE	111	ABCDE	133	ABCDE	154	ABCDE	185	ABCDE	213
ABCDE	4	ABCDE	19	A	35	ABCDE	58	ABCDE	89	ABCDE	118	ABCDE	134	ABCDE	156	ABCDE	188	ABCDE	220
ABCDE	5	ABCDE	23	A	36	ABCDE	59	ABCDE	94	ABCDE	119	ABCDE	136	ABCDE	159	ABCDE	190	ABCDE	221
ABCDE	6	ABCDE	25	BCDE	37	ABCDE	60	CD	98	ABCDE	120	ABCDE	138	A	165	ABCDE	199	ABCDE	223
ABCDE	8	ABCDE	26	ABCDE	39	ABCDE	61	CD	101	ABCDE	121	ABCDE	139	ABCDE	173	ABCDE	202	ABCDE	224
ABCDE	9	ABCDE	28	ABCDE	51	ABCDE	63	ABCDE	105	ABCDE	130	ABCDE	148	A C	175	ABCDE	203	ABCDE	225
ABCDE	10	ABCDE	29	ABCDE	52	ABCDE	86	ABCDE	106	ABCDE	131	ABCDE	151	B DE	176	ABCDE	211	ABCDE	226
ABCDE	12	ABCDE	32	ABCDE	53	ABCDE	87	ABCDE	108	ABCDE	132	ABCDE	153	ABCDE	184	ABCDE	212		

Mazda RX-3

miles in thousands	4	8	12	16	20	24	28	32	36	40	44	48	52	56	60	64	68	72	76	80	84
look for service code letter	A	B	C	A	B	C	A	B	D	A	B	C	A	B	C	A	B	D	A	B	C

Code	Job	Code	Job	Code	Job	Code	Job	Code	Job	Code	Job	Code	Job	Code	Job	Code	Job	Code	Job
ABCD	1	ABCD	18	ABCD	32	ABCD	52	BCD	81	D	101	ABCD	130	ABCD	159	ABCD	190	ABCD	221
ABCD	4	CD	19	ABCD	34	ABCD	54	BCD	83	ABCD	105	AB	131	CD	164	ABCD	200	ABCD	223
ABCD	5	ABCD	23	CD	35	CD	55	ABCD	85	ABCD	106	CD	132	CD	173	ABCD	202	ABCD	224
ABCD	6	ABCD	24	CD	36	AB	58	ABCD	86	ABCD	108	ABCD	133	AB	175	ABCD	203	ABCD	225
ABCD	8	ABCD	25	AB	37	ABCD	61	ABCD	87	ABCD	112	ABCD	153	CD	176	CD	211	ABCD	226
ABCD	9	BCD	26	ABCD	42	CD	63	ABCD	90	ABCD	118	ABCD	154	CD	184	CD	212		
ABCD	10	ABCD	28	ABCD	43	BCD	78	ABCD	94	CD	120	CD	155	ABCD	187	CD	213		
BCD	13	CD	29	ABCD	51	ABCD	79	D	98	ABCD	124	ABCD	156	ABCD	189	ABCD	220		

Renault R4

miles in thousands	3	6	9	12	15	18	21	24	27	30	33	36	39	42	45	48	51	54	57	60	63
look for service code letter	A	A	B	A	A	C	A	A	B	A	A	C	A	A	B	A	A	C	A	A	B

Code	Job	Code	Job	Code	Job	Code	Job	Code	Job	Code	Job	Code	Job	Code	Job	Code	Job	Code	Job
ABC	1	BC	18	ABC	34	BC	59	ABC	105	A	131	ABC	151	BC	166	A	175	ABC	202
ABC	2	BC	19	ABC	42	BC	60	ABC	106	BC	132	ABC	153	ABC	168	BC	176	BC	213
ABC	4	ABC	21	BC	43	BC	61	BC	108	BC	133	ABC	154	ABC	169	BC	184	ABC	220
ABC	6	ABC	22	ABC	51	BC	79	BC	113	ABC	134	C	155	ABC	170	BC	188	ABC	221
ABC	8	ABC	23	ABC	52	BC	85	BC	120	ABC	136	ABC	156	ABC	171	BC	190	ABC	223
BC	9	ABC	28	A	56	BC	89	BC	125	ABC	137	BC	158	ABC	172	BC	194	ABC	224
BC	15	ABC	29	BC	57	ABC	94	ABC	130	ABC	148	BC	161	ABC	173	ABC	199	ABC	226

Renault R5 845 cc

miles in thousands	3	6	9	12	15	18	21	24	27	30	33	36	39	42	45	48	51	54	57	60	63
look for service code letter	A	A	B	A	A	C	A	A	B	A	A	C	A	A	B	A	A	C	A	A	B

Code	Job	Code	Job	Code	Job	Code	Job	Code	Job	Code	Job	Code	Job	Code	Job	Code	Job
ABC	1	BC	19	ABC	42	BC	61	BC	113	ABC	136	BC	158	ABC	173	ABC	202
ABC	2	ABC	21	BC	43	BC	79	BC	120	ABC	137	BC	161	A	175	BC	213
ABC	4	ABC	22	ABC	51	BC	85	BC	125	ABC	148	BC	166	BC	176	ABC	220
ABC	6	ABC	23	ABC	52	BC	89	ABC	130	ABC	151	ABC	168	BC	184	ABC	221
ABC	8	ABC	28	A	56	ABC	94	A	131	ABC	153	ABC	169	BC	188	ABC	223
BC	9	ABC	29	BC	57	ABC	105	BC	132	ABC	154	ABC	170	BC	190	ABC	224
BC	15	ABC	32	BC	59	ABC	106	BC	133	C	155	ABC	171	BC	194	ABC	226
BC	18	ABC	34	BC	60	BC	108	ABC	134	ABC	156	ABC	172	ABC	199		

Renault R5-TL 956 cc

miles in thousands	3	6	9	12	15	18	21	24	27	30	33	36	39	42	45	48	51	54	57	60	63
look for service code letter	A	A	B	A	A	C	A	A	B	A	A	C	A	A	B	A	A	C	A	A	B

Code	Job	Code	Job	Code	Job	Code	Job	Code	Job	Code	Job	Code	Job	Code	Job	Code	Job
ABC	1	BC	19	ABC	42	BC	61	BC	113	ABC	136	BC	158	ABC	173	ABC	202
ABC	2	ABC	21	BC	43	BC	79	BC	120	ABC	137	BC	161	A	175	BC	213
ABC	4	ABC	22	ABC	51	BC	85	BC	125	ABC	148	BC	166	BC	176	ABC	220
ABC	6	ABC	23	ABC	52	BC	89	ABC	130	ABC	151	ABC	168	BC	184	ABC	221
ABC	8	ABC	28	A	56	ABC	94	A	131	ABC	153	ABC	169	BC	188	ABC	223
BC	9	ABC	29	BC	57	ABC	105	BC	132	ABC	154	ABC	170	BC	190	ABC	224
BC	15	BC	32	BC	59	ABC	106	BC	133	C	155	ABC	171	BC	194	ABC	226
BC	18	ABC	34	BC	60	BC	108	ABC	134	ABC	156	ABC	172	ABC	199		

Renault R6 845 cc

miles in thousands	3	6	9	12	15	18	21	24	27	30	33	36	39	42	45	48	51	54	57	60	63
look for service code letter	A	A	B	A	A	C	A	A	B	A	A	C	A	A	B	A	A	C	A	A	B

Code	Job	Code	Job	Code	Job	Code	Job	Code	Job	Code	Job	Code	Job	Code	Job	Code	Job
ABC	1	BC	19	ABC	42	BC	61	BC	113	ABC	136	BC	158	ABC	173	ABC	202
ABC	2	ABC	21	BC	43	BC	79	BC	120	ABC	137	BC	161	A	175	BC	213
ABC	4	ABC	22	ABC	51	BC	85	BC	125	ABC	148	BC	166	BC	176	ABC	220
ABC	6	ABC	23	ABC	52	BC	89	ABC	130	ABC	151	ABC	168	BC	184	ABC	221
ABC	8	ABC	28	A	56	ABC	94	A	131	ABC	153	ABC	169	BC	188	ABC	223
BC	9	ABC	29	BC	57	ABC	105	BC	132	ABC	154	ABC	170	BC	190	ABC	224
BC	15	ABC	32	BC	59	ABC	106	BC	133	C	155	ABC	171	BC	194	ABC	226
BC	18	ABC	34	BC	60	BC	108	ABC	134	ABC	156	ABC	172	ABC	199		

Renault — Toyota

Jobs to be done

Read page 40 before using these charts

Renault R6 1108 cc

miles in thousands	3	6	9	12	15	18	21	24	27	30	33	36	39	42	45	48	51	54	57	60	63
look for service code letter	A	A	B	A	A	C	A	A	B	A	A	C	A	A	B	A	A	C	A	A	B

Code	Job	Code	Job	Code	Job	Code	Job	Code	Job	Code	Job	Code	Job	Code	Job	Code	Job	Code	Job
ABC	1	BC	19	ABC	42	BC	61	ABC	106	BC	133	C	155	ABC	171	BC	194	ABC	226
ABC	2	ABC	21	BC	43	BC	79	BC	108	ABC	134	ABC	156	ABC	172	ABC	199		
ABC	4	ABC	22	ABC	51	BC	85	BC	113	ABC	136	BC	158	ABC	173	ABC	202		
ABC	6	ABC	23	ABC	52	ABC	86	BC	120	ABC	137	BC	161	A	175	BC	213		
ABC	8	ABC	28	A	56	ABC	87	BC	125	ABC	148	BC	166	BC	176	ABC	220		
BC	9	ABC	29	BC	57	BC	89	ABC	130	ABC	151	ABC	168	BC	184	ABC	221		
BC	15	ABC	32	BC	59	ABC	94	A	131	ABC	153	ABC	169	BC	188	ABC	223		
BC	18	ABC	34	BC	60	ABC	105	BC	132	ABC	154	ABC	170	BC	190	ABC	224		

Renault R8; R10

miles in thousands	3	6	9	12	15	18	21	24	27	30	33	36	39	42	45	48	51	54	57	60	63
look for service code letter	A	A	B	A	A	C	A	A	B	A	A	C	A	A	B	A	A	C	A	A	B

Code	Job	Code	Job	Code	Job	Code	Job	Code	Job	Code	Job	Code	Job	Code	Job	Code	Job
ABC	1	ABC	18	ABC	29	ABC	86	ABC	108	BC	133	ABC	154	BC	176	BC	213
ABC	3	BC	19	BC	32	ABC	87	ABC	113	ABC	134	ABC	156	BC	184	ABC	220
ABC	4	ABC	21	ABC	34	BC	90	BC	120	ABC	136	ABC	158	ABC	187	ABC	221
ABC	6	BC	22	ABC	51	BC	94	ABC	125	ABC	137	BC	161	ABC	189	ABC	223
ABC	8	ABC	23	ABC	52	C	95	ABC	130	ABC	148	BC	166	ABC	193	ABC	224
ABC	9	BC	27	A	56	ABC	105	A	131	ABC	151	ABC	173	ABC	199	ABC	226
ABC	12	ABC	28	BC	57	ABC	106	BC	132	ABC	153	A	175	ABC	202		

Renault R12 TL & TS

miles in thousands	3	6	9	12	15	18	21	24	27	30	33	36	39	42	45	48	51	54	57	60	63
look for service code letter	A	A	B	A	A	D	A	A	C	A	A	D	A	A	B	A	A	D	A	A	B

Code	Job	Code	Job	Code	Job	Code	Job	Code	Job	Code	Job	Code	Job	Code	Job	Code	Job
ABCD	1	BCD	18	ABCD	28	ABCD	52	BCD	87	BCD	113	ABCD	134	D	155	ABCD	184	ABCD	220
ABCD	2	BCD	19	BCD	29	ABCD	54	BCD	89	CD	120	BCD	136	ABCD	156	BCD	187	ABCD	221
ABCD	4	BCD	21	BCD	31	A	56	BCD	94	BCD	125	BCD	137	BCD	158	BCD	189	BCD	223
ABCD	6	BCD	22	ABCD	34	BCD	57	CD	95	BCD	130	BCD	148	BCD	161	BCD	190	BCD	224
ABCD	8	BCD	23	BCD	42	ABCD	61	ABCD	105	ABCD	131	BCD	151	BCD	173	ABCD	199	BCD	226
BCD	9	BCD	24	BCD	43	BCD	85	ABCD	106	ABCD	132	ABCD	153	A	175	ABCD	202		
BCD	12	BCD	25	ABCD	51	BCD	86	BCD	108	BCD	133	ABCD	154	BCD	176	BCD	213		

Renault R15-TL & TS

miles in thousands	3	6	9	12	15	18	21	24	27	30	33	36	39	42	45	48	51	54
look for service code letter	A	A	B	A	A	C	A	A	D	A	A	C	A	A	B	A	A	E

Code	Job	Code	Job	Code	Job	Code	Job	Code	Job	Code	Job	Code	Job	Code	Job	Code	Job
ABCDE	1	ABCDE	12	ABCDE	28	ABCDE	54	BCDE	89	BCDE	125	BCDE	137	ABCDE	159	BCDE	189	ABCDE	220
ABCDE	2	ABCDE	18	ABCDE	29	A	56	BCDE	94	ABCDE	130	BCDE	148	ABCDE	166	BCDE	190	ABCDE	221
ABCDE	4	ABCDE	19	BCDE	31	BCDE	57	ABCDE	105	ABCDE	131	BCDE	151	CDE	173	BCDE	199	BCDE	223
ABCDE	5	BCDE	21	ABCDE	34	ABCDE	61	ABCDE	106	BCDE	132	ABCDE	153	A	175	ABCDE	202	BCDE	224
ABCDE	6	BCDE	22	ABCDE	51	BCDE	85	BCDE	108	BCDE	133	ABCDE	154	BCDE	176	ABCDE	203	BCDE	225
ABCDE	8	BCDE	23	ABCDE	52	BCDE	86	BCDE	113	BCDE	134	D	155	BCDE	184	C E	204	BCDE	226
ABCDE	9	BCDE	24	ABCDE	53	BCD	87	BCDE	120	BCDE	136	ABCDE	156	BCDE	187	BCDE	213		

Renault R16-TL & TS

miles in thousands	3	6	9	12	15	18	21	24	27	30	33	36	39	42	45	48	51	54
look for service code letter	A	A	B	A	A	C	A	A	D	A	A	C	A	A	B	A	A	E

Code	Job	Code	Job	Code	Job	Code	Job	Code	Job	Code	Job	Code	Job	Code	Job
ABCDE	1	ABCDE	18	BCDE	31	BCDE	57	BCDE	94	ABCDE	131	ABCDE	153	BCDE	176	C E	204
ABCDE	2	ABCDE	19	ABCDE	34	BCDE	59	ABCDE	105	BCDE	132	ABCDE	154	BCDE	184	BCDE	213
ABCDE	4	BCDE	21	ABCDE	49	BCDE	60	ABCDE	106	BCDE	133	D	155	BCDE	187	ABCDE	220
ABCDE	5	BCDE	22	ABCDE	51	ABCDE	61	BCDE	108	BCDE	134	ABCDE	156	BCDE	189	ABCDE	221
ABCDE	6	BCDE	23	ABCDE	52	BCDE	85	BCDE	113	BCDE	136	ABCDE	159	BCDE	190	BCDE	223
ABCDE	8	BCDE	24	ABCDE	53	BCDE	86	BCDE	120	BCDE	137	ABCDE	166	BCDE	199	BCDE	224
ABCDE	9	ABCDE	28	ABCDE	54	BCD	87	BCDE	125	BCDE	148	CDE	173	ABCDE	202	BCDE	225
BCDE	15	ABCDE	29	A	56	BCDE	89	ABCDE	130	BCDE	151	A	175	ABCDE	203	BCDE	226

Toyota Crown 2300; 2600

miles in thousands	3	6	9	12	15	18	21	24	27	30	33	36	39	42	45	48	51	54	57	60
age of car in months	3	6	9	12	15	18	21	24	27	30	33	36	39	42	45	48	51	54	57	60
look for service code letter	A	B	A	C	A	D	A	E	A	B	A	D	A	B	A	E	A	D	A	C

Code	Job	Code	Job	Code	Job	Code	Job	Code	Job	Code	Job	Code	Job	Code	Job	Code	Job	Code	Job
ABCDE	1	ABCDE	19	D	55	BCDE	85	ABCDE	105	AB D	131	BCDE	149	C	167	ABCDE	203	BCDE	224
ABCDE	4	CDE	23	BCDE	58	ABCDE	86	ABCDE	106	CDE	132	BCDE	152	ABCDE	173	ABCDE	209	ABCDE	225
ABCDE	6	ABCDE	28	BCDE	61	ABCDE	87	ABCDE	108	BCDE	133	ABCDE	153	AB D	175	ABCDE	210	BCDE	226
ABCDE	8	ABCDE	29	BCDE	63	CDE	88	ABCDE	116	BCDE	135	ABCDE	154	CDE	176	CDE	213		
BCDE	9	BCDE	31	CDE	78	BCDE	89	BCDE	118	BCDE	136	CDE	155	CDE	184	ABCDE	215		
BCDE	11	ABCDE	51	ABCDE	79	ABCDE	94	BCDE	120	BCDE	141	ABCDE	156	BCDE	193	ABCDE	220		
BCDE	12	ABCDE	52	CDE	81	E	98	BCDE	126	BCDE	147	BCDE	159	BCDE	200	ABCDE	221		
ABCDE	18	ABCDE	54	CDE	83	E	101	BCDE	130	BCDE	148	BCDE	162	ABCDE	202	ABCDE	223		

Toyota – Vauxhall

Read page 40 before using these charts

Jobs to be done

Toyota 1600 Carina / 1600 Celica

	3	6	9	12	15	18	21	24	27	30	33	36	39	42	45	48	51	54	57	60
miles in thousands	3	6	9	12	15	18	21	24	27	30	33	36	39	42	45	48	51	54	57	60
age of car in months	3	6	9	12	15	18	21	24	27	30	33	36	39	42	45	48	51	54	57	60
look for service code letter	A	B	A	C	A	D	E	C	A	B	A	D	F	E	A	C	A	D	A	E

Code	Job	Code	Job	Code	Job	Code	Job	Code	Job	Code	Job	Code	Job	Code	Job
ABCDEF	1	BCDE	26	ABCDEF	52	CDE	85	BCDE	108	BCDE	136	CDE	173	BCDE	220
ABCDEF	4	ABCDEF	28	ABCDEF	53	ABCDEF	86	BCDE	116	BCDE	137	ABCDEF	175	BCDE	221
ABCDEF	6	ABCDEF	29	ABCDEF	54	ABCDEF	87	BCDE	118	BCDE	148	D	176	BCDE	223
ABCDEF	8	BCDE	32	D	55	CDE	88	BCDE	120	BCDE	151	CDE	184	BCDE	224
ABCDEF	9	ABCDEF	34	BCDE	58	ABCDEF	89	BCDE	126	BCDE	153	CDE	190	BCDE	225
ABCDEF	10	D	35	CDE	63	ABCDEF	94	BCDE	130	BCDE	154	BCDE	200	BCDE	226
ABCDEF	18	D	36	CDE	78	F	98	B DE	131	E	155	ABCDEF	202		
ABCDEF	19	BCDE	37	ABCDEF	79	F	101	CDE	132	ABCDEF	156	ABCDEF	203		
BCDE	23	BCDE	49	CDE	81	ABCDEF	105	ABCDEF	133	BCDE	159	CDE	211		
BCDE	25	ABCDEF	51	CDE	83	ABCDEF	106	BCDE	134	F	166	BCDE	213		

Toyota Corona Mk II

	3	6	9	12	15	18	21	24	27	30	33	36	39	42	45	48	51	54	57	60
miles in thousands	3	6	9	12	15	18	21	24	27	30	33	36	39	42	45	48	51	54	57	60
look for service code letter	A	B	A	C	A	D	A	E	A	B	A	D	A	B	A	E	A	D	A	C

Code	Job	Code	Job	Code	Job	Code	Job	Code	Job	Code	Job	Code	Job	Code	Job	Code	Job	Code	Job
ABCDE	1	ABCDE	23	BCDE	37	CDE	61	BCDE	87	BCDE	116	BCDE	136	BCDE	159	CDE	189	BCDE	223
ABCDE	4	ABCDE	24	BCDE	43	CDE	63	CDE	88	BCDE	118	BCDE	147	CDE	162	CDE	191	BCDE	224
ABCDE	6	BCDE	26	BCDE	49	CDE	78	BCDE	89	BCDE	120	BCDE	148	BCDE	167	BCDE	201	BCDE	225
ABCDE	8	ABCDE	28	ABCDE	51	CDE	79	BCDE	94	BCDE	126	BCDE	149	CDE	173	ABCDE	202	BCDE	226
BCDE	9	ABCDE	29	ABCDE	52	CDE	80	E	98	BCDE	130	BCDE	152	AB D	175	ABCDE	203		
BCDE	11	ABCDE	32	ABCDE	53	CDE	81	E	101	AB D	131	ABCDE	153	CDE	176	CDE	211		
BCDE	13	BCDE	34	ABCDE	54	CDE	83	ABCDE	105	CDE	132	ABCDE	154	BCDE	182	CDE	213		
ABCDE	18	D	35	D	55	ABCDE	85	ABCDE	106	BCDE	133	CDE	155	BCDE	186	BCDE	220		
BCDE	19	D	36	BCDE	58	BCDE	86	ABCDE	108	BCDE	135	ABCDE	156	BCDE	187	BCDE	221		

Vauxhall Firenza 1600

	3	6	9	12	15	18	21	24	27	30	33	36	39	42	45	48	51	54	57	60
age of car in months	3	6	9	12	15	18	21	24	27	30	33	36	39	42	45	48	51	54	57	60
look for service code letter	A	D	B	D	A	D	C	D	A	D	B	D	A	D	C	D	A	D	B	D

Code	Job	Code	Job	Code	Job	Code	Job	Code	Job	Code	Job	Code	Job	Code	Job	Code	Job
ABCD	1	ABCD	22	D	39	ABCD	79	ABCD	105	ABC	130	ABC	147	ABC	162	ABCD	203
D	4	ABCD	23	ABC	42	D	81	ABC	106	ABC	131	ABC	148	A D	175	BC	204
D	6	D	24	ABC	46	D	83	D	107	ABC	132	ABC	150	BC	176	ABC	213
D	8	BC	25	ABCD	51	ABCD	85	ABC	108	ABC	133	ABC	152	ABC	184	ABC	220
D	9	ABC	28	ABCD	52	ABCD	86	ABC	110	ABC	135	ABCD	153	ABC	187	ABC	221
D	12	ABC	29	ABC	58	ABCD	87	ABC	118	ABC	136	ABC	154	ABC	189	ABCD	223
D	18	ABC	32	ABC	61	ABC	92	ABC	119	ABC	141	C	155	ABC	190	ABC	224
D	19	D	34	ABC	63	ABC	94	ABC	120	ABC	144	ABCD	156	ABC	199	ABCD	225
ABCD	21	ABC	37	D	78	ABCD	101	ABC	129	ABC	146	ABC	159	ABCD	202	ABC	226

Vauxhall Ventora FD; FE

	3	6	9	12	15	18	21	24	27	30	33	36	39	42	45	48	51	54	57	60
age of car in months	3	6	9	12	15	18	21	24	27	30	33	36	39	42	45	48	51	54	57	60
look for service code letter	A	D	B	D	A	D	C	D	A	D	B	D	A	D	C	D	A	D	B	D

Code	Job	Code	Job	Code	Job	Code	Job	Code	Job	Code	Job	Code	Job	Code	Job	Code	Job	Code	Job
ABCD	1	D	19	ABC	31	ABC	63	ABC	92	ABC	118	ABC	134	C	155	ABC	188	ABC	220
D	4	ABCD	21	D	34	D	78	ABC	94	ABC	119	ABC	136	ABCD	156	ABC	193	ABC	221
D	5	ABCD	22	ABC	37	ABCD	79	ABCD	101	ABC	120	ABC	137	ABC	159	ABC	199	ABCD	223
D	6	ABCD	23	D	39	D	81	ABCD	105	ABC	129	ABC	139	ABC	162	ABCD	202	ABC	224
D	8	D	24	ABCD	51	D	83	ABC	106	ABC	130	ABC	148	A D	175	ABCD	203	ABCD	225
D	9	BC	25	ABCD	52	ABCD	85	D	107	ABC	131	ABC	151	BC	176	BC	204	ABC	226
D	12	ABC	28	ABC	58	ABCD	86	ABC	108	ABC	132	ABCD	153	ABC	184	ABC	213		
D	18	ABC	29	ABC	61	ABCD	87	ABC	110	ABC	133	ABC	154	ABC	185	ABCD	216		

Vauxhall Victor FD; FE 1600

	3	6	9	12	15	18	21	24	27	30	33	36	39	42	45	48	51	54	57	60
age of car in months	3	6	9	12	15	18	21	24	27	30	33	36	39	42	45	48	51	54	57	60
look for service code letter	A	D	B	D	A	D	C	D	A	D	B	D	A	D	C	D	A	D	B	D

Code	Job	Code	Job	Code	Job	Code	Job	Code	Job	Code	Job	Code	Job	Code	Job	Code	Job
ABCD	1	ABCD	22	D	39	ABCD	79	ABCD	105	ABC	130	ABC	147	ABC	162	ABCD	203
D	4	ABCD	23	ABC	42	D	81	ABC	106	ABC	131	ABC	148	A D	175	BC	204
D	6	D	24	ABC	46	D	83	D	107	ABC	132	ABC	150	BC	176	ABC	213
D	8	BC	25	ABCD	51	ABCD	85	ABC	108	ABC	133	ABC	152	ABC	184	ABC	220
D	9	ABC	28	ABCD	52	ABCD	86	ABC	110	ABC	135	ABCD	153	ABC	187	ABC	221
D	12	ABC	29	ABC	58	ABCD	87	ABC	118	ABC	136	ABC	154	ABC	189	ABCD	223
D	18	ABC	32	ABC	61	ABC	92	ABC	119	ABC	141	C	155	ABC	190	ABC	224
D	19	D	34	ABC	63	ABC	94	ABC	120	ABC	144	ABCD	156	ABC	199	ABCD	225
ABCD	21	ABC	37	D	78	ABCD	101	ABC	129	ABC	146	ABC	159	ABCD	202	ABC	226

Vauxhall Victor FD; FE 3·3 Estate

	3	6	9	12	15	18	21	24	27	30	33	36	39	42	45	48	51	54	57	60
age of car in months	3	6	9	12	15	18	21	24	27	30	33	36	39	42	45	48	51	54	57	60
look for service code letter	A	D	B	D	A	D	C	D	A	D	B	D	A	D	C	D	A	D	B	D

Code	Job	Code	Job	Code	Job	Code	Job	Code	Job	Code	Job	Code	Job	Code	Job	Code	Job	Code	Job
ABCD	1	D	19	ABC	31	ABC	63	ABC	92	ABC	118	ABC	134	C	155	ABC	188	ABC	220
D	4	ABCD	21	D	34	D	78	ABC	94	ABC	119	ABC	136	ABCD	156	ABC	193	ABC	221
D	5	ABCD	22	ABC	37	ABCD	79	ABCD	101	ABC	120	ABC	137	ABC	159	ABC	199	ABCD	223
D	6	ABCD	23	D	39	D	81	ABCD	105	ABC	129	ABC	139	ABC	162	ABCD	202	ABC	224
D	8	D	24	ABCD	51	D	83	ABC	106	ABC	130	ABC	148	A D	175	ABCD	203	ABCD	225
D	9	BC	25	ABCD	52	ABCD	85	D	107	ABC	131	ABC	151	BC	176	BC	204	ABC	226
D	12	ABC	28	ABC	58	ABCD	86	ABC	108	ABC	132	ABCD	153	ABC	184	ABC	213		
D	18	ABC	29	ABC	61	ABCD	87	ABC	110	ABC	133	ABC	154	ABC	185	ABCD	216		

Vauxhall — Volkswagen

Jobs to be done

Read page 40 before using these charts

Vauxhall Viscount

age of car in months	3	6	9	12	15	18	21	24	27	30	33	36	39	42	45	48	51	54	57	60
look for service code letter	A	D	B	D	A	D	C	D	A	D	B	D	A	D	C	D	A	D	B	D

Code	Job	Code	Job	Code	Job	Code	Job	Code	Job	Code	Job	Code	Job	Code	Job	Code	Job	Code	Job
D	1	D	19	A	37	ABC	58	ABCD	85	ABC	108	ABC	133	C	155	ABC	188	D	220
D	4	ABCD	23	BC	38	ABC	61	ABCD	86	ABC	110	ABC	134	ABCD	156	ABC	193	D	221
D	5	ABCD	25	BC	39	BC	63	ABCD	87	ABC	118	ABC	136	ABC	158	ABC	199	ABCD	223
D	6	ABCD	26	BC	41	BC	64	ABCD	89	ABC	119	ABC	137	BC	161	ABCD	202	BC	224
D	8	ABC	28	ABC	42	D	78	D	94	ABC	120	ABC	139	ABC	162	ABCD	203	BC	226
D	9	ABC	29	ABC	43	D	79	ABCD	101	BC	129	ABC	148	A D	175	BC	205		
D	12	ABC	31	ABC	46	D	80	ABCD	105	ABC	130	ABC	151	BC	176	ABC	211		
D	13	ABC	34	ABCD	51	D	81	ABC	106	ABC	131	ABCD	153	ABC	184	ABC	212		
ABCD	18	BC	36	ABCD	52	D	83	D	107	ABC	132	ABCD	154	ABC	185	ABC	213		

Vauxhall Viva HA 1159

age of car in months	3	6	9	12	15	18	21	24	27	30	33	36	39	42	45	48	51	54	57	60
look for service code letter	A	D	B	D	A	D	C	D	A	E	B	D	A	D	C	D	A	D	B	E

Code	Job	Code	Job	Code	Job	Code	Job	Code	Job	Code	Job	Code	Job	Code	Job	Code	Job	Code	Job
ABCDE	1	BC	19	ABC	34	ABC	61	E	97	ABC	119	ABC	136	ABCDE	156	BC	190	BC	226
DE	4	ABCDE	21	ABC	37	DE	78	E	101	ABC	120	ABC	138	ABC	158	ABC	199		
DE	6	ABCDE	22	ABC	42	DE	79	ABCDE	105	BC	129	ABC	139	BC	161	ABCDE	202		
DE	8	BC	23	ABC	43	DE	81	ABC	106	ABC	130	ABC	148	ABC	162	ABC	213		
BC	9	BC	25	ABC	46	DE	83	DE	107	ABC	131	ABC	151	BC	170	ABC	220		
BC	13	ABC	28	ABCDE	51	ABCDE	85	ABC	108	ABC	132	ABCDE	153	BC	176	ABC	221		
BC	14	ABC	29	ABCDE	52	ABC	89	ABC	110	ABC	133	ABCDE	154	ABC	184	ABCDE	223		
ABC	18	ABC	31	ABC	58	ABC	94	ABC	118	ABC	134	C	155	BC	189	BC	224		

Vauxhall Viva HB; HC 1159

age of car in months	3	6	9	12	15	18	21	24	27	30	33	36	39	42	45	48	51	54	57	60
look for service code letter	A	D	B	D	A	D	C	D	A	D	B	D	A	D	C	D	A	D	B	D

Code	Job	Code	Job	Code	Job	Code	Job	Code	Job	Code	Job	Code	Job	Code	Job	Code	Job	Code	Job
ABCD	1	ABCD	21	D	34	ABC	61	ABCD	87	ABC	110	ABC	133	C	155	ABC	189	ABC	221
D	4	ABCD	22	ABC	37	ABC	63	ABC	92	ABC	118	ABC	134	ABCD	156	ABC	190	ABCD	223
D	6	ABCD	23	D	39	D	78	ABC	94	ABC	119	ABC	136	ABC	159	ABC	199	ABC	224
D	8	D	24	ABC	42	ABCD	79	ABCD	101	ABC	120	ABC	138	ABC	162	ABCD	202	ABCD	225
D	9	BC	25	ABC	46	D	81	ABCD	105	ABC	129	ABC	148	BC	173	ABCD	203	ABC	226
D	12	ABC	28	ABCD	51	D	83	ABC	106	ABC	130	ABC	151	ABC	177	BC	204		
D	18	ABC	29	ABCD	52	ABCD	85	D	107	ABC	131	ABCD	153	ABC	184	ABC	213		
D	19	ABC	32	ABC	58	ABCD	86	ABC	108	ABC	132	ABC	154	ABC	187	ABC	220		

Vauxhall Viva HB GT; SL90 HC 1600

age of car in months	3	6	9	12	15	18	21	24	27	30	33	36	39	42	45	48	51	54	57	60
look for service code letter	A	D	B	D	A	D	C	D	A	D	B	D	A	D	C	D	A	D	B	D

Code	Job	Code	Job	Code	Job	Code	Job	Code	Job	Code	Job	Code	Job	Code	Job	Code	Job	Code	Job
ABCD	1	ABCD	22	D	39	ABCD	79	ABCD	105	ABC	130	ABC	147	ABC	162	ABC	198	ABCD	225
D	4	ABCD	23	ABC	42	D	81	ABC	106	ABC	131	ABC	148	BC	173	ABCD	202	ABC	226
D	6	D	24	ABC	46	D	83	D	107	ABC	132	ABC	150	A D	175	ABCD	203		
D	8	BC	25	ABCD	51	ABCD	85	ABC	108	ABC	133	ABC	152	BC	176	BC	204		
D	9	ABC	28	ABCD	52	ABCD	86	ABC	110	ABC	135	ABCD	153	ABC	183	ABC	213		
D	12	ABC	29	ABC	58	ABCD	87	ABC	118	ABC	136	ABC	154	ABC	186	ABC	220		
D	18	ABC	32	ABC	61	ABC	91	ABC	119	ABC	141	C	155	ABC	187	ABC	221		
D	19	D	34	ABC	63	ABC	94	ABC	120	ABC	144	ABCD	156	ABC	189	ABCD	223		
ABCD	21	ABC	37	D	78	ABCD	101	ABC	129	ABC	146	ABC	159	ABC	192	ABC	224		

Vauxhall VX 4/90 FD; FE

age of car in months	3	6	9	12	15	18	21	24	27	30	33	36	39	42	45	48	51	54	57	60
look for service code letter	A	D	B	D	A	D	C	D	A	D	B	D	A	D	C	D	A	D	B	D

Code	Job	Code	Job	Code	Job	Code	Job	Code	Job	Code	Job	Code	Job	Code	Job	Code	Job	Code	Job
ABCD	1	ABCD	22	D	39	ABCD	79	ABCD	105	ABC	130	ABC	147	ABC	162	ABC	198	ABCD	225
D	4	ABCD	23	ABC	42	D	81	ABC	106	ABC	131	ABC	148	BC	173	ABCD	202	ABC	226
D	6	D	24	ABC	46	D	83	D	107	ABC	132	ABC	150	A D	175	ABCD	203		
D	8	BC	25	ABCD	51	ABCD	85	ABC	108	ABC	133	ABC	152	BC	176	BC	204		
D	9	ABC	28	ABCD	52	ABCD	86	ABC	110	ABC	135	ABCD	153	ABC	183	ABC	213		
D	12	ABC	29	ABC	58	ABCD	87	ABC	118	ABC	136	ABC	154	ABC	186	ABC	220		
D	18	ABC	32	ABC	61	ABC	92	ABC	119	ABC	141	C	155	ABC	187	ABC	221		
D	19	D	34	ABC	63	ABC	94	ABC	120	ABC	144	ABCD	156	ABC	189	ABCD	223		
ABCD	21	ABC	37	D	78	ABCD	101	ABC	129	ABC	146	ABC	159	ABC	192	ABC	224		

Volkswagen Beetle 1200; 1300

miles in thousands	3	6	9	12	15	18	21	24	27	30	33	36	39	42	45	48	51	54	57	60
look for service code letter	A	B	A	B	A	B	A	B	A	B	A	C	A	B	A	B	A	B	A	C

Code	Job	Code	Job	Code	Job	Code	Job	Code	Job	Code	Job	Code	Job	Code	Job	Code	Job	Code	Job
BC	1	BC	15	ABC	30	BC	59	ABC	85	ABC	105	ABC	130	BC	148	BC	189	ABC	221
BC	3	BC	19	BC	42	BC	60	C	88	ABC	106	BC	131	BC	151	BC	193	BC	222
BC	4	BC	23	BC	43	BC	61	BC	90	BC	108	BC	132	BC	160	BC	199	ABC	223
BC	5	BC	25	ABC	51	BC	78	BC	94	BC	115	ABC	133	BC	162	ABC	202	BC	224
BC	6	BC	26	ABC	52	BC	79	C	99	BC	118	BC	134	BC	177	BC	211	BC	226
BC	8	ABC	28	B	56	BC	82	C	102	BC	120	BC	136	BC	184	BC	213		
BC	9	ABC	29	C	57	BC	83	C	104	BC	122	BC	137	ABC	187	ABC	220		

Volkswagen – Volvo

Read page 40 before using these charts

Jobs to be done

Volkswagen 1600 FB; Variant

miles in thousands	3	6	9	12	15	18	21	24	27	30	33	36	39	42	45	48	51	54	57	60
look for service code letter	A	B	A	B	A	B	A	B	A	C	A	B	A	B	A	B	A	B	A	C

Code	Job	Code	Job	Code	Job	Code	Job	Code	Job	Code	Job	Code	Job	Code	Job	Code	Job	Code	Job
BC	1	BC	19	BC	43	BC	78	BC	90	BC	108	ABC	133	BC	166	ABC	202	BC	226
BC	3	BC	23	ABC	51	BC	79	BC	94	BC	115	BC	134	BC	174	BC	211		
BC	4	BC	25	ABC	52	BC	82	C	98	BC	118	BC	136	BC	177	BC	213		
BC	5	BC	26	B	56	BC	83	C	99	BC	120	BC	137	BC	184	ABC	220		
BC	6	ABC	28	C	57	ABC	85	C	102	BC	122	BC	148	BC	187	ABC	221		
BC	8	ABC	29	BC	59	BC	86	C	104	ABC	130	BC	151	BC	189	BC	222		
BC	9	ABC	30	BC	60	BC	87	ABC	105	BC	131	BC	160	BC	193	ABC	223		
BC	15	BC	42	BC	61	C	88	ABC	106	BC	132	BC	162	BC	199	BC	224		

Volkswagen 411 LE; 412 LE Saloon & Variant

miles in thousands	3	6	9	12	15	18	21	24	27	30	33	36	39	42	45	48	51	54	57	60
look for service code letter	A	B	A	B	A	B	A	B	A	C	A	B	A	B	A	B	A	B	A	C

Code	Job	Code	Job	Code	Job	Code	Job	Code	Job	Code	Job	Code	Job	Code	Job	Code	Job
BC	1	ABC	18	BC	32	BC	59	BC	86	C	104	ABC	130	BC	151	BC	213
BC	3	ABC	19	BC	34	BC	60	BC	87	ABC	105	BC	131	BC	159	ABC	220
BC	4	BC	23	ABC	51	BC	61	C	88	ABC	106	BC	132	BC	164	ABC	221
BC	6	BC	25	ABC	52	BC	78	BC	90	BC	108	BC	133	BC	166	BC	222
BC	8	BC	26	ABC	53	BC	79	BC	94	BC	115	BC	134	BC	173	ABC	223
BC	9	ABC	28	ABC	54	BC	82	C	98	BC	118	BC	136	BC	177	BC	224
BC	10	ABC	29	AB	56	BC	83	C	99	BC	120	BC	137	ABC	202	BC	226
BC	12	ABC	30	C	57	ABC	85	C	102	BC	122	BC	148	BC	211		

Volkswagen K 70

miles in thousands	3	6	9	12	15	18	21	24	27	30	33	36	39	42	45	48	51	54	57	60
look for service code letter	A	B	A	F	A	D	A	E	A	C	A	D	A	B	A	E	A	D	A	F

Code	Job	Code	Job	Code	Job	Code	Job	Code	Job	Code	Job	Code	Job	Code	Job
BCDEF	1	ABCDEF	21	ABCDEF	43	BCDEF	81	BCDEF	108	ABCDEF	136	BCDEF	173	BCDEF	210
BCDEF	2	ABCDEF	22	ABCDEF	51	BCDEF	83	BCDEF	115	ABCDEF	141	ABCDEF	177	BCDEF	213
BCDEF	4	ABCDEF	23	ABCDEF	52	ABCDEF	85	BCDEF	118	ABCDEF	147	BCDEF	184	ABCDEF	220
BCDEF	5	ABCDEF	24	ABCDEF	54	ABCDEF	86	BCDEF	120	ABCDEF	149	BCDEF	187	ABCDEF	221
BCDEF	6	ABCDEF	25	D	57	ABCDEF	87	BCDEF	122	ABCDEF	152	BCDEF	189	BCDEF	222
BCDEF	8	BCDEF	28	BCDEF	59	E	88	BCDEF	130	BCDEF	153	BCDEF	200	ABCDEF	223
BCDEF	9	BCDEF	29	BCDEF	60	BCDEF	92	BCDEF	131	BCDEF	154	BCDEF	202	BCDEF	224
BCDEF	10	BCDEF	32	BCDEF	61	BCDEF	94	EF	132	ABCDEF	156	ABCDEF	203	ABCDEF	225
ABCDEF	18	BCDEF	34	BCDEF	78	BCDEF	106	BCDEF	133	BCDEF	159	ABCDEF	209	BCDEF	226
ABCDEF	19	ABCDEF	42	BCDEF	79	A	107	ABCDEF	135	BCDEF	162				

Volvo 120 range

miles in thousands	3	6	9	12	15	18	21	25	28	31	34	37	40	44	47	50	53	56	59	62	65	68	71	74
look for service code letter	A	B	A	C	A	B	A	F	A	B	A	E	A	B	A	F	A	B	A	C	A	B	A	G

Code	Job	Code	Job	Code	Job	Code	Job	Code	Job	Code	Job	Code	Job	Code	Job
BCDEFG	1	BCDEFG	25	BCDEFG	49	ABCDEFG	87	BCDEFG	122	ABCDEFG	153	BCDEFG	183	BCDEFG	213
BCDEFG	4	BCDEFG	26	ABCDEFG	58	E G	88	BCDEFG	130	BCDEFG	154	ABCDEFG	186	ABCDEFG	220
BCDEFG	6	ABCDEFG	28	BCDEFG	61	BCDEFG	92	BCDEFG	131	F	155	ABCDEFG	187	ABCDEFG	221
BCDEFG	8	ABCDEFG	29	BCDEFG	63	BCDEFG	94	BCDEFG	132	ABCDEFG	156	BCDEFG	189	BCDEFG	222
BCDEFG	9	ABCDEFG	31	BCDEFG	78	ABCDEFG	105	BCDEFG	133	BCDEFG	158	BCDEFG	192	ABCDEFG	223
BCDEFG	12	BCDEFG	34	BCDEFG	79	ABCDEFG	106	BCDEFG	134	BCDEFG	161	BCDEFG	198	BCDEFG	224
BCDEFG	18	D FG	36	BCDEFG	81	BCDEFG	108	BCDEFG	136	BCDEFG	162	ABCDEFG	202	BCDEFG	226
BCDEFG	19	ABC E	37	BCDEFG	83	BCDEFG	115	BCDEFG	137	D FG	174	ABCDEFG	203		
BCDEFG	23	D FG	38	BCDEFG	85	BCDEFG	118	BCDEFG	148	A	175	ABCDEFG	205		
BCDEFG	24	D FG	41	ABCDEFG	86	BCDEFG	120	BCDEFG	151	BCDEFG	176	ABCDEFG	211		

Volvo 142; 144; 145

miles in thousands	3	6	9	12	15	18	21	25	28	31	34	37	40	44	47	50	53	56	59	62	65	68	71	74
look for service code letter	A	B	A	C	A	B	A	F	A	B	A	E	A	B	A	F	A	B	A	C	A	B	A	G

Code	Job	Code	Job	Code	Job	Code	Job	Code	Job	Code	Job	Code	Job	Code	Job
BCDEFG	1	BCDEFG	25	BCDEFG	49	ABCDEFG	87	BCDEFG	122	ABCDEFG	153	BCDEFG	183	BCDEFG	213
BCDEFG	4	BCDEFG	26	ABCDEFG	58	E G	88	BCDEFG	130	BCDEFG	154	ABCDEFG	186	BCDEFG	220
BCDEFG	6	ABCDEFG	28	BCDEFG	61	BCDEFG	92	BCDEFG	131	F	155	ABCDEFG	187	ABCDEFG	221
BCDEFG	8	ABCDEFG	29	BCDEFG	63	BCDEFG	94	BCDEFG	132	ABCDEFG	156	BCDEFG	189	BCDEFG	222
BCDEFG	9	ABCDEFG	31	BCDEFG	78	ABCDEFG	105	BCDEFG	133	BCDEFG	158	BCDEFG	192	ABCDEFG	223
BCDEFG	12	BCDEFG	34	BCDEFG	79	ABCDEFG	106	BCDEFG	134	BCDEFG	161	BCDEFG	198	BCDEFG	224
BCDEFG	18	D FG	36	BCDEFG	81	BCDEFG	108	BCDEFG	136	BCDEFG	162	ABCDEFG	202	ABCDEFG	225
BCDEFG	19	ABC E	37	BCDEFG	83	BCDEFG	115	BCDEFG	137	D FG	174	ABCDEFG	203	BCDEFG	226
BCDEFG	23	D FG	38	BCDEFG	85	BCDEFG	118	BCDEFG	148	A	175	D FG	204		
BCDEFG	24	D FG	41	ABCDEFG	86	BCDEFG	120	BCDEFG	151	BCDEFG	176	ABCDEFG	211		

Volvo 164

miles in thousands	6·2	12·5	18·5	25	31	37	44	50	56	62	68	74	81	87	93	99
look for service code letter	A	A	A	D	A	C	A	D	A	A	A	A	E	A	A	A	D

Code	Job	Code	Job	Code	Job	Code	Job	Code	Job	Code	Job	Code	Job	Code	Job	Code	Job
ABCDE	1	ABCDE	19	ABCDE	34	ABCDE	54	ABCDE	94	ABCDE	130	ABCDE	153	ABCDE	183	B DE	208	ABCDE	225
ABCDE	3	ABCDE	21	BCDE	36	ABCDE	58	ABCDE	101	ABCDE	131	ABCDE	154	ABCDE	186	ABCDE	209	ABCDE	226
ABCDE	4	ABCDE	23	A C E	37	ABCDE	61	ABCDE	105	ABCDE	132	DE	155	ABCDE	187	ABCDE	210		
ABCDE	6	ABCDE	24	BCDE	38	ABCDE	63	ABCDE	106	ABCDE	133	ABCDE	156	ABCDE	189	ABCDE	213		
ABCDE	8	ABCDE	25	BCDE	41	ABCDE	66	ABCDE	108	ABCDE	134	ABCDE	159	ABCDE	192	ABCDE	220		
ABCDE	9	ABCDE	26	ABCDE	49	ABCDE	86	ABCDE	115	ABCDE	136	ABCDE	162	AB	198	ABCDE	221		
ABCDE	11	ABCDE	28	ABCDE	51	ABCDE	87	ABCDE	118	ABCDE	137	BCDE	174	ABCDE	202	ABCDE	222		
ABCDE	12	ABCDE	29	ABCDE	52	C E	88	ABCDE	120	ABCDE	148	A C E	175	ABCDE	203	ABCDE	223		
ABCDE	18	ABCDE	32	ABCDE	53	ABCDE	92	ABCDE	122	ABCDE	151	B DE	176	B DE	204	ABCDE	224		

Jacking up the car

Lifting the car off the ground safely

If the front is to be raised, release the handbrake. Jack up the car, making sure that the base of the jack remains squarely on the ground as the car is lifted. Apply the handbrake, to prevent the car from rolling once it has been raised.

If the rear of the car is being lifted, jack up the car and position chocks in front of and behind the front wheels.

Using the car jack There are two basic types of jack supplied with modern cars, a side jack or scissor jack.

The side jack fits into a socket in the car body, just

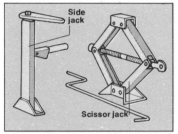

below the doors. There may be one or two sockets on each side.

If the lifting socket is immediately below the door, the jack will probably pre-

vent the door being opened once it is in position. If you need to open the door, do so before using the jack.

Scissor jacks have a peg in the jack platform, which locates in a hole in the body or suspension.

Position the jack under the car, in order that the base of the jack is parallel with the body—never use it with the base going across the car, as it can easily tip over. Screw the jack up by hand, until it is located under the lifting point. Fit the handle and jack up the car.

Using a bottle or trolley jack Bottle jacks can be either hydraulically operated or of the screw type. They all have threaded adjustable heads. Use a piece of 2 × 2 in. timber between the car and the head of the jack.

Screw the head of the jack up until it traps the timber. Position the lever in the side of the jack and pump it up and down on a hydraulic jack, or turn it on the screw type, to raise the car.

A trolley jack is the ideal type to use, because it can

move on its own wheels and, if it is positioned correctly, can lift the front or back of the car up in one operation. If necessary, use a piece of timber between the jack and the car, to protect it. Jack up the car.

Using axle stands Never work under a car that is mounted only on a jack. It is unsafe and could slip, resulting in a serious accident.

Fit axle stands under the car and lower the jack, so

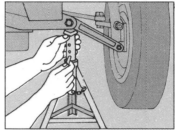

that the weight of the car is supported on the stands.

Using car ramps Ramps are ideal for lifting just the back or front of the car. Position a ramp either in front of each front wheel, or behind each rear wheel. Drive the car slowly and carefully forwards,

or backwards, on to the ramps.

Ramps cannot be used for carrying out repairs on the suspension system or wheels.

Garage pit A pit built in the floor of your garage is ideal for most servicing and repair jobs underneath the car. There are, however, several jobs that still require the car to be jacked up and mounted on stands—for example, suspension repairs.

DIY garage lifts If you have a do-it-yourself garage in your district, it is possible to hire a repair bay with a hydraulic lift.

There are two basic types of lift available. One is a simple drive-on platform lift. The more expensive type to hire is the 'wheel-free' lift, which has a platform on which the wheels stay, or can be converted to lift the car under the body so that the wheels hang free, enabling jobs on the wheels or suspension system to be carried out safely and in comfort.

The cost of hiring a garage repair bay with a hydraulic lift varies according to the district.

Where you can use a jack and axle stands

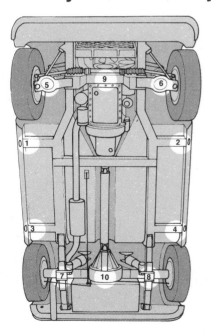

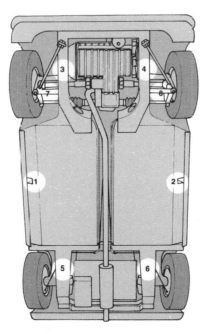

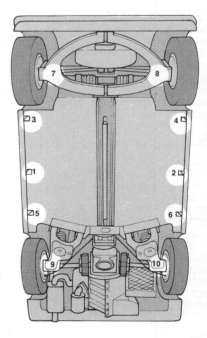

Front-engine rear-wheel drive Fit a side jack in the car body sockets—points 1, 2, 3 and 4. Scissor jacks fit holes in either the body or suspension units— points 1, 2, 3, 4, 5, 6, 7 and 8. Use a trolley or bottle jack under the front cross-member—point 9, or the rear axle casing—point 10. Position stands at points 5, 6, 7, 8, 9 and 10, or under side jacking points.

Transverse-engine front-wheel drive Use only the body side jack in the sockets provided—points 1 and 2. Do not attempt to use a scissor jack. If a bottle or trolley jack is being used, position it at points 3, 4, 5 and 6. Axle stands must be placed only under the official jacking points or at points 3, 4, 5 and 6; or under the lower suspension arm swivel—points 7 and 8.

Rear-engine rear-wheel drive Use the side jack at the two or four side points —points 1, 2, 3, 4, 5 and 6. If a bottle or trolley jack is used, jack up under the front suspension arms—points 7 and 8, and 9 and 10 at the rear. Position axle stands under the official jacking points, 1, 2, 3, 4, 5 or 6, so the suspension hangs free, or under the suspension—points 7, 8, 9 and 10.

1 Checking the underside for oil, water, petrol, fluid and exhaust leaks

Radiator Check the bottom of the radiator for leaks. If any of the seams are damaged, fit a new radiator (see p. 180). Make sure the drain tap or plug is not faulty. If it is, renew it.

Engine sump If the sump flange is leaking, tighten all the flange bolts (see p. 72). If this fails to cure the trouble, drain the sump and fit a new gasket. Check the drain plug. If it is leaking, drain the sump and fit a new sealing washer to the sump drain plug (see p. 72).

Brakes If there is fluid on the brake back-plate, the wheel cylinders are leaking. Fit new cylinder seals or a new cylinder (see p. 198).

Oil filter Check the oil filter bowl for leaks. If necessary fit a new sealing washer when you change the filter element (see p. 73).

Clutch housing If there is oil at the base of the clutch housing, the flywheel or gearbox oil seals may be faulty. Have them renewed.

Exhaust Run the engine and pass your hands across the exhaust pipes and silencer to feel for leaks. Do not touch the pipes. Have a damaged system repaired, or replaced, by a garage.

Crankshaft pulley Oil leaks behind the crankshaft pulley indicate a faulty timing-chain case seal. Have it renewed by a garage.

Steering rack Check the protective rubber boots on the steering rack. If they are split, oil will have leaked out. Renew them (see p. 70), and refill with oil.

Fuel pump and lines Check all the fuel pipes and pump flanges for leaks. Tighten all unions and renew any faulty parts.

Hydraulic clutch Check the slave cylinder on the side of the clutch for leaks. If necessary, overhaul or change the slave cylinder (see p. 219). Check the plastic pipe leading from the master cylinder (see p. 78).

Gearbox Check the gearbox for oil leaks at the drain plug and at the output shaft seal. If the drain plug is leaking, fit a new plug washer. If the seal is leaking, have it renewed by a garage.

Dampers Check all dampers for fluid leaks (see p. 69). If a unit is faulty, fit a new damper unit (see pp. 202-5).

Fuel tank Check the tank for leaks. Tighten any loose pipe unions and the nuts round the flange of the petrol-gauge sensor. Renew gaskets.

Half-shafts Heavy oil on the brake back-plate indicates a faulty half-shaft oil seal. Have the seals renewed by a garage.

Rear axle Check the rear axle for leaks round the casing and drain plug. If there is a leak, have a new gasket fitted. Fit a new plug washer.

2 Looking for underside leaks on front-engine front-wheel-drive cars

Check all the normal points for oil, water, fluid and petrol leaks (see above). If the gear casing is leaking, the engine will have to be taken out of the car and dismantled to fit a new casing gasket—a garage job. Oil leaks on these engines should be cured immediately, for if oil drips on the drive-shaft joints they may be damaged. Check all fuel and exhaust joints that may be under stress.

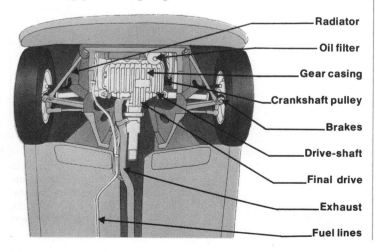

Radiator
Oil filter
Gear casing
Crankshaft pulley
Brakes
Drive-shaft
Final drive
Exhaust
Fuel lines

3 Looking for underside leaks on rear-engine rear-wheel-drive cars

Check all the normal points for oil, water, fluid and petrol leaks (see above). This type of car has a combined gearbox and final-drive assembly (transaxle). Oil leaks can damage both components. Check all the seals carefully. Check both the radiator and the water pump, which is separate from the engine, for leaks. Check the drive-shaft protective rubber boots for damage or deterioration.

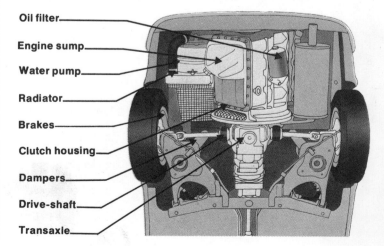

Oil filter
Engine sump
Water pump
Radiator
Brakes
Clutch housing
Dampers
Drive-shaft
Transaxle

4 Looking for exhaust faults

Check the whole system for leaks and rust. Rattles indicate faulty fixings.

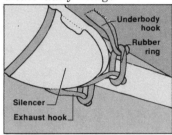

Type A Push up the exhaust, pull off the ring. Slip on new ring.

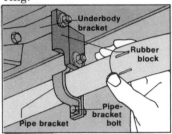

Type B Undo bolts to underbody and pipe brackets. Renew the hanger block. Renew pipe bracket and bolt if rusted or damaged by heat.

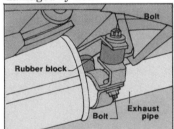

Type C Undo bolts to free block. Fit new mounting block. Make sure it is located correctly in the bracket.

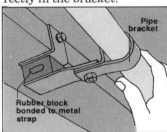

Type D Remove bolts holding block-and-strap assembly to brackets. Fit new assembly. Fit new bolts if rusted.

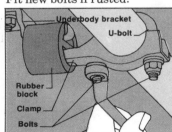

Type E Undo nuts, pull out U-bolt. Unhook block from clamp and underbody bracket. Renew block and reassemble.

5 Checking a multiple system

Leaks may be hard to locate in systems with multiple pipes, silencers and resonator boxes. Rev the engine and run your hand along close to the system feeling for escaping gas—do not touch hot pipes. Watch for leaks where components are joined by crimping, or where flanges are butted together with gaskets in between. If

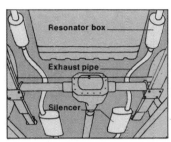

pipes or boxes are corroded or damaged, renew them.

A SINGLE EXHAUST SYSTEM

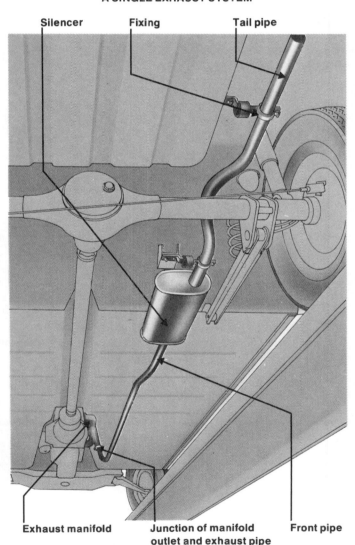

Silencer Fixing Tail pipe

Exhaust manifold   Junction of manifold outlet and exhaust pipe   Front pipe

6 Curing leaks from the manifold caused by loose nuts

Vibration often makes the nuts that hold the exhaust manifold work loose, so that gas leaks out through the joint. Hissing noises or a blackened manifold are signs of escaping gas.

You may need a socket with a universal joint to reach the nuts. Tighten them to the correct torque setting —ask a dealer what it is. If the leak persists, disconnect

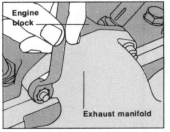

the down pipe, and remove the manifold. Fit a new manifold gasket (see p. 166).

7 Checking the exhaust from a transverse engine

Exhaust systems fitted to transverse engines may crack if the engine is not steady. Normally it should be prevented from rocking to and fro by a stabiliser bar that contains heavy rubber bushes. If the bushes split or become distorted, they must be replaced as soon as possible.

Undo the nuts and bolts that hold the stabiliser bar

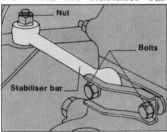

between the engine and bulkhead. Remove the bar. Push the damaged bushes out of the holes in the bar, and push

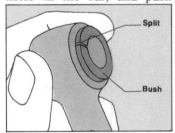

new ones in. Refit the bar and bolt it in place.

8 Checking the down-pipe attachment

Loosen the clamp that holds the exhaust pipe to the mani-

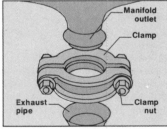

fold. Realign manifold and pipe, press them firmly together, and tighten the clamp.

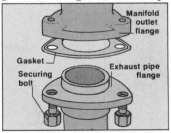

With flange attachments, undo the bolts, and remove the old gasket. Clean the flanges, and reassemble with a new flange gasket.

9 11

10

9 Checking the suspension before servicing

Any car's suspension system may be a combination of the main types for which servicing operations are given on these pages. If you are in doubt about the types on your car, identify them from the drawings or ask a dealer for details. The only systems that cannot be combined with others are hydrolastic and rubber cone suspensions.

Servicing operations include checks for wear in the suspension systems; for worn or damaged components are dangerous and may impair the car's ride or handling. Most servicing jobs should be carried out while the car is on axle stands (see p. 61), but there are two checks that can be made with the wheels on the ground.

Testing the dampers You can roughly check whether the dampers are badly worn by pressing down heavily on each front wing in turn. When you release the wing, the car should bounce up once, then return to the normal rest position. If it bounces more than that, the dampers may need to be renewed (see pp. 201-5). Repeat the test at the rear of the car to check the dampers.

Measuring the ride height The simplest way to check suspension wear is by measuring the ride height of the car. First make sure that it is parked on level ground. Measure from the centre of each wheel upwards to the centre of the wheel arch.

Compare the measurements for the two front wheels and the two rear wheels (front and rear measurements may be different). Then check your measurements with the measurements for the car's original ride height. A main dealer will tell you what this should be.

If the ride height has dropped by more than an inch, check the suspension for wear and the springs for sagging. Usually only leaf springs suffer from sagging, but coil springs can lose their tension. Renewing springs is a job for a garage. On some cars, Rovers for example, shims can be fitted under coil springs to restore the height.

10 Checking the condition of a MacPherson strut suspension

A MacPherson strut system combines a swivel pin, damper and coil spring in one unit. It is fitted at the front of the car and is fixed to the body at the top on a bearing. The bearing—which is mounted on a rubber-bonded block—is located on a plate fixed, by two or three bolts, to the body. At the bottom it is secured by means of a ball swivel joint.

Check the tightness of the cross-member bolts and the

top mounting nuts. Be particularly careful to check for rust round this mounting point. You can check from

A TYPICAL MACPHERSON STRUT ASSEMBLY

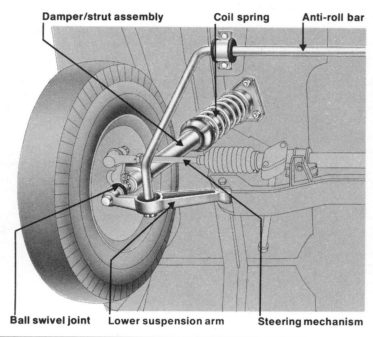

Damper/strut assembly   Coil spring   Anti-roll bar

Ball swivel joint   Lower suspension arm   Steering mechanism

above the car by looking under the bonnet.

If rust has weakened the inner wing metal, a strengthening plate can be bolted, or preferably welded, over the mounting point. This is a job for a garage.

Check that there are no oil leaks from the damper unit in the centre of the strut.

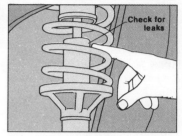

Any leaks normally result in having to fit a new damper unit, or change the whole strut (see pp. 204-5).

Some older units can be topped up. The filler plug is usually situated just below the coil spring. Use fluid recommended by the manufacturer. Except for early vehicles (usually before 1967) the ball swivel joints are sealed for life. If there is a nipple, lubricate with a grease gun (see p. 34).

These suspension systems have a tendency to transmit wheel imbalance. If you notice wheel wobble, have the wheels balanced by a garage. If the wobble persists, fit a new MacPherson strut assembly.

11 Lubricating and checking double wishbone coil spring suspension for wear

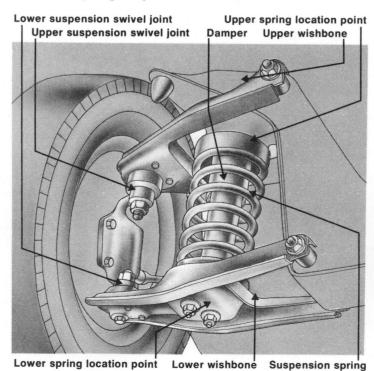

Lower suspension swivel joint   Upper spring location point
Upper suspension swivel joint   Damper   Upper wishbone

Lower spring location point   Lower wishbone   Suspension spring

Two wishbone-shaped arms at the top and bottom of each coil spring are attached to chassis pivot points.

Checking for wear
Lever between the chassis mounting point and the wishbone. If there is movement in the bearings, have new bushes fitted.

Lubrication
If the suspension pivots at the ends of the wishbones can be lubricated, nipples

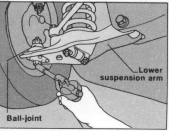

will be fitted to the pivot shafts. Fit a grease gun and pump in lubricant until it is forced out of the pivot points.

12 Checking coil spring suspension for wear and lubricating suspension points

There are two basic types of coil spring suspension—a coil spring mounted upright on a wishbone or swinging arm, and a coil spring that is mounted horizontally.

Coil springs are used in both front and rear suspensions. Horizontally mounted coil springs are used in the front suspension system of Rover 2000 body shapes, and in the front and rear of the Citroën Ami 6 and 8 and Dyane models.

Check the tightness of all nuts on the suspension linkages and pivot points. If they are secured by split-pins they cannot work loose as long as the pin is undamaged. If no split-pins are fitted, tighten to the torque recommended by the manufacturer.

Checking for wear

Check that all metalastic or rubber bushes on the upper and lower ends of the suspension struts are not cracked or contaminated with oil. Use a screwdriver to feel if they are springy (in good condition) or spongy (in poor condition). Replace any worn components.

On most modern cars the mounting plates supporting the struts are secured through the bodywork. You may have to remove the back seat squab or boot mat to check their condition. Refit the squab securely.

Lubricating

Lubricate the pivot points with light grease from a

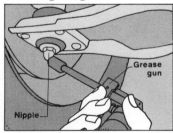

Nipple — Grease gun

grease gun, first wiping away any dirt round the nipples. If the ball-joints are protected by rubber boots, grease sparingly—use enough grease to fill the ball-joint, but not enough to force the boot off its seat.

On the smaller Triumph models, trunnion swivels at the base of the swivel pin should be lubricated only with a recommended heavy gear oil (for example 140 EP).

COIL SPRING WITH SINGLE WISHBONE SUSPENSION

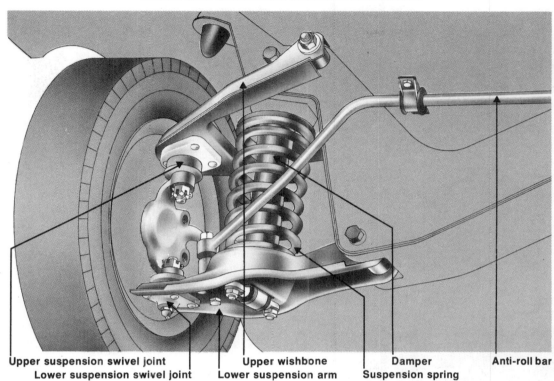

Upper suspension swivel joint
Lower suspension swivel joint
Upper wishbone
Lower suspension arm
Damper
Suspension spring
Anti-roll bar

HORIZONTALLY MOUNTED REAR SPRING

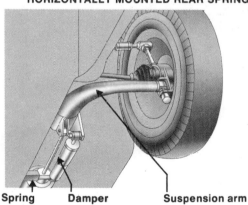

Spring Damper Suspension arm

HORIZONTALLY MOUNTED FRONT SPRING

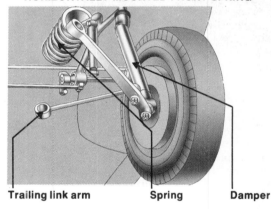

Trailing link arm Spring Damper

REAR INDEPENDENT COIL SPRING

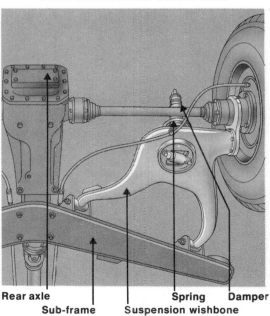

Rear axle
Sub-frame
Spring Damper
Suspension wishbone

REAR COIL SPRING SUSPENSION SYSTEM

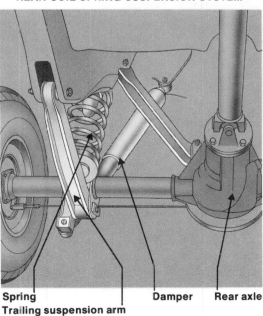

Spring
Trailing suspension arm
Damper Rear axle

13 Checking and lubricating semi-elliptic leaf springs

Leaf springs are usually used for rear suspension only. The semi-elliptic spring is fixed to a chassis member— at the front end by a metal-rubber bush and at the rear end by a swinging shackle. U-bolts hold the springs to the axle casing.

Check the tightness of the U-bolts, and also of any clamps

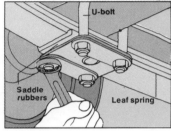

fitted to the leaves. Some manufacturers give specific torque settings for U-bolts: if so, do not overtighten, as the saddle rubbers may become distorted.

Inspect rubber bump stops and any check straps that are fitted. If the bump stops are perished, cracked or broken away from their backing plates, renew them. Renew the check straps if they are contaminated with oil, broken or frayed. Test for play in the bushes by using

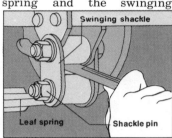

a lever between the leaf spring and the swinging

shackle at the rear, and the spring and bush at the front. If there is up and down movement, the bushes must be replaced by a garage.

Check the leaves for cracks. If there are any, take the car to a garage. Some springs have inserts between the leaves. If these are worn, have the springs replaced.

Use a stiff wire brush to remove any dirt or mud from the leaves and shackles. Lubricate the leaves with a lubricant recommended by the manufacturer. Do not use engine oil, which will cause the inserts to deteriorate. Use an aerosol spray or brush. Make sure that the lubricant soaks between the leaves.

If there are grease nipples in the shackle pins, lubricate with a grease gun.

TYPICAL LEAF-SPRING SUSPENSION

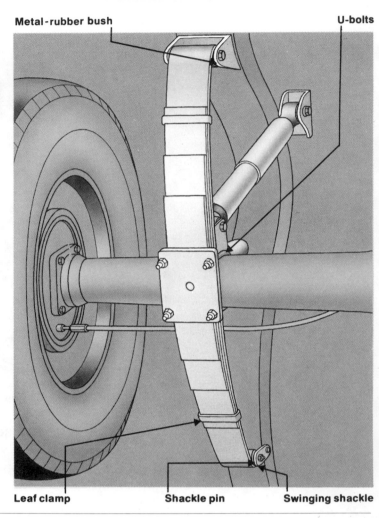

14 Checking and lubricating transverse leaf-spring suspension systems

A transversely mounted leaf spring may be incorporated in independent front or rear suspension. The spring is attached at its centre to either

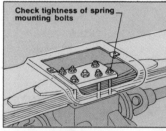

the axle or the body. At each end there is an eye fixed to the upper mounting of the wheel hub. If nipples are fitted to the

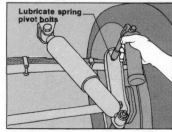

spring eye-pivot pins, use a pressure grease gun to lubricate them with grease. Check

the mounting bolts at the point where the spring is attached to the body or axle casing. If these are not tight the spring will move, causing wear to the component to which it is attached.

The spring itself needs no servicing. Use a grease gun to lubricate the trunnion

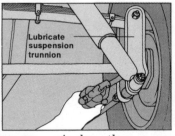

grease nipples—they are usually near the bottom.

On some cars a camber-compensating device is fitted, to reduce tyre wear. The camber compensator, if fitted, may have grease nipples where it is fixed to the suspension wishbone. If so, lubricate these points with grease, and tighten any anchor points.

TRANSVERSE LEAF-SPRING SUSPENSION

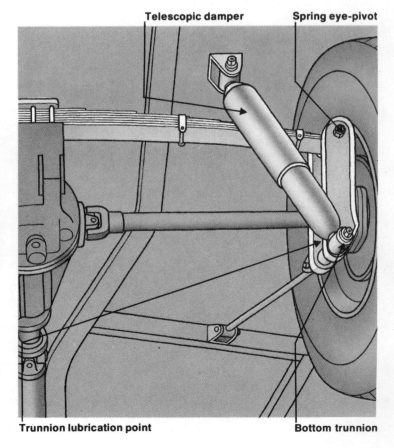

15 Checking and lubricating torsion-bar suspension systems

A torsion bar is usually used in an independent front or rear suspension system. It consists of either four or five metal leaves or a circular splined bar, and is fixed at one end to the body and at the other to a wishbone or swinging arm.

Check the tightness of all nuts on linkages and pivot points. If no split-pins are fitted, tighten to the torque recommended by the manu-

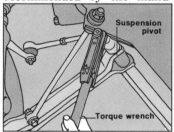

Suspension pivot

Torque wrench

facturer. Use a screwdriver to check that all metal-rubber or rubber bushes on the upper and lower ends of suspension struts are not cracked or oil-contaminated. Replace any

that are worn or that feel unusually spongy.

Use light grease from a grease gun to lubricate the pivot points, first wiping away any dirt round the nipples. Grease sparingly if the ball-joints are protected by rubber boots. Use enough to fill the joint but not to force the boot off its seat.

If the suspension becomes low on one side (checked by measuring the ride height— see p. 64), the torsion bar

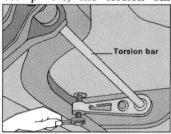

Torsion bar

needs adjustment. There is an adjusting bolt at the body end, but the bar must be correctly tensioned when it is adjusted – a garage job.

see p. 64

FRONT TORSION-BAR SUSPENSION

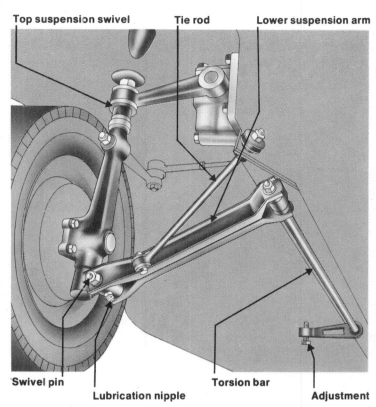

Top suspension swivel | Tie rod | Lower suspension arm

Swivel pin | Lubrication nipple | Torsion bar | Adjustment

REAR DOUBLE-ARM TORSION BAR

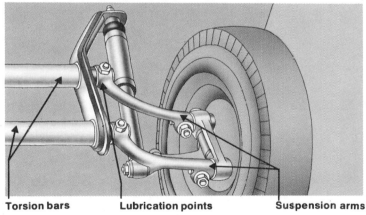

Torsion bars | Lubrication points | Suspension arms

REAR SINGLE-ARM TORSION BAR

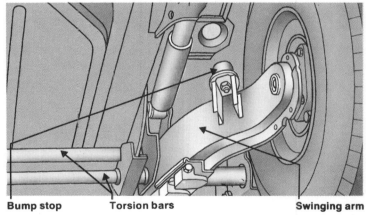

Bump stop | Torsion bars | Swinging arm

16 Topping up a de Dion tube suspension system

Remove the filler-level plug. Check the oil level and top up if necessary to the bottom of the filler hole. Use only the

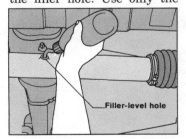

Filler-level hole

type of oil recommended by the car manufacturers. If the amount of topping up required is more than a few squirts from the syringe, look for oil leaks at the elbows and underneath the rubber boot.

If there are leaks, the oil seals in the tube are leaking; renewal must be done by a garage with specialist tools.

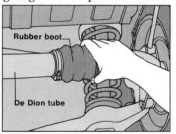

Rubber boot

De Dion tube

Check that the rubber boot protecting the swinging ends of the arms has not become dislodged or damaged. If it is damaged or contaminated with oil, have a new rubber boot fitted by a garage.

REAR DE DION TUBE SUSPENSION

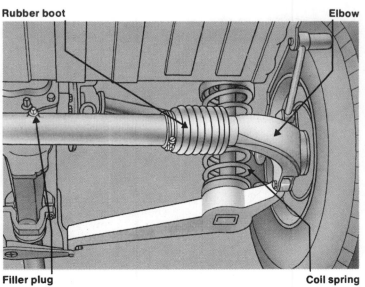

Rubber boot | Elbow

Filler plug | Coil spring

17

18

17 Checking hydrolastic and rubber cone suspension systems

Hydrolastic and rubber cone systems both provide independent suspension all round, and cannot be used in conjunction with other systems. They are always used separately. Rubber cones were first used on British Leyland Minis, replaced in 1964 by hydrolastic suspension, then reintroduced in 1970.

The two suspensions are basically the same, except that in the hydrolastic a displacer unit is used instead of a rubber cone. Hydrolastic suspension is in two parts — nearside and offside — which are independent of each other.

Lubricate the rear suspension radius arms, the nipple

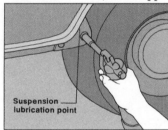

Suspension lubrication point

is just in front of the rear wheels, and the front ball swivel joints.

If the car's handling or ride appears to be defective in any way — such as dropping on one side, wallowing or unusual hardness or softness — it can be checked on both systems by measuring the ride height (see p. 64).

On hydrolastic suspension the system is pressurised through a normal type of tyre valve. Check that the valve is not leaking with an egg-cup of water. If it is, have a new valve fitted. Look also

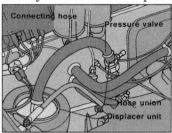

Connecting hose   Pressure valve

Hose union   Displacer unit

for fluid leaks. These are usually found around the pressurising valves or displacer units. Re-pressurising of the system can be carried out only by a garage with the necessary equipment.

On rubber cone systems, the cones tend to shrink with age, or they may deteriorate through oil contamination or general wear. Check their condition. If they are worn and the ride height is low, get them renewed at a garage.

On both systems, check for wear in the front tie rod by gripping it in the hand and

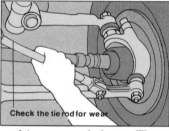

Check the tie rod for wear

pushing up and down. There should be no free play at all. If there is movement, check if the mounting rubbers are split or worn; if they are, renew them. If they are not, or if movement persists after fitting new rubbers, check the body mounting points. If they are damaged, have them repaired by a garage.

REAR HYDROLASTIC UNIT

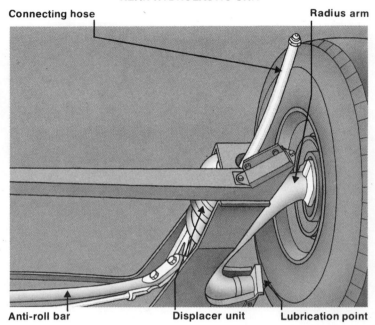

Connecting hose   Radius arm

Anti-roll bar   Displacer unit   Lubrication point

FRONT RUBBER CONE UNIT

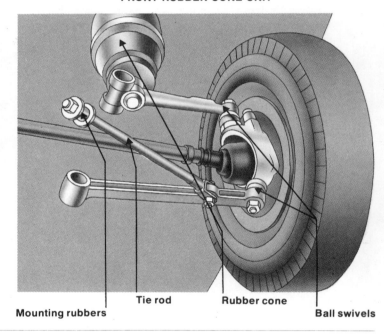

Mounting rubbers   Tie rod   Rubber cone   Ball swivels

18 Checking the anti-roll bars for wear or corrosion

An anti-roll bar is fitted to some front suspension systems. It consists of a steel bar, curved at each end, which is connected to the suspension and bodywork by rubber bushes. Use a screwdriver to poke the anti-roll bar pivots

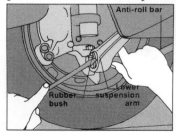

Anti-roll bar

Rubber bush   Lower suspension arm

and rubber bushes for signs of damage or perishing. If

they are in good condition, they will feel firm, if not they will feel spongy.

Examine mountings and the

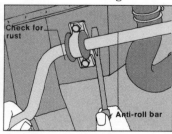

Check for rust

Anti-roll bar

chassis near by for rust. If there is any rust near the attachment points it must be dealt with immediately (see p. 232). If it is very bad, have it repaired by a garage.

TELESCOPIC DAMPER INSIDE SPRING

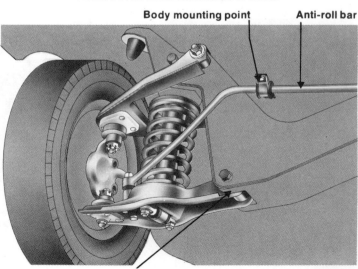

Body mounting point   Anti-roll bar

Suspension mounting point

19 Checking lever and telescopic dampers for tightness and leaks

Dampers are incorporated in all suspension systems. They operate hydraulically, and are usually either of the lever type or telescopic.

On some cars the mountings have a nut at the top and an eye at the bottom, on others the eye is at the top and the nut at the bottom. Some have either eyes or nuts at both ends. Tighten the top mounting nut and the nut securing the eye. If there is a recom-

Top mounting

mended torque for tightening, be careful not to overtighten. Tighten the lower mounting points also. Check that the rubber bushes are

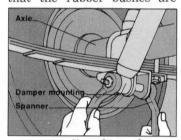

Axle

Damper mounting
Spanner

not protruding from the eye —indicating that they are perished, split or contaminated with oil. If they are damaged in any way, renew them (see p. 203).

Checking for leaks
On lever-type dampers, look for leaks at the point where

the lever arm emerges from the damper body. If there is

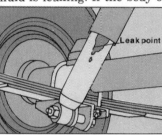

Leak point

Lever

a leak, the damper will have to be removed, and a new one of the same type fitted (see p. 202).

On telescopic dampers, look on the body for signs that the fluid is leaking. If the body or

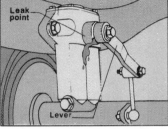

Leak point

piston rod has traces of fluid on it, a new damper must be fitted (see p. 203).

Checking for rust
With the sleeve raised on a telescopic damper, you will just be able to see inside to

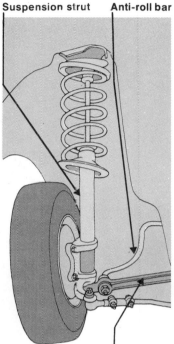

Piston rod

check for pitting or rusting of the piston rod. Check also

TYPICAL TELESCOPIC DAMPER LOCATIONS

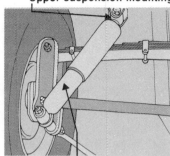

Suspension strut   Anti-roll bar   Upper suspension mounting

Telescopic damper

Upper swivel joint

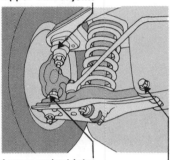

Lower suspension arm

Lower swivel joint

Suspension pivot point

the damper body. Clean it with a wire brush and make

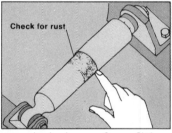

Check for rust

sure it is in good condition. If there is any sign of rust on the body or piston rod, fit a new damper (see p. 203).

Checking for wear
Make sure that the bump stops —fitted to the damper piston

rods—bushes, boots and dust seals have not split, cracked

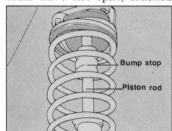

Bump stop

Piston rod

or perished. If rubber bump stops are worn down, the damper and spring will wear excessively on rough surfaces.

Check that all nuts are tight and any split-pins are in good condition. Renew any damaged components.

20 Topping up the fluid in a lever-type damper unit

Buy the fluid recommended by the car manufacturers. Carefully clean the damper body and round the filler plug with a wire brush. Remove the plug and make sure that

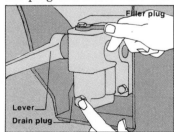

Filler plug

Lever
Drain plug

no dirt gets into the unit.

If it is impossible to top up while it is on the car, the damper will have to be re-

moved (see p. 202). Use an oil can to inject a small

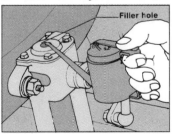

Filler hole

amount of fluid into the unit until it begins to trickle out.

Rock the car gently to expel any air from the damper, then refit and tighten the filler plug and clean any excess fluid carefully from the damper body.

A TYPICAL REAR LEVER DAMPER

Damper   Damper arm   Connecting link

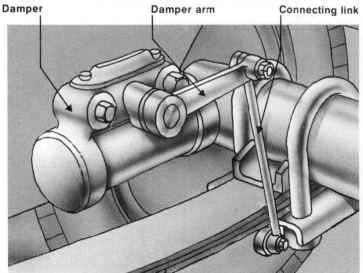

21	23
22	24

21 Checking the condition of rubber boots and seals

Look for oil leaks at both ends of the protective rubber boots on each side of the rack-and-pinion steering assembly. Check carefully the tightness of the retaining clips at the inner and outer ends of the two rubber boots.

If a boot is dirty, wash it in methylated spirit, which does not harm the rubber. Make sure that the moulding

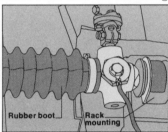

Rubber boot   Rack mounting

seam on the rubber boot is parallel to the rack housing. If it is twisted, loosen the retaining clip at one end and straighten it.

Examine the boot for signs of cracking or splitting. If it is damaged, fit a new boot (see p. 208).

22 Checking the rack-and-pinion mounting brackets

The rack-and-pinion steering assembly may be held to the chassis or car bodywork by U-bolts or specially shaped brackets. Check the tightness of the bolts or brackets to ensure that the rack assembly

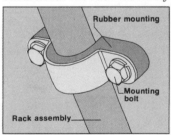

Rubber mounting

Mounting bolt

Rack assembly

cannot move. On BLMC transverse-engined cars, the U-bolt nuts are on the inside, either side of the steering column.

Some units are mounted on rubber bearing blocks between the rack housing and the body. Check the condition of the blocks. If they are damaged or contaminated with oil, fit new ones by undoing the mounting brackets, one at a time, and sliding new rubber blocks behind the rack-and-pinion assembly. If the job is too difficult, take the car to a garage and have them renewed.

23 Checking the ball-joints and seals for wear and lubricating the ball-joints

Check the condition of the ball-joint grease seals at the steering track rod ends.

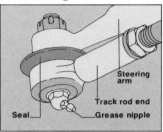

Steering arm

Track rod end

Seal   Grease nipple

If damaged fit new ball-joints.

To test a ball-joint, hold the arm to which the ball-joint pin is fitted, and get a

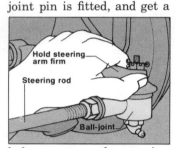

Hold steering arm firm

Steering rod

Ball-joint

helper to turn the steering wheel. Check the amount of movement in each ball-joint before it moves the arm you are holding. If there is any movement in the joint, it is worn. Remove it and fit a new one (see p. 207).

If there is a grease nipple in the base of each ball-joint, wipe the nipple clean

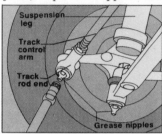

Suspension leg

Track control arm

Track rod end

Grease nipples

and fit a grease gun. Apply only three strokes of the grease gun to lubricate the joint. Make sure that you do not over-grease it, for the protective rubber seal can be pushed out by the pressure of the grease from the grease gun.

24 Checking the steering-column couplings

Some rack-and-pinion steering units have a coupling incorporated in the steering column. It is made of a composition rubber or canvas material, and normally is attached by bolts to splined flanges on the column and

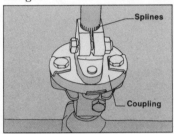

Splines

Coupling

on the rack-and-pinion shaft.

Wash the coupling in methylated spirit. If it is split or damaged, undo the coupling bolts, take the composition coupling from between the two flanges and fit a new one. Make sure the flange bolts are in good condition and fully tightened.

A TYPICAL RACK-AND-PINION STEERING SYSTEM

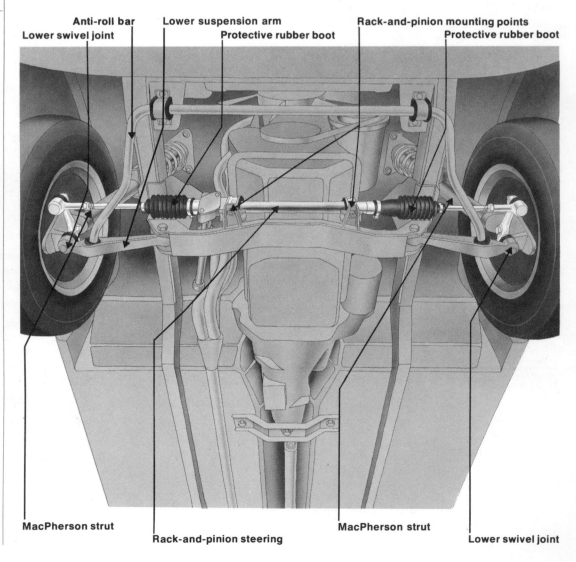

Anti-roll bar   Lower suspension arm   Rack-and-pinion mounting points
Lower swivel joint   Protective rubber boot   Protective rubber boot

MacPherson strut   MacPherson strut
Rack-and-pinion steering   Lower swivel joint

25 Checking and lubricating the steering swivel ball-joints

Check the upper and lower ball-joints on the front stub axles for wear. Remove the front road wheels. Fit a lever under the upper ball-joint and a suitable levering point. Move the lever up and down.

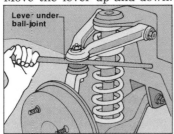

Lever under ball-joint

Check for any movement in the ball-joint. If it moves, the joint is worn and is dangerous to drive with. Have it replaced by a garage. Repeat this operation on the lower suspension ball-joint. If worn, have it renewed.

On suspensions using a MacPherson strut front-suspension assembly, there is only one ball-joint at the bottom. Use a lever under the lower suspension arm to

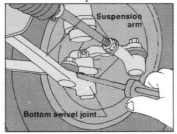

Suspension arm

Bottom swivel joint

check the ball-joint for wear.

Some cars have a top ball-joint and a threaded trunnion at the bottom. Check for wear in the top ball-joint and for

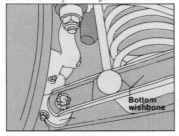

Bottom wishbone

looseness in the lower trunnion. If any of the parts are

worn, have them replaced by a garage.

Wipe all suspension joints clean and find out if they have grease nipples fitted. Many of the modern joints are pre-greased and sealed for life.

If there are grease nipples, clean them and apply three

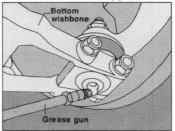

Bottom wishbone

Grease gun

shots of a grease gun to lubricate the joint. Get a helper to turn the steering wheel as the grease is being applied, to help circulate the lubricant. Do not over-grease a ball-joint, for the protective rubber seal around the top of the joint can be pushed out by the excess pressure of the grease gun.

26 Checking the steering and idler box mounting bolts

The bolts that hold the steering and idler boxes to the car

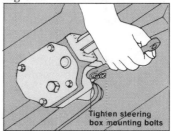

Tighten steering box mounting bolts

chassis must be kept tight to ensure safe steering.

Grip the idler drop-arm, and try to move it up and down and from side to side.

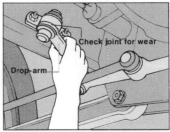

Check joint for wear

Drop-arm

If there is any movement, the idler bushes are worn. Have them replaced by a garage.

Check the tightness of the nuts that hold the drop-arms to the steering-box shaft and idler shaft. If the nut is castellated, remove the split-pin, check the tightness and fit a new pin.

27 Checking the king pins for wear, and lubricating

Some cars still use a king-pin swivel on the front suspension. The pin is fitted through bushed eyes at the top and bottom of the stub-axle, and it is held to a short centre axle by a cotter pin.

Clean the grease nipples fitted top and bottom at the sides of the stub axle. Fit a

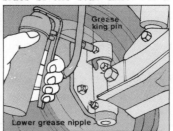

Grease king pin

Lower grease nipple

grease gun to the nipples, and pump in grease until it is seen being forced out.

Grip the road wheel at the top and bottom and rock it backwards and forwards. If there is any play, the king pins and bushes are worn. They are dangerous to drive with: have them replaced.

A STEERING BOX AND IDLER SYSTEM

Upper swivel joint   Steering box   Drop-arm   Drop-arm   Idler box   Upper swivel joint

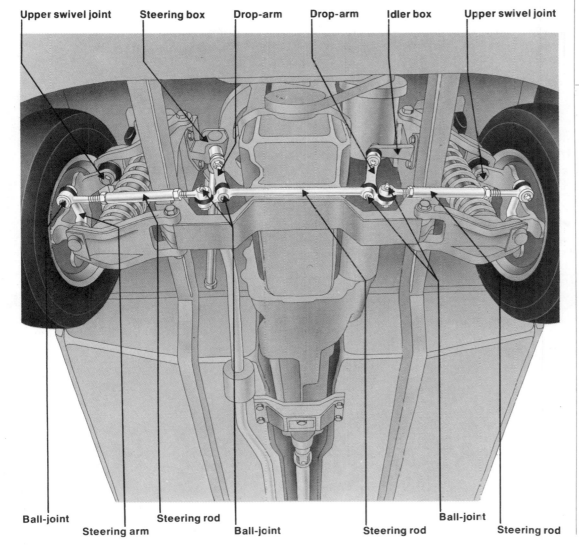

Ball-joint   Steering arm   Steering rod   Ball-joint   Steering rod   Ball-joint   Steering rod

28   30

29

28 Draining the lubricating oil from the engine sump

Run the engine to normal operating temperature, as warm oil drains more easily.

Switch off the engine and remove the oil filler cap.

Check the capacity of the sump (see chart, pp. 96-97), and have available enough containers to hold the drained oil. An old basin is ideal because it is shallow and will fit under the sump. Have sufficient new oil ready to refill both the engine sump and filter bowl if necessary (see pp. 96-97).

Find the drain plug and

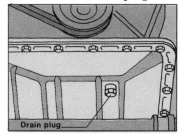

Drain plug

check that it is at the lowest point of the sump. If it is not, jack up the car to such an angle that all the sludge and the oil will drain out.

Clean round the drain hole with a rag. Put a container under the drain plug and undo the plug with a spanner or socket. It may be necessary to use a special sump plug removal tool if the plug has plain sides and internal faces.

Allow the oil to drain out for at least 10 minutes.

If the old oil is very dirty, it is advisable to flush the engine (see p. 73) to remove any accumulation of sludge. Check that the head of the plug is not

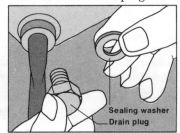

Sealing washer
Drain plug

damaged and that the washer is sound.

Take the old oil to a garage for disposal.

TYPES OF DRAIN PLUG

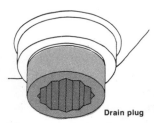

Drain plug

Most sump drain plugs can be removed with a combination male/female wrench (see p. 33). The plug that has a magnet to trap metal particles (below) in the oil, must be handled particularly carefully to avoid damage.

Magnetic drain plug

A TYPICAL FRONT-ENGINE LAYOUT

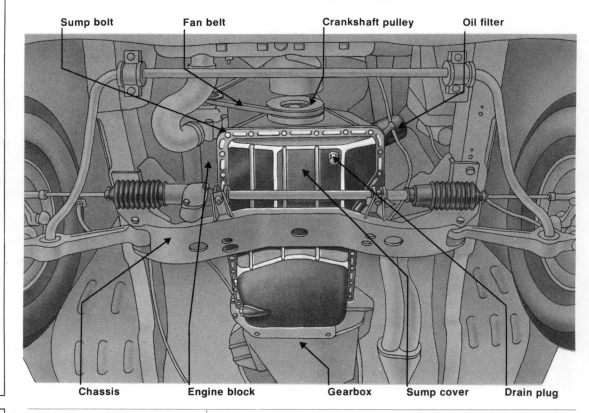

Sump bolt   Fan belt   Crankshaft pulley   Oil filter

Chassis   Engine block   Gearbox   Sump cover   Drain plug

TYPES OF SUMP FIXINGS

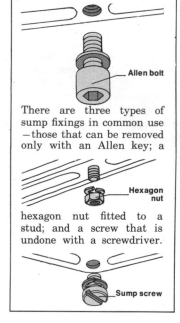

Allen bolt

There are three types of sump fixings in common use —those that can be removed only with an Allen key; a

Hexagon nut

hexagon nut fitted to a stud; and a screw that is undone with a screwdriver.

Sump screw

---

29 Checking the sump bolts

From underneath the car, check the tightness of the

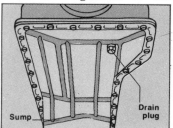

Sump   Drain plug

engine sump flange bolts. In most cases hexagon nuts are used, but some cars have screws or Allen bolts.

Use a ring or socket spanner, and do not apply too much pressure as this might distort or break the gasket. Tighten the bolts progressively on each side of the sump.

---

30 Cleaning the wire gauze oil strainer in the engine sump

After draining the oil, remove the six nuts which hold the

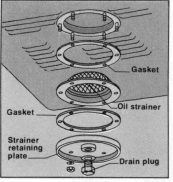

Gasket
Oil strainer
Gasket
Strainer retaining plate
Drain plug

strainer retaining-plate. The plate, strainer and two gaskets can then be removed.

Clean the strainer with paraffin or petrol. Use an old chisel or screwdriver carefully to scrape away all traces of the old gaskets.

Fit new gaskets on each side of the strainer flange.

Make sure the suction pipe is correctly seated in the strainer and, if necessary, slightly bend the strainer. Refit the strainer assembly. Fit new washers under the nuts.

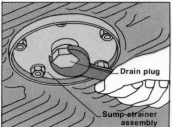

Drain plug
Sump-strainer assembly

Do not overtighten. Replace the sump drain plug.

31 Fitting a new paper element to an oil-filter bowl

The filter element is usually made of resin-impregnated paper that fits into a permanent housing on the engine. Renewing the element can

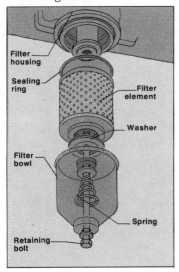

Filter housing
Sealing ring
Filter element
Washer
Filter bowl
Spring
Retaining bolt

be difficult because the housing is often inaccessible. It may be a job that can best be done from above the car.

The housing is secured with a long bolt through the centre.

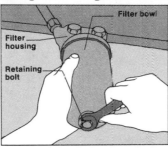

Filter bowl
Filter housing
Retaining bolt

Release the bolt, but before allowing the canister bowl to drop, tap it to break the seal. The bowl will be full of dirty oil, so have a container to catch the oil and filter (see pp. 96-97).

Separate the old element from the support washer and

spring. Clean the spring, washer, housing and bolt in clean petrol, and allow them to dry.

Reassemble the filter bowl on a bench. The spring goes in at the bottom with two washers, the shaped one on top. The new element fits on top of the shaped washer.

Clean the filter housing, and renew the seal in the top part of the housing. A new rubber seal is supplied with the filter

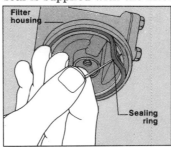

Filter housing
Sealing ring

element. You may have to dig out the old one with a thin,

sharp spike or needle.

The new seal has a square section; make sure that you do not twist or stretch it. Slot the seal into the groove in two or three places and press the rest home. Some manufacturers suggest filling the filter bowl with clean oil before replacing it, as the bearings could be starved until the engine has pumped oil into the filter, but this is not possible on side-mounted filters.

Hold the filter bowl, complete with its new element, in position against spring pressure while you fit the long bolt. Do up the bolt and, before it is tight, rotate the housing to make sure it sits against the new seal.

Fill the engine sump with oil (see pp. 96-97), and run the engine, slowly at first, to check oil pressure and make sure that there are no leaks.

32 Fitting a new cartridge type of oil-filter element

A cartridge filter, screwed to a threaded boss (male) or to

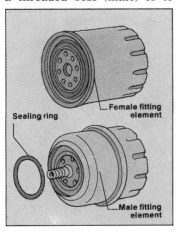

Sealing ring
Female fitting element
Male fitting element

a stud (female) at the side of the engine, can usually be unscrewed (anticlockwise) with two hands, but it may be necessary to use a strap spanner or to knock a screwdriver through the canister and use it as a lever. Some types have a hexagon cast on the base; use a spanner. Alternatively, the whole canister may be hexagon-shaped and a special spanner needed.

Clean the area and lightly grease the mating surfaces. Put a smear of clean engine oil on the washer which is supplied with the new filter. Fit the washer and filter.

33 Checking and cleaning a centrifugal type of oil-filter assembly

Slacken the generator bolts and remove the drive-belt. Undo the bolts that secure the crankshaft pulley and draw

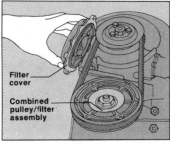

Filter cover
Combined pulley/filter assembly

off the combined crankshaft pulley and filter cover. Undo the centre nut and lift the complete filter assembly off the end of the crankshaft.

Wash the filter components

in clean petrol. Pay special attention to the inside of the filter cover, where all the oil

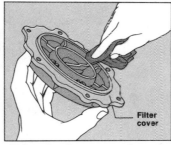

Filter cover

sludge is thrown, and to the filter strainer.

Reassemble the unit with new gaskets and seal, and a new tab locking-washer.

Refit and tighten the generator drive-belt (see p. 119).

FLUSHING OUT THE ENGINE

If the oil in the sump is particularly dirty, it is advisable to flush out the engine.

Paper-element filter
Drain the sump and replace the drain plug. Remove the filter bowl, discard the old element, clean the housing, fit a new oil seal to the housing and refit the bowl without the paper element.

Check the sump capacity (see pp. 96-97) and fill up with an engine-flushing oil. Start the engine and run it slowly. Check immediately for leaks around the filter. Let the engine warm up to normal running temperature, then switch off and drain the sump. Dispose of the flushing oil at a garage.

Remove the filter bowl, clean it and fit a new element. Refit the bowl and make sure that it sits on the oil seal correctly. Tighten.

Fill the engine with fresh oil to the Full mark on the dipstick. Start the engine and check for leaks.

Cartridge filter
Never flush the engine unless you are changing the filter. Drain the sump (see Job 28) and replace the drain plug. If the cartridge can be removed without damage, take it off, drain the dirty oil, and refit the filter canister. If it cannot be removed easily, leave

it, and have the filter and oil changed and the engine flushed by a garage.

Check the sump capacity (see pp. 96-97) and fill up with an engine-flushing oil.

Start the engine and run it slowly. If the cartridge was removed, check immediately for leaks around it. Warm the engine to normal running temperature, then switch off and drain the sump. Dispose of the oil at a garage.

Remove the cartridge and fit a new one. Fill the engine with fresh oil to the Full mark on the dipstick. Start up and check for leaks.

Centrifugal oil filters
Drain the sump and replace the drain plug. Remove the centrifugal oil filter, clean and replace it. Check the sump capacity (see pp. 96-97) and fill up with an engine-flushing oil. Start the engine and run it slowly. Check immediately for leaks round the filter assembly.

Warm the engine to normal running temperature, then switch off and drain the sump. Remove the centrifugal oil filter, clean and replace it.

Fill the engine with fresh oil (see pp. 96-97) to the Full mark on the dipstick. Start up and check lubrication system for leaks.

34	36
35	37

34 Checking the gearbox mountings

On front-engine rear-wheel-drive cars, the gearbox is fixed at the back by a rubber mounting to a cross-member, and at the front by the clutch-housing, which is bolted to an engine plate.

On most cars the clutch bell-housing bolts can be reached from underneath. On others it is necessary to remove a section of the floor.

Check and tighten the bolts round the clutch bell-housing. Check the bolts securing the mounting rubber to the cross-member, and the bolts holding

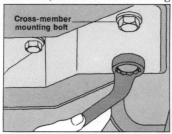

the cross-member to the body. If the rubber gearbox mounting bush is contaminated with oil, cracked or broken away from its backing-plate, fit a new one. Check the body-work where the cross-member

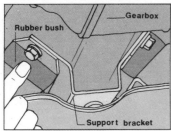

is bolted. If it is badly rusted have the area repaired by a garage. Do not try to treat the damage yourself.

35 Draining the oil from a conventional type of gearbox

It is advisable to drain the gearbox oil immediately after the car has been driven and when the oil is warm. This will ensure that it flows freely as it is draining.

Locate the level/filler plug on the side of the gearbox casing (see Job 37) and wipe the plug and area around it clean.

Remove the level/filler plug. Locate the drain plug in the base of the gearbox, and identify its type. Make sure a spanner of the correct type

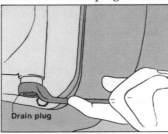

Drain plug

the plug and let all the oil drain out of the gearbox, into the pan.

If an overdrive is fitted, it

is used to undo it. Place a pan under the drain plug. Remove

will have to be drained separately (see Job 38).

Clean the drain plug and

Sealing washer · Drain plug

make sure that the sealing washer, if fitted, is in good condition. If necessary, fit a new sealing gasket. Replace the drain plug.

36 Refilling a gearbox and overdrive unit

Make sure all drain plugs are tight. Refill the gearbox with the recommended oil to the base of the level/filler plug hole. Allow any excess oil to trickle out. Clean the level/filler plug and refit it.

If an overdrive is fitted, the oil will run through from the gearbox to fill it. If a dipstick is used, place a funnel

Funnel in dipstick hole

in the dipstick hole and fill the gearbox with the correct quantity of oil—check this with your dealer. Allow it to settle and check the level. If necessary, top up a little, but do not overfill the unit.

A CONVENTIONAL GEARBOX

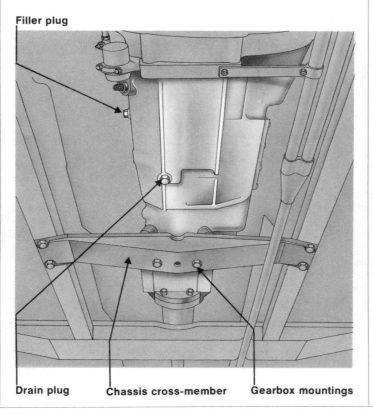

Filler plug

Drain plug · Chassis cross-member · Gearbox mountings

37 Topping up the gearbox oil level

Top up the gearbox with the grade of oil recommended by the manufacturers. This is usually the same grade of oil used in the engine. But if a different oil is recommended (check with your dealer if you are not sure), never mix the oils. Do not use ordinary lubrication oil in automatic transmissions. Special transmission fluid recommended by the manufacturer must be used.

Locate the level/filler plug on the side of the gearbox. This is usually reached from underneath the car. On some models there is a rubber or metal cover on the side of the

transmission cover, through which either a level/filler plug,

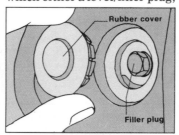

Rubber cover · Filler plug

or a dipstick/filler hole can be reached.

Thoroughly clean the area round the filler hole and remove the plug, or withdraw the dipstick. If a level/filler plug is fitted, the oil should be flush with the base of the

filler plug hole. If a dipstick is used, the oil should show on the high mark on the dipstick.

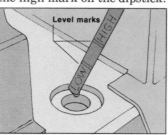

Level marks

If necessary, top up the oil level. On some cars it is possible to fit a small funnel in the filler hole and pour the oil into the funnel to top up. If a dipstick is used, fill the gearbox through a funnel placed in the dipstick hole until it reaches the high mark

on the dipstick. Use an oil syringe or a plastic dispenser

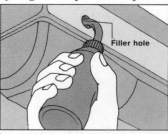

Filler hole

bottle if the hole is awkwardly positioned.

Clean and refit the level/filler plug, or wipe the dipstick clean and replace it. If the gearbox is fitted with an overdrive unit, drive the car for a few miles when you have finished the service jobs and recheck the gearbox oil level.

38 Draining the oil from a gearbox and overdrive unit

Check the base of the overdrive. It may have a hexagon plug, usually marked 'Drain'. Undo this and let the overdrive oil drain out. Do not

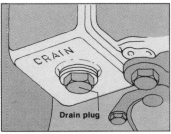

Drain plug

confuse this type of drain plug with other hexagon-headed

plugs found wired together. On some cars a circular plug, which has to be removed with a special 'C' spanner, will be found in the base of the unit.

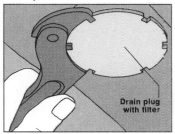

Drain plug with filter

Undo this and remove the plug and gauze filter behind

it. The third type of drain system is a filter plate in the base of the unit. This is held by screws round the edge of the plate. Undo the screws and remove the plate and filter gauze behind it. Wash any

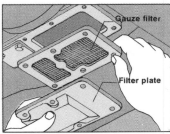

Gauze filter

Filter plate

filters in clean petrol and refit them before refilling (Job 36).

40 Lubricating a column gear-change linkage

Open the bonnet of the car and trace the linkage down the steering column. The first pivot points will be found at the base of the steering column. In most cases this is more easily reached from underneath the car. Thoroughly clean the pivot points in petrol to remove any dirt. Lubricate all metal

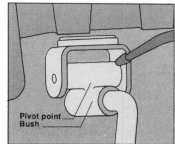

Pivot point Bush

pivot points with light machine oil. Check the pivot points on the linkage going into the gearbox. Some gearboxes use a cross-shaft mounted in rubber bushes between the chassis and the gearbox. Check the condition of the rubber bushes. Renew them if necessary.

Check all bolts, clevis pins or clips securing the linkage for wear. Many of the con-

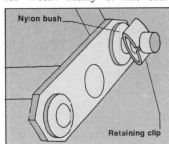

Nylon bush

Retaining clip

necting rods operate in nylon or plastic bushes. Check for wear, and renew if necessary.

39 Lubricating a floor-mounted gear linkage

Lubricate the gear-lever pivot ball if it is stiff.

Undo the screws holding the plate that secures the protective rubber boot round the base of the gear lever. Slide the rubber boot up the gear lever.

Release the locking washer that secures the plastic or steel domed cap at the base of the lever. Unscrew the cap and lift out the gear lever.

Lubricate the pivot ball with a high-melting-point grease. Refit the gear lever and rubber boot.

Some cars—the Vauxhall Victor range for example—have external linkages from the floor-mounted gear lever to the side of the gearbox. From underneath the car, clean and lubricate the pivot points with oil. If the pivot points are worn, have them replaced by a garage. Do not attempt the repair yourself.

COLUMN-MOUNTED GEAR LINKAGE

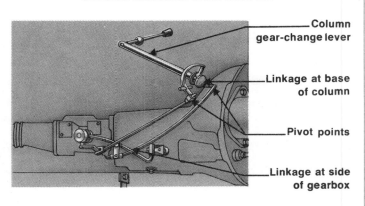

Column gear-change lever

Linkage at base of column

Pivot points

Linkage at side of gearbox

FLOOR-MOUNTED GEAR LINKAGE

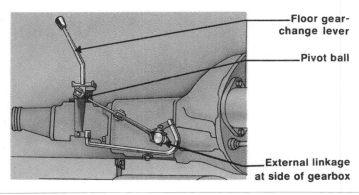

Floor gear-change lever

Pivot ball

External linkage at side of gearbox

41 Cleaning the filters in an overdrive unit

If the filter on the overdrive unit is part of the draining system, wash the filter in clean petrol and reassemble.

If a normal drain plug is used, the filter is located behind a plate on the side of

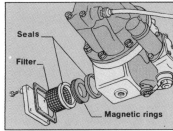

Seals

Filter

Magnetic rings

the overdrive. Undo the screws and remove the plate,

gasket, filter, magnetic rings and seals. Clean the filter and magnetic rings. If necessary, fit new sealing washers and gasket. Some overdrives have two filters, one on the

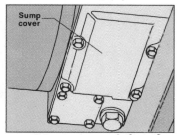

Sump cover

overdrive sump and the other on the relief valve. Remove the sump cover and the cover

gasket and lift out the rectangular filter assembly. Clean the filter gauze in petrol. Fit

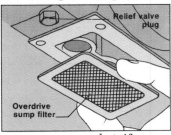

Relief valve plug

Overdrive sump filter

a new cover gasket if necessary—some filters have a gasket on each side of the filter. Lay the gasket and filter on the cover and fit the second gasket. Reassemble. To clean the relief valve filter, remove the relief valve

plug and its sealing ring from the base of the overdrive unit. Pull the relief valve down about ½ in. and slide off the cylindrical filter. Check the

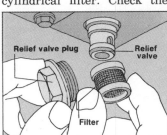

Relief valve plug

Relief valve

Filter

filter for damage, and wash it in clean petrol. Clean the relief valve plug, fit a new sealing ring, replace the cleaned filter and reassemble the valve unit.

42 Checking and lubricating mechanically operated clutch linkages

The clutch linkage can be either cable or rod-operated.

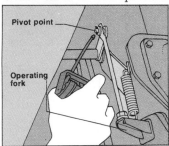

Lubricate all the pivot points on a rod-operated clutch and check the condition of the pivot pins. If the pins are worn, fit new ones.

On cable-operated clutches ensure that the inner cable runs smoothly in its outer casing. If necessary, disconnect the cable at the pedal end and trickle oil down the inner cable to lubricate it. Oil the shaft that the clutch

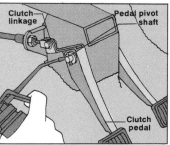

pedal pivots on. Check that the return spring is not broken. If it is, renew it.

43 Checking and adjusting free play at the clutch pedal

The free play is the distance the pedal travels before it operates the clutch. Hold a ruler against the toe-board, inside the car, and alongside the clutch pedal. Press the pedal until the initial move-

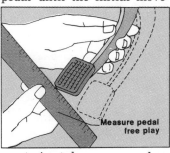

ment is taken up, and a greater effort is needed to

push it further. Measure the distance it moves.

Check the free play. If it is more than recommended, release the lock-nut on the adjus-

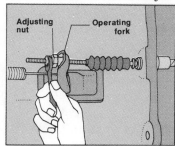

ter under the car. Undo the adjuster to reduce the travel. Screw the adjuster in to increase it. Tighten the lock-nut.

44 Adjusting clutch free play on a Ford Cortina Mk III

The clutch on the Cortina Mk III is cable-operated. The earlier Cortinas used hydraulically operated clutches. Undo the lock-nut on the clutch adjuster under the car at

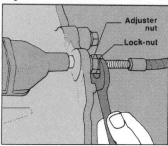

the clutch fork. Get a helper to press the clutch pedal down as far as it will go inside the car. Pull the adjuster away from its housing. Measure the

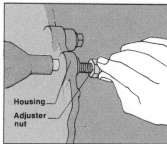

distance between the adjuster nut and its housing with feeler blades. Turn the nut until the correct clearance (·124-·144 in.) is obtained. Hold the adjusting screw in this position and tighten the lock-nut.

If clutch action is stiff, disconnect the clutch cable at the pedal and pull it through into the engine compartment. Hold it up and trickle oil down the inner cable to lubricate it.

MECHANICAL CLUTCH LINKAGE

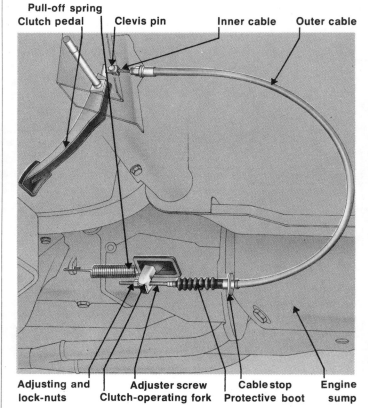

Pull-off spring
Clutch pedal
Clevis pin
Inner cable
Outer cable

Adjusting and lock-nuts
Adjuster screw
Clutch-operating fork
Cable stop
Protective boot
Engine sump

45 Adjusting the clutch free play on the Ford Escort range

The Ford Escort range of cars uses a cable-operated clutch. Unlike most other mechanically operated clutches there is no evident free play at the clutch fork.

Both the clutch and brake pedal should be level. If the clutch pedal is slightly lower than the brake pedal, release the lock-nut on the adjuster screw under the car at the clutch fork.

Turn the adjuster screw in until both clutch and brake

pedals are level. When the pedals are level, hold the

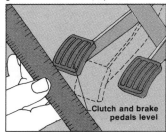

adjuster screw in this position and tighten the lock-nut to secure it.

46 Checking and adjusting the Vauxhall clutch

The pedal free play on mechanically operated Vauxhall clutches is measured at the clutch operating fork end, under the car.

Unhook the pull-off spring from the clutch fork. Pull the

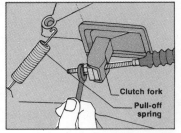

end of the fork away from the adjusting screw. Check the clearance with a ruler between the clutch fork and the lock-nut (see chart). To

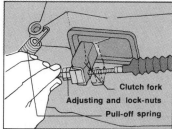

adjust the clearance, loosen the lock-nut and turn the adjuster screw to give the correct clearance. Tighten the lock-nut and reconnect the spring.

Vauxhall clutch clearances	
Viva HA/HB/HC	$\frac{1}{4}$ in.
Victor FC	$\frac{1}{8}$ in.
Victor FD/FE (4-cyl.)	$\frac{3}{16}$ in.
Victor FD/FE (6-cyl.)	$\frac{1}{8}$ in.
VX 4/90	$\frac{3}{16}$ in.
Ventora FD/FE	$\frac{1}{8}$ in.
Viscount	$\frac{1}{8}$ in.
Firenza HC	$\frac{1}{4}$ in.

47 Bleeding a Lockheed hydraulic clutch system

Clean the hydraulic reservoir cap and remove it. Top up the reservoir with Lockheed fluid.

Locate the clutch slave cylinder, usually fitted to the right-hand side of the clutch housing. On British Leyland transverse-engine cars, however, the cylinder is under the bonnet.

Clean the end of the bleed nipple and fit a bleed spanner to it. Attach a rubber bleed

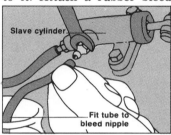

Slave cylinder

Fit tube to bleed nipple

tube to the nipple, and immerse the other end of the tube in a clean jar containing about 1 in. of clean hydraulic

fluid. Undo the bleed nipple one complete turn and get a

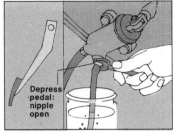

Depress pedal: nipple open

helper to depress the clutch pedal slowly. Just before it reaches the end of its travel,

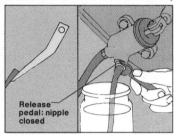

Release pedal: nipple closed

tighten the bleed nipple. Allow the pedal to return un-

assisted. Repeat the operation, closing the bleed nipple at the end of each stroke of the clutch pedal.

When air bubbles stop rising from the end of the tube, lock up the bleed nipple and remove the bleed tube.

Get the helper to keep the hydraulic reservoir topped up with clean hydraulic fluid during the operation. Never let the fluid run low. When the clutch has been bled, top

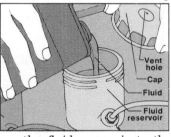

Vent hole
Cap
Fluid
Fluid reservoir

up the fluid reservoir to the correct level (see p. 130). Clean the vent hole in the cap. Replace and tighten the reservoir cap securely.

48 Adjusting the British Leyland clutch clearance

The clearance is measured with feeler blades between the clutch-operating arm and the adjustable stop.

Disconnect the pull-off spring from the top of the clutch-operating arm. Pull the

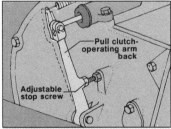

Pull clutch-operating arm back

Adjustable stop screw

arm back and measure the gap between the adjustable stop screw and the arm. The correct clearance is ·020 in.

If the gap is too small, undo the lock-nut and turn the

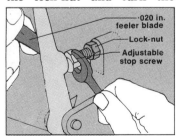

·020 in. feeler blade
Lock-nut
Adjustable stop screw

stop screw clockwise to increase it. If the gap is too great, turn the stop screw anticlockwise to reduce it.

When the correct clearance has been obtained, tighten the lock-nut and refit the clutch pull-off spring.

HYDRAULIC CLUTCH SYSTEM

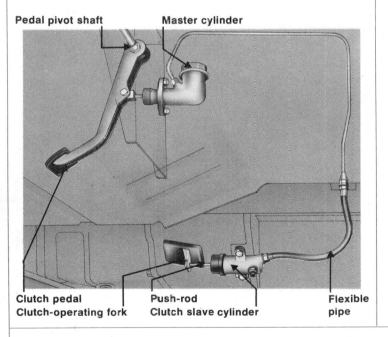

Pedal pivot shaft   Master cylinder

Clutch pedal
Clutch-operating fork   Push-rod
Clutch slave cylinder   Flexible pipe

49 Adjusting the clearance on hydraulic clutches

Most hydraulic clutches have spring-loaded slave cylinders (see p. 219), which are self-adjusting. Others, however, can be adjusted. They have an adjuster on the slave cylinder push-rod, between the cylinder and clutch fork. Disconnect the clutch pull-off spring, positioned between the operating fork and the clutch housing. Push the operating fork away from the push-rod, and check the clearance between the end of the

push-rod and the operating fork. The gap should be at

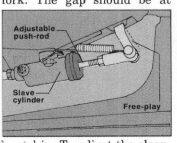

Adjustable push-rod
Slave cylinder
Free-play

least ⅛ in. To adjust the clearance, use two spanners, one to hold the push-rod still and

50 Bleeding a Girling hydraulic clutch system

Clean the hydraulic reservoir cap and remove it. Top up the reservoir with new fluid recommended by the manufacturers. Locate the clutch slave

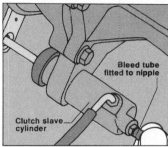

Bleed tube fitted to nipple
Clutch slave cylinder

cylinder, fixed to the side of the clutch housing under the car. Take off the bleed nipple dust cover. Fix a bleed spanner over the nipple and attach one end of a rubber tube to the nipple. Immerse the other end of the tube in a jar containing about 1 in. of new

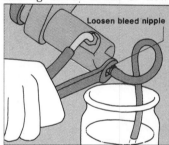

Loosen bleed nipple

hydraulic fluid. Turn the nipple anticlockwise to loosen it. Get a helper to operate the clutch pedal slowly. Make sure the helper keeps the fluid reservoir topped up with new fluid.

Watch the end of the tube in the jar. When the air bubbles stop rising from the tube, get your helper to hold the clutch pedal down while you close the bleed nipple. Remove the bleed tube and replace the dust cover. Top up to the correct level and refit the cap.

the other to undo the lock-nut. Loosen the lock-nut on

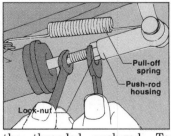

Pull-off spring
Push-rod housing
Lock-nut

the threaded push-rod. To increase the clearance, screw the rod in, and to reduce it, screw the rod out. Tighten the lock-nut after adjustment.

51 Checking the flexible hoses in the braking system

Check for signs of chafing, cracks or perishing, and renew any hose that is worn or damaged (see p. 197). If a hose seems particularly vulnerable to chafing—perhaps because it is near a moving part—buy a coiled-wire guard at an accessory shop and fit it to the hose.

Get a helper to press the brake and clutch pedals inside the car, and check all unions, joints and seals under-

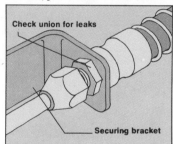

Check union for leaks

Securing bracket

neath for leaks. If you find leaks, tighten joints. If leaks persist, dismantle any faulty sections and renew hoses or pipes (see p. 197). Check that all the brackets that hold the hoses are tight.

52 Checking the metal pipes in the braking system

Look for signs of rusting or damage caused by stones, and renew the metal pipes if necessary (see p. 197).

If pipes have been covered by underbody compound, scrape it off so that you can examine them properly.

Wipe all the joints linking metal pipes or flexible hoses and pipes together, and check

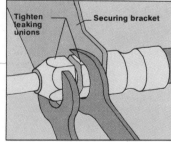

Tighten leaking unions

Securing bracket

them for tightness and signs of leaking. Check other unions for leaks, and replace any faulty pipe or joint.

Look for kinks in metal pipes underneath the car. If any sections appear faulty, replace them (see p. 197). Check that all the brackets holding the pipes are sound and tight, and that they have not been displaced by the movement of the car.

TYPICAL LAYOUT OF HYDRAULIC PIPES

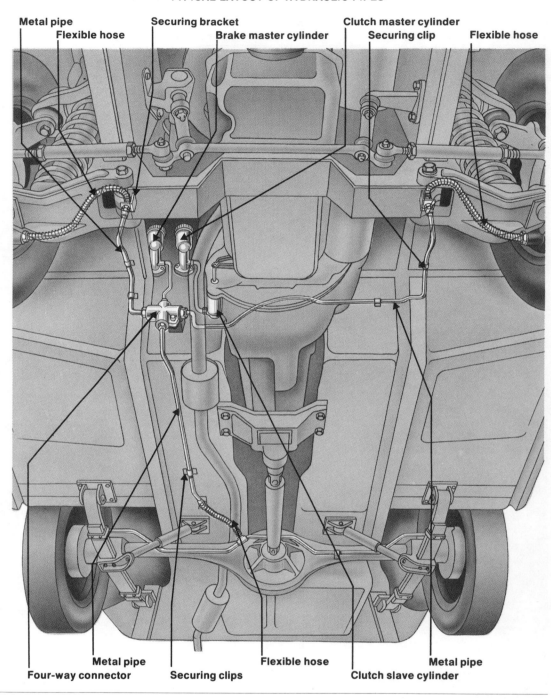

Metal pipe
Flexible hose
Securing bracket
Brake master cylinder
Clutch master cylinder
Securing clip
Flexible hose

Metal pipe
Four-way connector
Securing clips
Flexible hose
Clutch slave cylinder
Metal pipe

53 Checking the pipes and hoses in the clutch hydraulic system

Plastic pipes are often used in clutch systems, because pressures are lower than in the brake lines. Check all the

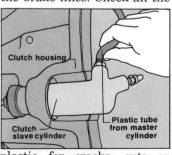

Clutch housing

Clutch slave cylinder

Plastic tube from master cylinder

plastic for cracks, cuts or perishing, and renew any pipes that are faulty. Make sure that all the securing

clips are tight and are holding pipes well away from exhaust

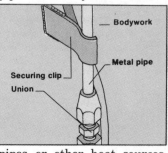

Bodywork

Metal pipe

Securing clip

Union

pipes or other heat sources.

The connection between the clutch master cylinder and the slave operating cylinder on the gearbox, is usually a metal pipe with a

flexible section at the lower end. Check the tightness of the joints at both ends and examine for leaks. Do not overtighten any joint.

Check any rubber hoses

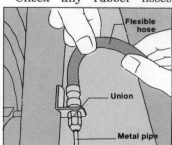

Flexible hose

Union

Metal pipe

for perishing by bending them sharply, particularly near the ends. If any surface cracks show, renew the hoses.

54 Checking a dual braking system

A dual-line braking system provides separate hydraulic circuits for the front and rear brakes. If one circuit fails, the other is unaffected and can be used to stop the car.

Clean the pipes under the master cylinder, depress the

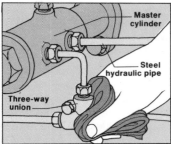

brake pedal, and look for leaks. If there are any, check that the joint is tight and, if necessary, renew the faulty section (see p. 197).

Make sure that the supply pipes from the reservoir to

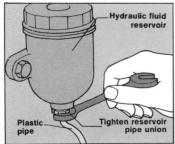

the master cylinder in the engine compartment have not deteriorated, and check that the brackets holding the pipes are tight. Check that all unions and joints under the car are tight, but do not overtighten, as unions fracture easily. Renew any faulty unions or pipes if necessary (see p. 197).

55 Draining and filling a final-drive unit combined with the rear axle

If you have to drain the rear axle, run the car first to ensure that the oil is warm. Place a tray that can hold about 8 pints under the drain plug, usually near the back.

Clean around the filler-level plug and remove it with a spanner. Use a ring spanner or socket to remove the drain

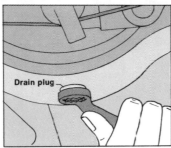

plug, and leave it until all the old oil has poured out into

a tray. Wash the drain plug in solvent and replace it. Use a plastic dispenser bottle to

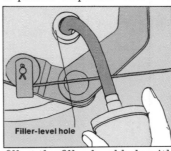

fill at the filler-level hole with oil recommended by the car manufacturer. Fill until the oil just trickles out of the filler hole.

Make sure that you do not overfill the rear axle; excess oil can cause the hub seals to fail prematurely. Wipe off the

surplus oil and make sure that the filler-plug sealing washer (if fitted) is in good condition. If the oil level drops significantly between one service and another, there may be a leakage at the pinion oil seal, the hub seals or the gas-

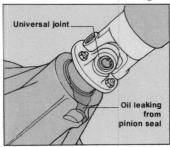

ket between the differential housing and its cover-plate. Identify the area that is leaking and have a new gasket or seal fitted. Do not attempt to fit it yourself.

56 Topping up a gearbox/final-drive unit

Use a ring spanner or socket to take the filler plug from the gearbox. The oil should reach the base of the hole.

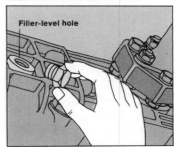

If not, use an oil syringe or plastic dispenser to top up with recommended oil. Do not overfill. Let excess trickle out. Clean and replace plug.

REAR AXLE LUBRICATION

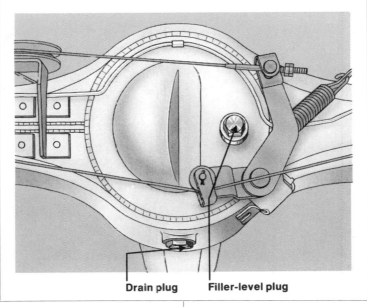

Drain plug   Filler-level plug

57 Draining and refilling a combined gearbox and final-drive unit

Place a container able to hold 8 pints of liquid under the drain hole, usually at the lowest point of the gearbox. Remove both the filler-level plug (on the side of the gear-

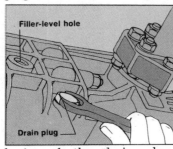

box) and the drain plug. Leave until the oil stops draining into the container. Clean and refit the drain plug.

Use an oil syringe or plastic dispenser to inject the oil recommended by the car

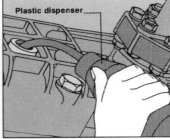

manufacturer at the filler hole. Never overfill; allow any excess oil to trickle out until the level is at the base of the filler hole.

Clean the filler-level plug and replace it.

58 Topping up a final-drive unit at the rear axle

To check the axle oil, make sure that the car is level on the axle stands. The filler plug is usually either on the side or at the back of the differential casing. Clean

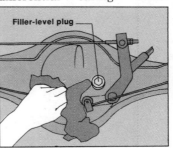

round the plug to make sure no dirt gets in, and remove it with a spanner. If no oil spills out, use an oil syringe

or plastic dispenser to top up with the oil recommended by the car manufacturer.

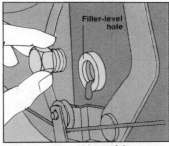

Fill until oil trickles out. Wipe away the excess oil and make sure that the plug sealing washer (if fitted) is in good condition. Renew it if necessary and refit and tighten the plug.

59 Checking drive-shaft couplings for tightness, wear and deterioration

Check the bolts on rubber doughnut couplings for tightness. Check the rubber for

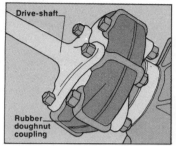

Drive-shaft

Rubber doughnut coupling

signs of deterioration, cracking, swelling or oil contamination. If these couplings are defective, fit new ones (see pp. 212-213). The constant-velocity joints on front-wheel-drive cars do not usually have bolts. But if the drive-shaft is joined to the final-drive assembly by a rubber spider joint, make sure that the U-bolts are not loose and rubbing against the gear casing. Check the tight-

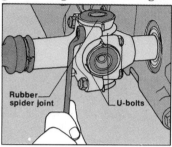

Rubber spider joint   U-bolts

ness of the U-bolt nuts; if a torque setting is given, use a

torque wrench to tighten them.

Front-engine rear-wheel-drive cars, with independent rear suspension have a universal joint on the drive-shaft.

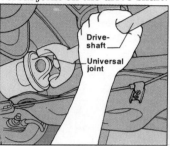

Drive-shaft

Universal joint

Hold the drive-shaft near the joint and try to move it up and down. If there is any free play in the joint, a new universal joint will have to be fitted (see p. 212).

62 Lubricating the drive-shaft universal joints

Clean the grease nipple and pump in lithium-based grease.

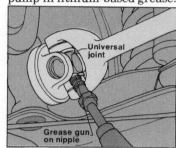

Universal joint

Grease gun on nipple

If the nipple is blocked, fit a new one (see p. 34). Many universal joints do not have grease nipples; they are sealed for life and further lubrication is unnecessary.

60 Checking the drive-shaft protective rubber boots

Constant-velocity joints each have a protective rubber boot to keep out dirt and grit. Joints do not need maintenance, but check the rubber boots for splits or deterioration. If they

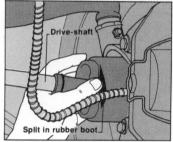

Drive-shaft

Split in rubber boot

are worn, renew them (see pp. 214-215). If road dirt gets into the joint it turns into a fine grinding paste. A split rubber boot, therefore, means that the joint will wear rapidly. Some manufacturers advise overhauling the joint if a rubber boot is damaged.

61 Checking the final-drive oil seals

There is an oil seal in the final-drive housing at the inboard end of any drive-shaft. An oil leak here will need im-

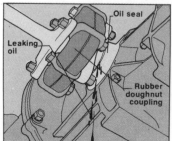

Oil seal

Leaking oil

Rubber doughnut coupling

mediate attention. Special tools are needed, so it is a job for a garage.

FRONT-ENGINE FRONT-WHEEL DRIVE

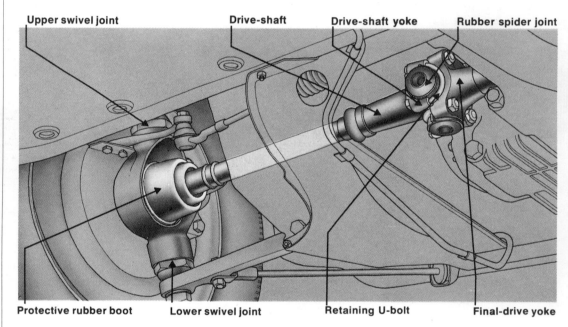

Upper swivel joint   Drive-shaft   Drive-shaft yoke   Rubber spider joint

Protective rubber boot   Lower swivel joint   Retaining U-bolt   Final-drive yoke

REAR-ENGINE REAR-WHEEL DRIVE

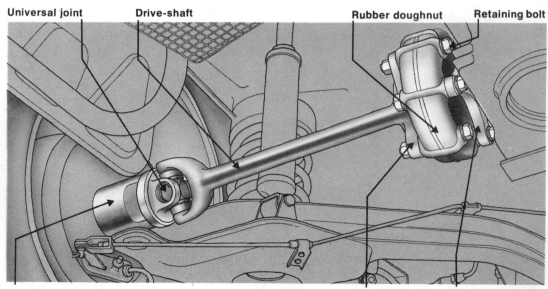

Universal joint   Drive-shaft   Rubber doughnut   Retaining bolt

Rear-wheel hub   Drive-shaft flange   Final-drive flange

63 Checking the propeller-shaft universal joints for wear

Hold the universal-joint flange firmly with one hand and grip the propeller shaft with the

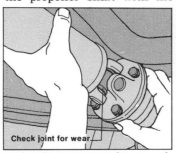

Check joint for wear.

other. Try moving the propeller shaft from side to side. If there is movement, the joint is worn and will need renewing (see p. 212). Check that the flange nuts and bolts are tight. If castellated nuts are used, remove the split-pins,

tighten the nuts and bolts and fit new split-pins. Bend

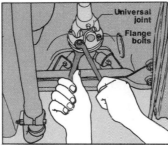

Universal joint

Flange bolts

the ends of the pin round the sides of the nut.

There are no propeller-shaft universal joints on Daf cars. Check the rubber bushes at each end of the propeller shaft. If they are cracked or contaminated with oil, have new ones fitted.

64 Lubricating the propeller-shaft splines

Clean the grease nipple on the sliding joint with a dry cloth, and pump in a lithium-

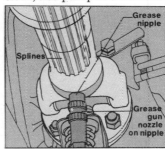

Grease nipple

Splines

Grease gun nozzle on nipple

based grease. If you have to renew a blocked grease nipple (see p. 34), make sure the new nipple is the same size as the old one. Remove the old nipple and screw the new one in firmly.

65 Lubricating the propeller-shaft universal joints

Clean the grease nipple in the centre of the joint with a dry cloth, and pump in a

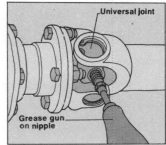

Universal joint

Grease gun on nipple

lithium-based grease from a grease gun until grease oozes from the joint. If the nipple is blocked, fit a new one. If you notice any wetness from behind the final-drive flange,

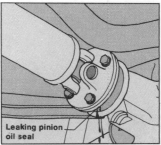

Leaking pinion oil seal

a pinion oil seal may be leaking. Renewal is a job for a garage.

Many universal joints have no grease nipples, as they are sealed for life and cannot be lubricated.

66 Checking the propeller-shaft centre bearing

On cars which have two-piece propeller shafts, check the tightness of all mount-

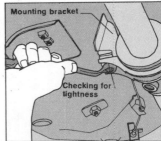

Mounting bracket

Checking for tightness

ing bolts and brackets. Check the rubber mountings for cracks, swelling or oil contamination. Any parts that are worn or deteriorated must be replaced.

To check for wear in the centre bearing, hold the shaft near the bearing and try to move it up and down. If there is any free play, the bearing is worn and a new one must be fitted. These are normal universal-type joints (see p. 212).

FRONT-ENGINE REAR-WHEEL DRIVE

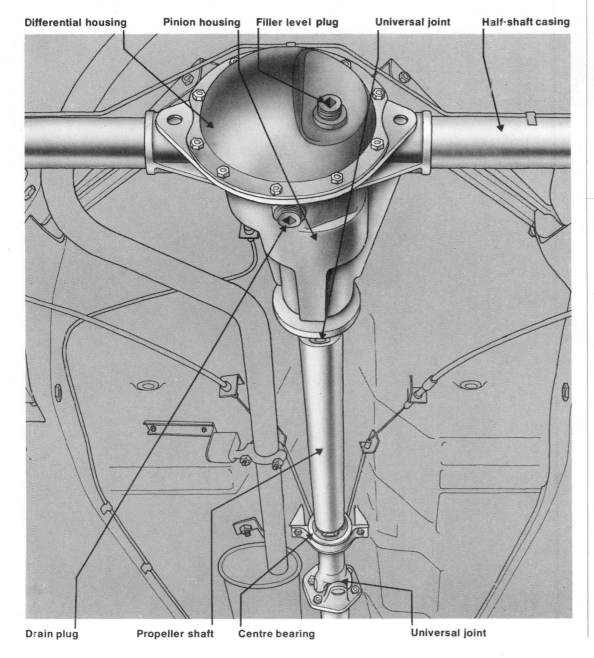

Differential housing   Pinion housing   Filler level plug   Universal joint   Half-shaft casing

Drain plug   Propeller shaft   Centre bearing   Universal joint

67 Removing the protective transmission undertrays

To inspect the Variomatic transmission, first remove the undertrays. If necessary, jack up the car and reposition the axle stands under the suspension units, so that the weight of the car rests on the suspension. Undo the

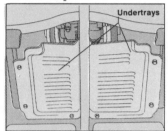

seven bolts that hold each undertray to the bodywork.

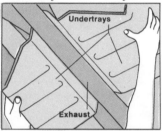

Fold down the tray on each side of the exhaust pipe, and unclip them.

VARIOMATIC TRANSMISSION

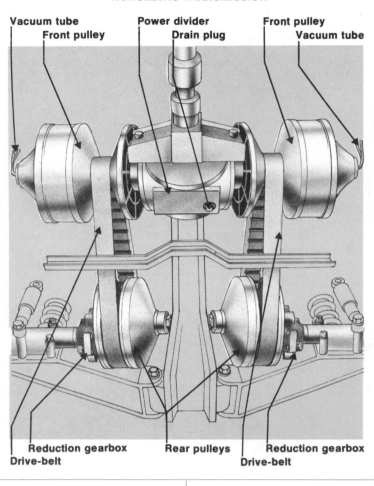

Vacuum tube
Front pulley
Power divider
Drain plug
Front pulley
Vacuum tube

Reduction gearbox
Drive-belt
Rear pulleys
Reduction gearbox
Drive-belt

68 Draining and refilling the power divider

Place a container under the drain plug of the power divider. Remove the filler/level plug from the side of

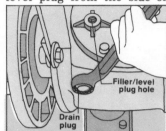

the unit, and the drain plug from the base of the casing.

Allow the oil to drain out. Wipe the drain plug clean and replace it. Fill the casing with oil (see chart) to the base of the filler/level

plug hole. Replace the filler/level plug.

69 Draining and refilling the reduction gears

On the Daf 33, 44 and 55 models there are two reduction gearboxes, one serving each rear wheel. They are positioned level with and on the outside of the rear secondary pulleys.

Place a container under both reduction gear casings. Remove the filler/level plug from the side of the casings

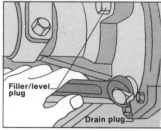

and the drain plugs from the base of the casings. Allow the oil to drain out.

Wipe the drain plugs clean and replace them. Fill both reduction gear casings to the base of the filler/level plug holes, with new oil (see chart—p. 83).

Allow any excess oil to trickle out. Wipe the filler/level plugs clean and replace them.

70 Draining and refilling the reduction gearbox

On the Daf 66 there is only one reduction gearbox—positioned just behind and between the rear secondary pulleys.

Place a container under the reduction gearbox. Remove the filler/level plug from the front of the box and the drain plug from the

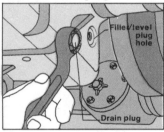

base of the gearbox. Wait until all the oil has drained out into a container.

Wipe the drain plug clean and replace it. Tighten the plug fully. Fill the reduction gearbox, with the oil recommended by the manufacturers (see chart—p. 83), to the base of the plug hole.

Allow any excess oil to trickle out of the filler hole. Wipe the filler/level plug clean and replace it.

71 Topping up the oil level in the power divider

Remove the filler/level plug from the side of the power-divider casing. Check the level of the oil in the casing

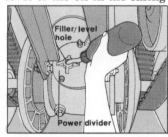

through the filler/level hole. If oil is not level with the bottom of the hole, top up the unit with the oil recommended by the manufacturers (see chart—p. 83).

Allow any excess oil to

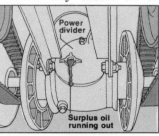

trickle out of the filler hole. Wipe the filler/level plug clean and replace it.

72 Topping up the reduction gears— Daf 33, 44 and 55

Remove the filler/level plugs from the sides of the reduction boxes on each side of the rear secondary pulleys. Check the level of the oil in the casings through the

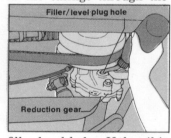

filler level holes. If the oil is not level with the bottom of the holes top it up (see chart—p. 83).

Allow any excess oil to trickle out of the filler holes.

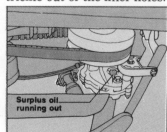

Wipe the filler/level plugs clean and replace them.

73 Topping up the reduction gearbox on the Daf 66

Remove the filler/level plug from the side of the reduction gearbox. Check the level of the oil in the casing through the filler/level plug hole. If necessary, top up

with oil (see chart). Allow excess oil to trickle out. Wipe the filler/level plug clean and replace it tightly.

74 Checking the condition of the drive-belts

From underneath the car, check the condition of both belts for wear. If any of the teeth in the driving surface of the belts are

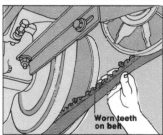

chipped or cracked, or if the sides of the belt are worn and are beginning to 'flake' or craze, fit two new belts (see pp. 216-17).

75 Checking and adjusting the pulley flange clearance on a Daf 66 model

Check the clearance between the rear pulley flanges with a feeler blade of the right size (see chart). If it is incorrect, slacken the four self-locking nuts that secure the reduction

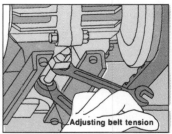

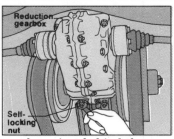

gearbox—just behind the rear pulleys—to the chassis. Loosen the lock-nut on the adjusting bolt at the front of the reduction gear casing.

Turn the rear wheels backwards and forwards to ensure the belts ride at the highest point on the rear pulleys. If the clearance is too wide, turn

the adjusting bolt anticlockwise, to reduce the clearance. If the clearance is too small, turn the adjusting bolt clockwise, to draw the belts further into the pulley flanges. After turning the bolt, rotate the wheels to ensure that the belt is in the correct position for adjustment. Check again with the feeler blade.

After adjusting the belts, tighten the adjusting bolt lock-nut and tighten the nuts holding the reduction gearbox to the car's chassis.

76 Checking and adjusting the clearance between the secondary pulley flanges

If the car was driven into position, before it was jacked up, the position of the drive-belt on the rear pulleys will be correct. But if the wheels have been turned or the belts disturbed since, turn the rear wheels backwards and forwards until the belts are riding on the top of the pulleys. With feeler blades of the correct thickness (see chart),

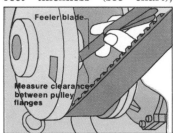

check the clearance between the flanges of the two rear pulleys. If they are incorrect adjust them. On the 33, 44 and 55 models, slacken the four bolts holding the power-

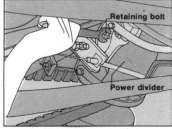

divider unit to the chassis. Slacken the lock-nut on the horizontal adjusting bolt at the back of the power divider.

If the clearance is too great, turn the adjusting bolt anticlockwise. This will move the power divider closer to the secondary unit and allow the drive-belts to ride higher on

the pulleys, thus reducing the clearance between the pulley flanges.

If the clearance is too small, turn the adjusting bolt clockwise. This will pull the belt deeper in between the pulley

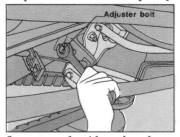

flanges and widen the clearance between the flanges.

The flanges of each pulley should be adjusted so that the feeler blade is a tight sliding fit between them.

When the pulleys have been correctly set, tighten the adjusting bolt lock-nut. Tighten the four bolts securing the

power divider to the chassis.

To ensure that the power divider is square in the chassis, pull the propeller shaft forwards against spring pressure and release it. It should return to its normal operating position.

If it does not, loosen the power divider belts, realign the unit and retighten the belts.

77 Checking the condition of the flexible vacuum pipes

There are four short flexible vacuum pipes—two to each of the pulley units at the side of the primary (front) pulley units. If these are damaged, the engine kickdown and braking will be affected.

Loop a piece of rag round the vacuum pipes and pull

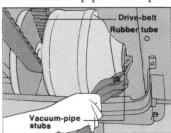

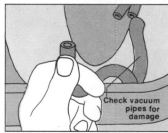

them off their connections on the pulley units. Check the

flexible pipes for deterioration. If they are cracked, split

or covered in oil fit new ones.

One of the flexible vacuum pipes, each side, is slightly larger in diameter than the other. Make sure the flexible pipe is fitted to its correct connection. Push it fully home on to the stub to ensure that it does not leak.

Oil type and capacity		Pulley clearances	
Daf 33 — ATF type A/A		**New belts**	
Power divider	400 cc	Daf 33	1-1·5 mm.
Reduction gears	140 cc	Daf 44	3-4 mm.
		Daf 55	3-4 mm.
Daf 44 and 55 — SAE 80		Daf 66	3-4 mm.
Power divider	475 cc		
Reduction gears	250 cc	**Used belts**	
		Daf 33	1-1·5 mm.
Daf 66 — SAE 80		Daf 44	2-3 mm.
Power divider	475 cc	Daf 55	2-3 mm.
Reduction gear	430 cc	Daf 66	2-3 mm.

78 Releasing the brake shoes to remove the brake drums

To remove the brake drum in order to service the brakes, it may be necessary to release or to back off the brake shoes.

Most front drum brakes have twin leading shoes, which means that both brake shoes

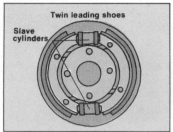

contact the drum at the same time. They are pulled into

closer contact by the rotation of the drum when the brake pedal is applied.

All rear and some front drum brakes have a leading and trailing shoe—which

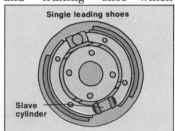

means that although both shoes contact the drum at the same time, only the leading

shoe is pulled into closer contact by the drum rotation. When the car is being reversed, the trailing shoe is drawn into closer contact with the drum. This system provides equal braking effort in both directions.

On single leading shoe brakes—as illustrated on these pages—there is only one adjuster which compensates for both shoes. On twin leading shoe brakes there are two adjusters, one for each brake shoe. These are opposite one another, either inside the drum or on the brake back-plate.

The type of adjuster fitted varies enormously between manufacturers and even with-

in the same range of models. Identify the type fitted to your car from the illustrations.

Always make sure that the brakes are off before attempting to release the shoes.

Press the brake pedal to centralise both shoes in each drum. Undo the adjusters fully to give maximum clearance between shoes and drum.

All adjusters should turn or move easily. If they are too tight, apply a few drops of penetrating oil to ease them.

Never lubricate any adjuster that is controlled by a friction device. If you do, the friction effect will be lost and the brake shoes would lose their adjustment.

79 Identifying the type of brake adjuster on your car

If there is no hole in the back-plate or drum and no obvious adjusting nut, the shoes are adjusted automatically by a self-compensating device controlled by the handbrake (see Job 80).

Adjusters mounted on the brake back-plate

A square thread nut on the

brake back-plate indicates a split-wedge adjuster (A).

A hexagonal bolt-head near the wheel cylinder is a friction-type adjuster (B).

If there is a lever on the back-plate tensioned by a spring clip, the adjuster is a Girling expanded push-rod spring-clip adjuster (C).

A Girling expanded push-

rod plastic button adjuster has a button protruding from the back-plate (D).

Adjusters reached through back-plate holes

Remove a rubber plug from the hole. The Lockheed cylinder adjuster has the disc incorporated into the wheel cylinder (E), and the serrated disc adjuster is incorporated into the shoe pivot (F).

If you can see two toothed plates meshed together it is a serrated-plate adjuster (G).

Adjusters reached through holes in the drum

Remove the plug. A slot indicates a snail-cam type adjuster (H). You can see the disc on a knurled disc adjuster (I). A serrated disc supporting a lever is a Girling cylinder adjuster (J).

A. Split-wedge adjusters

Most cars have a manual adjuster—usually a square nut on the outside of the brake back-plate. It is located on the opposite side of the plate to the wheel cylinder. If the adjusting nut is fully screwed in, there will be little lining left on the shoe.

To contract the brake shoes, use a brake adjusting spanner to turn the adjuster anticlockwise until the drum turns freely, or until the adjuster can be turned no further.

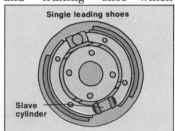

Return spring
Adjusting nut

B. Friction adjusters

Two hexagonal back-off adjusters are mounted on the brake back-plate. The bolts operate as cams pushing against the edge of the shoe. The maximum adjustment is by turning the bolt-head through 180°.

Use a special brake adjusting spanner to turn both adjusters anticlockwise until the wheel is just turning freely. Make sure that both hexagonal bolt-heads are turned by the same amount, or as far as they will go.

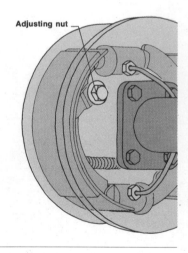

Adjusting nut

C. Expanded push-rod spring-clip adjusters

Some Girling brakes—for example on the Hillman Avenger—have a spring-clip adjuster. When the handbrake is off, the handbrake lever rests on a spring clip in the brake back-plate.

To release the brake shoes, move the handbrake lever backwards and forwards to release the tension of the clip. Remove the clip to allow the handbrake lever to move closer to the back-plate, when the handbrake is in the off position. Check that the wheel can turn freely.

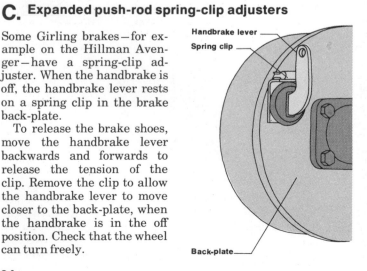

Handbrake lever
Spring clip
Back-plate

D. Expanded push-rod plastic button adjusters

A plastic button which protrudes through a hole in the back-plate acts as a stop to the handbrake's internal lever.

Use a screwdriver to push the plastic button off its seat. Slacken the handbrake adjustment until the internal lever touches the back-plate. Replace the button on reassembly.

On the Cortina Mk III, Granada and Consul, the plastic plunger is a handbrake adjuster gauge. Never remove it. The gap between the gauge and lever is 0·20 to 0·39 in.

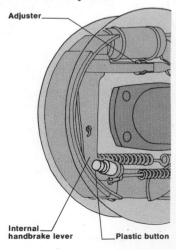

Adjuster
Internal handbrake lever
Plastic button

E. Lockheed cylinder adjusters

On early Rootes cars, and on the Austin Westminster Mk II and its successors, a square hole in the back-plate gives access to the brake adjuster lever which is engaged with a toothed wheel.

On some cars, access to the adjusting mechanism is through a hole in the brake drum itself.

Use two screwdrivers—one to push the lever away from the wheel and the other to turn the wheel anticlockwise to release the brake shoes.

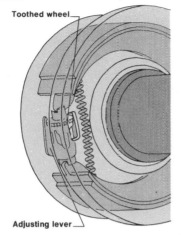

F. Serrated disc adjusters

The brake mechanism on Vauxhall models has a knurled adjuster which is held in position by the brake-shoe return spring.

The spring acts as a locking device on the adjuster. The cylinder slides on the back-plate, and must always be free to centralise the shoes.

To release the shoes, push a screwdriver through a hole in the brake back-plate and flick the nut round anticlockwise until the brake shoes are released and the drum is free.

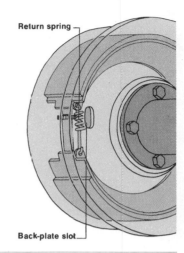

G. Lockheed serrated-plate adjusters

The Triumph 2·5 PI, the Triumph Stag and recent models in the Chrysler (Rootes) Hunter range have these Lockheed serrated-plate adjusters.

The access hole in the brake back-plate or drum is blocked by a rubber plug. Remove the plug and push in a screwdriver. Use the screwdriver to swing the adjuster plate away from its sister plate, which is attached to the leading brake shoe, to release the shoes.

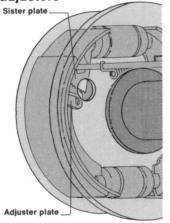

H. Snail-cam adjusters

A slotted adjuster can be reached through a hole in the drum with a screwdriver. There is usually a hole in the wheel as well, so that the wheel does not have to be removed to reach the adjuster. If you do take off the wheel make sure the holes line up when you replace it. Push a screwdriver through the hole until it is located in the adjuster slot. Turn the screwdriver anticlockwise, as far as it will go, to retract the shoes.

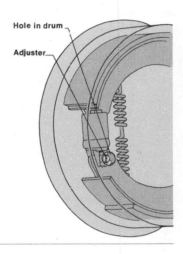

I. Knurled disc adjusters

These are held in place by the brake shoe return spring. The spring acts as a lock and the cylinder, which slides on the back-plate, must always be free to centralise the shoes.

To reach the adjuster, push a screwdriver through a hole in the brake drum and flick the nut anticlockwise, against spring pressure, until the drum can rotate freely.

Be careful not to damage the serrations on the nut when backing off the shoes as this will cause difficulty when the drum is refitted.

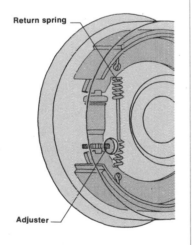

J. Girling cylinder adjusters

The Ford Cortina Mk II, Capri Mk I, Corsair and the British Leyland MGC, Triumph 1500 and Marina 1800 have Girling cylinder adjusters. The backing-off mechanism is reached through a hole in the brake drum. Push a small screwdriver through the hole in the drum and lift the adjuster lever off its toothed wheel. Rest the lever on a ledge in the casting and turn the toothed wheel with the screwdriver anticlockwise to release the shoes. Check that the drum turns freely.

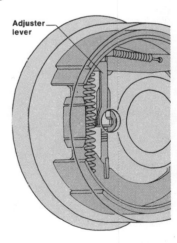

80 Checking automatically operated brake adjusters

Automatic adjusters may be connected to the footbrake or handbrake. The shoes are adjusted as the brakes are applied. This should mean that the brakes are correctly adjusted at all times, and you should be able to remove the drums without backing off the adjusters. However, if the drums are difficult to remove back off the adjuster.

The adjuster often fitted to Girling rear brakes is typical. The handbrake lever arm is pivoted, and actuates a lever pawl which engages a ratchet on the adjuster wheel at the end of the piston assembly. Inside the wheel is a screw with a slotted head fitting against the shoe.

As the linings wear, the lever pawl clicks into the next position and turns the adjuster wheel when the brake is released. The screw moves out to compensate for lining wear

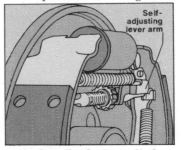

as the handbrake is applied.

To back it off, push a screwdriver through the hole in the drum and turn the adjuster inwards. To check the adjusters spin the rear drums. Apply the handbrake and check that it locks the drums. Do this several times to make sure the maximum adjustment has been made.

Where the adjuster is operated by the footbrake, follow the same procedure with the brake pedal. The distance the pedal travels will decrease as the shoes are adjusted.

81 Removing separate brake drums

If the brake drum has drum retaining screws or a locating flange centralising the inside edge of the drum to the hub, it is separate from the wheel hub.

Clean the face of the drum with a wire brush. Mark a line across the face of the drum and the centre hub cap, to ensure that the drum can be refitted in the same place without upsetting the balance of the drum and wheel.

When you have slackened the brake-shoe adjuster (see Job 78), remove the countersunk screws that hold the drum to the hub. Pull off the drum.

If it is a very tight fit, tap the protruding rim of the drum lightly with a hide or a plastic mallet and turn the drum at the same time. This should break the seal holding the drum and ease removal.

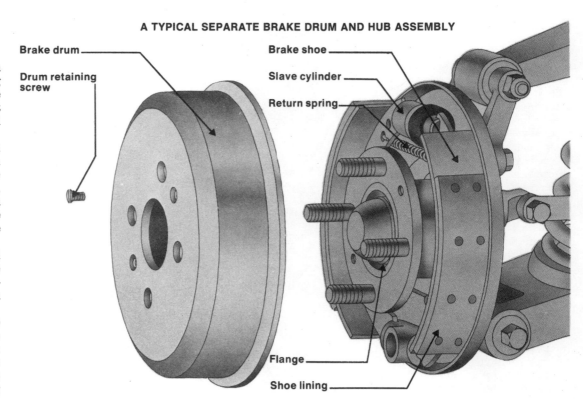

A TYPICAL SEPARATE BRAKE DRUM AND HUB ASSEMBLY

Brake drum

Drum retaining screw

Brake shoe

Slave cylinder

Return spring

Flange

Shoe lining

82 Removing brake drums combined with the hubs

When the brake drum is integral with the wheel hub, prise the grease cap away from the hub centre with a heavy screwdriver. Remove the split-pin that secures the castellated hub nut and undo the nut. The nut may be very tight, so use a long bar and socket to remove it.

Remove the spacing washer and the outer tapered roller bearing. Lift off the combined hub and brake drum.

On some rear drums—for example, on the British Leyland 1100 and 1300 range and most Daf models—a special pulling tool is needed to draw off the drum. Hire one, to suit your car, from your local dealer.

Fit the puller to the wheel studs, and fit the wheel stud nuts to secure it. Turn the centre bolt of the puller to

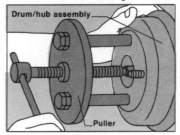

Drum/hub assembly

Puller

draw the drum and hub assembly from the stub axle.

Note that the nearside hub nut has a left-hand thread—turn it clockwise to free it.

On some rear brake drums the inner hub bearing may come apart as the drum is drawn off, leaving the inner track on the axle. Use another puller to draw the track off the hub, and remove the oil seal and outer track.

Reassemble and grease the bearing (see p. 104). Fit it with a new oil seal.

INTEGRAL DRUM AND HUB ASSEMBLY

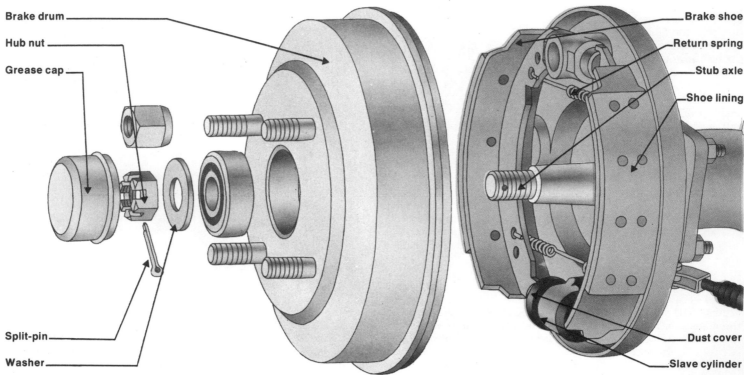

Brake drum

Hub nut

Grease cap

Brake shoe

Return spring

Stub axle

Shoe lining

Split-pin

Washer

Dust cover

Slave cylinder

83 Checking the brake drums, slave cylinders and brake linings

Clean inside the brake drums with a rag or soft brush soaked in methylated spirit. Never blow lining dust away. Care-

Score marks

fully check the condition of the braking surface inside

A TYPICAL DRUM-BRAKE ASSEMBLY

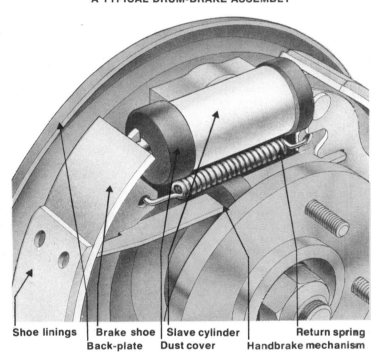

| Shoe linings | Brake shoe | Slave cylinder | Return spring |
| Back-plate | Dust cover | Handbrake mechanism |

the drum. If it is badly scored or discoloured, or cracked radially by the build-up of heat inside the drum, fit a new drum. Once the face of the drum is scored, the efficiency of the brake will decline and new linings will quickly become worn.

Check the brake linings. Minor wear on the brake linings can be compensated by tightening the brake adjusters. Replace linings that are two-thirds worn—less than $\frac{1}{16}$ in. thick above the shoe or

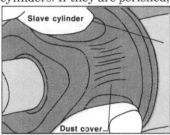

1/16" minimum thickness

Brake lining

1/16" minimum thickness

rivet head. Never rivet new linings to old shoes. If the linings are worn, loose or contaminated by oil, fit new shoes (see p. 193).

Squeeze the rubber dust covers that protect the wheel cylinders. If they are perished,

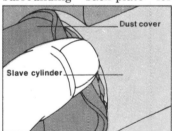

Slave cylinder

Dust cover

remove the brake shoes (see p. 193), slide off the damaged covers and fit new ones. Pull back the dust cover and examine the cylinder and the surrounding back-plate for

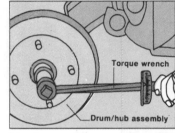

Dust cover

Slave cylinder

any signs of hydraulic fluid. If the fluid has been leaking

past the cylinder seals, you must either renew the seals and the dust covers or fit a complete new wheel cylinder unit (see p. 198). The brake shoes will have to be removed for this job (see p. 193).

To replace the brake drums, reverse the dismantling procedure (see p. 193). Use a new split-pin if a castellated hub nut is removed. If the hub has taper-roller wheel bearings, make sure that the bearings are correctly adjusted during replacement (see p. 93).

Some hubs require the use of a torque wrench to obtain the correct pre-load on the

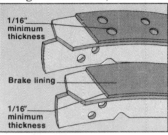

Torque wrench

Drum/hub assembly

bearings. If a collapsible spacer is used between the bearings, that too must be replaced (see p. 93).

Note that the Audi 100 hub bearing requires a dial gauge to set up the permissible bearing free-play. Do not attempt this yourself but take the car to a garage.

When you have reassembled the drum or integral hub assembly, adjust the brake shoes (see Job 84 or 85). If the hub grease cap was removed, refit it (see Job 95).

84 Adjusting the brakes on Daf models

On Daf models it is difficult to turn the rear wheels because of the drag on the transmission. Adjust the brakes (see Job 85) until the drum cannot be turned. Back off the adjuster slightly—by one or

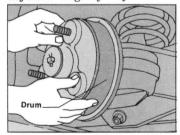

Drum

two clicks—until the slight movement, known as backlash, between the cogs in the reduction gear can be felt at the drum.

Check the handbrake adjustment (see pp. 90-91).

85 Adjusting the drum brakes on front and rear wheels

Spin each front drum, and apply the footbrake to ensure that the brake shoes are centralised. Release the footbrake. Adjust each wheel separately.

Identify the type of adjuster fitted to your car (see Job 72). Check the number of adjusters on each drum. All rear and some front drums have

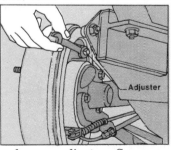

Adjuster

only one adjuster. Screw up the adjuster until the drum is locked. Back off the adjuster

two clicks and check that the drum revolves freely. If the drum is still binding, back the adjuster off further until it is free.

If there are two adjusters opposite each other, complete

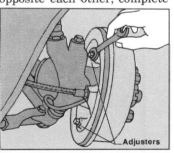

Adjusters

the adjustment on one, then adjust the second. If after adjusting there is a slight rubbing as the drum is turned, press the brake pedal to centralise the shoes.

Adjust the rear brakes in

the same way, but make sure the handbrake is off.

Check the handbrake adjustment (see pp. 90-91).

When you have replaced the wheels, test the car on the road to check that the brakes are adjusted evenly. Brake sharply on a clear road at a speed of about 25 mph.

If the adjustment is correct, the car will pull up evenly. If the car pulls to one side, this indicates incorrect adjustment. Readjust the brakes and retest.

If the brake shoes are left binding through incorrect adjustment, extensive overheating of the brake drums will cause the grease in the hubs to melt, thus contaminating the linings. This will also accentuate brake fade and glazing of the brake drum, and you will soon have to fit new brake shoes.

86 Checking the pads and discs

Disc brakes are self-adjusting but the pads and discs must be checked regularly for wear. Slacken the road wheel nuts. Jack up the car (see p. 61) and support it on axle stands so that the wheels can turn.

Remove the wheels on the axle being checked, except if the car—for example the Rover 2000—has inboard disc brakes.

1 Inspect both brakes on the same axle, so you can see if the pads are wearing at the same rate. Check the thick-

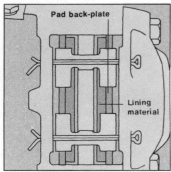

Pad back-plate

Lining material

ness of material left on the pad through the opening in the caliper.

Recommended minimum thickness of pads is: Lockheed $\frac{1}{8}$ in.; Girling $\frac{1}{8}$ in.; Girling S1H $\frac{1}{16}$ in. Some continental manufacturers give similar recommendations for their brakes—consult your dealer.

With swinging caliper brakes the pads are wedge shaped. They become flatter with wear. If the pads are worn parallel and are be-

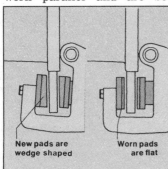

New pads are wedge shaped   Worn pads are flat

tween $\frac{1}{8}$ and $\frac{1}{16}$ in. thick; fit new ones.

Inboard pads may wear more quickly than outer pads. Always fit new pads (see p. 197) when even one is below the recommended thickness.

If a pad is not replaced before it is worn out completely, the disc itself will become damaged and will have to be replaced.

Remember, that after renewing pads on any disc-

FIXED-CALIPER DISC BRAKE

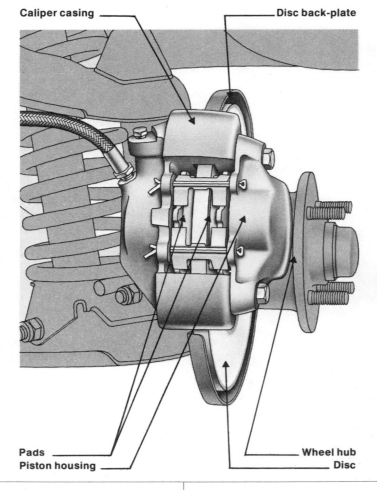

Caliper casing

Disc back-plate

Pads
Piston housing

Wheel hub
Disc

SLIDING CALIPER

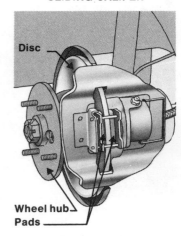

Disc

Wheel hub
Pads

SWINGING CALIPER

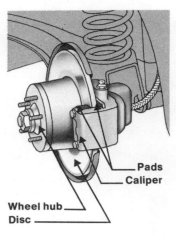

Pads
Caliper

Wheel hub
Disc

brake assembly, you must pump the brake pedal before driving the car, to restore normal pressure.

2 Check the condition of the braking area on the disc. It should be polished, though it is not unusual to find rust round the outer edge. If one face is rusty, the caliper piston on that side is probably stuck and must be freed (see p. 201).

Check that the disc turns freely without dragging. Run your fingernail over the surface of the disc. Light irregu-

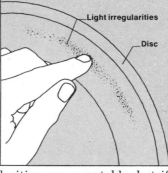

Light irregularities

Disc

larities are acceptable, but if there is any sign of deep scoring, pitting or cracking, the disc must be skimmed or renewed.

87 Checking the condition of the pistons in a disc-brake system

Jack up the end of the car you need to work on, and support it on axle stands so that the wheels are free to turn (see p. 61).

Get a helper to apply the brake pedal gently.

Observe the actions of the pistons on each wheel in turn. They should move out evenly and press the pads against the disc.

1 With the brakes off, check to see if there is a clearance between the pad and disc.

In most cases the disc and the pad should be in light contact, or nearly so.

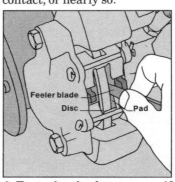

Feeler blade

Disc   Pad

2 Test the brake to see if it nips a thin feeler blade

between the pad and the disc. If the pad does not move, overhaul the brake (see p. 201).

If there is a significant gap on one pad only, the piston

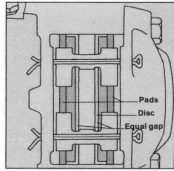

Pads
Disc
Equal gap

is sticking. Remove that pad (see p. 197) and try to push the piston back into place. If it is tight, the caliper will have to be overhauled (see p. 201). Do not press the brake pedal while any of the pads are removed.

3 Lift the dust covers. If there is any sign of brake fluid, the seals are faulty and will have to be renewed (see p. 201). Make sure no dirt gets into the system.

SEQUENCES FOR BLEEDING BRAKES

All drum or all disc brakes

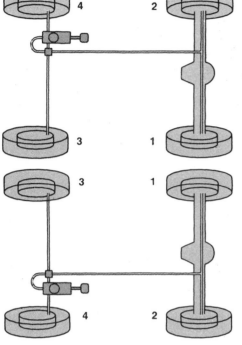

Right-hand drive
Nearside rear;
offside rear;
nearside front;
offside front

Left-hand drive
Offside rear;
nearside rear;
offside front;
nearside front

Disc brakes on the front, drum brakes on rear

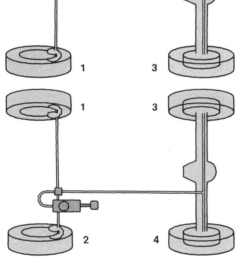

Right-hand drive
Nearside front;
offside front;
nearside rear;
offside rear

Left-hand drive
Offside front;
nearside front;
offside rear;
nearside rear

Inboard rear disc brakes

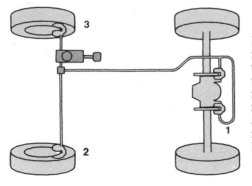
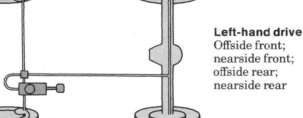

Bleed first the two rear brakes from the one nipple; then the nearside front for a car with right-hand drive and the offside front for a car with left-hand drive

88 Renewing the hydraulic fluid completely in the braking system

To change the fluid completely in a hydraulic braking system, 'bleed' all the brakes to flush out the old fluid, but keep topping up the master cylinder reservoir in the front compartment with new fluid of a type recommended by the car manufacturer.

Only one brake should be bled at a time—starting usually with the one furthest from the master cylinder reservoir and working round to the nearest brake. The sequence for various combinations is shown left.

Remove the carpet from beneath the brake pedal to en-

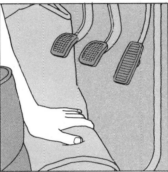

sure that the pedal can be depressed fully.

Lift the bonnet and wipe the top of the hydraulic brake

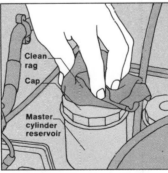

reservoir. Remove the cap.

Jack up the first wheel to be bled. Place an axle stand under the car to support it.

Clean the brake bleed nipple on the back-plate of the first brake in the sequence. Fit a ring spanner over the hexagon head of the nipple. Slide the

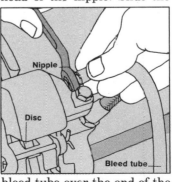

bleed tube over the end of the nipple and put the other end

of the tube in a glass jar. Fill the glass jar with about ½ in. of clean brake fluid. Make sure the end of the tube is submerged.

Turn the spanner anticlockwise to open the bleed nipple.

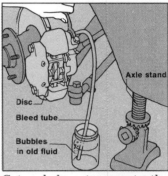

Get a helper to operate the brake pedal.

If the car has a vacuum servo unit fitted, get your helper to operate the brake pedal several times before starting. This will destroy the part vacuum in the unit.

While the brake pedal is being operated, fill the master cylinder reservoir frequently

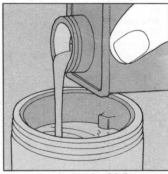

with new fluid. Make sure that the fluid is not allowed to splash on to the paintwork: it is highly damaging.

Never refill the hydraulic reservoir with used fluid. Make sure the handbrake is off before bleeding the brake.

Watch the fluid being injected into the jar. When the old fluid has stopped flowing and clean fluid, free of air bubbles, can be seen, get your helper to push down the brake pedal while you tighten the nipple on the back-plate. Repeat on each of the other wheels.

Note There are special brake bleeding kits that remove the need for continually topping up the master cylinder reservoir, and make brake-bleeding a one-man operation. There are also special bleed nipples, which can be fitted, that shut off automatically. For advice on approved types, consult your AA regional office.

89 Checking and adjusting a single cable with rods

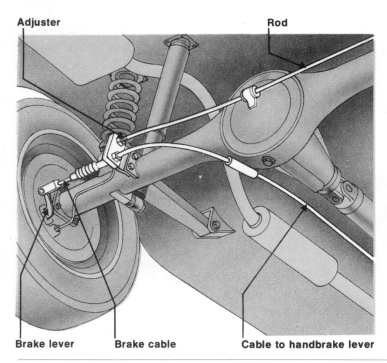

Adjuster — Rod

Brake lever — Brake cable — Cable to handbrake lever

On cars with rear drum brakes the handbrake is adjusted automatically when the shoes are adjusted (see p. 85). Extra adjustment is needed only to compensate for any stretch or slack in the cable and rods.

Release the handbrake lever inside the car. Brush off any dirt round the brake mechanism under the car. Remove the split-pin and clevis—some

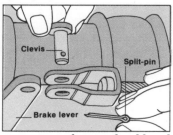

Clevis — Split-pin — Brake lever

cars may have shouldered bolts—securing the rod or cable to the lever on the brake back-plate. Adjust the rear-wheel brake shoes so that the

drum is locked on (see p. 84).

To adjust, free the lock-nut on the adjuster—which is inserted into the cable—and turn the adjuster until the cable or rod will just fit the brake lever on the back-plate. Tighten the lock-nut. Clean the clevis or shouldered bolt, and the yoke on the end of the cable or rod. Grease the clevis and refit the cable or rod to the brake lever. Use

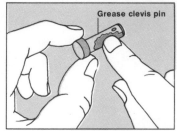

Grease clevis pin

a new split-pin in the clevis to secure it. Adjust the brakes (see p. 87). Apply the handbrake inside the car and make sure both rear wheels lock.

90 Checking and adjusting double cable linkages

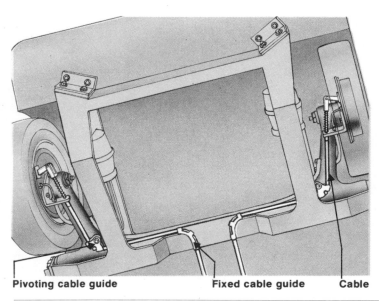

Pivoting cable guide — Fixed cable guide — Cable

On handbrakes with twin cables, one to each rear wheel, the cables should be adjusted individually by threaded adjusters at the base of the handbrake lever inside the car.

Make sure that the handbrake is released. Check the condition of the cables under the car. If they are frayed, fit new cables. Clean any guides through which the

Oil pivot shaft

cables pass, and lubricate the pivot shaft with light machine

oil. Make sure that the guides move freely.

Adjust the cables one at a time. Loosen the lock-nut and

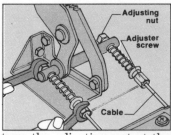

Adjusting nut — Adjuster screw — Cable

turn the adjusting nut at the base of the handbrake lever until the rear wheel is locked. Back off the adjuster until the wheel just revolves freely. Tighten the lock-nut. Repeat this operation on the other cable. Apply the handbrake inside the car and make sure both rear wheels lock.

91 Checking and adjusting cables with an equaliser and roller

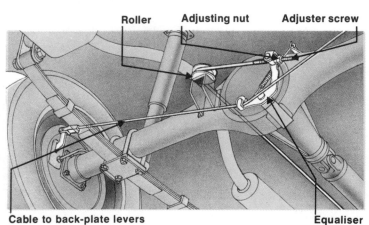

Roller — Adjusting nut — Adjuster screw

Cable to back-plate levers — Equaliser

The brake equaliser and roller unit is mounted on the rear axle casing. A single cable runs from the handbrake lever inside the car, round a roller, and is connected to the equaliser by an adjuster screw. A second cable, attached to the equaliser, is connected between the levers on the brake back-plate.

Make sure that the handbrake is released. Check the condition of the cables. If they are frayed, fit new ones. Make sure the roller turns freely. If necessary, lubricate the roller shaft with light machine oil. Some roller shafts

have a grease nipple. Fit a grease gun to the nipple and lubricate the shaft.

Loosen the lock-nut. Tighten the adjusting nut until all

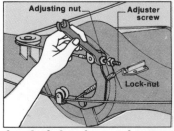

Adjusting nut — Adjuster screw — Lock-nut

the slack has been taken out of the cables. Check that the road wheels rotate freely. Tighten the adjuster lock-nut.

92 Checking and adjusting a cable with a rod and roller

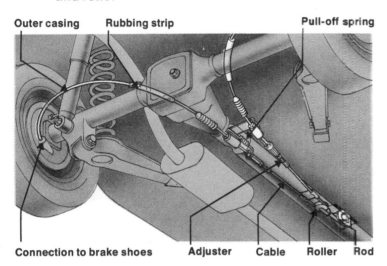

Outer casing Rubbing strip Pull-off spring

Connection to brake shoes Adjuster Cable Roller Rod

A short rod with a roller attached is connected to the bottom of the handbrake lever under the car. A cable, passing round the roller, goes to each rear wheel. Each length of cable has its own adjuster and pull-off spring.

Make sure that the handbrake is released. Check the condition of the cable where it passes round the roller. If it is frayed, fit a new cable (see p. 200).

Make sure the clevis at the base of the handbrake lever, under the car, moves freely. If necessary, remove the clevis, clean it with emery cloth, grease and replace it.

Loosen the adjuster lock-

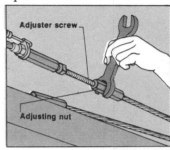

Adjuster screw

Adjusting nut

nuts, and turn the adjusters equal amounts until the two

rear wheels are locked. Back off the adjusters an equal number of turns each until the wheels revolve freely. Apply the handbrake inside the car and make sure both rear wheels are locked. Tighten the lock-nuts.

93 Checking and adjusting the linkage on early Jaguar cars with disc handbrakes

The early Mk II Jaguars used a mechanically operated disc handbrake. If the handbrake lever travel is excessive, and the disc pads are properly adjusted, the cable has stretched and needs to be adjusted.

Release the handbrake inside the car. Screw in the

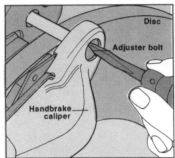

Disc

Adjuster bolt

Handbrake caliper

handbrake adjuster bolt on each rear-brake caliper until the wheels are locked.

Remove the clevis pin securing the forked end of the main

cable to the bottom of the compensator, which is attached

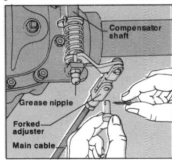

Compensator shaft

Grease nipple

Forked adjuster

Main cable

by a bracket to the final-drive casing.

Slacken the lock-nut on the adjuster, and screw the forked end further on the cable. When the end is fitted to the compensator and the clevis pin replaced, there should be no slack in the main cable or the two cables going to the brake calipers.

Refit the clevis and secure it with a new split-pin. Fit a

grease gun to the nipple at the base of the compensator shaft, and lubricate the shaft until grease is forced out between the sides of the compensator.

Unscrew the caliper adjuster bolts. Place a ·004 in. feeler blade between the handbrake caliper pad and the

disc. Tighten the caliper adjuster bolt until the blade is just pinched. Repeat this operation on the other rear handbrake caliper. Test the action of the handbrake lever inside the car. Make sure it locks and releases the rear wheels as it is pulled on and off.

JAGUAR DISC-BRAKE LINKAGE

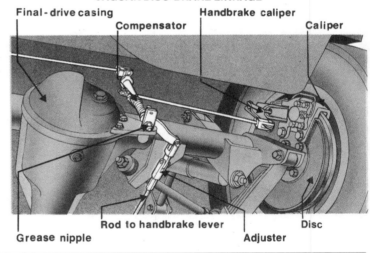

Final-drive casing Handbrake caliper

Compensator Caliper

Rod to handbrake lever Disc

Grease nipple Adjuster

94 Checking and lubricating guides, cables and linkages

From underneath the car, clean all the cable pivot points and guides with a wire brush. On some pivot points or rollers grease nipples are supplied, to lubricate the shafts. Put a grease gun on all these points

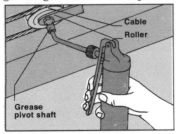

Cable Roller

Grease pivot shaft

and make sure they are properly lubricated. Check the

condition of the cables, especially where they run round a roller or guide. Clean the cable, and lubricate it with oil where it runs through the roller. Apply the handbrake several times. If a cable is

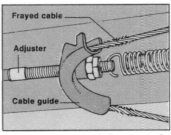

Frayed cable

Adjuster

Cable guide

showing signs of fraying, fit a new one (see p. 200), or it

could let you down. Some cables that run through an outer casing have a grease nipple fitted to the outer case. Fit a grease gun to the nipple

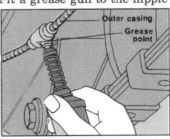

Outer casing

Grease point

and thoroughly grease the inner cable.

Check all clevis pins and shouldered bolts, especially those that connect a cable or rod to the lever on the brake

back-plate. If they appear rusty, remove them and clean the shank of the clevis with emery cloth. Grease the clevis

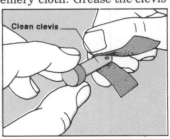

Clean clevis

and refit it. Use a new split-pin to secure the clevis; splay the ends of the split-pin to hold it in place.

Inside the car, lubricate the handbrake-lever pivot point with clean engine oil.

95	97	99
96	98	

95 Lubricating front-wheel bearings without dismantling

Wheel bearings should be dismantled, the old grease removed, and the bearings reassembled with fresh grease at the intervals recommended by the manufacturers. It is, however, possible to grease front-wheel bearings while they are still on the car.

Remove the wheel hub cap, and prise the grease cap from

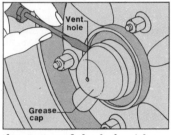

the centre of the hub with an old chisel or a blunt screwdriver.

Clean out the old grease from inside the cap, and make sure that the small vent hole in the end of the cap is completely clear.

Wipe away any hardened grease from the centre of the hub assembly. Press fresh

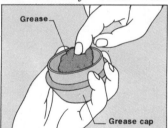

grease, of the type recommended by the manufacturers, into the hub centre, and fill the cap to within ⅛ in. of the edge. Fit the grease cap to the hub centre and tap it with a hide or wooden mallet. Do the same on the other hub.

96 If the bearings have grease nipples

A few cars—for example the Jaguar range—have a grease nipple on the hub bearings.

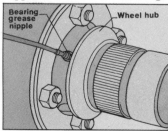

Do not apply more than two or three strokes of the grease gun. Too much grease will damage the grease seal.

97 Dismantling front-wheel bearings on hubs with drum brakes

Remove the hub cap and prise the dust-cover from the hub centre with an old chisel or a screwdriver. Slacken the brake adjuster (see pp. 84-85) so that the drum can be easily removed.

Remove the countersunk screws that secure the brake

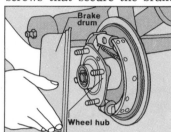

drum to the hub assembly, and lift off the drum. (On some cars, the drums are combined with the hub assembly and are removed with the hub.)

Remove the split-pin from the castellated hub nut (or the nut retainer, if one is

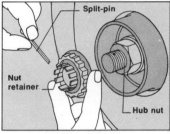

fitted), and undo the hub nut. On some models a self-locking nut is fitted to the hub.

Draw the hub forwards until the front tapered roller bearing falls out. If ball or straight roller bearings are fitted they will remain inside the hub. Lift off the hub.

To remove the rear bearing, turn the hub over, wheel studs downwards, prise out the grease seal and lift out the

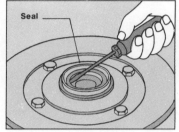

tapered bearing. If the roller or ball races are straight, tap out one bearing race with a drift. Remove the spacer and tap out the other.

98 Dismantling front-wheel bearings on hubs with disc brakes

Remove the hub cap and prise off the grease cap from the centre of the hub.

It may be possible, if the flexible hydraulic pipe is long enough, to remove the disc-brake caliper without disturbing the hydraulic pipe. But, if so, make sure that you support the caliper carefully (see p. 199), to prevent straining the flexible hydraulic pipe.

Alternatively, you may

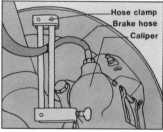

have to clamp the hydraulic pipe—to prevent loss of fluid—and undo the pipe at the caliper. If you do this, you will have to bleed the brakes after the caliper has been assembled (see p. 199).

To remove the caliper, bend back the tabs of the locking washers that secure

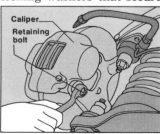

the heads of the caliper mounting-bolts. Undo and remove the mounting-bolts and lift the caliper away

from the disc. Make a note of any shims fitted between the caliper and its mounting.

Insert a wedge between the disc-brake pads in the caliper, to hold the caliper pistons in position. Never press the brake pedal once the caliper has been removed.

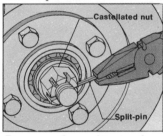

Remove the split-pin from the castellated nut (or the nut retainer), and undo the hub nut. On some models a self-locking nut is fitted. Undo it and set it aside.

Draw the hub forwards until the tapered bearing falls out. (If straight ball or roller-bearing races are fitted, they will remain inside

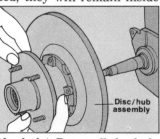

the hub.) Draw off the hub.

To remove the rear tapered bearing, prise out the grease seal and lift the tapered bearing out. If straight rollers or ball races are fitted, gently tap out one of the bearings with a drift.

99 Removing Volkswagen front-wheel hub bearings

On the Volkswagen range of small cars, disc or drum brakes may be fitted, but the wheel hub is secured to the stub axle in the same way—by two nuts with a locking washer between them.

Bend up the two tabs of the locking washer that secure

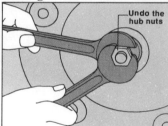

the front and back nuts. Hold the back nut with a spanner and undo the front nut with another. Remove the locking washer and undo the back nut. On drum brakes the hub and drum are integral. Fit a hub

puller to the wheel studs and tighten the puller centre bolt to draw the drum off.

Slide the assembly off the stub axle. Lift out the front tapered roller bearing. Prise out the grease seal and lift out the back tapered roller bearing. When reassembling, fit a new grease seal and locking washer.

100 Removing the hub assembly on a British Leyland front-wheel-drive car

Remove the hub caps. Remove the road wheel and prise off the grease cap in the centre of the hub. Remove the brake drum (see pp. 84-85) or the disc caliper if the car has front disc brakes (see p. 199).

Wipe any grease off the axle and remove the split-pin from the castellated nut, or take off any nut retainer that is fitted. On some models a self-locking nut may be used.

Disconnect the track-rod

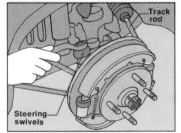

arm (see p. 207), and release the upper and lower suspension

ball-joint swivels in the same way. Undo and remove the

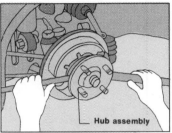

centre hub nut. Place levers behind the hub assembly and prise the hub and swivel assembly off the splined drive-

shaft. Turn the hub assembly over and prise out the grease

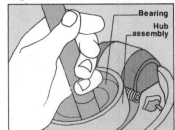

seal. Mount the hub on a wooden block and tap the bearing race out of the hub with a

drift. Remove the hub spacer. Turn the hub over and tap out the back bearing race.

101 Cleaning, greasing, refitting and adjusting tapered roller bearings

Wash both tapered roller bearings in clean petrol. Allow them to dry, and examine each race for signs of wear—for example, pitting on the rollers, discoloration or scoring. Hold the race between the thumb and forefinger and spin it round. If it feels rough as it spins, buy and fit a pair of new bearings.

Remove the grease from the hub centre and examine the inner tracks still fitted to

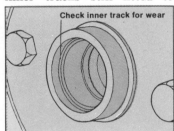

the hub. If they are cracked, new tracks will have to be fitted. Do not attempt to remove them: special tools are needed. Take the faulty hub to a garage and get them to fit new tracks and supply new tapered races to suit the hub.

Knead the grease recom-

mended by the manufacturers thoroughly between the tapered rollers and the bearing cage.

Place the hub on the bench, with the wheel studs downwards. Replace the inner bearing and make sure that it sits squarely in its track. Fit a new grease seal, with the lip facing downwards, to hold the bearing in place. Make sure that it

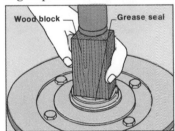

is lined up evenly, and tap it gently into position with a

hardwood block and a mallet, until the seal is flush with the edge of the housing.

Turn the hub over, and coat the space inside the hub between the bearings with fresh grease. But do not over-pack the hub with grease: leave an air space to allow the grease to circulate. If it is overfilled, the bearing may run hot and the grease will melt and run out, causing bearing failure.

Clean the stub axle and caliper mounting-plate, if there is one. Make sure that there is no grease on the disc —or on the brake drum on a combined drum/hub assembly. Refit the hub to the stub axle.

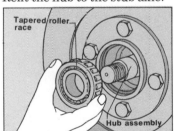

Slide the greased front tapered race into position on the stub axle. Fit the thrust washer and hub nut. If a self-locking nut was used,

fit a new nut. Tighten the hub nut gradually, and periodic-

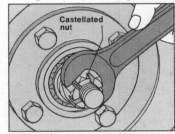

ally turn the hub assembly. When the hub becomes hard to turn, turn the nut in the opposite direction until the hub moves freely again, but without any play.

If a castellated nut is used, make sure the slots in the nut line up with the split-pin hole. If not, tighten the nut slightly until they do.

If a nut retainer is used, fit the retainer to the hub nut.

Always use a new split-pin to secure the hub nut. Fit the pin and bend its ends across the flats on the nut and the end of the stub axle. Pack the cap with grease and refit it to the hub (see Job 95).

Fit the drum or caliper and, if the pipe was removed, bleed the brakes (see p. 197).

A TAPERED ROLLER-BEARING ASSEMBLY

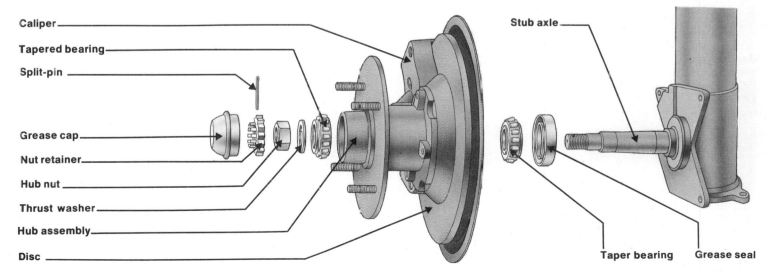

102 Cleaning, greasing, refitting and adjusting ball or straight roller races

Wash both races in clean petrol. Hold them between the thumb and forefinger and spin them. If they feel rough, buy and fit a pair of new races.

Remove all the old grease from the centre of the hub. Carefully knead fresh grease, recommended by the manufacturer, into the two races, and make sure that they are well packed. Fit the back race in the hub and tap it gently

into position with a hardwood block. When it is level with the edge of the hub use a drift to drive it home.

Refit the back grease seal, with the lip of the seal facing

the back bearing. Tap the seal flush with the edge of the hub.

Turn the hub over and fit a new spacer to the hub centre. Pack the centre of the hub with fresh grease, but leave an air gap to allow the grease to circulate when

the hub becomes warm. Fit the outer race and tap it into the housing.

Fit the reassembled hub to the stub-axle. Fit the thrust-washer and the nut.

Tighten the nut to the torque specified by the manu-

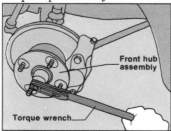

facturer. (Check what this should be with your dealer.) If the split-pin holes do not line up, tighten it further until they do. If a nut retainer or a self-locking nut is used, tighten only to the specified torque figure.

Fit the nut retainer, if one is used, and fit a new split-pin. Never use the old pin. Bend the ends of the pin round the flats of the nut and stub-axle.

Fit the brake drums (see p. 87), or caliper (see p. 199). Bleed the brakes if necessary.

Pack the cap with grease

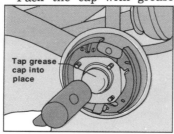

and tap it securely into position on the hub.

A STRAIGHT ROLLER-RACE ASSEMBLY

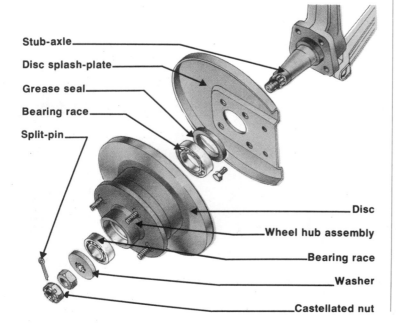

103 Cleaning, greasing, fitting and adjusting wheel bearings on front-wheel-drive cars

Clean the two races in petrol and remove all the old grease from the centre of the hub. Hold the races between the thumb and forefinger and spin them. If they 'rumble' or sound rough, fit new races.

Grease the races by 'kneading' the grease between the

balls and the cage. Fit the back race to the suspension swivel/hub assembly. Tap the race into the housing with a drift. Fit the new seal, with the lip facing the bearing. Tap

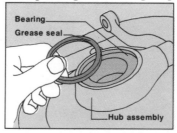

in the seal until it is flush.

Fit the new spacer to the centre of the hub and pack

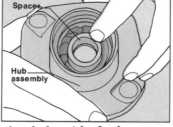

the hub with fresh grease. Leave space in the hub to

allow the grease to circulate.

Refit the front race flush with the edge of the housing. Tap it in further so that the seal can be fitted.

Check the condition of the splines in the hub assembly and on the actual drive-shaft.

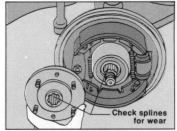

If the splines are worn, have the shaft and the hub renewed at a garage.

Refit the hub to the drive-shaft. Fit the thrust-washer and the nut. Tighten the nut to the torque specified by the manufacturers—check the correct tightness with your local garage. If the slots in the castellated nut do not line up with the hole in the stub axle, tighten until they do.

Fit a new split-pin. Bend the ends of the pin round the nut and stub-axle. Pack the

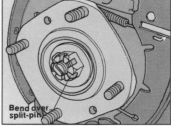

cap with grease and fit it to the hub and tap it into place (see Job 95). Refit the road wheels and lower the car to the ground. Check that all the wheel nuts are tight.

BALL-RACE ASSEMBLY ON FRONT-WHEEL DRIVE

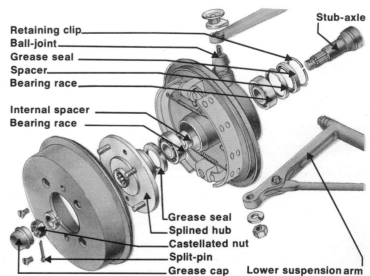

104 Lubricating and adjusting rear-wheel bearings

The rear-wheel bearings on the half-shafts fitted to live rear axles (see p. 201) are maintenance-free. The bearings are automatically lubricated by the oil in the axle casing.

On independent suspension rear-wheel-drive cars, using separate drive-shafts, the hub bearings can be greased and adjusted.

Remove the wheel hub cap and prise off the centre grease

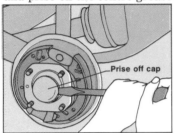
Prise off cap

cap with an old chisel or a screwdriver.

Take out the split-pin holding the castellated hub nut. Tighten the nut to the torque specified, check this with

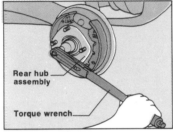
Rear hub assembly
Torque wrench

your local franchised dealer.

Make sure the slots in the castellated nut line up with the hole in the axle. If not, tighten the nut a fraction more until they do. Fit a new

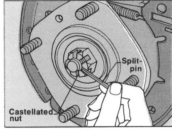
Split-pin
Castellated nut

split-pin, and bend the ends over the flat of the nut and the stub-axle.

Pack the grease cap with fresh grease, recommended by the manufacturers, to within ⅛ in. of the edge. Tap the cap back into place in the centre of the hub.

Do not attempt to dismantle rear-wheel bearings, or you may damage them. Special tools and pullers are needed. If the bearings cannot be adjusted, take the car to a garage and have them overhauled.

105 Checking the condition of all the wheels and tyres

Check the condition of the side walls, especially the inside wall, which may have been overlooked in routine

Wear on inside wall

servicing (see pp. 36-37). Look for cracks and scuffing, and for bulges that indicate a weak tyre carcass. If any damage is discovered, have the tyre checked by a dealer.

Check the depth of the tyre tread. The legal requirement is a minimum depth of 1 mm, but a deeper tread is advisable.

Carefully examine the wheel round the stud holes.

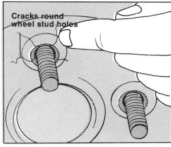
Cracks round wheel stud holes

If there are hair-line cracks, fit a new wheel rim.

Check the wheel rim for damage—often caused by

striking the kerb. It may be possible to tap out a minor dent in the rim, but any severe rim distortion must be repaired by a specialist.

Look around the rim to ensure there are no balance weights missing—indicated by a clean area. If a weight is

Weight missing

missing, have the wheel balanced again. Check the wheel nuts for tightness.

Kerb scrubbing
Continuous brushing against the kerb will wear the side wall, create a horizontal split and cause the tyre to blow out.

Kerb bumping
Driving up and down the kerb will bruise the side wall which will eventually split in two places, causing the tyre to blow out.

Over-inflation If only the centre of the tread has worn, the tyres are over-inflated. Keep the tyres at the correct pressure (see p. 37).

Under-inflation If the outside tread of a tyre is worn, the tyres have been under-inflated. Keep the pressure correct (see p. 37).

Neglected cut A cut in the tyre tread will let in water, which will rot the plies and cause a chunk to peel off. Have cuts treated.

Wheel balance Uneven tyre wear at one or more spots on the tread is caused by out-of-balance wheels. Have the wheels balanced.

Incorrect camber
Severe wear on one side of the tyre tread only is caused by incorrect camber angle. Have the angle checked.

Suspension wear
Regular wear across the tread is due to faulty suspension. Check springs, dampers and bearings (see pp. 201-5).

Flat spots Tread wear at one point only is caused by the brakes locking. Check brake condition (see pp. 84-89).

Feathering If the tread is rippled on the outside edge of the tyre, the track is incorrect. Have it checked (see p. 131).

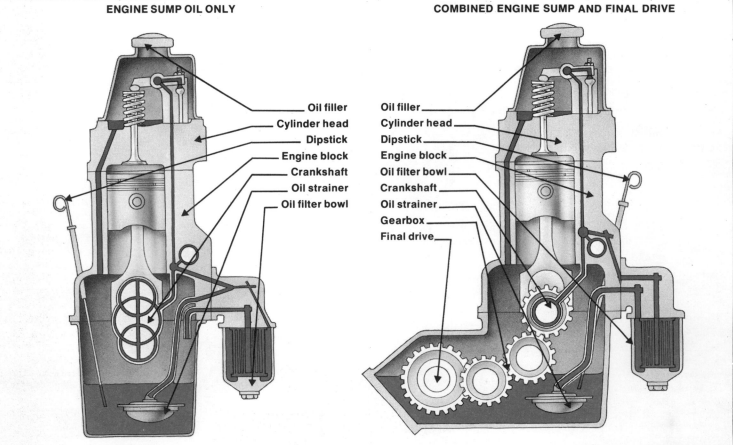

ENGINE SUMP OIL ONLY	COMBINED ENGINE SUMP AND FINAL DRIVE

Oil filler
Cylinder head
Dipstick
Engine block
Crankshaft
Oil strainer
Oil filter bowl

Oil filler
Cylinder head
Dipstick
Engine block
Oil filter bowl
Crankshaft
Oil strainer
Gearbox
Final drive

The conventional sump, which provides lubricating oil for the engine only, is found on front-engine rear-wheel-drive cars. The gear-box and final drive—which is in the rear axle—have their own lubricating oil.

On most transverse-engined front-wheel-drive cars—for example, BLMC Minis, 1100s and Maxis—the gearbox and final drive are housed in the engine sump and lubrica-ted by the same oil. There is one dipstick.

ENGINE SUMP AND OIL FILTER CAPACITIES

	Pints without filter	Pints with filter
AUDI		
100 LS		7
100 LS Automatic	Change	7
100 GL	filter	7
100 GL Automatic	with	7
Coupé S	oil	7
Coupé S Automatic		7
BRITISH LEYLAND BLMC		
Austin		
A40 Farina	5½	6½
A60	6¾	7½
A110 Mk II	12	12¾
Maxi 1500	8¾	9¾
Maxi 1750	8¾	9¾
Austin/Morris		
1100	7½	8½
1100 Automatic	11	12
1300	7½	8½
1300 Countryman	7½	8½
1300 GT	7½	8½
Mini 850	7½	8½
Mini 1000	7½	8½
Mini Clubman	7½	8½
Mini Cooper S	7½	8½
1800 Mk II	9	10¼
1800 S	9	10¼
2200	16	17
2200 Automatic	9	10¼
Midget	5½	6½
Sprite	5½	6½

	Pints without filter	Pints with filter
Morris		
Minor 1000	5½	6½
Marina 1·3	6½	7
Marina 1·8	7	8
Marina 1·8 TC		6⅜
MGB without oil cooler	Change	7½
MGB with oil cooler	filter	8¼
MGC without oil cooler	with	12½
MGC with oil cooler	oil	14½
MG 1100	7½	8½
Riley		
Elf	7½	8½
Wolseley		
Hornet	7½	8½
Jaguar		
2·4	11	13
3·4	11	13
3·8	11	13
3·8 S type	11	13
Rover		
2000 SC	8	9
2000 SC Automatic	8	9
2000 TC	9	10
Triumph		
Herald 1200	6½	7
Herald 12/50	7	7½
Herald 13/60	7	8
Vitesse Mk I	8	9

	Pints without filter	Pints with filter
Triumph cont'd.		
Vitesse Mk II	8	9
1300	6¼	7¼
1500	6¼	7¼
2000	8	9
Toledo 1300	7	8
Dolomite	7	8
Spitfire Mk I	7	8
Spitfire Mk II	8	9
Stag	8	9
GT-6	8	9
TR 4	9	10
TR 4A	9	10
TR 5	8	9
TR 6	8	9
BMW		
1600	7	7½
1800	7	7½
2000	7	7½
2002	7	7½
2500	8¾	10
2800	8¾	10
CHRYSLER RANGE		
Rootes		
Imp	4½	5½
Chamois	4½	5½
Stiletto	4½	5½
Sunbeam Sport	4½	5½
Avenger	6	7
Avenger GT	6	7

	Pints without filter	Pints with filter
Rootes cont'd.		
Hillman Minx 1500	7	7½
Hunter 1500	7	7½
Hunter 1725	7	7½
Singer Gazelle	7	7½
Singer Vogue	7	7½
Humber Sceptre	7	7½
Sunbeam Rapier	7	7½
Sunbeam Alpine	7	7½
Chrysler 180	7	8
Simca		
1000	Centrifugal filter only	4⅓
1100	4½	5¼
1100 S	4½	5¼
1301	7	7¾
1301 Automatic	7	7¾
1501	7	7¾
1501 Automatic	7	7¾
CITROËN		
Dyane	3½	4
Ami 6	4	4½
Ami 8	4	4½
DAF		
33	No filter sump	3½
44	Strainer only	3½

106 Refilling the engine sump with clean oil

Wipe the oil filler cap clean to prevent dirt dropping into

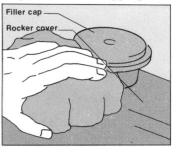

the oil filler hole. Remove the oil filler cap.

Use the correct amount of new engine oil recommended by the manufacturers (see chart) to fill the sump. Allow enough to fill the filter bowl, if a new oil filter element has been fitted (see chart).

If the oil filler cap has a gauze filter in it, wash it thoroughly in a suitable solvent (see Job 171). Refit the filler cap.

Start the engine and check that the oil-pressure light goes out, or that a suitable pressure is registered on the oil-pressure gauge, if one is fitted. If the light stays on, or the gauge fails to record a pressure within 10 seconds, switch off immediately and investigate.

Check for oil leaks round the filter assembly, and any

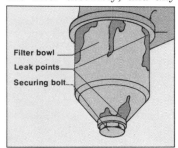

other part of the engine that might be a potential leak point. Tighten the filter assembly or any other leak points. Stop the engine and allow the oil to settle. Check the level of the oil on the dip-

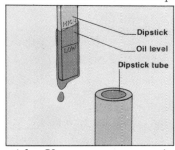

stick. If necessary, pour in more oil until the level in the sump reaches the Full mark on the dipstick. Wipe away any oil spilt round the filler hole and refit the cap.

107 Topping up the oil in the engine sump

Make sure the car is on level ground. Check the oil when the car has been standing for some time and the oil has settled in the engine sump.

Remove the dipstick and wipe it with a lint-free rag.

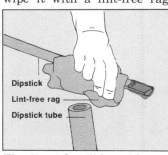

The dipstick will be calibrated with Full or High and Low marks. Replace the dipstick and remove it again. Inspect

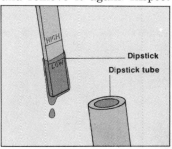

the position of the mark left by the engine oil on the dipstick. If the level is below the Full mark, replace the dipstick, wipe the oil filler cap clean and remove it. Pour in

new oil of the correct grade until it reaches the Full mark on the dipstick.

Do not overfill the sump. As a rule, approximately 2 pints of oil are necessary to raise the level from the Low to the Full mark. If the sump is overfilled it will cause unnecessary crankcase pressure, resulting in oil leaks.

If the oil consumption is high—for example, less than 200 miles to a pint—the cylinder bores or piston rings may be worn, allowing the oil to by-pass the piston rings and enter the combustion chamber. This may be indicated by blue smoke emitted from the exhaust. If this happens the engine is worn and will need overhauling. That is a specialist garage job.

ENGINE SUMP AND OIL FILTER CAPACITIES

	Pints without filter	Pints with filter
Daf cont'd.		
55	4	4½
66	4¾	5¼
DATSUN		
Cherry 100A range	5¼	6¼
Cherry 120	4¾	5½
Sunny 1200 range	4¾	5½
Bluebird 160B	6½	7½
Bluebird 160B Automatic	6½	7½
Bluebird 180B	6½	7½
Bluebird 180B Automatic	6½	7½
Bluebird 180SSS	6½	7½
240Z Sports	7¼	8¾
260C Custom de luxe	8¾	10
260C Custom de luxe Automatic	8¾	10
FIAT		
500	Centri-	3¾
600D	fugal	5¼
850	filter	5¾
124	Change filter with oil	6⅔
124S		6⅔
125	6⅔	7⅔
127	7	8
128	6⅛	7½
FORD		
Anglia 105E	4½	5½
Anglia 123E	4½	5½

	Pints without filter	Pints with filter
Ford cont'd.		
Escort	5¾	6½
Cortina Mk I 1200 cc	4	4½
Cortina Mk I 1500 cc	4½	5½
Cortina Mk II to 1968	7	7¼
Cortina Mk II 1968/70	7	7¼
Cortina Mk III	5¼	6¼
Corsair 120E	6	6½
Corsair 120E GT	6	6½
Corsair V4 1700 cc	6	7
Corsair V4 2000 cc	6	7
Classic Capri 109E	5¾	6¼
Classic Capri 109E GT	5¾	6¼
Zephyr/Zodiac Mk III	7	8
MAZDA		
RX3	3½	10¼
RENAULT		
R4	4½	5
R5 845 cc	4½	5
R5 TL 596 cc	5¼	5¾
R6 845 cc	4½	5
R6 1108 cc	5¼	5¾
R8	4½	5
R10	4½	5
R12 TL & TS early '73	4½	5¼
R12 TL & TS late '73	4½	5¼
R15 TL	5¼	5¾
R15 TS	7	7½
R16 TL & TS	7	7½
R16 Automatic	7	7½
R17 TL	8½	9

	Pints without filter	Pints with filter
Renault cont'd.		
R17 TS	8½	9
TOYOTA		
Corolla 1100	4¾	5¾
Corolla 1200	4¾	5¾
Corolla 1200 SL	4¾	5¾
Corona 1500	6¼	7¼
Corona 1900 Mk II	7¼	8¾
Corona 2000 Mk II	7¼	8¾
Carina 1600	5	5½
Celica 1600	5	5½
Crown 2300	8½	9¾
Crown 2600	8½	9¾
VAUXHALL		
Viva HA	4½	5
Viva HB 1159 cc	4½	5
Viva HB 1600 cc	4½	5
Viva HB GT	7½	8
Viva HB SL90	4½	5
Viva HC 1159 cc	4½	5
Viva HC 1600 cc	7½	8
Victor FC	6	6½
Victor FD 1600 cc	7½	8
Victor FD 2000 cc	7½	8
Victor FD 33 (Estate)	8	8¾
Victor FE 1800 cc	7½	8
Victor FE 2000 cc	7½	8
Victor FE 3·3 (Estate)	8	8¾
VX4/90 FC	6	6½
VX4/90 FD	7½	8
VX4/90 FE	7½	8

	Pints without filter	Pints with filter
Vauxhall cont'd.		
Ventora FD	8	8¾
Ventora FE	8	8¾
Viscount	8¼	9
Firenza 1600 cc	7½	8
Firenza 2300 cc	7½	8
VOLKSWAGEN		
Beetle 1200	No filter	4½
Beetle 1302	sump	4½
Beetle 1600	strainer	4½
1600 FB	only	4½
1600 Variant		4½
411 LE Saloon	5¼	6¼
411 LE Variant	5¼	6¼
412 LE Saloon	5¼	6¼
412 LE Variant	5¼	6¼
K70	6¼	7
VOLVO		
120	5¾	6½
142	5¾	6½
144	5¾	6½
145	5¾	6½
164	9¼	10½

WARNING
Never overfill the sump: too much oil creates excessive pressures in the crankcase and can result in leaks and damaged seals. Use only the type of oil recommended by the car manufacturer.

108

109

108 Checking the condition and renewing the distributor contact points

If the distributor contact points are burnt, pitted or incorrectly gapped, misfiring will be experienced, engine performance will be poor and petrol consumption heavy.

The servicing procedure for all distributors is similar, but each type has slight variations in the way the points are fitted and how they are adjusted.

To reach the points, prise back the two clips holding the distributor cap to the distributor body and remove the cap. Place it out of the way, so that the distributor can be worked on without difficulty.

Stage 1
Remove the rotor arm, and rotate the engine—by the fan belt or a spanner on the crankshaft pulley nut, or by putting the car in top gear and rocking it backwards and forwards—until the contact points open.

Stage 2
Inspect the contact faces for signs of pitting, burning or contamination. If the contact faces are badly damaged, fit a complete new set of contact points.

Stage 3
New contact faces are protected with a wax film. Clean them with a petrol-moistened rag.

Make sure that the new points are fitted in exactly the same way as those removed. See that all the insulating washers are replaced, and that the low-tension leads are tucked out of the way of the moving contact point.

Stage 4
To adjust the points gap, slightly loosen the one or two screws that hold the fixed contact point to the distributor base-plate. Place a screwdriver in the points adjusting slot. Turn the screwdriver so that the contact points open wide enough to enable a feeler blade, of the correct thickness, to slide snugly between the contacts.

Retighten the screws holding the fixed contact point to the base-plate. Turn the engine crankshaft one full turn, until the points are fully open, and recheck the points gap. If necessary, readjust.

Refit the distributor rotor arm and replace the cap.

109 Checking and renewing the points on a Lucas distributor

Stage 1 Removing the rotor arm
The rotor arm on a Lucas distributor is a push-fit on the distributor shaft. To remove the rotor arm, simply pull it off the shaft. If it is tight, gently lever it off with a screwdriver placed below the boss of the insulator. Avoid damaging the insulation.

Carefully examine the arm for signs of burning on the edge of the brass contact, or for cracked insulation. If it is damaged, fit a new rotor arm.

When you are refitting the rotor arm, make sure that the lug on the rotor arm is located in the distributor-shaft keyway. Push it down as far as it will go.

Stage 2 Checking the contact faces
Turn the engine so that the fibre heel of the moving contact point is on the peak of the distributor cam, and the points are fully open. Check the contact-point faces.

If they are dirty clean them with a lint-free rag. If they are badly burnt or pitted, it will be impossible to set the points gap accurately. Fit a new set of contact points.

Stage 3 Fitting new points
Undo and remove the pillar nut above the moving contact-

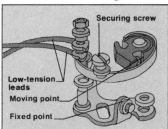
Securing screw · Low-tension leads · Moving point · Fixed point

point spring. Lift off the plastic insulating cap and the two low-tension leads.

Remove the moving contact point and the insulating washer below the spring eye. Undo the two screws holding the fixed contact point to the base-plate. Clean the base-plate.

Fit the new fixed contact to the base-plate, but do not fully tighten the screws. Lightly grease the pivot shaft on which the moving point fits.

Fit the insulating washer to the spring pillar and fit the moving contact point. Fit the boss of the plastic cap through the eyes of the low-tension leads and fit the cap over the pillar, through the spring eye. Refit and tighten the nut.

One-piece points
Most modern Lucas contact-point sets are in one piece to eliminate the need for indi-

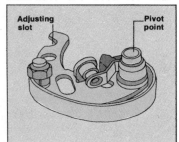
Adjusting slot · Pivot point

vidual insulating washers. Remove the old points and simply fit a new one-piece contact set to the pivot post. Replace the low-tension leads, locating them over the insulated base of the contact set, and secure them with the plastic nut. Adjust the points gap in the conventional way.

WHERE YOU SHOULD CHECK

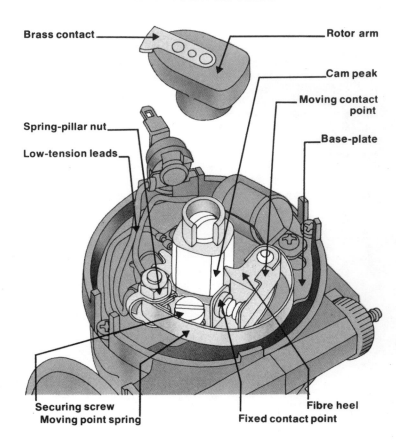

Brass contact — Rotor arm
Cam peak
Moving contact point
Spring-pillar nut
Low-tension leads — Base-plate
Securing screw · Moving point spring — Fibre heel · Fixed contact point

Stage 4 Adjusting the gap
Make sure that the contact points are fully open and that the base-plate screws are loose. Fit a screwdriver into the adjusting slot and turn

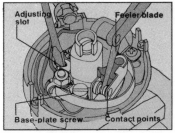
Adjusting slot · Feeler blade · Base-plate screw · Contact points

the screwdriver to open the points. Slide a ·015 in. feeler gauge between the faces of the contact points. Turn the screwdriver clockwise to close the points on the feeler blade, until the blade is just pinched. Avoid closing the gap too far, or an incorrect clearance will then be obtained.

When the correct gap is achieved, tighten the screws holding the fixed contact points to the base-plate. Turn the engine one full turn and recheck the gap.

Points gap
All Lucas distributors have a points gap of between ·014 and ·016 in.

110 Checking and renewing the points on an AC Delco distributor

Stage 1 Removing the rotor arm
Because the centrifugal advance weights are above the contact points, the rotor arm is round. Undo the screws holding the arm to the plate. Lift off the arm. Check the arm contact for signs of pitting or burning. Bend the centre electrode, to ensure that it contacts the carbon brush.

When refitting the rotor arm, note that there is a square and a round locating leg on the underside. Make sure these are located correctly in the holes on the centrifugal base-plate. If the arm is damaged, fit a new one.

Stage 2 Checking the contact faces
Turn the engine so that the contact points are fully open. Examine the contact faces. If they are dirty, clean them with a lint-free rag. If they are pitted, fit a new contact set.

Stage 3 Fitting new points
The moving contact point and low-tension leads are secured by a plastic clip. Push the spring of the moving point in towards the distributor shaft, to disengage it from the plastic clip. Lift off the point. Undo the base-plate screws and lift out the point.

Fit the fixed point to the base-plate, but do not fully tighten the screws. Lubricate the pivot post with high-melting-point grease. Fit the new plastic clip to the side bracket and position the two low-tension cables—one fits from the top and the other from the side. Fit the moving point and make sure that the spring fits the peg on the plastic sleeve to hold the leads in place.

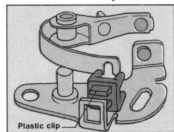
Plastic clip

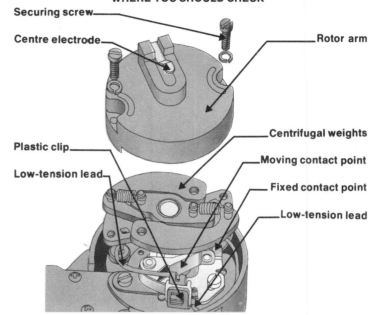

WHERE YOU SHOULD CHECK

Securing screw
Centre electrode
Rotor arm
Plastic clip
Low-tension lead
Centrifugal weights
Moving contact point
Fixed contact point
Low-tension lead

Stage 4 Adjusting the gap
Turn the engine so that the fibre heel of the moving contact point is on the peak of the cam, and the points are fully open. Put a screwdriver in the adjusting slot and move the fixed point until a feeler blade, of the correct thickness, fits snugly between the contact faces. Tighten the screws holding the fixed point to the base-plate. Turn the crankshaft one full turn and recheck the gap. If necessary, readjust the clearance.

Points gap
The clearance on all AC distributors is between ·019 and ·021 in.

111 Checking and renewing the points on a Motorcraft or Autolite distributor

Stage 1 Removing the rotor arm
The rotor arm is a push-fit on the distributor shaft: pull it off. Check the contact area for signs of pitting or burning. If it is damaged, fit a new rotor arm. Make sure the sprung centre electrode is pulled up enough to contact the carbon brush in the distributor cap. Check the insulation for signs of cracking.

When refitting the arm, make sure it is located in the distributor-shaft keyway.

Stage 2 Checking the contact faces
Turn the engine crankshaft until the plastic heel is on the peak of the distributor cam, and the points are fully open. Check the contact faces. If they are dirty, clean them with a lint-free rag. If they are pitted, fit new points.

Stage 3 Fitting new points
The contact points, fitted to a Motorcraft (Autolite) distributor, are a one-piece set. Undo the cross-headed screw holding the two low-tension leads to the side of the contact-breaker points. Lift the low-tension leads carefully out of the way.

Undo and remove the two contact screws holding the combined fixed point and moving contact points to the distributor base-plate. Lift out the complete contact set.

Clean the contact faces of the new points with a petrol-moistened rag to ensure that you remove the protective film.

Lubricate the pivot post with a high-melting-point grease. Fit the new contact set to the distributor base-plate. Fit the base-plate screws, but do not fully tighten the screws at this time.

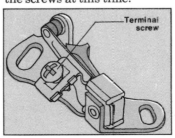
Terminal screw

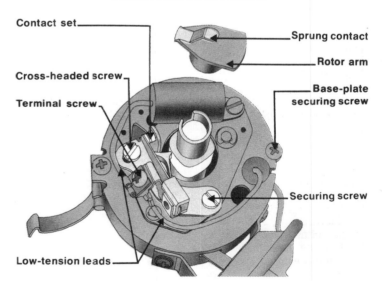

WHERE YOU SHOULD CHECK

Contact set
Sprung contact
Rotor arm
Cross-headed screw
Terminal screw
Base-plate securing screw
Securing screw
Low-tension leads

Stage 4 Adjusting the gap
Turn the engine so that the heel of the contact set is on the peak of the distributor-shaft cam, and the points are fully open. Place a screwdriver in the adjusting slot and turn the screwdriver anticlockwise to open the gap. Place a feeler between the contact faces, and close the points until the feeler blade is just pinched between the contact faces.

Tighten the base-plate screws to hold the contact points in their correct position. Turn the engine crankshaft one full rotation and check the points gap again. If necessary, readjust the gap to the correct clearance.

Points gap
Anglia; Cortina Mk I; Corsair; Zephyr/Zodiac: ·015 in. Escort; Cortina Mk II and III; Classic/Capri 109E: ·025 in.

112 Checking and renewing the points on a Toyo Kogyo distributor

Stage 1 Removing the rotor arm

There are two identical distributors on Mazda rotary-engined cars. The rotor arms have a contact arm on each side. Pull the arm off the distributor shaft. Check both contact faces for signs of pitting. If the rotor arm is damaged, fit a new one. Check the centre of the brass contact arm for signs of carbon deposit from the brush in the distributor cap. Clean it with a petrol-moistened rag. When refitting, locate the rotor arm on the distributor shaft keyway.

Stage 2 Checking the contact faces

Turn the engine crankshaft until the contact points are fully open. If the faces are dirty, clean them with a lint-free rag. If they are pitted, fit a complete contact set.

Stage 3 Fitting new points

Loosen the low-tension terminal screw at the side of the distributor body. Lift off the low-tension lead attached to the spring blade of the moving contact point, from the distributor terminal.

Remove the two screws holding the fixed contact to the distributor base-plate. Lift the complete contact set out over the distributor shaft.

Clean the faces of the new contact points with a petrol-moistened rag to remove the protective film. Fit the new set over the distributor shaft and loosely fit the two securing screws. Reconnect the low-tension lead to the terminal on the side of the distributor, making sure it is insulated from the distributor body. Tighten the terminal screw.

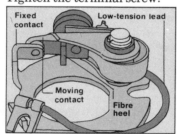

Stage 4 Adjusting the gap

With the fixed-point securing screws loose, fit a screwdriver in the head of the adjusting slot, just behind the contact face of the fixed point. Turn the engine until the heel of the moving point is on the peak of the cam. Turn the screwdriver so that the contact faces just pinch a feeler blade of the correct thickness. Tighten the securing screws in the base-plate to hold the points.

If you are in doubt about the car's performance after setting the points, have them checked by a garage.

Points gap
On both distributors the gap is ·018 in.

WHERE YOU SHOULD CHECK

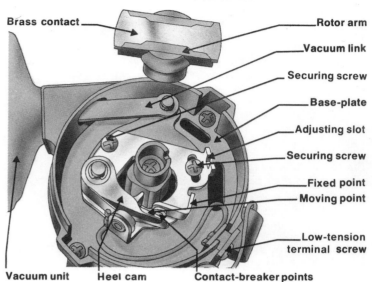

Brass contact — Rotor arm — Vacuum link — Securing screw — Base-plate — Adjusting slot — Securing screw — Fixed point — Moving point — Low-tension terminal screw

Vacuum unit — Heel cam — Contact-breaker points

113 Checking and renewing the points on a Ducellier distributor

Stage 1 Removing the rotor arm

The Ducellier rotor arm is a push-fit on the distributor shaft. Pull it up to remove it. If the face of the brass contact is burnt, fit a new rotor arm. Check the top of the brass contact where it meets the carbon brush in the distributor cap. If it is dirty, clean it with a petrol-moistened rag.

When refitting the rotor arm, make sure that it fits firmly into the keyway in the distributor shaft.

Stage 2 Checking the contact faces

Turn the engine crankshaft until the contact points are fully open. Check the condition of the contact faces. If they are pitted, fit a complete new set of points. If they are dirty, clean them with a dry, lint-free rag.

Stage 3 Fitting new points

A Ducellier distributor uses a two-piece contact set. Undo the low-tension terminal nut on the side of the distributor body and loosen the terminal base nut. Slide out the low-tension lead attached to the spring blade of the moving point. Remove the spring clip that holds the moving point to its pivot post. Lift out the moving contact point.

Remove the single screw that holds the fixed point to the base-plate and remove the fixed point. Locate the elongated slot in the end of the fixed point over the peg in the base-plate, and fit the single retaining screw. Fit the moving contact to its pivot post and replace the spring clip retaining it. Connect the low-tension lead to the distributor terminal.

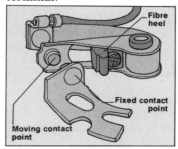

Stage 4 Adjusting the gap

A special tool, which has a peg that fits a hole in the base-plate, is recommended for adjusting the points gap. As the tool is turned it moves the fixed point.

If one of these tools is not available from your local dealer, try to do the job with a screwdriver.

Make sure the heel of the moving contact is on the peak of the cam. Move the fixed point until a feeler blade, of the correct thickness, fits snugly between the contact-point faces. Tighten the fixed-point base-plate screw to secure the points.

Points gap
In most cases, between ·017 and ·019 in. On Simca 1301 and 1501, ·018 to ·021 in.

WHERE YOU SHOULD CHECK

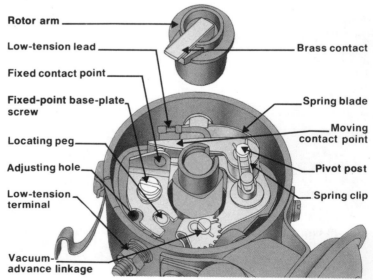

Rotor arm — Low-tension lead — Fixed contact point — Fixed-point base-plate screw — Locating peg — Adjusting hole — Low-tension terminal — Vacuum-advance linkage — Brass contact — Spring blade — Moving contact point — Pivot post — Spring clip

114 Checking and renewing the points on a Marelli distributor

Stage 1 Removing the rotor arm

The rotor arm on the Marelli distributor is fitted to the centrifugal base-plate, and the centrifugal weights are above the contact points. Remove the two screws and lift the arm off. If the brass contact is pitted, fit a new rotor arm. Clean the centre of the brass contact with a petrol-moistened rag and check the insulation for signs of cracking.

Stage 2 Checking the contact faces

Turn the engine crankshaft so that the contact points are fully open. Check the contact faces, and clean with a lint-free rag. If the faces are pitted, fit a new contact set.

Stage 3 Fitting new points

Loosen the low-tension terminal nut on the side of the distributor body and remove the low-tension lead fixed to the moving contact point. The contact points are a one-piece set. Remove the single screw that holds the contact set to the distributor base-plate and lift out the contact-point set.

Clean the faces of the new contact points with a petrol-moistened rag, to remove the protective film. Make sure they are dry. Slide the new contact set under the centrifugal weights and locate the back of the fixed point on its peg in the base-plate. Refit the single screw to retain the contact points, but do not fully tighten it at this stage.

Fit the low-tension lead to the terminal on the side of the distributor, and tighten the terminal nut fully to hold it in position.

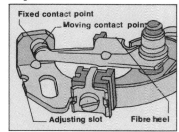

WHERE YOU SHOULD CHECK

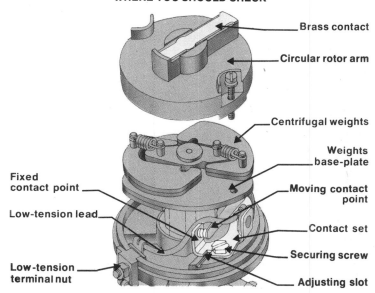

Brass contact

Circular rotor arm

Centrifugal weights

Weights base-plate

Moving contact point

Fixed contact point

Low-tension lead

Contact set

Securing screw

Low-tension terminal nut

Adjusting slot

Stage 4 Adjusting the gap

Turn the engine crankshaft and make sure that the fibre heel of the moving point is on the peak of the distributor cam, and that the points are fully open. Fit a screwdriver in the adjusting slot and turn it until a feeler blade of the correct thickness fits snugly between the contact faces. Tighten the single screw holding the fixed point to the distributor base-plate.

Turn the engine crankshaft one full turn, so that the points are fully open again, and re-check the clearance.

Points gap

Between ·018 and ·020 in. On Fiat 850 coupé, ·017 and on Fiat 127 and 128, ·016 in.

115 Checking and renewing the points on a Bosch distributor

Stage 1 Removing the rotor arm

The rotor arm on Bosch distributors is a push-fit on the distributor shaft. It also retains a condensation shield. Pull off the rotor arm and remove the condensation shield. Check the contact edge for signs of pitting. If it is damaged fit a new rotor arm. Make sure that the centre of the brass contact is in good condition. Clean it with a petrol-moistened rag.

When refitting the rotor arm, make sure that the boss fits through the condensation plate and locates in the keyway on the distributor shaft.

Stage 2 Checking the contact faces

Turn the engine crankshaft until the contact points are fully open. Clean the faces with a lint-free rag. If the faces are burnt or badly pitted, fit a new set of contact points.

Stage 3 Fitting new points

A two-piece contact set is fitted to Bosch distributors. Remove the spring clip that holds the moving contact to its pivot post. Push the contact spring blade inwards and lift off the moving contact. Lift off the low-tension lead from the plastic clip on the side of the fixed point. Undo the single screw that holds the fixed point to the base-plate and take out the contact point.

Fit the new fixed contact point over the peg in the base-plate and refit the single screw. Fit the low-tension lead to the peg on the plastic clip and fit the new moving point.

Make sure that the spring blade fits the plastic clip and holds the lead in place. Fit the spring clip to the pivot post.

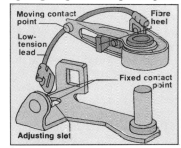

WHERE YOU SHOULD CHECK

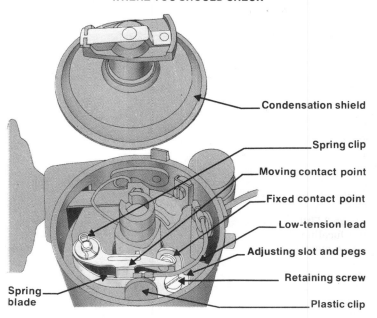

Condensation shield

Spring clip

Moving contact point

Fixed contact point

Low-tension lead

Adjusting slot and pegs

Retaining screw

Plastic clip

Spring blade

Stage 4 Adjusting the gap

When the fixed-point base-plate screw is loose, insert a screwdriver between the pegs on the base-plate and into the adjusting slot on the fixed contact point. Make sure that the points are fully open and turn the screwdriver until the contact faces just pinch a feeler blade of the correct thickness. Tighten the base-plate screw. Turn the engine crankshaft one full turn, until the contact points are open, and re-check the gap with a feeler blade.

Points gap

The correct clearance for all Bosch distributors is ·016 in.

116 Checking and renewing the points on a Nippondenso distributor

WHERE YOU SHOULD CHECK

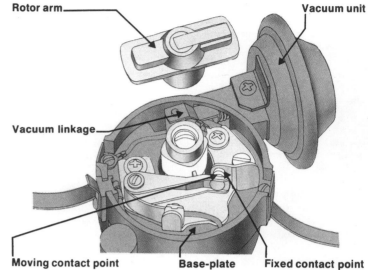

Rotor arm

Vacuum unit

Vacuum linkage

Moving contact point   Base-plate   Fixed contact point

Stage 1 Removing the rotor arm

The rotor arm is a plastic moulding with the brass contact standing above the arm boss. It is a push-fit on the shaft. Pull off the arm.

Check the edge of the brass contact for signs of pitting or burning. If it is damaged,

fit a new arm. Clean the centre of the brass contact to remove any carbon deposits from the contact brush in the distributor cap.

When refitting the rotor arm, make sure it is located in the keyway on the shaft.

Stage 2 Checking the contact faces

Turn the engine crankshaft so that the contact points are fully open. Check the condition of the contact faces. If

they are dirty, clean them with a lint-free rag. If the faces are badly pitted or burnt, fit a new contact set.

Stage 3 Fitting new points

The Nippondenso distributor uses a one-piece contact set. Loosen the low-tension terminal nut on the side of the distributor body. Lift off the low-tension lead attached to the spring blade of the moving contact. Undo the two screws holding the fixed contact point to the base-plate. Lift out the complete contact set. Fit the new set in position and secure it with the base-plate screws. Do not fully tighten the screws.

Reconnect the low-tension

lead, from the contact blade, to the terminal on the side of the distributor, making sure it is insulated from the distributor body. Tighten the terminal nut.

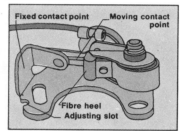

Fixed contact point   Moving contact point

Fibre heel
Adjusting slot

Stage 4 Adjusting the gap

Turn the engine crankshaft so that the fibre heel of the moving contact point is on the peak of the distributor cam. Put a screwdriver in the adjusting slot just behind the fixed-point face. Place a feeler blade, of the correct thickness, between the contact faces.

Turn the screwdriver to move the fixed point so that it

just pinches the feeler blade between the contact faces. Tighten the two base-plate screws to hold the points in this position.

Contact gap

The clearance between the contact faces, when open, on all distributors is between ·018 and ·020 in.

---

117 Checking and renewing the contact points on a Citroën Ami 8

WHERE YOU SHOULD CHECK

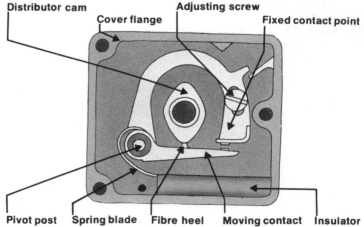

Distributor cam   Adjusting screw

Cover flange   Fixed contact point

Pivot post   Spring blade   Fibre heel   Moving contact   Insulator

Stage 1 Removing the distributor cover

Undo the self-tapping screws and remove the radiator grille. Remove the centre bolt that holds the cooling fan to the shaft and lift out the fan.

Undo the seven screws and remove the distributor splash shield. This reveals the distributor cover. Undo the three screws and lift off the cover.

Stage 2 Checking the contact faces

Turn the engine crankshaft, by the flywheel, so that the distributor contact points are fully open. Examine the faces

of the points. If they are dirty, clean them with a lint-free rag. If they are badly pitted or burnt, fit a new contact set.

Stage 3 Fitting new points

The contact breaker is a two-piece set, held by one external and one internal screw. Remove the screw in the bottom of the contact-breaker housing that holds the low-tension lead and the spring blade of the moving contact. Slide the spring blade out of the insulator and lift it off its pivot post. Undo the single screw that holds the fixed point to the distributor base-plate.

Clean the contact faces of the new points to remove the protective film. Slide the fixed-point eye over the pivot post and loosely fit the base-plate securing screw.

Lightly grease the pivot post and fit the moving point to the post. Slide the spring blade into the insulator and fit the external screw holding the low-tension lead to the spring blade. Put a thin film of high-melting-point grease on the face of the cam lobes to lubricate them.

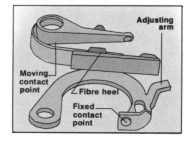

Adjusting arm

Moving contact point

Fibre heel

Fixed contact point

Stage 4 Adjusting the gap

Turn the engine crankshaft by the flywheel, so that the heel on the moving contact point is on the peak of the distributor cam. Insert a screwdriver in the adjusting slot of the fixed point and fit a feeler blade, of the correct thickness, between the two contact faces.

Turn the screwdriver so that the contact faces just pinch the feeler blade. Tighten the base-plate screw.

Turn the engine on the flywheel so that the second cam lifts the moving point. Check

the clearance between the two faces.

If the gap is greater than ·018 in. or less than ·014 in., the cam is worn and will have to be renewed. This is a job for a garage.

If on removing the cam, which is held by a central screw, and turning it through 180 degrees, you find that the gap is the same, the shaft is distorted. Fit a new distributor.

Points gap

The exact clearance on all Ami 8 distributors is ·016 in.

118 Checking the distributor's ignition advance mechanism

Remove the distributor cap and rotor arm to give access to the vacuum link attached to

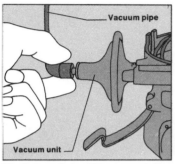

the base-plate. Disconnect the vacuum pipe from the end of the vacuum diaphragm unit attached to the side of the distributor body. If the pipe

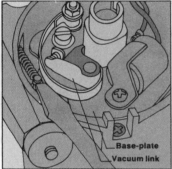

Base-plate

Vacuum link

is plastic it is a push-fit. If a steel pipe is used, it is usually

screwed firmly into place.

Use a screwdriver to rotate the contact-breaker base-plate so that the vacuum advance link is pushed towards the vacuum unit. Push it as far as it will go against the pressure of the vacuum-unit return spring, and hold it in this position. Place a

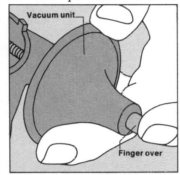

Vacuum unit

Finger over

finger over the end of the vacuum unit, where the vacuum pipe is attached, and release the base-plate. If the unit is in good condition, the finger should be gripped by the suction in the vacuum unit. If it is not, the vacuum diaphragm in the unit is perforated and a new assembly will have to be fitted to the distributor (see pp. 162-3).

RETARDING AND ADVANCING THE IGNITION

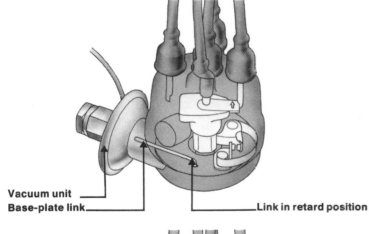

Vacuum unit
Base-plate link ————————— Link in retard position

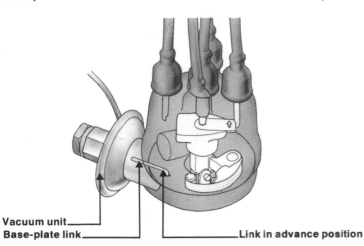

Vacuum unit
Base-plate link ————————— Link in advance position

119 Checking vacuum units with external linkages

On Motorcraft and some AC Delco distributors there is an external link connecting the diaphragm in the vacuum unit to the contact-breaker base-plate. With the engine running, rev it up slightly and observe the link. If it moves as the engine speed is altered, the vacuum unit is working correctly. If the distributor is difficult to reach, check the unit by removing the vacuum pipe from the carburettor. Suck on the pipe and place your tongue over the end. The tongue should be held by suction.

WHERE YOU SHOULD CHECK

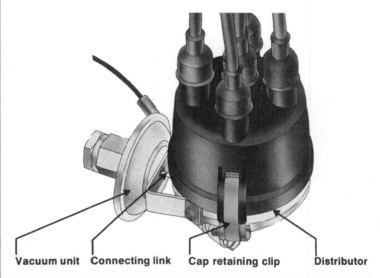

Vacuum unit   Connecting link   Cap retaining clip   Distributor

120 Checking the centrifugal advance mechanism

An accurate check of the centrifugal mechanism can be made only with specialist equipment. It is, however, possible to check that the centrifugal weight tension springs are connected, and that the weights are free and moving smoothly on their pivots.

Remove the distributor cap and check the rotation of the distributor rotor arm. Most rotor arms have an arrow marked on them. If not, put

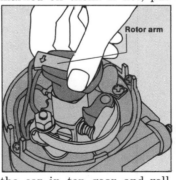

Rotor arm

the car in top gear and roll it forwards to find the direction in which the rotor arm rotates. Grip the rotor arm between two fingers and turn it in the direction of the arrow, or of the normal rotation, determined by moving the car in gear.

Release the rotor arm. It should spring back under the

pressure of the centrifugal weight tension springs. If

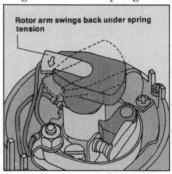

Rotor arm swings back under spring tension

not, the springs are broken or the weights are sticking. Renew or clean the mechanism as necessary (see p. 161).

On distributors with circular rotor arms, with the centrifugal weights above the base-plate, undo the screws holding the rotor arm and lift the rotor arm off. Turn the distributor shaft so that the springs on the centrifugal weights are under tension. Use a thin screwdriver to check that the centrifugal weights move freely on their pivot pins. On some distributors the weights will only move as the cam is turned. If they are tight, remove them, clean the pivot posts, lubricate them with high-melting-point grease, and reassemble.

121 Lubricating the shaft and mechanism on a Motorcraft (Autolite) distributor

With the rotor arm removed (see Job 111), clean the distributor base-plate and cam lobes with a dry cloth.

Never over-lubricate a distributor. Lightly smear the lobes of the cam with high-melting-point grease. Put a few drops of engine oil on to the cam felt in the centre of the distributor shaft. Trickle oil down the distributor shaft, between the shaft and the base-plate. Lubricate the advance link pivot, on the base-plate, with a light machine oil.

Wipe away any excess oil or grease.

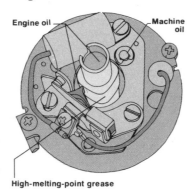

122 Lubricating the shaft and mechanism on a Bosch distributor

With the rotor arm removed (see Job 115), clean the base-plate and cam lobes with a dry cloth. Put one drop of engine oil on the felt ring in the contact-breaker base-plate. Lubricate the centre of the distributor shaft with two drops of oil. Put one drop of oil on the moving contact pivot post. Smear the face of the cam lobes with a light film of high-melting-point grease. Lubricate the advance link pivot with two drops of oil. Wipe away any excess

lubricant or grease before re-assembling the distributor.

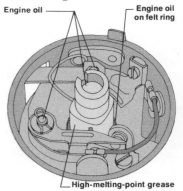

123 Lubricating the shaft and mechanism on a Marelli distributor

Early models Wipe the base-plate clean with a dry cloth. Lightly oil the moving contact pivot post. Smear a thin film of high-melting-point grease on the cam lobes, and oil the external lubricator wick protruding from the side of the distributor body.
Later models Wipe the base-plate and cam lobes clean with a dry cloth. Smear the cam lobes with a film of high-melting-point grease. Oil the cam felt pad and the centrifugal weight pivot points,

above the contact-breaker plate. Wipe away excess.

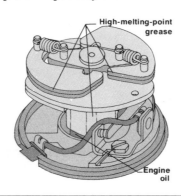

124 Lubricating the shaft and mechanism on a Toyo Kogyo distributor

There are two distributors on the Mazda rotary-engine cars: lubricate in the same way. With the rotor arm removed (see Job 112), wipe the base-plate and cam lobes with a dry cloth. Smear the lobes of the cam with a thin film of high-melting-point grease. Put two drops of oil in the centre of the distributor shaft, and one drop of oil on the moving contact pivot post. Lubricate the vacuum advance pivot post where it is attached to the base-plate. Wipe away any

excess oil or grease before reassembling the distributor.

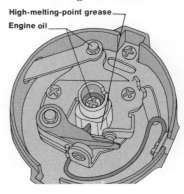

125 Lubricating the shaft and mechanism on a Ducellier distributor

With the rotor arm removed (see Job 113), clean the base-plate and cam lobes with a dry cloth. Put a few drops of engine oil on the felt pad in the centre of the distributor cam, to lubricate the cam bush and distributor shaft. Lightly smear the cam lobes with a thin film of high-melting-point grease. Put one drop of oil on the moving contact pivot post —avoid getting any oil on the low-tension lead from the moving contact spring blade to the low-tension terminal.

Wipe away any excess oil or grease before reassembling.

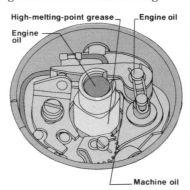

126 Lubricating the shaft and mechanism on a Nippondenso distributor

With the rotor arm removed (see Job 116), wipe the base-plate and cam lobes clean with a dry cloth. Never over-lubricate a distributor: lightly smear the lobes of the cam with a thin film of high-melting-point grease. Put two drops of oil on the felt in the centre of the distributor shaft, to lubricate the cam bearing. Put one drop of oil on the moving contact pivot post and on the vacuum advance pivot post on the base-plate. Wipe away any excess oil or grease from the

distributor base-plate or contacts, before reassembling.

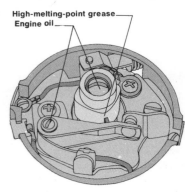

127 Lubricating the shaft and mechanism on a Citroën Ami 8 distributor

When the cover is off the distributor (see Job 117), you can see only the shaft, cam and contact-breaker points. The rotor arm is on the other end of the shaft. Wipe the base-plate, cam lobes and contact-breaker mechanism with a dry cloth. Trickle two drops of engine oil on to the distributor shaft, so that it runs down inside. Put one drop of oil on the moving contact

pivot point, and lightly smear the face of the cam lobes with a thin film of high-melting-point grease. Carefully wipe away any excess oil or grease from the distributor base-plate.

Because the distributor is vertical, any surplus lubricant will run to the bottom of the distributor housing and could cause a short-circuit where the spring blade is

attached to the insulator. When refitting the cover, make sure a new gasket is used. The old one may be

saturated in oil, which could cause a short-circuit between the contact points and result in ignition failure.

128 Lubricating the shaft and mechanism on a Lucas distributor

Thoroughly clean the base-plate and cam lobes with a dry cloth. Lubricate the cam face with a film of high-melting-point grease. Put two drops of oil through the gap between the distributor shaft and the base-plate. Apply a few drops of oil to the screw holding the cam to the distributor shaft, and put one drop of oil on the moving contact pivot post.

On one-piece contact sets (see Job 109), apply a smear of petroleum jelly to the hollow pivot post.

Wipe away any excess oil or grease.

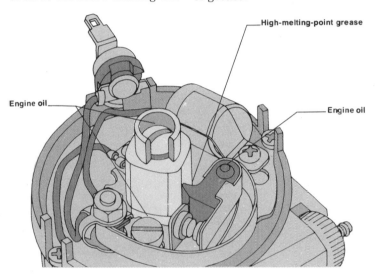

129 Lubricating the shaft and mechanism on an AC Delco distributor

Circular rotor arms With the rotor arm removed (see Job 110), wipe the base-plate and cam lobes with a dry cloth. Inject a few drops of light machine oil through the hole in the distributor base-plate. Put a single drop of oil on each advance weight pivot, and smear the cam lobes with high-melting-point grease.

Other models Put a few drops of oil on the felt pad in the centre of the cam. Pour a teaspoonful of engine oil through the hole in the base-plate. Smear the cam lobe with high-melting-point grease.

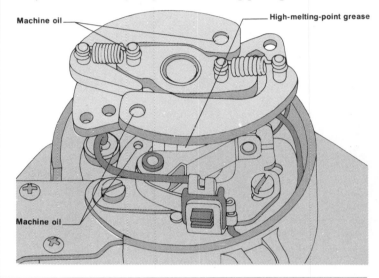

130 Checking the high-tension leads, distributor cap and rotor arm

Label each high-tension lead with the appropriate cylinder number (No. 1 nearest the radiator), so that they can be refitted correctly. Disconnect the high-tension leads from the spark-plugs.

Clean all the high-tension leads with a dry cloth. Inspect the leads, the connectors and the moisture seals for signs of cracking, perishing or burning. If any damage is evident, fit a new set of high-tension leads. Check the coil high-tension and low-tension leads also.

There are two types of lead that may be fitted; a wire core or a carbon core. The carbon core leads are automatically suppressed to prevent radio interference. With the distributor cap removed, wipe inside and outside with a clean, dry cloth, to remove any carbon dust or moisture from the inside of the cap. Examine the electrodes on the inside of the distributor cap for signs of pitting or burning. Inspect the cap for 'tracking' — a forked-lightning effect on the polished bakelite surface between the electrodes. If you find signs of either condition, fit a new distributor cap and leads. Check the carbon contact in the centre of the cap. If it is fixed, and worn flush with the cap, fit a new cap. If it is spring loaded, fit a new carbon brush and spring, if necessary.

Remove the rotor arm and clean it with a dry cloth. Examine the rotor-arm contact for excessive corrosion or carbon build-up. Use neat methylated spirit to remove any carbon deposits.

Refit the rotor arm. Check that it does not tilt or rotate out of true on the distributor shaft. If it does, it may strike the electrodes in the distributor cap. If the rotor arm incorporates a spring contact blade, make sure that it is in contact with the carbon brush in the centre of the distributor cap.

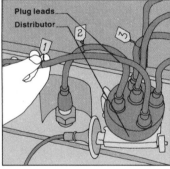
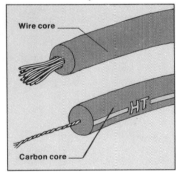
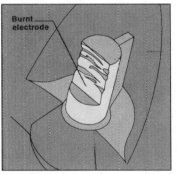
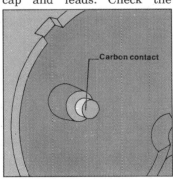
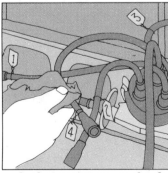
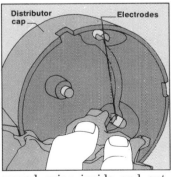

TYPES OF ROTOR ARM

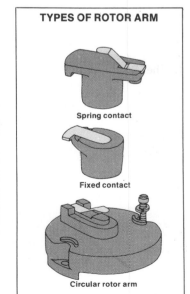

Spring contact

Fixed contact

Circular rotor arm

131 Cleaning and adjusting spark-plugs

Warning Some cars, especially those with emission-control equipment, are fitted with air surface gap spark-plugs. These have three heavy earth electrodes instead of the conventional single electrode, and they must not be cleaned or adjusted in any way.

Before removing the plugs on conventional engines, label

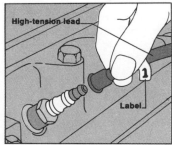

each lead with its cylinder number so that it can be re-fitted correctly.

Remove the leads and unscrew each plug half a turn

with a box or plug spanner fully pushed home. Use the right spanner or it may damage the ceramic insulator.

Clean round the spark-plug

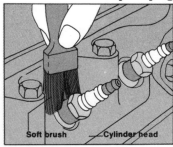

with a soft, dry brush so that dirt does not fall into the cylinder when the plug is removed. Blow out with an airline if possible. Be particularly careful not to allow particles to enter the plug holes on rotary engines—the seals are more easily damaged.

Remove each plug and, at the same time, renew its

sealing washer if you find that it is distorted. If the plugs have

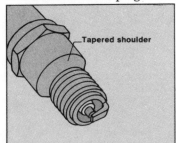

tapered shoulders they do not have sealing washers. Check the condition of the plugs. A

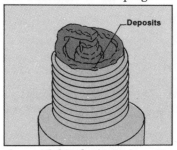

plug with black, sooty deposits has been running with over-

rich carburation. A plug with a white, powdery deposit has been running with weak carburation. Adjust the carburettor (see pp. 128-9). If the electrodes are covered with very heavy deposits or are badly eroded, discard them and fit new ones.

Clean the ceramic insulator and check for cracks. If the ceramic part is damaged, discard the plug. It will almost certainly cause misfiring. The

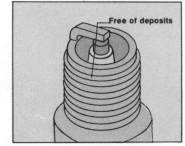

electrodes must be clean. If possible, have the plugs sand-blasted at a garage to remove any deposits.

FINDING THE RIGHT PLUG AND GAP FOR YOUR CAR

Plug makes
AC=AC Delco M=Marchal
B=Bosch Ma=Marelli
Ch=Champion Mo=Motorcraft
L=Lodge N=NGK

	Make	Type	Gap
AUDI			
100 GL	B	W240-T2	·024-·027 in.
100 GL Automatic	B	W240-T2	·024-·027 in.
100 LS	B	W225-T2	·024-·027 in.
100 LS Automatic	B	W225-T2	·024-·027 in.
Coupé S	B	W240-T2	·024-·027 in.
Coupé S Automatic	B	W240-T2	·024-·027 in.
BMW			
1600	B	W200-T30	·025 in.
1800	B	W200-T30	·025 in.
2000	B	W200-T30	·025 in.
2002	B	W200-T30	·025 in.
2500	B	W175-T2	·025 in.
2800	B	W175-T2	·025 in.
BRITISH LEYLAND			
Austin			
A40 Farina	Ch	N5	·025 in.
A60	Ch	N5	·025 in.
A110	Ch	N12Y	·025 in.
Maxi 1500	Ch	N9Y	·025 in.
Maxi 1750	Ch	N9Y	·025 in.
Austin/Morris			
1100	Ch	N5	·025 in.
1300	Ch	N9Y	·025 in.
1300 Countryman	Ch	N9Y	·025 in.
1300 GT	Ch	N9Y	·025 in.
1800 Mk II	Ch	N9Y	·025 in.
1800 S	Ch	N9Y	·025 in.
2200	Ch	N9Y	·025 in.
Midget (1275 cc)	Ch	N9Y	·025 in.
Midget (1098 cc)	Ch	N12Y	·025 in.
Midget (948 cc)	Ch	N12Y	·025 in.
Mini 850 (pre 1970)	Ch	N5	·025 in.
Mini 850 (post 1971)	Ch	N9Y	·025 in.

	Make	Type	Gap
Austin/Morris cont'd			
Mini 1000 (pre 1970)	Ch	N5	·025 in.
Mini 1000 (post 1971)	Ch	N9Y	·025 in.
Mini Clubman (pre 1970)	Ch	N5	·025 in.
Mini Clubman (post 1971)	Ch	N9Y	·025 in.
Mini Cooper S	Ch	N9Y	·025 in.
Sprite (1275 cc)	Ch	N9Y	·025 in.
Sprite (1098 cc)	Ch	N12Y	·025 in.
Sprite (948 cc)	Ch	N12Y	·025 in.
Jaguar			
2·4	Ch	N5	·025 in.
3·4	Ch	N12Y	·025 in.
3·8	Ch	N12Y	·025 in.
3·8 S type	Ch	N12Y	·025 in.
Morris			
Marina 1·3	Ch	N9Y	·025 in.
Marina 1·8	Ch	N9Y	·025 in.
Marina 1·8 TC	Ch	N9Y	·025 in.
MG1100	Ch	N9Y	·025 in.
MGB	Ch	N9Y	·025 in.
MGC	Ch	N9Y	·025 in.
Minor 1000 (pre 1970)	Ch	N5	·025 in.
Minor 1000 (post 1971)	Ch	N9Y	·025 in.
Riley			
Elf	Ch	N5	·025 in.
Rover			
2000 SC	Ch	N9Y	·025 in.
2000 SC Automatic	Ch	N9Y	·025 in.
2000 TC	Ch	N9Y	·025 in.
Triumph			
1300	Ch	N9Y	·025 in.
1500	Ch	N9Y	·025 in.
2000	Ch	N9Y	·025 in.
Dolomite	Ch	N9Y	·025 in.
GT-6	Ch	N9Y	·025 in.
Herald 1200	L	CNY	·025 in.
Herald 12/50	L	CNY	·025 in.
Herald 13/60	Ch	N9Y	·025 in.
Spitfire	Ch	N9Y	·025 in.
Stag	Ch	N9Y	·025 in.

	Make	Type	Gap
Triumph cont'd			
Toledo 1300	Ch	N9Y	·025 in.
TR 4	L	CNY-NN	·025 in.
TR 4A	L	2HN-CN	·025 in.
TR 5	Ch	N9Y	·025 in.
TR 6	Ch	N9Y	·025 in.
Vitesse Mk I	Ch	N9Y	·025 in.
Vitesse Mk II	Ch	N9Y	·025 in.
Wolseley			
Hornet	Ch	N5	·025 in.
CHRYSLER			
Chrysler Rootes			
Avenger	Ch	N7Y	·025 in.
Avenger GT	Ch	N7Y	·025 in.
Chamois	Ch	N9Y	·025 in.
Chrysler 180	Ch	N7Y	·024 in.
Hillman Minx 1500	Ch	N9Y	·025 in.
Humber Sceptre	Ch	N9Y	·025 in.
Hunter 1500	Ch	N9Y	·025 in.
Hunter 1725	Ch	N9Y	·025 in.
Imp	Ch	N9Y	·025 in.
Singer Gazelle	Ch	N9Y	·025 in.
Singer Vogue	Ch	N9Y	·025 in.
Stiletto	Ch	N9Y	·025 in.
Sunbeam Alpine	Ch	N9Y	·025 in.
Sunbeam Rapier	Ch	N9Y	·025 in.
Sunbeam Sport	Ch	N9Y	·025 in.
Chrysler Simca			
1000	Ch	N7Y	·025 in.
1100	Ch	N7Y	·025 in.
1100 S	Ch	N7Y	·025 in.
1301	Ch	N7Y	·025 in.
1301 Automatic	Ch	N7Y	·025 in.
1501	Ch	N7Y	·025 in.
1501 Automatic	Ch	N7Y	·025 in.
CITROËN			
Ami 6	M	345	·025 in.
Ami 8	M	345	·025 in.
Dyane	M	345	·025 in.
DAF			
33	B	W175-T1	·034 in.
44	B	W175-T1	·034 in.
55	Ch	L87Y	·026 in.
66	Ch	L87Y	·026 in.

Check that the electrodes on the clean plugs are in good condition, with no great

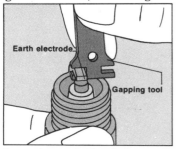

loss of metal. Bend the earth electrode back with a gapping

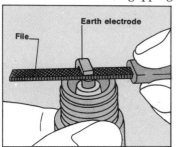

tool, and with a points file gently remove irregularities

and square off the electrodes. Gently bend back the electrode, and reset the gap between the earth and centre electrodes with a feeler blade. On most modern plugs this should be between ·023 in. and ·030 in. See the chart for the recommended gap for your car. The gap should be set so that the blade of the feeler gauge can just be inserted.

Make sure that the plug threads are clean and carefully screw the plug by hand into the plug hole. The washers should not be removed from plugs. Doing so will distort them. Tighten with a plug spanner—but not too tightly. If you use a torque wrench, follow the manufacturer's instructions for tightening.

On cars with aluminium cylinder heads, it is advisable to clean and to grease the plug threads with a graphite-based grease, to avoid any possible damage to the head.

132 Buying and fitting a new set of spark-plugs

When buying new spark-plugs, specify the year, make, model and engine size of the car. Manufacturers often change the plug specifications when engine power is increased or a larger engine is installed.

Before removing the old plugs, label the high-tension leads so that they can be replaced in the correct order when the new plugs are fitted.

Loosen the spark-plug half a turn and clean round it with a soft, dry brush so that dirt does not fall into the cylinder when the plug is removed. Blow out with an air-line if possible.

Unscrew the plug with a box spanner or socket. Discard the old plugs and sealing washers. New washers are supplied with new plugs. Tapered-shoulder plugs do not have washers.

Set the gap by inserting the

recommended size of feeler blade—between ·023 in. and

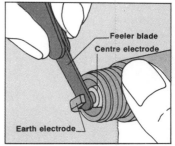

·030 in. on most cars (see chart). It should just fit. If it is too tight, reset the plug gap (see Job 131).

Make sure that the sealing washers are flush on to the plugs and then carefully screw them by hand.

Tighten with a box or plug spanner. Spark-plugs must not be too tight. If you use a torque wrench, follow the plug manufacturer's instructions for tightening.

FINDING THE RIGHT PLUG AND GAP FOR YOUR CAR

	Make	Type	Gap		Make	Type	Gap		Make	Type	Gap
DATSUN				**MAZDA**				**Vauxhall cont'd**			
240Z Sports	N	BP6ES	·033 in.	RX3	N	B7EM	·035 in.	Viva HB 1159 cc	AC	42XLS	·030 in.
260C Custom	N	BP6ES	·033 in.					Viva HB 1600 cc	AC	42TS	·030 in.
260C Custom Auto	N	BP6ES	·033 in.	**RENAULT**				Viva HB GT	AC	41T	·030 in.
Bluebird 160B	N	BP5ES	·025 in.	R4	AC	43FS	·020-·028 in.	Viva HB SL90	AC	42XLS	·028 in.
Bluebird 160B Auto	N	BP5ES	·025 in.					Viva HC 1159 cc	AC	42XLS	·030 in.
Bluebird 180B	N	BP5ES	·025 in.	R5 845 cc	AC	43FS	·024-·028 in.	Viva HC 1600 cc	AC	R41TS	·030 in.
Bluebird 180B Auto	N	BP5ES	·025 in.	R5 TL 956 cc	AC	42FS	·024-·028 in.	VX4/90FC	AC	42XLS	·030 in.
Bluebird 180SSS	N	BP5ES	·033 in.	R6 845 cc	AC	43FS	·025 in.	VX4/90FD	AC	42TS	·030 in.
Cherry 100A range	N	BP5ES	·025 in.	R6 1108 cc	AC	42FS	·025 in.	VX4/90FE	AC	R42TS	·030 in.
Cherry 120	N	BP5ES	·025 in.	R8	AC	43FS	·024 in.				
Sunny 1200 range	N	BP5ES	·025 in.	R10	M	36	·024 in.	**VOLKSWAGEN**			
				R12 TL & TS	Ch	L87Y	·024-·028 in.	Beetle 1200	B	W145T1	·028 in.
FIAT				R15 TL & TS	AC	42FS	·024-·028 in.	Beetle 1302	B	W145T1	·028 in.
124	Ma	CW7LP	0·6 mm.	R16 Automatic	AC	4	·028 in.	Beetle 1600	B	W145T1	·028 in.
124S	Ma	CW7LP	0·6 mm.	R16 TL	AC	42XLS	·028 in.	1600 FB	B	W145T1	·028 in.
125	Ma	CW7LP	0·6 mm.	R16 TS	AC	44XLS	·028 in.	1600 Variant	B	W145T1	·028 in.
127	Ma	CW7LP	0·6 mm.	R17 TL	Ch	N2G	·024-·028 in.	411 LE Saloon	Ch	N7Y	·028 in.
128	Ma	CW7LP	0·6 mm.					411 LE Variant	Ch	N7Y	·028 in.
500	Ma	CW6N	0·6 mm.	R17 TS	Ch	N2G	·024-·028 in.	412 LE Saloon	Ch	N7Y	·028 in.
600D	Ma	CW6N	0·6 mm.					412 LE Variant	Ch	N7Y	·028 in.
850	Ma	CW6LP	0·6 mm.					K70	Ch	N7Y	·028 in.
				TOYOTA							
FORD				Carina 1600	N	BPR5ES	·031 in.	**VOLVO**			
Anglia 105E	Mo	AG 32	·025 in.	Celica 1600	N	BPR5ES	·031 in.	120	B	W175T35	·028-·032 in.
Anglia 123E	Mo	AG 32	·025 in.	Corolla 1100/1200	N	BPR5ES	·031 in.	120S	B	W200T35	·028-·032 in.
Classic Capri 109E	Mo	AG 32	·025 in.	Corolla 1200 SL	N	BPR5ES	·031 in.	142	B	W175T35	·028-·032 in.
Classic Capri 109E GT	Mo	AG 32	·025 in.	Corona 1500	N	BP6ES	·031 in.	142S	B	W200T35	·028-·032 in.
Corsair 120E	Mo	AG 32	·025 in.	Corona 1900 Mk II	N	BP6ES	·031 in.				
Corsair 120E GT	Mo	AG 32	·025 in.	Corona 2000 Mk II	N	BP6ES	·031 in.	142GL	B	W225T35	·028-·032 in.
Corsair V4 1700 cc	Mo	AG 22	·025 in.	Crown 2300	N	BP6ES	·031 in.	144	B	W175T35	·028-·032 in.
Corsair V4 2000 cc	Mo	AG 22	·025 in.	Crown 2600	N	BP5ES	·031 in.	144S	B	W200T35	·028-·032 in.
Cortina Mk I 1200 cc	Mo	AG 32	·025 in.	**VAUXHALL**							
Cortina Mk I 1500 cc	Mo	AG 32	·025 in.	Firenza 1600 cc	AC	42TS	·030 in.	144GL	B	W225T35	·028-·032 in.
Cortina Mk II	Mo	AG 32	·025 in.	Firenza 2300 cc	AC	R41TS	·030 in.	145	B	W175T35	·028-·032 in.
Cortina Mk III (ohv)	Mo	AG 22	·025 in.	Ventora FD/FE	AC	42XLS	·030 in.	145S	B	W200T35	·028-·032 in.
Cortina Mk III (ohc)	Mo	BF 32	·025 in.	Victor FC	AC	42XLS	·030 in.	145GL	B	W225T35	·028-·032 in.
Escort	Mo	AG 22	·025 in.	Victor FD 1600 cc	AC	42TS	·030 in.				
Escort RS 1600	Mo	AG 12	·025 in.	Victor FD 2000 cc	AC	41T	·030 in.	164	B	W200T35	·028-·032 in.
Zephyr/Zodiac Mk III	Mo	AG 22	·025 in.	Victor FD 3·3 (Estate)	AC	42XLS	·030 in.				
				Victor FE 1800 cc	AC	R41TS	·030 in.				
				Victor FE 2000 cc	AC	R42TS	·030 in.				
				Victor FE 3·3 (Estate)	AC	42XLS	·030 in.				
				Viscount	AC	42XLS	·030 in.				

133 Checking the ignition timing with a strobe lamp when the engine is running

Make sure that the timing marks (see p. 164) on the crankshaft pulley and timing chain cover, or the flywheel and bell-housing, are clean

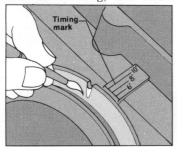

Timing mark

and easily visible. Mark them if necessary with a dab of white paint or chalk.

On some engines the vacuum advance should be disconnected and the end of the pipe plugged; on other cars the vacuum advance remains in operation (see chart below).

Connect the strobe lamp (see p. 35) and start the engine. If the car has a tachometer, check that the engine speed is within the range specified below.

Aim the strobe lamp at the timing marks. If the light shows the pulley, or flywheel, timing mark to be in line

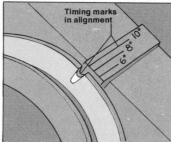

Timing marks in alignment

with the static timing mark, the timing is correct. If it

does not, get a helper to loosen the distributor clamp bolt and turn the distributor body slightly until the marks are level. Tighten the distributor clamp bolt.

When you have set the timing, get your helper to press the accelerator pedal gradually, to increase the engine speed, while you check the timing marks with the strobe

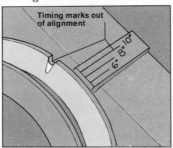

Timing marks out of alignment

lamp. The marks on the pulley or flywheel should appear to move steadily backwards as

engine speed increases, and return to alignment with the static mark when the engine speed returns to idle. This proves that the centrifugal advance mechanism is working correctly. If the mark does not move, overhaul the centrifugal weights and tension springs (see p. 161).

With the strobe light still directed at the timing marks, get your helper to increase the engine speed, using the accelerator, to approximately 2000 rpm. Hold the revs steady and disconnect and connect the vacuum advance pipe several times. The timing mark on the pulley should move quickly backwards each time the pipe is connected, showing that the vacuum unit is working properly. If it does not do this, fit a new vacuum unit (see p. 162).

STROBOSCOPIC IGNITION TIMING

Distributor vacuum:
D—Disconnected
C—Connected
N—None fitted

	Revs per minute	Vacuum	Degrees before tdc		Revs per minute	Vacuum	Degrees before tdc		Revs per minute	Vacuum	Degrees before tdc
AUDI				**Wolseley**				**RENAULT**			
100 GL/Automatic	3000	D	5	Hornet	600	D	8	R4	650-675	D	tdc±1
100 LS/Automatic	3000	D	14					R5 845 cc	650-675	D	5-7
Coupé S/Automatic	3000	D	14	**CHRYSLER**				R5 TL 956 cc	675-725	D	5-7
				Chrysler Rootes—Garage job				R6 845 cc	650-675	D	tdc±1
BMW				Chrysler Simca—Garage job				R6 1108 cc	650	D	tdc±1
1600/1800/2000/2002	1400	D	25					R8	675	D	tdc
2500/2800	1700	D	25	**CITROËN**				R10	675	D	tdc
				Ami 6/8			garage	R12 TL/TS early '73	650-675	D	tdc±1
BRITISH LEYLAND				Dyane			job	R12 TL/TS late '73	650-675	D	5-7
Austin								R15 TL	750-800	D	tdc±1
A40 Farina	600	D	6	**DAF**				R15 TS	625-675	D	2-4
A60	600	D	8	33/44	900	D	5	R16 Automatic	625	D	5-7
A110	650	D	8	55/66	800	D	tdc	R16 TL/TS	675	D	tdc±1
Maxi 1500 HC/1750	1000	D	13					R17 TL	625-675	D	5-7
Maxi 1500 LC	1000	D	12	**DATSUN**				R17 TS	1100	D	14-18
				240Z Sports	650	D	17				
Austin/Morris				260C Custom dl	550	D	10	**TOYOTA**			
1100	600	D	5	260C Custom dl Auto.	650	D	10	Carina 1600	600	D	16
1300/Countryman	600	D	10	Bluebird 160B	600	D	10	Celica 1600	600	D	18
1300 GT	1000	D	9	Bluebird 160B Auto.	650	D	10	Corolla 1100/1200	600	D	13
1800 Mk II HC	600	D	12	Bluebird 180 B	600	D	10	Corolla 1200 SL	600	D	13
1800 Mk II LC/1800 S	600	D	17	Bluebird 180B Auto.	650	D	10	Corona 1500	550	D	13
2200	1000	D	12	Bluebird 180SSS	650	D	14	Corona 1900 Mk II	600	D	18
Midget/Sprite	1000	D	13	Cherry 100A range	700	D	8	Corona 2000 Mk II	600	D	13
Mini 850	600	D	3	Cherry 120	600	D	7	Crown 2300	600	D	15
Mini 1000/Clubman	600	D	8	Sunny 1200 range	600	D	7	Crown 2600	600	D	11
Mini Cooper S	600	D	4								
				FIAT				**VAUXHALL**			
Jaguar				124/124S/125/127	1000	N	12	Firenza 1600/2300	650-700	C	9
2·4	600	D	8	128/500/600D/850	1000	N	12	Ventora FD/FE	500-550	C	9
3·4/3·8 S type	600	D	2					Victor FC	600-650	C	9
3·8	600	D	4	**FORD**				Victor FD 1600 cc	500-550	C	9
				Anglia 105E	700-800	C	10	Victor FD 2000 cc	650-700	C	9
Morris				Anglia 123E	700-800	C	6	Victor FD 3·3 (Estate)	500-550	C	9
Marina 1·3	650	D	12	Classic Capri 109E	700-800	C	8	Victor FE 1800/2000	650-700	C	9
Marina 1·8	800	D	14	Classic Capri 109E GT	700-800	C	10	Victor FE 3·3 (Estate)	500-550	C	9
Marina 1·8 TC	800	D	11	Corsair 120E	700-800	C	8	Viscount	500-550	D	9
MG 1100	1000	D	9	Corsair 120E GT	700-800	C	10	Viva HA	600-650	C	9
MGB	600	D	13	Corsair V4 1700 cc	700-800	C	8	Viva HB 1159 cc	600-650	C	4½
MGC	1000	D	2	Corsair V4 2000 cc	700-800	C	10	Viva HB 1600 cc/GT	650-700	C	9
Minor 1000	600	D	6	Cortina Mk I 1200 cc	700-800	C	8	Viva HB SL90	800-850	C	9
				Cortina Mk I 1500 cc	700-800	C	8	Viva HC 1159 cc	600-650	C	4½
Riley				Cortina Mk II to 1968	700-800	C	8	Viva HC 1600 cc	650-700	C	9
Elf	600	D	8	Cortina Mk II 1968/70	700-800	C	10	VX4/90 FC	600-650	C	9
				Cortina Mk III	700-800	C	6	VX4/FD/FE	650-700	C	9
Rover				Escort	700-800	C	6				
2000 SC/Automatic	550-600	D	4	Zephyr/Zodiac Mk III	700-800	C	8	**VOLKSWAGEN MODELS**			
2000 TC	700-750	D	6					Check with your VW dealer			
				MAZDA							
Triumph models				RX3	700	D	See p. 164	**VOLVO**			
Recommended static timing only (see p. 164)								120/142/144/145/164	Check with your dealer		

134 Removing the rocker cover on an overhead-valve engine

Disconnect any water heater hoses attached to the top of the rocker cover and push them to one side. Undo the hose between the rocker cover

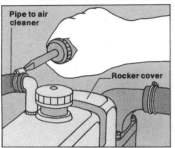

Pipe to air cleaner

Rocker cover

and the air cleaner. Remove the air cleaner (see p. 123). If necessary, disconnect the

carburettor linkage and disengage any high-tension leads from the clip on the rocker cover. Undo the rocker cover

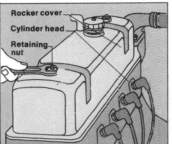

Rocker cover

Cylinder head

Retaining nut

nuts or bolts—either in the centre or around the flange—or the retaining clips. Lift off the cover.

135 Removing the cover on an overhead-camshaft engine

In most cases the cover that protects the camshaft is not obstructed. On the Hillman Imp range, however, the petrol pump is fixed to the cover. Remove the fuel pipes. Undo

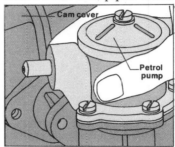

Cam cover

Petrol pump

the two securing nuts and remove the pump and the pump

spacer gasket. Remove the nuts that secure the cover to

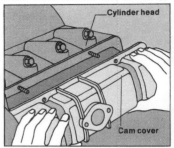

Cylinder head

Cam cover

the cylinder head and lift off the cover.

On twin-overhead-camshaft engines, remove the air cleaner and take off the cam covers and their gaskets.

136 Identifying when the inlet and exhaust valves are open and closed

The clearances for inlet and exhaust valves are usually different. To find the inlet valves, trace the inlet manifold from the carburettor to the cylinder head. Find the exhaust valves by following the exhaust manifold.

The clearance on each valve must be set with the valve

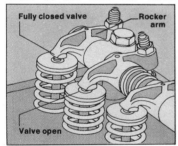

Fully closed valve

Rocker arm

Valve open

fully closed. It is difficult to tell when a valve is fully closed, but easy to see if it is fully open, because the engine can be turned forwards (clockwise) to find the point at which a rocker arm pushes down on the valve stem to the greatest extent.

Use a spanner on the crankshaft pulley nut to turn

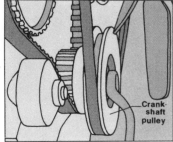

Crankshaft pulley

the engine until the valve to be adjusted is fully open, then rotate the crankshaft through a further 360 degrees. The valve will then be fully closed.

Never turn an engine backwards; it can slacken the

timing chain on some units or damage the bearings.

The rule of nine

On in-line engines, when one valve is fully open a corresponding valve is fully closed—so the effort of turning over the engine to adjust each valve clearance can be avoided. There is a simple method of 'pairing' valves called the 'rule of nine' which can be used on four-cylinder in-line engines with valves positioned in the most common

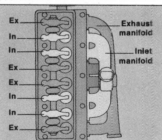

Exhaust manifold

Inlet manifold

Ex
In
In
Ex
Ex
In
In
Ex

sequence: exhaust, inlet, inlet, exhaust, exhaust, inlet, inlet, exhaust. Count the valve nearest the radiator as No. 1 and number the others consecutively so that the valve furthest away is No. 8.

If valve No. 1 is fully open, valve No. 8 is fully closed and in the right position to be adjusted (1+8=9). If valve No. 4 is open, valve No. 5 is closed (4+5=9); and so on.

A similar rule, the 'rule of 13', can be applied to six-cylinder in-line engines with the same sequence. If valve No. 1 is fully open, valve No. 12 is fully closed (1+12=13).

Crossflow engines

On some crossflow engines, such as Fords, the exhaust

and inlet valves alternate. With the crossflow design, use

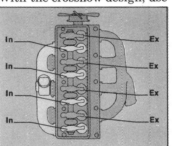

In
In
In
In
Ex
Ex
Ex
Ex

one of the two charts below.

Four-cylinder in-line engine

Valve		open, valve		closed
	7	open, valve	1	closed
,,	8	,,	,,	2	,,
,,	5	,,	,,	3	,,
,,	6	,,	,,	4	,,
,,	3	,,	,,	5	,,
,,	4	,,	,,	6	,,
,,	1	,,	,,	7	,,
,,	2	,,	,,	8	,,

Six-cylinder in-line engine

Valve		open, valve		closed
	11	open, valve	1	closed
,,	12	,,	,,	2	,,
,,	9	,,	,,	3	,,
,,	10	,,	,,	4	,,
,,	7	,,	,,	5	,,
,,	8	,,	,,	6	,,
,,	5	,,	,,	7	,,
,,	6	,,	,,	8	,,
,,	3	,,	,,	9	,,
,,	4	,,	,,	10	,,
,,	1	,,	,,	11	,,
,,	2	,,	,,	12	,,

Chrysler Avenger

On the Chrysler Avenger engine, the inlet and exhaust valves of each cylinder must be adjusted when both are closed, with the piston at top-dead-centre on its compression stroke.

To check that the piston is on the compression stroke, remove the distributor cap and turn the engine until the points are just opening. Then note to which segment inside the distributor cap the rotor arm is pointing.

Trace the lead from that segment to the engine. The piston in that cylinder will then be at top-dead-centre. This is accurate enough for setting the clearances.

Volvo engines

On four-cylinder models, valves 1, 2, 3 and 5 are adjusted when No. 1 piston is on top-dead-centre, and valves 4, 6, 7 and 8 are set when No. 4 piston is on top-dead-centre.

On six-cylinder Volvo engines, valves 1, 2, 3, 6, 7 and 10 should be adjusted when No. 1 piston is on top-dead-centre, and 4, 5, 8, 9, 11 and 12 when No. 6 is on top-dead-centre.

ADJUSTING V-ENGINE VALVE CLEARANCES

When a valve is open, turn the crankshaft 360 degrees to close it

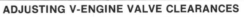

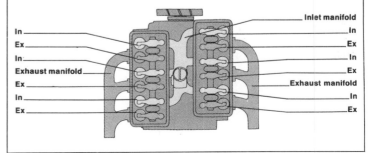

In
Ex
In
Exhaust manifold
Ex
In
Ex

Inlet manifold
In
Ex
In
Ex
Exhaust manifold

137 Adjusting the valve clearances on overhead-valve engines with rocker shafts

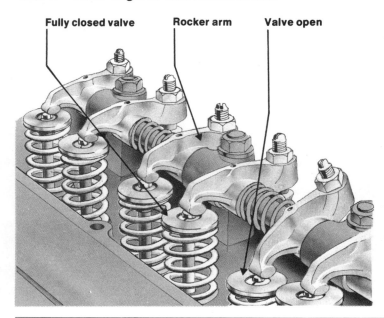

Fully closed valve   Rocker arm   Valve open

On engines with a rocker shaft and rocker arms, the valve clearance is adjusted between the arm and the valve stem.

Using the rule of nine, if possible (see p. 109), turn the engine until No. 1 valve is fully closed. Insert the recommended size of feeler blade

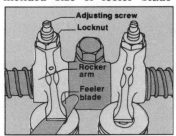

between the rocker arm and the tip of the valve stem.

If the blade is not an exact fit—it should slide between the two surfaces under slight pressure of the fingers—use a

spanner to slacken the rocker-arm locknut.

Inside the locknut is an adjusting screw. Turn this with a screwdriver until the

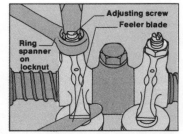

feeler blade is just nipped, then hold the screw still while you tighten the locknut. Insert the blade again. If the gap is incorrect, slacken the locknut and readjust it.

If the gap closes slightly when the locknut is tightened, adjust the gap with a thicker feeler blade. Tighten the lock-

FINDING THE CORRECT VALVE CLEARANCE

	INLET VALVES		EXHAUST VALVES			INLET VALVES		EXHAUST VALVES	
	Setting when hot	Setting when cold	Setting when hot	Setting when cold		Setting when hot	Setting when cold	Setting when hot	Setting when cold
	in. mm.	in. mm.	in. mm.	in. mm.		in. mm.	in. mm.	in. mm	in. mm.
AUDI					**Rover**				
100 range	·006 0·15		·016 0·4		2000, SC, SC Automatic, TC		·008–·010		·013–·015
BMW					**Triumph**				
1600		·006 0·15		·006 0·15	1300, 1500, 2000		·010		·010
1800		·008 0·2		·008 0·2	Dolomite		·008		·018
2000		·008 0·2		·008 0·2	GT6		·010		·010
2002		·008 0·2		·008 0·2	Herald 1200, 12/50,				
2500		·010 0·25		·010 0·25	13/60		·010		·010
2800		·012 0·3		·012 0·3	Spitfire		·010		·010
					Stag		·006–·008		·006–·008
BRITISH LEYLAND					Toledo 1300		·010		·010
Austin					TR4, TR4A, TR5, TR6		·010		·010
A40 Farina		·012		·012	Vitesse Mk I, Mk II		·010		·010
A60		·015		·015					
A110		·012		·012	**Wolseley**				
Maxi 1500		·016–·018		·020–·022	Hornet		·012		·012
1750		·016–·018		·020–·022					
					CHRYSLER				
Austin/Morris					**Chrysler Rootes**				
1100, 1300, 1300 GT		·012		·012	Avenger		·008		·016
1300 Countryman		·012		·012	Avenger GT		·010		·016
1800 Mk II, 1800 S		·015		·015	Chamois		·004–·006		·006–·008
2200		·016–·018		·020–·022	Chrysler 180		·010		·014
Mini 850, 1000		·012		·012	Hillman Minx 1500	·012		·014	
Mini Clubman		·012		·012	Humber Sceptre,				
Mini Cooper S		·012		·012	Hunter 1500, 1725	·012		·014	
Sprite		·012		·012	Imp		·004–·006		·004–·006
					Singer Gazelle, Vogue	·012		·014	
Jaguar					Stiletto		·006–·008		·013–·015
2·4, 3·4, 3·8, 3·8 S					Sunbeam		·006–·008		·013–·015
type		·004		·006	Sunbeam Alpine,				
					Rapier		·013		·013
MG					Sunbeam Sport		·006–·008		·013–·015
Midget		·012		·012					
1100		·012		·012	**Chrysler Simca**				
MGB, MGC		·015		·015	1000, 1100, 1100S		·012 0·3		·014 0·35
					1301, 1301 Automatic		·008 0·2		·010 0·25
Morris					1501, 1501 Automatic		·008 0·2		·014 0·35
Marina 1·3		·012		·012					
Marina 1·8		·013		·013	**CITROËN**				
Marina 1·8 TC		·013		·013	Ami 6, Ami 8, Dyane		·006 0·15		·006 0·15
Minor 1000		·012		·012					
					DAF				
Riley					33, 44		·004 0·1		·006 0·15
Elf		·012		·012	55, 66		·006 0·15		·008 0·2

nut and check the gap with the correct-sized blade.

As a final check, try the gap with blades one size smaller and one size larger. The smaller blade should be loose.

Daf engines
The method of adjustment varies. The 55 and 66 models have a raised oblong adjusting screw. A special spanner is needed to grip the screw.

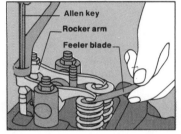

Early 33 models have adjusters with an Allen-key head.

Later models of the 33 and 44 have a slot for a screwdriver in each adjuster.

Ford four-cylinder, in-line
British Ford four-cylinder in-line engines made since April 1970 have an adjusting nut on the push-rod end of the rocker arm. Insert the recommended size of feeler blade between the rocker-arm pad and the tip of the valve stem, with the valve fully closed. If the blade is not an exact fit,

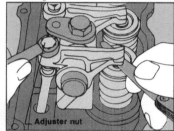

with the valve fully closed. If the blade is not an exact fit,

use a ring spanner to turn the self-locking adjusting nut until the blade is just pinched between the two surfaces. Remove the feeler blade.

Fiat engines
The adjusters are square-headed, and the manufacturers recommend the use of two special spanners, one a socket spanner shaped like a

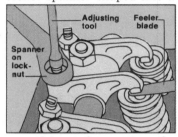

screwdriver, for setting the valve clearances. Slacken the locknut, and use the special

socket tool to turn the adjuster until the correct size of feeler blade fits into the gap.

Volkswagen engines
The adjusters are over the springs. The clearance on both valves of each cylinder can be set at the same time. Adjust

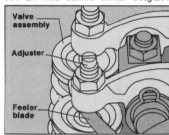

with the engine turned until the piston is at top dead centre, at the end of its compression stroke (see p. 164), when both valves will be closed. Repeat for each cylinder.

FINDING THE CORRECT VALVE CLEARANCE

	INLET VALVES		EXHAUST VALVES			
	Setting when hot	Setting when cold	Setting when hot	Setting when cold		
	in. mm.	in. mm.	in. mm.	in.	mm.	
DATSUN						
240Z Sports	·010 0·25		·012 0·3			
260C Custom de luxe	·010 0·25		·012 0·3			
260C Custom de luxe Automatic	·010 0·25		·012 0·3			
Bluebird 160B, 160B Automatic	·011		·011			
Bluebird 180B, 180B Automatic	·010 0·25		·012 0·3			
Cherry range	·014 0·35	·010 0·25	·014 0·35	·010	0·25	
Sunny range	·014 0·35	·010 0·25	·014 0·35	·010	0·25	
FIAT						
124		·006 0·15		·008	0·2	
124S		·008 0·2		·008	0·2	
125		·018 0·45		·02	0·5	
127		·006 0·15		·008	0·2	
128		·012 0·3		·016	0·4	
500, 600D		·006 0·15		·006	0·15	
850		·006 0·15		·008	0·2	
FORD						
Anglia 105E, 123E	·010		·017			
Classic Capri 109E		·010		·020		
Classic Capri 109E GT		·011		·023		
Corsair 120E		·008		·018		
Corsair 120E GT		·012		·022		
Corsair V4 1700 cc, 2000 cc		·012		·020		
Cortina Mk I, 1200 cc, 1500 cc		·008		·018		
Cortina Mk II to 1968	·010		·017			
Cortina Mk II 1968/70	·010		·020			
Cortina Mk III ohv	·010		·020			
Cortina Mk III ohc	·008		·010			
Escort	·010		·017			
Escort GT	·012		·022			
Zephyr, Zodiac Mk III		·014		·014		
RENAULT						
R4, R5, R5TL, R6, R8		·006 0·15		·008	0·2	
R10		·008 0·2		·012	0·3	
R12, TL, TS, R15 TL		·006 0·15		·008	0·2	
R15 TS, R16, R17 TL		·008 0·2		·010	0·25	
R17 TS		·010 0·25		·012	0·3	
TOYOTA						
Carina 1600	·008 0·2		·013 0·33			
Celica 1600	·008 0·2		·013 0·33			
Corolla 1100, 1200, 1200 SL	·008 0·2		·012 0·3			
Corona 1500, 1900 Mk II, 2000	·008 0·2		·014 0·33			
Crown 2300	·007 0·18		·010 0·25			
Crown 2600	·007 0·18		·010 0·25			
VAUXHALL						
Firenza 1600, 2300 cc	·007–·010		·015–·018			
Ventora FD	·013		·013			
Ventora FE	·013		·013			
Victor FC	·013		·013			
Victor FD 1600	·007–·010		·007–·010			
Victor 2000	·007–·010		·007–·010			
Victor FD 3·3 Estate	·013		·013			
Victor FE, 1800 cc, 2000 cc	·007–·010		·015–·018			
Victor FE 3·3 Estate, Viscount	·013		·013			
Viva HA	·006		·010			
Viva HB 1159 cc	·006		·010			
Viva HB 1600 cc	·007–·010		·015–·018			
Viva HB GT	·007–·010		·015–·018			
Viva HB SL 90, HC 1159 cc	·008		·008			
Viva HC 1600 cc	·007–·010		·015–·018			
VX 4/90 FC	·013		·013			
VX 4/90 FD	·007–·010		·015–·018			
VX 4/90 FE	·007–·010		·015–·018			
VOLKSWAGEN						
Beetle 1200		·008 0·2		·012	0·3	
Beetle 1300		·004 0·1		·004	0·1	
Beetle 1600, FB Variant 411, 412 ranges		·006 0·15		·006	0·15	
K70		·008 0·2		·008	0·2	
VOLVO						
120	·016–·018		·016–·018			
142	·016–·018		·016–·018			
144	·016–·018		·016–·018			
145	·016–·018		·016–·018			
164	·020–·022		·020–·022			

138 Adjusting the valve clearances on overhead-valve engines without rocker shafts

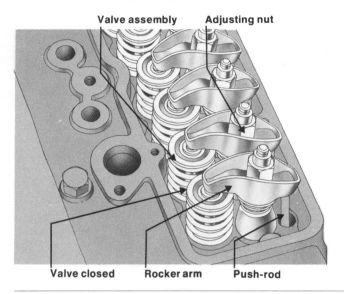

Valve assembly   Adjusting nut

Valve closed   Rocker arm   Push-rod

On some engines, the rocker arms are mounted on individual studs. This system is used on British Ford V4 and V6 engines, and the Vauxhall Viva. Set the valve clearance on Ford engines with the engine running (see Job 139).

With the valve to be adjusted fully closed (see p. 109),

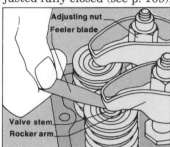

Adjusting nut
Feeler blade

Valve stem
Rocker arm

insert the recommended size of feeler blade (see p. 110) be-

tween the rocker arm and valve stem. If the blade is not a tight fit, turn the adjusting nut clockwise, with a socket or

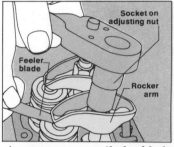

Socket on adjusting nut

Feeler blade

Rocker arm

ring spanner, until the blade is pinched.

Remove the blade and check the clearance with blades one size smaller and one size larger. The smaller one should be a loose fit, the larger one should not enter the gap at all.

139 Adjusting the valve clearances while the engine is running

Some engine manufacturers recommend setting the valve clearances while the engine is running.

Use a strip feeler gauge, which is longer than normal and made of hardened steel to withstand the hammering of the rocker arm and valve mechanism.

Undo the throttle stop screw slightly (see pp. 128-9) so

that the engine is running at its slowest idling speed. Switch off the engine and remove the rocker cover. Restart the engine.

Start at No. 1 cylinder (see p. 109) and use a ring spanner to slacken the locknut that holds one end of the rocker arm to the top of the push-rod. Leave the spanner attached to the nut.

Hold the correct size of feeler blade (see p. 110) in one hand

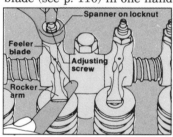

Spanner on locknut

Feeler blade

Adjusting screw

Rocker arm

and a screwdriver, on the adjusting screw, in the other.

Insert the feeler blade into the gap between the rocker arm and the tip of the valve stem. Turn the adjusting screw inside the locknut until the feeler blade is just pinched. Hold the screwdriver firmly, put down the feeler gauge and tighten the locknut.

The engine can be kept running while all the valves are adjusted, but never have more than one locknut or adjusting screw loose at the same time.

140 Adjusting the valve clearances when the rocker arms are worn

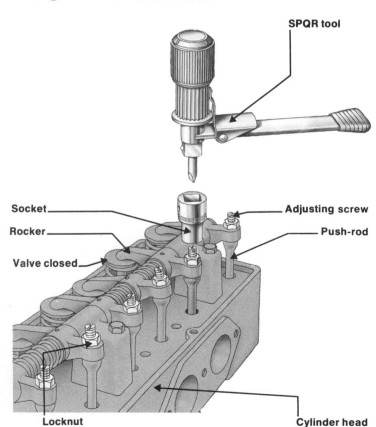

SPQR tool

Socket

Rocker

Valve closed

Adjusting screw

Push-rod

Locknut   Cylinder head

An SPQR Tappet Adjuster is particularly useful if any of the rocker arms are worn, and

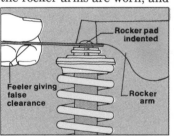

Rocker pad indented

Feeler giving false clearance

Rocker arm

a feeler blade gives a false reading. The tool consists of a screwdriver bit and interchangeable sockets.

Check that the valve you are adjusting is fully closed (see p. 109). Select a socket of the correct size and fit the tool over the locknut. Hold down

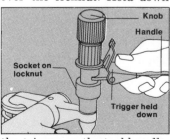

Knob

Handle

Socket on locknut

Trigger held down

the trigger on the tool handle, and turn the knob until the

screwdriver bit fits into the adjusting screw.

Keep holding the trigger down and turn the tool handle anticlockwise—just enough to slacken the locknut.

With the trigger still held down, turn the knob clockwise until you hear a loud click. This indicates that the adjusting screw has been screwed down until it is in contact with the top of the push-rod.

Release the trigger. Consult the chart supplied with the tool, to find out how many clicks are needed to give the

Turn knob correct number of clicks

correct clearance. Turn the knob anticlockwise the correct number of clicks. Hold the knob to retain this setting.

Hold down the trigger and turn the handle clockwise to tighten the locknut.

141 Adjusting the valve clearances on overhead-camshaft engines

There are two basic types of overhead-camshaft engine—a direct-acting camshaft and an indirect-acting camshaft. In both types the camshaft is clearly seen, and it is easy to position the cam lobes so that each valve is fully closed.

Direct-acting camshaft engines

The cam lobes bear directly on to the cam followers, which are fitted over the valves. Adjustment is usually made by adding or removing shims,

between the cam follower and the valve stem (see Job 142),

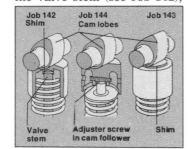

Job 142 Shim   Job 144 Cam lobes   Job 143

Valve stem   Adjuster screw in cam follower   Shim

or between the cam follower and the cam lobe (see Job 143). But on Vauxhall engines, the

gap is adjusted by turning a screw in the side of the cam follower (see Job 144).

Camshafts with the shims set between the valve and the follower have to be removed, so that the shims can be changed to give the correct gap (see Job 142).

Indirect-acting camshafts

On an indirect-acting assembly, the camshaft operates a finger that bears on the valve.

In all cases it is possible to set the valve clearance without removing the camshaft. On some engines there is an

adjusting screw at the end of the finger (see Job 146). On

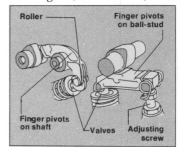

Roller   Finger pivots on ball-stud

Finger pivots on shaft   Valves   Adjusting screw

others a roller is used (see Job 145). Valve adjustment on these engines is relatively simple, and no special tools are needed.

142 Adjusting the valve clearances when the shims are inside the cam followers

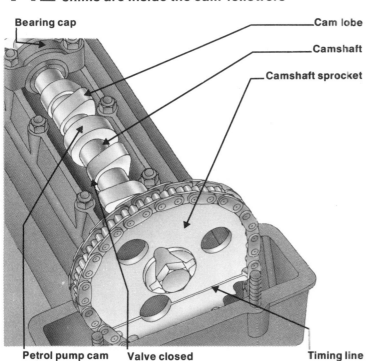

Bearing cap   Cam lobe

Camshaft

Camshaft sprocket

Petrol pump cam   Valve closed   Timing line

On Jaguar and Hillman Imp engines, the adjusting shims are fitted inside the cam

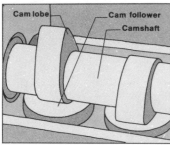

Cam lobe   Cam follower   Camshaft

followers, which are mounted on top of the valve stem.

To adjust the clearances the camshaft must be removed and, after it has been refitted, the valve timing reset correctly (see pp. 176-7).

On twin-overhead-camshaft engines, one camshaft should never be rotated while the other is in place. This would

cause the valves to clash. Remove one camshaft while turning and adjusting the clearances on the other.

Write down a list of the valves in order, counting the one nearest to the radiator as No. 1.

The clearance between each follower and cam must be

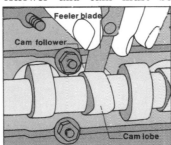

Feeler blade

Cam follower

Cam lobe

measured with the valve closed—when the cam base is nearest its follower and the cam lobe points upwards,

directly away from the valve.

Turn the engine over to close each valve. Measure the clearance between the base of each cam and its follower, by inserting feeler blades of different sizes until you find one that is an exact fit. Write the sizes of the clearances on your list of the valves.

When your list of measurements is complete, write down the clearance recommended for each valve by the engine manufacturer (see pp. 110-11).

The list will now show which valves must be adjusted—which is done by putting thicker or thinner shims inside the cam follower.

Turn the engine so that No. 1 piston is at top dead centre (see p. 164). Mark the position of the camshaft on its sprocket or timing chain, then remove it (see p. 169). Never turn the engine while the camshaft is out of the car.

Lift off the cam follower and take out the shims. Keep them in the correct order.

The shims may have their sizes etched in their surfaces. If not, carefully measure each of them with a micrometer (see p. 34).

To find out the sizes of the shims needed to adjust the clearance, do a sum for each valve. For example:

Actual valve clearance .022 in.
Deduct the recommended valve clearance . . . .017 in.
This equals excess valve clearance . . . .005 in.
Add thickness of existing shim, say . . . .090 in.
Which means that the thickness of shims required for correct clearance is . . . .095 in.

To get the correct clearance on that particular valve, you would need a shim or shims

totalling .095 in. thick. Use shims removed from another tappet where possible, to save buying more new ones than necessary.

Insert shims of the correct size in all the cam followers

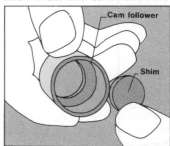

Cam follower

Shim

and refit them to the engine. Replace the camshaft, but do not reconnect the timing chain. Tighten the bolts to the manufacturer's torque setting (check if necessary at a dealer's).

Rotate the camshaft to close each valve in turn, and use feeler gauges to check the clearances again. If any of them are incorrect, remove the camshaft again and correct them.

When all the clearances are correct, turn the camshaft so that it is in the same position as it was before it was removed.

On Jaguar twin-camshaft engines use the special timing

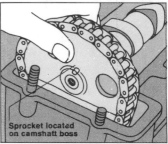

Sprocket located on camshaft boss

plate (see p. 177) supplied by the makers. Fit the timing chain to the sprocket, and position the sprocket on the camshaft to reset the valve timing (see pp. 176-7).

143 Adjusting the valve clearances on a Fiat engine with shims outside the cam followers

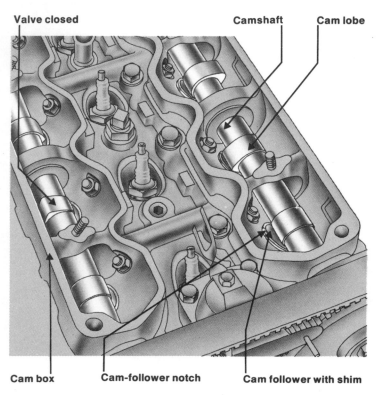

Valve closed   Camshaft   Cam lobe

Cam box   Cam-follower notch   Cam follower with shim

Fiat overhead-camshaft engines have shims fitted into recesses on top of the cam followers: the movement of the valves depends on the thickness of the shims.

Make a list of the valves, counting the one nearest the radiator as No. 1. The clearance between the base of the cam and the shim is measured with the valve fully closed. See that the base of the cam is nearest the shim, with the cam lobe pointing directly upwards away from it.

Measure the clearance between the base of the cam and the shim by inserting feeler

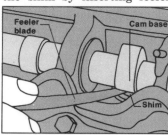

blades of different sizes, until one fits. Write down each clearance in turn.

When the list is complete, write down the clearance recommended for each valve. Deduct one figure from the other and you will know the valves that need to be adjusted, and the shims required.

On the valves that need to be adjusted, turn the cam follower so that the notch is visible. Use a special forked tool, obtainable from a Fiat

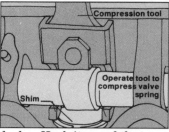

dealer. Hook it round the camshaft, to push down the edges

of the cam follower against the pressure of the valve

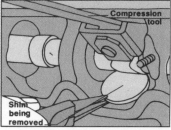

spring. Use pliers to pull out the shim.

Check the size stamped on the shim or measure its thickness with a micrometer (see p. 34).

Calculate the shims you need to give the correct thickness. For example:

Actual clearance:	·022 in.
Correct clearance:	·017 in.
Equals excess of:	·005 in.
Existing shim:	·090 in.
Plus excess:	·005 in.
New shim needed:	·095 in.

To get the correct clearance on that particular valve, you will need shims totalling ·095 in. thick. Buy new shims as they are required, but where possible use shims removed from other cam followers.

Put the new shims of the correct thickness into the top of the cam follower. Release the compression tool and repeat the operation on all valves.

144 Adjusting the valve clearances on a Vauxhall overhead-camshaft engine

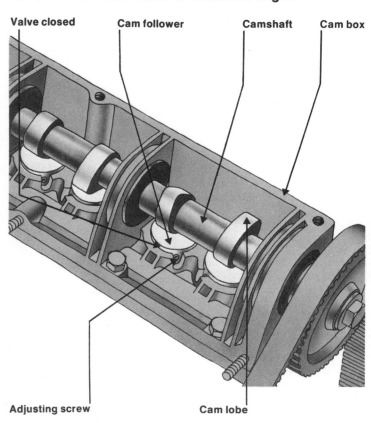

Valve closed   Cam follower   Camshaft   Cam box

Adjusting screw   Cam lobe

The valve clearances on the Vauxhall overhead-camshaft engines are adjusted by a tapered screw fitted to the side of the cam follower, just below the camshaft.

Turn the engine to close the valve you are working on —the cam base must be close to the cam follower, with the cam lobe pointing directly upwards away from the cam follower. Turn the cam follower, on the closed valve, in its

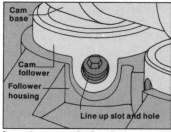

housing until the hole in its face is lined up with the slot in the follower housing.

Insert the recommended size of feeler blade between the cam base and the top of the follower, to check the valve clearance.

Fit a ⅛ in. Allen key into the

slot in the cam follower. Turn the Allen key until you feel

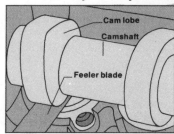

the feeler blade just pinched.

Each full turn of the key will alter the gap by ·003 in.

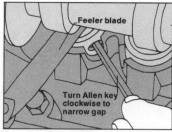

Since the valve clearances have a ·003 in. tolerance (see p. 110), they can always be adjusted in this way within the range recommended by the manufacturer. Turn the engine one full turn and re-check the gap.

145 Adjusting the valve clearances on BMW engines

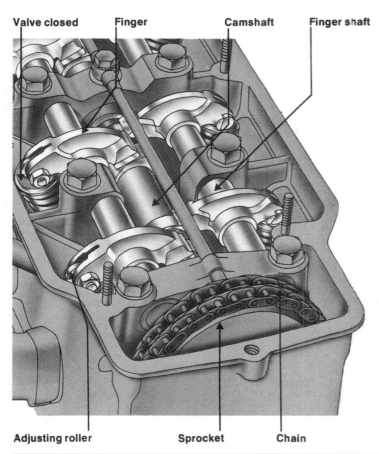

Valve closed · Finger · Camshaft · Finger shaft

Adjusting roller · Sprocket · Chain

Valve adjustment on BMW overhead-camshaft engines is by a roller that bears on the top of the valve stem. The roller is attached to a finger which pivots on its own shaft, and is operated by the engine's camshaft.

Turn the engine so that the valve you want to adjust (see p. 109) is fully closed. The base of the cam must be nearest to the finger, with the cam lobe pointing directly upwards away from the finger.

Insert the recommended size of feeler blade (see p. 109)

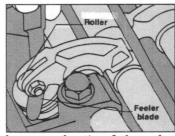

between the tip of the valve stem and the roller.

If it is not an exact fit, the blade should be just pinched and resistance should be felt when sliding it between the two surfaces.

To adjust the valve clear-ance, loosen the locknut at the side of the roller with a span-

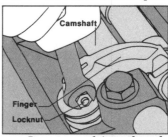

ner. Insert a rod into the ad-justing hole and turn it to

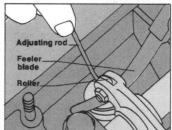

rotate the roller until the blade is just pinched. Hold the rod to keep the setting while you tighten the locknut.

Check the gap again. If it has narrowed as the locknut was tightened, repeat the adjustment—if necessary use a slightly thicker blade to allow for closing the gap. Tighten the locknut.

146 Adjusting the valve clearances on indirect overhead-camshaft Ford and Datsun engines

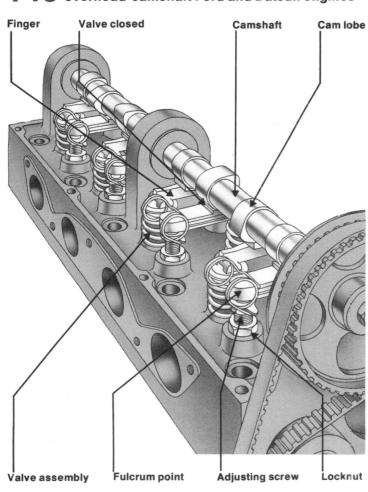

Finger · Valve closed · Camshaft · Cam lobe

Valve assembly · Fulcrum point · Adjusting screw · Locknut

On Ford and Datsun overhead-camshaft engines, with in-direct-acting shafts, the lobes of the cams push down fingers that open the valves. The gap is adjusted by raising or lower-ing the fulcrum point on which the finger pivots. (This system is used particularly on the British and some German and American Fords, the Datsun 'L' series engines and the Mercedes overhead-cam-shaft engines.)

Turn the engine so that the first valve to be adjusted is closed (see p. 109), with the base of the cam nearest the finger and the lobe pointing upwards. Insert a feeler blade

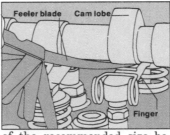

of the recommended size be-tween the cam base and the finger.

To adjust, loosen the lock-nut on the adjusting screw. Put an open-ended spanner on the adjusting nut and turn it to lower or raise the ful-crum point, until the feeler blade is just pinched. On some

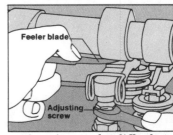

engines it may be difficult to use an open-ended spanner: a special shaped spanner may be needed. Hold the ad-justing nut firmly, to keep the

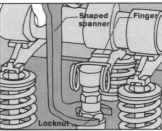

setting accurate, while you tighten the locknut.

Check the gap again. If it has closed as the locknut was tightened, repeat the adjust-ment. If necessary, use a slightly thicker blade to allow for closing. Repeat the opera-tion on all the valves.

Recheck the gaps after turn-ing the engine one full turn.

147 Adjusting the valve clearances on overhead-camshaft engines with inclined valves

Engines with fingers that operate inclined valves have adjusting screws at the end of

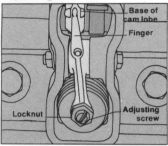

the finger nearest to the valve. (Cars fitted with this type include the Chrysler 180; Datsun 200L; NSU Prinz; Peugeot 104, 204 and 304; some Toyota Corona and Crown models and the Volkswagen K70.)

In most cases the engine has a single cam cover and gasket, which have to be re-

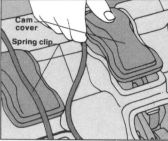

moved. The exception to this is the VW K70, which has individual covers, held by spring clips, over each valve. Release the clips and lift off the covers and gaskets.

Turn the engine over so that the valve to be adjusted is fully closed—with the base of the cam nearest the finger and the lobe pointing away from it (see p. 109).

If the camshaft cannot be

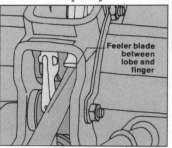

seen—say, on the Peugeot 304—turn the engine so that the valve is fully open (see p. 109). Use a spanner on the crankshaft pulley nut and turn the engine through 360 degrees. The valve to be adjusted will now be fully closed.

Insert the recommended size of feeler blade (see pp. 110-11) into the gap between the end of the finger and the base of the cam lobe. If the blade is not an exact fit between the two surfaces, the

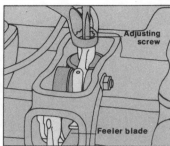

clearance must be adjusted. Loosen the locknut on the adjuster screw with a ring spanner. Turn the adjuster screw with a screwdriver until the feeler blade is pinched. Hold the screw in this position and tighten the locknut. Check the gap again. If it closed as the locknut was tightened, repeat the adjustment and, if necessary, use a blade ·001 in. thicker.

Turn the engine one full turn and recheck.

A TYPICAL OVERHEAD CAMSHAFT

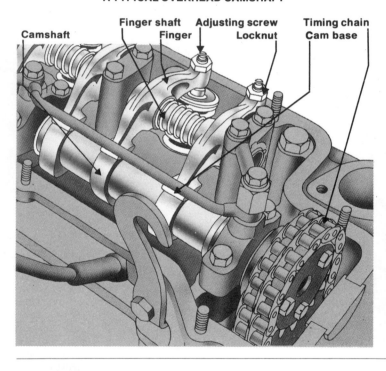

THE VOLKSWAGEN K70 OVERHEAD CAMSHAFT

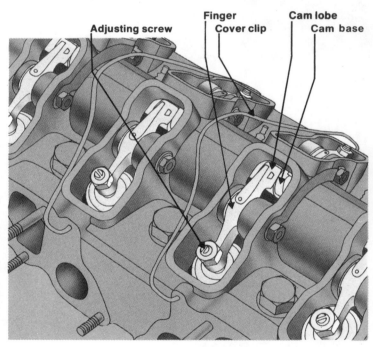

148 Checking for wear on the valve-operating mechanism

If the valve clearances on an overhead-camshaft engine have to be repeatedly checked and altered, some part of the valve-operating mechanism is probably worn and will have to be replaced.

This is usually caused when the hardened surface of a component wears, and the softer metal beneath it is constantly compressed by the action of the mechanism.

On engines that use cam followers with the adjusting shims between the followers and the valve stem, check the

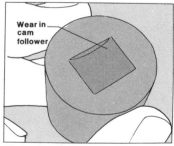

contact face of the follower where it meets the cam lobe.

If it is indented, fit a new set of cam followers.

On Vauxhall engines, check also on the condition of the

adjusting screws and renew them if needed. Special replacement screws are available from Vauxhall dealers.

On the finger type of cam mechanism, check the finger

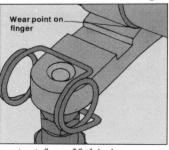

contact face. If this is worn or showing signs of 'chipping' fit

a new set of fingers. On all assemblies, check the condition of the camshaft lobes. If they are crazing on the tip of

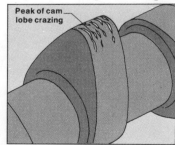

the lobe, the hard surface has become soft and a new camshaft will have to be fitted—a garage job.

149 Checking for wear on the shafts and sprockets of an overhead-camshaft engine

If a drive-chain is worn, it can upset the valve timing, it could slip off the sprockets—which might damage the valves and pistons—and it could cause poor running.

Check the chain for wear, make sure that it is under tension and fitted correctly to all the sprockets. Turn the engine clockwise (see p. 164) to apply the correct tension.

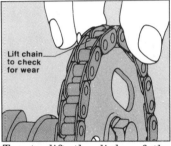
Lift chain to check for wear

Try to lift the links of the chain away from the teeth of the camshaft sprocket. If the chain can be lifted off the sprocket teeth, it is badly

worn and should be renewed.

Most chains are endless—without a joining link—and the whole timing chain case has to be dismantled to remove it. This is a garage job.

While checking the chain, remove the sprocket from the camshaft boss and slip it out of the timing chain (see p. 169). Check the condition of the camshaft-sprocket teeth. If they are pointed

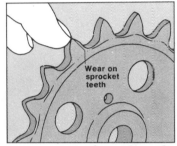
Wear on sprocket teeth

or worn at the sides, the chain will not ride evenly over them. Fit a new camshaft sprocket.

150 Checking the rate of wear on overhead-camshaft drive-belts

Sprockets on a belt-driven overhead-camshaft engine rarely wear, but the drive-belt itself—made of a composition material—may deteriorate. If the belt is worn it is likely to break, which could stop the camshaft and damage the engine.

Check the condition of the belt every time the cover is removed to check the valve clearances. Examine the belt closely. Signs of cracking in

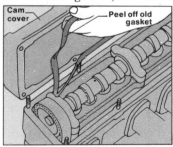
Drive belt starting to crack

the belt material are good indications that it has weakened and should be renewed. Make

sure that none of the teeth on the belt is missing or chipped.

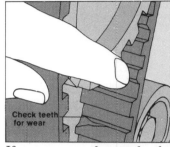
Check teeth for wear

If some are damaged, the sprocket could slip round inside the belt and upset the timing. Fit a new belt to the drive mechanism.

When you fit a new belt, clean all the teeth on the sprocket with methylated spirit to remove any particles of the old belt that might be stuck to them.

Ensure that each sprocket is timed correctly (see pp. 176-7) before you fit the new belt in position.

151 Reassembling the rocker cover and components on an overhead-valve engine

Refit the rocker cover with the gasket that was removed. Start the engine and run it to its normal operating temperature. Listen for tappet noise. If one valve is noisy, check and readjust it.

If all the clearances are correct, stop the engine and remove the rocker cover. Peel off the old gasket and clean inside the rocker cover and the mating flange on the cylinder head.

Soak a new cork rocker-cover gasket in water to make

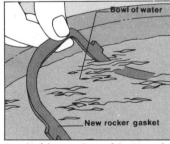
Bowl of water
New rocker gasket

it pliable, and enable it to be shaped to the contours of the rocker cover. Smear both the rocker cover and cylinder-head flanges with high-melting-point grease.

Lay the gasket in position and make sure that it matches the contours of the flange. Fit the rocker cover.

If the cover is held by screws round the flange, fit each screw and tighten them, half a turn at a time.

If the cover is held by two, or three, centre nuts, the nuts will probably have two cup washers with a rubber sealing washer between them. Renew the rubber sealing washers if they are cracked or badly compressed.

If the cover is held by a spring clip, make sure that it is correctly positioned before engaging the clip to secure it.

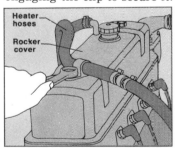
Heater hoses
Rocker cover

Refit the heater hoses and connect the carburettor linkage, if necessary. Replace the

Air cleaner

carburettor air cleaner (see p. 123). Top up the radiator. Start the engine and check the gasket for oil leaks.

152 Reassembling the covers and components on an overhead-camshaft engine

Not all covers on overhead-camshaft engines use a gasket. Check to see if a cover gasket was fitted originally.

Replace the cover with any gasket that was removed. Temporarily connect any necessary parts—for example, the fuel line—and start the engine. Run it until it reaches its normal working temperature. Check to make sure all the valves are quiet. If not, locate the noisy ones and readjust them.

Remove the cover and strip off the old gasket, if one is

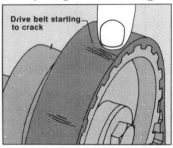
Cam cover
Peel off old gasket

fitted. Clean the faces of the cam cover and the mating flange. If the engine has an alloy cover, clean it only with methylated spirit: do not use a steel scraper or a wire brush.

If the cover has a cork gasket, coat both sides of the gasket in high-melting-point grease and lay it in position. Refit the cover.

In many cases the cover

gasket is thick paper. Coat the two mating surfaces with a soft sealing compound (see p. 166). Position the paper gasket over the cover studs

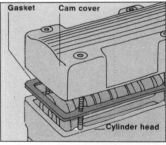
Gasket
Cam cover
Cylinder head

and press it down in position. Fit the cover and tighten the nuts to the recommended torque setting.

Refit the heater hoses. Replace the carburettor air cleaner and connect the breather hose cleaner.

On the Hillman Imp range refit the petrol pump, and

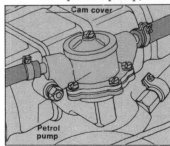
Cam cover
Petrol pump

make sure that the pump operating trigger fits over the camshaft. Connect the fuel line and top up the radiator.

153 Check radiator and heater hoses

Look for fine cracks and hardening of the hoses, which indicate that the rubber is perishing. Either bend the

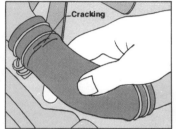

hoses sharply, or squeeze them. Make sure that cables or metal parts have not been rubbing on the hoses. Check the hose clips for tightness.

154 Check the radiator pressure cap

The radiator cap incorporates a primary seal closed with a spring. If pressure builds up in the radiator, the seal opens, and water and steam escape through the radiator overflow. Inspect the seals and

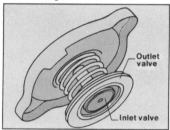

the spring and make sure that the cap's rating, marked in pounds per square inch on the

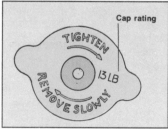

top of the cap, is as recommended in the car handbook.

155 Flush out the radiator block

Remove the radiator cap, unscrew the drain tap, and let the water out. Remove the bottom hose. Run water through a garden hose into the top of the radiator. Let the water run for about five minutes. When clean water is flowing out, turn off the water, refit the bottom hose and tighten the clip. Top up the radiator and replace the cap.

A TYPICAL WATER-COOLED SYSTEM

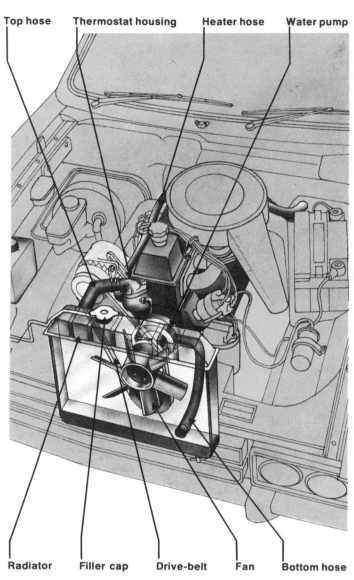

Top hose   Thermostat housing   Heater hose   Water pump

Radiator   Filler cap   Drive-belt   Fan   Bottom hose

156 Points to watch when topping up the radiator

If your car has a semi-sealed system with an overflow reservoir, inspect the level in the reservoir. This is often

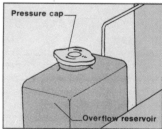

of transparent plastic. If the level is low, undo the filler cap and top up with clean water. In standard radiators, the water level should be about 1 in. below the neck, but it should always cover the core or come up to the level plate.

Where possible, use soft water for topping up the radiator. Hard water tends to build up a 'fur' deposit

which causes overheating.

If a large quantity of water is needed for topping up, allow the engine to cool, or use warm water.

The radiator cap should not be taken off when the engine is hot—the boiling water could gush out and scald you. But if the cap must

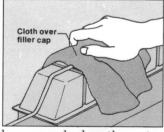

be removed when the water is hot, cover it with a cloth and turn it gently, gradually releasing the pressure. Top up the radiator, but never use cold water if the engine is hot. Replace the cap.

157 Water-pump lubrication

Find the grease nipple, if fitted, in the water-pump cas-

ing and lubricate with a grease gun containing high-melting-

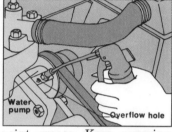

point grease. Keep pumping until grease emerges from the side overflow hole.

For pumps with a blanking plug on top, buy a special

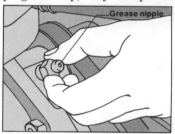

nipple. Screw it into the hole and insert grease until it emerges from the side overflow. Remove the nipple and replace the plug.

If the lubrication hole has a screw, undo it and apply a

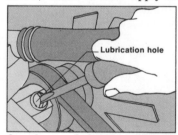

few drops of clean engine oil.

Some pumps are sealed for life, and generally require no maintenance. If it is necessary,

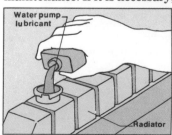

however, a water-pump lubricant can be obtained to pour into the radiator.

158 Adjusting the tension on a dynamo drive-belt

To adjust a dynamo drive-belt, you must move the dynamo. But always bear in mind that if the belt is too tight, the dynamo bearings will have suffered and a new dynamo will have to be fitted.

Loosen the two pivot bolts that hold the dynamo to the

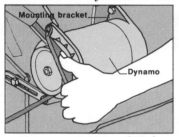

engine mounting bracket. Slacken the adjusting bolts that secure the sliding ad-

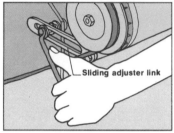

juster link to the engine and dynamo. Put a strong screwdriver or lever between the en-

gine block and the dynamo body. Lever the dynamo away from the engine so that the belt

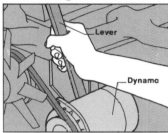

is tightened. Tighten the bolts just enough to hold the dynamo in position. Check the tension of the belt—there

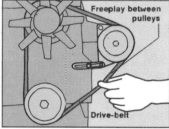

should be about ¾ in. of slack on the longest run of the belt between two of the pulleys.

Once the correct tension has been achieved, fully tighten all the mounting bolts and check the tightness of the drive-belt again.

159 Adjusting the tension on an alternator drive-belt

Because the front and rear bearings on an alternator are ball-races, the drive-belt can be tensioned more tautly than the belt on a dynamo.

If it is too slack, an alternator belt will slip, producing a low charge rate and causing excessive wear. Loosen the two pivot bolts that hold the alter-

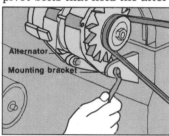

nator to the engine mounting bracket. Slacken the two bolts holding the sliding adjuster

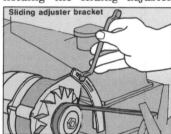

link to the engine block and alternator, so that the alter-

nator can be moved and adjusted.

Place a strong screwdriver or lever between the body of the alternator and the engine block. Lever the alternator

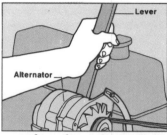

away from the engine until the drive-belt is tight. Do up the bolts on the mounting bracket and check the tightness of the drive-belt—there should be

only very slight movement on the longest length of belt between pulleys. Tighten all the mounting bolts.

160 Adjusting a dynamo drive-belt on a Volkswagen

Dynamo belt adjustment on the air-cooled Volkswagen engine is different from that on other makes of car: you have to fit or remove spacer

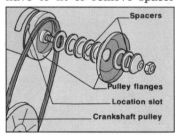

washers between the flanges of the dynamo pulley to increase or decrease the pulley radius.

Turn the engine so that the slot in the rear pulley

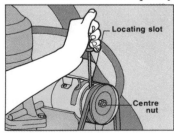

flange is at the top. Wedge a screwdriver in the slot, hold the pulley still and remove the

pulley centre nut. Remove the washers in front of the pulley

flange, and lift off the front pulley flange.

If the drive-belt is slack—with more than ½ in. of play between the dynamo and crankshaft pulleys—remove some of the washers from be-

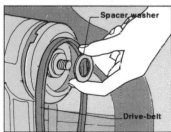

tween the pulley flanges. Put the front pulley flange back in position and fit all the spare spacer washers in front of the flange. Refit the centre nut.

Hold the rear pulley flange still, and tighten the nut.

Fit a spanner on the crank-

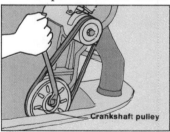

shaft pulley nut and turn the engine over, this will centralise the drive-belt. Check the

belt tension. If it is still too slack, remove more washers. If the belt is too tight, fit some spare washers from the front of the pulley to reduce the pulley diameter and slacken the tension of the drive-belt. There should be no more than ½ in. belt free play between pulleys.

161 Lubricating a dynamo bearing

Many dynamos require no maintenance, but some have a small oil hole in the protruding end of the rear bush casing. Inside the housing is a felt pad which absorbs the oil and keeps the bearing lubricated. Place the nozzle of an oil can in the lubrica-

ting hole and inject two or three drops of clean lubricating oil: engine oil will do. Lack of oil causes premature wear of the bronze bush and makes the generator less efficient.

Avoid over-lubricating the bush. Too much oil can contaminate the interior of the dynamo and cause the unit to fail completely. If this happens it cannot be cleaned, and you will have to fit a new dynamo (see p. 186).

162 Cleaning an AC-type mechanical petrol pump

There are two types of AC pump, one with a glass bowl,

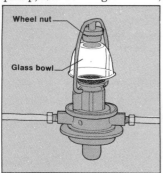

Wheel nut
Glass bowl

the other all steel. To clean them, unscrew the small

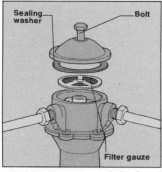

Sealing washer
Bolt
Filter gauze

wheel nut on top of the bowl in the glass type, and undo the bolt at the top of the steel model. Lift off the glass bowl or steel domed cap.

Remove the sealing washer and filter gauze and wash the

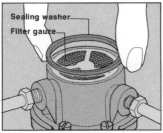

Sealing washer
Filter gauze

gauze thoroughly in a bowl of clean petrol. Remove any sediment which may be lying at the bottom of the filter housing. Replace the filter gauze and check that the sealing washer has not perished. If it shows signs of perishing, fit a new sealing

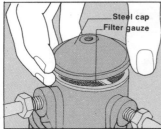

Steel cap
Filter gauze

washer. Replace the bowl or steel cap and tighten the small wheel or bolt. Take care not to overtighten the bolt, otherwise the thread in the pump body may be damaged.

163 Checking and cleaning an SU mechanical petrol pump

Pull the fuel line from the outlet pipe. Remove the securing screws and lift off the top.

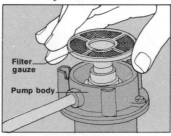

Pump top and outlet pipe
Washer
Filter gauze
Securing screw
Inlet pipe

Take out the washer and filter gauze, and wash the

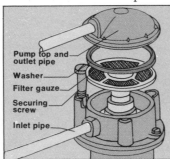

Filter gauze
Pump body

gauze in a bowl of petrol. Clean any sediment from the body of the filter housing. Check that the filter washer has not perished. Refit the gauze and washer. Replace the cap, screws and fuel line.

A TYPICAL FUEL SYSTEM

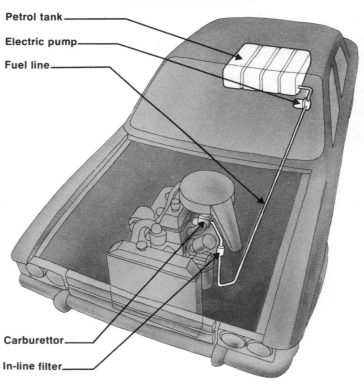

Petrol tank
Electric pump
Fuel line
Carburettor
In-line filter

164 Cleaning and checking an electric fuel pump

Remove the pump (see p. 143) and block off the fuel line with a rubber plug or clamp, or keep the line above the petrol level in the tank. Lift out the pump and undo the two retaining screws. Lift

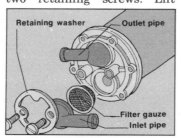

Retaining washer
Outlet pipe
Filter gauze
Inlet pipe

off the retaining washer and remove the inlet feed section to expose the filter gauze. Re-

move the gauze and wash it in a bowl of clean petrol. Remove any sediment from the inlet section. Replace the gauze

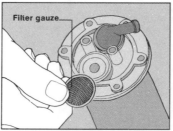

Filter gauze

and reassemble the pump. Take care not to overtighten the screws in the pump body. Refit the pump to the car, unblock the fuel line from the tank and reconnect it.

165 Cleaning the filter on a Ford petrol pump

Remove the top screw and lift off the filter cap and seal-

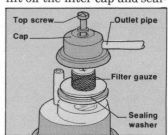

Top screw
Cap
Outlet pipe
Filter gauze
Sealing washer

ing washer. Lift out the filter and wash it in clean petrol. Wipe the housing area with a lint-free rag, and reassemble.

166 Replacing an in-line fuel filter

In-line filters are sealed and cannot be cleaned. To fit a

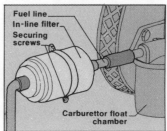

Fuel line
In-line filter
Securing screws
Carburettor float chamber

new one, pull off the fuel lines at the filter and block off the tubes. Undo the securing screws and fit the new unit. Replace the screws and the fuel lines.

167 Cleaning a glass filter bowl

Undo the wheel nut and slide the securing bracket to one

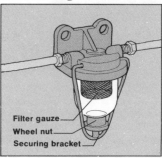

Filter gauze
Wheel nut
Securing bracket

side. Remove the bowl and sealing washer to gain access to the filter gauze. Remove it and wash it in clean petrol. Wash out the filter bowl.

Remove any sediment in the base of the filter bowl. If necessary, scrape it out with the blade of a small screwdriver. Replace the gauze and check that the washer has not perished. Replace the glass bowl and bracket, and tighten the wheel nut.

168 Checking the breather pipe

Undo the hose-retaining clips and remove the hose between the rocker or cam

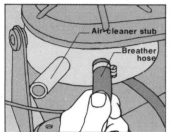

cover and the air cleaner. Check that the hose is clear and check it for cracks. If it is damaged, fit a new hose. Tighten the clips carefully.

169 Checking the flame trap breather unit

Disconnect the hose between the air cleaner and the flame trap unit. Remove the unit

from the top of the rocker or cam cover. Clean the inside, removing all oil and carbon deposits, and refit.

170 Cleaning a dipstick engine breather unit

Remove the dipstick. Unscrew the breather unit from

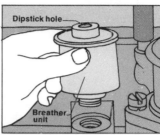

the engine block. Wash the cleaner in petrol to remove the oil sludge. Dip in clean engine oil, allow to drain off, and refit.

171 Cleaning an oil filler cap breather unit

A wire gauze filter is incorporated in the filler cap. Remove the cap from the

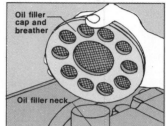

rocker or cam cover. Wash the cap in petrol to remove sludge. Oil it lightly, let it drain off and refit the cap.

172 Renewing a felt filter in a crankcase breather unit

This type of filter, used for example on the Austin Maxi,

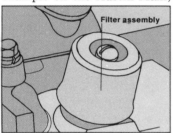

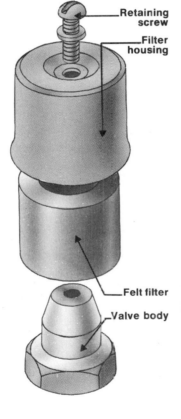

is bolted to the crankcase. The felt filter contained in the filter housing can be renewed. Undo the centre retaining screw and lift off the filter housing. Remove the felt filter and discard it.

Thoroughly clean the inside of the filter housing and the valve body which is screwed into the engine crankcase.

Fit the new felt over the top of the valve body. Slide the filter housing over the felt and secure it with the retaining screw. Tighten the screw fully to secure the cover. Wipe clean the area round the filter assembly.

173 Checking an engine with a closed-circuit ventilation system

The breather control valve, which is fitted to many BLMC cars, is between the crankcase and the inlet manifold.

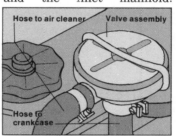

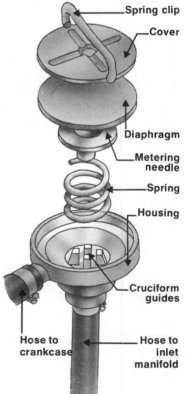

Remove the spring clip and lift off the cover. Remove the diaphragm, metering needle and spring. Clean all the metal parts in petrol. Wash the diaphragm in methylated spirit and check it to make sure it is not perforated. Do not use any abrasive material to clean the valve components. If the diaphragm, or any other part, is worn, renew it. Remove the hose connecting the valve assembly to the crankcase, and make sure it is clean. Reassemble the valve unit in its correct order.

174 Checking a box-type crankcase ventilation breather unit

The box type of breather unit, fitted to small Ford engines, is close to the petrol pump

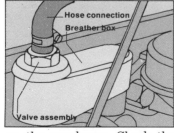

on the crankcase. Check the condition of the hose between the breather box and the air

cleaner. If it is cracked or perished, renew it.

Unscrew and pull the valve assembly from the rubber grommet in the top of the filter box. Remove the circlip from the base of the valve and lift out the sealing washer, valve assembly and spring.

Wash all the parts thoroughly in petrol. If any parts are obviously worn or damaged, fit new ones. Reassemble the valve, fit it to the filter box and reconnect the hose.

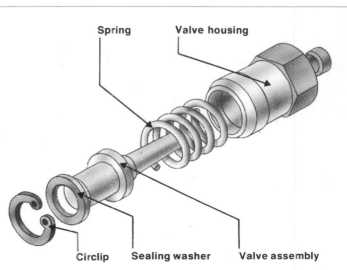

THE MAIN TYPES OF CARBURETTOR AIR CLEANER

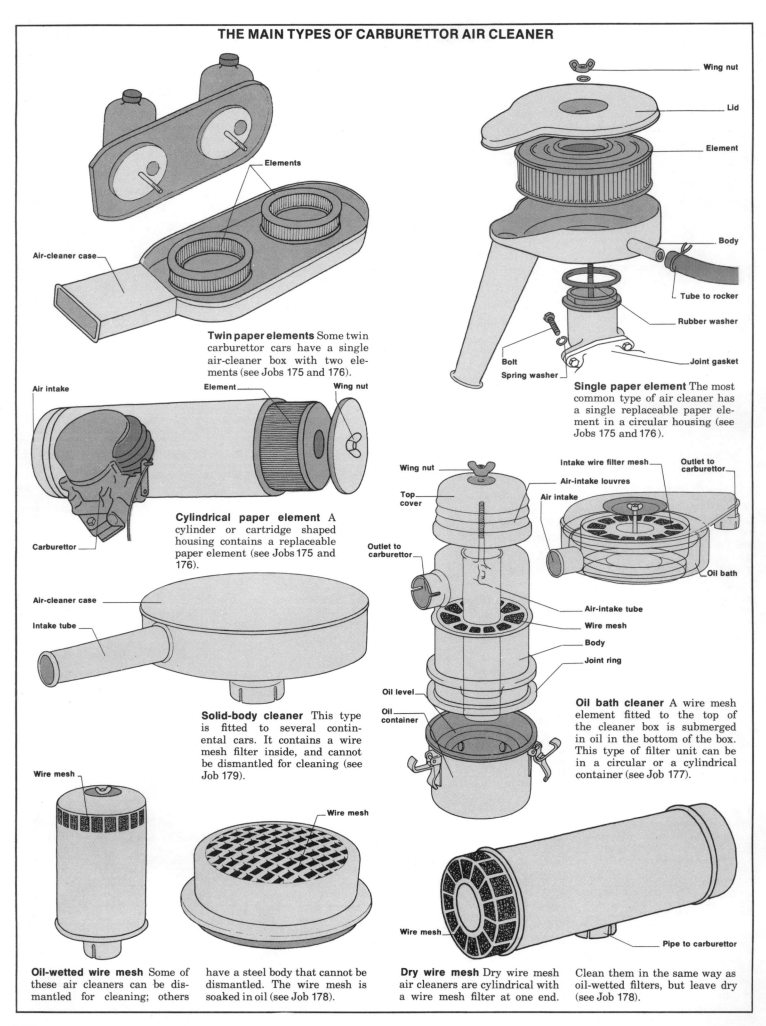

Elements

Air-cleaner case

Twin paper elements Some twin carburettor cars have a single air-cleaner box with two elements (see Jobs 175 and 176).

Air intake

Element

Wing nut

Carburettor

Cylindrical paper element A cylinder or cartridge shaped housing contains a replaceable paper element (see Jobs 175 and 176).

Air-cleaner case

Intake tube

Solid-body cleaner This type is fitted to several continental cars. It contains a wire mesh filter inside, and cannot be dismantled for cleaning (see Job 179).

Wire mesh

Wire mesh

Oil-wetted wire mesh Some of these air cleaners can be dismantled for cleaning; others have a steel body that cannot be dismantled. The wire mesh is soaked in oil (see Job 178).

Wing nut

Lid

Element

Body

Tube to rocker

Rubber washer

Bolt

Spring washer

Joint gasket

Single paper element The most common type of air cleaner has a single replaceable paper element in a circular housing (see Jobs 175 and 176).

Wing nut

Top cover

Outlet to carburettor

Intake wire filter mesh

Air-intake louvres

Air intake

Outlet to carburettor

Oil bath

Air-intake tube

Wire mesh

Body

Joint ring

Oil level

Oil container

Oil bath cleaner A wire mesh element fitted to the top of the cleaner box is submerged in oil in the bottom of the box. This type of filter unit can be in a circular or a cylindrical container (see Job 177).

Wire mesh

Wire mesh

Pipe to carburettor

Dry wire mesh Dry wire mesh air cleaners are cylindrical with a wire mesh filter at one end. Clean them in the same way as oil-wetted filters, but leave dry (see Job 178).

175 Cleaning and refitting a replaceable paper element

Corrugated paper elements are impregnated with resin and trap particles of dirt. Undo the bolt or wing nut attaching the air-cleaner

Dirty element

assembly to the carburettor. Take out the element and tap it lightly to remove dirt particles. Blow carefully with an air line or tyre pump in the reverse direction to the normal air flow (usually from inside) to remove dirt and dust.

If, despite cleaning, the element remains clogged or saturated, discard it and fit a replacement of the same type as the old one.

Clean the cover and the back-plate. Replace the element, turning it so that a clean section is opposite the air inlet tract.

Make sure that any rubber washers are correctly located in each half of the air-cleaner cover and reassemble the unit on the carburettor. Fit and tighten the retaining screw or nut. Renew any flame jacket fitted between the air cleaner and carburettor.

176 Fitting a new paper element to an air cleaner

A paper element should be renewed at the recommended mileage, or sooner if you drive in dusty conditions or if it shows signs of being clogged.

Undo the bolts or wing nuts that hold the air cleaner to the carburettor. Remove the unit and discard the old paper element.

Clean the casing and check the rubber seals. If any are damaged, replace them with new sealing rings, sometimes supplied with the new ele-ment. Reassemble the air cleaner with the new element.

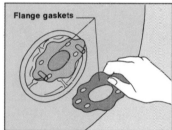

Flange gaskets

Use a new flange gasket when you refit it to the carburettor, if it is the bolt-on type.

177 Cleaning the filter and refilling an oil bath cleaner

Undo the wing nut or bolt which secures the cleaner to

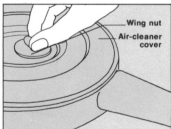

Wing nut
Air-cleaner cover

the carburettor. Undo the cleaner cover and remove the whole unit. Take out the

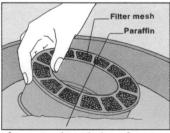

Filter mesh
Paraffin

element, rinse it in solvent or petrol and dry it with a clean, lint-free cloth. Clean out the element bowl, make sure all sediment is removed from the bowl, and fill it to the level

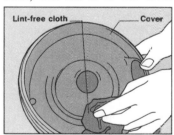

Lint-free cloth   Cover

mark with clean engine oil. Replace the element and cover.

On Volkswagens, the upper element does not need clean-ing, but make sure the inlet

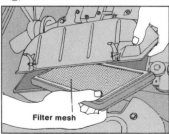

Filter mesh

holes, leading into it, are not clogged.

178 Cleaning an oil-wetted wire mesh cleaner

An oil-wetted, wire mesh cleaner element is in a hous-ing bolted to the carburet-tor intake. Undo the bolt, nut or wing nut holding the cover of the filter to its

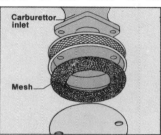

Carburettor inlet

Mesh

housing. Lift off the front cover and remove the cir-cular wire mesh filter ele-ment. Wash it in solvent or petrol to remove the dirt. Allow it to dry. Dip the filter in clean engine oil, allow it to drain, and replace it. Bolt the cover to the filter housing.

180 Checking and changing the filters in an emission control cleaner

Many engines are fitted with a crankcase breathing system (see p. 121) to prevent fumes reaching the atmosphere.

If, on your car, the system vents the crankcase to the air cleaner, through a tube from the rocker or cam cover, it is necessary to disconnect the vacuum pipe and the evapor-ative emission hose in order to remove the air cleaner for servicing.

Take off the two sleeve nuts and the hot-box hose. Once the assembly has been dis-mantled change the cleaner element (see Jobs 175-9). Re-

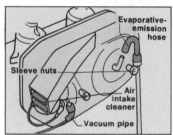

Evaporative-emission hose

Sleeve nuts

Air intake cleaner

Vacuum pipe

assemble the unit in reverse order.

179 Cleaning a solid-body air cleaner

A solid-body type cleaner unit, which has a wire mesh interior, cannot be taken apart to be cleaned. Undo the clip holding the cleaner unit to the carburettor in-take. Lift off the complete

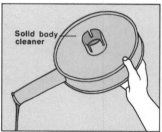

Solid body cleaner

cleaner assembly. Fill a basin with clean petrol and dip the cleaner in it. Fill the air intake with petrol and swill it around inside.

Tip it up to empty out the petrol and remove the dirt and dust from the wire mesh interior.

181 Checking and setting the position of the pre-heating controls

Most air cleaners have season-al settings, to ensure that hot air is drawn into the car-burettor in the winter and cool air in the warmer months.

On some cars the air-cleaner body should be turned so that the intake spout faces the exhaust manifold or the cold-air stream passing across

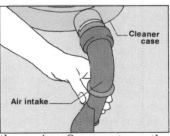

Cleaner case

Air intake

the engine. On some types the air intake spout is fixed, but a moveable nozzle at the end of the spout can be turned to give the correct setting. On other cars there are flaps marked 'winter' and 'summer'.

Flap with seasonal markings

Make sure that the flap is correctly positioned. In win-ter the warm air helps to vaporise the fuel and to warm up the engine quicker. In summer the colder air flow helps prevent over-fast vapor-isation and helps in cooling the carburettor. Leaving it wrongly adjusted will waste petrol in summer and winter.

182 Cleaning the float chamber bowl on an SU carburettor

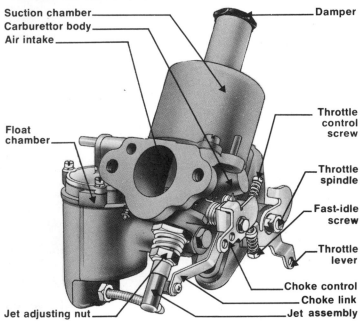

Suction chamber
Carburettor body
Air intake
Damper
Throttle control screw
Float chamber
Throttle spindle
Fast-idle screw
Throttle lever
Choke control
Choke link
Jet adjusting nut
Jet assembly

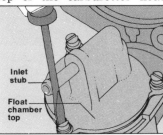

Inlet stub
Float chamber top

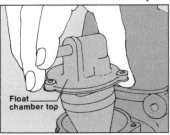

Float chamber top

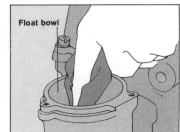

Float bowl

Remove the fuel line from the top of the carburettor float chamber. Undo the three screws that secure the top to the float chamber body and lift off the top, complete with the float assembly. Clean inside the float chamber bowl with a dry rag. Scrape out any sediment from the bottom of the bowl with a small screwdriver, and wash it out in clean petrol.

Check the paper gasket between the float chamber and the top. If it is damaged, fit a new one. Refit the top, making sure the fuel inlet pipe faces the correct way. Tighten the three securing screws and refit the fuel line to the chamber top.

183 Cleaning the float chamber bowl on a Stromberg CD carburettor

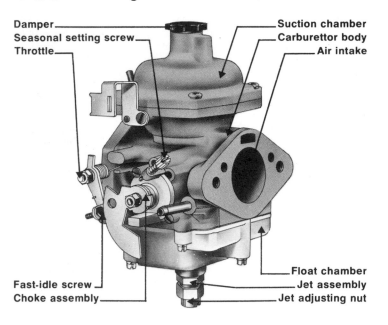

Damper
Seasonal setting screw
Throttle
Suction chamber
Carburettor body
Air intake
Fast-idle screw
Choke assembly
Float chamber
Jet assembly
Jet adjusting nut

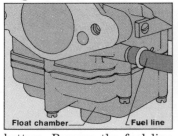

Float chamber
Fuel line

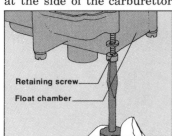

Retaining screw
Float chamber

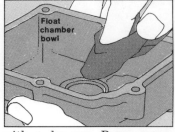

Float chamber bowl

The float chamber on a Stromberg CD carburettor is at the bottom. Remove the fuel line at the side of the carburettor body. Undo the six screws that hold the float chamber bowl to the carburettor body. Pull the bowl downwards to remove it. Clean inside the bowl with a dry rag. Remove any sediment from the base of the bowl. Wash out the bowl in clean petrol.

Refit the bowl, but make sure that you do not foul the floats, which will be hanging down from the body of the carburettor. Push the float chamber bowl tight against the carburettor body. Refit and tighten the six screws. Replace the fuel pipe.

184 Cleaning the float chamber bowl on a fixed-jet carburettor

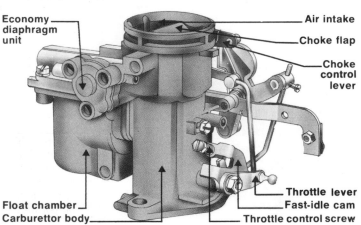

Economy diaphragm unit
Air intake
Choke flap
Choke control lever
Float chamber
Throttle lever
Fast-idle cam
Carburettor body
Throttle control screw

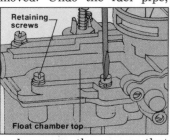

Retaining screws
Float chamber top

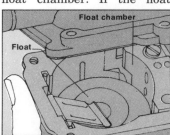

Float chamber
Float

On some fixed-jet carburettors, the float is attached to the top, and the chamber is part of the body casting. On others, the float chamber bowl drops down and can be removed. Undo the fuel pipe, and remove the screws that hold the float chamber or top.

Lift off the top or remove the float chamber. If the float chamber comes off, turn it upside-down and remove the float. On others, the float is fixed to the top. Clean the chamber with a dry rag. Reassemble and tighten the screws. Refit the fuel pipe.

185 Checking the operation of the hot-spot valve between inlet and exhaust manifold

Cars with a combined inlet/exhaust manifold have a thermostatically controlled hot-spot valve—to assist vaporisation—in the exhaust manifold, just below the point

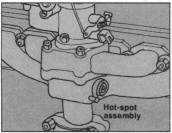

where the two manifolds join. It can be identified by

the short shaft that protrudes from the side of the exhaust manifold, and is linked to a stop by a coil spring.

Check that the shaft is free to turn. If not, disconnect

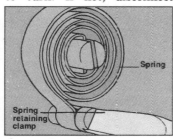

the spring from its anchor point and free it from the slot

in the valve shaft. If the shaft will not turn, soak it in penetrating oil and rotate

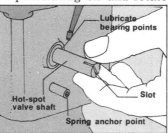

it backwards and forwards until it is free. Reconnect the spring. Twist the shaft and make sure it returns under spring tension. If the spring has lost its tension, buy and fit a new one.

187 Lubricating carburettor cable controls and linkages

A carburettor's cable controls start at the accelerator pedal.

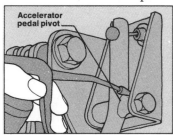

Squirt oil on the pedal pivot shaft and make sure that it moves freely.

Trickle oil on the inner cable. Work the pedal by hand to ensure that the lubricant is spread between the inner and outer cables. Make sure

that the cable stop on the carburettor grips the casing.

Carefully lubricate, with light machine oil, all the pivot points on the cable mechanism and the carbur-

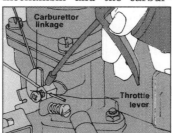

ettor. Work the pedal again and make sure that the throttle valve closes.

If a pivot plate is used in

the linkage, check that the plate is free to turn and that the 'ball-joint' con-

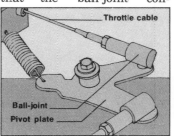

nections on the end of the cable move freely when the accelerator pedal is operated.

If the linkage is allowed to stiffen, it is difficult to get a good idling speed, and fuel is wasted. Strip and clean the linkage to get the mechanism moving and returning freely.

186 Topping up the dashpot oil level

Unscrew the cap on top of the carburettor suction chamber

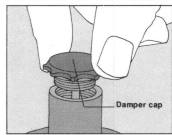

and withdraw the damper unit. Pour in light oil—SAE 20 on SU carburettors, and a special Zenith dashpot oil on a Stromberg CD unit.

Fill the suction piston guide rod to within $\frac{1}{4}$ in. of the top of the rod. Gently replace the

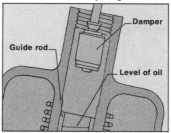

damper, push it slowly down and screw the cap fully home.

Check the action of the piston by lifting the air valve through the air intake opening. It should resist the lift and rise slowly under pressure if the oil is at the correct level and the damper in good condition. If not, fit a new damper assembly.

188 Lubricating and adjusting carburettor rod linkages

Most carburettor rod linkages have a ball-jointed head, attached to the throttle valve lever, which threads on to the linkage rod to the accelerator pedal. Adjust the length to give the correct throttle opening. How the ball-joint is secured varies:

Tubular clip To remove the rod from the throttle lever, slide the tubular clip off the

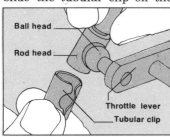

end of the rod. Pull the rod off the ball fixed to the lever.

Screw the head clockwise to shorten and anticlockwise

to lengthen it. Put a smear of grease round the ball, push the rod head on to the ball and refit the tubular clip.

Spring strap Lift the two clips on the strap round the ball head. Slide the strap off the ball head and pull the head

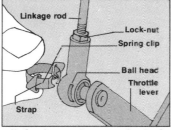

off the lever. Loosen the lock-nut on the linkage rod and screw the ball head up or down to adjust it.

Spring-loaded sleeve To remove a spring-loaded sleeve, lift it against the spring

pressure and pull it off. Lubricate the ball with grease to

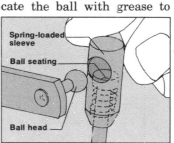

ensure it moves freely, and press the head back in position.

Spring clip A spring clip may secure the ball on the throttle

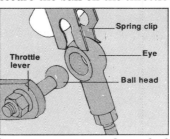

lever to an eye on the end of the linkage rod. Pull off the

clip and slide the ball out of the eye. Screw the eye up or down the linkage rod to increase or reduce the length. Grease the ball head and reassemble.

Locating clip On some carburettors, a cranked lever is fitted to the throttle spindle.

The linkage rod is held to the lever with a locating clip.

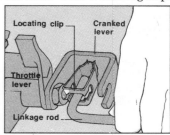

No adjustment is possible, but check that the clip is not cracked, and that it grips the rod and fits properly into the cranked carburettor lever. Lubricate all pivot points on the linkage.

189 Adjusting the throttle cable

Check that the outer cable of the throttle is firmly gripped and cannot move in its clamp. Loosen the clamp screw and move the outer cable so that

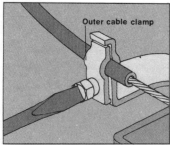

Outer cable clamp

it is tight. Tighten the clamp screw to hold it firmly.

Loosen the inner cable clamp screw and pull the inner cable through the clamp, without moving the lever attached to the throttle spindle—so that the inner cable is tight.

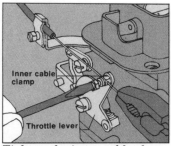

Inner cable clamp

Throttle lever

Tighten the inner cable clamp screw to hold the cable.

Check the action of the accelerator pedal. The throttle valve should open and close fully, without sticking at any point.

190 Checking and adjusting the manual choke operation on a fixed-jet carburettor

Remove the air cleaner from the top of the carburettor intake (see pp. 122-3).

Check that the choke flap in the top of the carburettor intake is vertical and fully

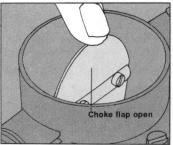

Choke flap open

open. Pull out the choke control knob and check that the

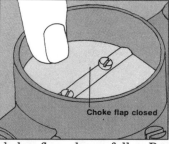

Choke flap closed

choke flap closes fully. Release the choke control knob and make sure that the choke flap returns to the vertical position.

If it stays partly closed, disconnect the choke cable and the connecting link. Work the choke flap by hand and lubricate the spindle sparingly at the same time with penetrating oil. Carbon build-up

round the spindle will cause it to stick.

If the spindle is worn, renew it (see p. 147).

On some carburettors, the connecting link between the choke lever and the throttle lever is adjustable.

Loosen the screw that holds the link to the choke lever. Operate the manual choke control and start the engine. Turn the throttle stop screw in to achieve a fast idle.

Pull the interconnecting link through its clamp on the choke lever and tighten the clamp screw fully.

When the engine is hot, release the choke and adjust the idling speed. The connecting link will now open the throttle the correct amount to give a fast-idling speed when the choke is in operation. On some carburettors the connecting link is a preset length that cannot be adjusted. Pull the choke knob fully out and check that the link is opening the throttle slightly. If the engine idles too fast the link is probably bent. Fit a new link arm, which is usually held between the throttle and choke levers by small split-pins. Always fit new split-pins.

CHECKING THE CONNECTING LINK

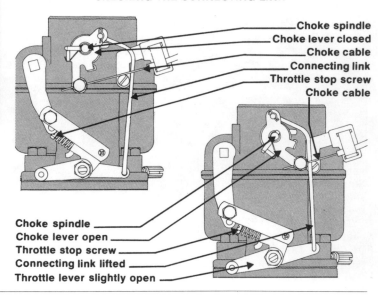

Choke spindle
Choke lever closed
Choke cable
Connecting link
Throttle stop screw
Choke cable

Choke spindle
Choke lever open
Throttle stop screw
Connecting link lifted
Throttle lever slightly open

191 Checking and adjusting the choke operation on an SU carburettor

The choke on an SU carburettor is operated by a cable that draws down the jet to increase the flow of fuel through the carburettor. As the jet is drawn down, so a fast-idle cam opens the throttle valve slightly to produce a fast idle.

Operate the choke control knob and check that the jet drops down and returns fully when the choke knob is released. Lubricate the jet lever

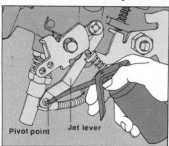

Pivot point   Jet lever

pivot point, where it is fixed to the jet, with light machine

oil. Disconnect the choke inner cable from its clamp in the choke lever, and reconnect it with $\frac{1}{16}$ in. free play. Pull out the choke knob until the choke lever just starts to move the jet.

Start the engine and run it until it reaches operating temperature. Adjust the fast-idle screw to give a speed of

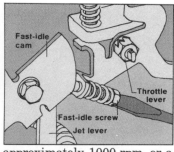

Fast-idle cam

Throttle lever

Fast-idle screw
Jet lever

approximately 1000 rpm, or a fast-idle speed.

When the choke is operated on cold starting, this will open the throttle valve sufficiently to give a fast idle.

WHERE YOU SHOULD CHECK

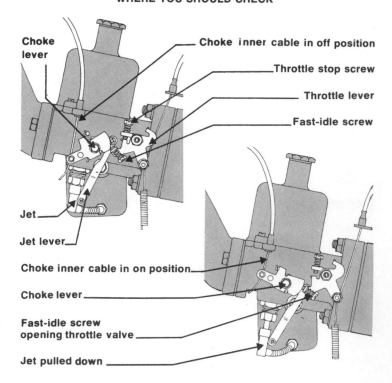

Choke lever

Choke inner cable in off position
Throttle stop screw
Throttle lever
Fast-idle screw

Jet
Jet lever

Choke inner cable in on position

Choke lever

Fast-idle screw opening throttle valve

Jet pulled down

192 Checking and adjusting the choke operation on a Stromberg CD carburettor

The choke cable on a Stromberg CD carburettor is connected to a cam lever which, in turn, is attached at its centre to a special petrol metering valve built into the body of the carburettor.

As the choke knob is pulled out, so the lever turns. The

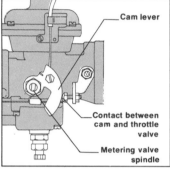

cam face of the lever contacts the throttle valve and opens the valve slightly to provide a fast idle. The centre of the arm turns the metering valve spindle, which provides a richer petrol/air mixture to the carburettor.

Check that the lever lifts when the choke knob is pulled, and that the lever returns to its stop on the carburettor

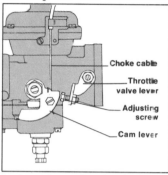

body when the knob is released.

Loosen the clamp that holds the end of the choke cable to the cam lever. Make sure the

lever is against its stop, and reconnect the choke cable. Pull the choke knob out and start the engine. It should run at a fast idle. If not, or if it is running too fast, adjust the screw that is attached to the throttle valve lever, and which touches the edge of the fast-idle cam lever.

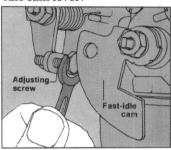

Turn the screw clockwise to decrease the fast-idle speed and anticlockwise to increase it. When adjusted properly, the engine should run at about 1000 rpm when cold and first started under choke.

193 Checking that the automatic choke mechanism works correctly

To engage an automatic choke, kick the accelerator pedal down and check that the choke flap closes. By kicking the pedal a second time you should release it.

The action of the choke assembly can be checked with the engine running. If the choke engages and the engine runs at a fast idle, it should falter if the accelerator pedal is kicked down to disengage the choke.

If it does not work, check the marks on the choke housing, heat shield and carburettor body. They should

all be in line. If not, loosen the housing screws and turn

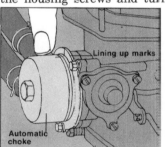

each component so that the marks line up.

Re-check the action of the choke. If it still fails, repair it (see pp. 154-5).

194 Checking and cleaning carburettor in-line fuel filters

Some carburettors, mainly the older SU type, have a petrol filter installed in the petrol line, where it is attached to the carburettor. These can be identified by the extra large union nut that secures the petrol pipe.

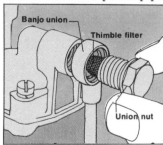

Undo the union nut and take care that the two seal-

ing washers, one on each side of the pipe banjo, are not lost. Pull the union nut out and remove the small thimble-shaped mesh filter.

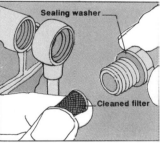

Wash it in clean petrol and make sure that all the sediment and globules of water are removed. Reassemble the filter and reconnect the pipe.

195 Checking the line filter on a Weber carburettor

On Weber twin-choke carburettors there is a petrol filter set into the carburettor float chamber top, just above the needle-valve assembly. Undo the brass plug in the

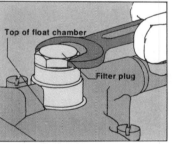

top of the float chamber. Remove the plug and lift out the barrel-shaped gauze filter.

Wash the filter in clean petrol and make sure that all sediment and water globules are removed. Shake the filter dry. If the filter gauze is split

or damaged, fit a new filter unit. Drop it back into its chamber with the plain end facing upwards. Check the plug sealing washer and replace the brass plug.

196 Adjusting an SU starter carburettor

A starter carburettor is a small, solenoid-operated unit

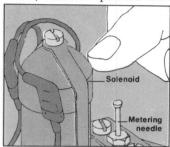

between the main carburettors. By operating the manual choke control, you activate the unit and bleed an extra charge of petrol directly into the inlet manifold.

Get a helper to operate the choke. At the same time listen carefully at the starter carburettor for a click, which indicates that the solenoid has been activated.

If there is no click, check the power supply to the unit by short-circuiting the terminal on the thermostatic manifold control to earth with a screwdriver blade or test lamp. If the electric current flows, the solenoid is faulty, fit a new one to the starter carburettor (see p. 156).

Check the adjustment of the petrol-metering needle. Start the engine and run it to working temperature. When the solenoid switches itself off, reactivate it by shorting out the manifold switch terminal. With the starter carburettor reactivated, and the engine running regularly, the colour of the exhaust smoke should be black.

If the smoke is not black, the mixture is too weak. Turn

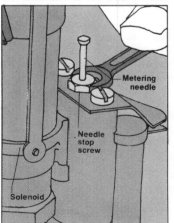

the needle stop screw anticlockwise to enrich it.

If the engine runs erratically, the mixture is too rich. Turn the needle stop screw clockwise to weaken it.

197 Checking the adjustment and tuning an SU-type carburettor

Start the engine and run it until it reaches normal operating temperature. Stop the engine and remove the air cleaner. Undo the throttle

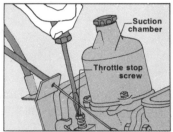

stop screw until it is just clear of its stop, and the throttle valve is closed. Rotate the stop screw one and a half turns clockwise, so that the throttle valve is just open. Mark the side of the piston suction chamber and the side of the carburettor body, so that they can be realigned correctly

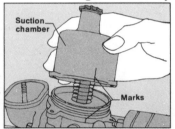

later. Undo the screws and remove the suction chamber

and piston assembly. Turn the jet adjusting nut at the base of the carburettor until the jet

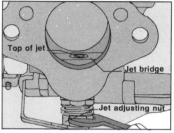

is level with the jet bridge. Clean the piston assembly with methylated spirit and check that the shoulder of the

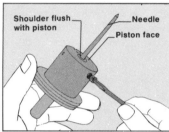

jet needle, in the base of the piston, is level with the bottom face of the piston. Clean inside the suction chamber.

Refit the piston assembly and locate the needle in the jet. Refit the suction chamber, line up the marks on the chamber and carburettor body and fit and tighten the screws.

Remove the damper from the top of the dashpot. Lift the piston with a screwdriver blade, through the air intake, and let it fall. You should hear a click as it strikes the jet bridge. If not, centralise the jet (see p. 153). Top up the dashpot with oil (see Job 186) and refit the damper.

Turn the jet adjusting nut down two complete turns and restart the engine. Run it to its operating temperature.

Turn the throttle stop screw clockwise to get a fast-idle speed. Turn the jet adjusting

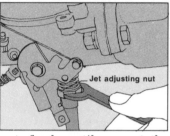

nut slowly until you get the fastest idle speed that is consistent with even running.

To check, look at the exhaust smoke. An irregular engine note, splashy misfire and colourless exhaust indicate a weak mixture: turn the jet adjusting nut down to enrich the mixture.

A regular or rhythmical misfire and blackish smoke

indicate that the mixture is too rich: turn the jet adjusting nut up to weaken it.

If the mixture is too weak, the speed will decrease and the engine will stall. If too rich, the speed will increase.

A regular, even note indicates the correct mixture. Check again by lifting the piston $\frac{1}{32}$ in. The engine should speed up slightly then settle at its idling speed if the mixture is correct.

When you have achieved the correct mixture strength, adjust the throttle stop screw to give a slow, smooth idling speed. Refit the air cleaner.

HD type Use the same method for tuning the larger HD range of carburettors. The

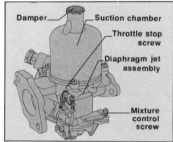

main difference is that you adjust the mixture strength with a screw attached to a diaphragm, which controls the jet assembly.

198 Checking the adjustment and tuning a Stromberg CD-type carburettor

Remove the carburettor air cleaner (see p. 123). Unscrew the dashpot damper and take

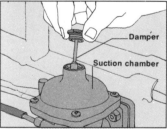

it out. Push a pencil inside the top of the dashpot and hold the air valve down against the jet bridge in the carburettor

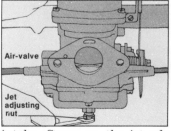

intake. Screw up the jet adjusting nut at the base of the carburettor until the jet comes into contact with the underside of the air valve.

Turn the jet adjusting nut down three full turns. Top up the dashpot with oil (see Job 186) and refit the damper.

Start the engine and run it until it has reached its normal operating temperature. Turn the throttle stop screw to give a fast-idle speed.

With the engine running, push a long thin screwdriver through the air intake and lift the air valve $\frac{1}{32}$ in. If the mixture strength is correct, the engine speed should rise slightly and then settle to its original idling speed.

If the engine speed rises appreciably, the strength of the mixture is too rich. Turn up the jet adjusting screw to weaken it. If the engine falters and stalls, the mixture is too weak. Turn down the jet adjusting screw to enrich it. When you have established the mixture strength, turn the throttle adjusting screw anticlockwise until the slowest, smooth idling speed is achieved. Refit the carburettor air cleaner assembly.

199 Checking the adjustment and tuning a fixed-jet carburettor

Before starting to tune a fixed-jet carburettor, remove the carburettor air cleaner and check that the choke flap opens and closes (see Job 190).

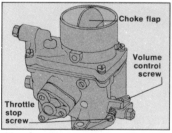

Check also that the throttle valve opens fully when the accelerator pedal is pressed.

There are two main adjusting screws on a fixed-jet car-

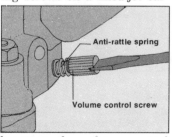

burettor: the volume control screw, which has a long

knurled head, and screws into the carburettor body, and the

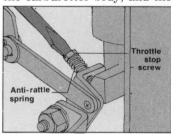

throttle stop screw. Both screws have anti-rattle springs.

Refit the air cleaner, start the engine and run it to operating temperature.

Turn the throttle stop screw clockwise until the engine is running at a fast idle. Turn the volume control screw anticlockwise until the engine starts to run erratically. Slowly turn the volume control screw back until the engine runs evenly. Readjust the throttle stop screw to give the slowest, smooth idling speed.

If the engine will not run smoothly, the jets may be blocked. Clean them with a foot pump (see p. 148).

200 Checking the adjustment and tuning a progressive twin-choke carburettor

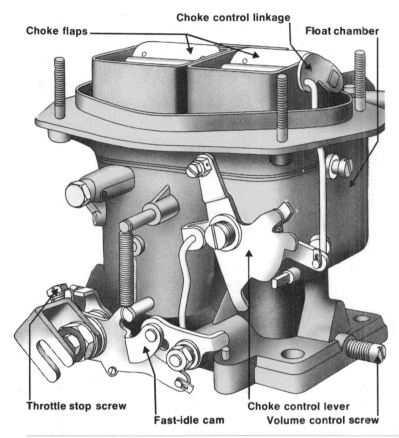

Choke control linkage

Choke flaps

Float chamber

Throttle stop screw

Fast-idle cam

Choke control lever

Volume control screw

Remove the air cleaner (see p. 123) and look down the barrel of each choke. Get a helper to press the accelerator pedal, and make sure that both throttle valves open fully when the accelerator pedal is pressed right down.

The primary flap begins to open before the secondary flap, but both flaps must be fully open at the same time.

While the air cleaner is off, operate the manual choke control and make sure that both choke flaps close and

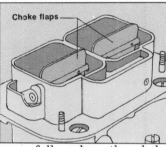

Choke flaps

open fully when the choke knob is released. If not, adjust the choke linkage (see pp. 126-7). Refit the air cleaner to the top of the carburettor.

Start the engine and run it until it reaches normal work-

ing temperature. Turn the throttle stop screw so that

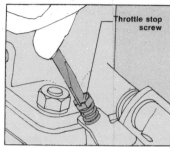

Throttle stop screw

the engine is at a fast idle. Undo the volume control screw on the carburettor

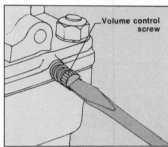

Volume control screw

flange until the engine starts to run erratically. Turn the screw back until you get an even idle speed. If the engine refuses to run smoothly the jets may be blocked. Clean them (see pp. 126-7).

201 Checking the adjustment and tuning multi-SU-type carburettors

Slacken the two throttle spindle clamps that hold the interconnecting rod to the carburettor throttle valve spindles. Slacken the two choke spindle clamps that hold the jet control interconnecting rod. Disconnect the choke cable.

Check and tune both car-burettors individually (see p. 128), start the engine and run it until it reaches its

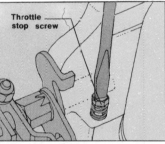

Throttle stop screw

normal working temperature. Turn the throttle stop screws to give a fast-idle speed. Fit

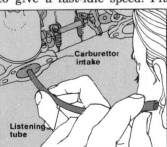

Carburettor intake

Listening tube

a piece of tubing on each carburettor intake and listen to the intensity of the hiss from each. Adjust the individual throttle stop screws until the hissing sounds the same on all carburettors.

Check the mixture strength by lifting each piston $\frac{1}{32}$ in. Adjust the mixture as necessary (see p. 128). Turn each

throttle stop screw an equal amount until the correct idling speed is achieved. Set the throttle interconnecting clamp

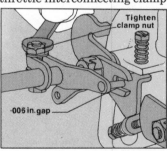

Tighten clamp nut

·006 in. gap

levers so that the link pin is ·006 in. above the lower edge of the fork. Tighten the clamp.

With both jet levers at their lowest position, set the clamps so that both jets open together.

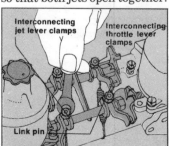

Interconnecting jet lever clamps

Interconnecting throttle lever clamps

Link pin

Tighten the clamp bolts. Reconnect the choke cable. Operate the manual choke control until the jets on both car-burettors are about to move. Adjust the fast-idle screws by equal amounts.

TWIN CARBURETTOR LINKAGE

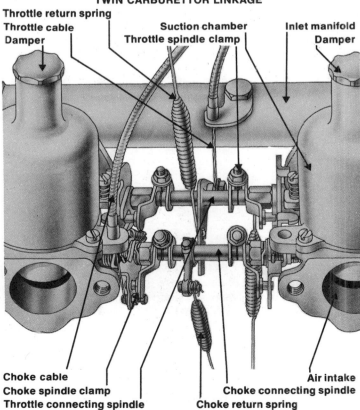

Throttle return spring

Throttle cable

Damper

Suction chamber

Throttle spindle clamp

Inlet manifold

Damper

Choke cable

Choke spindle clamp

Throttle connecting spindle

Choke connecting spindle

Choke return spring

Air intake

202 Topping up the brake and clutch hydraulic fluid reservoirs

The reservoirs that supply hydraulic fluid to the brake and clutch master cylinders are mounted in the engine compartment on front-engined cars, and the boot compartment on rear-engined cars. They are identical in appearance, with the brake fluid reservoir nearer the side of the car and usually larger than the clutch fluid reservoir. Clean the reservoir cap

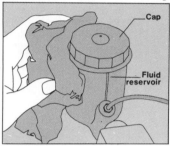

before removing it, to prevent dirt getting into the system. Top up, with the hydraulic fluid recommended by the car manufacturer, to the level

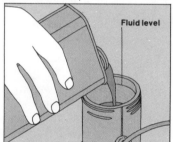

mark on the inside of the reservoir. If there is no mark,

top up to within ¼ in. of the top.

Take care not to spill any fluid on the paintwork when topping up, as it will strip off the paint. If any is spilt, wipe it away immediately with a lint-free rag.

Before replacing the cap, wipe it and make sure the small vent hole in the top of

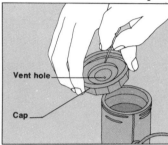

the cap is clear. Probe it clear with a steel needle if it is blocked.

Wipe the pipe connection at the master cylinders. Get a helper to apply the brake and clutch pedal a few times, while you check all the connections for leaks.

If the fluid needs frequent topping up, check the disc pads for wear. Renew them if necessary (see p. 195). On the clutch assembly, check the flexible pipe between the clutch master cylinder and the slave cylinder attached to the clutch housing. If either a pipe union or the slave cylinder is leaking, it must be renewed (see p. 196).

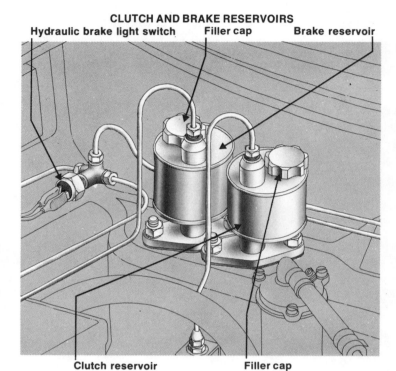

CLUTCH AND BRAKE RESERVOIRS

Hydraulic brake light switch — Filler cap — Brake reservoir

Clutch reservoir — Filler cap

WHEN THERE IS A FLUID-LEVEL WARNING LIGHT

Some brake reservoir caps are fitted with a float-actuated switch that operates a brake warning light inside the car when the fluid in the reservoir falls below the safe limit.

When removing the reservoir cap, there is no need to disconnect the switch wires. But as the cap is undone and lifted out, hold a clean rag under the float unit to prevent brake fluid dripping on to the surrounding paintwork. Top up the reservoir to

the level marked and refit the float assembly and the cap.

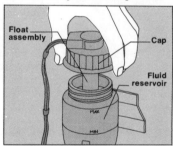

203 Checking the brake servo for leaks

A servo unit uses the partial vacuum at the inlet manifold to boost the hydraulic pressure in the braking system. A pipe, connecting the manifold to the servo unit, has a non-return valve at one end which retains the vacuum in the servo unit when the car is decelerated.

If the vacuum pipe is cracked or perished it will upset the braking balance of the unit. Check the pipe carefully, and if damaged, renew it (see p. 197).

If the servo unit is separate from the master cylinder, check the hydraulic pipe connections between the two. Tighten the union nuts.

On a combined master cylinder and servo unit, the hydraulic connections are internal and need no attention. If the unit is sluggish, check the air filter (see p. 131).

COMBINED SERVO AND MASTER CYLINDER
Fluid reservoir — Vacuum pipe to inlet manifold

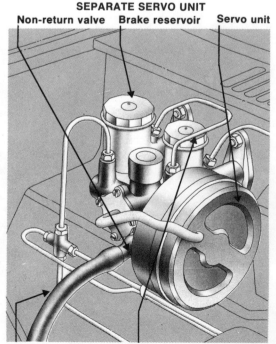

Hydraulic pipes — Combined master cylinder and brake servo

SEPARATE SERVO UNIT
Non-return valve — Brake reservoir — Servo unit

Vacuum pipe to inlet manifold — Fluid pipe between servo and master cylinder

204 Renewing the filter in a Lockheed direct-acting and a Girling Supervac servo

The filter assembly is in the barrel of the servo hydraulic cylinder just behind the brake pedal. To gain access to it, disconnect the pedal push-

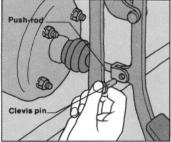

rod from the top of the brake pedal. It may be connected by a clevis pin or a shouldered

bolt. Slide back the protective rubber boot and the filter retainer. Hook out the filter. In some cases there are two filters, one felt and the other

of a foam material. Cut the filters to remove them from the push-rod.

Take the new filter and cut through it from the edge

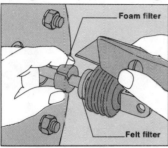

to the centre. Slide it over the push-rod. If there are two filters, fit the foam filter first, followed by the felt filter. Press them into the neck of the valve body. Make sure that they are pushed in past the end of the body, and fit the filter retainer.

Slide the protective rubber boot back into position. If the boot is split or damaged, it will have to be stretched and removed from the end of the push-rod and a new boot fitted. Lubricate the neck of the new boot, where it contacts the push-rod, with brake grease or clean hydraulic fluid.

205 Fitting a new filter element to a Girling Powerstop servo unit

The standard Girling brake servo unit—for example, the Mk IIB—or the Girling Powerstop, which is fitted as an

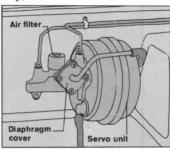

accessory, has an external filter on top of the servo unit.

Replacement air-filter kits, consisting of a filter element and a base washer, can be bought from most dealers. The filter assembly is held

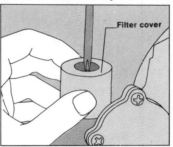

to the servo unit by a single centre screw. Undo the screw

and lift off the filter cover. Remove the filter element and the base washer below it. Clean the housing, to which the filter fits, with methylated spirit. Make sure the filter cover is also clean before reassembling.

Fit the base washer in position and replace the filter

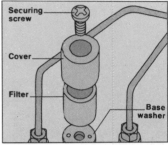

element. Fit the cover over the element and fit and tighten the securing screw. Wipe the area around the filter unit clean with a dry rag.

When buying a new kit, give the dealer the make and model of car to which it is to be fitted, to ensure that correct replacement parts are obtained. If you are in doubt, take the old parts to your dealer so that he can match them accurately.

206 Fitting a new filter element to a Lockheed servo unit

The Lockheed servo unit has an air filter on top of the dia-

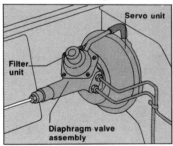

phragm valve assembly. A new air-valve assembly can be bought, but always state the make and model of car, to ensure getting the correct filter parts.

The cover retaining the filter assembly is held to the

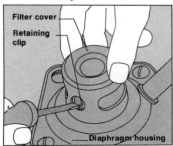

diaphragm valve by a spring clip. To release it, push in

the clip through a small opening in the cover with a screwdriver. Lift off the cover.

Remove the spring, guide, filter element and gasket.

Clean the guide and spring and inside the filter housing with methylated spirit. Clean the cover and make sure the air-intake slots round the side of the filter housing are not blocked.

Slide the new gasket over the valve housing. Fit the new filter element. Replace the guide, locating it over the end of the valve. Fit the spring and cover.

Make sure the cover engages the spring retaining clip on the diaphragm valve and is held securely in position on the servo unit.

207 Cleaning the servo air filter on a unit using a vacuum reservoir tank

The conventional type of servo unit is connected in line with a vacuum reservoir tank,

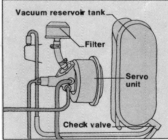

which provides power-assisted braking even when the engine is stopped. The filter unit is fitted to a tube attached to the top of the air-valve assembly and bolted to the engine bulkhead. Undo the hose clip

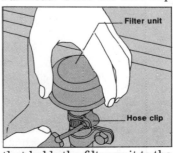

that holds the filter unit to the tube. Pull the filter unit out of

the end of the hose. Place the filter in a pan of clean methylated spirit and let it soak for about an hour.

After soaking, clean the gauze in the top of the filter with a stiff brush. Swill it

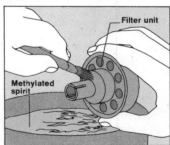

round in clean methylated spirit to remove any dirt that might have accumulated. Leave the filter to dry and then soak it in clean brake fluid. Hang it up until all the surplus brake fluid has drained away from the filter gauge. Check that the hose between the filter and servo is clean and not perished.

Fit the filter unit back on to the hose and tighten the clip that secures it. Start the engine and check that the servo works.

208 Renewing a power-steering filter unit

Renew the replaceable cartridge filter in the power-steering fluid reservoir.

Carefully wipe the top of the reservoir. Undo the nut or retaining clips holding the

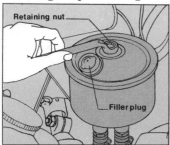

reservoir lid in position and lift off the lid.

Remove the coil spring that holds down the pressure-plate. Lift off the plate and remove

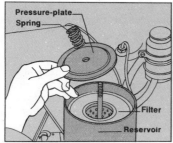

the cartridge filter. Fit the new filter and replace the plate, spring and reservoir lid. Tighten the nut, or refit the clips. Remove the filler plug. Top up with fluid to the level specified (see Job 209).

POWER-ASSISTED RACK-AND-PINION STEERING

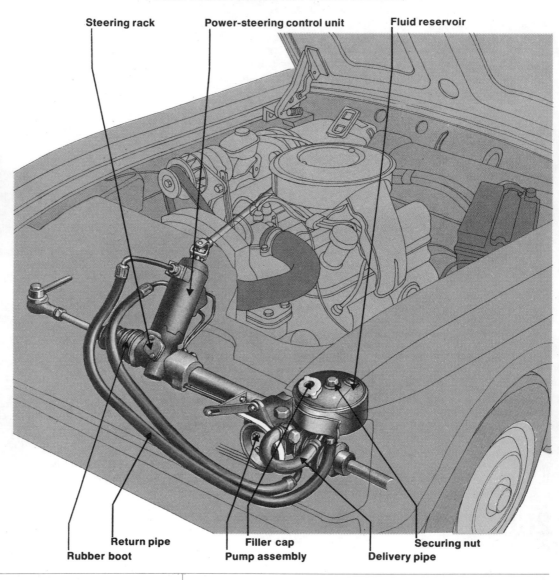

Steering rack   Power-steering control unit   Fluid reservoir

Return pipe   Filler cap   Securing nut
Rubber boot   Pump assembly   Delivery pipe

209 Topping up the fluid reservoir in a power-assisted steering system

Check the fluid level in the power-steering reservoir and, if necessary, top up to the level specified by the maker.

To ensure that the system stays clean, wipe the filler cap and surrounding area. Remove the filler cap. Some

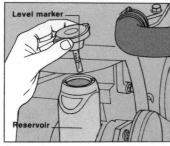

filler caps have a dipstick with a level mark on it.

Always use the fluid recommended by the manufacturers. Top up to the level mark indicated on the dipstick or, if the reservoir has a filter, until the fluid is just above the filter pressure-plate. This can be

seen through the top of the filler hole. Wipe the cap clean and fit it firmly back on the

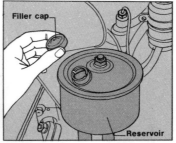

reservoir. The need for continuous topping up between recommended service intervals indicates a leaking seal or a loose hose union.

Never run the engine if the fluid reservoir is empty. In an emergency a car can certainly be driven and the steering will respond, but using it will almost certainly damage the pump mechanism, which will result in an expensive repair bill.

210 Checking the hoses and drive-belts on a power-assisted steering system

If the reservoir fluid level is correct and the steering fails to respond, the drive-belt that controls the delivery pump may be slipping. Check the drive-belt tension. There should be only ½ in. free movement on the longest run of belt between the pump and drive pulleys. If the pump is

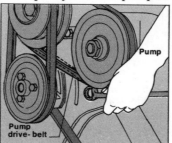

driven by the generator belt, move the generator to tension the belt (see p. 119).

If the pump has its own drive-belt, loosen the securing bolts and pull the pump back against the belt until

there is ½ in. free movement.

Check the hose connections. If they show signs of slight

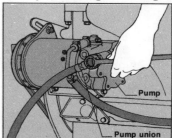

leaks, wipe the unions clean and tighten them. Do not overstrain a union nut. If a leak persists after you have tried to tighten a connection, take the car to a garage and have the system checked.

Do not attempt to renew any faulty hoses yourself. Check the rubber boots on rack-and-pinion units for splits or deterioration. If a rubber boot is damaged, it must be renewed (see p. 208).

211 Topping up the oil level in the steering box on the driver's side of the car

The steering box is mounted at the bottom of the steering column, inside the engine compartment.

Wipe the top of the box clean with a paraffin-soaked rag. The filler plug, which is a square or hexagonal nut, is fitted into the top of the box. (If there is a nut in the centre with a stud that has a screwdriver slot, do not dis-

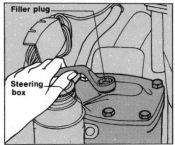

turb it.) Remove the plug and top up the level with oil recommended by the manufac-

turers. Fill to the bottom of the filler-plug hole. If access is difficult, use a plastic dispen-

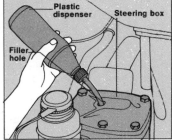

ser with a filler tube attached. Replace and tighten the filler plug and wipe away any surplus oil.

A continuously low oil level indicates a leak from the bottom of the box where the drop arm is attached. Wipe the area clean and check for signs of leaking. If an oil seal is damaged, it will have to be replaced by a garage.

212 Topping up or greasing the steering idler on the opposite side of the car

The steering idler is bolted to the engine compartment bulkhead, on the opposite side of the car to the steering box. A drop arm at the base of the idler connects with the front-wheel steering arm on its own side of the car and, through a steering rod, with the drop arm on the steering box on the other side of the car.

Wipe the top of the unit and remove the plug. Use only oil

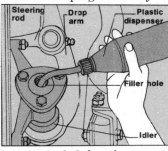

recommended by the manufacturers to top up the idler

to the base of the filler-plug hole. Refit the plug and wipe the idler clean.

On an oil-filled idler, look for leaks at the bottom of the unit where the drop arm is attached. If it is leaking, the oil seal is damaged. Take the car to a garage and have a new seal fitted.

Some idlers should be lubricated with grease. If there is

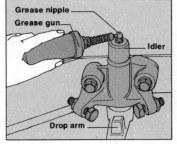

a lubrication nipple on top of the idler, fit a grease gun and grease it thoroughly.

213 Checking the steering track

The front wheels of most cars are not parallel, but are at a slight angle to each other, to compensate for any inherent slackness in the steering and suspension systems. On rear-wheel-drive cars, the front wheels are usually angled inwards—called toe-in. On front-wheel-drive cars, they are angled outwards—called toe-out. On some cars, the tracking is neutral, and a few have either toe-in or toe-out on the rear wheels.

The steering is set accurately when the car leaves the factory and normally needs little attention. But major work on steering or suspension may upset the track of the front wheels, and they should be realigned. As the amount of toe-in or toe-out is seldom more than $\frac{1}{8}$ in., it is impossible for the do-it-yourself motorist to do this accurately. Take the car to a garage that has wheel-aligning equipment.

On many recent models the camber and castor angles of the front suspension can be adjusted, but on older models these angles are set.

The steering design of each car is a compromise between handling, roadholding, comfort and tyre wear.

Incorrectly tracked wheels cause poor handling, strain on the steering and suspension systems, and uneven and costly tyre wear.

TRACKING THE FRONT WHEELS

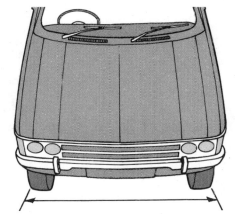

Toe-out
The front wheels are set so that they point slightly outwards at their front edges. This is found on some front-wheel-drive cars where the power is applied to the steered wheels.

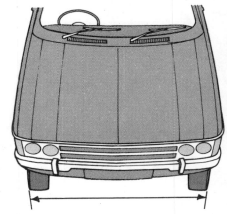

Toe-in
The front wheels are set so that the front edges of the wheels point slightly inwards. This type of tracking is normal on wheels that are not being driven (rear wheel drive).

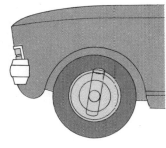

Castor angle
Castor is the angle at which the king pin or steering swivel leans backwards from the vertical at the top. The centre axis of the pin meets the ground in front of the tyre. This provides self-centring when the steering wheel is released after cornering.

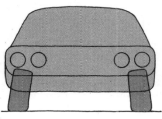

Negative camber

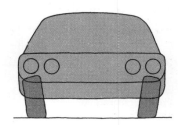

Positive camber

Camber angle
The camber is the angle at which the wheels are tilted from the vertical when seen from the front.

On negative camber—which is associated with cars that have sports characteristics—the wheels are further apart at the bottom. Roadholding

is improved, but tyre wear is likely to be uneven.

On positive camber the wheels are closer together at the bottom—this is common on cars with soft suspension—so that when the car is fully loaded the wheels are vertical.

214 Topping up Borg Warner Type 35 and ZF automatic transmission

Run the car for at least 5 miles so that the transmission fluid is warm, and all selector positions have been used. Park on level ground, apply the handbrake and select Park and switch off the engine. Remove the dipstick, wipe it

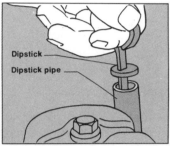

Dipstick
Dipstick pipe

clean and dip it immediately. The difference between 'high' and 'low' on the dipstick is 1 pint. Top up through the dipstick pipe with the recommended fluid. Do not let dirt enter the system. When filled, check the level again.

Use a wire brush to clean the gauze or nylon screen shielding the gearbox air inlet on the torque converter housing. If you cannot reach

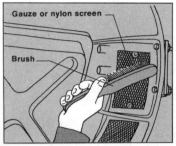

Gauze or nylon screen

Brush

it from above, jack up the front of the car and clean it from underneath. Top up the ZF automatic in the same way.

If the transmission needs frequent topping up, and no leaks are visible, the gearbox may be overheating because an oil cooler was not fitted before the car was used for towing a heavy load.

216 Topping up a General Motors automatic transmission

Run the car for at least 5 miles so that the gearbox fluid is warm, and all selector positions have been used. Park on a level surface and apply the handbrake. Select 'low', let the engine idle for two minutes and leave it running. Remove the dipstick, wipe it and dip it immediately. The

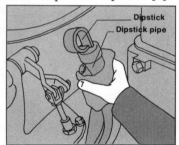

'Low'
'High'

difference between 'high' and 'low' on the dipstick, is 1 pint.

Do not let dirt enter the system. Wipe the dipstick pipe

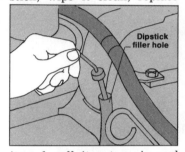

Dipstick
Dipstick pipe

clean, then top up with the recommended fluid through a funnel inserted in the tube.

If the car is used for towing heavy loads, frequent topping up may be needed, but check that no leaks are visible. Ask your garage about having a gearbox oil cooler fitted to the transmission.

218 Topping up an automatic transmission system

Run the car for a few miles to circulate and warm the oil. Park on level ground, apply the handbrake, select N and switch off the engine. Allow the oil to settle for one minute.

Remove the dipstick, wipe it clean and dip it immediately. Top up through the oil filler if necessary.

On the Austin Maxi the transmission fluid can be checked hot or cold, but it is better to check it hot. The dipstick has two 'full'

marks and two 'low' marks. Check on one—full—when the

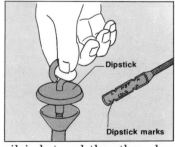

Dipstick

Dipstick marks

oil is hot and the other—low—when the oil is cold.

215 Topping up the Toyoglide automatic transmission system

The fluid level in a Toyoglide automatic transmission—fitted to the Toyota range—can be checked hot or cold. But the manufacturers recommend checking it hot.

Run the car for about 5 miles, making sure all the gear selector positions are used. Stop on level ground and with the handbrake on select the P or Park position.

Wipe the neck of the transmission dipstick with a clean lint-free rag. Pull out the dipstick, wipe it clean, replace

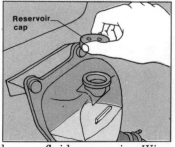

Dipstick
filler hole

it and pull it out again and check the dipstick fluid level.

If it needs topping up, fit a

clean funnel in the dipstick hole and fill the transmission with a fluid recommended by Toyota, to the 'hot' level on the dipstick.

Replace the dipstick, remove it again and make sure that the fluid is now up to the

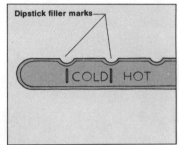

Dipstick filler marks

COLD HOT

correct level mark on the dipstick. If the level has to be checked when the fluid in the transmission is cold, run the engine for two minutes to distribute the lubricant. Check in the same way as described above. The fluid should reach the 'cold' mark. If not, top up as necessary and check again. If in doubt, check when hot.

217 Topping up a Nissan 3N automatic transmission system

Though there are 'hot' and 'cold' marks on the transmission fluid dipstick, it is advisable to check the fluid after a 5 mile run.

Stop the car and let it idle for about two minutes. With the engine still running, put the gear selector lever in the P or Park position. Wipe the gearbox filler/dipstick tube clean with a lint-free rag.

Remove the dipstick, wipe it clean and replace it. Remove it again, and check that the oil level indicated on the marker area of the dipstick reaches the 'hot' mark.

If not, fit a clean funnel into the filler dipstick hole and top

up as necessary. Use only the transmission fluid recommen-

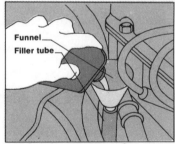

Funnel
Filler tube

ded by the car manufacturers.

After topping up, allow the engine to run for about two minutes—to distribute the fresh oil—and check the level again to make sure it is correct. Replace the dipstick.

219 Topping up the torque converter on a semi-automatic transmission

The torque converter on a semi-automatic transmission

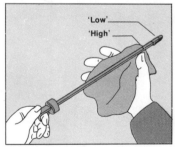

Reservoir cap

has a fluid reservoir. Wipe the reservoir cap·and remove

it. Use the recommended fluid, and top up to the level

Reservoir

marked on the side of the transparent reservoir.

220 Checking the securing bolts on the exhaust and inlet manifolds

The bolts holding manifolds are often difficult to reach, so you may need a box spanner or a socket to undo and tighten them.

Get a helper to rev the engine, or do it yourself by moving the throttle linkage near the carburettor. Watch and listen for 'blowing' at the exhaust manifold where it joins the cylinder head. If the manifold and exhaust flanges of the gasket and surrounding areas are discoloured, or if

any gas can be felt escaping, the gasket must be renewed.

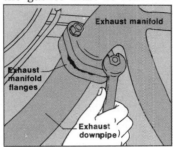

Check the tightness of the joint between the exhaust

manifold and the downpipe. Check the inlet manifold

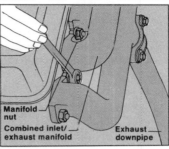

gasket for damage. Tighten the nuts or bolts, working from the centre outwards. Some carburettors are very

heavy, and can cause a severe strain on their mountings. This can distort the joint surfaces, so that unwanted air gets in and weakens the fuel and air mixture to the engine.

Some carburettors use rubber 'O' rings between the carburettor flange and the inlet manifold, to prevent fuel frothing in the carburettor body. Do not tighten them down too much, because it will cause misfiring.

Tighten every joint and make sure they are completely sealed against air leaks.

EXHAUST MANIFOLD

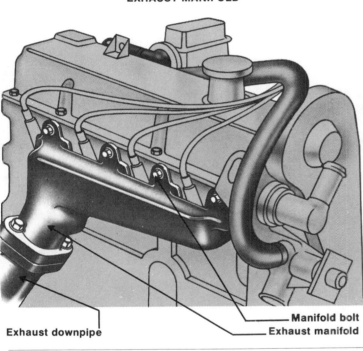

Exhaust downpipe

Manifold bolt
Exhaust manifold

COMBINED INLET AND EXHAUST MANIFOLDS

Carburettor

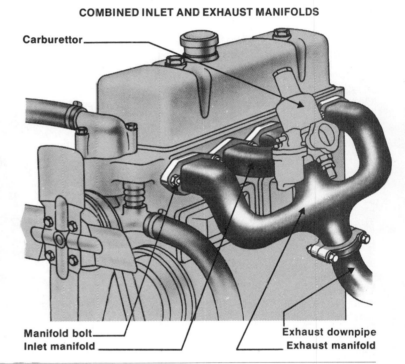

Manifold bolt
Inlet manifold

Exhaust downpipe
Exhaust manifold

221 Checking the condition of the engine mountings

Carefully check the rubber mountings between the engine and the body. If these become impregnated with oil, they lose their shock-absorbing properties. Check the tightness of the bolts and, if necessary, tighten them. Undue vibration will cause engine fittings to shake loose and fall off. The manifold joint is usually the first to suffer. If the mountings are damaged, renew them.

Place a jack under the engine sump, with a piece of

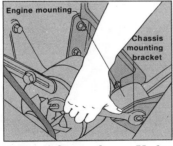

wood between the sump and the jack. Operate the jack until it just contacts the sump pan. Undo the engine mounting bolts. Jack up the engine high enough to enable the mountings to be removed. Take care not to put undue strain on bolts, carburettor linkages, etc. Some of these items may have to be disconnected, to allow the engine to be raised high enough to clear the mountings.

Slide the new mountings into position and carefully lower the engine. Make sure the bolt holes or studs on the mountings line up with the mounting brackets of the engine. Refit the securing bolts, tighten them securely; lower and remove the jack. **Note:** Renewing engine mountings on the Audi is a garage job, as engine alignment is adjusted at the mountings.

222 Checking the compression pressures of the cylinders

If the engine performance is poor and normal tuning fails to improve it, have the compression pressures checked by a garage. Alternatively, you can do it yourself with one of the hand-held compression testers available from accessory shops or dealers.

These testers will help in diagnosing any faults caused by differences in cylinder compressions: worn cylinders, pistons and rings; faulty valves, seatings and springs; or a leaking cylinder-head gasket will be indicated.

To use the tester, run the engine up to normal operating temperature and switch off. Remove the spark-plugs and the carburettor air cleaner to give unrestricted air flow to the engine. Connect the tester to No. 1 cylinder.

Spin the engine on the starter with the throttle

fully open. The dial on the instrument will record the

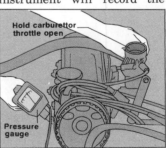

maximum pressure reached. This should be within the limits specified by the manufacturer but, if the figures are not available, the following is a rough guide: over 110 psi—excellent; 90-110 psi—very good; 70-90 psi—satisfactory; but if below 70 psi—poor.

If the pressures vary by more than 20 psi between any cylinders, take the car to a garage for a complete engine overhaul.

223 225
224 226

223 Cleaning door drain holes

All car doors have some form of drain hole along the bottom to allow any water that seeps between the window and sealing rubber to drain away. When servicing or washing

the car, make sure the holes are clear. Wipe the door edge.

224 Lubricating door locks

On some cars a small hole is drilled in the door frame to give access to the lock mechanism. Lubricate with four

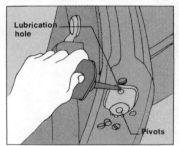

or five drops of thin oil. Oil the tips and the central pivot below the oil hole. If the striker-plate is made entirely of

metal, lubricate with fine oil. If it has nylon parts, use a special lubricant that is harmless on nylon, rubber and plastic. Again, use only four or five drops of oil. Wipe away

any surplus lubricant to prevent getting it on your clothes when you use the car.

225 Clearing the drain hose in an air-extractor system

Some cars are fitted with an air ventilation and extraction system. This provides a circulation of fresh air inside the car without having to open the windows.

The inlet control is on the fascia panel inside the car, and the outlet grilles are usually situated just behind the rear side windows. The grilles are exposed to the weather. To protect them, internal hoses are fitted to allow rain water to drain away. The

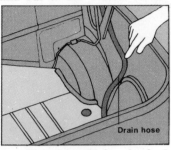

hoses run through the boot and out of the bottom of the car. They should be checked for signs of damage or perish-

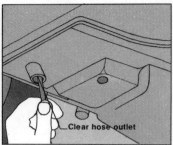

ing. If there is any sign of a leak, replace the hose. They must be kept clear and in good condition. To clear them, probe the tube with a strong flexible wire.

CLEANING AND LUBRICATION POINTS

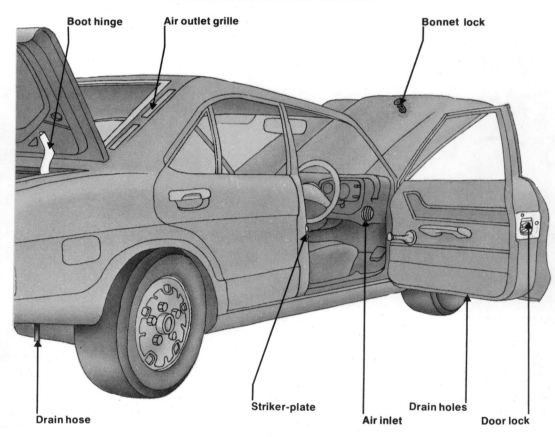

Boot hinge   Air outlet grille   Bonnet lock

Striker-plate   Air inlet   Drain holes   Door lock

Drain hose

226 Lubricating the hinges on the boot, bonnet and doors

Lubricate all the door, bonnet and boot hinges at the points where they pivot. Use a water-repellent lubricant.

There are two types of door hinges—internal and external.

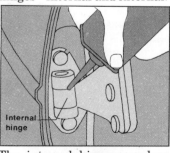

The internal hinges are less exposed to the weather, so

they should be lubricated less frequently than the exposed external hinges. The striker-

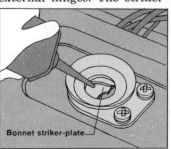

plate of the bonnet lock, situated close to the front of the top of the radiator, should be lubricated. Oil the striker pin, situated on the bonnet, and

all the bonnet hinges at the same time.

Boot hinges may be external or internal. The same in-

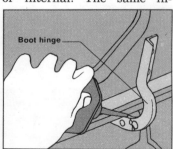

structions apply as for door hinges, but external hinges need special attention. Apply a few drops of light machine oil to the boot latch mechanism and to the actual lock.

Repairing your car

Starter motor/1

WHEN THE CAR WILL NOT START

Symptom	Check	Symptom	Check
Starter motor does not turn and lights do not come on	Battery condition – pp. 36-37 Battery earth connections – pp. 36-37	Starter motor does not turn but lights are bright	Ignition/starter switch – p. 190 Defective starter – p. 140 Ignition wiring – pp. 188-9 Gear lever position (automatic cars) Solenoid – this page Starter engagement – p. 139
Starter motor does not turn and lights dim	Battery condition – pp. 36-37 Battery earth connections – pp. 36-37 Starter motor pinion jammed or not engaging – p. 139 Engine seized – consult a garage		
Solenoid switch clicks. Engine turns slowly but will not start	Battery condition – pp. 36-37	Engine starts but starter does not disengage, making a noise	Engine earth strap – p. 37 Battery condition – pp. 36-37 Cable connections – p. 189 Starter motor – p. 140

Checking the starter motor solenoid

There are two basic types of starter motor; the inertia type and the pre-engaged type. Both use a solenoid to activate them. If they fail to turn the starter motor, first check that the battery lead terminals are making good contact. Clean the battery earth lead where it is attached to the car bodywork (see p. 37).

Pre-engaged type The solenoid on a pre-engaged starter motor is on the motor body. As the solenoid is activated by the ignition switch, the drive is put into mesh with the fly-wheel ring gear before the motor starts to turn. The drive pinion, attached to the motor shaft, is mounted on a free-wheel clutch, to prevent the engine driving the motor when it has fired. If the motor fails to turn, first check the solenoid (see different types below).

Inertia type When the ignition switch is turned on, a light current flows through the solenoid. A plunger in the solenoid makes contact between the main battery and starter motor leads, attached to the solenoid body. A heavy current, direct from the battery, then flows to the starter motor. The motor spins, and the drive mechanism on the end of the motor shaft is pushed, by inertia, into mesh with the starter ring gear. If the motor fails to turn, check that the solenoid is working.

PRE-ENGAGED STARTER

INERTIA STARTER

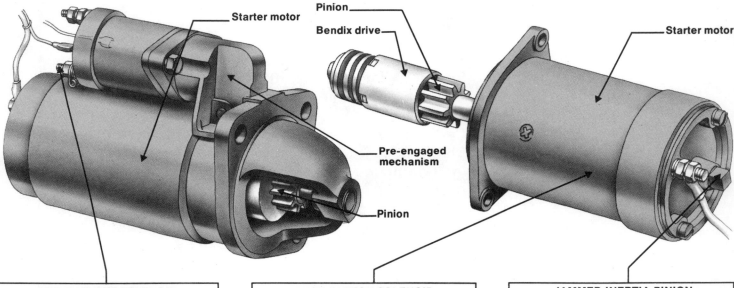

Starter motor

Pinion

Bendix drive

Pre-engaged mechanism

Pinion

Starter motor

PRE-ENGAGED SOLENOID

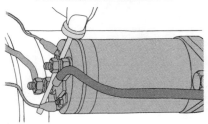

Remove the rubber caps from the solenoid terminals. Use an insulated screwdriver to short-circuit the two main terminals and take the battery power straight to the motor windings. If the motor turns, the solenoid is faulty. Have a new solenoid fitted. If the motor fails, overhaul it.

PUSH-BUTTON SOLENOID

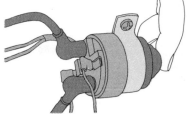

Press the rubber-covered solenoid button. If the starter motor does not turn, lift off terminal caps. Use an insulated screwdriver to short-circuit the two terminals. If the motor turns, fit a new solenoid unit. If the motor fails to turn, overhaul the starter motor (see p. 140).

JAMMED INERTIA PINION

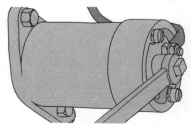

If the starter motor pinion jams (see chart above) and the motor fails to turn the engine, remove the centre cover on the starter motor end-plate, to expose the motor shaft. Fit a spanner to the squared end of the shaft. Turn it clockwise to wind the pinion out of mesh.

If the starter motor drive is sticking

If the starter spins without turning the engine, the drive is sticking and the complete unit must be removed from the car for checking.

1 Remove the battery leads and disconnect the power cable. Undo the two or three bolts that hold the starter in place. A socket-wrench may be needed (see p. 32). Make sure that when you unscrew the nut that holds the power lead, you do not turn the whole connecting bolt, or the field winding connections may be damaged. Remove the starter motor.

2 Check the operation of the pinion. (It should slide back smoothly to the

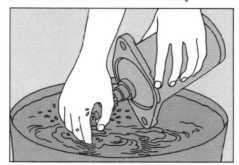

buffer spring.) Remove any dirt by working the pinion back and forth in

a bath of methylated spirit or petrol. Wipe off excess fluid and check the action again when it is dry. Do not oil the assembly.

3 If any components of the drive assembly are obviously damaged — if, for example, the return spring is broken or the pinion teeth are badly worn — they must be replaced or a new drive unit must be fitted.

4 Clean the starter motor, but do not strip it unless you have considerable mechanical experience.

Repairing a Bendix drive unit

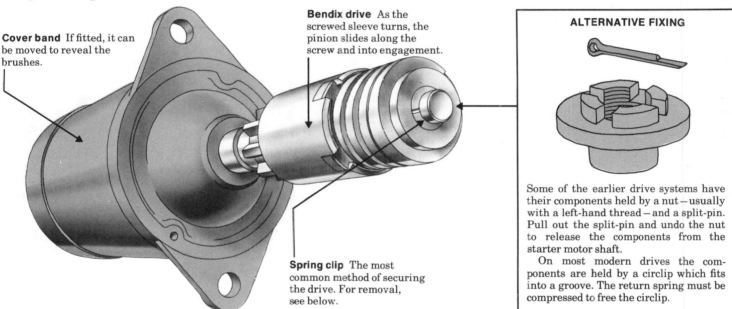

Cover band If fitted, it can be moved to reveal the brushes.

Bendix drive As the screwed sleeve turns, the pinion slides along the screw and into engagement.

Spring clip The most common method of securing the drive. For removal, see below.

ALTERNATIVE FIXING

Some of the earlier drive systems have their components held by a nut — usually with a left-hand thread — and a split-pin. Pull out the split-pin and undo the nut to release the components from the starter motor shaft.

On most modern drives the components are held by a circlip which fits into a groove. The return spring must be compressed to free the circlip.

If all the recommended methods of freeing the pinion fail, it will have to be dismantled. The cause may be a broken return spring, which can be examined only with the pinion removed from the shaft. If the pinion teeth have been 'chewed up' by constant contact with the ring gear of the flywheel, fit a new pinion.

Tools: Valve-spring compressor; carborundum stone; screwdriver.
Materials: New return spring; new pinion.

1 To remove the circlip from its groove at the end of the shaft, start

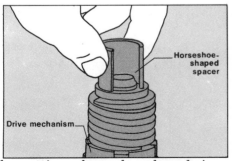

Horseshoe-shaped spacer

Drive mechanism

by putting a horseshoe-shaped piece of metal — bent from any piece of

metal more than $\frac{1}{16}$ in. thick, or cut and shaped from a piece of tubing of the correct diameter — on the end of the drive unit.

2 Hook one end of a valve-spring compressor under the pinion, so that the other end bears on a bridge piece — a spare piece of mild steel strip — which in turn bears on the horseshoe-shaped piece of metal.

3 Tighten the compressor to squeeze the buffer spring slightly. Prise out

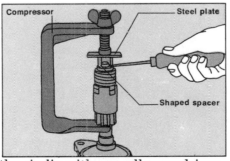

Compressor

Steel plate

Shaped spacer

the circlip with a small screwdriver. Release the compressor and slide the pinion assembly off the shaft.

4 A broken return spring prevents a pinion from disengaging when the engine starts. It is possible to fit a new return spring.

5 A new pinion is more expensive, but if it is worn fit a new one. It is cheap compared with the cost of renewing a starter motor.

6 Before reassembling the unit, examine the splines of the starter

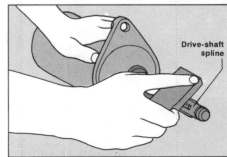

Drive-shaft spline

shaft and remove any burrs with a small carborundum stone. Fit the pinion, compress the spring and fit the circlip back in its groove. Make sure that the pinion moves freely.

Starter motor /2

Renewing the starter motor brushes

The brushes of a starter motor must be renewed if they are worn down to less than $\frac{3}{8}$ in. — measured from the top of the brush, where the terminal lead is attached, to the bottom of the brush where it contacts the commutator.

Disconnect the main lead to the starter motor terminal. Unbolt the motor and remove it from the engine.

Tools: Screwdriver; electric soldering iron; pliers or wire cutters.
Materials: Starter motor brushes; fine glass-paper; resin-core solder; methylated spirit.

1 Undo the fixing nut, washers and spacer from the terminal stud. Keep them in their correct order.

2 Unscrew the two long bolts from the end-plate and pull them out. Draw off the casing surrounding the armature. Clean the segments of the

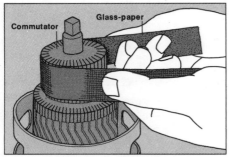

Commutator   Glass-paper

commutator with fine glass-paper, and wash it in methylated spirit. If it is badly worn, fit a new motor.

3 A set of new brushes consists of two with uninsulated plaited leads, and two plaited leads that are insulated. One of the insulated leads is longer than the other.

4 The brushes with insulated leads have to be connected to the armature windings, but the leads are copper and the windings are aluminium, which means that they cannot be joined with ordinary solder. To do

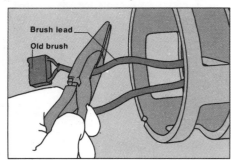

Brush lead
Old brush

the job at home, cut through the existing brush leads with pliers. Make sure that you leave at least $\frac{1}{2}$ in. of the old lead attached. Clean the ends of the old and new leads, and hook the remnant of the old lead through the loop of the new

---

FACE-TYPE COMMUTATOR

On most modern starter motors, the brushes are held in a plastic moulding attached to the commutator end-plate. The commutator segments are mounted vertically on the end of the armature. Clean the commutator with methylated spirit. Do not use any form of abrasive paper because the segments are thinner than on the drum-type commutator. New brushes are simply pressed into the holder, but the field winding brush leads have to be soldered into place.

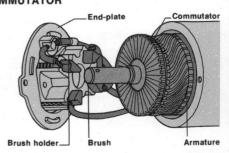

End-plate   Commutator

Brush holder   Brush   Armature

DRUM-TYPE COMMUTATOR

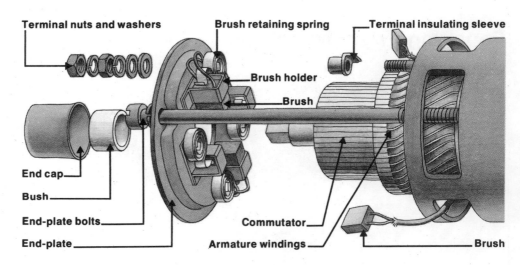

Terminal nuts and washers   Brush retaining spring   Terminal insulating sleeve

Brush holder

Brush

End cap

Bush

End-plate bolts   Commutator

End-plate   Armature windings   Brush

---

brush leads. Flow resin-core solder over the ends of the wires. Heat the joint with a soldering iron and join the new and old leads securely with resin-core solder.

5 Use pliers to cut through the two old leads on the end-plate brushes,

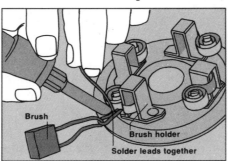

Brush
Brush holder
Solder leads together

and solder the two new brushes with uninsulated leads to the old leads.

6 On drum-type commutators, fit new brushes in their holders. Jam them temporarily by resting the clock springs on the sides.

7 Refit the casing and the end-plate. Each has a locating notch so that they come together correctly.

8 Make sure the nylon insulating sleeve is fitted to the screw terminal connected to the main feed wire, or the terminal may touch the end-

plate and cause a short circuit. Refit the terminal nut washers and through-bolts. With drum-type commutators, use a small screwdriver to move each clock spring so that it

Lever brush spring up

bears on top of a brush and pushes it into contact with the commutator.

9 Hold the starter motor body against the car body to earth it. Connect the starter motor terminal by a

lead to the live terminal post on the battery. The motor should turn.

Engine performance

WHEN ENGINE PERFORMANCE CAUSES PROBLEMS

Symptom	Check	Symptom	Check
Engine performance		Coughs and splutters, often backfiring	Fuel starvation – p. 142 Water in fuel – p. 124
Engine turns normally but will not fire	Ignition system – pp. 157-163 Carburettor – pp. 146-156 Fuel pump and lines – pp.142-5	Engine pinks	Incorrect fuel – p. 8 Ignition timing – pp. 108, 164-5 Distributor advance mechanism – pp. 161-3 Overheating – pp. 180-1 Spark-plug overheating – pp. 106-7 Excessive deposits in combustion chamber – p. 171
Engine backfires or bangs through carburettor	Ignition timing – pp. 108, 164 Distributor cap – p. 159		
Engine fires but fails to keep running	Ignition system – pp. 157-163 Fuel pump and lines – pp. 142-5 Carburettor – pp. 146-156	Water drips from exhaust	Blown cylinder-head gasket – pp. 166-175 Cracked or warped cylinder head – garage job
Cold engine stalls	Choke – pp. 126-7, 154-6		
Hot engine stalls	Idle speed – pp. 128-9 Fuel/air mixture – pp. 127-9 Pilot air jet – p. 148 Choke – pp. 126-7, 154-6 Contact points – pp. 98-102, 160 Carburettor – pp. 146-156 Inlet manifold – p. 166	Engine misses at high speed	Loose or dirty ignition connections – pp. 159-160 Contact-breaker points – pp. 98-102, 160 Spark-plugs – pp. 106-7 Dirt in carburettor – p. 124 Coil – p. 160 Valve clearances – pp. 109-177 Air-cleaner – pp. 122-3
Rough idle	Idle mixture – pp. 128-9 Contact points – pp. 98-102, 160 Ignition timing – pp. 108, 164-5 Inlet manifold – p. 166	Engine falters, picks up and stops	Lack of petrol – pp. 142-153
Engine stalls on acceleration	Accelerator pump – p. 148 Choke – pp. 126-7, 154-6 Fuel supply – p. 142 Distributor – pp. 157-163 Air-cleaner – pp. 122-3 Variable-jet carburettor piston – pp. 150-3	Engine falters and stops when hot	Vaporisation in fuel lines – p. 142
		Engine does not seem to reach normal operating temperature	Thermostat – p. 181 Temperature gauge or sensor – garage job
Poor acceleration	Ignition timing – pp. 108, 164 Inlet manifold – p. 166 Fuel supply – p. 142 Accelerator linkage – pp. 125-6 Valve clearances – pp. 109-117 Engine compression – p. 135 Distributor advance mechanism – pp. 161-3	Engine uses too much petrol	Carburettor – pp. 146-156 Air-cleaner – pp. 122-3 Choke – pp. 146-156
		Engine backfires when pulling	Fuel starvation, water in fuel – pp. 124, 142 Inlet manifold – p. 166 Ignition timing – pp. 108, 164-5 Centrifugal weights – p. 161
Engine misses or surges	Spark-plugs – pp. 106-7 Ignition circuit – pp. 157-163 HT leads – p. 159 Inlet manifold – p. 166 Fuel starvation – p. 142 Flooding carburettor – pp. 147, 151-3 Restricted exhaust – garage job	**Engine noises**	
		Light tapping	Valve clearances – pp. 109-117 Worn cams, followers or rocker arms – pp. 174-5
Engine lacks power	Ignition timing – pp. 108, 164-5 Distributor advance mechanism – pp. 161-3 Inlet manifold – p. 166 Valve clearances – pp. 109-117 Engine compression – p. 135 Fuel starvation – p. 142 Throttle linkage – p. 125	Light tap varying with engine speed	Small-end bush – garage job Broken piston rings – garage job
		Heavy knock varying with engine speed or load	Big-end bearings – garage job
		Rattle or grind when clutch is used	Clutch release bearings – pp. 218-224
Engine cuts out when car stops	Throttle adjustment – pp. 128-9 Pilot air jet – p. 148 Inlet manifold – p. 166	Squeal or whine	Water pump seals – p. 182 Slack generator belt – p. 119
Engine runs on when switched off	Overheating – pp. 180-1 Spark-plug overheating – pp. 106-7 Excessive deposits in combustion chamber – p. 171 Valve clearances – pp. 109-117 Inlet manifold – p. 166	Hissing pop as throttle is opened	Exhaust manifold leak – p. 166 Damaged silencer – garage job
		Rattle during tick-over	Timing chain or tensioner – garage job
		Hiss varying with engine speed	Inlet manifold – p. 166
Engine coughs and splutters	Water or dirt in fuel system – p. 124 Low fuel level in carburettor – pp. 146-153	Heavy irregular tapping	Seized valve – pp. 167-175 Broken valve spring – pp. 167-175 Bent push-rod – p. 174

Fuel pump/1

Identifying your fuel pump

Every car has a fuel pump which pushes petrol from the tank to the carburettor. The first hint of fuel pump trouble may be lack of performance at full throttle, because the pump cannot keep pace with the demands of the carburettor. Similarly, if there is petrol in the tank and the engine staggers to a halt—rather than cutting out suddenly—the fault is probably in the pump.

First find out if your car has a mechanical or an electric pump.

Electric pumps are usually mounted in the boot near the fuel tank. But some are under the car or in the engine compartment. They are powered from the ignition circuit.

After long use, the diaphragm, which pushes petrol through the pump, and the valves, through which the petrol flows, will begin to leak. Pump manufacturers sell overhaul kits which include a new diaphragm and valve assembly. Pumps with one-piece bodies cannot be serviced, except for filter cleaning. If one of these fails completely, you can only fit a new unit.

Mechanical pumps are bolted to the side of the engine block, and are usually operated by a special lobe on the camshaft. The pump has a divided chamber containing a filter and sediment bowl and petrol valves.

AC Delco mechanical pumps have either a glass dome fixed by a clip, or a metal cap fastened with a bolt through the top of the cap. The pump has an inlet and outlet valve.

SU-type mechanical pumps have a domed metal cap, fastened by bolts around the perimeter of the dome. It has only one self-return valve.

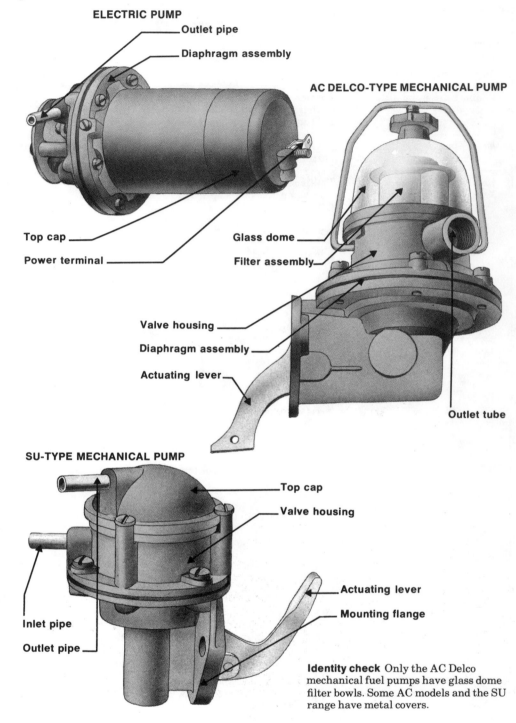

ELECTRIC PUMP
Outlet pipe
Diaphragm assembly
Top cap
Power terminal

AC DELCO-TYPE MECHANICAL PUMP
Glass dome
Filter assembly
Valve housing
Diaphragm assembly
Actuating lever
Outlet tube

SU-TYPE MECHANICAL PUMP
Top cap
Valve housing
Actuating lever
Mounting flange
Inlet pipe
Outlet pipe

Identity check Only the AC Delco mechanical fuel pumps have glass dome filter bowls. Some AC models and the SU range have metal covers.

Clearing blockages in fuel lines

If you suspect fuel pump trouble, first check that there is fuel in the tank and that the fuel line is clear. If the filler cap has a vent hole, make sure that it is not blocked.

Look along the length of the fuel line—from tank to carburettor—for signs of leaking. Tighten any loose joints, and renew any broken or hardened sections of pipe.

1 Make sure that petrol is reaching the carburettor. Disconnect the fuel line from the carburettor—depending on the make of car, you may have to unscrew a clamp or a nut before removing it.

2 With the car in neutral, hold the end of the petrol pipe over a cup.
Electrical pumps Turn on the ignition switch. Petrol should be pumped continuously from the end of the pipe. If petrol is not pumped out, the petrol pump is faulty or the petrol pipes are blocked. Bubbles in the petrol indicate a leak in the line.
Mechanical pumps Turn the engine on the fan belt. As the pump is activated, petrol should be pumped out of the pipe.

3 Disconnect the inlet pipe from the pump. Connect a tyre pump or a garage air line to the end of the

pipe. Remove the filler cap and get a helper to listen at the petrol tank. Air forced through the line should be heard bubbling in the tank.

4 Check that the filter is clean. If it looks dirty, carefully remove it (see p. 120). Wash it in petrol and replace it. If it is damaged, fit a new filter.

5 Vapour locks in the fuel line can occur when the pipe is too close to the exhaust system or the engine block. To prevent this, move the pipe away from the hot spot, fit a protective shield, or wrap the pipe in asbestos string.

Checking an electrical fuel pump

First make sure there is fuel in the tank, and that it is reaching the carburettor.

1 Disconnect the fuel line at the carburettor. Direct the disconnected

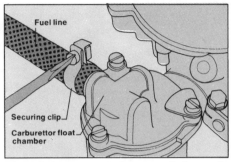

pipe into a container and keep it well away from the engine and the exhaust system, particularly if the engine is hot. Switch on the ignition and check that fuel is delivered into the container.

2 If no fuel comes out, find the pump itself and switch on the ignition. A working pump will tick—rapidly at first, and then settle down to about one beat a second. If the pump ticks without delivering fuel, check it for leaks and blockages (see p. 142).

3 If the pump remains silent, tap it lightly with the handle of a screwdriver—the points may be sticking. If this fails, there may be a power-supply fault. Switch off the ignition.

4 Disconnect the power input lead from the pump terminal. Connect one wire from a test lamp to the disconnected lead, and the other to the pump terminal. Switch on the ignition; the bulb should light.

5 If the lamp fails to light, disconnect the test lead from the pump

terminal. Connect the free wire to a good earth point on the chassis or

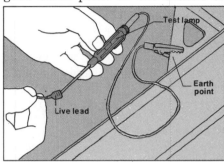

body. If the lamp then lights, the trouble is in the earth wire between the pump body and the chassis. Check and tighten all connections. Replace a broken earth wire.

6 If the lamp fails to light with a good earth, the fault is in the supply lead from the battery. Check the wiring (see p. 189).

Repairing an SU electrical fuel pump

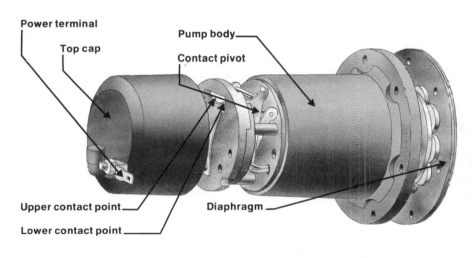

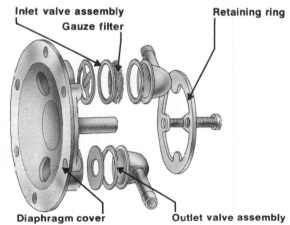

If the pump has fuel and power and still does not work, check the condition of its contact-breaker points and the pump filter.

Tools: Screwdrivers and pliers; contact file.
Materials: Outer sealing ring for the filter.

1 Disconnect the power supply. Remove the rubber boot, if one is fitted, from the plastic end cover of the pump. Undo the nut and pull

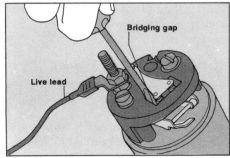

the cover off. Reconnect the power input lead to the terminal. Bridge

the edges of the contact-breaker points with the blade of a small screwdriver. If the pump gives only one stroke with the ignition switched on, the points are not making contact and the point faces are either dirty or badly corroded.

2 Remove the upper point and clean it with a fine contact file. The lower point is usually harder to reach, but it may be possible to get at it through an opening in the plastic moulding, using a small contact file or a piece of glass-paper.

3 If the pump still does not work, one of the valves may be obstructed by dirt. Undo the inlet pipe and plug it to prevent petrol leaking from the fuel tank.

4 Remove the retaining ring over the plastic valve covers. Take off the

cover of the inlet valve. Remove the outer sealing ring over the wire-gauze filter, and carefully prise out the gauze filter with a small screwdriver.

5 Lift out the valve and wash it thoroughly in petrol. Make sure it is refitted in the same position. Remove the outlet valve—which faces in the opposite direction—and clean and refit it.

6 If the pump still does not work, the diaphragm is probably damaged, or the magnet winding is faulty. It is a waste of time and effort to attempt further repairs, as factory-reconditioned units are reliable and comparatively cheap.

To fit a new pump, remove the two bolts holding the old unit. Bolt on the new pump and connect it to the fuel and power supplies.

Fuel pump/2

Taking a mechanical fuel pump off the car

The first step in overhauling a faulty mechanical fuel pump is to take it out of the car.

Disconnect the fuel lines from the pump and plug the one that leads from the petrol tank, so that fuel does not escape. Undo the nuts holding the pump to the engine block. Note the position of any spacers between the pump and the block, so that you refit them in their correct order.

Mark the upper and lower body castings with the edge of a file so they can be reassembled in the same position.

Tools: Spanners; screwdriver; flat-ended punch; light hammer; vice.
Materials: Pump overhaul kit to suit make and model; clean cloths; engine oil.

Repairing an SU-type mechanical fuel pump

1 Undo the screws holding the domed cover, and take it off. Remove the gauze filter and clean it with petrol to remove any sediment. Clean inside the pump cover in the same way.

2 Undo the ring of screws around the dome casting, so that you can separate the upper and lower halves.

3 Use one of the cover screws to push out the pivot pin of the rocker arm. The arm rests against the cam-shaft lobe and operates the pump.

4 Hold the pump carefully as you take out the rocker arm, otherwise the small coil spring will jump out. As it is removed the rocker arm disengages from the diaphragm rod and the diaphragm. The spring is underneath—it will push up the diaphragm rod and the diaphragm.

5 Try not to disturb the oil seal under the diaphragm, but if oily deposits are found on the diaphragm the seal is leaking. Buy a new seal and seal retaining cup.

6 The seal is secured by a cup, which is held in place by a slight distortion in the casting. Tap gently with a flat-ended punch and a light

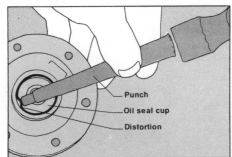

Punch
Oil seal cup
Distortion

hammer to remove the distortion. Lever out the cup and oil seal.

7 Coat a new seal in engine oil. Drop it into place and position a new cup with its edges upwards.

8 Use a socket of a suitable size from a socket set to push the cup in squarely. Assemble the parts in a vice, and gently tighten the jaws so that the socket presses on the cup.

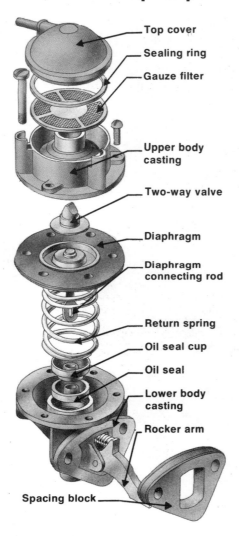

Top cover
Sealing ring
Gauze filter
Upper body casting
Two-way valve
Diaphragm
Diaphragm connecting rod
Return spring
Oil seal cup
Oil seal
Lower body casting
Rocker arm
Spacing block

9 When the cup is fully home in its seat on top of the oil seal, use the hammer and the punch and gently distort the casting again so that the cup is locked in place.

10 Push the new diaphragm and spring into the lower casting so that

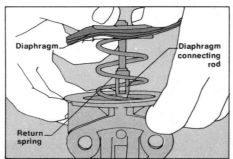

Diaphragm
Diaphragm connecting rod
Return spring

the eye of the diaphragm rod faces the rocker aperture. Refit the rocker-

A ONE-PIECE PUMP

Top cover
Outlet pipe
Filter
Inlet pipe
Actuating lever
Pump body

Pumps with one-piece bodies cannot be dismantled, but the filter and the sediment bowl can be cleaned. If the pump is defective, fit a new one.

FITTING AN OIL SEAL AND CUP

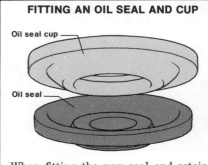

Oil seal cup
Oil seal

When fitting the new seal and retaining cup, make sure the centre boss of the seal fits into the centre of the cup. Distort the casting to secure it.

arm assembly to engage with the eye of the diaphragm rod.

11 Squeeze the flexible valve from underneath and pull it out of the pump chamber. Clean the seating and fit the new valve by hand.

12 Reassemble the upper and lower castings of the pump body so that the file marks are in line.

13 Press the rocker arm slightly to hold the diaphragm level while the short screws are finger tightened.

14 Fit the filter, sealing ring and top cover, using the long screws. Gently tighten the short screws until they are fully tight; then fully tighten the long ones.

Repairing an AC Delco-type mechanical pump

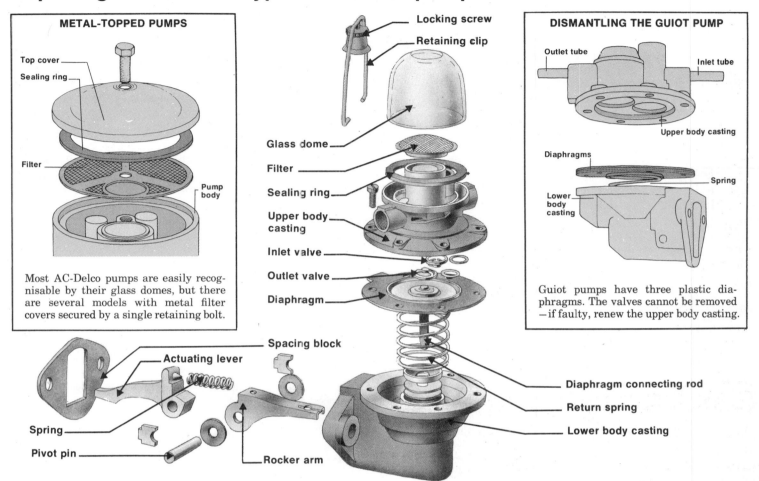

METAL-TOPPED PUMPS

Top cover
Sealing ring
Filter
Pump body

Most AC-Delco pumps are easily recognisable by their glass domes, but there are several models with metal filter covers secured by a single retaining bolt.

Locking screw
Retaining clip
Glass dome
Filter
Sealing ring
Upper body casting
Inlet valve
Outlet valve
Diaphragm

DISMANTLING THE GUIOT PUMP

Outlet tube
Inlet tube
Upper body casting
Diaphragms
Spring
Lower body casting

Guiot pumps have three plastic diaphragms. The valves cannot be removed — if faulty, renew the upper body casting.

Spacing block
Actuating lever
Spring
Pivot pin
Rocker arm

Diaphragm connecting rod
Return spring
Lower body casting

1 Undo the locking screw on top of the pump, take off the clip and remove the glass bowl and filter. Mark the two castings. Undo the screws and separate the two castings.

2 The diaphragm rod has a notch in the end which engages in a fork on

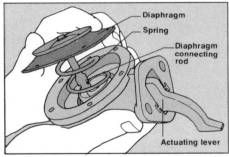

Diaphragm
Spring
Diaphragm connecting rod
Actuating lever

the rocker arm. To remove the diaphragm, turn it through a right angle. Do not remove the rocker.

3 AC pumps have two valves, and the same type is used for inlet and outlet; it is turned upside-down to reverse its function. Note the direction in which the old valves face before removing them — if you fit a new valve the wrong way up, the pump will not work. Take the valve retaining screws out of the upper casting. Remove the retainer plate, the two valve assemblies and the paper gasket.

4 Some AC pumps have no retainer plate; the valve assemblies fit directly into the casting. They are held in place by slight distortions on the edge of the casting. Scrape away these high spots with a steel scraper. Do not damage the casting.

5 Lever out the old valves with a small screwdriver. It does not matter

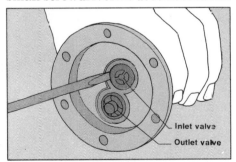

Inlet valve
Outlet valve

if you damage the valves while removing them.

6 Push in the new valves with a piece of metal tube with an internal diameter of $\frac{9}{16}$ in. and an external diameter of $\frac{3}{4}$ in. — for example, a short piece of electrical conduit, or a socket from a socket wrench. Make sure the valves fit squarely.

7 Put the assembly in a vice and tighten it slowly so that the metal tube presses the valves home.

8 Lightly tap the casting with a small punch to make notches that will secure the valves.

9 If the oil seal on the diaphragm connecting rod is worn, fit a new one. On most pumps, the seal and its retaining ring are held in place by distortions in the casting. On those with a retaining collar, undo the screws. Fit a new seal and secure it.

10 Refit the diaphragm and connecting rod. Turn the assembly through 90 degrees to engage the rocker arm. Put the castings together, line up the marks and fit the screws.

11 Hold the rocker arm up, to draw the diaphragm inwards, level with the edge of the casting flanges. Tighten the casting screws. Refit the filter and glass bowl, fit the clip and tighten the locking screw to secure the bowl. On pumps with metal tops, tighten the cover screw.

12 Fit the spacers to the engine block studs. Position the pump so that the actuating lever is on top of the pump cam. Half tighten the fixing nuts and press the pump body against the engine. The rocker arm spring will push it back if it is fitted correctly. Fit the fuel lines.

Carburettor/1

Faults you may find on a fixed-jet carburettor

On fixed-jet carburettors, made by Zenith, Solex, Weber, Motorcraft (Ford) and the Japanese Nikki, the flow of petrol to the engine is controlled by a series of jets that prevent the mixture of air and petrol becoming too rich to burn. These jets are mounted in the emulsion block, which is open to the atmosphere, where the petrol is emulsified (mixed with air) before it enters the engine. As the throttle valve is opened, air rushes into the engine and sucks petrol with it. The wider the valve is opened the greater the fuel flow.

To provide an extra burst of mixture for rapid acceleration, the carburettor has an accelerator pump which is connected to the throttle linkage. Sudden pressure on the accelerator pedal opens the accelerator pump, which squirts an extra charge of petrol into the carburettor.

For cruising, the carburettor has an economy device—a diaphragm operated by reduced pressure in the inlet manifold. This restricts the flow of petrol.

Poor starting, a steady rise in petrol consumption, irregular tick-over and poor acceleration are all symptoms of a worn carburettor.

The main wear point is the throttle spindle and its bearings.

Wear here creates an air leak, upsetting the petrol/air mixture and causing uneven running.

High fuel consumption may be due to a perforated diaphragm in the economy device. The diaphragm can be replaced (see p. 148).

Poor acceleration can be attributed to a fault in the accelerator pump. There are two basic types of pump: the diaphragm type, used in Fords and the older Solex carburettors, and the piston type used in the modern Zenith.

If the piston type is worn, there may also be wear in the carburettor body. Fit a replacement carburettor.

PISTON ACCELERATOR PUMP

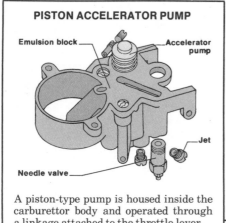

Emulsion block · Accelerator pump · Jet · Needle valve

A piston-type pump is housed inside the carburettor body and operated through a linkage attached to the throttle lever.

DIAPHRAGM ACCELERATOR PUMP

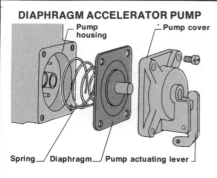

Pump housing · Pump cover · Spring · Diaphragm · Pump actuating lever

A diaphragm assembly is mounted outside the carburettor and is operated by an arm attached to the throttle. The diaphragm is returned by a spring.

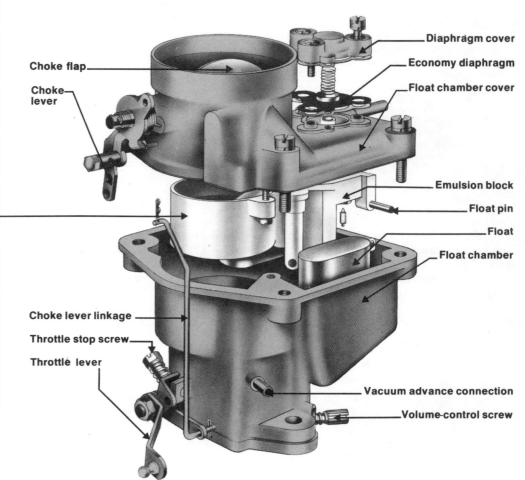

Choke flap · Choke lever · Diaphragm cover · Economy diaphragm · Float chamber cover · Emulsion block · Float pin · Float · Float chamber · Choke lever linkage · Throttle stop screw · Throttle lever · Vacuum advance connection · Volume-control screw

TYPES OF EMULSION BLOCK

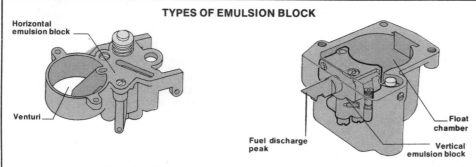

Horizontal emulsion block · Venturi · Fuel discharge peak · Float chamber · Vertical emulsion block

A horizontal emulsion block is screwed to the top casting of the carburettor. It has a venturi to match the carburettor intake, and houses all the carburettor jets and the float mechanism. A vertical emulsion block is bolted to the outside of the float chamber and has a fuel discharge peak that protrudes into the carburettor venturi. Note that Motorcraft (Ford) carburettors do not have an emulsion block.

FLOAT ASSEMBLY

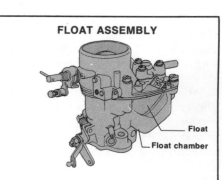

Float · Float chamber

The fuel level in the float chamber must be at the correct height (check this with your dealer) for the jets to meter the correct flow of fuel. The level is controlled by a needle valve.

Renewing the throttle spindle and throttle valve

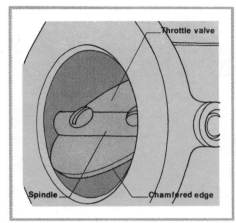

Disconnect the operating cable or rod from the throttle lever. Grip the end of the throttle spindle and try to move it up and down. If there is any play, the spindle or carburettor body is worn. The most usual wear point is the spindle, which can be renewed. But if the carburettor body itself is worn, fit a replacement carburettor.

When renewing the spindle, always fit a new throttle valve. On some carburettors, the plate fits against a flat section on the spindle. On others it fits into a slot.

Tools: Screwdriver; punch; pin-hammer.
Materials: ·Spindle; butterfly; screws; 320-grit wet-and-dry paper.

1 Remove the carburettor air cleaner (see p. 123). Disconnect the choke control linkage, vacuum advance pipe and fuel pipe. Undo the nuts holding the carburettor to the inlet manifold, and remove it.

2 Note the position of the linkage between the throttle lever and the accelerator pump and choke flap. There may be alternative mounting

holes, and you must ensure that the linkage is refitted correctly. Discon-

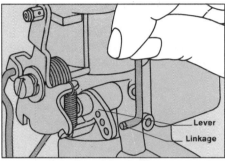

nect the linkage, which is usually secured by split-pins.

3 Undo the nut or screw that holds the throttle lever to the spindle. Re-

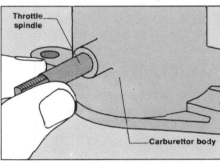

move the lever. Turn the spindle so that the screws holding the throttle

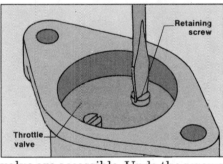

valve are accessible. Undo the screws and remove the throttle valve. If

the valve fits in a slot in the spindle, turn the spindle until the valve is vertical and remove it. Use the wet-and-dry paper to rub off any burrs on the spindle, they might score the bearings in the carburettor body. Slide the worn spindle out of the carburettor bearings.

4 Fit the new spindle to the carburettor body. Position the throttle valve so that its chamfered edge fits the body. Replace and tighten the

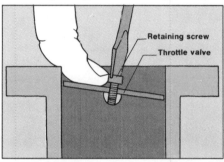

two throttle valve screws. Turn the valve so that the screw heads are inwards. Fix a small punch in a vice and fit the carburettor over it so that the punch contacts the head of the screws. Use a small hammer

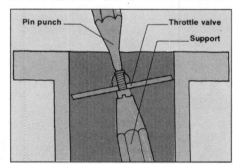

to burr over the ends of the screws. Turn the valve back to its original position.

Renewing the needle valve

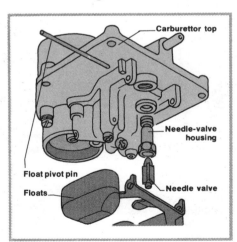

1 Remove the air cleaner (see p. 123). Disconnect the choke cable and the linkage between the throttle and the accelerator pump and choke flap. Undo the fuel pipe, remove the

screws that hold the top of the carburettor, and lift off the top.

2 Remove the float pivot pin and lift off the float. Never operate the

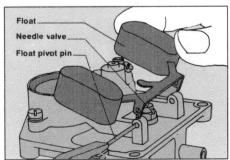

accelerator linkage when the top is off the carburettor.

3 Check and shake the float. If it is copper, it may have become perfor-

ated and contain fuel. If so, replace it with a plastic float. Undo the needle-valve assembly. Fit new assembly,

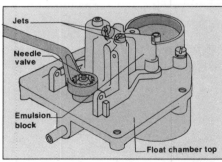

using a washer of the same thickness under the head of the needle-valve housing. Replace the float and check the height when the float arm is resting on the needle (see p. 149). Adjust by bending the arm, and reassemble.

Carburettor/2

Cleaning the jets on a fixed-jet carburettor

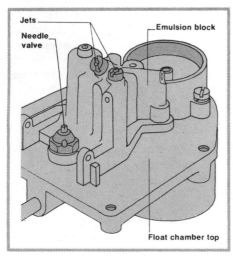

Jets
Needle valve
Emulsion block
Float chamber top

1 Remove the top of the carburettor (see p. 147). Undo the screws securing the emulsion block to the carburettor body. On carburettors with horizontal emulsion blocks the needle-valve assembly may have to be removed (see p. 146).

2 Unscrew the jets one at a time and blow them clean with an air line, or probe them clear with a brush

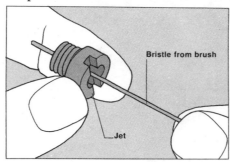

Bristle from brush
Jet

bristle. Never use wire to clear a blocked jet. If new jets are needed, make sure you fit jets of the correct size. Blow clean the delivery holes in the emulsion block.

3 Check the flatness of the face of the block by rubbing it lightly on a

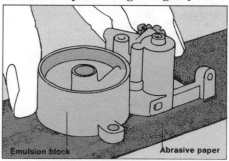

Emulsion block
Abrasive paper

sheet of 320-grit wet-and-dry abrasive paper placed on plate glass. If the face is flat it will be shiny all over. Reassemble with new gaskets and 'O' ring seals, where fitted.

Overhauling an accelerator pump

Piston-type pumps are located in the emulsion block or float chamber casting. Diaphragm pumps are mounted outside on the chamber.

1 Remove the emulsion block (see p. 146) or float chamber (see p. 147).

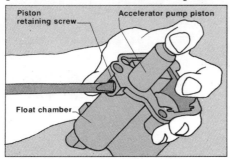

Piston retaining screw
Accelerator pump piston
Float chamber

Release the retaining screw and withdraw the piston assembly. Hold the piston between thumb and forefinger to test the piston action. If it

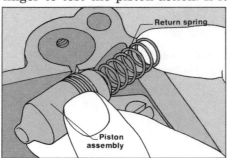

Return spring
Piston assembly

sticks, or the spring is weak, fit a new piston assembly.

2 Check the piston and bore in the casting for scoring. If the bore is damaged, fit a replacement carburettor. Remove the circlip holding the non-return ball-valve in the bore in the carburettor body. Clean the ball. Reassemble the parts.

Diaphragm pump Remove the screws holding the diaphragm pump cover. Lift out the diaphragm and

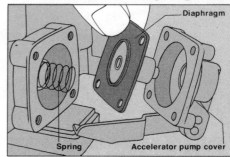

Diaphragm
Spring
Accelerator pump cover

spring. Clean and reassemble the unit with a new diaphragm.

Fitting a new economy diaphragm

At cruising speeds the economy diaphragm lifts to allow extra ventilation to the jets, weakening the mixture. If fuel consumption is heavy, fit a new economy diaphragm.

1 Undo the three or five screws that secure the diaphragm cover to the

Cover
Spring

body of the carburettor. Lift off the cover and remove the spring and diaphragm. Note that there are gaskets on top and below the diaphragm.

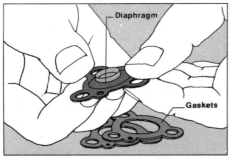

Diaphragm
Gaskets

Check that the spring is undamaged. Fit a new one if necessary.

2 Fit the new diaphragm so that the bleed holes line up with the hole in the carburettor casting. Make sure the cup is facing upwards. Refit the spring and replace the cover.

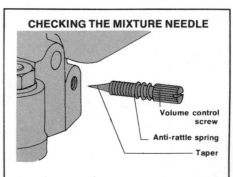

CHECKING THE MIXTURE NEEDLE

Volume control screw
Anti-rattle spring
Taper

Remove the slow-running mixture (volume control) screw from the side of the carburettor. Check that the taper is not ridged, scored or bent. If there is any damage, fit a new needle. Make sure that the anti-rattle spring is fitted on the mixture needle, and screw the needle into the carburettor body. Tighten the needle and unscrew it about two full turns. Adjust the carburettor (see p. 128).

Checking and cleaning a twin-choke carburettor

The two most popular makes of twin-choke carburettors are the Weber and Solex. Other makes work on the same basic principles.

The most common type is the progressive-choke carburettor. A primary choke, operated by a linkage, opens first, feeding a mixture of petrol and air to the engine. Then a secondary choke, operated by a diaphragm sensitive to the air pressure in the manifold, also opens. Both chokes become fully open at the same time. The two chokes have different-sized jets: do not mix them when you overhaul the carburettor.

The second type has two throttle butterflies on a common spindle, so the chokes open simultaneously. The jets are identical.

The main wearing parts are the same as in a fixed-jet unit (see pp. 147-8), but major overhaul is best left to a garage.

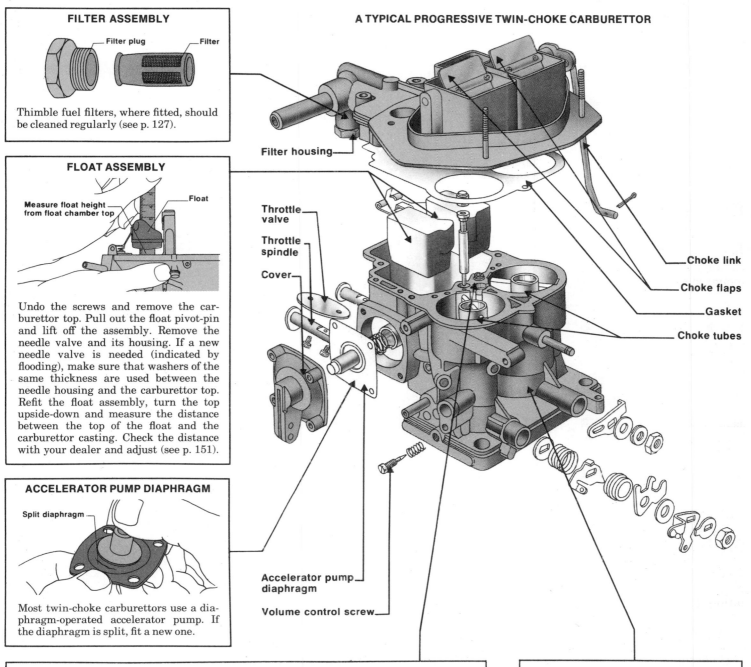

A TYPICAL PROGRESSIVE TWIN-CHOKE CARBURETTOR

FILTER ASSEMBLY

Filter plug — Filter

Thimble fuel filters, where fitted, should be cleaned regularly (see p. 127).

FLOAT ASSEMBLY

Measure float height from float chamber top — Float

Undo the screws and remove the carburettor top. Pull out the float pivot-pin and lift off the assembly. Remove the needle valve and its housing. If a new needle valve is needed (indicated by flooding), make sure that washers of the same thickness are used between the needle housing and the carburettor top. Refit the float assembly, turn the top upside-down and measure the distance between the top of the float and the carburettor casting. Check the distance with your dealer and adjust (see p. 151).

ACCELERATOR PUMP DIAPHRAGM

Split diaphragm

Most twin-choke carburettors use a diaphragm-operated accelerator pump. If the diaphragm is split, fit a new one.

Filter housing

Throttle valve
Throttle spindle
Cover

Choke link
Choke flaps
Gasket
Choke tubes

Accelerator pump diaphragm
Volume control screw

REMOVING THE JETS ON TWIN-CHOKE CARBURETTORS

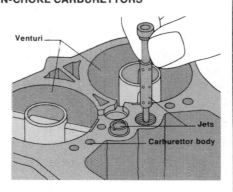

Do not remove all the jets or emulsion tubes from a progressive twin-choke carburettor at the same time: the jets are different sizes and may get mixed up. Some jets are reached from inside the float chamber, and others are accessible from the outside, after removing jet blanking plugs. Clean any jets by blowing through them with an air line or probing them clear with a brush bristle. Never probe them clear with a piece of wire. On most twin-choke carburettors the discharge valves are situated in the lower body of the unit and sealed with 'O' rings. Fit new rings and gaskets when reassembling the carburettor.

Venturi

Jets
Carburettor body

THROTTLE GEAR LINKAGES

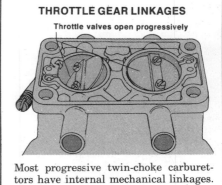

Throttle valves open progressively

Most progressive twin-choke carburettors have internal mechanical linkages. Do not try to overhaul these.

Carburettor/3

Overhauling an SU variable-jet carburettor

The SU carburettor has a tapered needle that slides in an adjustable jet to increase or decrease the petrol flow. The needle is attached to a piston assembly which slides up and down the suction chamber. As the throttle butterfly opens, air is drawn through the piston assembly from the suction chamber above the piston. The piston rises, lifts the tapered needle out of the jet, and increases the flow.

An oil-filled damper assembly in the top of the suction chamber limits the speed at which the piston rises. If there is no oil in the damper, the piston will rise quickly, causing engine hesitation and stalling. Check the damper oil-level regularly and top up if necessary (see p. 125).

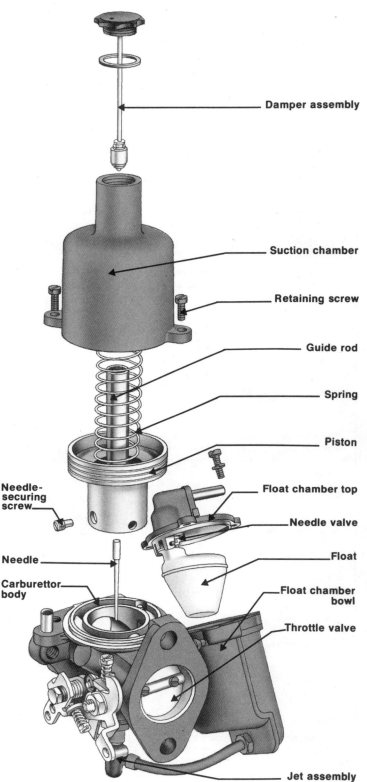

- Damper assembly
- Suction chamber
- Retaining screw
- Guide rod
- Spring
- Piston
- Float chamber top
- Needle valve
- Float
- Float chamber bowl
- Throttle valve
- Jet assembly
- Needle-securing screw
- Needle
- Carburettor body

HS JET ASSEMBLY

The most commonly used SU carburettor is the HS series. Fuel from the float chamber enters the main jet through a feed pipe—usually a flexible nylon tube—attached to it. A tapered needle, attached to the bottom of the piston assembly—which in itself is lifted by suction—moves in and out of the jet, thus increasing or decreasing the flow of fuel according to the engine's requirements.

The jet is carried in a jet holder. To remove a jet, disconnect the fuel feed pipe from the bottom of the float chamber and draw the jet out. When you fit a new jet, remember that it will have to be centralised in the jet holder (see p. 151).

To enrich the mixture for cold starting, the choke draws the jet down from the tapered needle, and provides a wider opening from which the fuel can flow.

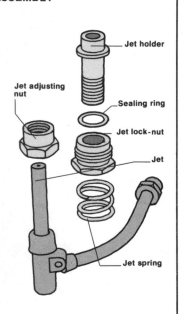

- Jet holder
- Jet adjusting nut
- Sealing ring
- Jet lock-nut
- Jet
- Jet spring

HD JET ASSEMBLY

HD series carburettors are used on Rover 2000 and most Jaguar models. The basic principle of operation is the same as the HS series (above). But in the HD the fuel is carried to the base of the carburettor through a casting that is part of the float chamber. It is contained in the base by a diaphragm that carries the jet assembly. In both types the operation of the choke moves the jet downwards to enrich the mixture, and at the same time opens the throttle butterfly slightly to achieve a cold fast-idle setting.

On this carburettor a mixture screw controls the jet adjusting lever. Turn the screw clockwise to enrich the mixture, and anti-clockwise to weaken it. Operation of the choke control moves the jet adjusting lever to enrich the mixture and operates a fast-idle cam that controls the throttle butterfly.

To adjust the HD carburettor (see p. 128) there is a volume control screw as well as mixture control and throttle stop screws.

The main wear points are the needle and jet, and possibly the diaphragm assembly in the base of the unit. Replacements can be obtained from an SU dealer.

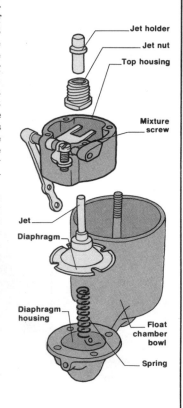

- Jet holder
- Jet nut
- Top housing
- Mixture screw
- Jet
- Diaphragm
- Diaphragm housing
- Float chamber bowl
- Spring

FLOAT NEEDLE VALVE

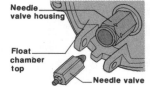

- Needle valve housing
- Float chamber top
- Needle valve

The needle valve is in the top of the float chamber of an SU carburettor. To change it, remove the top, dismantle the float and unscrew the valve.

FLOAT ASSEMBLY

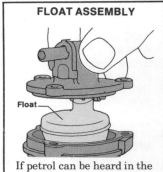

- Float

If petrol can be heard in the float when it is shaken, fit a new float assembly.

Fitting a new needle and jet to improve fuel consumption

The tapered needle in an SU carburettor moves in and out of the jet to regulate the flow of fuel. If the needle is worn the fuel consumption will increase; fit a new needle and jet. If the throttle spindle is worn, renew it (see p. 147).

Tools: Screwdriver; adjusting nut spanner.
Materials: New needle; new jet; clean rag; methylated spirit.

1 Unscrew and remove the damper from the top of the suction chamber. Mark a line across the base of the

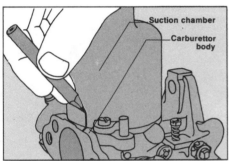

suction chamber and the body of the carburettor. This provides a guideline so the suction chamber can be replaced in the correct position.

2 Undo the screws holding the suction chamber to the body of the car-

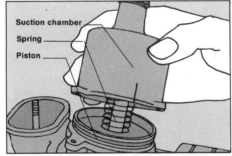

burettor and lift it off. Remove the piston return spring and lift out the piston. The tapered needle is held

by a securing screw to the base of the piston air valve.

3 Loosen the needle-securing screw in the side of the piston air valve and withdraw the needle. Fit a new needle. Make sure that the shoulder is flush with the base of the piston air valve. If a spring-loaded needle is fitted, make sure the spring housing is flush with the base of the

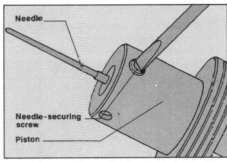

piston air valve. Tighten the needle-securing screw. Clean the sides of the piston and air-valve assembly with methylated spirit to remove any dirt or carbon deposits.

4 Remove the cross-head screw that holds the carburettor choke linkage to the base of the jet. Undo the flexible petrol pipe from the bottom of

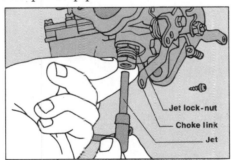

the float chamber. Loosen the jet lock-nut and withdraw the jet from the carburettor jet holder.

5 Remove the jet adjusting nut and the spring. Replace only the nut, and screw it up as far as it will go. Push the new jet into position. Replace the piston assembly, lightly oil the guide rod and fit the suction chamber. Push the piston down with a

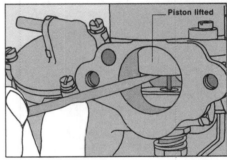

pencil to centralise the jet. Tighten the jet lock-nut.

6 Lift the piston and let it drop. If you do not hear a metallic click as

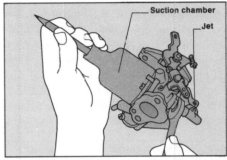

the piston strikes the jet bridge, repeat the centralising procedure.

7 When the jet is centralised, remove it. Undo the jet adjusting nut and refit the spring and the nut. Refit the jet. Set it by undoing the nut two full turns.

8 Remove the suction chamber and refit the spring. Replace the chamber, making sure the marks line up.

Checking and adjusting the float level for economy

If the float level is incorrect, too much petrol flows into the float chamber and is wasted.

Tools: Screwdriver; test bar or ruler.
Materials: New float, if necessary.

1 Disconnect the fuel line at the top of the float chamber. Undo the screws that hold the float chamber top, and lift off the top. Hold the top, inverted, in the palm of your hand.

2 Make sure the needle valve moves freely. Push it fully home to close it and insert a test bar—$\frac{5}{16}$ in. diameter for HS carburettors, and $\frac{7}{16}$ in. diameter for HD models—between the rim of the float chamber

top and the radius of the float lever. When the float lever is on the bar it

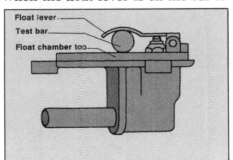

should just be in contact with the top of the needle.

3 If necessary, bend the lever at the start of the radius until it contacts the top of the needle valve.

Nylon float If the float is nylon with a brass lever, the clearance should be between $\frac{1}{8}$ in. and $\frac{3}{16}$ in. Measure between the lip of the float chamber top and the bottom of the float with

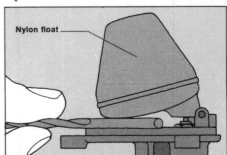

the shank of a drill bit. The gap is the same for a spring-loaded valve—without the needle valve depressed.

Carburettor /4

Overhauling a Stromberg CD carburettor

Like the SU carburettors (see p. 150), the Stromberg CD range regulates the fuel flow by moving a tapered needle in and out of an adjustable jet. The needle is fixed to the base of the air valve, which is moved by a diaphragm.

The diaphragm is fitted to the air-valve body and the outside flange of the carburettor body, to form a seal between the carburettor intake and the suction chamber at the top. If a diaphragm becomes perforated or damaged, the seal is broken and the air valve cannot lift; engine response is slowed considerably.

MANUAL CHOKE CONTROL

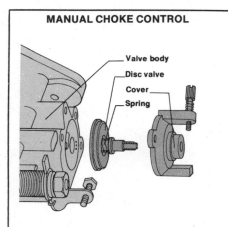

When the choke control on the car's instrument panel is pulled out, it operates an enrichening valve on the side of the carburettor body, and a fast-idle cam opens the throttle slightly to increase the engine speed.

If dirt is able to get into the system it can block off the fuel regulating holes and make cold starting difficult. Strip and clean the enrichening valve.

Some Stromberg CD carburettors use a water-heated automatic choke. If this fails, overhaul it (see p. 155).

1 Disconnect the choke cable from the side of the carburettor. Undo the nut holding the fast-idle cam to the spindle of the enrichening valve.

2 Lift off the fast-idle cam and remove the cam return spring. Note how the spring is fitted. It is important to replace the spring in the correct position.

3 Undo the two screws that hold the enrichening valve to the carburettor body, and lift out the valve assembly. This will reveal a light spring and 'C' washer.

4 Remove the 'C' washer that holds the valve disc spring, and remove the spring. This enables the two parts of the disc valve to be moved apart for cleaning. Do not try to take the discs off the spindle. The end of the spindle is burred over to secure them.

5 Make sure that the fuel regulating holes in the disc are clear. Wash the disc valve in clean petrol. Dry the valve and reassemble it so that the small regulating holes are at the bottom of the housing when the choke is in the 'on' position.

DAMPER ASSEMBLY

If the damper piston is worn, remove the circlip with pliers and fit a new piston on the rod.

JET ASSEMBLY

The jet is spring-loaded and the assembly is sealed with 'O' rings. To realign the jet, turn the jet adjusting screw.

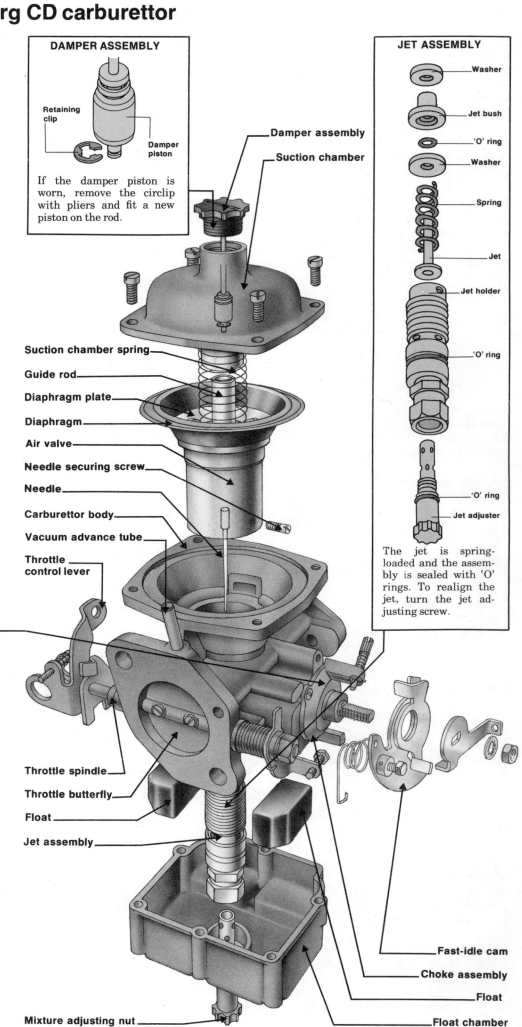

Fitting a new needle, jet or diaphragm

Fitting a new throttle spindle and butterfly involves the same procedure as for a fixed-jet carburettor (see p. 147). If the diaphragm, needle or jet need renewing, the carburettor has to be dismantled.

Tools: Screwdrivers; spanners to fit the jet holder nut; pliers.
Materials: New jet; set of carburettor gaskets and seals; new diaphragm, if necessary.

1 Scribe a line across the suction chamber and the carburettor body,

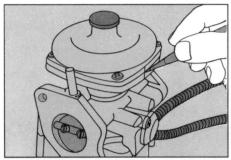

so that it can be refitted in the correct position. Undo the four cross-headed screws on the top of the carburettor and lift off the chamber. Remove the air-valve return spring.

2 Lift out the air valve and the diaphragm assembly. Hold the dia-

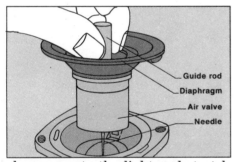

phragm up to the light and stretch it to check if it is perforated. If so,

a new diaphragm will have to be fitted to the air valve.

3 Undo the four screws through the centre diaphragm plate. Lift off the

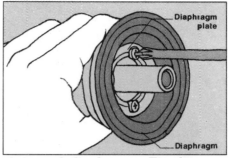

plate and diaphragm. Fit the new diaphragm and tighten the screws.

4 Loosen the needle securing screw, and remove the needle from the air

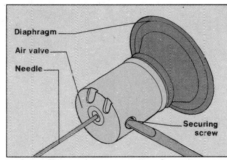

valve. Fit a new needle, keeping its shoulder flush with the air-valve base. Tighten the securing screw.

5 Turn the carburettor upside-down and remove the jet adjusting screw. Undo the larger of the two nuts at the base of the float chamber and remove the jet holder, jet, jet spring and brass bush.

6 Fit a new jet and spring to the brass bush. Fit the assembly to the

jet holder, with new washers and 'O' sealing rings. Screw the jet

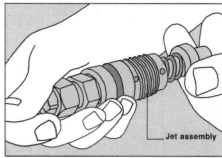

holder assembly into the body of the carburettor.

7 Fit the air-valve assembly, and make sure that the lug on the lip of the diaphragm fits into the groove on the body of the carburettor. Make sure that the needle on the bottom of the air valve fits squarely into the jet. Fit the suction chamber and tighten the chamber screws.

8 Lift the air valve and let it drop. If it does not give a metallic click as it strikes the jet bridge, loosen the jet

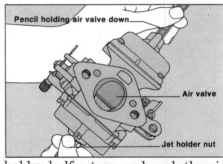

holder half a turn and push the air valve down with a pencil. This will centralise the jet. Once the air valve falls freely, tighten the jet holder nut. Fit the damper and adjust the carburettor (see p. 127).

Renewing the float needle valve

Tools: Screwdriver; spanner to fit the needle-valve housing; pliers.
Materials: New needle valve; washers.

1 If fuel floods from the float chamber, undo the six float chamber

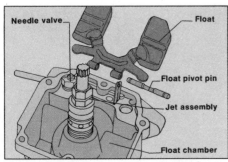

screws and remove the float chamber. Remove the float pivot pin.

Lift off the two floats to gain access to the hexagon-shaped needle-valve housing in the carburettor body.

2 Undo the housing and remove the complete assembly from the car-

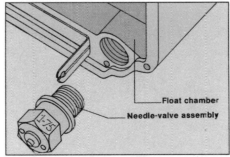

burettor body. The size of the needle valve is marked on the flat section on the hexagon head of the housing.

3 Use washers of the same thickness as those removed. Fit and tighten the new needle-valve assembly. Refit the float assembly and turn the complete unit upside-down.

4 Use a ruler to measure the distance between the top of the float—the highest part—and the body of the carburettor. It should be 16 mm. If it needs adjusting, gently bend the float arm extension until it just touches the needle valve and gives the correct float-level height. Note that the float arm extension is springy, so bend it slightly past the required point. Measure the distance and adjust if necessary. Reassemble the float chamber. Start the engine and check for flooding.

Carburettor/5

How an automatic choke works

When the engine is cold, press the accelerator pedal once before switching on the ignition. This operates a mechanism by which a coil spring in the choke housing can hold the choke flap closed, and the throttle butterfly is opened slightly to provide a fast idle when the engine is first started.

The spring in the choke housing is controlled either by water temperature, by hot air from a 'hot-box' attached to the exhaust manifold, or an electric element. As the engine warms, the heat of the water, air or element, expands the coil spring and the choke flap opens.

The choke flap is also controlled by a piston or diaphragm inside the choke housing. At low engine speeds, when inlet manifold depression is high, the piston or diaphragm opens the choke flap against the pressure of the coil spring. If the engine load is increased the manifold depression (suction) is reduced and the piston or diaphragm rises, allowing the coil spring to close the choke flap.

Dirt or carbon inside the choke housing may jam the mechanism, so keeping the choke closed.

Tools: Pliers; screwdriver; twist drill of the correct diameter (·040 to ·060 in.); spanners. **Materials:** New diaphragm; petrol.

Overhauling a Zenith hot-air choke

The spring that controls the choke flap is operated by air from the exhaust 'hot-box'. Remove the carburettor (see p. 147). Allow it to cool before dismantling the choke.

1 Clean the choke unit and check that the white line on the serrated cover coincides with the casting mark on the choke body. If no marks can be seen, scribe a line across both surfaces to establish their positions.

2 Hold one spanner on the centre nut of the assembly and, using

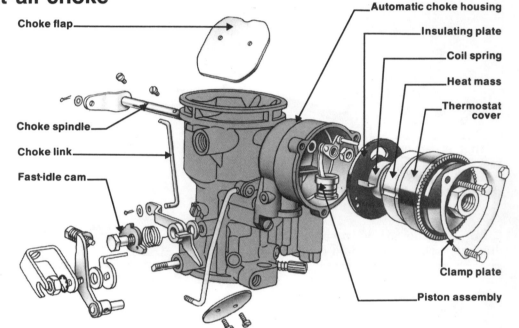

Choke flap — Automatic choke housing — Insulating plate — Coil spring — Heat mass — Thermostat cover — Choke spindle — Choke link — Fast-idle cam — Clamp plate — Piston assembly

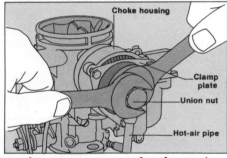

Choke housing — Clamp plate — Union nut — Hot-air pipe

another spanner, undo the union nut securing the hot-air pipe. Remove the screws that hold the clamp plate and lift out the thermostat cover, heat mass and coil spring. Remove the heat insulating plate.

3 Check the fast-idle cam and choke flap spindle for free operation. If they are tight, clean them with a lint-free cloth and lubricate them.

4 Check the operation of the piston in the choke housing. It should

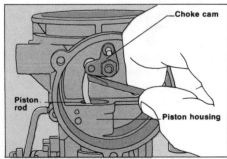

Choke cam — Piston rod — Piston housing

move freely inside its cylinder. If it is tight, remove and clean it. It

should be level with the top of the cylinder on 42 WIAT carburettors, and ·040 in. below the top of the piston on 42 VNT carburettors.

5 Thoroughly clean the inside of the choke housing with methylated spirit or clean petrol. Remove any dirt or carbon deposits. Dry the housing and oil the piston lightly.

6 Some automatic chokes have a diaphragm-mounted unit attached

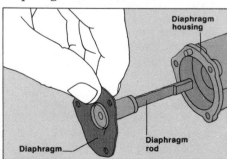

Diaphragm housing — Diaphragm — Diaphragm rod

to the side of the choke housing. Undo the three screws holding the diaphragm cover and remove the diaphragm from the housing. Stretch the diaphragm to see if it is holed or damaged. If the diaphragm is faulty, fit a new one.

7 Check the choke spindle for play —there should be none. If it is worn, remove the choke flap and fit

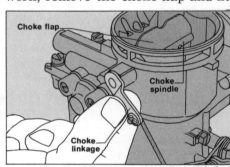

Choke flap — Choke spindle — Choke linkage

a new spindle (see p. 147). Make sure the choke linkage is refitted the correct way.

8 Reassemble the unit. Fit the heat insulating plate and the coil spring. Make sure that the spring engages the operating peg on the mechanism inside the choke housing. Fit the heat mass and thermostat cover. Replace the retaining plate. Make sure that the marks on the plate and choke housing line up. Do up the securing screws and refit the pipe from the exhaust 'hot-box'. Make sure that all the carburettor linkage moves freely (see p. 125).

Overhauling a Ford water-heated choke

Ford chokes are water-controlled. On ohv engines the water inlet and outlet tubes are on the same side of the choke water jacket. On ohc engines the inlet and outlet tubes are on opposite sides of the jacket.

1 Disconnect the water hoses from the water jacket at the choke assembly. Undo the three screws that hold the water jacket to the body of the choke.

2 Lift off the housing and note the position of the end of the thermo-

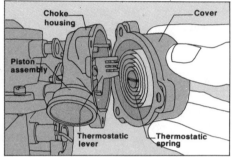

stat spring. It can fit in one of three positions in the thermostatic lever.

3 Make sure that the piston valve moves freely in its cylinder. If necessary, disconnect the piston linkage, remove the piston and clean it. Refit the piston.

4 Push the piston down until you can see the bleed port in the piston cylinder. Insert a length of bent

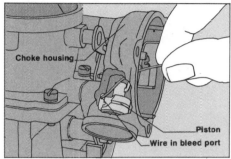

wire, ·040 in. thick, into the bleed port and allow the piston to return against it.

5 Open the throttle until the fast-idle tab clears the cam. Close the choke plate until its movement is

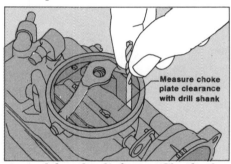

stopped by the linkage. Check the gap between the choke flap and body

with a drill shank, or rod of the correct diameter. Ask your Ford dealer to specify the clearance for the type and model of carburettor fitted to your car.

6 Release the throttle and check that the fast-idle tab is in the first step of the cam. To adjust the clearance, increase the bend in the rod

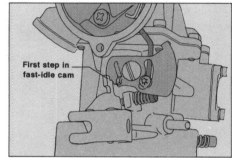

to the fast-idle cam until the tab is in the first step of the cam. Press the accelerator pedal twice to ensure that the adjustment is correct.

7 Remove the wire from the piston bleed port. Clean inside the choke housing and reassemble the mechanism. Make sure that the thermostat spring is located in the correct slot in the lever. If in doubt, engage it in the centre slot. Refit the water jacket and reconnect the hoses.

Overhauling a Solex electric heater-element choke

Some Solex chokes—especially on Volkswagen engines—have a bi-metallic thermostat spring which is controlled by an electric element. When the spring is cold, the choke is closed. As the element heats the spring, it expands and opens the choke. The choke also has a piston or diaphragm vacuum unit.

1 Disconnect the terminal lead. Undo the three screws holding the retaining plate to the body, and remove the plate.

2 Lift off the cap that contains the bi-metallic spring and element.

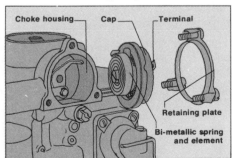

Connect the lead to the element terminal, turn on the ignition and earth the cap. The heater element

should get hot. If not, the element is damaged and a new unit is needed. Turn off the ignition.

3 Make sure that the vacuum piston moves freely in its cylinder.

If a diaphragm vacuum unit is fitted, remove the screws holding the diaphragm cover to the side of the

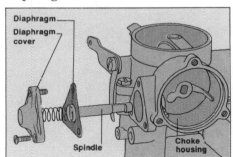

choke body. Lift off the cover and remove the diaphragm. If the diaphragm is perforated or damaged, fit a new one.

4 Make sure that the choke spindle moves freely. If necessary, lubricate the spindle bearings to ensure that it can turn easily. Check the linkage between the other end of the choke spindle and the fast-idle cam

which is attached to the throttle butterfly spindle.

5 On diaphragm-operated units only, refit the plastic cap that protects the diaphragm. Fit the choke element and cover. Make sure that the bi-metallic spring engages with the choke lever, and that the marks on the cover line up with the

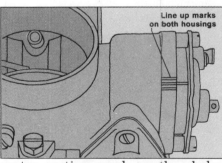

centre casting mark on the choke housing. Fit the retaining plate.

6 Run the engine and check that the choke flap is fully open when the engine is warm, and that the idling speed stop-screw is resting in the last notch of the fast-idle cam. Adjust the idle speed (see p. 128) to give a normal hot-engine tick-over.

Carburettor/6

Overhauling a Stromberg water-heated choke

The choke flap is open during normal running, but a richer mixture is needed for cold starts. When the engine is cold, the flap is held closed by a bi-metallic spring, controlled by water temperature. As the engine warms up, the water heats and the spring expands, closing the flap.

1 Disconnect the inlet and outlet water pipes from the water jacket on

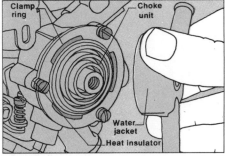

the choke unit. Undo the centre bolt and remove the water jacket.

2 Remove the three screws and clamp ring. Carefully remove the finned heat mass and coil spring.

3 Remove the heat insulator. Clean inside the choke housing. Check that

the metering needle moves freely. If not, prise off the choke spindle

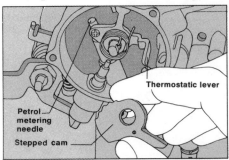

clip and remove the stepped cam, spring and thermostat lever. Undo the housing plug and remove the metering needle. Clean the needle and reassemble it. Undo the three

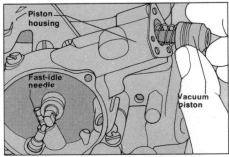

screws holding the piston cover. Remove the cover and piston. Clean

the piston and refit it. Reassemble the lever, spring and stepped cam to the choke spindle. Refit the retaining clip to secure them.

4 Rotate the thermostat lever anticlockwise. Use a feeler blade to measure the distance between the

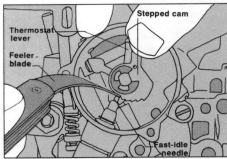

base of the stepped cam and the fast-idle needle. (Check the clearance with your dealer.)

5 Fit the heat insulator. Make sure that the peg on the thermostat lever fits through the slot in the insulator. Refit the coil spring and heat mass. Line up the marks on the heat mass, body casting and retaining plate. Fit the plate screws. Replace the water jacket and hoses.

Overhauling an SU auxiliary starter carburettor

Cars with more than one SU carburettor may have a starter unit operated by a solenoid. The unit is controlled by a thermostatic switch in the inlet manifold water jacket. Starting difficulty is caused by a faulty starter carburettor.

1 Remove the lead from the solenoid terminal. Switch on the choke and check the supply at the lead with a test bulb (see p. 189). If the bulb lights, the solenoid is damaged.

2 Remove the top of the solenoid and lift out the solenoid unit, spring

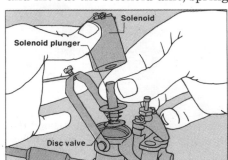

and disc valve. Fit a new unit. Replace the top and connect the wire to the terminal. Check the solenoid (it should click as it rises).

3 If the test bulb does not light, short-circuit the terminal on the

manifold switch by holding a screwdriver across the terminal and inlet

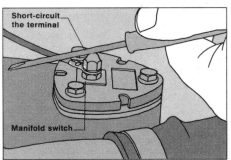

manifold. If the solenoid then operates, the switch is faulty.

4 Remove the three screws that hold the switch unit to the manifold. Lift

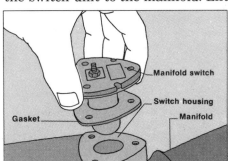

out the unit. Remove the old gasket from the face of the manifold switch housing. Clean the face of the housing with a steel scraper to remove any particles of the old gasket.

5 Grease both faces of the new gasket and lay it in position on the manifold. Fit the new switch unit and screw it firmly into position. Reconnect the lead to the switch terminal and check the solenoid.

6 To adjust the starter carburettor needle, run the engine until it reaches working temperature and the solenoid is switched off. Activate the solenoid, with the engine running, by shorting out the switch.

7 Ideally the exhaust smoke should now be discernibly black, with the engine running regularly. If the smoke is not black, the mixture is too weak. Turn the needle stopscrew anticlockwise to enrich the mixture. If the engine runs irregu-

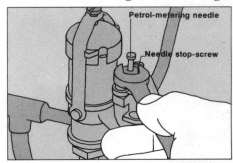

larly, turn the needle stop-screw clockwise to richen the mixture.

Distributor / 1

How the sparks are produced in the engine

It is essential when tracing a fault in the ignition system to know how the system works, because each component has to be checked in turn.

The ignition system produces the sparks necessary to burn the petrol-air mixture in the engine combustion chambers. It consists of a switch, battery, coil, distributor and spark-plugs.

The battery produces low-tension current (usually 12 volts) which, when the ignition is switched on, flows to the coil. The coil boosts this low-tension current, transforming it into high-tension current (up to 30,000 volts). Its primary winding is connected between the battery and the contact-breaker points in the distributor. As current flows through the primary winding, which is wrapped round a soft iron core, a magnetic field is created. This regularly collapses as the low-tension circuit is switched on and off by the opening and closing of the contact-breaker (CB) points. This collapse generates the high-tension current in the secondary winding in the coil, which is connected by a high-tension lead to the distributor cap.

Once this high voltage is produced, the distributor sends it to each spark-plug in turn to produce a spark at the correct time in each piston's four-stroke cycle.

The spark-plug has two electrodes —live and earth—with a gap (usually ·025 in.) between them, and the spark is produced when the high-tension current jumps the gap.

Low-tension circuit
Low-tension current flows into the coil's primary winding at a terminal usually marked SW (or +) for 'switch'. Another terminal, marked CB (or −) leads to the contact-breaker assembly in the distributor. When the LT circuit is broken, the magnetic field created by it collapses—inducing high-tension current in a secondary winding in the coil.

High-tension circuit
The high-tension current flows to the centre terminal in the distributor cap, where it is passed to the rotor arm. Cables from the cap then carry HT pulses to each spark-plug in turn. Because of the high voltage, the HT leads are thick and heavily insulated. Modern leads have carbon centres and act as radio and television interference suppressors.

Battery and ignition switch
A fully charged battery puts out only 6 or 12 volts when the ignition is switched on. This low-tension (LT) current flows to the coil, where it is boosted to high-tension (HT) current of about 16,000 volts, but sometimes up to 30,000 volts. HT current is needed to provide the sparks that will fire the mixture in the combustion chambers and so turn the engine.

Distributor and plugs
The contact-breaker points in the distributor control the timing of the spark. Its size is controlled by the gap between the electrodes at the tip of each plug. This is small (usually about ·025 in.), but the high voltage of the current from the distributor cap, ranging from 16,000 to 30,000 volts, enables it to jump the gap, and produce the necessary spark.

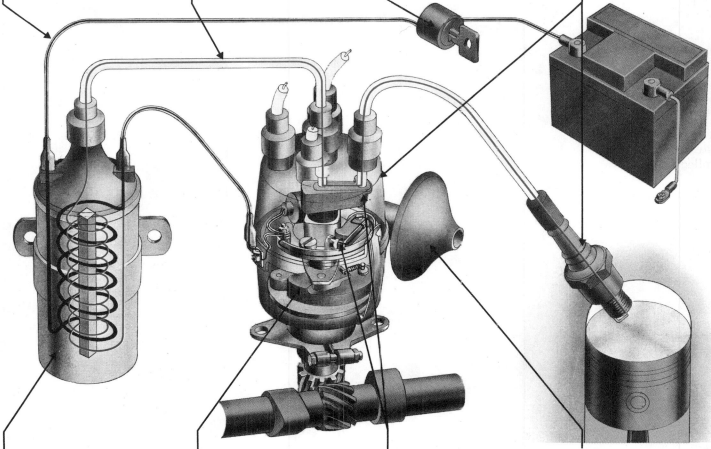

Coil
To do its job of transforming low-tension into high-tension current, the coil depends upon the contact-breaker. When the points open, LT current ceases to flow in the coil's primary winding (darker coils) and HT current is induced in the secondary winding (lighter coils). This flows to the distributor. The points close again, and the process is repeated.

Centrifugal advance
As engine speed increases and pistons move faster, the petrol-air mixture must be ignited earlier, so timing of the spark has to be advanced. This is done through two weights linked to the distributor shaft. At increased speed they are thrown outwards and pull the cam, attached to them, round the shaft to open the points earlier and provide advanced ignition.

CB points and rotor arm
The rotor arm transmits HT current to electrodes lining the inside of the distributor cap as it turns on the distributor shaft. The HT pulses are passed on to each spark-plug in turn. The contact-breaker points beneath the rotor arm are opened by one of the high points on the distributor shaft cam, and closed again by a spring blade on the moving contact point.

Vacuum advance
On distributors such as the Lucas, suction in the manifold acts on a diaphragm that pulls the contact-breaker assembly forward so that the cam opens the CB points even earlier. When the throttle is wide open, suction is low and the CB assembly returns to normal. If it did not, the spark would occur too soon and perhaps cause over-advanced ignition.

Distributor /2

Parts of a typical distributor and some variations

Distributor cap
The cap houses the carbon brush and segments that carry high-tension current from the coil, through high-tension leads to the distributor's rotor arm and the spark-plugs.

Rotor arm
When the arm rotates, current flows through its electrode from the central brush, sparks across a gap to each segment in the cap and passes through leads to the plugs.

Capacitor or condenser
A condenser is placed across the points to help reduce wear and store an electrical charge which speeds up the passage of the high-tension current to the spark-plugs.

Contact-breaker points
One contact-breaker point is fixed and the other movable. Points open to break the low-tension current to the primary winding in the coil. A spring closes them again and current is restored.

Base-plate
The base-plate links the cam and contact-breaker assembly with the centrifugal weights which help to advance the ignition as engine speed increases. It is also attached to the vacuum-advance unit.

Cam
The movable CB point is pushed away by a lobe of a cam, which is mounted on the distributor shaft. The cam is controlled by centrifugal weights.

Centrifugal advance
The two weights spin out as engine speed increases, and move the cam round to open the points earlier. They are returned by tension springs.

Vacuum advance
This mechanism helps the cam to open points even earlier. It is operated by manifold suction, and pulls the points forward as speed increases.

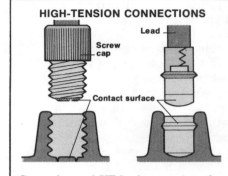

HIGH-TENSION CONNECTIONS

Some plug and HT leads screw into the distributor cap (left). Others snap into place (right).

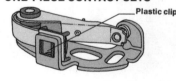

CENTRIFUGAL WEIGHTS

On some AC-Delco and Marelli units, the weights are above the contact-breaker plate. The square and round pegs of the rotor arm must fit correctly.

ONE-PIECE CONTACT SETS

There are no nuts on AC-Delco points. The LT leads are held by a plastic clip.

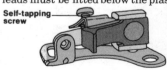

On Lucas points, the LT terminal leads must be fitted below the plastic nut.

On Ford points, the LT lead is secured to the contact by a self-tapping screw.

LINKS TO CAMSHAFT

Two types of distributor drive. Left, a skew gear drive, which twists into place. Right, slightly off-set tongues that can be replaced in only one way.

1 Checking the distributor cap and rotor arm

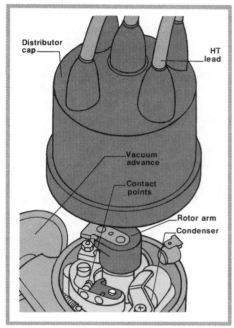

When an engine will not start, it may be that high-tension current is not reaching the plugs, due to a faulty distributor cap or rotor arm.

1 Release the spring clips and lift off the distributor cap.

2 Disconnect the central HT lead from the cap. If you cannot disconnect the HT lead easily, hold the side of a screwdriver to earth and

place the tip close to the central pip or carbon brush inside the distributor cap. If the lead can be re-

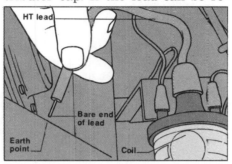

moved, hold it by its insulation, so that the metal end is close to a good earth (the engine block).

3 Switch on the ignition and flick open the contact-breaker points. If there is no spark, the coil is faulty. If a spark jumps between the HT lead and earth (or the screwdriver and cap), the coil is producing HT current but it is leaking away before reaching the plugs. Look for breaks in the HT cables that might be causing the current to short-circuit.

4 If the cables are undamaged, the cap or rotor arm is faulty. Clean the cap with a dry rag, to remove any dirt or carbon dust that might be causing a short-circuit.

5 Look carefully inside the cap for any cracks or for signs of 'tracking' —fine lines that look like forked lightning. They mark paths along which HT current is leaking between the segments in the distributor cap. Check also for corrosion at the centre terminal. If there is any damage, fit a new cap.

Rotor arm Cracks and punctures are usually too small to see, but they may allow current to earth on the distributor cam. Check the boss of the rotor arm for cracks.

Hold the HT lead from the coil close to the electrode on the rotor

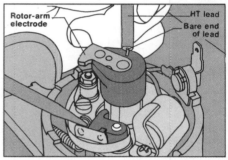

arm. Switch on the ignition and flick the points. If there is a spark, the rotor arm is faulty. Fit a new one. If there is no spark, the rotor arm is serviceable, so check the LT circuit and coil for faults.

2 Checking for damp and condensation

Ignition trouble is mainly caused by rain and condensation. Damp can short-circuit HT current to earth.

1 Look for water droplets on HT cables. Wipe off any water with a

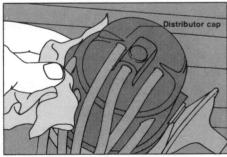

dry cloth, or coat the cables with a water-repellent spray. Switch on the ignition and try to start the engine.

2 If the car still will not start, pull each plug cover in turn off its spark-

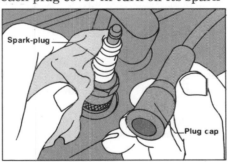

plug. Dry the ceramic insulator with a clean cloth and replace the cable before moving to the next plug. Make sure that the top of the coil is dry.

3 Press the spring clips that hold the distributor cap, pull them out

and down, and take off the cap. Then dry it thoroughly inside and out.

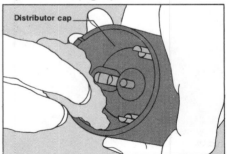

Replace it, and make sure that none of the wires is obviously disconnected or damaged.

4 Try to start the car again. If it will not start, check to see whether a spark is being produced or not.

3 Checking that there is a spark

1 Take the HT lead off one of the plugs. Grip it by its insulation and hold the end close to a good earth point, such as the cylinder head (not the rocker box cover or carburettor). The plug cover can be removed from the lead to establish better contact, if necessary.

2 Make sure the battery is fully charged. Get someone to switch on the ignition and turn the engine on the starter.

3 If a spark does not jump from lead to earth, check the contact-breaker points (see p. 160). If there is a

spark, make sure it is reaching the plug electrodes.

4 Take out the plug. Reconnect it to its lead and lay it on the cylinder head. Have the engine turned over again. If there is no spark, the plug itself may be faulty (see p. 106).

Distributor /3

4 Checking the contact-breaker points

1 Release the spring clips and lift off the distributor cap.

2 Take off the rotor arm, which is 'keyed' to the top of the distributor

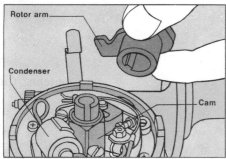

shaft. In some distributors it is a push fit on the shaft and can be pulled off. On others it is held by screws. **Note** Most distributors have the centrifugal weights below the base-

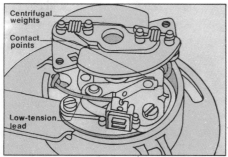

plate. But on the AC distributor fitted, for example, to overhead-

camshaft Vauxhall Victors, the weights are mounted directly below a circular rotor arm above the contact-breaker assembly. The rotor arm in such a case is held by two screws, which must be removed.

3 Beneath the rotor arm located on the distributor base-plate are the

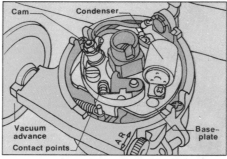

contact-breaker points, the condenser, the LT cable to the spring blade and the contact-breaker cam, which here has four lobes to operate a four-cylinder engine.

4 The rubbing block that carries the movable contact point may have become worn by rubbing against the cam, so that the points no longer open to the correct gap. To check that the points will open, put the car in top gear and push it forward with the wheels turned on a slight lock.

5 Check the gap between the points with a feeler gauge. Reset the points if necessary (see pp. 98-103).

6 If the contact points are blackened, the cause may be a wrongly adjusted voltage regulator, wrongly adjusted points, the presence of oil or a faulty condenser. Badly burnt points indicate condenser failure. Remove the condenser, which is usually fixed to

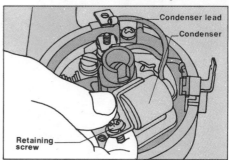

the base-plate or distributor body by a single screw. Disconnect the condenser wires from their terminals and fit a new condenser. Replace the blackened points. After fitting new points, always check that the ignition timing is correct (see p. 108).

7 In rare cases, the cable from the distributor's LT terminal to the CB spring blade may have broken. Check and replace if necessary.

5 Checking the low-tension circuit and coil

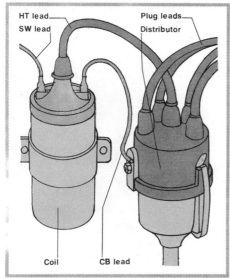

A jump lead with a test light is needed to check the low-tension circuit and the coil.

The coil has two LT terminals. One is connected to the ignition switch, and usually marked SW, the other to the contact-breaker points and marked CB.

On negative-earth cars, the coil switch terminal may be marked + and the contact-breaker terminal −. On positive-earth cars these sym-

bols are reversed, so that the switch terminal bears the − sign, and the contact-breaker terminal the + sign.

1 Lift off the distributor cap, put the car in top gear and push it forward until a lobe of the cam opens the contact-breaker points fully. Do this on level ground with the wheels turned on a slight lock.

2 Earth one end of the jump lead to the distributor body and connect the other end to the contact-breaker LT terminal. Switch on the ignition.

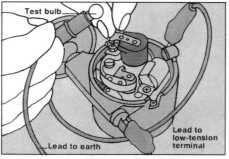

If the lamp lights, the LT circuit is in order. If it does not light, there may be a fault in the line between the ignition switch and coil.

3 Connect one end of the jump lead to the coil's SW terminal and earth the other end. If current is reaching the coil, the bulb will light. If it does not, check the battery and its LT connections to the coils.

4 Disconnect the LT lead from the coil's CB terminal. Connect one end of the jump lead to that terminal and earth the other end.

If the test bulb lights up, the coil is in good working order. If it fails to light, the coil is faulty and must

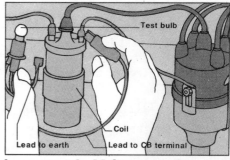

be renewed. Make sure that you connect the replacement coil the right way round. If you connect it wrongly the coil will still work, but it is better not to do so as it will strain the ignition system.

Gaining access to the centrifugal weight tension springs

Poor acceleration, 'pinking' and overheating may be caused by a broken spring in the centrifugal timing advance mechanism. Check by twisting the rotor arm in the normal direction of rotation (see p. 159). If the rotor arm does not return to its normal position when it is released, a spring may have broken.

Some tension springs are above the base-plate. On others the base-plate has to be removed.

Tools: Thin-nosed pliers; small crosshead and bladed screwdrivers; BA spanner; feeler blade.
Materials: Weight springs; emery cloth.

AC DELCO

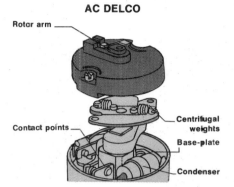

Undo the two screws that hold the rotor arm to the centrifugal advance plate and lift off the rotor. The weights and springs are just below it, above the contact-breaker points.

DUCELLIER

Remove the rotor arm, contact-breaker points and screws that secure the base-plate. Disconnect the vacuum operating arm. Lift off the distributor base-plate.

NIPPONDENSO

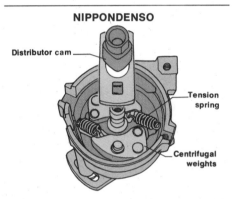

Remove the rotor arm and the contact-breaker points. Disconnect the vacuum advance arm from the base-plate pillar. Undo the securing screws and remove the base-plate.

BOSCH

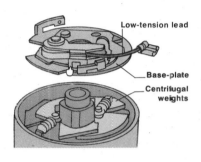

Remove the rotor arm and condensation shield. Undo the screw that secures the base-plate to the body. Pull off the LT lead terminal and lift out the plate.

MARELLI

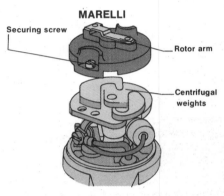

Undo the two screws that hold the rotor arm to the centrifugal advance plate and lift off the rotor. The weights and springs are just below it, above the contact-breaker points.

LUCAS

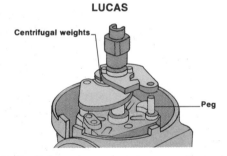

Pull off the rotor arm and remove the contact-breaker points. Disconnect the vacuum return spring at the base-plate pillar. Undo the two small base-plate screws set in the distributor clip recesses and lift off the base-plate. The tension springs, attached to the weights, are just below the base-plate.

TOYO KOGYO

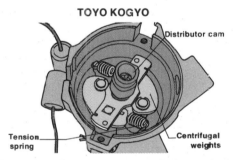

Remove the rotor arm, and the contact-breaker points. Undo the screws that secure the base-plate to the body. Remove the circlip that holds the vacuum advance operating arm to the plate and disconnect the arm from its locating peg. Lift off the plate. The weights and springs are below.

MOTORCRAFT

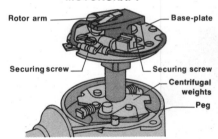

The contact-breaker points and condenser can be left. Remove the circlip that secures the vacuum advance operating arm to the base-plate. Undo the screws that hold the plate to the distributor body. Pull the LT lead through the distributor body to remove the plate and get at the springs.

Changing the centrifugal weight tension springs

Each centrifugal weight is attached to its own spring. One spring is usually slightly stronger than the other, and is a loose fit between the anchor post and the peg on the weight, when the weights are at rest. This is normal, so do not attempt to tighten the long fixing loop.

While the base-plate is off, check to make sure that the weights are free to move on their pivots. If they are tight, lift them off and clean the pivot post with fine emery cloth. Refit the weights and lubricate the posts with clean engine oil.

1 Use a pair of thin-nosed pliers to lift the eyes of the springs from their

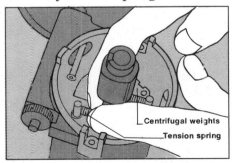

grooves on the mounting pegs. Make sure the centrifugal weights

pivot freely. Fit the new springs by hand. Make sure that they are located in the grooves in the top of the mounting pegs. Be careful not to stretch them too much.

2 Reassemble the parts of the distributor by reversing the dismantling procedure.

3 Use a feeler blade to re-gap the contact-breaker points (see pp. 98-103). Refit the rotor arm to the distributor shaft and tighten its screws (if fitted). Replace the cap.

Distributor / 4

Replacing a vacuum unit

To check that the vacuum advance mechanism is working, disconnect the assembly. Take off the pipe at the distributor side of the diaphragm chamber and fit a length of tubing in its place. Suck on the tube, then block the end with your tongue. You can also test for suction by pressing a finger over the stub pipe and pushing forward the peg on which the vacuum return spring is secured. Suction should be felt for at least 10 seconds. If it is not, fit a new unit.

Tools: Thin-nosed pliers; cross-head and bladed screwdrivers; 2 and 4 BA spanners.
Materials: New vacuum advance unit.

Vacuum unit on a Lucas distributor

1 Use pliers to lift the vacuum return spring off its peg on the dis-

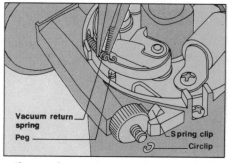

tributor base-plate and remove the small circlip from the end of the threaded vernier shaft.

2 Undo the vernier screw from the shaft and count the number of clicks made as it is removed. Lift

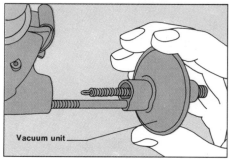

out the spring clip. Withdraw the vacuum assembly from the dis-

tributor body. Slide the new unit into position and refit the spring clip in position and the vernier screw on to the shaft. Make sure it is tightened by the same number of clicks it took to remove it. If you fail to do this, you may find that the fine setting of the ignition timing has been upset when you have replaced the unit. Refit the circlip to the end of the shaft.

3 Reconnect the return spring to the base-plate peg. Replace the rotor arm, distributor cap and reconnect the vacuum pipe.

Vacuum unit on an AC Delco distributor

There are two basic types of AC Delco distributor—one with weights below the base-plate, and the other with weights above the contact-breaker points.

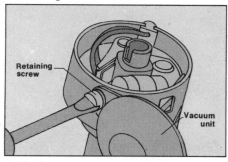

1 Undo the screw holding the vacuum unit to the distributor

body and unhook the unit's other arm from the slot in the side of the

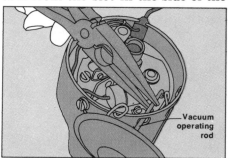

body. Disconnect the vacuum operating rod from the base-plate.

2 Remove the unit and slide in the new one. Connect the vacuum

operating rod to its hole in the base-plate. Make sure it is secure.

3 Fix one arm of the vacuum-unit bracket into its hole. Screw the other arm to the distributor body.

4 Reconnect the vacuum pipe to the new unit. Refit and re-gap the contact-breaker points (see pp. 98-103). Replace the rotor arm and the distributor cap.

5 The distributor with weights above the contact-breaker points is similar in design, but the vacuum arm is fixed to the distributor base-plate by a screw.

Vacuum unit on an Autolite (Ford) or Motorcraft distributor

There is no vernier adjuster on this distributor. The return spring is attached to the vacuum unit.

1 Remove the condenser, which is held by a screw. Lift off the circlip

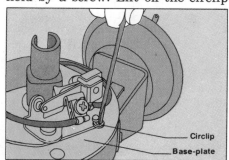

on the vacuum-unit pivot post. Undo the two screws holding the

contact-breaker base-plate assembly to the distributor body. Lift out the assembly.

2 Undo the two cross-head screws that hold the vacuum diaphragm

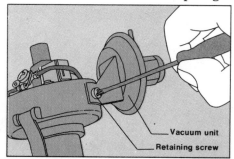

assembly bracket to the side of the distributor body, and remove the

complete vacuum assembly from the distributor.

Note: On another type of Ford distributor the operating arm from the vacuum unit fits over a peg on the base-plate, and it is not necessary to remove the base-plate. Remove the circlip. Undo the screws holding the unit to the distributor body. Lift the operating arm off the base-plate peg. Remove the unit.

3 When refitting either type, slide the unit into position and locate the operating arm over the peg on the distributor base-plate. Refit the retaining circlip and make sure that it is in its groove.

Vacuum unit on a Bosch distributor

Do not remove the contact-breaker points on the Bosch distributor. Lift off the condensation cover.

1 Remove the circlip that holds the vacuum operating arm to the peg on the distributor base-plate. Do not

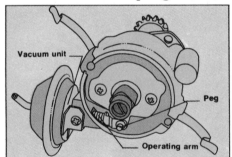

lose the circlip or allow it to drop inside the distributor body.

2 Lift the arm off the peg. Undo the two screws that hold the vacuum

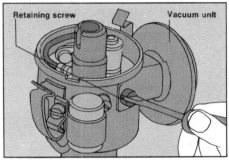

unit to the side of the distributor body. Remove the vacuum unit.

3 To fit the new vacuum unit, slide the operating arm over the peg in the base-plate and screw the vacuum unit to the distributor body. Fit the

circlip to the peg on the base-plate. Refit the condensation cover, the rotor arm, cap and vacuum pipe.

Note: Some Bosch distributors have a return spring, instead of a circlip, retaining the vacuum operating arm.

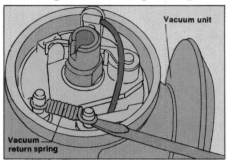

Prise off the spring to remove the unit. Fit a new unit in reverse order.

Vacuum unit on a Nippondenso distributor

1 On the Nippondenso distributor, the vacuum return spring is incor-

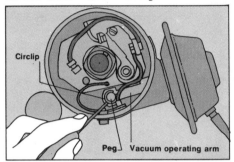

porated in the actual vacuum assembly and does not need to be touched. It comes away with the rest of the unit. Undo the two screws that

hold the vacuum assembly unit to the side of the distributor body. Disconnect the vacuum operating arm from the peg on the distributor

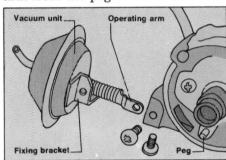

base-plate. Remove the vacuum unit from the side of the distributor body.

2 When fitting the new vacuum unit, make sure that the operating arm is properly located on its base-

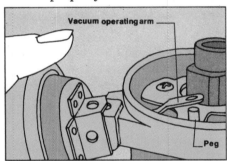

plate peg. Refit and tighten the screws holding the unit to the body. Fit the pipe to the vacuum unit.

Removing and refitting a distributor

Some distributors, fitted in awkward positions for example, have to be removed from the engine for repair. Start by turning the engine so that it is on its firing stroke on number 1 cylinder (see p. 164). Remove the distributor cap and check that the rotor arm is pointing towards the number 1 plug lead segment in the distributor cap. Lay the distributor cap to one side.

Disconnect the low-tension supply lead from the terminal on the side of the distributor body. If the distributor has a vacuum advance unit fitted, either pull the plastic pipe—fitted between the vacuum unit and the inlet manifold —away from its connection on the unit, or unscrew the pipe-union from the vacuum unit.

Tools: Spanners to fit distributor securing bolts; sharp pointer to scribe line on distributor.

1 Mark the base of the distributor body and the engine block, so that

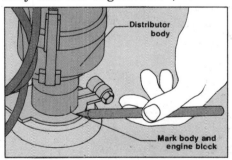

they can be realigned exactly when the distributor is refitted.

2 Do the same with the rotor arm and the distributor body. Do not disturb the clamp bolt in the plate that holds the distributor to the engine. Unbolt the plate itself from the engine. Remove the distributor.

Note: On a car with a distributor linked to the camshaft by skew gears

—such as the Vauxhall—the rotor arm will turn a few degrees when the distributor is moved. Note how much it turns. To refit, wind the rotor back

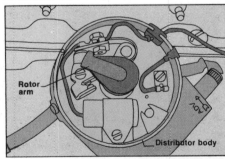

through the same angle. When the skew gears meet, they will turn the distributor shaft and bring the rotor arm back to the correct point.

3 On all types of distributor, line up the marks on the distributor body and the engine. Refit the securing bolts and reconnect the low-tension wire, vacuum pipe and cap.

Ignition timing

How to set and check the static ignition timing

The ignition timing—which ensures that the spark occurs in each cylinder at the correct moment for combustion—should normally need no attention. But if the distributor has been moved, check it, for faulty timing wastes petrol.

All cars have timing marks that are designed to be in line when the piston in the engine's timing cylinder (usually No. 1, but sometimes Nos. 4 or 6—check with your dealer) is at or near top dead centre—that is, the top of its compression stroke.

One fixed mark is usually on the cover of the timing chain or belt, or on the flywheel housing; the other is on the movable crankshaft pulley or flywheel. If the timing is not set at top dead centre, there may be additional marks on the pulley or flywheel to show degrees before or after top dead centre.

There are four stages: finding the compression stroke in the timing cylinder; lining up the timing marks at or near top dead centre; making sure that the rotor arm is pointing to the distributor cap segment that serves the timing cylinder; and checking with a test lamp.

Tools: Spanner to fit crankshaft; test lamp; cardboard; protractor; pencil; mirror.

1 Remove the spark-plugs and ask a helper to cover the timing cylinder's spark-plug hole with his thumb. Put the car in neutral and use a spanner to rotate the crankshaft (turn clockwise to avoid slackening the nut).

If this is difficult, put the car on level ground, engage top gear and move the car forwards. Turn the engine until pressure forces the thumb off. This shows that the piston is on its compression stroke.

2 Keep turning the engine until the fixed pointer lines up with the top-dead-centre mark or the appropriate timing mark. If there is only a top-dead-centre mark when an advance mark is needed, take a semi-circle

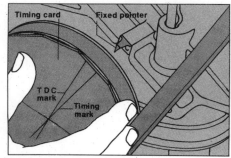

of cardboard and draw a line at right angles from the centre to the

Cylinder spark-plug hole To find the compression stroke, cover the hole with a thumb and turn the engine until the thumb is forced off.

Timing cylinder On most cars, the timing is set when the No. 1 cylinder is on its compression stroke.

Coil Connect a test lamp between the low-tension terminals on the coil when checking the ignition timing.

Rotor arm The arm must point exactly at the segment in the distributor cap that serves the timing cylinder.

Contact-breaker points The points should be just open, to allow high-tension current to flow to spark-plug.

Fixed timing marks Fixed marks are usually pointers on the timing chain case, belt cover or flywheel housing.

Moving timing marks Moving marks are either on the crankshaft pulley or the flywheel. All cars with transverse engines have moving and fixed timing marks on the flywheel and flywheel housing. Hold a mirror against the hole in the housing to see the marks.

top edge to indicate top dead centre. Use a protractor and pencil to mark the number of degrees before tdc (see p. 165) to the right of the mark on the edge of the disc. Hold the disc against the front of the crankshaft pulley, and line up the disc's top-dead-centre mark with the top-dead-centre mark on the pulley. Turn the engine until the disc's second mark lines up with the fixed pointer.

3 Align the rotor arm with the segment in the distributor cap that serves the timing cylinder spark-plug. Fit the distributor's D-shaped offset tongue or slot to the camshaft drive. (If the linkage is through skew gears, the rotor arm may not point directly at the segment. With-

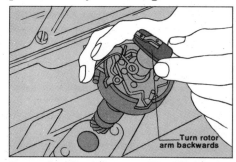

draw the distributor. Wind back the rotor arm to allow for its movement as the gears mesh with the camshaft and refit it.)

4 Bolt the distributor in place. Connect a test lamp to the two low-tension terminals on the coil, and

check again that the rotor arm points to the proper segment. Switch on the ignition: the test lamp will

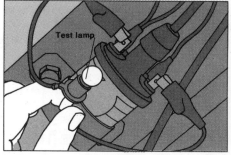

light. Twist the body of the distributor inside its clamp until the lamp goes out. Tighten the clamp.

5 Check finally by turning the engine over once. The test light should go out when the timing mark lines up with the fixed pointer. For fine adjustment, turn the distributor with the Vernier screw at the side. If no screw is fitted, slacken

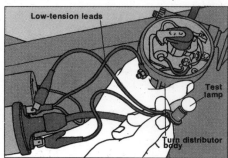

the clamp and turn the distributor clockwise to advance the timing, anti-clockwise to retard it.

STATIC IGNITION TIMING

Degrees before top dead centre ... *Degrees before top dead centre* ... *Degrees after top dead centre* ... *Degrees before top dead centre*

AUDI
100 GL
100 GL Automatic
100 LS — Timed by a strobe light only (see p. 108)
100 LS Automatic
Coupé S
Coupé S Automatic

BMW
1600 _ _ _ _ _ _ _ _ _ _ 3
1800 _ _ _ _ _ _ _ _ _ _ 3 — After initial setting, check timing with strobe light (see p. 108)
2000 _ _ _ _ _ _ _ _ _ _ 3
2002 _ _ _ _ _ _ _ _ _ _ 3
2500 _ _ _ _ _ _ _ _ _ _ 3
2800 _ _ _ _ _ _ _ _ _ _ 3

BRITISH LEYLAND

Austin
A40 Farina _ _ _ _ _ _ _ 3
A60 _ _ _ _ _ _ _ _ _ _ 5
A110 _ _ _ _ _ _ _ _ _ 5
Maxi 1500 _ _ _ _ _ _ _ 10
Maxi 1750 _ _ _ _ _ _ _ 10

Austin/Morris
1100 _ _ _ _ _ _ _ _ _ 3
1300 _ _ _ _ _ _ _ _ _ 8
1300 Countryman _ _ _ 8
1300 GT _ _ _ _ _ _ _ 2
1800 Mk II _ _ _ _ _ _ 9
1800 S _ _ _ _ _ _ _ _ 9
2200 _ _ _ _ _ _ _ _ _ 9
Midget _ _ _ _ _ _ _ _ 7
Mini 850 _ _ _ _ _ _ _ tdc
Mini 1000 _ _ _ _ _ _ _ 5
Mini Clubman _ _ _ _ _ 5
Mini Cooper S _ _ _ _ _ 7
Sprite _ _ _ _ _ _ _ _ 7

Jaguar
2·4 _ _ _ _ _ _ _ _ _ 8
3·4 _ _ _ _ _ _ _ _ _ 2
3·8 _ _ _ _ _ _ _ _ _ 4
3·8 S type _ _ _ _ _ _ 4

Morris
Marina 1·3 _ _ _ _ _ _ 9
Marina 1·8 _ _ _ _ _ _ 10
Marina 1·8 TC _ _ _ _ 7
MG 1100 _ _ _ _ _ _ _ 5
MGB _ _ _ _ _ _ _ _ 10
MGC _ _ _ _ _ _ _ _ 8
Minor 1000 _ _ _ _ _ _ 3

Riley
Elf _ _ _ _ _ _ _ _ _ 5

Rover
2000 SC _ _ _ _ _ _ _ 4
2000 SC Automatic _ _ _ 4
2000 TC _ _ _ _ _ _ _ 6

Triumph
1300 _ _ _ _ _ _ _ _ _ 9
1500 _ _ _ _ _ _ _ _ _ 10
2000 _ _ _ _ _ _ _ _ _ 8
Dolomite _ _ _ _ _ _ _ 11
GT-6 _ _ _ _ _ _ _ _ 10
Herald 1200 _ _ _ _ _ _ 15
Herald 12/50 _ _ _ _ _ 15
Herald 13/60 _ _ _ _ _ 9
Spitfire _ _ _ _ _ _ _ 6
Stag _ _ _ _ _ _ _ _ 14
Toledo 1300 _ _ _ _ _ _ 10
TR 4 _ _ _ _ _ _ _ _ 4
TR 4A _ _ _ _ _ _ _ _ 4
TR 5 _ _ _ _ _ _ _ _ 11
TR 6 _ _ _ _ _ _ _ _ 11
Vitesse Mk I _ _ _ _ _ 10
Vitesse Mk II _ _ _ _ _ 10

BRITISH LEYLAND cont'd

Wolseley
Hornet _ _ _ _ _ _ _ _ 5

CHRYSLER

Chrysler Rootes
Avenger _ _ _ _ _ _ _ 9-11
Avenger GT _ _ _ _ _ _ 9-11
Chamois _ _ _ _ _ _ _ 3-5
Chrysler 180 _ _ _ _ _ 10
Hillman Minx 1500 _ _ _ _ 7-9
Humber Sceptre _ _ _ _ 7-9
Hunter 1500 _ _ _ _ _ 7-9
Hunter 1725 _ _ _ _ _ 7-9
Imp _ _ _ _ _ _ _ _ 3-5
Singer Gazelle _ _ _ _ _ 7-9
Singer Vogue _ _ _ _ _ 7-9
Stiletto _ _ _ _ _ _ _ 3-5
Sunbeam Alpine _ _ _ _ 6-10
Sunbeam Rapier _ _ _ _ 6-8
Sunbeam Sport _ _ _ _ 3

Chrysler Simca
1000 _ _ _ _ _ _ _ _ 10
1100 _ _ _ _ _ _ _ _ 12
1100S _ _ _ _ _ _ _ 12
1301 _ _ _ _ _ _ _ _ 12
1301 Automatic _ _ _ _ 12
1501 _ _ _ _ _ _ _ _ 12
1501 Automatic _ _ _ _ 12

CITROËN
Ami 6 _ _ _ _ _ _ _ _ 8
Ami 8 _ _ _ _ _ _ _ _ 8
Dyane _ _ _ _ _ _ _ _ 8

DAF
33 up to Aug. '73 _ _ _ _ 5
33 after Aug. '73 _ _ _ _ _ _ _ 5
44 up to Aug. '73 _ _ _ _ 5
44 after Aug. '73 _ _ _ _ _ _ _ 5
55 _ _ _ _ _ _ _ _ _ tdc
66 _ _ _ _ _ _ _ _ _ tdc

DATSUN
240Z Sports
260C Custom de luxe
260C Custom de luxe Auto
Bluebird 160B
Bluebird 160B Automatic
Bluebird 180B — Timed by a strobe light only (see p. 108)
Bluebird 180B Automatic
Bluebird 180SSS
Cherry 100A range
Cherry 120
Sunny 1200 range

FIAT
124 _ _ _ _ _ _ _ _ _ 10
124S _ _ _ _ _ _ _ _ 10
125 _ _ _ _ _ _ _ _ _ 10
127 _ _ _ _ _ _ _ _ _ 10
128 _ _ _ _ _ _ _ _ _ 10
500 _ _ _ _ _ _ _ _ _ 10
600D _ _ _ _ _ _ _ _ 10
850 _ _ _ _ _ _ _ _ _ 10

FORD
Anglia 105E _ _ _ _ _ _ 10
Anglia 123E _ _ _ _ _ _ 6
Classic Capri 109E _ _ _ 8
Classic Capri 109E GT _ _ 10
Corsair 120E _ _ _ _ _ 8
Corsair 120E GT _ _ _ _ 10
Corsair V4 1700 cc _ _ _ 8
Corsair V4 2000 cc _ _ _ 8
Cortina Mk I 1200 cc _ _ 6
Cortina Mk I 1500 cc _ _ 8
Cortina Mk II to 1968 _ _ 6

FORD cont'd
Cortina Mk II 1968/70 _ 10
Cortina Mk III _ _ _ _ _ 6
Escort _ _ _ _ _ _ _ _ 6
Zephyr/Zodiac Mk III _ _ 8

MAZDA
RX3 — leading distributor tdc / trailing distributor 5 atdc

RENAULT
R4 _ _ _ _ _ _ _ _ _ tdc±1
R5 845 cc _ _ _ _ _ _ 5-7
R5 TL 956 cc _ _ _ _ _ 5-7
R6 845 cc _ _ _ _ _ _ tdc±1
R6 1108 cc _ _ _ _ _ _ tdc±1
R8 _ _ _ _ _ _ _ _ _ tdc
R10 _ _ _ _ _ _ _ _ _ tdc
R12 TL & TS early '73 _ tdc±1
R12 TL & TS late '73 _ tdc±1
R15 TL _ _ _ _ _ _ _ tdc±1
R15 TS _ _ _ _ _ _ _ 2-4
R16 Automatic _ _ _ _ _ 5-7
R16 TL & TS _ _ _ _ _ tdc+1
R17 TL _ _ _ _ _ _ _ 5-7
R17 TS _ _ _ _ _ _ _ 7-9

TOYOTA
Carina 1600 _ _ _ _ _ 10
Celica 1600 _ _ _ _ _ _ 8
Corolla 1100 _ _ _ _ _ 8
Corolla 1200 _ _ _ _ _ 8
Corolla 1200 SL _ _ _ _ 10
Corona 1500 _ _ _ _ _ 8
Corona 1900 Mk II _ _ _ 10
Corona 2000 Mk II _ _ _ 7
Crown 2300 _ _ _ _ _ _ 8
Crown 2600 _ _ _ _ _ _ 8

VAUXHALL
Firenza 1600 cc _ _ _ _ 9
Firenza 2300 cc _ _ _ _ 9
Ventora FD _ _ _ _ _ _ 9
Ventora FE _ _ _ _ _ _ 9
Victor FC _ _ _ _ _ _ 9
Victor FD 1600 cc _ _ _ 9
Victor FD 2000 cc _ _ _ 9
Victor FD 3·3 (Estate) _ _ 9
Victor FE 1800 cc _ _ _ 9
Victor FE 2000 cc _ _ _ 9
Victor FE 3·3 (Estate) _ _ 9
Viscount _ _ _ _ _ _ _ 9
Viva HA _ _ _ _ _ _ _ 9
Viva HB 1159 cc _ _ _ 4½
Viva HB 1600 cc _ _ _ 9
Viva HB GT _ _ _ _ _ _ 9
Viva HB SL90 _ _ _ _ _ 9
Viva HC 1159 cc _ _ _ 9
Viva HC 1600 cc _ _ _ 9
VX4/90 FC _ _ _ _ _ _ 9
VX4/90 FD _ _ _ _ _ _ 9
VX4/90 FE _ _ _ _ _ _ 9

VOLKSWAGEN
Beetle 1200
Beetle 1300
Beetle 1600
1600 FB
1600 Variant
411 LE Saloon — Check with your Volkswagen dealer
411 LE Variant
412 LE Saloon
412 LE Variant
K70

VOLVO
120
142
144 — Timed by a strobe light only. Check with your dealer
145
164

165

Gaskets

Choosing the right gasket for the job

Gaskets are fitted between two mating surfaces, to seal the joint so that liquid or gas cannot escape. Different materials are used, depending on the function of the gasket.

The cooling system has paper or cork gaskets. To seal joints where there is oil, you need paper, cork, rubber or copper gaskets. Metal and asbestos are fitted in hot places such as the exhaust system. Metal shims or copper and asbestos gaskets are used on some cylinder heads.

Leaking gaskets soon become obvious. An oil leak makes the engine dirty. A leak at the inlet manifold reduces performance. Exhaust leaks are noisy and may release fumes into the car. Cooling system leaks cause over-heating, and the coolant needs frequent topping up. Fuel leaks can be detected by the smell of petrol. Always buy new gaskets from a dealer who specialises in your make of car. Tell him exactly which gasket you need.

To ensure a leak-proof seal, coat cork gaskets with a thin layer of high-melting-point grease. Coat paper gaskets with gasket cement. Use soft cement on a joint which is likely to be disturbed—the sump, for instance—and hard cement where a joint is unlikely to be disturbed—for example, the gearbox.

WHERE GASKETS STOP LEAKS

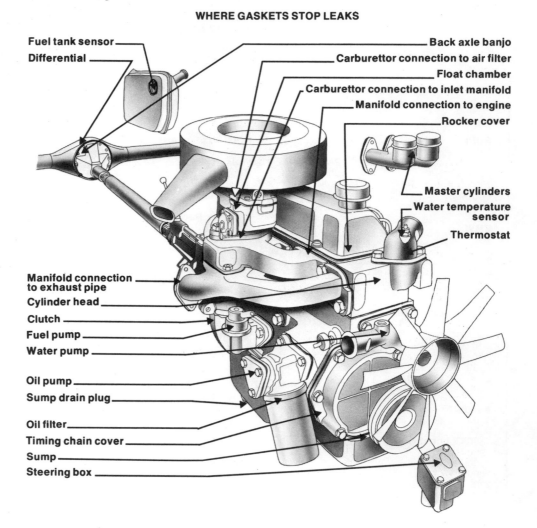

- Fuel tank sensor
- Differential
- Back axle banjo
- Carburettor connection to air filter
- Float chamber
- Carburettor connection to inlet manifold
- Manifold connection to engine
- Rocker cover
- Master cylinders
- Water temperature sensor
- Thermostat
- Manifold connection to exhaust pipe
- Cylinder head
- Clutch
- Fuel pump
- Water pump
- Oil pump
- Sump drain plug
- Oil filter
- Timing chain cover
- Sump
- Steering box

Changing a gasket to avoid leaks

Always fit a new gasket whenever a joint has been disturbed. A used gasket may leak.

Tools: Spanners to fit the components.
Materials: New gasket to match the joint; grease or cement.

1 Remove the component which fits on top of the gasket. Inspect the old gasket for spots where it has not

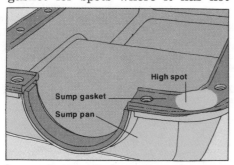

been flattened between the two mating surfaces. These spots indicate distortion in the surfaces where leaks could occur. Have the surfaces flattened at a garage.

2 Scrape off any pieces of old gasket cemented to the metal. If the components are steel or iron, use a steel scraper or a blunt chisel; if they are alloy, use a hardwood scraper. Take care not to scratch the surface.

3 Clean both mating surfaces with petrol or paraffin. Let them dry.

4 Draw a metal straight edge across each mating surface. If you see day-

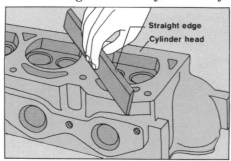

light between surface and straight edge, the surface is distorted. Have it refaced at a machine shop.

5 Fit the new gasket, using high-melting-point grease if it is cork, and cement if it is paper. Some gaskets have 'Top' or 'Front' marked on them to ensure correct fitting;

others have tabs which project when the assembly is complete. In general, a correctly fitted gasket does not block any passages—for air, water or oil—formed by the mating surfaces. Some cylinder-head gaskets are, however, designed to block passages that are not needed.

6 Fit the metal component on top of the new gasket. Insert the retaining bolts. Then tighten them fully, screwing down each bolt one turn at a time so that the metal component is not distorted. In some cases—for example the cylinder head—bolts may have to be tightened in a special sequence and to a specified torque with a torque wrench (see p. 32).

7 Take the car on the road for a test-drive to make sure that the new gasket is not leaking. If there is a leak, the mating surfaces may be distorted—strip the components, clean the surfaces, and have them flattened at a garage. After running the car for some miles, check the torque on the bolts.

Cylinder head / 1

Clearing the engine compartment for an overhaul

A cylinder-head overhaul is necessary only if engine performance is poor and routine servicing fails to make any improvement.

The cause could be either burnt or badly pitted valves and seats, or carbon build-up on the valves, cylinder-head combustion chambers and piston crowns.

Remove the spark-plugs and check their condition (see p. 106). If they are very badly oiled up, the pistons and cylinder bores may be worn and

the engine will need to be overhauled. This is a garage job. If they are only slightly coated with oil, the wear could be in the valve guides. Check the engine condition with a compression gauge (see p. 135). If the readings are low and unbalanced, overhaul the cylinder head.

The preliminary work of clearing the engine compartment to allow access to the cylinder head is similar for all cars, whether ohv (overhead valve) or ohc (overhead camshaft).

Tools: Selection of ring and open-ended spanners to fit the manifold, rocker or cam cover, carburettor, air-filter nuts and bolts; screwdriver; wood or steel scraper; valve-grinding tool; valve-spring compressor; electric drill and selection of rotary wire brushes; stepped valve guide drift.
Materials: A cylinder head overhaul kit with all the necessary gaskets and seals for your engine (Rovers and BMWs need special equipment; they recommend leaving the work to a garage); valve-grinding paste; new valves, possibly only exhaust; emery cloth; valve guides, if necessary, to suit the engine.

Battery Disconnect the battery leads. Remove the battery if it is in the engine compartment.

Carburettor connections Remove the air cleaner (see p. 122). Disconnect the fuel pipe, choke and accelerator linkage (see pp. 146-153). Remove the distributor vacuum pipe from the side of the carburettor. Undo the bolts or nuts holding the carburettor to the inlet manifold. Remove the carburettor (see pp. 146-153).

Manifolds Undo the inlet and exhaust manifold nuts or bolts and lift off the manifolds. On Vauxhall 4-cylinder ohc engines, remove the thermostat for access to a nut inside the manifold. Release the exhaust downpipe from the exhaust manifold (see p. 135).

Temperature gauge Remove the temperature gauge wire from the terminal on the cylinder-head sensor.

Flexible hoses Disconnect the top radiator, by-pass and heater hoses from the cylinder head. (On Vauxhalls, remove also the radiator bottom hose.) On cars with a temperature-regulated automatic choke, disconnect the water hoses at the carburettor. Remove the hoses from the water-heated inlet manifolds.

Cooling system Remove the radiator cap and open the drain plugs or taps in the engine block and radiator. Drain the coolant (see p. 179). Keep the water if it contains antifreeze.

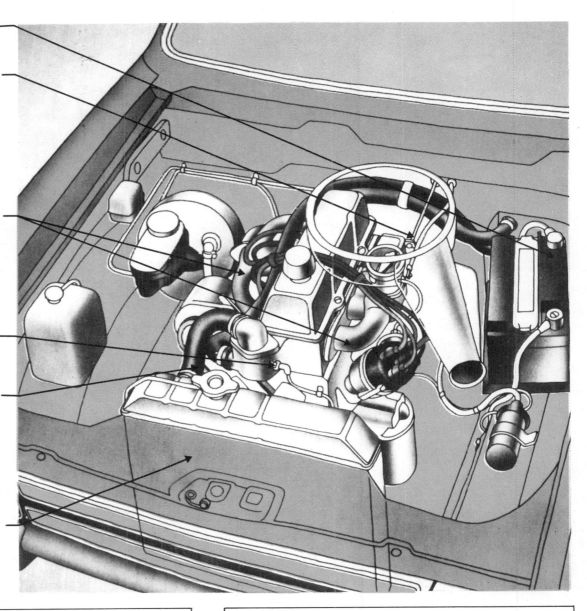

AIR-COOLED ENGINES

Because of the ducting round the engine, it is not always possible to get at the cylinder head while the engine is in the chassis — for example, on Volkswagens and Dafs. Removal is a garage job.

On a Fiat 500, remove the air hoses and ducting to give access to the cylinder head.

The cylinder-head dismantling procedure is the same as for a water-cooled engine.

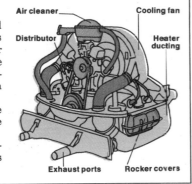

REAR WATER-COOLED ENGINES

The layout of a water-cooled rear-engined car is similar to that of a front-engined car, but the radiator and fan assembly are on one side of the engine.

Drain the cooling system. Disconnect the hoses between the engine and the cooling system.

Dismantling the cylinder head itself is the same as for front-engined cars.

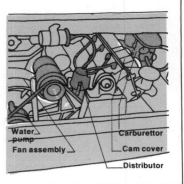

Cylinder head/2

Types of rocker assembly on overhead-valve engines

Two basic types of rocker assembly are fitted to overhead-valve engines. Check which type your car has.
Shaft-mounted rocker arms The rocker arms, which are either cast or pressed steel, pivot on shafts that are mounted in brackets bolted to the cylinder head. The rocker arms are lubricated by oil pumped through the centre of the shaft and out through small delivery holes.
Stud-mounted rocker arms Each pressed-steel rocker arm is mounted on its own stud pressed into the cylinder head. The rocker arm is spring-loaded against a pivot ball and is retained by a self-locking nut. Lubrication is by oil mist from the engine crankcase. There are usually no lubrication problems and few wear points.

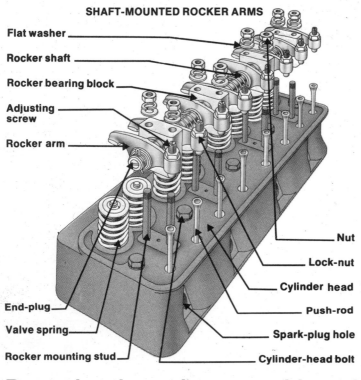

SHAFT-MOUNTED ROCKER ARMS

Flat washer
Rocker shaft
Rocker bearing block
Adjusting screw
Rocker arm
End-plug
Valve spring
Rocker mounting stud

Nut
Lock-nut
Cylinder head
Push-rod
Spark-plug hole
Cylinder-head bolt

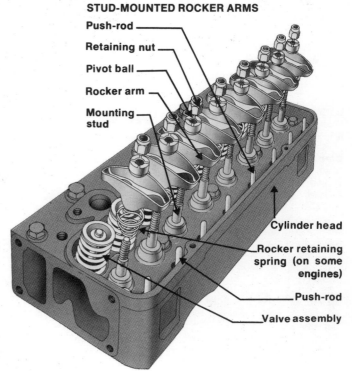

STUD-MOUNTED ROCKER ARMS

Push-rod
Retaining nut
Pivot ball
Rocker arm
Mounting stud

Cylinder head
Rocker retaining spring (on some engines)
Push-rod
Valve assembly

Removing the rocker assembly and push-rods

Before removing the rocker assembly and the push-rods, get a piece of card and make small holes in it to correspond with the number of push-rods on the engine (twice the number of cylinders). When the push-rods are removed, push them through the card to keep them in their correct order.

Tools: Spanners to fit the rocker mounting bolts or nuts, and external oil feed pipe unions if fitted.

Shaft-mounted rocker arms
1 Check if there is an external oil feed pipe to the rocker assembly.

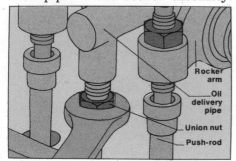

Rocker arm
Oil delivery pipe
Union nut
Push-rod

This is usually screwed into a mounting bracket. Unscrew the feed pipe.

2 Undo the mounting bolts or nuts half a turn at a time—starting at the ends on both sides of the cylinder head and working towards the centre—until the valve-spring tension is relieved.

3 Remove all the bolts or nuts. Lift the rocker assembly slightly, and make sure that the head of the ad-

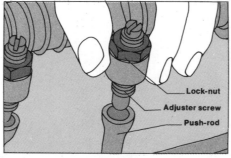

Lock-nut
Adjuster screw
Push-rod

justing screw is clear of the cup in the top of each push-rod. Oil collects in these cups. If the rocker assembly is lifted straight out, it could pull up a push-rod and dislodge the cam follower at the bottom.

4 To break the oil seal between the push-rod and cam follower, lift each rod slightly and twist it clear of the cam follower. Remove the rods one at a time, and push them through a numbered piece of card to ensure that they are kept in their correct order, ready for reassembly.

Stud-mounted rocker arms
1 Undo each self-locking nut from the centre of the rocker arms. Lift

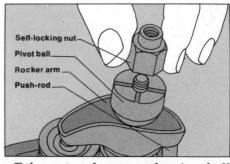

Self-locking nut
Pivot ball
Rocker arm
Push-rod

off the nut and remove the pivot ball beneath it. Keep the nuts and pivot balls in the order in which they were removed.

2 Remove each rocker arm and spring individually. Lay the rocker arms and springs down in the order in which they were removed, so that they can be refitted in the same order when reassembling.

3 To break the oil seal between the push-rods and the cam followers, lift each rod slightly and twist it, to clear the cam follower, as it is being removed. Push the rods, in their correct order, through a numbered piece of card, ready for reassembly.

When the engine has an overhead camshaft

On an overhead-camshaft engine, the camshaft is above the valves in the cylinder head, and is driven by a belt or chain from the engine crankshaft. If the cylinder head has to be removed, the drive-belt or chain must be disconnected. This will upset the valve timing (see p. 176) unless the crankshaft is turned to a set position first.

How the cylinder head is dis- mantled depends on the design of the overhead camshaft. There are two basic types—direct-acting and indirect—and either may be belt or chain-driven.

Direct-acting camshaft Valve clearances are adjusted by shims mounted above or below the cam follower over the valve, or—for example, on Vauxhalls—by an adjusting screw set in the side of the cam follower. If shims are used, do not lose them or mix them up when dismantling. They can be measured with a micrometer and used again.

Indirect-acting camshaft The camshaft is set to one side and operates the valves through fingers mounted on a separate shaft or on ball pivots. When the camshaft has been removed, the fingers can be twisted to one side to give access to the valves.

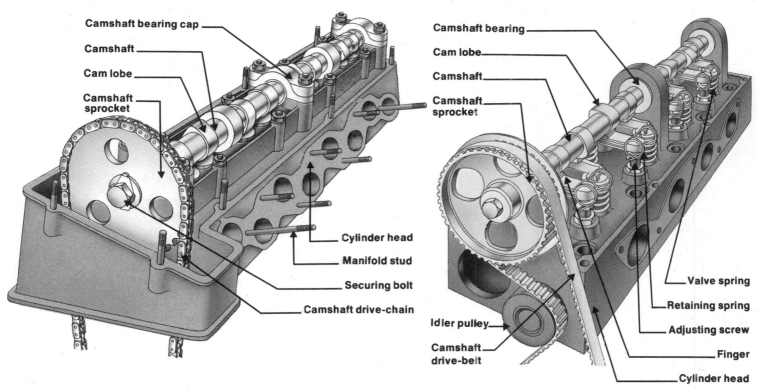

DIRECT-ACTING CAMSHAFT

Camshaft bearing cap
Camshaft
Cam lobe
Camshaft sprocket
Cylinder head
Manifold stud
Securing bolt
Camshaft drive-chain

INDIRECT-ACTING CAMSHAFT

Camshaft bearing
Cam lobe
Camshaft
Camshaft sprocket
Valve spring
Retaining spring
Adjusting screw
Finger
Cylinder head
Idler pulley
Camshaft drive-belt

Removing the camshaft from the cylinder head

Removing the camshaft to allow the cylinder head to be dismantled is the same for direct and indirect-acting camshafts. At this stage the differences depend on whether it is belt or chain-driven.

Tools: Spanners to fit the cam-sprocket bolts, bearing caps or cam covers; chain tensioner if necessary.

1 Turn the engine so that the crankshaft or flywheel timing marks line up with the top-dead-centre mark on the casing (see p. 164). Check that the timing mark on the auxiliary pulley is also correctly positioned (see p. 176).

2 Chain-driven camshafts Use a special tool to release the chain tension. If a tool is not available, push a bar between the chain and the chain casing on the tensioner side. Lever towards the chain to compress the tensioner. Slide the chain off the tensioning sprocket.

Turn up the locking washer on the sprocket centre-bolt and undo the bolt. Lift the sprocket and chain off the boss of the camshaft. Take care

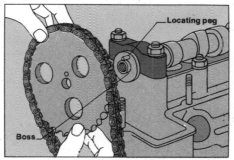

Locating peg
Boss

not to disturb the locating peg in the camshaft boss. Lay the sprocket and chain carefully over the side of the chain casing.

2 Belt-driven camshafts Loosen the idler pulley centre-bolt and push the pulley against spring pressure away from the belt. Slide the belt off the pulley and tighten the centre-bolt to hold the pulley.

3 Undo the bolts or nuts holding the camshaft bearing caps. Lift off

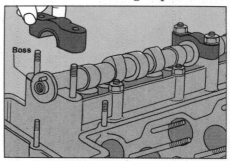

Boss

the bearing caps and remove the camshaft. On some engines—for example, Vauxhalls and Fiats—it is possible to unbolt the camshaft box and lift off the box, complete with the camshaft.

Indirect-acting camshaft
Remove the camshaft in the same way. Lift fingers off the pivot balls or twist the fingers on their shaft to get access to the valves in the cylinder head.

Cylinder head /3

Removing the cylinder head from the engine block

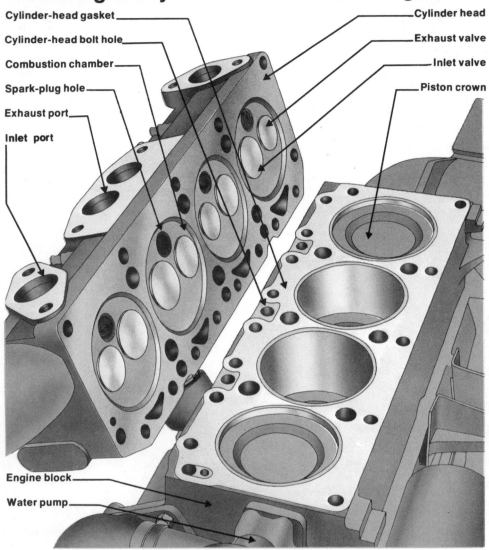

Cylinder-head gasket
Cylinder-head bolt hole
Combustion chamber
Spark-plug hole
Exhaust port
Inlet port
Cylinder head
Exhaust valve
Inlet valve
Piston crown
Engine block
Water pump

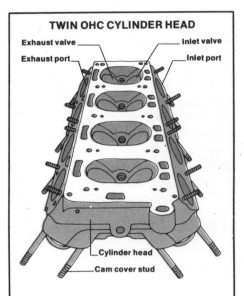

TWIN OHC CYLINDER HEAD

Exhaust valve
Exhaust port
Inlet valve
Inlet port
Cylinder head
Cam cover stud

Twin overhead-camshaft engines are of a cross-flow design—with the inlet manifold on one side of the cylinder head and the exhaust manifold on the other. The combustion chamber is hemispherical, and the valves are inclined outwards at the top.

When the camshafts have been removed (see p. 169), undo the cylinder-head bolts or nuts progressively. Start with the centre bolts and loosen them diagonally outwards, working first one side of the centre and then the other.

When the bolts or stud nuts have been removed, lift the head off the engine block. If it is tight, tap it gently with a wooden mallet to free it. Though angled slightly, the engine valves are fitted in the same way as in any other engine.

The cylinder head may be made of cast iron or aluminium. When you remove it, take care not to damage the surface between the cylinder head and engine block.

1 Disconnect the spark-plug lead from the top of each plug. Loosen the spark-plugs in the cylinder head, but do not remove them at this stage (to ensure no damage is done to the threads or piston if anything should be dropped against the plug hole).

2 Follow the sequence recommended by the manufacturer and slacken the cylinder-head retaining bolts or

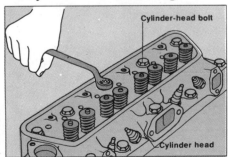

Cylinder-head bolt
Cylinder head

nuts. If you do not have that information, start at the centre bolts.

Loosen them half a turn at a time, working diagonally outwards on each side from the centre. When the head is no longer under tension, undo and remove the bolts or nuts. Lift off any flat and spring washers used on cylinder-head studs.

3 Remove the head with a direct pull. It is sometimes necessary to free the seal between the head and block by tapping the cylinder head with a wooden or hide mallet. In

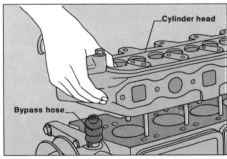

Cylinder head
Bypass hose

extreme cases, gently drive tapered hardwood wedges between the head and the block. Slide a knife under the gasket to free it. (On some engines the cylinder head is located on two dowels, in opposite corners

of the block. Make sure that these dowels do not move or come away with the cylinder head.)

4 If the engine has an overhead camshaft, do not turn it over when you have removed the head. To do so would upset the valve timing (see p. 176) and may disengage the drive chain.

5 If the engine is wet-linered—that is, with cylinders set loosely in the block—turning could dislodge the liners and cause water leaks into the sump after reassembly. Fit bars

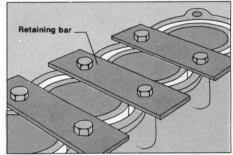

Retaining bar

across the block and use the cylinder-head bolts to secure them firmly, to keep the wet liners in place.

How the engine valves are assembled and removed

Burnt or badly seating valves cause loss of engine power, and increase petrol consumption. Those most likely to suffer damage are the exhaust valves, which are continuously subjected to the very high temperature of the combustion chamber. The inlet valves suffer less because they are cooled by the incoming mixture of air and petrol.

The valve assembly consists of the valve—which moves up and down in a guide in the cylinder head—a valve stem oil seal, valve spring, a spring retaining cap and two collets or collars, which hold the cap and ensure that the spring is under compression. The collets themselves may be held in place by spring clips.

On overhead-camshaft engines you must use a proper valve-spring compressor to remove the valves. On an overhead-valve engine a home-made compressor can be used. If the valves are badly burnt or pitted, fit new ones. When overhauling a cylinder head it is wise to fit a new set of valve springs.

MAKING AND USING VALVE-SPRING COMPRESSORS

Making a spring compressor
A valve-spring compressor can be made, for overhead-valve push-rod engines only, from a few simple pieces of material. Dimensions depend on the size of engine, but the compressor detailed below is suitable for most conventional 4-cylinder and many 6-cylinder engines.

Materials: Stout piece of chain about 9 in. long with ½ in. wide links; piece of ¼ in. plate steel 1½ in. wide and 7 in. long, ¼ in. nut and bolt.

1 Drill a ¼ in. hole in the steel bar, ½ in. from the end. At a point 2 in. from the same end drill a hole—about ⅜ in. diameter—big enough to fit over the two retaining

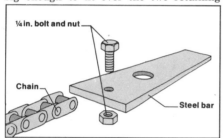

collets on the valve stem. Bolt one end of the chain to the first hole in the steel bar. Round off the edges of the other end of the steel bar to form a handle.

2 Fit one of the links of the chain over a rocker stud and screw on the stud nut, or

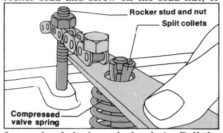

fit a rocker bolt through the chain. Pull the piece of steel down against the spring cap

Using a production compressor
1 Fit the valve-spring compressor so that its forked end straddles the valve-spring cap

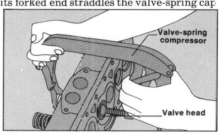

and the flat end fits against the valve head. (Note that Audi cars need a special compressor available from a dealer.)

---

1 Tighten the compressor screw to draw the spring coils together. If it is difficult to move, tap the forked end of the tool with a hammer.

2 Remove the split collets. Release the compressor tool and lift off the

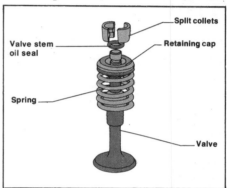

spring retaining cap, valve spring or springs, and slide the oil seal off the valve stem. Withdraw the valve from its guide in the cylinder head. As you remove the remaining valves, number them and keep them in their original order.

Decarbonising the cylinder head and pistons

Lay the cylinder head on a bench with the combustion chambers facing upwards. Make sure that the valve seats in the head are not scratched when the carbon is being removed. Do not use steel scrapers or rotary wire brushes on alloy cylinder heads.

1 On a cast-iron cylinder head, use a steel scraper to remove the hard pieces of carbon from the combustion chambers. On an alloy head, first soak the combustion chambers and ports in paraffin to soften the carbon deposits.

2 Fit a rotary wire brush to the chuck of an electric drill, and remove the smaller deposits of carbon from the combustion chambers. Push the rotary brush up the inlet and exhaust ports of the cylinder head. Make sure that all the carbon is removed.

On alloy cylinder heads, use only a wooden scraper to remove the carbon from the combustion chambers and the inlet and exhaust ports.

3 Wrap fine emery cloth round a piece of flat wood. Draw it back-

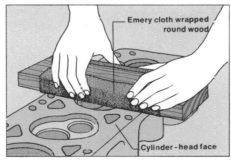

wards and forwards across the surface of the cylinder head, to remove any particles of the old head gasket.

4 Wash the cylinder head in paraffin and let it dry.

5 Remove any carbon build-up from the piston crowns with a wooden scraper. But leave ⅛ in. ring of carbon round the edge of the

piston crown, and do not remove the ring of carbon inside the top of the

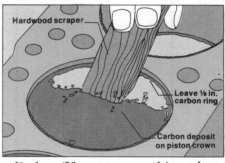

cylinder. (If you remove this carbon, engine oil consumption will increase until the ring has re-formed with use.)

6 Clean the face of the engine block with fine emery cloth wrapped round the piece of wood. Blow out the carbon dust from the tops of the pistons with an air-line or tyre pump.

7 Wipe the piston crowns, cylinders and face of the block clean with a paraffin-soaked rag.

Cylinder head/4

Checking the valves, guides and seats

Check the condition of the valves very carefully. If they are burnt or badly pitted, fit new ones. If not, they can be re-ground to match their seats in the cylinder head.

1 Scrape all the carbon deposits from the head, throat and stem of

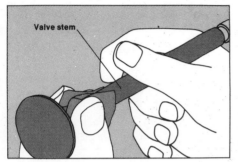

the valve. Clean the head and throat with a piece of fine emery cloth. Do not clean the valve seat.

2 Check the seat of each valve. Light pitting is acceptable and will be removed when the valve is re-ground to the seat in the cylinder head. If the pitting or burning is severe, new valves are needed.

3 If the valve is to be used again, check that the valve stems are a

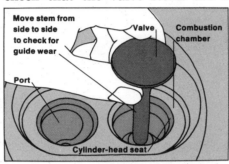

good fit in their guides. Renew the guides if the valve stems can be

moved sideways. Worn inlet valves increase fuel consumption.

4 Check the condition of the matching seats in the cylinder head. If

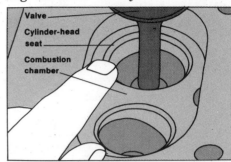

they are badly burnt they will have to be recut with a special tool. (A kit of valve-seat cutting tools can be hired, but if you do not want to undertake the work yourself, take the head and its valves to a garage.)

How to fit a new set of valve guides

On some engines, the valves fit directly into precisely machined holes in the head; in others, separate valve guides are fitted in holes in the cylinder head.

If your engine is of the first type, the machined hole has to be bored slightly larger to take new valves

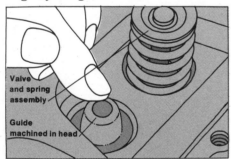

with wider stems—a garage job. But if you have the other type, you can fit new guides.

Do not buy new guides until you have removed one of the old ones, so that you can make sure that they are the same height. Buy or borrow a special tool—a stepped drift that fits the guide and prevents burring the edge. If the cylinder head is alloy, heat it in an oven to a temperature of 200°C (392°F).

1 Raise the cylinder head on wooden blocks. Fit the stepped drift into

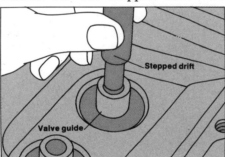

one of the end guides and tap the guide out of the head. Do the same to the other end guide.

2 Buy the new set of guides and check the height. Turn the cylinder head over and replace it on the blocks. Smear two of the new guides with engine oil, and fit one at one end of the head. Tap it in gently with a mallet and stepped drift. Do the same at the other end. If the new guides have shoulders, keep tapping until they will go no further. If they have no shoulder, you must measure their height against the old guides still in the head. Turn the cylinder head over.

3 Lay a straight-edge between the two end guides. If they are still

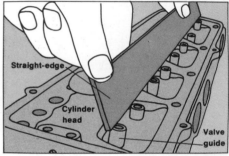

below the level of the old guides, continue tapping them home.

4 When the two new end guides are correctly positioned, remove all the

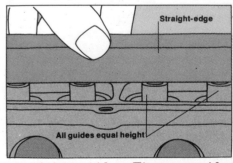

remaining guides. Fit new guides to the level of the two end guides.

Recutting the valve seats in the cylinder head

A valve-seat cutting kit consists of the angled seat cutter, a mandrel to fit the valve guides, to ensure that the seat is cut evenly, and a turning bar.

1 Select the mandrel that fits the valve guide. There should be no slack or sideways movement. Choose

the seat cutter of the correct angle. (Check the seat angle with your local dealer.) Fit the cutter to the turning bar and the mandrel to the bottom of the cutter.

2 Before cutting, push the mandrel through a piece of brown paper. The paper picks up the pieces of

metal cut away from the seat and avoids rippling on the valve seat.

3 Locate the mandrel in the valve guide and push it down so that the cutter contacts the seat. Turn the bar clockwise two full turns and check the seat condition. Continue cutting until the pitting is removed.

Grinding in new or old valves

Even when the cylinder-head valve seats have been recut, or when new valves are fitted, they have to be ground into the seats. If the old valves are being used, grind in first with coarse grinding paste and finish off with fine paste. With new valves or recut seats, use only fine paste.

1 Smear a thin layer of grinding paste on the seat of the valve and slide the light spring over the valve stem. Place the valve in its guide.

2 Moisten the rubber suction cap of the grinding tool and press it on to the valve head.

3 Press down on the grinding tool, against the light valve-spring pressure, so that the face of the valve seat contacts the matching seat in the cylinder head.

4 Rotate the grinding tool backwards and forwards between the

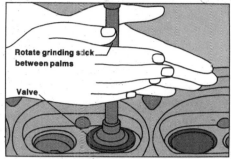
Rotate grinding stick between palms

Valve

palms of the hands and keep it pressed down. Occasionally relieve the pressure and allow the spring to lift the valve off its seating. Half turn the valve and continue grinding until you can no longer feel any resistance between the two surfaces.

5 Lift out the valve and clean the grinding paste from the valve and cylinder-head seats. The seats should have a matt grey finish without any signs of pitting. If necessary, continue grinding. If coarse grinding paste has been used, change to fine

paste when all the pitting has been removed.

6 Clean the valve and head seats with paraffin to make sure that all the grinding paste is removed. Draw pencil lines $\frac{1}{8}$ in. apart across the

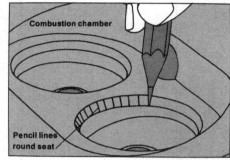
Combustion chamber

Pencil lines round seat

surface of the cylinder-head seat. Replace the valve in the guide and, with a slight downward pressure, rotate it one quarter turn. Lift it out and make sure all the pencil lines have been cut where the valve seat meets the seat in the cylinder head. If not, continue grinding.

Refitting the valves in the cylinder head

Clean the valve ports in the cylinder with paraffin. Smear the combustion chambers with a film of oil.

When you replace the valves in the cylinder head, make sure that each is fitted to its own seat.

1 Clean the valves and lightly lubricate the stems with oil. Drop

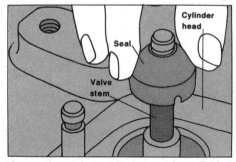
Cylinder head

Seal

Valve stem

the valves into their guides. Drop the spring base-plate into position (if

one is fitted) and fit the valve spring or springs over the valve stem. Slip the oil seal over the stem, and fit the spring retaining cap in position over the spring.

2 Fit the valve spring compressor so that its forked end straddles the collar and the other end is against

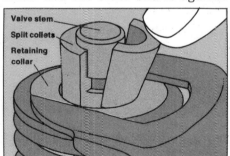
Valve stem

Split collets

Retaining collar

the head of the valve. Tighten the compressor screw to close the spring

far enough to enable the split collets to be fitted to the valve stem.

3 Make sure that the collets locate in the groove round the top of the valve spring. If the collets have a retaining clip, fit the clip to hold them in position. If not, dab grease on each collet. Gently release the valve-spring compressor. Make sure that the collets are not pushed out.

4 Do the same to the remaining valves. When they have all been fitted, put the cylinder head on the bench, combustion chambers downwards, and tap each valve stem lightly with a hammer. This bounces the valve spring and makes sure that the collets are properly seated. Check that all the oil and water channels in the cylinder head are clean.

Refitting the cylinder head

Refitting the cylinder head is similar for ohv and ohc engines, but it is sometimes possible to check the valve clearance and reassemble the overhead camshaft (see p. 175) before fitting the head.

1 Make sure that the faces of the cylinder head and engine block are perfectly clean. On cast-iron heads smear the two surfaces lightly with clean oil. If any rubber oil seal 'O' rings are used between the two surfaces, fit new ones.

2 If the block has no location dowels and the cylinder head is bolted on, put a punch in the bolt holes in opposite corners of the block. Fit the new cylinder-head gasket. It will be marked 'Top' or 'Front'.

3 On Vauxhall Vivas and Victors, early Rovers and all cars with alloy cylinder heads, use a sealing compound recommended by the makers.

4 Position the cylinder head correctly and fit the head bolts. Re-

move the punches. Fit the washers and nuts to the head studs.

5 Tighten the head bolts a turn at a time. Follow the same sequence as for slackening, or start at the centre and move diagonally outwards in both directions. Turn all the nuts or bolts until they are just tight against the cylinder head.

6 Tighten with a torque wrench set to the figure recommended by the manufacturers (check with a dealer).

Cylinder head /5

Overhauling the rocker assembly on an overhead-valve engine

Any wear in the rocker mechanism of an overhead-valve engine will make it difficult to adjust valve clearances accurately and eliminate noise. On shaft-mounted rocker arms, the assembly will have to be dismantled to determine the extent of wear. On stud-mounted rocker arms, the wear can be easily seen.

Shaft-mounted rocker arms

1 Remove the shaft retaining clip, screw or split-pin.

2 Slide the components off the shaft and lay them out in the order in which they are removed.

3 Check the shaft for wear at the points where the rocker arms pivot. This is indicated by a groove in the

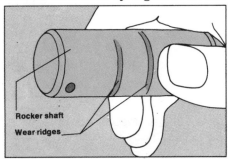

Rocker shaft
Wear ridges

top surface of the shaft. If there is a groove, fit a new shaft and a set of rocker arms.

4 If the shaft is in good condition and the rocker-arm bushes are not

worn, check the ends of the arms, where they contact the top of the

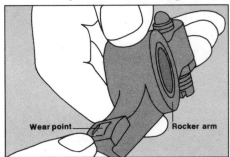

Wear point   Rocker arm

valve stem; look for indentations. If the arms are worn, fit new ones.

5 Remove the end-plug from the rocker shaft, and check that the oil gallery and the oil delivery holes to each rocker are clear. Wash in clean petrol and dry. Lubricate the shaft and refit the end-plug.

6 Reassemble the rocker shaft and make sure that the mounting blocks, tension springs and rocker arms are in their correct positions. Fit the shaft retaining clip.

Stud-mounted rocker arms

1 If the ends of the arms are worn at the point where they contact the valve stem, fit new arms.

2 Check the tightness of the self-locking nut on the rocker stud. It should need at least 3 lb./ft with a torque wrench to turn it.

RELEASING THE ROCKER SHAFT

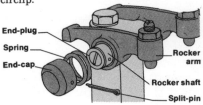

Rocker shaft
End-plug
Spring
Circlip
Rocker arm

Circlip On some types a circlip fitting into a groove in the rocker shaft holds the components in position. Remove the circlip.

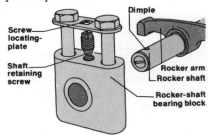

End-plug
Spring
End-cap
Rocker arm
Rocker shaft
Split-pin

Split-pin A split-pin, fitting through a matching hole in a collar and the shaft may be used. Close the ends of the pin and pull it out.

Dimple
Screw locating-plate
Shaft retaining screw
Rocker arm
Rocker shaft
Rocker-shaft bearing block

Retaining screw A square-headed screw, which threads into the top of a mounting bracket and is located in a dimple in the shaft, has to be unscrewed.

Refitting the rocker arms and push-rods

Before refitting the push-rods to the engine, make sure that they are undamaged. Roll them along the edge of the bench. If they are seen to be bent, fit new ones.

Shaft-mounted rocker arms

1 Fit the push-rods into place. Make sure they fit snugly in the cups of

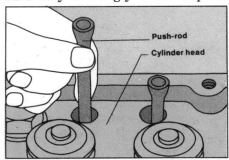

Push-rod
Cylinder head

the cam followers inside the engine. If the rocker shaft has not been dismantled for overhaul, remove the end-plug and clean the oilway.

2 Lubricate the rocker shaft with engine oil and refit the end-plug. Fit

the assembled shaft so that the dome on the base of each adjusting screw

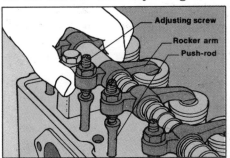

Adjusting screw
Rocker arm
Push-rod

fits into the cup at the top of each push-rod.

3 Fit the bolts through the mounting brackets and screw them into the cylinder head. If the mounting brackets are stud fitted, fit the flat and spring washers and nut.

4 Tighten the nuts, or bolts, progressively half a turn at a time, until the mounting brackets are tight against the cylinder head. Check the adjusters and lock-nuts for tight-

ness. Check and adjust the valve clearances (see pp. 109-117).

5 Fit a new gasket and the rocker cover. Refill the cooling system and sump, and run the engine to operating temperature. Check for leaks, and retighten, if necessary.

Stud-mounted rocker arms Slip the spring and arm over the stud; and fit the pivot ball and centre adjusting nut. Tighten the nut to

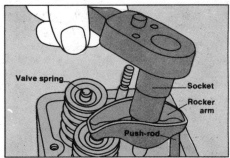

Valve spring
Socket
Rocker arm
Push-rod

give the correct valve clearance (see pp. 109-117). Refit the rocker cover (see **5** above).

Refitting a camshaft to an overhead-camshaft engine

Camshafts that are mounted in bearings on top of the cylinder head (see p. 169) can be fitted, and the valve clearances can be set, before the head is bolted to the engine block.

If the camshaft is contained in a cam box that bolts to the cylinder head, fit the cylinder head (see p. 173) to the engine and bolt the cam box into position (see below).

1 Clean the camshaft bearing shells and make sure the oil delivery holes

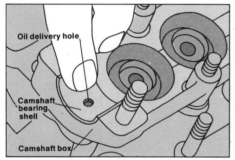

are clear. Lubricate the shells with clean engine oil.

2 Slide the camshaft into position and fit the bearing caps. Tighten the bearing-cap nuts to their recommended torque figure. Check the valve clearances (see pp. 109-117).

3 Adjust the valve timing (see p. 176). Turn the camshaft so that the timing marks line up. The cam lobes on the firing cylinder should both point upwards.

4 Refit the cylinder head to the engine block (see p. 173). Make sure it is positioned correctly, and fit and tighten the head nuts or bolts to the torque figure recommended by the engine manufacturer.

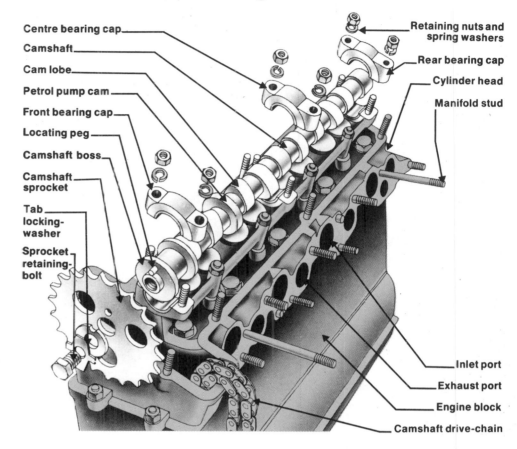

Centre bearing cap
Camshaft
Cam lobe
Petrol pump cam
Front bearing cap
Locating peg
Camshaft boss
Camshaft sprocket
Tab locking-washer
Sprocket retaining-bolt

Retaining nuts and spring washers
Rear bearing cap
Cylinder head
Manifold stud
Inlet port
Exhaust port
Engine block
Camshaft drive-chain

5 Check that the timing marks on the crankshaft or flywheel line up with the casing marks (see p. 164).

On chain-driven shafts, fit the chain to the cam sprocket and fit the sprocket to the camshaft boss, so that the valve timing marks line up. Check the chain for wear; if it is worn, have it renewed.

On belt-driven shafts, check the condition of the belt. If it has cracked, or the teeth on the inside of the belt are damaged, fit a new one. Make sure the belt is located correctly on the sprockets.

6 Tension the chain or belt (see p. 176) and rotate the crankshaft one

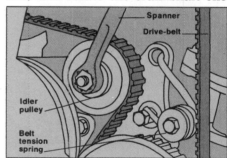

Spanner
Drive-belt
Idler pulley
Belt tension spring

full turn. Check again that the timing marks all line up.

When the camshaft is box-mounted

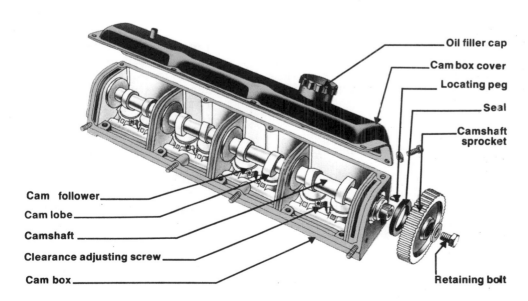

Oil filler cap
Cam box cover
Locating peg
Seal
Camshaft sprocket
Cam follower
Cam lobe
Camshaft
Clearance adjusting screw
Cam box
Retaining bolt

Box-mounted camshafts can be removed and replaced without disturbing the camshaft bearings.

1 Turn the camshaft in the cam box so that the timing marks line up, or so that the two cam lobes on the firing cylinder are pointing directly upwards.

2 Fit the cam box assembly to the cylinder head and secure the bolts.

3 Make sure the timing marks are still in alignment, including those on the auxiliary shaft driving the fuel pump and the distributor. Connect the drive-belt or chain, as previously described, and check the valve clearances (see pp. 109-117).

Cylinder head /6

Timing the valves on overhead-camshaft engines

To adjust the timing of the valves on any ohc engine, you must first find out on which cylinder the timing should be established. In most cases it is timed on No. 1 cylinder, but consult your dealer, to find out if your car is different.

To establish top dead centre (see p. 164) remove the distributor cap and check that the rotor arm points towards the plug lead segment of the timing cylinder. Check that the top-dead-centre marks on the crankshaft (or flywheel) are in line with the static marks on the casing.

If the camshaft has already been fitted, avoid turning the engine before the driving chain (or belt) has been fitted. To do so could damage valves and piston crowns.

These general rules apply to all ohc engines—single or twin-cam—but variations for individual makes are given below.

In the case of Rovers, the manufacturers advise that timing should be carried out only by authorised dealers, because of the method used to lock the camshaft in position and the need for special tools.

Similarly, BMW recommend that all work on the cylinder head should be left to official dealers.

Ford

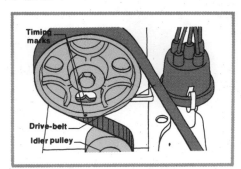

1 Before fitting the cylinder head, turn the camshaft so that the pulley key—on the camshaft boss—is at the top. Fit the pulley on the camshaft boss key. Check that the timing mark at the base of the pulley is in line with the dot on the camshaft housing.

2 Fit the toothed drive-belt and release the spring-loaded idler pulley to tension the belt. Turn the shaft one revolution and recheck the timing.

Toyota

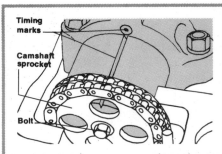

1 Position the camshaft so that the 'V' in the flange is in line with the hole in the front camshaft bearing cap. Fit the camshaft sprocket to the chain and locate the sprocket on the peg in the camshaft flange.

2 Fit a new locking washer to the sprocket-securing bolt and tighten the bolt to a torque of between 47 and 54 lb./ft. Bend over the lock tabs to secure the bolt. Refit the camshaft cover.

Datsun

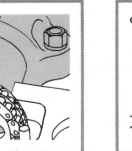

1 Turn the assembled camshaft so that the sprocket keyway is at the top—twelve-o'clock position.

2 Fit the camshaft sprocket to the chain, so that the timing mark on the sprocket lines up with the marked link on the timing chain.

3 Fit the sprocket and chain to the camshaft, locating the sprocket on the camshaft key. Fit and tighten the sprocket-securing bolt.

Fiat

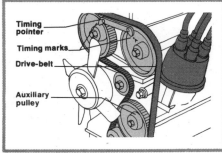

1 Turn the two camshaft sprockets so that the dots, or holes, on the face of the sprocket line up with the two pointers on the timing bracket. Refit the cam-boxes to the cylinder head (see p. 175). Turn the auxiliary pulley until the timing dot is at 34 degrees from the vertical in a clockwise direction.

2 Fit the toothed belt and tension the spring-loaded idler pulley by releasing the pulley lock-nut and retightening it. Fit a spanner to the pulley nut and turn the shaft once. Recheck the timing marks.

Volkswagen

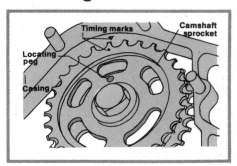

1 Fit the thrust-plate to hold the camshaft in position. Put the sprocket on the shaft, locating it on the peg in the camshaft boss.

2 Turn the sprocket so that the timing dot lines up with the 'V' on the surface of the timing case.

3 Lift off the sprocket—without disturbing the position of the camshaft. Fit the chain to the sprocket and replace the sprocket. Fit and tighten the sprocket bolt and refit the camshaft cover and timing chain cover to the engine.

Hillman Imp

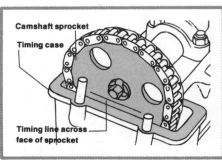

1 Refit the camshaft so that the No. 1 cylinder cam-peaks are the same distance above the cylinder head cover face. Fit the camshaft bearing caps and tighten with a torque wrench set at 6 lb./ft.

2 Position the camshaft sprocket in the timing chain so that the timing line across the sprocket face is parallel with the top edge of the timing cover. Tighten the sprocket-securing bolt to a torque of 19 lb./ft.

3 Bend the tabs of the securing bolt lock-washer. Refit the camshaft cover.

Vauxhall

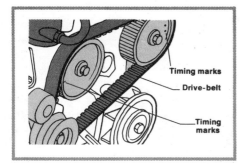

1 Fit the camshaft (see p. 175) so that the timing marks on the camshaft pulley are at approximately the two o'clock position.

2 Turn the auxiliary shaft pulley so that the timing marks are furthest away from the camshaft pulley. Line up the pulleys, so that a straight edge passing through the centre of both shafts lines up with the two sets of timing marks.

3 Fit the drive-belt and temporarily adjust the spring-loaded idler pulley to tension the belt. Fit a spanner on the crankshaft pulley nut and turn the shaft one full revolution. Recheck the alignment of the timing marks with the straight edge. Check that the top-dead-centre crankshaft timing marks are also in line.

4 Always turn the crankshaft in a clockwise direction to ensure the correct belt tension between camshaft and crankshaft. Tension the belt on the idler pulley. Take the car to a garage and have the belt tension checked. There should be a deflection of ·003 in. under a load of 10 lb.

Jaguar

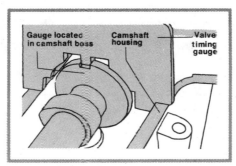

1 Turn the engine until No. 6 (front) piston is at top dead centre. Then tension the top timing chain.

2 Remove the locking wire from the setscrews holding the cam sprockets —some can be reached only by turning the crankshaft. Remove all the setscrews and return the engine to top dead centre on No. 6.

3 Remove the sprockets from the camshaft flanges. Position the camshafts with a valve timing gauge and check that the top-dead-centre marks line up.

4 Release the adjuster plates from their circlips and press them forwards until the serrations disengage. Replace the sprockets on the camshafts and align exactly the holes in the adjuster plate with the tapped holes in the camshaft flanges.

5 Re-engage the serrations of the adjuster plate and the sprockets. Refit the circlips and setscrews. Recheck the chain tension and secure the cam-sprocket retaining screws with new locking wire.

British Leyland Maxi

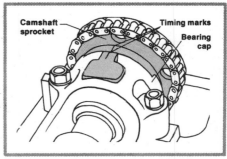

The valve clearances can be established and the camshaft fitted to the cylinder head before the head itself is refitted to the engine block.

1 Turn the camshaft so that the cam-sprocket locating peg is at the top. Refit the cylinder head (see p. 173). Fit the cam sprocket to the timing chain. Position the sprocket on the camshaft and make sure that the peg fits the sprocket hole.

2 Line up the camshaft timing marks on top of the front camshaft bearing cap and the back of the cam sprocket. Ensure the $\frac{1}{4}$ in. top-dead-centre mark on the flywheel lines up with the mark on the flywheel housing. (No. 1 cylinder on firing stroke.)

3 Fit the sprocket-securing bolt and washer. Tighten the bolt to a torque of 35 lb./ft. Slacken the lock-nut on the adjuster screw of the left-hand chain guide. Turn the adjuster until the chain is tight, but not taut, and tighten the lock-nut. Make sure the front cover dowel bolt engages in the lower end of the right-hand chain guide.

Refitting the parts around the engine

1 When reassembling any type of engine, make sure all the parts are absolutely clean. Dirty parts can allow grit into the engine and cause more rapid wear. Use plenty of clean engine oil on all moving parts, to avoid dry metal-to-metal contact when the engine is first started after an overhaul. When

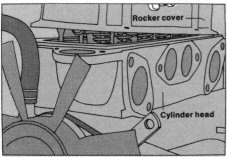

the cylinder head and rocker gear, or overhead camshafts have been

fitted, position the rocker or camshaft gasket and fit the covers. Fit new manifold gaskets, and bolt the manifolds into position.

2 Fit the spark-plugs (see p. 106), and reconnect the spark-plug leads. Make sure that they are fitted to the correct plugs. Refit the car-

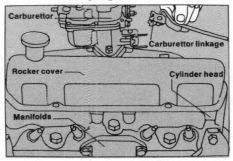

burettor and the carburettor connections, throttle and choke linkages.

3 Fit the hoses on water-controlled automatic chokes. Refit the hoses to

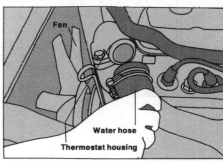

the radiator, manifold and heater unions. Fill the radiator.

4 Start the engine and check all the hose connections for leaks. Once the engine has reached operating temperature, adjust the carburettor (see pp. 124-9) and, if necessary, check the ignition system.

Cooling system /1

WHEN THE COOLING SYSTEM GOES WRONG

Symptom	Check	Symptom	Check
Overheating	Coolant level – p. 36 Fan-belt tension – p. 119 Hoses – p. 179 Pressure cap – p. 181 Clogged system – p. 180 Water pump – p. 182 Thermostat – p. 181 Expansion tank pipe – p. 180 Radiator air passages – p. 180 Ignition timing – p. 108 Distributor advance – p. 164 Thermostatically controlled fan – garage job	Loud screech on starting from cold	Fan-belt tension – p. 119 Frozen water pump – p. 182 Water-pump bearings – p. 182 Generator bearings – p. 119 Power-steering pump – garage job
		Radiator continually needs water	Rust stains on hoses – p. 179 Cylinder-head gasket – p. 166 Radiator matrix – p. 179
		Heater remains cool	Water control valve – p. 183 Thermostat – p. 181 Heater element – p. 183
Leaks from water pump	Seals or gaskets – p. 182	Heater cools suddenly	Coolant level – p. 36 Fan belt – p. 119 Water control valve – p. 183 Heater hose – p. 183
Continuous bubbling and overheating	Cylinder-head gasket – p. 166		

How the engine cooling system works

Car engines are cooled by either water or air. In water-cooled engines, which are fitted to most cars, water absorbs heat as it is pumped through the engine block. The hot water passes to the radiator, where it is cooled by air drawn or blown through the radiator by a fan.

Most cars have fans driven by a belt from a pulley on the front of the engine block. Some manufacturers use thermostatically controlled fans which allow the engine to reach its working temperature more quickly and prevent over-cooling.

On some transverse-engined cars the radiator is mounted at the side near the road wheel. Because of this, it may get dirty very quickly.

Overheated systems increase fuel consumption and may cause pinking and engine seizure. If the engine runs too cool, fuel is wasted and the heater is inefficient.

Air-cooled engines

Air-cooled engines have fins on their cylinder blocks to increase the surface area for dissipating heat. Air is blown over the fins by a fan. As long as the fan-belt tension is correct and the fins are clean, the system is usually trouble-free.

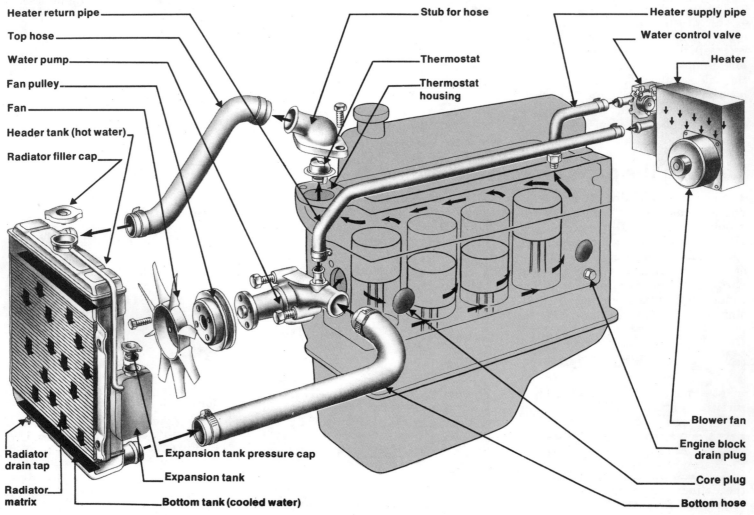

Heater return pipe
Top hose
Water pump
Fan pulley
Fan
Header tank (hot water)
Radiator filler cap
Radiator drain tap
Radiator matrix
Expansion tank pressure cap
Expansion tank
Bottom tank (cooled water)
Stub for hose
Thermostat
Thermostat housing
Heater supply pipe
Water control valve
Heater
Blower fan
Engine block drain plug
Core plug
Bottom hose

Locating and curing leaks in the system

The weak links between the radiator and the engine are the flexible hoses, which may leak because they have perished, cracked, worn or split. Leaks may also occur at the clips which secure the hoses to the radiator or engine stubs.

Never work on the cooling system if the water is likely to be hot: let the engine cool down.

Tools: Buckets; screwdriver; knife or hacksaw.
Materials: New hoses if necessary.

Draining the system
1 If there is antifreeze in the system, get enough buckets ready to save the liquid. The handbook will tell you how much liquid is required to fill the system.

2 Remove the radiator cap and put large buckets beneath the block and radiator. Undo the radiator and engine block drain taps or release the bottom radiator hose.

3 Clear blockages in the taps with a piece of thin wire.

Removing the old hose
1 Undo the clips holding both ends of the hose and gently pull it off the radiator and engine stubs.

2 If the hose is stuck and cannot be pulled off a stub, cut through the

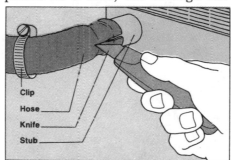

Clip
Hose
Knife
Stub

end of the hose with a knife or a hacksaw to remove it.

3 Clean both stubs with fine emery cloth and lubricate them with soap.

Fitting a new hose
Slide the clips over the hose and push it on to the stubs. Avoid twists in the hose and tighten clips.

Refilling the system
1 Close the drain taps. Refill the system and replace the radiator cap.

2 Run the engine to its working temperature. If the joints leak, tighten the clips further.

3 Check the water level (see p. 36) and replace the radiator cap.

TYPES OF HOSE CLIP

Jubilee clips

Wire clip

Split-pin clip

Various clips are used to fix hoses to the stubs on the engine and radiator. They include the Jubilee, wire, split-pin (as on Simca and Renault) and the knurled Jubilee for finger adjustment. All work on the same principle and can usually be interchanged, provided that the clip's diameter is similar to that of the hose. Do not overtighten a clip, particularly if it is made of wire: it may cut the hose.

Mending a leak in the radiator matrix

Matrix leaks should be left to a garage with specialist equipment, unless a proprietary sealant will stop them. Leaks in the header tank or bottom tank can be soldered.

Tools: Large soldering iron; screwdrivers; spanners for mounting bolts; wire brush.
Materials: Abrasive paper; flux; solder.

1 Run the engine to its normal working temperature, mark the leak and drain the system. Remove the radiator by releasing hoses, mounting bolts and, where necessary, the shroud. Lift the radiator clear.

2 Clean around the leak with a wire brush and abrasive paper to

reveal the metal. Coat the surface with flux to ensure an even run of solder. Put an even coating of solder on the metal, covering $\frac{1}{2}$ in. around the leak. Put the radiator back in the car, bolt it in place and reconnect the hoses. Refill the system. Run the engine for a few minutes to check for leaks.

Removing and fitting engine core plugs

Core plugs are secured in the cylinder block and head casting. They may rust from inside and cause leaks. If a plug leaks, fit a new one.

Tools: Hammer; old chisel or screwdriver; flat punch; thin punch.
Materials: New core plug; sealing compound.

1 Drain the cooling system. Hammer an old cross-cut chisel or screwdriver through the centre of the plug and prise it free. Take care not to damage the sides of the hole or any other part of the casting. Some Rover models have threaded plugs, use the chisel to turn them anti-clockwise. After removing the **plug, flush out the system** (see p. 180).

2 Clean the wall of the hole in the cylinder block and coat it with sealing compound. The usual type of core plug is a steel disc, convex on one side and concave on the other.

3 Press the new plug into the hole, concave side inwards, until it comes against the inner lip. Tap it home with a flat punch which is just smaller than the plug—this will force the outer rim of the plug into a groove in the hole.

4 Fit a threaded plug by coating it in sealing compound.

5 Some cars have holes without grooves. The core plugs to fit these

are straight-sided. Coat the rim of the plug with sealing compound and

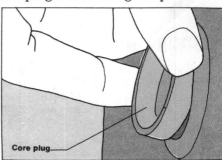

Core plug

tap it into place with a hammer. Use a thin punch and a hammer to bend over the lip of the hole in two or three places. Refill the system with coolant and check for leaks with the engine running.

Cooling system /2

Flushing the radiator and engine block

If the cooling system does not drain, or if the engine is overheating for no identifiable reason, the radiator and block should be flushed.

Tools: Screwdriver; spanners to fit thermostat housing.
Materials: Flushing agent.

1 Remove the engine-block tap or plug and probe the hole with a wire. Refit the engine drain-tap or plug and fill with a flushing agent.

2 Run the engine for ten minutes, after reaching working temperature.

3 Then empty the radiator and block. Fill and empty the system with clean water. Repeat until clean water runs from the radiator.

Backflushing
1 A normal flushing clears only the radiator sediment. Backflushing will remove more corrosion, debris and dirt from the radiator and from the waterways in the head and engine

block. Drain the system and disconnect the bottom hose from its stub on the radiator (pp. 178-9).

2 Run a garden hose from the mains water supply into the bottom of the radiator. Disconnect the top hose

Garden hose

or remove the radiator cap. Turn on the water supply. Allow the water to run until clear liquid flows out.

3 Reconnect the bottom hose to the radiator and disconnect its other end from the engine block.

4 Remove the thermostat and its gasket. Then push the garden hose

into the block at the thermostat mounting, and allow the water to

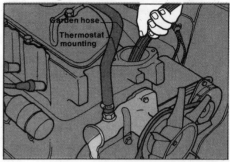
Garden hose
Thermostat mounting

run through until it drains clear from the bottom hose stub.

5 Repeat, allowing short periods between each flushing, then refit the thermostat and bottom hose. Run the engine for a few minutes to check for any leaks.

Checking the expansion tank
Run the engine to its normal working temperature, mark any leaks and drain the system. If the tank is metal, solder over the leaks. If the pressure cap leaks, fit a new one.

Curing an airlock in the cooling system

If an airlock develops—perhaps when the system is refilled—it is simpler to bleed the water through the heater return pipe than through the radiator hoses.

Tool: Screwdriver.

1 Switch the heater to 'on', check that the radiator is topped up, and run the engine until the top radiator hose heats suddenly as hot water reaches it—indicating that the thermostat has opened.

2 Switch off the engine and loosen the heater return pipe at the joint with the bottom radiator hose or the water pump. This joint is usually near the fan—so for safety, the engine must be stopped.

3 Restart the engine and allow it to tick over. Taking care to avoid the fan, pull the heater pipe clear.

4 When a steady stream of water comes through (usually after only a few seconds), stop the engine—to

Heater pipe
Fan

avoid putting a hand near the moving fan—and refit the pipe. Tighten the joint and top up the radiator.

AIRLOCKS ON AN IMP

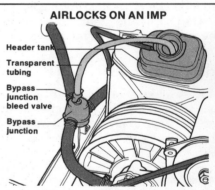
Header tank
Transparent tubing
Bypass junction bleed valve
Bypass junction

The method of bleeding the cooling system on the Hillman Imp differs from the usual, because a bypass junction and valve are fitted. You need a 2 ft length of transparent tube with an internal diameter of $\frac{3}{16}$ in. Keep the bleed valve on the radiator itself closed—it must not be used.

1 Close the drain taps and fill the system with coolant containing the recommended inhibitor or antifreeze.

2 Fit the tubing to the bleed valve on the bypass junction, and put the other end into the header tank.

3 Open the bleed valve, move the heater control on the fascia to hot, and run the engine at about 2000 rpm.

4 Top up the system as the level drops. Wait for air bubbles to stop running through the tube. Rev the engine for a moment and close the bleed valve.

5 Stop the engine, remove the tube and refit the radiator cap.

Removing the radiator for cleaning

A radiator clogged with dirt will cause the water to boil, and may eventually damage the engine.

Tools: Screwdriver and spanner to fit mounting bolts.
Materials: Warm water; washing-up liquid.

1 Drain the system and undo the radiator hoses and retaining bolts. Remove the radiator.

2 Spray the back of the radiator with a hose on medium pressure to

remove any dirt, dead flies or leaves that may be in the honeycombing.

3 Hose the radiator from the rear to force water through the matrix, but do not scrape off dirt—you may damage the matrix.

4 Allow the radiator to dry. Refit it and refill the system.

5 If a blockage persists after cleaning, consult a garage.

Removing and testing a thermostat

The thermostat (usually fitted in a cast housing on to which the top hose fits) is a valve which allows the cooling system to reach its working temperature before it opens to bring the radiator into operation.

There are two types of thermostat: one that shuts the valve when it fails, causing overheating; the other that opens the valve when it fails, causing the engine and heater to run cool.

A suspect thermostat of either type can be roughly checked by running the engine until the top hose heats up suddenly – this shows that the valve has opened.

If the hose heats gradually, the valve may be failing and should be replaced. A more accurate check can be made by removing the thermostat from its housing.

Tools: Spanner to fit housing bolts; saucepan; long-nosed pliers; thermometer.
Materials: Thermostat-housing gasket; high-melting-point grease; emery cloth.

1 Drain about 3 pints of coolant from the radiator (see p. 179). If the job is done in winter, drain the coolant into a container so that it can be used for refilling the radiator. Undo the thermostat housing bolts and lift off the cover. With cast-

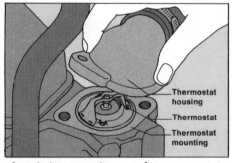

Thermostat housing
Thermostat
Thermostat mounting

aluminium engines, take care not to prise the cover free.

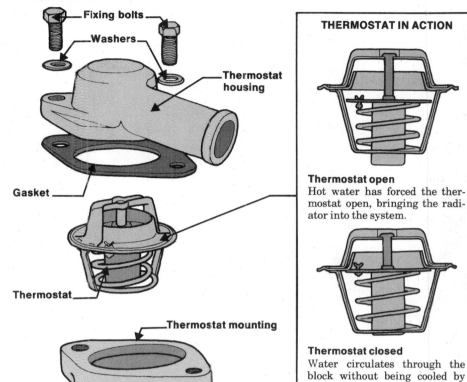

Fixing bolts
Washers
Thermostat housing
Gasket
Thermostat
Thermostat mounting

THERMOSTAT IN ACTION

Thermostat open
Hot water has forced the thermostat open, bringing the radiator into the system.

Thermostat closed
Water circulates through the block without being cooled by the radiator.

2 Peel off the old gasket and any sealing compound which may have been used, and lift out the thermostat. Clean the thermostat housing and the cylinder head with fine emery cloth.

3 Inspect the thermostat valve, which should be shut tight. If it is not, discard the thermostat.

4 If it is shut, look for a stamp mark on the thermostat valve which will indicate the temperature at which the valve should open to bring the radiator into the system.

5 Heat a saucepan of water on the kitchen stove to within 11°C (20°F)

of the marked temperature. Stir the water as it heats, to ensure that the temperature is uniform.

6 Hold the thermostat in the water with a pair of long-nosed pliers. Do not let it touch the pan – the metal will be hotter than the water.

7 Increase the heat, and the valve should begin to open within 3°C (5°F) of the marked temperature. It should be fully open when it reaches the temperature specified. If the thermostat fails this test, discard it. If it passes the test, refit the unit. Always use a new housing gasket, and smear it liberally with high-melting-point grease.

Checking and renewing a radiator cap

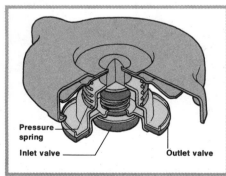

Pressure spring
Inlet valve
Outlet valve

The spring loading of the cap keeps the cooling system under pressure, and raises the boiling point of water so that it does not boil at the working temperature of the engine. When the coolant heats and expands,

air or water escapes through an outlet valve into an expansion tank or overflow pipe. When the coolant cools and contracts, air or water is drawn in through an inlet valve.

1 To check the cap, run the engine until it is warm, but not too hot. Stop the engine. Put a cloth over the cap to protect your hand from scalding steam. Unscrew the cap a quarter turn. There should be a slight hiss as you undo the cap. If there is not, fit a new cap.

2 The new cap must have the same dimensions as the old one – take the old one with you when you go to buy

it. Check the pressure marking stamped on top of the cap. The new cap must have the same pressure

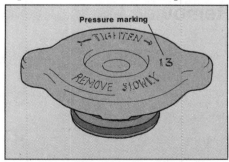

Pressure marking

marking as the old, or the engine will run at the wrong temperature. This could lead to overheating or uneconomic fuel consumption.

Cooling system /3

Removing and fitting a water pump

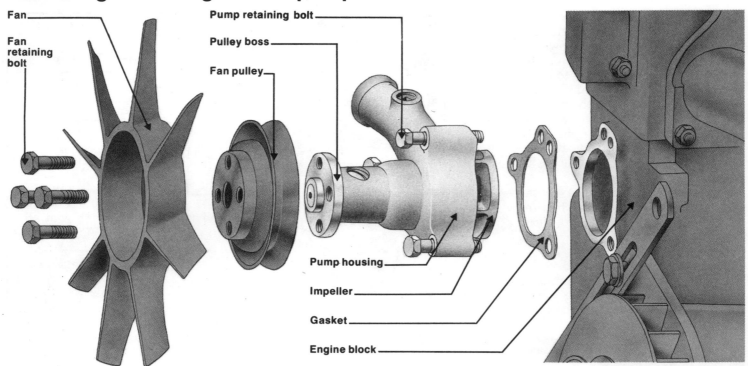

Fan

Fan retaining bolt

Pump retaining bolt

Pulley boss

Fan pulley

Pump housing

Impeller

Gasket

Engine block

If the temperature of the coolant is consistently high and cannot be lowered by servicing the thermostat (see p. 181), the water pump is faulty. The usual cause of failure is wear in the bearings or the impeller, so that the pump is no longer able to circulate water efficiently. A failing pump may be very squeaky and lubrication (see p. 118) will not quieten it. When a water pump is leaking or has failed, fit a new one that is guaranteed by the maker, or have the leaking pump overhauled.

Tools: Spanners to fit generator bolts; fan blades and water-pump fixing bolts; screwdriver.
Materials: Replacement water pump; pump gasket; new by-pass hose, if fitted; gasket cement.

1 Drain the cooling system. If the pump is situated in a place that is difficult to reach, undo the top and bottom radiator hoses, remove the radiator retaining bolts and lift out the radiator.

2 Slacken the generator bolts so that you can move it to allow the

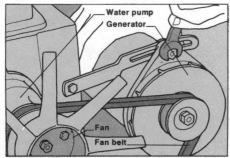

Water pump
Generator
Fan
Fan belt

fan belt to be loosened and slipped off the pulleys.

3 If you are not certain that the pump is leaking, find out if the bearings are worn by gripping the fan

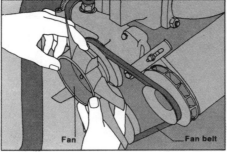

Fan
Fan belt

blades and trying to rock the impeller shaft backwards and forwards. If there is play, remove the pump.

4 Unbolt the fan and remove it. Slide off the pulley and remove any spacers from the shaft.

5 Undo the four or five bolts that secure the pump. Some bolts may be longer than others; note their positions.

6 Ease the pump off its locating dowels. Use a screwdriver as a lever

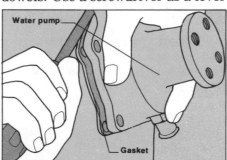

Water pump
Gasket

if necessary, but be careful not to damage the surface. Do not use a screwdriver on an aluminium hous-

ing. If the pump is not to be overhauled, discard it.

7 Clean any remains of gasket and compound from the cylinder block with a screwdriver. Be very careful not to damage the metal by gouging. Complete the cleaning by rubbing down with fine emery cloth.

8 Coat both sides of a new gasket with a non-setting jointing compound (see p. 166). (The compound is not necessary on the VW K70.)

9 Fit the gasket to the pump and bolt the pump in position. Tighten

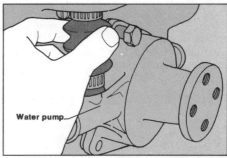

Water pump

the bolts evenly. If there is a by-pass hose, fit it at this stage.

10 Refit any spacers and the pulley and fan. Replace the fan belt and check the tension (see p. 119).

11 If the radiator was removed, replace it. Refill the cooling system. If you are using fresh water, add the correct amount of antifreeze.

12 Run the engine for a few minutes and check that there are no leaks from the pump or the hose.

Heating system

Tracing a fault in the heating system

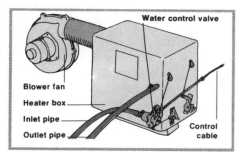

Water control valve
Blower fan
Heater box
Inlet pipe
Outlet pipe
Control cable

If a heater fails to work, first check the temperature of the engine coolant in the radiator with a small thermometer. If the temperature is low, the thermostat is probably faulty and will have to be renewed (see p. 181). Check the condition of the heater hoses (see p. 179). If they are perished or kinked, the water flow will be restricted. Renew any damaged hoses as soon as possible. An airlock is often to blame for restricted water flow through the heater. The most likely time for an airlock to happen is after the coolant has been changed.

Tools: Crosshead and bladed screwdrivers.
Materials: Length of plastic hose.

1 Undo and remove the heater return-hose from the heater box.

2 Connect a length of plastic hose to the return stub on the heater box.

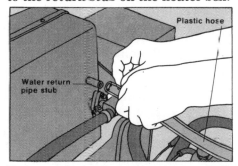

Plastic hose
Water return pipe stub

Remove the radiator cap (see p. 179) and lead the other end of the hose into the top of the radiator. Switch on the ignition and start the engine.

3 Move the heater lever in the car to 'Hot', and check that water flows from the end of the plastic hose.

4 Rev the engine to make the water circulate more quickly to clear any airlocks in the system.

5 Turn the heater lever to 'Off', and check that the flow stops.

6 If there is no water flow at all, or very little, the heater box or the water control valve is faulty. Remove the control valve and blow through the plastic hose. Once the water in the box has been cleared, you should be able to blow without any resistance. If not, the box is blocked. Take the car to a garage to have the box replaced.

Fitting a new water control valve

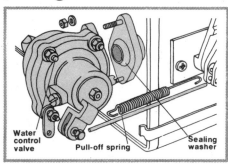

Water control valve
Pull-off spring
Sealing washer

If the heating system is still faulty after any airlock has been eliminated, fit a new water control valve. On some heaters, it is mounted at the side; on others, it fits directly on the engine block.

Tools: Screwdrivers; ⅜ in. ring spanner.
Materials: New water control valve and seal or flange gasket; emery cloth.

1 Disconnect the linkage from the side of the water control valve. On valves mounted on the engine block, undo the cable that controls the valve lever.

2 Remove the water hose from the valve inlet stub. Some water may be lost from the cooling system.

3 Undo the nuts or screws holding the water control valve to the heater or to the engine block.

4 Lift off the water control valve. Those fitted to the side of the heater have a rubber 'O' sealing ring on the valve stub. Those fitted to the engine block have a flange gasket.

5 If a new gasket has to be fitted, clean the face of the engine block with fine emery cloth. Remove the old gasket or sealing compound.

6 Renew the sealing ring or the gasket and fit the new control valve.

7 Reconnect the rods or cable, and fit the hoses. Top up the radiator with coolant (and antifreeze).

CHECKING THE BLOWER FAN

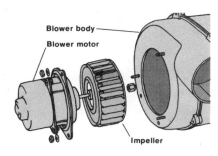

Blower body
Blower motor
Impeller

If the heater blower fan fails to work, carry out the following systematic checks to determine the fault.

Tools: Screwdrivers; ⅜ in. ring spanner; test lamp.
Materials: New motor.

1 Remove the leads from the heater fan in the engine compartment. Connect a test bulb across the leads. Turn on the fan switch inside the passenger compartment. If the bulb lights, the fault is in the fan.

2 If the bulb does not light, then the wiring circuit is at fault and will have to be checked thoroughly—probably in stages—with a circuit-tester (see pp. 188-9).

3 If the fan assembly is faulty, undo the nuts or bolts holding the motor to the heater box. Lift out the complete motor/fan unit.

4 Few new motors are sold with a fan impeller. Measure the distance between the fan and its housing. On older assemblies the impeller is bolted to the shaft: undo the nut and slide the impeller off the shaft. On more recent models, the fan is held by a locking clip: remove the clip and slide the fan off the shaft.

5 Fit the old fan impeller to the new motor. Make sure that it is secured in the same position on the shaft, so that when working it does not foul the fan housing.

6 Refit the motor/fan assembly to the housing and reconnect the wiring.

CLEARING THE DRAIN TUBES

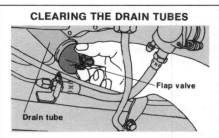

Flap valve
Drain tube

Cars with horizontal air intakes just below the windscreen have drain tubes from the base of the intake box. As a precaution against blockages, they should be cleaned occasionally.

1 To clean the tubes, jack up the car and mount it on axle stands.

2 Locate the drain tube. Some cars have two—one on each side of the housing.

3 Remove the flap valve from the end of the tube and probe the tube clear with a screwdriver, removing any leaves or dirt. Replace the flap valve.

Electrical system /1

How the car's electrical system works

A car's electrical system is divided into separate circuits—the ignition and starting circuit; the charging circuit; and the lighting and accessory circuits.

The current for all the electrical circuits is taken from the battery, which is kept charged by a generator—either an alternator or a dynamo. The generator is linked to the battery through a control box, on dynamos, or a regulator, on alternators. This prevents the battery discharging back through the generator and regulates the flow of current from the generator to the battery, ensuring that it is correctly charged. If a dynamo control box or an alternator regulator fails, take the car to an auto-electrician—it is not a job for home mechanics.

From the battery, current flows through feed wires to the components. The circuits are not completed by wires running back to the battery's earth terminal; instead,

the components are connected to the car's steel bodywork, which acts as an earth return and completes the circuits. This reduces the amount of wiring needed and makes it easier to trace faults. The circuits are protected by fuses and are usually controlled by switches.

The battery is earthed to the car's bodywork either from its positive terminal (positive earth) or from its negative terminal (negative earth). Connecting the battery the other way round reverses the flow of current; this will damage the generator control box, the alternator, and accessories such as radios which contain transistors and other electronic devices. Reversing the battery earth connection will also make some heaters and wiper motors run backwards. Look at the battery to see whether the + or − terminal is connected to earth, and make sure that it is always reconnected in the same way.

SUPPRESSED COMPONENTS

If a car has a built-in radio, taking current directly from the battery, many of the car's electrical components may have suppressors fitted to eliminate radio interference.

A suppressor is a small cylinder with a wire protruding from one end. The suppressor body is earthed to the car chassis or component and the wire is connected, by a tag, to the terminal of the component it is suppressing.

The components that most need suppressing are the generator and coil, but suppressors are also used to eliminate interference from electric clocks and windscreen-wiper motors. If a component has to be changed or removed for repair, make a note of the terminal to which the suppressor lead is attached, and make sure that it is refitted correctly when reassembling the component.

WHEN THE ELECTRICAL SYSTEM GOES WRONG

Symptom	Check	Symptom	Check
All lamps fail to light	Battery—pp. 36-37 Switch—pp. 189-190	All accessories on same fuse fail	Fuse—p. 189 Fuse holder—p. 189 Wiring (supply to fuse)—pp. 188-9
All lamps go out completely when starter is operated	Battery terminal connections—pp. 36-37	Battery goes flat (charge rate too low)	Fan belt tension—p. 119 Battery electrolyte level very low—pp. 36-37 Control box—garage job
Lamps controlled by main lighting switch fail to operate	Fuse (if fitted)—p. 189 Wiring—pp. 188-9 Switch—pp. 189-190	Generator not charging	Fan belt broken—p. 119 Generator connections—p. 119 Generator brushes—pp. 185-7 Control box—garage job
One lamp of pair (or set) fails to light	Bulb—p. 192 Earth connection—pp. 36-37 Bulb-holder contact—p. 192 Wiring—pp. 188-9	Erratic charging	Control box—garage job Generator brushes—pp. 185-7
Panel lamp fails to light	Fuse (if fitted)—p. 189 Bulb—p. 192 Switch—pp. 189-190 Wiring—pp. 188-9 Rheostat (if fitted)—garage job	Noisy dynamo	Mounting bolts or pulley—p. 119 Bearings—pp. 186-7
Side and rear lamps fail, but flashers and stoplights work	Fuse (if fitted)—p. 189 Wiring—pp. 188-9 Switch—pp. 189-190 Bad earth at bulb holder—p. 192	Horn failure	Fuse—p. 189 Wiring and connections—pp. 188-9, 192 Adjustment—garage job
Interior lamp fails to work when door is opened	Fuse—p. 189 Bulb—p. 192 Switch contact dirty or broken—p. 190	Horn volume low or intermittent	Connections—p. 192 Adjustment—garage job
All lights dim when car is stationary or at low speed	Fan belt tension—p. 119 Battery condition—pp. 36-37 Low charge rate—garage job	Difficulty in turning engine	Battery discharged—pp. 36-37 Dirty battery connections—pp. 36-37 Engine to chassis earth strap loose or missing—p. 135 Faulty starter motor—p. 138
All lights dim when car is running at moderate to high speed	Fan belt tension—p. 119 Generator faulty—pp. 119, 185-7 Control box—garage job	Failure of direction indicators	Fuse and fuse holder—p. 189 Flasher control unit—p. 191 Wiring and connections—pp. 188-191
Poor lighting from one or more lamps	Dirty lens—p. 192 Earth connection—p. 192 Bulb—p. 192	Dashboard warning light not flashing or unit not ticking when indicators are operated	Blown or faulty bulb—p. 192 Wiring and connections—pp. 188-192
Lamps flicker or get brighter when generator is charging	Battery condition—pp. 36-37 Fan belt tension—p. 119	Dashboard light flashes too quickly or slowly	Blown or faulty bulb—p. 192 Flasher unit faulty—p. 191

The difference between a dynamo and an alternator

The battery is charged by a generator which is driven by a belt from the engine crankshaft pulley. The generator will be either a dynamo, producing direct current (DC), or an alternator, which produces alternating current (AC).

An alternator can produce more current, at the same engine speed, than a dynamo, and can generate current while the engine is idling. But alternators are delicate instruments and few faults, apart from worn brushes, can be handled by the

do-it-yourself motorist. Dynamos are less complicated and more robust, and it is possible for a motorist to carry out his own repairs (see pp. 186-7). But make sure that any new parts bought for the repair are of the correct type and manufacture.

Renewing the brushes on two types of alternator

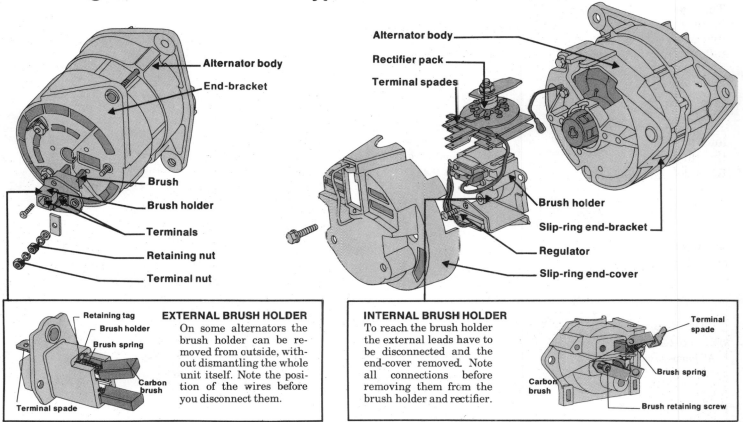

EXTERNAL BRUSH HOLDER
On some alternators the brush holder can be removed from outside, without dismantling the whole unit itself. Note the position of the wires before you disconnect them.

INTERNAL BRUSH HOLDER
To reach the brush holder the external leads have to be disconnected and the end-cover removed. Note all connections before removing them from the brush holder and rectifier.

There are two main types of brush fitting on alternators. On one, the brush holder can be detached from the end-bracket without dismantling the whole unit. On the other, you have to remove a black plastic slip-ring end-cover to get access to the carbon brushes.

Always make a note of which wires go to which terminals on the brush holder.

Tools: Bladed and cross-head screwdrivers; BA sockets and bar.
Materials: New set of brushes.

Loosen the alternator mounting bolts and remove the drive-belt. Remove the bolts and lift the alternator out of the car.

Internal brush holder
1 If the alternator has a black plastic slip-ring end-cover, it has an internal brush holder. Remove the screws that hold the cover.

2 Note the position of the wires between the rectifier pack and the brush holder and remove the wires.

Undo the screws that hold the brush holder to the alternator, and then remove the brush holder.

3 Undo the four screws through the terminals and remove the brushes. One brush has an anti-rattle plate. Slip the new brushes and the anti-rattle plate into place and refit the screws.

External brush holder
1 If there is no cover, undo the screws that hold the brush holder to the body. Lift out the brush holder. Depress the retaining tag on the

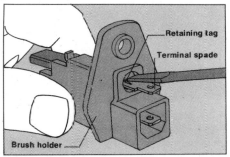

terminal spade and push the terminal out of its slot.

2 Press down the retaining tag on the new terminal spade and push it

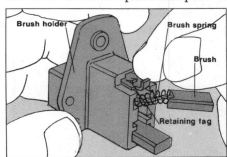

into the holder. Pull the spade through from the other side with a pair of pliers or your fingers.

3 Refit the holder to the alternator and connect the wires in the correct order. Replace the end-bracket.

4 Fit the alternator to the engine. Make sure the belt is adjusted properly (see p. 119). Check the battery connections. If the wrong terminal is earthed (the positive terminal of a negative-earth battery, or vice versa) a short-circuit will damage the alternator.

Electrical system /2

Removing and dismantling the dynamo

If your ammeter shows that the battery is not recharging, or if a red warning light comes on, then the dynamo may be faulty. Remove it from the car and inspect the brushes, armature and commutator.

If there is solder spattered over the armature windings, repair at home is impossible. Part-exchange the dynamo for a reconditioned or new unit. Remove the pulley from the old generator, as exchange units rarely have a pulley fitted.

Tools: Two spanners; screwdrivers; vice.
Material: Piece of wood—if needed.

1 Disconnect the leads from the dynamo terminals. Gently ease off the connectors, undo the adjusting bolt and swing the dynamo towards the engine to slacken the fan belt.

2 Remove the fan belt from the pulley wheel and take out the two remaining dynamo fixing bolts. Lift out the dynamo and take it to a bench or clean working surface.

3 Unscrew and remove the two long retaining bolts. If the bolts are too tight to be released with a screwdriver, grip the head of each in turn

in a vice and rotate the dynamo carefully to loosen it.

4 The commutator end-bracket, which holds the carbon brushes, can usually be pulled off. If it is tightly fixed, loosen it by tapping it lightly with a piece of wood.

5 Put the end-bracket on a clean, dry surface. If the dynamo has a distance washer on the armature shaft, lay it aside safely. Inspect the brushes which pick up the current from the commutator, and check the commutator segments for wear.

REMOVING THE PULLEY

Undo the pulley retaining nut until it is just above the end of the dynamo shaft. Support the underside of the pulley in one hand and strike the nut gently and squarely with a hammer to break the pulley-to-shaft joint. Remove nut. If the dynamo is going to be exchanged, remove the Woodruff key which locks the pulley to the shaft.

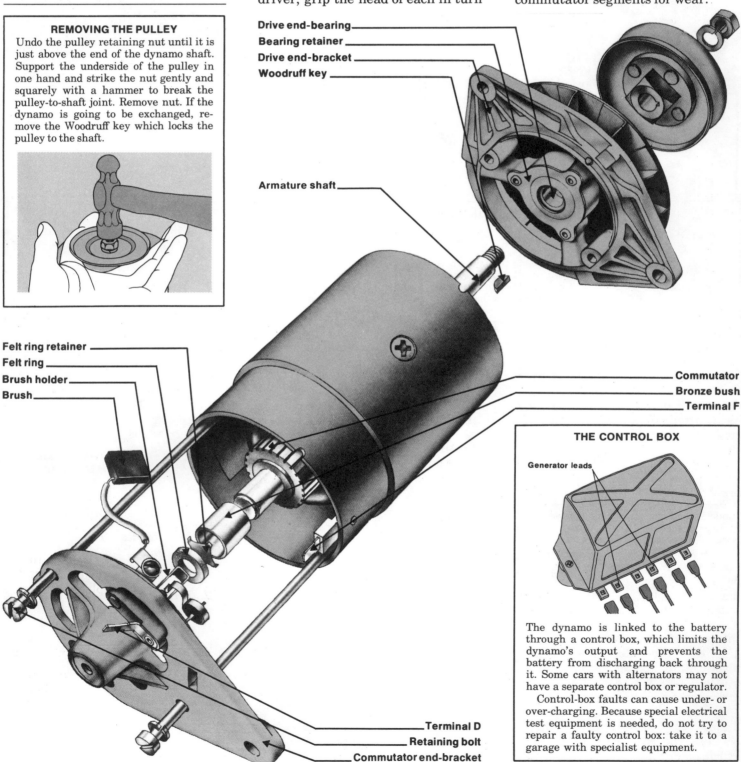

Drive end-bearing
Bearing retainer
Drive end-bracket
Woodruff key
Armature shaft
Felt ring retainer
Felt ring
Brush holder
Brush
Commutator
Bronze bush
Terminal F
Terminal D
Retaining bolt
Commutator end-bracket

THE CONTROL BOX

Generator leads

The dynamo is linked to the battery through a control box, which limits the dynamo's output and prevents the battery from discharging back through it. Some cars with alternators may not have a separate control box or regulator.

Control-box faults can cause under- or over-charging. Because special electrical test equipment is needed, do not try to repair a faulty control box: take it to a garage with specialist equipment.

Changing the brushes in the dynamo

New dynamo brushes are about $\frac{3}{4}$ in. long. Fit new brushes if they are worn to $\frac{1}{4}$ in. or less.

Tools: Screwdrivers; fine file; stiff brush.
Materials: Petrol-moistened rag; fine glass-paper; new brushes; brush springs.

1 The brushes, which are in holders in the commutator end-bracket, are pressed against the commutator by clock springs. Lift up each spring and rest its end on the holder so that the brushes can be taken out.

2 Deal with one brush at a time. Undo the terminal screw and carefully pull out the brush and its wire from the guide.

3 Clean the guide with a stiff brush and wipe with petrol and a rag.

4 Check the brush springs. If one is much stronger than the other, fit two new springs.

5 Insert the new carbon brush into its guide on the commutator end-bracket. If it does not slide freely, use a fine file to remove high spots. Tighten the terminal screw. Fit the second brush in the same way.

6 Check that the new brushes conform to the curve of the commutator. If not, wrap fine glass-paper round the commutator, with the rough side outwards. Twist the end-bracket backwards and forwards over the glass-paper to shape the brushes. Remove the paper. Clean away any carbon dust with a rag soaked in methylated spirit.

7 When refitting the end-bracket, wedge the springs against the side

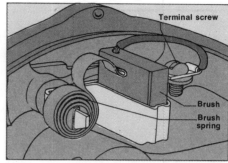

of the brushes to hold them clear of the commutator.

8 Position the springs on top of the brushes only after the dynamo has been assembled. Push a thin screwdriver through the end-bracket vents and lift each spring into place.

Checking and cleaning the commutator

Tools: Calipers; hacksaw blade.
Materials: Fine glass-paper; cleaning rag.

1 Remove the armature assembly from the dynamo casing and examine the commutator. Use a

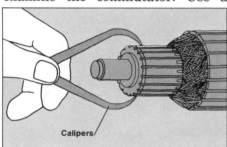

pair of calipers to check that the commutator is evenly round. Fix

them in one position, then make sure that the same adjustment fits exactly all round the commutator.

2 If the commutator appears to be in good condition, clean it with a

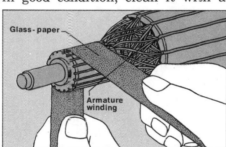

strip of fine glass-paper (not emery cloth, which contains destructive

metal particles). Wipe away any dust with a clean dry rag.

3 Use a worn hacksaw blade to cut the commutator segment channels to a depth of about $\frac{1}{16}$ in. Clean the

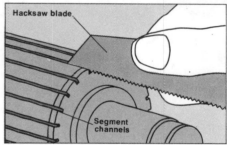

assembly with a dry rag and refit it in the dynamo casing.

Changing the commutator end-bracket bush

Inspect the commutator end-bracket before refitting it on the dynamo casing. Wash the bracket in petrol and look for damage.

Tools: Screwdrivers; hammer; vice.
Materials: Dowelling; engine oil.

1 If the bronze bush, through which the armature shaft fits, is

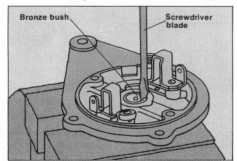

worn, remove both brushes (see above). Chip out the bush with an

old screwdriver and a light hammer. Do not damage the alloy bracket.

2 On old dynamos, block the oil hole in the bearing casing with a matchstick and lay the casing on the bench. Fill the centre of the

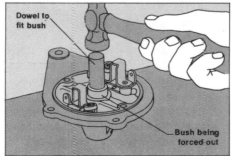

bush with grease. Insert a piece of dowelling to fit the bush, and strike it with a hammer. The grease will then force the bush up and out under hydraulic pressure.

3 Lubricate a new bush by soaking it in cold engine oil for 24 hours, or in hot oil (100°C) for 2 hours. Alternatively, place the bush in a tray of oil and press both ends together with your finger and thumb until oil is forced through the bush.

4 Line up the new bush with the hole in the end-bracket. Press the bush gently into place against a block of wood in a vice. Fit the shaft and check that the commutator rotates freely.

5 Refit the brushes and replace the end-brackets on the commutator. Fit it to the dynamo casing. Replace the retaining bolts, push a thin screwdriver through the cooling vents in the bracket and lift each brush spring back into place, so that the brushes contact the commutator.

Electrical system /3

Understanding a car's wiring system

An electrical circuit may fail for any one of many reasons—chafed wires, a blown fuse, loose connections at battery or component, a faulty switch, relay or solenoid and, most frequently, burnt-out bulbs.

The wiring diagrams in the owner's handbook or workshop manual show the electrical circuits

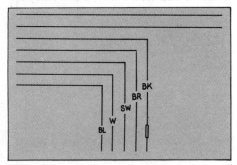

of the car as straight untangled lines, with the colours indicated by letters.

When you look under the bonnet, however, you will see no such orderly arrangement. Instead, the wires emerge from a bunched harness, or

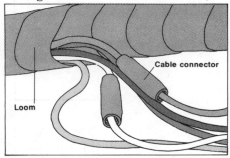

loom. It is usually only after the wires leave the loom that they are likely to be chafed and the insulation worn, so that a short circuit is eventually caused.

The circuit wires have coloured insulating material to help with identification. Most manufacturers show the colours in their owner's handbook with a letter or numeral code. (The majority of British manu-

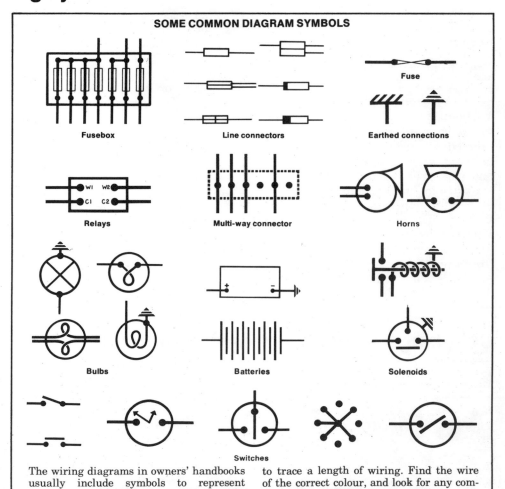

SOME COMMON DIAGRAM SYMBOLS

Fusebox
Line connectors
Fuse
Earthed connections
Relays
Multi-way connector
Horns
Bulbs
Batteries
Solenoids
Switches

The wiring diagrams in owners' handbooks usually include symbols to represent components or connections. They can be useful guide points when you are trying to trace a length of wiring. Find the wire of the correct colour, and look for any component or connection indicated in the area you are inspecting.

facturers use the Lucas code, in which B=black, R=red, U=blue. But Ford use a different code—SW=black, GE=yellow.) Always check in the handbook or ask your dealer for advice before trying to work on the wiring.

The insulation of some wires has a thin strip of contrasting colour running the entire length of the wire. This is called a tracer colour. In handbook diagrams the main

insulating colour is given first: for example, a wire with yellow insulation and a red tracer strip is identified as Y/R.

Normally there is only one feed wire from the battery, via the fuse box, to each electrical component. The components are connected to the car body, which provides the earth return as the other earth terminal of the battery is also connected to the car's body.

Tracing a fault in the wiring system

When changing a fuse fails to correct a fault, suspect a fault in a component or in the wiring.

Use the wiring diagram to identify and trace as much of the wire as possible. Look for chafing at any points where the wire passes through metal clips and holes in the bulkhead. Also check that any connections on the circuit are clean.

Components, such as the starter motor, which are attached to the engine are earthed through a flexible metal strap between the engine and the car body. If the earth strap is faulty, the starter will not

work. Unbolt the strap, clean it with emery cloth, and reconnect.

Most components are attached to the body and are earthed by either direct contact or a short earth lead.

If a component continuously fails, check its wiring with a circuit tester (see p. 189).

1 Use a tester with a pointed probe and connect the clip to a good clean earth point on the body. Switch on the electrical system being tested.

2 Disconnect the supply wire from the terminal on the component and

touch the end with the tester probe. If the tester bulb lights, the wire is

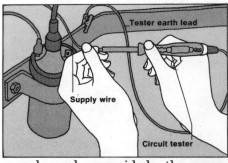

sound and, provided the component is adequately earthed, the fault must be in the component. If

Checking the fuses

For most circuits, 25 or 35 amp fuses are needed. To calculate the minimum rating of fuse required, divide the wattage of all the components on the circuit by the battery voltage and fit a fuse one size up. For example, if the components on a circuit consume 60 watts and the car has a 12 volt battery, the current flowing in the circuit is $60 \div 12 = 5$ amps. But if a 5 amp current runs continuously through a fuse rated at 5 amps, the fuse will quickly melt. So a stronger fuse—a 10 amp one—should be fitted. Do not use a fuse that is too strong for the circuit.

Replacing a fuse

The most common reason for a blown fuse is a short circuit in a component. When a component fails, find its circuit in the wiring diagram and check that its fuse has not failed.

Some cars have several fuses, each protecting one circuit; on others one fuse may cover several circuits. When fitting a new fuse, use a piece of fine emery cloth to clean the ends and holder in the fuse box.

If a new fuse fails immediately after you have fitted it, check for a fault in the component.

TYPES OF FUSES AND FUSE SYSTEMS

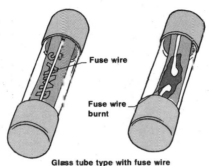

Glass tube type with fuse wire

Labels: Fuse wire; Fuse wire burnt

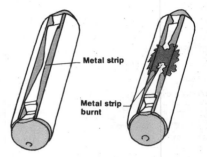

Ceramic type with metal strip

Labels: Metal strip; Metal strip burnt

Two types of fuses are used in cars. In one, the fuse wire runs between two metal endcaps inside a glass tube. The other fuse is ceramic and has a strip of metal in a recess down one side.

In both cases, if the fuse has blown, the wire/metal will have melted.

Cars with two fuses

If a car has just two fuses, each protecting a number of circuits, replace the blown fuse with a new one of the correct rating and then operate the components on each circuit protected by the fuse. If a component fails, you will have traced the fault in the circuit. When a fault cannot be traced, have the circuits checked by a garage.

Cars with no fuses

Some cars do not have fuses. If a component fails to work, check its earth connection and power supply. If there is a fault which causes the wiring to burn out, the whole circuit will have to be replaced.

Fusible link

Modern Vauxhall cars incorporate a high-resistance fuse in the main battery feed, in addition to the usual fuses.

This 'fusible link' protects the entire electrical system (except the starter motor) by means of a length of copper wire that will melt under an electrical overload. If it blows, all the electrical circuits will fail. A replacement can be fitted only by a dealer.

Circuit breaker

Many Vauxhall cars have a thermal circuit breaker which protects lights not connected to any fuse. An electrical overload activates the circuit breaker and this makes the lights flicker on and off. If this happens you must immediately find the fault in the wiring, or your battery will run down.

FITTING A LINE FUSE

If you fit an accessory such as a radio or tape-player, protect it with its own line fuse. A plastic holder, into which the fuse fits, must be set into the supply wire to the accessory. If the fuse fails, remove it from the holder and fit a new fuse.

Tools: Soldering iron; pliers.
Materials: Line fuse holder; fuse of the correct rating; solder.

1 To fit this type of fuse, first cut the wire at a convenient, accessible point between the supply feed and the accessory.

2 Bare about ⅛ in. of the two ends of the cut wire. Unscrew the plastic insulated fuse

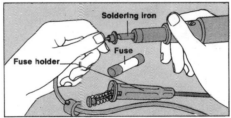

Labels: Soldering iron; Fuse; Fuse holder

holder. Slide the largest part of the holder on to one cut end of wire. Then slide the spring on to the wire. Use a soldering iron to coat the end of the wire with a thin film of solder (called tinning).

3 Fit one of the flat-headed nipples to the end of the wire and solder it in position. This acts as a stop and keeps the spring and the holder on the wire.

4 Slide the other part of the fuse holder on to the cut wire and solder on the nipple.

5 Fit the fuse in the holder and snap the two parts of the holder together.

the bulb does not light, however, there is a fault in the wiring.

3 In this case check the supply line back to the switch. The most likely fault would be a dirty or loose 'bullet' or snap connector. Check their positions on the owner's handbook wiring diagram. Push the tester through the wire's insulation just before and just after each connector. Make sure it touches the wire.

4 If the bulb lights on only one side but not the other, clean the connector with fine emery cloth. If that

does not work, you must fit a new connector (see p. 191).

5 To check the switch, turn on the switch, put the point of the tester on the input and output terminals —identified by the colour of the cables attached to the terminals (see p. 188). The switch is faulty if the tester bulb lights when placed on the input terminal, but fails to light when placed on the output terminal.

If no fault can be found, it is likely that the component is faulty and it will have to be repaired.

USING A CIRCUIT TESTER

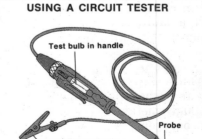

Labels: Test bulb in handle; Probe; Crocodile earth clip

Connect the clip of the lead to a good earth point, and use the probe end to make contact with the live lead of the circuit being tested.

Electrical system /4

Repairing a damaged or broken wire

If a wire is broken it is possible, as a temporary measure, to join the two ends by twisting the strands together and then covering the joint with insulating tape. But for a permanent repair, use a socket-type line connector which has two bullet-shaped nipples that fit into a small metal tube inside a rubber sleeve.

The electrical system uses many different types of wires. Each has a separate job, so if any wires have to be renewed make sure that the correct grade of cable is used: the wrong type may overheat.

Car wiring is graded by the number and thickness of strands in the cable. Four main grades are used: 65/0.3 (65 strands of 0.3 mm. diameter each)—connecting the starter to the starter solenoid; 44/0.3—connecting the dynamo, battery and control box; 28/0.3—for headlamps and heater fans; and 14/0.25—for interior lights, flashers and sidelights.

If you cannot identify the grade needed from the manufacturer's handbook, find out the current required by the component. Double that number and buy the wire with the nearest number of strands above it. For example, if a component has a rating of 12 amps, 2×12=24. Buy a 28-strand wire—28/0.3.

Tools: Pliers, with side-cutters or cable stripper; core solder; soldering iron; line connector.
Materials: Fine emery cloth; insulating tape.

1 To fit the connector, trim one end of the broken wire and strip ⅛ in. off the insulation. Clean the bared wire with emery cloth.

2 Use the soldering iron to tin the end of the wire. Wipe the wire with a clean rag while the solder is still hot to give a smooth end.

3 Push the tinned end of the wire through the hole in one of the

nipples so that it protrudes through the other end. Solder the wire to the end of the nipple, making sure that both wire and nipple receive direct

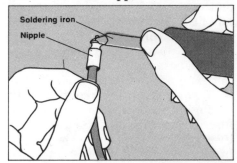

heat from the soldering iron and become hot enough for the solder to flow to a smooth globule.

4 Fit the other nipple to the other cut wire by the same method. Press the nipples into each end of the sleeve until they snap into place. The sleeve may have to be slightly loosened before the nipples can be pushed in.

How to remove and test a switch

If an electrically operated component fails and the fuse has not blown (see p. 189), check the appropriate switch. This can be done with the switch in place if its wiring is accessible, but usually the switch has to be removed. Disconnect the battery before working on a switch.

The simplest form of switch has two wires at the back—one from the power supply and the other to the component it controls. To test it, disconnect the two wires and join them temporarily. Use a spare piece of wire to make the connection if they are too short to meet. Reconnect the battery (and switch on the ignition if the power to the component is controlled by the ignition circuit). If the component now works, the fault is in the switch. Discard it and fit a new one.

Switches that control more than one component have several wires behind. If one component is not working, use the wiring diagram in the car handbook (see p. 188) to identify which wire takes the power to the switch and which feeds that component. Join these wires and find out if the component then works.

Some switches have an indicator bulb. If the bulb fails, remove it and stand it on one of the battery terminals. Connect the metal bayonet fitting with a piece of wire to the other battery terminal. If the bulb does not light, fit a new one.

Rocker switches

Rocker switches are normally clipped into the dashboard. Reach behind the dashboard, squeeze up the clips (usually on the side of the switch) and push the assembly through the dashboard.

On some models the switch can be removed towards you by pushing the switch body alternately at each end and simultaneously easing it out of the instrument surround.

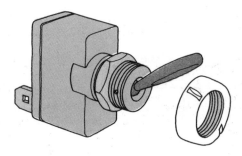

Tumbler switches

Tumbler switches are fitted from behind the dashboard. A threaded section protrudes through a hole, and a nut holds it in place. Undo the nut and push the switch out backwards. If these switches control more than one circuit, identify the wires before testing.

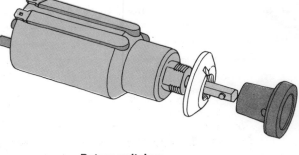

Rotary switches

The knob on a rotary switch may do two jobs. On a washer-wiper switch, for example, turning the knob operates the wipers and pushing it works the washers. To remove the switch take off the knob, which is usually held by a spring-loaded pin. (This should be pressed in with a sharp implement.) With the knob removed, undo the nut holding the switch.

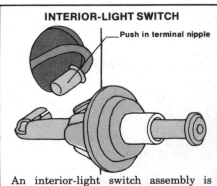

INTERIOR-LIGHT SWITCH

Push in terminal nipple

An interior-light switch assembly is either screwed into the door pillar or pushed into a hole where it jams in position. The switch is a small piston which is pushed in when the door is closed. This puts out the interior lights by disconnecting the earth wire. When the door is opened the piston moves out.

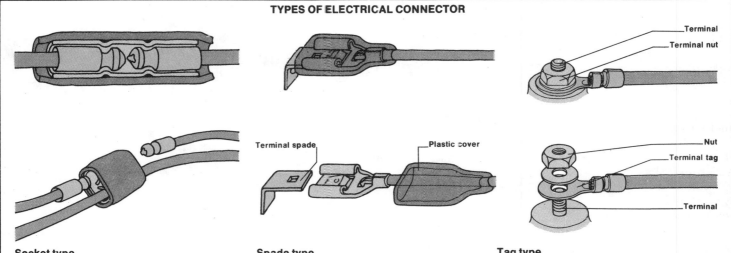

TYPES OF ELECTRICAL CONNECTOR

Terminal
Terminal nut
Terminal spade
Plastic cover
Nut
Terminal tag
Terminal

Socket type

An insulated rubber sleeve fits over bullet-like nipple connectors. They may be single or multiple to fit any number of wires. The nipples themselves are fitted over the ends of the wires until the insulation is inside the nipples. The nose of the nipples should then be soldered where the wires have come through. If no solder is available, simply wrap the excess wire back over the nipples.

Spade type

The flat, interlocking spade connector – the Lucar type – is the most commonly used. There are two sizes: a large one for heavy current connections – for example, generator output – and a small one for almost every other sort of situation. The male side of each connector is fitted to the component, and the push-on female connector is attached to the end of the connecting wire.

Tag type

A tag-type connector should always be used when making a connection to a terminal. A terminal tag is a metal eye soldered to the end of a wire, which is held in place on a component by a stud, passing through the eye, and nut. Some connections are fixed to wires with a special crimping tool. If you do not have such a tool, use solder. Tag connectors may be single or multiple.

Dismantling a multiple switch on a steering column

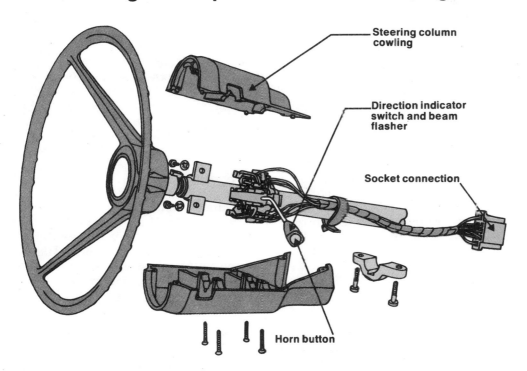

Steering column cowling

Direction indicator switch and beam flasher

Socket connection

Horn button

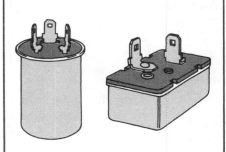

DIRECTION INDICATORS

A flashing indicator is operated by an automatic make-and-break switch housed in a metal canister, known as the flasher unit. The unit, which is sealed, is situated either in the engine compartment or under the instrument panel. The flasher unit will be box-shaped or cylindrical, and has either two or three connections.

When the indicators are working properly the unit ticks and a dashboard light flashes. The indicator should flash at a rate of between 60 and 120 times a minute to comply with the law.

If the indicators do not work, or if they flash erratically, check that none of the wires connected to the unit is loose. To test the unit, disconnect the wires and join them together. Then, with the ignition turned on, move the indicator switch, first to the left and then to the right position. If all the flasher bulbs light, the flasher unit is faulty and should be replaced.

If any of the flasher lights do not come on with the switch in either position, a bulb has blown or there is a wiring fault. Check both possibilities.

Stalk-type switches on the steering column can operate several components – for example, light flashers, dip and beam, direction indicators, horn, wipers and washers.

Some multiple switches can be removed by undoing the holding screw after the cowling has been taken off the steering column. The wiring usually runs into a plug-and-socket connection which can be pulled apart for inspection.

Other multiple switches can be removed only after the steering wheel has been taken off – usually a job for a specialist. But on some cars the removal of the steering wheel centre exposes the wheel retaining-nut which, when undone, allows the steering wheel to be removed. In most cases a special puller is needed: consult a dealer.

If you remove the steering wheel, make sure that the front road wheels are pointing straight ahead when the steering wheel is refitted.

Electrical system /5

Changing headlamp and sidelight bulbs

1 To change a headlight bulb, undo the screw at the bottom of the

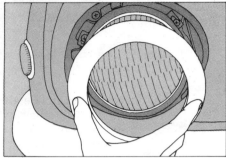

chrome lamp rim. Pull the bottom of the rim out and lift off the rim and the rubber sealing ring.

2 Push the lamp unit in against spring pressure. Twist the unit so that it is freed from the screws, then lift it from its back shell.

3 Unplug the wires at the bulb-holder assembly. Remove the spring

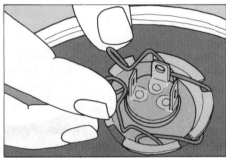

clips holding the assembly to the reflector and lift out the combined bulb and holder. Discard it.

4 Fit a new assembly. Check that the wires are in good condition. Note that the combined bulb and holder assembly is specially shaped to prevent its being fitted incorrectly in a position that would alter the dipper beam.

5 Refit the unit to the car and replace the rubber sealing ring after

COMBINED BULB AND HOLDER

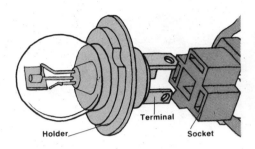

Holder Terminal Socket

BAYONET FITTING

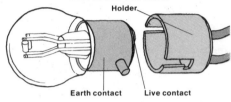

Holder

Earth contact Live contact

checking that it is in good condition. Then switch on the lights and check that they work on beam and dip.

Sealed-beam units

The reflector and lens all form part of one large bulb in sealed-beam headlights. The beam is considered sealed because the positions of the filaments, reflector and lens have been set during manufacture and cannot be altered.

Sealed-beam units have to be replaced as a whole and are connected by a push-on plug. Remove a failed sealed-beam unit by the same method as for an ordinary headlamp unit, and fit a replacement.

Some sealed-beam units have a connection for a sidelight bulb.

Side, rear and flasher lights

Bulbs for most sidelights, rear-lights and flashing indicator lights have bayonet fittings like household electric bulbs.

Rear-light bulbs often have two

SEALED-BEAM UNIT

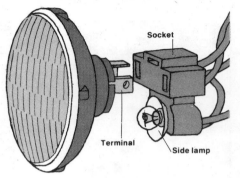

Socket

Terminal Side lamp

CONTACT BULB

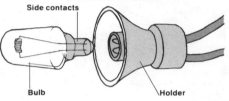

Side contacts

Bulb Holder

filaments, one for the rear-lights and one for the stoplights. To ensure that the connections are right, these bulbs will fit in only one way.

To change a sidelight bulb, remove the screws holding the glass cover. Discard the old bulb, and before fitting a new one check the connections. If necessary remove any corrosion with fine emery cloth.

Some sidelight bulbs are all glass on the outside and have no brass cap. Fit by pressing into the socket.

On some cars the rear-light/flasher bulbs are located inside the boot to save unscrewing the external assembly. On other cars it may be necessary to remove it.

Panel bulbs

Never try to change a failed bulb in an instrument panel; have it done by an expert. On most cars the panel and instrument lights are connected by flexible printed circuits. Handling by someone who is not experienced could damage a circuit.

QUARTZ-HALOGEN BULBS

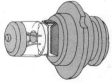

Quartz-halogen bulbs should be handled only by their metal parts because oils in the skin damage the quartz.

1 Remove the failed lamp unit, using the same method as for an ordinary headlight bulb.

2 Fit the new bulb unit, making sure it is locked correctly. There is an indentation on the bulb-holder unit that matches a pip on the reflector.

IF THE HORN IS FAULTY

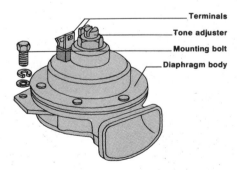

Terminals
Tone adjuster
Mounting bolt
Diaphragm body

Most cars have a simple electric diaphragm-type horn. Others have wind-tone horns, usually fitted in pairs to larger models.

The diaphragm and wind-tone horns work in a similar way. An electric current passes

through a pair of contact points making and collapsing a magnetic field which cause a diaphragm to vibrate and produce a loud noise.

Different noises are produced in the diaphragm-type horn by variation in the size of the diaphragm, and in the wind-tone type by varying the shape of the horn. It is illegal to fit horns so that they emit a two-tone note, similar to those used by ambulances or police cars.

The horn is often exposed to water and salt thrown up off the road, and the main problem is keeping the terminal connections in good condition. Disconnect the leads and rub the terminals with emery paper.

To replace a faulty horn, unbolt the unit from its mounting, disconnect the leads and fit a suitable replacement.

WHEN THE BRAKES GO WRONG

Symptom	Check	Symptom	Check
Brakes judder	Linings—this page Back-plate spring U-bolts, swivel pins and bushes—garage job	Pedal spongy or needs pumping	Air in system—p. 197 Leaks—p. 62 Master cylinder—p. 196
Car pulls to one side	Tyre pressures—p. 37 Brake adjustment—p. 84 Oil on linings—p. 87 Wheel cylinder piston—p. 198	Brakes drag or fail to release	Brake adjustment—p. 84 Shoe pull-off springs—this page Handbrake cables—pp. 90 and 200 Air vent in reservoir cap—p. 130 Wheel cylinder piston—p. 198 Pedal to master cylinder—p. 196 Hydraulic cylinder seals—pp. 198-9
Too much pedal travel	Brake adjustment—p. 84 Master cylinder push-rod—p. 196		
Vibration when you press the pedal	Condition of drums—p. 87 Disc alignment—p. 195	Brakes grab	Shoes, linings and return springs—this page
More pedal effort needed than usual	Linings—this page Wheel cylinder units—p. 198 Servo vacuum supply—garage job	Brakes overheat and fade	Shoes—this page
		Brakes fail suddenly	Consult a garage

Fitting replacement brake shoes

Fit new brake shoes if the linings are worn to within $\frac{1}{16}$ in. of the rivets, or if they are only $\frac{1}{16}$ in. thick on bonded shoes. Never re-line shoes.

Always fit new shoes to both wheels on the same axle.

Tools: Screwdriver; Mole grips; mallet.
Materials: Replacement brake shoes; brake grease.

1 Mount the car on axle stands (see p. 61). Back off the adjusters and remove the drums (see p. 84).

2 To remove the hold-down springs and pins: **A** compress and twist the

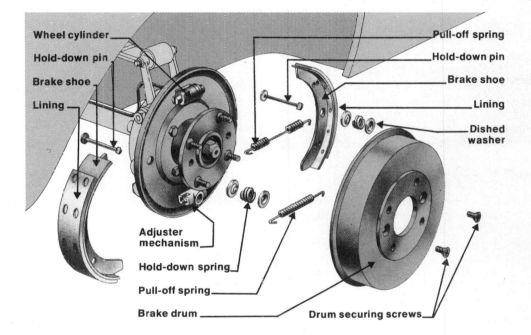

Wheel cylinder / Hold-down pin / Brake shoe / Lining / Adjuster mechanism / Hold-down spring / Pull-off spring / Brake drum / Pull-off spring / Hold-down pin / Brake shoe / Lining / Dished washer / Drum securing screws

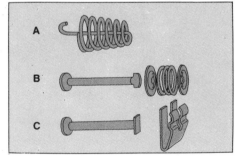

spring, or **B** compress the spring and twist the dished washer, or **C** withdraw the clip.

3 Note the position of the shoes, so that the new ones can be fitted

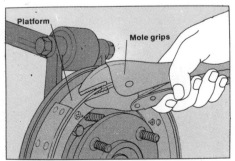

Platform / Mole grips

correctly. Fit Mole grips to the shoe platforms and lever them out.

4 Remove the pull-off springs and lift the shoes away from the brake

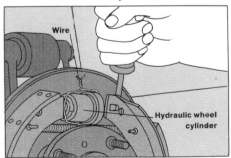

Wire / Hydraulic wheel cylinder

assembly. Wire the wheel cylinder to retain the piston. Clean the backplate, cylinder and pivot point with a rag and methylated spirit.

5 Remove the adjuster mechanism, if possible (see p. 198), and lubricate the threads and piston with brake

grease. Reassemble the mechanism. Refit it and make sure the adjuster is fully retracted.

6 Fit the lower pull-off spring between the two new brake shoes. Spread the shoes and fit their ends into the slots on the lower adjuster or wheel cylinder unit. Position the opposite end of one shoe in the slot of the upper adjuster or wheel cylinder and fit the top pull-off spring. Lever the other brake shoe so that it engages in its slot.

7 Refit the hold-down springs. Remove the wire holding the piston and fit the drum and road wheel. Adjust the brakes (see p. 84). Press the brake pedal to centralise the shoes and check the adjustment again.

Brakes /2

Identifying different disc-brake systems

The design of disc-brake units varies, but the principle is always the same. Two friction pads are pushed by hydraulic pressure against metal discs on the wheel hubs.

There are three types of disc unit:
Fixed caliper: each pad is operated by its own cylinder.
Swinging caliper: a single cylinder operates one pad and a hinged caliper pushes the other against the disc.
Sliding caliper: a single cylinder has two pistons. One applies one pad and the other operates a yoke that works the second pad.

Always use the correct replacement pads: avoid cheap substitutes.

Some rear disc calipers incorporate a handbrake mechanism. A special tool is needed to release and remove the pads — a job for a garage. But other types have a scissor-type caliper with its own pads which can be renewed by the do-it-yourself motorist (see p. 195).

Tools: Pliers; punch; small hammer; piston retraction tool or a flat piece of hard wood.
Materials: New pads; anti-squeal or rattle shims; brake grease.

Removing the pads from fixed calipers

1 On Girling units the pads are held in place by pins secured by spring clips. Pull out the clips and withdraw the retaining pins. If the pins are rusted or tight, clean them with a wire brush and tap them out with a punch and hammer. Lockheed use pins with split ends. Close the ends and push out the pins.

2 Grip the pad backing plates with pliers and pull out the pads. Remove any anti-squeal shims between the pad backing plate and the piston.

3 Scrape the inside of the pad housing with a screwdriver, to remove any dirt. Check the condition of the cylinders, disc, dust seals and pads (see p. 195).

4 Open the bleed nipple in the caliper and push the piston back evenly with a retraction tool or piece of wood. Tighten the bleed nipple when the pistons are fully retracted.

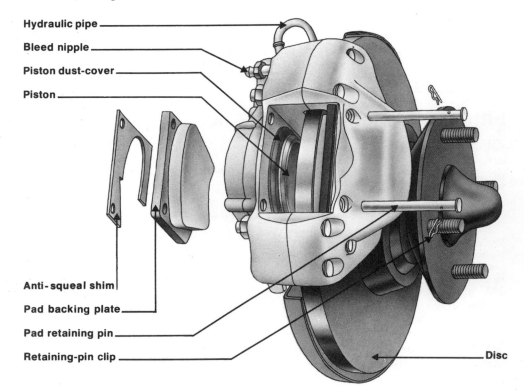

Hydraulic pipe — Bleed nipple — Piston dust-cover — Piston — Anti-squeal shim — Pad backing plate — Pad retaining pin — Retaining-pin clip — Disc

Removing the pads from swinging calipers

1 Straighten the ends of the pad retaining pins and withdraw the pins from the caliper housing. Remove the pad retaining springs.

2 Grip the pad backing plates with pliers and pull out the pads. Remove any anti-squeal shims from between each backing plate and piston.

3 Dip a clean, lint-free cloth into new brake fluid. Thoroughly clean the exposed faces of the pistons. Wipe them dry and coat the piston surface with special disc-brake grease. Do not over-lubricate.

4 Inspect the caliper, disc, dust seals and brake pads (see p. 195).

5 Open the caliper bleed nipple and push the single piston back into its caliper, either with a special retraction tool or by half-inserting an old pad and levering against the piston end. Tighten the bleed nipple.

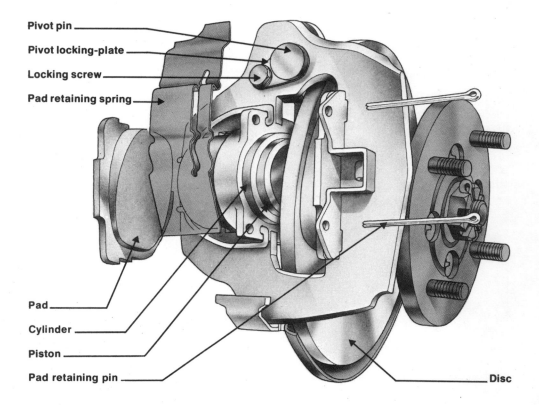

Pivot pin — Pivot locking-plate — Locking screw — Pad retaining spring — Pad — Cylinder — Piston — Pad retaining pin — Disc

Removing the pads from sliding calipers

1 Remove the pad retaining-pin clip, and draw out the two disc pad retaining pins with pliers.

2 Pull the pads out of the caliper. Check the disc, sliding yoke and brake pads (see below).

3 Check that the yoke slides and that the yoke spring is not broken.

4 Open the bleed nipple and retract the pistons. Tighten it when the pads are fully retracted.

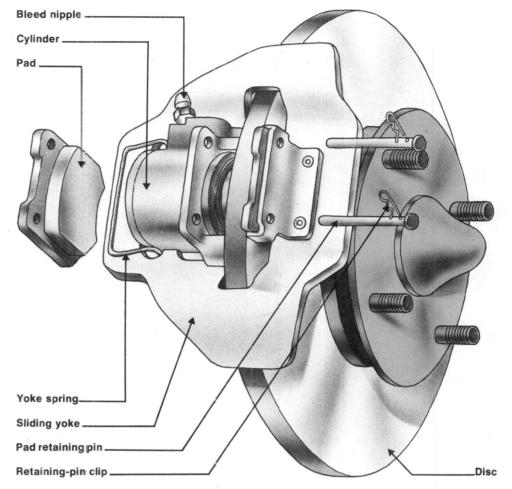

Bleed nipple

Cylinder

Pad

Yoke spring

Sliding yoke

Pad retaining pin

Retaining-pin clip

Disc

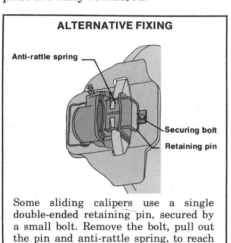

ALTERNATIVE FIXING

Anti-rattle spring

Securing bolt

Retaining pin

Some sliding calipers use a single double-ended retaining pin, secured by a small bolt. Remove the bolt, pull out the pin and anti-rattle spring, to reach the pads.

Checking the disc and fitting new pads

Disc pads should normally be replaced if they have worn below $\frac{1}{8}$ in. thick, but some manufacturers advise changing them sooner.

Note that new pads for swinging-caliper units are wedge-shaped. Fit new ones when the angled surfaces of the two pads have worn parallel to each other.

1 Clean the inner surface of the caliper and carefully check the rubber dust-covers for signs of cracking or perishing of the rubber. Lift the edge of the rubber dust-cover and check round the pistons for signs of fluid leaks. If a caliper is leaking, it should be overhauled (see p. 199).

2 Check the disc. A certain amount of scoring is permissible, but the marks should not be so deep as to drag on the fingertips. Renew a disc if the scoring is deep. This means unbolting the disc from the hub assembly and fitting a new one. Rust on the braking area of the disc face indicates a seized caliper piston: overhaul the caliper to free the piston (see p. 199). A ring of corrosion above the braking surface of the disc is common. Tap the edge of the disc with a wooden mallet and clean the

rusty surface with a file or coarse emery cloth.

3 Before fitting the new disc pads, check the disc for distortion. Spin the disc and measure the greatest gap between the inside of the caliper housing and the disc face with

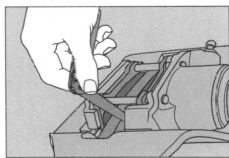

a feeler gauge. The maximum permissible side-to-side movement is ·005 in. If it is greater, check the adjustment of the wheel hub bearing (see p. 92). If that is correct, the disc is distorted. Fit a new disc.

4 Fit the new pads. Lightly lubricate the anti-squeal shims with brake grease and insert them between the back-plate and the piston. If the shims have arrows stamped on them, face the arrows in the direction of wheel rotation. If the

retaining pins have splayed ends, fit new ones. On Girling units clean and grease the pins.

5 Pump the brake pedal to locate the pads. Top-up with clean fluid, and check that the discs spin.

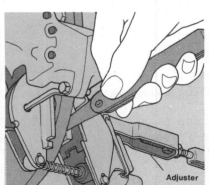

HANDBRAKE CALIPER

Adjuster

Most handbrakes are self-adjusting, but some have a screw-thread adjuster on the handbrake cable under the car.

1 Put the handbrake lever in the off position. Turn the adjuster to bring the pads into contact with the discs.

2 Release the adjuster and measure the clearance between the face of the pads and the disc. There should be a maximum clearance of ·003 in.

195

Brakes/3

Dealing with different types of hydraulic systems

All hydraulic brake systems work on the same principle: pressing the brake pedal operates a master cylinder which pushes the brake fluid along pipelines to slave cylinders at the wheels. The cylinders contain pistons which are pushed out by the movement of the fluid, to apply the brake shoes or pads.

Most systems are single-line, but some cars have divided-line systems in which a double-barrel master cylinder operates two independent systems. If there is a failure in one, the other will provide enough braking to stop the car. The components of a dual system are similar to those of a single circuit.

MASTER CYLINDER

Several types of master cylinder are fitted, but in most cases the fluid reservoir is part of the master cylinder.

1 Divided-line cylinder. **2** Centre-valve (CV). **3** Compression-barrel (CB).

FLEXIBLE PIPES

Check that the pipes are not chafing against suspension units.

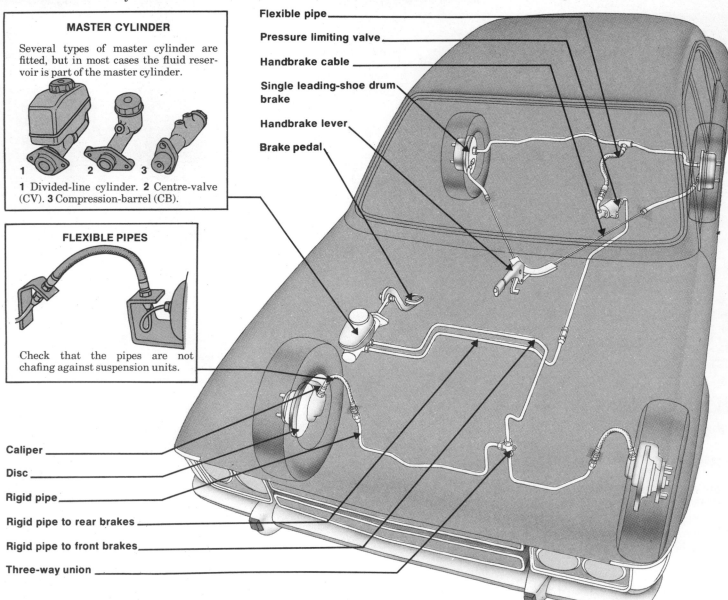

Flexible pipe

Pressure limiting valve

Handbrake cable

Single leading-shoe drum brake

Handbrake lever

Brake pedal

Caliper

Disc

Rigid pipe

Rigid pipe to rear brakes

Rigid pipe to front brakes

Three-way union

Fitting a new master cylinder in the engine compartment

If the master cylinder is leaking, fit a new one. Make sure a correct replacement is purchased. Do not attempt to use an overhaul kit, since internal wear is difficult to detect.

Tools: Spanners to fit the securing nuts and bolts and the pipe union nuts.
Materials: New master cylinder; hydraulic fluid.

---

1 Undo the union between the brake pipe and the master cylinder. Let the hydraulic fluid drain. Do not allow it to run on to the paintwork.

2 Inside the car, disconnect the master cylinder push-rod from the

brake pedal. This is usually secured with a clevis pin or a shouldered

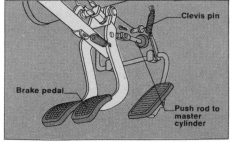

Clevis pin

Brake pedal

Push rod to master cylinder

bolt and nut. Make sure the push-rod is clear of any obstruction.

3 Undo the bolts holding the master cylinder to the bulkhead. Draw out the master cylinder.

4 Slide the new master cylinder into position and secure it lightly. Check that the push-rod is clear and fit

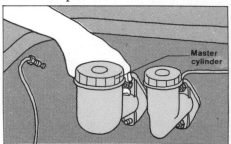

Master cylinder

the rod to the brake pedal. If it is secured by a clevis, fit a new split-pin. Tighten the master cylinder, reconnect the hydraulic pipes and fill and bleed the system (see p. 197).

Renewing flexible and rigid brake pipes

Check the brake pipes regularly (see p. 78). Bend the flexible pipes and look for cracks or signs of deterioration. Check rigid pipes for signs of rusting, corrosion or damage caused by stones. Block off the reservoir filler cap with polythene (see p. 199) to retain the brake fluid.

Tools: Spanners to fit the brake pipe union nuts.
Materials: New flexible or rigid pipes of the correct length and type.

1 To remove a flexible pipe, hold the hexagon steady and undo the acorn nut on the metal pipe first. Remove the lock-nut that holds the flexible pipe to the mounting bracket. Undo the other end of the flexible pipe from the caliper or wheel cylinder.

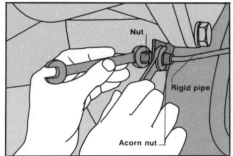

If it has a washer, buy a new one.
On metric-threaded pipes no sealing washer is used because they do not tighten down on to the caliper or wheel cylinder housing.

2 Screw the new pipe into the wheel cylinder first, and tighten.

3 Pass the pipe end through the bracket and secure it with the lock-nut. Make sure that the pipe is correctly bent before tightening the lock-nut. It must not be twisted or strained when the wheels are turned lock-to-lock. There must be enough to allow suspension movement.

4 Refit the rigid pipe to the end of the flexible pipe.

Renewing rigid pipes

1 If a rigid metal pipe has to be fitted, it must be of the correct length, and bent to the shape of the pipe it is replacing.

2 If a pipe has to be made up, make sure that the dealer puts the correct

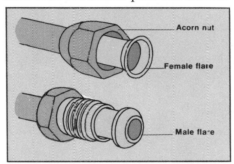

'flare' on the end of the pipe. If a rigid pipe is to match a flexible

pipe the end must have a female flare. If it is to fit a master cylinder, wheel slave cylinder or a three-way connector, a male flare has to be formed on the end.

3 If a new pipe has to be bent to a given shape, bend it gently round a

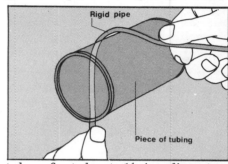

tube of at least 1½ in. diameter. Check after bending that the pipe has kept its roundness, that it is not in any way distorted and that there is no crack in the metal. Never fit a pipe which you suspect is damaged.

4 To ensure that dirt cannot enter the new pipe, cover its end with masking tape before threading it into position under the car. Check that it fits correctly without distortion. Connect the pipe at both ends and make sure that the union nuts are tight.

5 When new pipes have been fitted, always bleed the brakes.

Bleeding the hydraulic system

The sequence in which brakes can be bled depends on the type of system fitted on the car.
All-drum brakes Slacken off twin-leading shoe adjusters and lock-on single leading shoes (see p. 84). Start bleeding at the wheel furthest from the master cylinder and finish at the nearest one.
Front discs, rear drums Bleed the discs first, starting furthest from the master cylinder, followed by the drum brakes.
Girling divided-line On this twin system bleed the rear brakes first, then the front brakes, in the same order as 'all drums'.
Lockheed divided-line On this twin system the offside front and rear brakes are bled together, followed by the nearside front and rear brakes.

Tools: Bleed-spanner; jar; rubber tube.
Materials: New hydraulic brake fluid.

1 Wipe the top of the master cylinder reservoir and remove the cap.

2 Fit the bleed tube to the first nipple and place the other end of the

tube in a jar with about 1½ in. clean fluid in it. Make sure the end of the tube is below the level of the fluid in the jar. Fit the bleed-spanner to the nipple. Release the nipple by gently

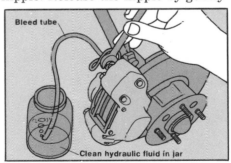

turning the spanner anticlockwise half a turn.

3 Get a helper to press the brake pedal. The method of applying the brake pedal varies according to the type of master cylinder fitted.
Girling CV Depress the pedal fully once, then apply three short, quick strokes and allow the pedal to return quickly. This will expel air that can become trapped behind the seals in the master cylinder.

Girling CB Depress the pedal slowly as far as it will go, and allow it to return only slowly.
Lockheed Depress the pedal slowly and allow it to return quickly.

4 Keep the master cylinder reservoir constantly topped-up with clean fluid of the type recommended by the brake manufacturers. Never allow it to get low, or air will enter.

5 As the pedal is being depressed, watch for signs of air bubbles at the end of the tube. When the fluid is clear of air bubbles, get the helper to hold the brake pedal down, and tighten the bleed nipple. Transfer the tube to the next wheel and repeat the operation.
Never top-up the hydraulic reservoir with fluid that has been expelled from the system. It may have been contaminated with water and other impurities and it is likely to contain a certain amount of air. When bleeding has been completed, top-up the reservoir to the level indicated on it and replace the cap.

Brakes /4

Removing a slave cylinder on drum brakes

Twin leading shoe brakes have two cylinders in each drum. Single leading shoe brakes use only one cylinder (see p. 84). In some, the cylinders are fixed to the back-plate: others slide. If a cylinder leaks, remove and overhaul it.

Tools: Screwdriver; hammer; spanners.
Materials: Brake grease; new wheel cylinder.

Dealing with fixed cylinders

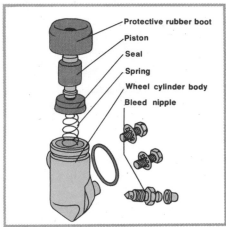

Protective rubber boot
Piston
Seal
Spring
Wheel cylinder body
Bleed nipple

1 Remove the brake drum and the brake shoes (see pp. 84 and 193).

2 Remove the fluid reservoir cap in the engine compartment, place a small sheet of polythene over the reservoir and refit the cap. Disconnect the flexible pipe from the rigid pipe and remove the flexible pipe.

3 If the cylinder is secured by a circlip, spring off the clip. If it is held by nuts, undo them. Remove the wheel cylinder from the back-plate.

Dealing with sliding cylinders

1 Remove the brake drum, shoes and flexible pipe. Disconnect the handbrake linkage. Pull back the

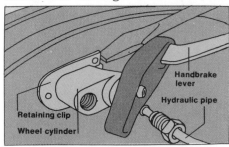

Handbrake lever
Hydraulic pipe
Retaining clip
Wheel cylinder

rubber dust cover and tap out the retaining clip on the cylinder.

2 Slide out the retaining plate and disengage the handbrake lever from

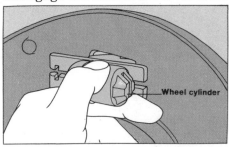

Wheel cylinder

the wheel cylinder. Remove the wheel cylinder from inside the brake back-plate.

3 Some sliding cylinders have two Y-shaped securing plates retaining a

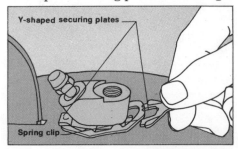

Y-shaped securing plates
Spring clip

spring clip. Slide one of the Y-shaped plates towards the handbrake lever.

4 Push the second Y-shaped plate inwards so that the leg can be eased under the spring clip and pulled out.

5 Lift the spring clip and first Y-shaped securing plate off the wheel

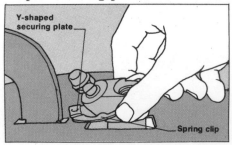

Y-shaped securing plate
Spring clip

cylinder. Remove the cylinder and examine it to identify the worn parts. Fit new parts as necessary.

6 When you reassemble, lubricate the parts with brake grease.

Renewing the rubber seal in a slave cylinder

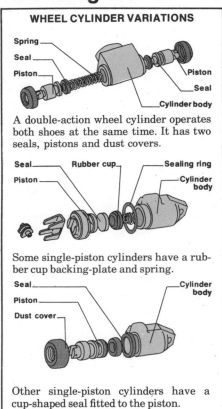

WHEEL CYLINDER VARIATIONS

Spring
Seal
Piston
Piston
Seal
Cylinder body

A double-action wheel cylinder operates both shoes at the same time. It has two seals, pistons and dust covers.

Seal
Rubber cup
Sealing ring
Piston
Cylinder body

Some single-piston cylinders have a rubber cup backing-plate and spring.

Seal
Cylinder body
Piston
Dust cover

Other single-piston cylinders have a cup-shaped seal fitted to the piston.

1 Peel off the rubber dust covers and pull out the pistons. If a single piston sticks, reconnect it to the brake pipe and press the pedal.

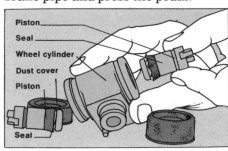

Piston
Seal
Wheel cylinder
Dust cover
Piston
Seal

2 Wash the cylinder in new brake fluid. Check the cylinder bore for

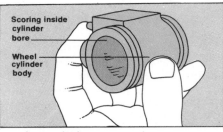

Scoring inside cylinder bore
Wheel cylinder body

scoring, pitting, corrosion or a wear ridge. If it is damaged, fit a new

unit. Prise off the old seal and wash the piston in brake fluid.

3 Soak the new seal in clean brake fluid and fit it to the piston with the cupped face pointing inwards.

4 Dip the piston and seal in clean brake fluid and slide the assembly into the cylinder. Make sure that the lip does not turn back on itself.

5 Coat the inside of the dust cover with brake grease and fit the cover

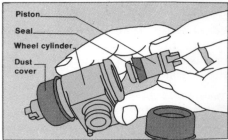

Piston
Seal
Wheel cylinder
Dust cover

to the groove round the wheel cylinder. Refit the cylinder, connect the hydraulic pipe and reassemble the shoes and drum.

Overhauling a disc-brake hydraulic system

When you push down the brake pedal, hydraulic fluid in the brake system, because it cannot be compressed, is displaced and forces the piston in the brake calipers towards the disc. The fluid is retained by seals fitted in grooves either round the circumference of the piston or round the piston bores in the caliper. If fluid leaks can be seen round the pistons, fit new seals.

To do this, you must first take the caliper assembly off the car. If the pistons are damaged or scored, fit new ones. Piston and seals can be renewed with the caliper in one piece: never split the caliper.

Tools: Spanners to fit the brake-hose union; caliper mounting bolts; screwdriver; hammer; jack; axle stand; compression tool.
Materials: New piston seals; brake grease; clean brake fluid; thin polythene sheet.

1 Jack up the front of the car and mount it on axle stands (see p. 61). Remove the road wheels and lift out the disc pads (see p. 195).

2 Depress the brake pedal gently to force out the pistons slightly. Remove the hydraulic reservoir cap, place a piece of clean polythene over reservoir to seal the air vent and restrict fluid loss. Replace the cap.

3 Disconnect the brake pipe at the union and plug the open end of the rigid pipe. Undo the caliper mounting bolts and note any shims between the caliper and stub-axle lugs.

4 Remove the piston dust covers and pull the pistons out of the caliper

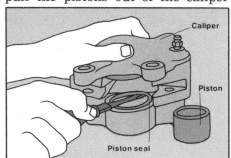

cylinders. Carefully prise out the piston seals and seal retaining rings.

5 Thoroughly wash the caliper and piston assembly in clean brake fluid. Check all components for signs of wear. Carefully examine the outer surface of the pistons. If they show signs of etching—light crazing of the surface—fit new pistons.

6 Clean out the grooves that secure the seals or retaining rings. Wash inside the cylinder with clean fluid.

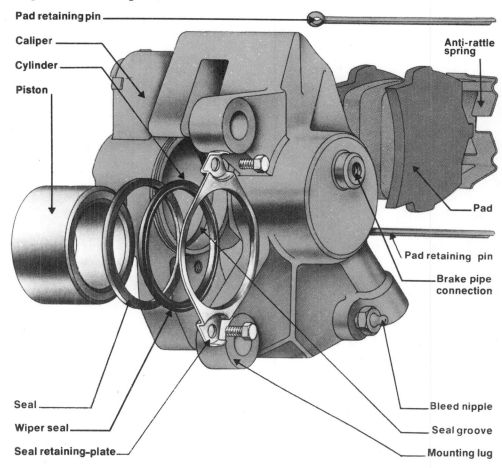

Pad retaining pin
Caliper
Cylinder
Piston
Seal
Wiper seal
Seal retaining-plate

Anti-rattle spring
Pad
Pad retaining pin
Brake pipe connection
Bleed nipple
Seal groove
Mounting lug

7 Soak the new seals in clean brake fluid and fit them to the pistons or caliper cylinders. Lubricate the pistons with brake fluid and fit them in the caliper cylinders. Make sure that they are pressed in evenly.

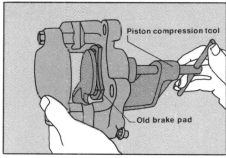

Retaining rings that fit flush with the end of the cylinders can be pressed into position with a brake pad and a piston compression tool.

8 Replace any dust covers that were fitted. Make sure that the inner lip of the cover fits securely in the groove round the piston.

9 Refit the caliper to the stub-axle lugs and replace any shims. Fit the caliper bolts with a new tab locking-washer. Tighten the bolts and bend the ends of the tabs. Lubricate the face of the piston with brake grease. Refit the pads (see p. 195), connect the pipes and bleed the system (see p. 197).

SWINGING AND SLIDING CALIPERS

Swinging caliper Remove the pads and press the pedal to force the pistons out of the cylinders. Disconnect the brake pipe. Remove the clip or clips holding

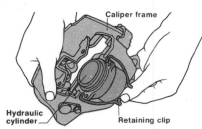

the cylinder to the caliper frame. Remove the cylinder. Draw out the piston and fit new seals. Check the caliper pivot pin for wear. Renew it if it is worn.

Sliding caliper Remove the pads and the caliper. Grip the caliper yoke in a vice, press the piston into the cylinder and push the cylinder downwards, against

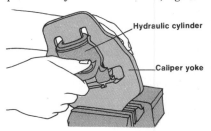

spring pressure, to remove it. Overhaul the cylinder assembly. Check the sliding faces of the cylinder and yoke for wear. Renew any worn parts.

Brakes /5

Checking the operation of the handbrake

When the handbrake is applied, brake shoes, or pads, operate on two wheels—usually the rear wheels.

There are two basic systems. In one, two cables—one for each wheel—are connected to the handbrake lever. In the other, a single cable connects the handbrake lever to a compensator or equaliser mechanism. Rods or cables run from the equaliser to the wheels. Check the connections at the handbrake lever

and under the car to establish which type you have to deal with.

Most handbrakes have some means of adjustment to compensate for any stretching in the cable during use. When no further adjustment is possible (see p. 90), buy and fit a new cable to match the car.

If the brake cable is found to be frayed or rusted, renew it.

Before fitting a new cable, make sure that the drum brake mechan-

ism is operating correctly (see p. 84). If the hydraulic wheel cylinder is of the single-piston sliding type, it should move freely in the brake back-plate. Lubricate it with brake grease (see p. 87). Check the action of any automatic adjuster, especially one operated by the handbrake (see p. 91). Make sure that it is free and that the operation of the handbrake lever moves the mechanism to adjust the shoes correctly.

Renewing a worn or stretched handbrake cable

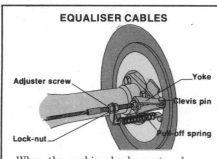

EQUALISER CABLES

Adjuster screw · Yoke · Clevis pin · Lock-nut · Pull-off spring

When the parking brake system has an equaliser mechanism, individual adjusters and pull-off springs are fitted to the brake cables or rods.

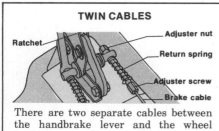

TWIN CABLES

Ratchet · Adjuster nut · Return spring · Adjuster screw · Brake cable

There are two separate cables between the handbrake lever and the wheel brakes. Each cable has to be adjusted at the lever end—usually inside the car.

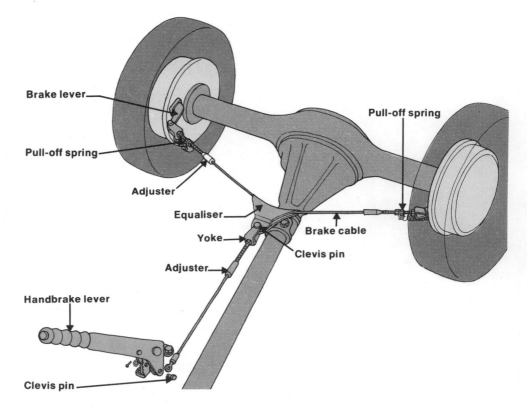

Brake lever · Pull-off spring · Pull-off spring · Adjuster · Equaliser · Yoke · Brake cable · Clevis pin · Adjuster · Handbrake lever · Clevis pin

Before fitting a new brake cable, make sure that the shoes on the drum brakes are properly adjusted (see p. 84). Disc brakes are self-adjusting and do not normally need to be corrected.

Tools: Pliers; spanners to fit the adjusting nuts; jack and axle stands.
Materials: New brake cable to suit the car; new clevis pins and split-pins; new shouldered bolts and nuts, if used.

1 Jack up the back of the car and mount it on axle stands (see p. 61). Release the handbrake lever.

2 Remove the split-pins from the clevis pins on the wheel brake levers, or from the equaliser unit.

3 Remove the clevis pins, if fitted. On some cars the cables are held by shouldered bolts and nuts. Remove the nuts and lift out the bolts.

4 At the front of the car, disconnect the cable from the handbrake lever. Twin cables are attached to the base of the handbrake lever inside the car. A single cable is attached to the lever under the car by a clevis pin or bolt. Remove the cable.

5 If the cable is threaded round pulleys or cable guides, make sure

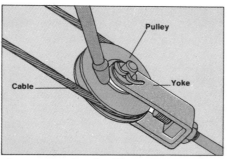

Pulley · Cable · Yoke

they move freely. If necessary, clean them with a wire brush and lubricate them with penetrating oil. If they are still stiff or corroded, it is

advisable to have them replaced by a skilled mechanic.

6 If the new brake cable has an outer casing, trickle oil down inside the casing to ensure that it is suitably lubricated.

7 Fit the new cable to the handbrake lever first. Use a new clevis pin and secure it with a new split-pin. If it was held by a shouldered bolt, fit a new bolt and coat the bolt shank with grease.

8 Run the cable through its guides or pulleys and connect it to the brake lever in the back-plate. Use new clevis pins, or bolts, and always secure the clevis with a new split-pin to ensure that it is safe.

9 Adjust the handbrake cable (see p. 90). Make sure that the lock-nuts are tightened.

Suspension /1

Identifying the dampers on your car

Dampers—often wrongly called shock absorbers—may be telescopic or lever-arm type. Both are hydraulically operated, and their job is to damp vibrations so that the springs—the true shock absorbers—do not go on flexing.

The dampers are located under the car between body and axle at the rear, and between body and lower suspension arm at the front. In the case of some lever-type dampers, the lever itself is the top wishbone of the suspension.

Weak dampers cause unsteady cornering, violent dipping and rock-ing when braking, and severe bumping when the car is on the move.

If there are fluid leaks on the body of the telescopic damper, renew it. Renew lever-type dampers when there are fluid leaks at the point where the lever arms are attached to the side of the damper.

FRONT DAMPER (MACPHERSON STRUT)

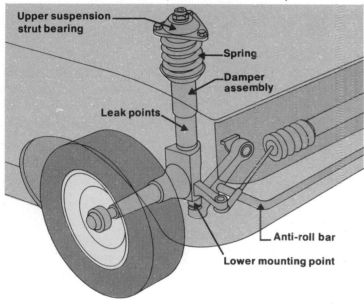

REAR DAMPER (TELESCOPIC)

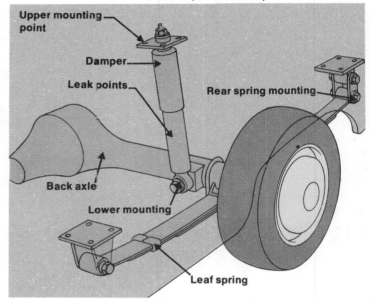

OTHER TYPES OF DAMPER FITTED ON THE FRONT SUSPENSION

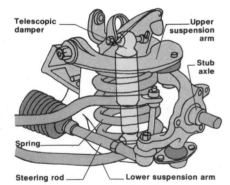

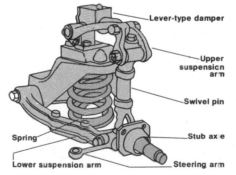

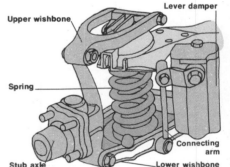

Telescopic damper in spring With double-wishbone front suspension, a telescopic damper is fitted inside a coil spring between the lower wishbone and the bodywork.

Lever damper and suspension arm On some cars the lever attached to the damper unit forms the upper suspension arm. It may have a double or single arm.

Separate lever damper Some damper units are bolted to the chassis and connected by an arm to the lower wishbone. The system is sometimes also used on rear suspensions.

WHEN THE DAMPERS GO WRONG

Symptom	Check	Symptom	Check
Car low on one side	Tyre pressures – p. 37 Hydrolastic pressure – garage job Weak or broken spring – garage job Torsion bar – garage job Uneven loading – p. 30	Car tilts to one side when cornering	Weak or broken spring – garage job Hydrolastic pressure – garage job Damper units – pp. 202-5 Chassis damage – garage job
Car low front or rear	Damper units – pp. 202-5 Weak or broken spring – garage job	Hard or rough ride	Tyre pressures – p. 37 Defective tyre – p. 95 Damper units – pp. 202-5 Uneven loading – p. 30 Weak spring – garage job Anti-roll bar – p. 64
Car low rear or one wheel	Uneven loading – p. 30		
Car low one wheel only	Weak or broken spring – garage job Damaged suspension – garage job	Car sways violently	Damper units – pp. 202-5 Weak spring – garage job Anti-roll bar – p. 64 Roof-rack loading – p. 30

Suspension /2

Replacing front lever dampers

Lever dampers on the front may include the upper suspension arm or wishbone or be connected to the lower suspension wishbone by a ball-jointed link. The damper body is bolted to the car body.

Remove encrusted dirt and check the damper body for leaks (see p. 201). If topping up fails to cure handling problems, replace the unit.

Tools: Spanners to fit the suspension arm nuts and ball-jointed link nuts; spring clamp; hammer and cold chisel.
Materials: New damper unit; link arms, if necessary; rubber bushes.

1 Jack up the car and place axle stands under the body box-sections, so that the suspension hangs free (see p. 61). Remove the road wheels.

2 Place a bottle-jack under the lower wishbone. Jack up the suspension to compress the spring.

3 Use a hammer and cold chisel to tap down the locking tab that re-

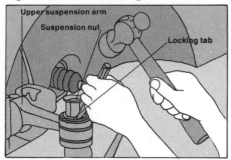

tains the upper suspension arm nut. Remove the nut and the tab.

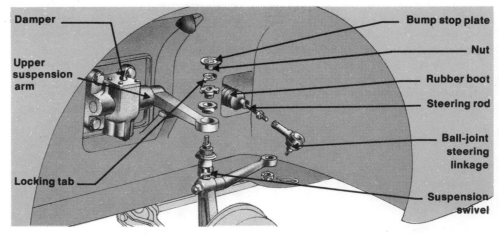

4 Lift off the top suspension collar and remove the rubber bush below it. Push the damper arm up and

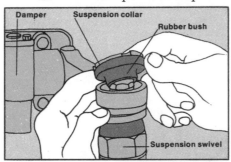

away from the suspension swivel. Remove the rubber bush below it.

5 From under the bonnet undo the four nuts holding the damper to the bodywork. Lift out the damper unit.

6 A new damper unit comes complete with the suspension arm. Fit the damper to the car body.

7 Always renew the rubber bushes. Position the lower rubber bush on the suspension swivel. Pull the lever arm down on to the boss of the lower

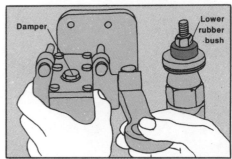

rubber bush. Fit the top rubber bush, collar, lock-washer and nut. Tighten the nut fully, and bend the tab of the lock-washer against the head of the nut to make sure that it is secure.

8 Refit the road wheels and lower the car to the ground.

Replacing rear lever dampers

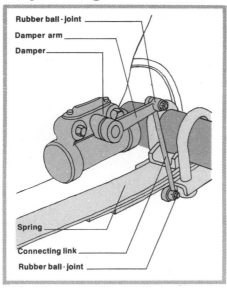

Rear lever dampers are connected to the axle housing or rear suspension by a link mounted on rubber ball-jointed ends. If the rubber has deteriorated fit a new arm.

Tools: Spanners to fit the ball-joint nuts and the damper mounting nuts and bolts; ball-joint pin extraction tool; wire brush; grease; jack and axle stands.
Materials: New damper unit; ball-joint connecting link, if necessary.

1 Jack up the car and mount it on axle stands (see p. 61). Remove the road wheels.

2 Undo the nuts that hold the connecting link to the damper arm and the mounting on the rear axle or suspension unit.

3 Use an extraction tool (see p. 207) to remove the tapered pin of the ball-joint from the end of the arm.

4 Pull the arm out of the damper and away from the axle. Check the condition of the rubber ball-joint ends. If they are damaged, fit a new connecting link.

5 Undo the nuts and bolts holding the damper unit to the car body. Lift the damper from under the wing.

6 There are left and right-hand damper units. Be sure they are fitted to their correct sides. Bolt the new damper to the car body. If the bolts have self-locking nuts, fit new ones.

7 Draw the damper arm down so that it meets the connecting link. Fit the pins of the connecting link to the eye on the damper arm and the axle mounting at the same time, to avoid straining the rubber ball-joints.

8 Hold the tapered pins firmly in position and fit and tighten the nuts. If the old link is being used, clean the pin threads with a wire brush and smear them with grease.

9 Refit the road wheels. Lower the car off the axle stands.

Renewing a telescopic damper

Telescopic dampers may be fitted to the front or rear suspension. Each damper is a cylinder containing a piston on a rod. The cylinder is attached to the axle, or to the lower suspension arm, at the bottom, and the end of the piston rod is attached to the bodywork at the top. On some front suspensions the unit may be incorporated in the MacPherson strut (see p. 201), or it may be surrounded by a suspension spring. In this case spring compressors are needed (see p. 204).

Look for fluid leaks round the body of the damper, and on the rubber mounting bushes. If either shows signs of leaking, fit new dampers.

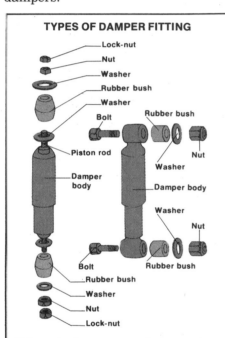

TYPES OF DAMPER FITTING

Telescopic dampers may have a rod at the top and bottom, secured by a nut and lock-nut (left); or eyes at each end with rubber bush inserts, bolted to brackets on suspension and bodywork (right); or a combination of the two.

Tools: Spanners to fit damper nuts; screwdriver; sockets and extension bar; brakepipe clamp and plug; punch; hammer; spring compressors; axle stands; jack; wire brush.
Materials: New dampers; grease; brake fluid.

1 Jack up the car and mount it on axle stands (see p. 61). Remove the road wheels.

2 Locate the top mounting-point. If it is an eye mounting it will be under the wing. If it is a threaded rod it may be in the boot, behind the rear seat squab or under the bonnet.

3 Eye mountings are secured by a bolt and nut. Undo the nut and

remove the bolt. Rod fixings are threaded and have a screwdriver

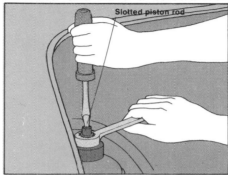

slot or square to hold them while the lock-nut and base nut are undone.

4 Lift off the top-plate and the upper rubber bush on the rod type. Those with an eye fixing can be pushed out of their mounting brackets.

5 Undo the nut and bolt or nuts that secure the bottom of the damper to the axle or suspension bracket.

6 Pull the damper away from its bottom mounting and draw it down-

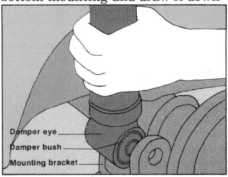

wards away from its top mounting in the bodywork.

7 Prime the new unit by moving the piston rod up and down, ensuring that air and hydraulic fluid inside the cylinder are in their correct compartments. Do not lay the unit on its side after priming.

8 Where eye-type fixings are used, clean the shank and threads of the

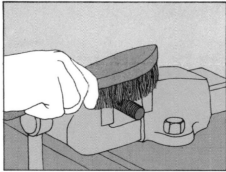

bolts and coat the threads in grease. If the rubber bushes are not part of the damper, fit new bushes to the damper eyes at this stage.

9 If the damper has rod fittings, undo the nuts at each end and remove

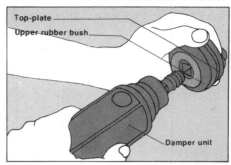

the washers and rubber bushes. Brush the rods clean.

10 Fit the damper eye to the bracket on the axle casing and slide the bolt

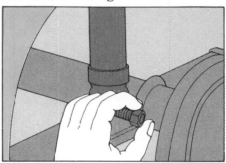

into place from the outside. If the damper has to be removed at any time it is easier to drive it out from the inside where there is more room to swing a hammer. Fit the spring washer and nut to the bolt. Repeat this operation on the damper eye where it fits on to the top bracket. Tighten the nut fully against the mounting brackets.

11 If the damper has a rod fixing, attach the bottom first. Push the rod

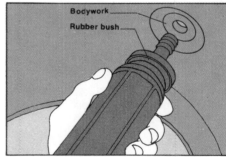

through the hole in the bodywork. Make sure the boss on the lower rubber bush locates in the hole.

12 Fit the upper rubber bush to the piston rod, with the boss facing downwards and contacting the boss on the lower rubber bush. Fit the plate and tighten the nut fully until it makes metal-to-metal contact on the shoulder. Tighten the lock-nut.

13 Refit the road wheels and lower the car off the axle stands. Make sure all the wheel nuts are tight.

Suspension/3

Dismantling and fitting a complete MacPherson strut

If fluid leaks down the side of a MacPherson strut and the car handles badly on corners, it is possible either to fit a new strut or overhaul the existing one (see p. 205). Note that a new strut is supplied without the suspension spring, so spring compressors are needed.

It is dangerous to attempt to dismantle a strut without compressing the suspension spring. If home-made compressors are used, fit them before you remove the strut. Commercial compressors can be fitted after the unit is removed.

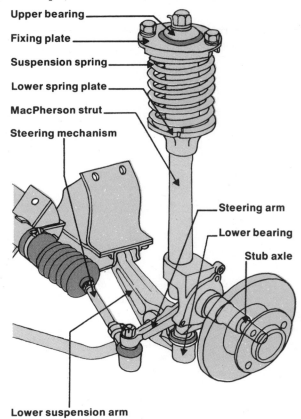

Upper bearing
Fixing plate
Suspension spring
Lower spring plate
MacPherson strut
Steering mechanism
Steering arm
Lower bearing
Stub axle
Lower suspension arm

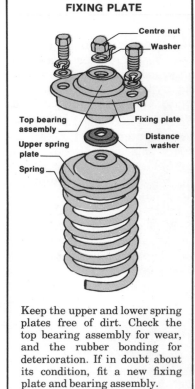

FIXING PLATE

Centre nut
Washer
Top bearing assembly
Fixing plate
Upper spring plate
Distance washer
Spring

Keep the upper and lower spring plates free of dirt. Check the top bearing assembly for wear, and the rubber bonding for deterioration. If in doubt about its condition, fit a new fixing plate and bearing assembly.

MAKING SPRING COMPRESSORS

Suspension spring
Spring compressor

To compress the spring of a MacPherson strut unit, take three pieces of $\frac{3}{8}$ in. diameter rod or $\frac{3}{4}$ in. wide steel plate, about 9 in. long. Bend each end so that they hook over the second top and second bottom coils when the spring is compressed (see **2** below). Tie the three straps together for safety with wire when the work is being done.

Tools: Spanners to fit the suspension nuts and bolts; spring compressors; brake-pipe clamp and plug; jack and axle stands; wire brush.
Materials: New strut; tab locking-washer; grease; top bearing, if necessary.

1 Jack up the front of the car and mount it on axle stands (see p. 61). Remove the wheels.

2 If a home-made spring compressor is used, jack up the suspension strut to compress the spring. Fit the three compressors over the spring and lower the jack.

3 Open the bonnet. Wire-brush the threads on the top of the strut fixing plate. Lubricate with penetrating oil and slacken the centre nut. Do not undo the nut fully.

4 Undo the bolts that hold the fixing plate to the bodywork.

5 From under the wing, clamp the flexible brake hose to save fluid. Some brake manufacturers make a special clamp for brake hoses. If you use an ordinary G-clamp, make

sure that the edges are rounded enough not to damage the hose.

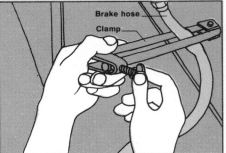

Brake hose
Clamp

Undo the rigid brake-pipe union nut and pull the pipe away from the hose. Plug the end of the rigid pipe.

6 Remove the nut holding the flexible brake hose to the bracket on the suspension strut, and free the hose. Release the track-rod ball-joint from the steering arm (see p. 207). Bend

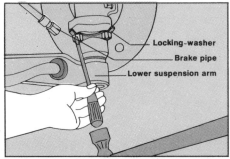

Locking-washer
Brake pipe
Lower suspension arm

back the tabs of the locking-washer at the strut base, or cut the wire.

7 Remove the bolts holding the strut to the end of the lower suspension arm. Pull down the strut

assembly to free it from its top mounting. Lift out the spring and strut assembly. Hold the strut in a

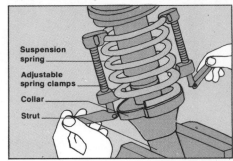

Suspension spring
Adjustable spring clamps
Collar
Strut

vice. If bought compressors are being used, fit and tighten them.

8 Remove the centre nut on the top fixing plate. Lift off the washer, top bearing assembly, distance washer, spring plate, spring and bump rubber. Renew the top bearing and the rubber if damaged. Fit the clamped suspension spring on the new lower spring plate.

9 Slide the new strut into the bodywork, and fit the upper spring plate. Refit the top bearing assembly, and bolt the assembly to the bodywork.

10 Connect the bottom of the strut to the lower suspension arm. Use a new locking-washer. Tighten the bolts and bend over the tabs. If wire was used, wire the bolt heads together. Connect the brake hoses. Bleed and top-up the brakes (see p. 197). Fit the road wheels.

Fitting an insert to a damaged MacPherson strut

If the outer casing of a MacPherson strut is sound but the strut is leaking, it is cheaper to fit an insert, rather than a complete new strut assembly. The insert is a sealed self-contained unit, complete with valves and hydraulic fluid, designed to fit inside the original outer casing. This eliminates the need to refill the strut casing on reassembly with fresh hydraulic damper fluid.

To fit an insert, the complete strut assembly has to be removed from the car (see p. 204). If, after you dismantle the suspension spring and clean the outer casing of the strut, the strut body is found to be dented, damaged or badly rusted, it is advisable to fit a complete new strut assembly (see p. 204).

Tools: Hammer; punch; 'C' spanner, or a pair of stilsons to fit the collar; thin-nosed pliers; wire brush; vice.
Materials: Damper insert; grease; oil.

1 Grip the strut in a vice. Do not damage the casing. Prise out the small indentation that secures the locking collar in the strut.

2 Use a 'C' spanner, stilsons or a hammer and punch to undo the lock-

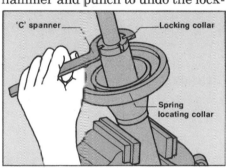

ing collar. Slide it off the piston rod. Pull out the piston rod and valve assembly from the strut. Remove the strut from the vice and pour out the old hydraulic fluid.

3 Replace the strut in the vice and clean the casing with a wire brush. Remove any dirt from the lower spring plate. Clean inside the strut with paraffin, and dry it.

4 Check the top of the strut. Clean the threads with a wire brush and—with a pair of thin-nosed pliers—pull out the slight indentation, where it was tapped in to lock it on the collar. Try the new locking collar. If it does not screw easily

borrow a thread cutter or have the threads recut at a garage.

5 Slide the new insert into the strut casing. Fit the sealing ring and screw the new locking collar into position. Tighten the collar down as far as it will go.

6 Centre-punch one point, at the top of the strut body, against the

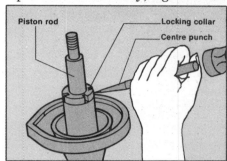

threads of the locking collar to hold it in place and ensure that it cannot unscrew.

7 Hold the complete strut assembly vertical. Pump the piston rod up and down a few times to prime the unit.

8 Fit the bump rubber to the piston rod and position the clamped suspension spring in the lower spring locating plate. Position the upper spring plate. Make sure that it fits

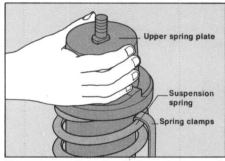

the squared end of the piston rod. Fit the upper bearing assembly, washer and nut. Hold the upper spring plate to stop the rod turning and tighten the nut.

9 Refit the complete strut assembly to the car (see p. 204). Clean and

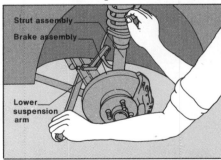

grease the threads of the bolts that hold the bottom of the strut to the lower suspension arm. Reconnect the brake hoses and bleed the brakes (see p. 197). Check the brake lines for leaking. Fit the road wheels and lower the car off the axle stands.

To fit a new hydraulic damper insert in a MacPherson strut, remove the complete strut from the car. Make sure the body is sound.

Labels (exploded diagram): Bump rubber; Locking collar; Sealing ring; Piston rod; Damper insert; Lower spring plate; Strut casing; Brake assembly

Steering / 1

Identifying different types of steering units

Before working on the steering system, find out which of the two main types—rack-and-pinion or steering box—is on your car.

If you have a steering-box system, there is little that you can do without specialist garage equipment. And even on a rack-and-pinion unit, which can to some extent be repaired or replaced by the do-it-yourself motorist, use only replacement parts recommended by the car manufacturer and have the car checked afterwards by a garage.

How rack-and-pinion works

In a rack-and-pinion system, the pinion is a short shaft with a gear wheel which engages with a toothed shaft, called the rack. The steering wheel moves the pinion which in turn moves the rack horizontally inside its housing. The road wheels are attached, through ball-jointed arms, at each end of the rack. Complete replacement is possible if there are serious faults, but there are also four repairs that can be undertaken —the rubber boots, the pinion, the yoke and the ball-joints.

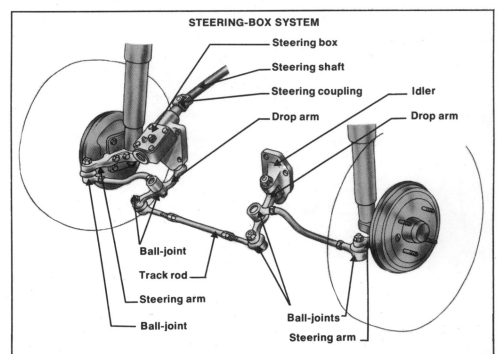

STEERING-BOX SYSTEM

- Steering box
- Steering shaft
- Steering coupling
- Idler
- Drop arm
- Drop arm
- Ball-joint
- Track rod
- Steering arm
- Ball-joint
- Ball-joints
- Steering arm

The steering wheel moves a mechanism inside the steering box which is joined to a shaft, called a rocker arm. This shaft is attached to a lever, the drop arm, at the base of the steering box. Rods, with ball-joints on their ends, transmit the steering-box movement to the road wheels. Worn ball-joints can be replaced (see p. 207), but to cure steering-box faults special tools are needed. Take the car to a garage for such repair work.

PINION PRE-LOAD

Movement in the steering column is a sign of insufficient pinion pre-load. Remove the unit (see p. 209).

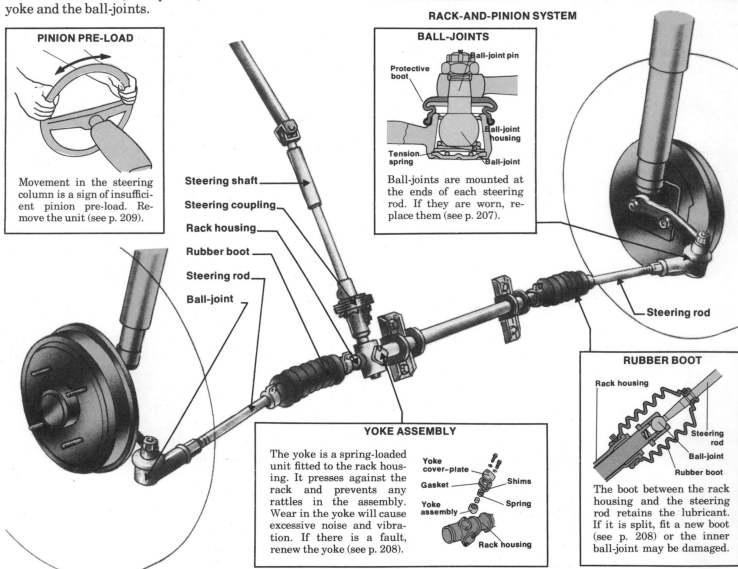

RACK-AND-PINION SYSTEM

- Steering shaft
- Steering coupling
- Rack housing
- Rubber boot
- Steering rod
- Ball-joint
- Steering rod

BALL-JOINTS

- Ball-joint pin
- Protective boot
- Tension spring
- Ball-joint housing
- Ball-joint

Ball-joints are mounted at the ends of each steering rod. If they are worn, replace them (see p. 207).

YOKE ASSEMBLY

The yoke is a spring-loaded unit fitted to the rack housing. It presses against the rack and prevents any rattles in the assembly. Wear in the yoke will cause excessive noise and vibration. If there is a fault, renew the yoke (see p. 208).

- Yoke cover-plate
- Gasket
- Yoke assembly
- Shims
- Spring
- Rack housing

RUBBER BOOT

- Rack housing
- Steering rod
- Ball-joint
- Rubber boot

The boot between the rack housing and the steering rod retains the lubricant. If it is split, fit a new boot (see p. 208) or the inner ball-joint may be damaged.

WHEN THE STEERING GOES WRONG

Symptom	Check	Symptom	Check
Car wanders	Tyre pressures – p. 37 Uneven loading – p. 30 Steering linkage – garage job Steering box – garage job Front-wheel bearings – pp. 92-95 Springs – garage job	Excessive play in steering	Steering box – garage job Ball-joints – this page King-pins – garage job Pinion pre-load – p. 209
Steering hard to turn	Tyre pressures – p. 37 Lubrication – p. 63 Adjustment – p. 133 Front-wheel alignment – p. 133 Steering box – garage job Pinion pre-load – p. 209	Car pulls to one side	Tyre condition – p. 95 Brakes binding – p. 84 Springs – garage job Front-wheel alignment – p. 133 Rear axle fault – garage job Steering rattles (rack-and-pinion) – p. 208 Worn yoke – p. 208

Renewing a ball-joint when the steering is slack

An accurate check to ensure there is no excessive play in a steering ball-joint can be made only with specialist garage equipment. But if that kind of fault-finding indicates that a ball-joint needs renewing, you can do the job yourself.

Tools: Spanners to fit the ball-joint nut and the steering rod lock-nuts; pin-removal tool; pliers; wire brush; jack and axle stands.
Materials: New ball-joint assemblies; new split-pin or a new self-locking nut; medium grease; penetrating oil.

1 Remove the wheel on the side of the faulty ball-joint. Brush the threads above the ball-joint nut and lubricate them with penetrating oil.

2 If the nut is castellated, remove the split-pin that secures it. Dis-

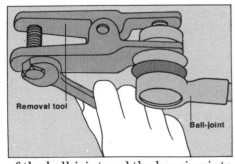

card a split-pin that has been used: buy new split-pins. Undo the nut.

3 Fit the fork end of the ball-joint pin-removal tool between the top

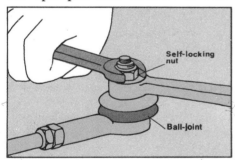

of the ball-joint and the housing into which the pin fits. Position the flat

end of the tool over the threaded end of the pin. Tighten the screw on the tool handle with a spanner to close the jaws and force the tapered ball-joint pin from its housing. If the pin is tight, tap the top of the tool with a hammer to release it.

4 Pull the steering rod away from the pin-housing, so that the pin is drawn out. This action should also release the pin-removal tool.

5 Hold one spanner on the lock-nut on the steering rod and another on the ball-joint adjusting nut next to

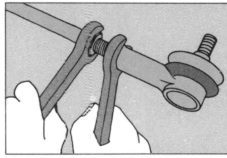

it. Turn only the ball-joint adjusting nut. Do not disturb the lock-nut, otherwise a new ball-joint cannot be fitted in the same position.
Steering-box track-rods Note that the left-hand ball-joint has a left-hand thread and the right-hand ball-joint a right-hand thread.

6 Count and note the number of turns it takes to unscrew the ball-joint from the steering rod.

7 To ensure that your repair is completely safe, it is advisable to buy only the car manufacturer's recommended replacements. Clean and grease the threads on the end of the steering rod, and on the new ball-joint pin. Screw the new ball-joint on to the steering rod. Count the number of turns, so that it is in the same position as the

original joint. Use two spanners, one on the steering-rod lock-nut

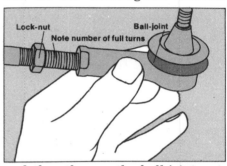

and the other on the ball-joint nut, and tighten the steering-rod lock-nut on to the ball-joint assembly.

8 Fit the tapered pin into the housing. Fit and tighten the ball-joint nut. If the nut is self-locking, hold the pin firmly in position in its

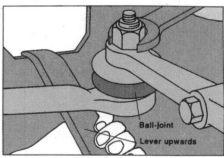

housing with a bar pressed against the base of the ball-joint. This prevents the pin turning when the thread reaches the nylon insert in the nut. If a castellated nut is used, fit a new split-pin and turn the pin ends around the flat sides of the nut. Most modern ball-joints are pre-packed with grease and need no lubrication. If the joint has a grease nipple, however, apply grease carefully with a gun (see p. 34).

9 When the new ball-joint has been fitted, take the car to a garage and have the track of the road wheels checked and, if necessary, reset on specialist equipment (see p. 133).

Steering /2

Renewing a rubber boot on the steering rod

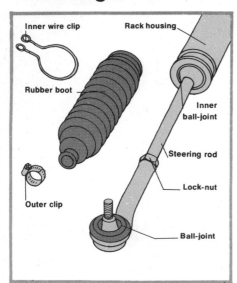

Cracks and splits in a protective rubber boot allow lubricant to leak out and dirt and grit to enter. In time the inner ball-joint in the rack housing will suffer and a new rack will be needed. To save money, fit a new boot at the first signs of wear.

Tools: Spanners to fit ball-joint assembly nuts and steering rod lock-nut; pin-removal tool; wire brush; pliers; wire cutters; jack; axle stands.
Materials: New rubber boot; new clips; water-repellent grease; EP90 oil.

1 If both boots are damaged, fit them one at a time. Jack up the car on one side and mount it on axle stands (see p. 61). Remove the road wheel. Wipe all parts near the boot with a petrol or paraffin-soaked rag.

2 Remove the ball-joint (see p. 207), and undo the lock-nut from the end of the steering rod. Always count

the number of turns it takes to remove the lock-nut.

3 Remove the clip or cut the wire that secures the rubber boot to the rack housing.

4 Remove the plastic cap (if fitted) from the end of the outer clip screw

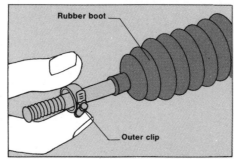

thread. Undo the screw that holds the clip and remove the clip.

5 Slacken the inner clip that holds the boot to the rack housing. Lift

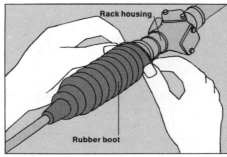

the boot out of the recess in the housing and slide it off the rod.

6 Grease the sealing surfaces of the new boot and slide it over the rod. Note that the inner ends of left and right boots have different diameters.

7 Position the lip of the inner end in the recess in the rack housing.

8 Slide the outer end of the boot into the recess on the steering rod. Refit and tighten the securing clip or wire to the outer end.

9 Raise the inner end of the boot and fill it with $\frac{1}{3}$ pint of EP90 oil.

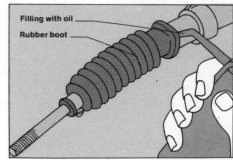

Make sure that the boot is seated properly and fit the retaining clip or wire at the inner end.

10 Refit the ball-joint lock-nut, counting the number of turns to position it correctly, and replace the

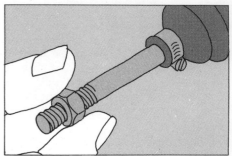

ball-joint. Tighten the lock-nut and fit the ball-joint pin and nut. Take the car to a garage and have the road wheel track checked for safety.

Renewing a rack-and-pinion yoke

The yoke cover is held by bolts. Shims are fitted under the cover to give the correct clearance. If a new

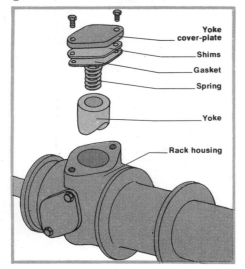

yoke is required, use one identical to the one removed.

On manual steering units the yoke may be plastic or sintered steel. On power-assisted units the yokes are always sintered steel.

Tools: Spanners to fit the yoke-plate bolts; feeler gauges; clean rag.
Materials: New yoke cover-plate; yoke; shims; cover gasket; sealant; EP90 oil.

1 In some cases it may be necessary to remove the entire rack-and-pinion unit from the car. But if the yoke cover-plate can be seen from underneath the car, undo the bolts holding the plate to the base of the rack housing. Remove the cover-plate, shims and gasket. Note whether the gasket is fitted above or below shims. Remove the spring and yoke.

2 Check the position of the two lines across the curved face of the yoke where it contacts the body of the

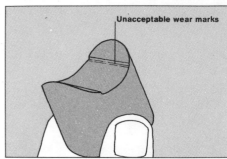

rack. The lines should be thin and about half-way up the face. If the lines are wide, and towards the bottom, fit a new yoke.

3 Use a clean, dry lint-free rag to wipe the yoke and the mating sur-

Adjusting the steering pinion pre-load

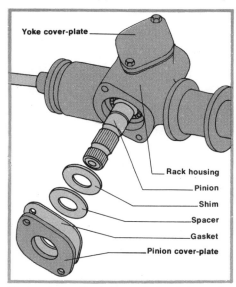

Yoke cover-plate

Rack housing
Pinion
Shim
Spacer
Gasket
Pinion cover-plate

To ensure that the pinion stays in correct contact with the horizontally moving rack and is not too loose or too tight (see p. 206), shims are placed between the pinion cover and the rack housing. To adjust the pinion clearance, remove the complete rack-and-pinion steering assembly from the car.

Tools: Spanners to fit the ball-joint pin nut, pinion and yoke-plate cover-bolts; rack securing nuts or bolts; pin-removal tool; straight-edge; Mole grips; feeler gauges; jack and axle stands.
Materials: Shims; cover-plate gasket; pinion-shaft seal; sealant.

1 Jack up the car and mount it on axle stands (see p. 61). Undo the steering rod ball-joints (see p. 207). Remove the pinch bolt that holds the pinion on the steering column. Undo the clamps or U-bolts that hold the rack assembly and lift it out.

2 Loosen the yoke cover-plate bolts to relieve pressure on the rack.

3 Undo and remove the two or three bolts that hold the pinion cover-plate. Slide the cover-plate carefully over the splines on the end of the pinion shaft. Do not disturb the pinion shaft.

4 Remove the pinion spacer. Rotate the pinion slightly to lift the shims out of their recess, but do not lift it so far that it disengages from the rack —this could upset the pinion-shaft block serrations and make engagement with the steering column diffi-

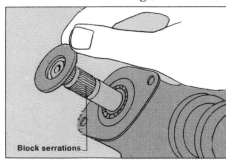

Block serrations

cult. Check the condition of all the bearings. If even only one bearing is slightly damaged, it is advisable, for safety, to fit a complete new rack-and-pinion steering assembly.

5 Clean the faces of the rack housing and the cover-plate. Make sure that the pinion is engaged with the rack and fit new shims. Replace the spacer and fit a new gasket.

6 Lay a straight-edge across the spacer and the rack housing. With a feeler gauge, measure between the

straight-edge and the top of the rack housing. If the gap is more than

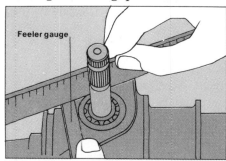

Feeler gauge

·004 in. or less than ·002 in., remove or add shims.

7 Fit a new gasket in the pinion cover-plate. Grease the gasket and refit the plate. Dip the bolts in sealant and tighten to a torque of between 12 and 15 lb.ft.

8 Tighten the yoke-plate bolts. Hold the end of the pinion shaft in a pair of Mole grips and turn the pinion to make sure it travels freely

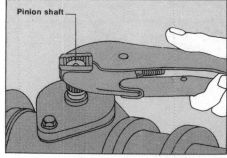

Pinion shaft

across the full length of the rack. If it feels tight, add a ·001 in. shim.

9 Refit the rack assembly to the car. Fit and tighten the pinch bolt and reconnect the ball-joints.

---

faces of the rack housing and the yoke cover-plate.

4 Replace the yoke, yoke tension spring, new shims and gasket.

5 Cut a section out of the old yoke cover-plate, sufficiently close to the

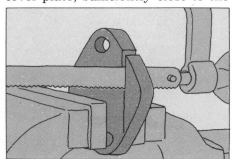

bolt holes to give access to the inside of the yoke assembly. Bolt this

cover in position over the shims and spring (or gasket).

6 Measure the clearance between the top of the yoke and the base of the cover-plate. The gap must not be

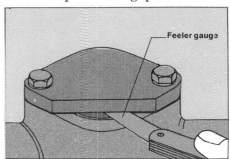

Feeler gauge

less than ·002 in., and not greater than ·005 in. With a ·002 in. feeler gauge in position, get a helper to turn the steering wheel from lock

to lock. The feeler gauge must not be pinched at any time the wheel is being turned. Now try a ·005 in. feeler gauge. The gauge should be pinched firmly between the yoke and cover-plate all the time that the helper is moving the rack.

7 If the clearance is incorrect, remove shims to narrow the gap or add shims to widen it. Check again across the travel of the rack to ensure that the gap is correct.

8 Once the correct clearance has been established, remove the cut cover-plate and fit the new, complete plate. Dip the retaining bolts in a sealant before fitting them. Refill the rack housing with about $\frac{1}{3}$ pint of EP90 oil.

Transmission /1

Identifying what repairs are possible on a transmission system

The faults that can develop in a transmission system and the repairs that are possible for the do-it-yourself mechanic depend on the basic design of the transmission.

In rear-wheel-drive cars with the engine at the front, power from the engine is transmitted through the clutch and gearbox and then along the propeller shaft to the final-drive unit at the rear. The propeller shaft has universal joints (see p. 212) at both ends—and sometimes in the middle—to allow for the up-and-down movement as the car goes over bumps in the road.

Universal joints are also used on the shafts that drive the wheels. On cars with a live rear axle—that is where the final-drive unit and the half-shafts are in a rigid axle casing—repairs call for garage equipment.

On the other type of rear-wheel drive—independent rear suspension, where the final-drive unit is attached to the car independently of the drive-shafts—there may be two different kinds of universal joint (see p. 212). Both can be replaced without garage equipment, but you must take care to distinguish between a conventional Hardy Spicer joint and a rubber doughnut type.

On front-engine, front-wheel-drive cars, universal joints are used on the inner ends of the drive-shafts. But a third type of joint—called a constant-velocity joint—is fitted on the outer ends of the drive-shafts. Constant-velocity joints can also be repaired by the do-it-yourself motorist (see p. 214).

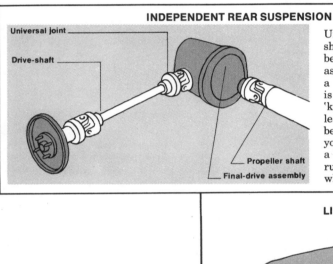

INDEPENDENT REAR SUSPENSION

Universal joint
Drive-shaft
Propeller shaft
Final-drive assembly

Universal joints on the drive-shaft enable the power to be maintained to each wheel as the suspension flexes. If a drive-shaft universal joint is worn, it will cause a 'knock' as the clutch is released. Universal joints can be renewed (see p. 212), but you must distinguish between a Hardy Spicer joint and the rubber-encased type on front-wheel-drive cars.

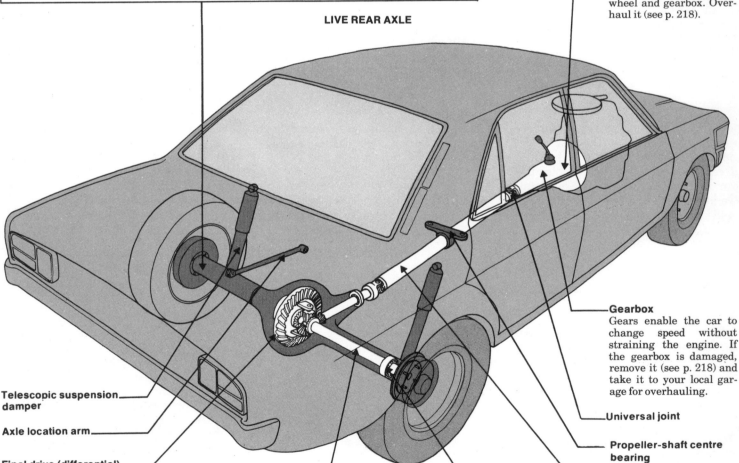

LIVE REAR AXLE

Clutch
When the clutch is engaged, a friction disc transmits the engine power to the gearbox. A worn clutch may slip, increase fuel costs and cause damage to the fly-wheel and gearbox. Overhaul it (see p. 218).

Gearbox
Gears enable the car to change speed without straining the engine. If the gearbox is damaged, remove it (see p. 218) and take it to your local garage for overhauling.

Universal joint

Propeller-shaft centre bearing

Propeller shaft
On front-engine, rear-wheel-drive cars, the propeller shaft transmits the drive from the gearbox to the final drive assembly. If the universal joints are worn renew them (see p. 212).

Telescopic suspension damper

Axle location arm

Final drive (differential)
The final-drive gear arrangement directs the power from the engine to the wheels and enables road wheels to turn at different speeds. Apart from topping-up and checking oil levels (see p. 79), repairs are a garage job.

Half-shafts
Two shafts transmit the power from the final-drive assembly to the road wheels. If one shaft breaks, drive is lost. It must be repaired by a garage.

Half-shaft bearing

FRONT-ENGINE, FRONT-WHEEL DRIVE

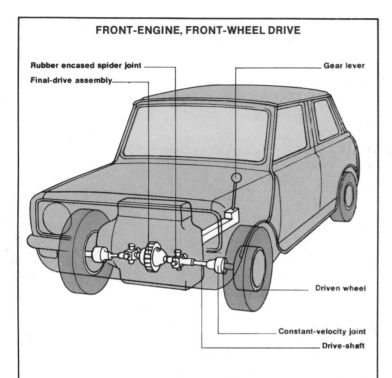

Rubber encased spider joint
Final-drive assembly
Gear lever
Driven wheel
Constant-velocity joint
Drive-shaft

At the final-drive end of the shaft, two types of universal joint may be used: a conventional Hardy Spicer joint, using small needle rollers, or a rubber-encased spider joint. These joints are secured by U-bolts to shaped coupling flanges on the drive-shaft and the final-drive assembly.

At the road wheel end of the drive-shaft a constant-velocity joint is used. This works on the principle of one sphere rotating within another and enables the wheel to be steered while power is transmitted. The joint can cope with an angle of 30 degrees between the drive-shaft and the hub-shaft leading to the wheel.

REAR-ENGINE, REAR-WHEEL DRIVE

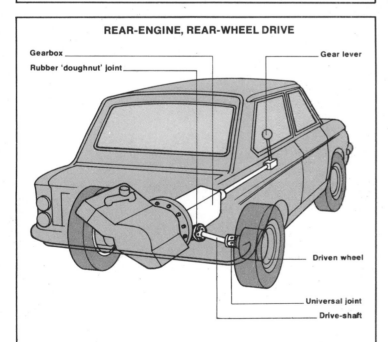

Gearbox
Rubber 'doughnut' joint
Gear lever
Driven wheel
Universal joint
Drive-shaft

Some manufacturers fit a rubber doughnut joint between the drive-shaft and the final-drive assembly. This type of universal joint has three functions. It transmits the drive from the final-drive unit to the drive-shaft; it acts as a buffer, damping out the initial shock as the drive is taken up; and it flexes to allow for the up-and-down movement of the suspension.

On some suspension systems that do have this type of joint, a conventional Hardy Spicer universal joint is fitted at the other end of the drive-shaft. Other manufacturers, however, fit Hardy Spicer joints at both ends of the drive-shafts.

WHEN THE TRANSMISSION GOES WRONG

Symptom	Check
Car vibrates	Wheel balance – garage job Wheel nuts – p. 95 Universal joints, prop-shaft and drive-shafts – p. 212 Fan blades – p. 118 Front wheel bearings – p. 92
Engine runs but prop-shaft does not turn	Clutch free play – p. 76 Automatic gearbox – p. 134 Clutch friction disc – p. 220
Prop-shaft turns but car does not move	Half-shaft or rear axle – consult a garage
Difficulty in engaging gear	Idling speed – pp. 128-9 Clutch free play – p. 76 Clutch reservoir – p. 130 Clutch pressure-plate and friction disc – p. 220
Difficulty in engaging gear after car has not been used	Clutch friction disc – p. 220
Clutch slips	Clutch adjustment – p. 76 Friction disc – p. 220 Oil on linings – p. 220
Clutch judders	Pressure-plate – p. 220 Engine mountings – p. 135
Clutch noisy with engine running and pedal all the way out	Clutch linkage – p. 76
Clutch noisy with pedal depressed	Clutch release bearing – p. 220 Flywheel spigot bearing – p. 220
Thud or 'clunk' when clutch engages	Prop-shaft and drive-shaft universal joints – p. 212 Rear axle or half-shaft splines – garage job
Clutch pedal will not come all the way back	Clutch linkage – p. 76
Gear lever rattles or makes buzzing noise	Gear lever tightness – p. 75 Gear lever damper – garage job Remote-control linkage – p. 75 Engine and gearbox mountings – p. 135 Idling speed – pp. 128-9
Gears grind when engaged, car not moving	Idling speed – pp. 128-9 Clutch engagement – p. 218
Grinding when changing gear	Clutch adjustment – p. 76 Synchromesh or gearbox bearings – garage job
Gear slips out of engagement	Engine and gearbox mountings – p. 135 Gearbox wear – garage job
Transmission noisy in forward gears	Lubricant level – p. 79 Alignment – garage job Internal components – garage job
Noisy in reverse	Reverse idler gear or shaft – garage job
Transmission sticks in gear	Lubricant level – p. 79 Gear-change linkage – p. 75 Internal fault – garage job Friction disc – p. 220
Little increase in road speed although engine revs increase	Clutch free play – p. 76 Oil on linings – p. 220

Transmission /2

Overhauling a Hardy Spicer universal joint

The most common type of universal joint—fitted to all propeller shafts but also to some drive-shafts—is the Hardy Spicer. It has a four-armed cross piece, or spider, held in two sets of bearings mounted in jaws, or yokes, which are held at right angles to each other.

If the joint on a propeller shaft or drive-shaft is worn, renew the spider and bearing assemblies. The job illustrated is on a propeller shaft. Use the same procedure for a drive-shaft joint.

If the propeller shaft vibrates when the car is driven after repair, take it to a specialist garage and have the shaft dynamically balanced.

A special kind of universal joint is found on some British Leyland cars —for example, the Maxi range. Although similar in principle, the joint—called a pot-joint—is packed with a special grease and is sealed in a rubber cover.

The most likely cause of failure is that the cover has been damaged or worn, allowing the grease to escape. Because repair can involve dismantling the final-drive unit, it is advisable to take the car to a garage if a pot-joint is faulty.

Tools: Jack; axle stands; screwdriver; spanners to fit the flange nuts and bolts, and centre bearing if fitted; shallow pan; circlip pliers; soft-faced hammer; large vice; sockets and ratchet or lever bar; wire brush. **Materials:** New universal joint assembly; paraffin; high-melting-point grease; spare grease nipple if necessary; gearbox oil.

1 Jack up the back of the car and mount it on axle stands; this minimises the loss of gearbox oil.

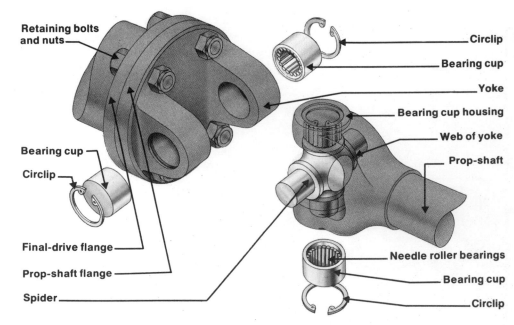

Retaining bolts and nuts · Bearing cup · Circlip · Final-drive flange · Prop-shaft flange · Spider · Circlip · Bearing cup · Yoke · Bearing cup housing · Web of yoke · Prop-shaft · Needle roller bearings · Bearing cup · Circlip

2 Check whether the universal joint has a circlip in each of the four bearing housings. A joint with only two circlips cannot be overhauled.

3 To check for wear, push a large screwdriver between the spider and

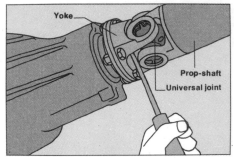

Yoke · Prop-shaft · Universal joint

the yokes and try to lever the spider away from each yoke in turn. If you can move the spider and yoke apart, overhaul the joint.

4 Scribe a line across the flanges of the propeller shaft and the final drive so that they can be refitted in the same position. If the shaft has a centre bearing, scribe a line round the bearing housing.

5 Undo the four nuts and bolts that secure the propeller shaft

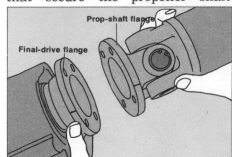

Prop-shaft flange · Final-drive flange

flange to the flange on the final drive. Pull the flanges apart and

Checking drive-shaft joints and fitting a new rubber doughnut

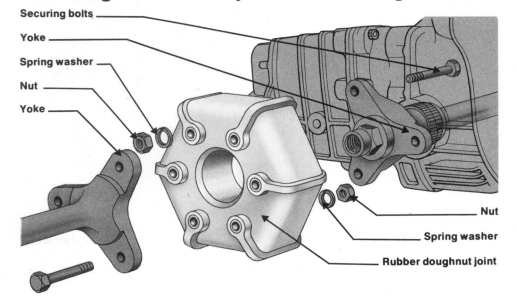

Securing bolts · Yoke · Spring washer · Nut · Yoke · Nut · Spring washer · Rubber doughnut joint

The separate drive-shafts on cars that have independent rear suspension may have a Hardy Spicer type of universal joint at one end or at both ends. Clicking when the car goes round a corner is usually an indication that one of the joints is worn or loose.

Check the spiders (see above) and if they are faulty, overhaul them in the same way as for joints on a propeller shaft.

Some cars, however, have a rubber doughnut joint at the final-drive end of the shaft. Check the rubbers for signs of cracking, contamination from oil, swelling or sponginess. Renew the joint if the rubber is damaged.

These joints have metal strips

lower the propeller shaft. Lay a shallow tray under the gearbox to catch oil, and draw out the shaft.

6 Squeeze the ends of each circlip together with circlip pliers. Use the same pliers to draw the circlips out of their yokes. If a circlip is

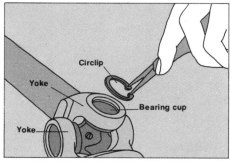

rusted or broken, chip it out in small pieces with a screwdriver blade.

7 Strike the web of the yoke, just below the bearing cup housing, with a soft-faced mallet. This will jar

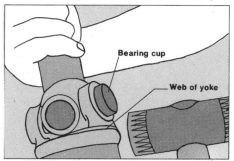

the bearing cup and its needle rollers out of the yoke housing. Lift the cup out. Twist the shaft through 180 degrees and strike the web again to drive out the opposite bearing cup. Lift the cup out from the housing, leaving the spider loose in its yoke.

8 Turn the central spider to free it from the yoke on the shaft and pull the two yokes apart. Rest the yoke, with the spider still attached, in the jaws of the vice and strike the webs

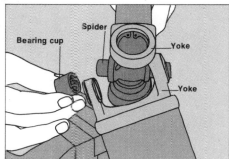

of the yoke on both sides with a soft-faced mallet to remove the remaining bearing cups and needle rollers. Pull the cups out of their housings and discard them.

9 Remove the central spider. Wash the yokes in paraffin and scrape any dirt from the circlip grooves. If a grease nipple is fitted to the yoke, make sure the grease hole in the yoke is clear. Attach a grease gun to the nipple and pump it to make sure that the nipple is letting grease through.

10 The new spider assembly has its bearing cups ready assembled with the needle rollers and is pre-greased. Remove two opposite bearing cups and thread the bared ends of the spider into one of the two yokes.

11 Make sure the needle rollers are positioned round the inner surface of each bearing cup. If necessary, hold them in place with extra grease.

12 Position the cups in the yoke-bearing housings and place the

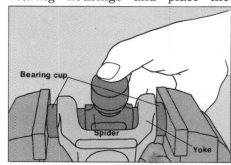

whole assembly between the jaws of the vice. Tighten the jaws to squeeze the bearing cups into the yoke. Move the spider back and forth and rotate it, to ensure that the needle rollers stay securely in place in their bearing cups.

13 The vice can press the cups only flush with the yokes. Place two sockets between the cups and vice jaws. Tighten the vice to press the cups below the level of the circlip grooves in the yokes. Check frequently to make sure the cups are not pressed too far in.

14 Refit the circlips. Make sure that they are seated in their grooves.

15 Fit the spider to the other yoke and repeat the procedure.

16 Slide the propeller shaft into the gearbox housing. Line up the scribed marks on the flanges at the final drive. Refit and tighten the flange bolts.

17 Take the car off the axle stands and lower to the ground.

---

bonded into the rubber. Make sure that they have not worked loose. If they have, fit a new doughnut.

Check the bolt holes in the two yokes and make sure that they have not become elongated. Fit new yokes if necessary.

Make sure that you always use a set of new nuts and bolts when you do any work on a doughnut joint.

Tools: Jack; axle stands; two spanners to fit the nuts and bolts securing the joint; screwdriver.
Materials: New rubber doughnut joint; set of six new bolts, nuts and washers.

1 Jack up the back of the car and mount it on axle stands. Remove any dirt round the bolts securing the rubber doughnuts to the yokes.

2 Undo the nuts and bolts. Slide the rubber doughnut joint from between the two yokes. Clean the yoke faces with a wire brush.

3 Slide the new doughnut between the yokes and refit the nuts and bolts. Tighten the bolts alternately on each side. Remove the band round the outside of the doughnut.

Temporary removal When an undamaged doughnut has to be temporarily removed—for work on the gearbox or final drive, for example—compress it with a clamp before undoing it. Otherwise the rubber may flex out of shape and be difficult to replace. A suitable clamp, to compress the rubber joint, can be

made from two large Jubilee hose clips. Undo the two clips and stretch them out. Connect the serrated end

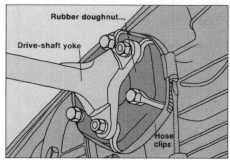

of one clip to the adjusting screw of the other, to make one long clip. Wrap the clip round the rubber joint and fix them together. Tighten the clip adjusting screw to draw the clip tightly round the joint.

Transmission/3

Problems that may affect front-wheel-drive cars

The joints at the ends of the drive-shafts on front-wheel-drive cars have to accommodate both the vertical movement of the suspension and the swivelling action of the steering. At the wheel end of the shaft, this is achieved by a special kind of joint, called a constant-velocity joint. A worn constant-velocity joint produces 'knocking' when driven on full lock.

On the other end of the shaft—called the inboard end—there is fitted a rubber doughnut joint, a Hardy Spicer type joint (see p. 212) or a rubber-encased spider joint. Worn inboard joints produce a 'knocking' which is loudest when you accelerate hard.

Rubber-encased joints are the most vulnerable—oil can contaminate the rubber, making it swell and break away from the spider. When you deal with this type of joint, you must draw the drive-shaft away from the final-drive housing.

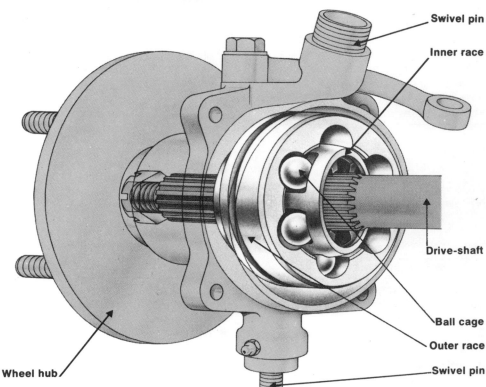

Swivel pin

Inner race

Drive-shaft

Ball cage

Outer race

Swivel pin

Wheel hub

Renewing a rubber-encased spider joint

The sequence on this page shows particularly how to change the rubber-encased spider joints on the drive-shaft of a British Leyland Mini. The same principle applies to other cars that use drive-shafts with these types of joints.

But if you are in doubt after inspecting the underside of your car, it is advisable to ask your dealer whether your model involves any special difficulties or calls for special equipment. In many cases, dealers are willing to give advice and hire the equipment needed.

Tools: A 1 in. thick block of wood; hub-cap key; socket, to fit the hub nut; long extension bar; wheel brace; axle stands; large and small screwdrivers; ball-joint pin remover; copper or hide mallet; round file; large vice; torque wrench.
Materials: Rubber-encased spider; new U-bolts; U-bolt nuts and spring washers.

1 Turn the steering to full lock and remove the bolt on the bump rubber.

Bump rubber

Upper suspension arm

Remove the rubber and lay it aside. If it is worn, buy a new one.

2 Wedge a block of wood between the upper suspension arm and the rebound platform. Remove the hub cap and the grease cap in the centre.

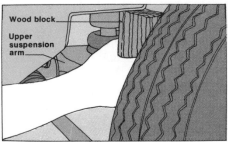

Wood block

Upper suspension arm

3 Straighten the split-pin and draw it out of the hub nut. Loosen the hub nut with a long extension bar and socket, but do not undo it fully.

4 Loosen the road wheel nuts. Jack up the car and mount it on stands so that the suspension hangs down.

5 Remove the eight nuts on the universal-joint U-bolts and prise the

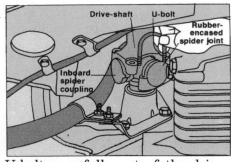

Drive-shaft   U-bolt

Rubber-encased spider joint

Inboard spider coupling

U-bolts carefully out of the drive-shaft yokes.

6 Remove the road wheels. Undo the ball-joint nut at the end of the

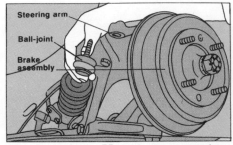

Steering arm

Ball-joint

Brake assembly

steering arm. Use a remover (see p. 207) to free the ball-joint pin from the steering arm.

7 Remove the nut from the lower steering swivel pin. Use the taper breaker to remove the pin from the lower suspension arm.

8 Press down the lower suspension arm. Swing out the hub assembly.

9 Prise the inboard yokes apart with a screwdriver—the drive-shaft is able to telescope a little on the sliding splines—and remove the rubber-encased spider.

10 Slide the new rubber-encased spider between the two yokes, draw the yokes together and fit the four U-bolts. Fit and tighten the U-bolt nuts. Reassemble the drive-shaft hub assembly in the reverse order that it was dismantled. Refit the road wheels and lower the car off the axle stands.

Overhauling a constant-velocity joint

To overhaul a constant-velocity joint, first dismantle and remove the inboard rubber-encased spider joint (see p. 214). Then undo the nut securing the drive-shaft to the wheel hub. This is a castellated nut, tightened to a specific torque figure and secured with a split-pin.

Ask your dealer for the correct torque figure for your car and use a torque wrench to tighten the nut when you replace it.

Some cars also need a hub-puller to draw the hub off the shaft. This may be difficult, so have the joint renewed by a garage in such cases.

Tools: Socket to fit hub nut; copper or hide mallet; two small screwdrivers; pliers; large vice; torque wrench; long extension bar.
Materials: Constant-velocity-joint kit; sachet of special grease; a new protective rubber cover, 18 swg soft wire for the rubber cover; new split-pin for the hub nut.

1 Remove the drive-shaft centre-nut, lower the end of the drive-shaft and tap the shaft out of the hub.

2 Use a large screwdriver to break the metal or wire bands securing the inner and outer ends of the rubber cover on the shaft and hub. Have new wires ready for reassembly.

3 Hold the drive-shaft upright, with the joint at the bottom. Strike the edge of the joint sharply with a mallet to knock it off the shaft.

4 Discard the old joint. Pack the new joint, which is dry when it is sold, with the special grease supplied by the dealer.

5 Slide the new rubber cover over the shaft, small end first. Keep it clear of the splined end of the shaft.

6 Make sure the locking ring, fitted to the groove in the splined end of the shaft, is sound. If necessary, fit a new locking ring to the shaft.

7 Compress the locking ring into its groove on the shaft with two small screwdrivers. At the same time, get a helper to ease the new

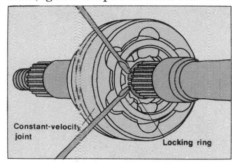

Constant-velocity joint
Locking ring

joint on to the shaft. Push the drive-shaft and the new joint together as far as they will go.

8 Use a mallet to tap the new joint firmly on to the shaft. The locking ring will expand into a groove inside the joint and lock it to the shaft.

9 Make sure that the lips of the rubber cover are located in the grooves on the joint and shaft. Wrap two turns of 18 swg soft wire round

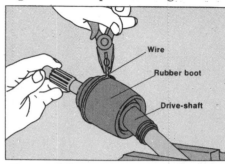

Wire
Rubber boot
Drive-shaft

the rubber cover. Twist the ends together with pliers to tighten the

wire and bend the ends flat, away from the direction of shaft rotation.

10 Reassemble the shaft back on the hub, locating the shaft splines with those inside the hub.

11 Refit the inboard-end of the shaft to the final-drive housing. Reassemble the suspension. Tighten the lower swivel-pin nut to a torque of between 35 and 40 lb.ft. Refit the steering ball-joint and tighten the nut to between 20 and 24 lb.ft.

12 Fit the centre hub nut and the road wheel. Lower the car to the ground. Tighten the road wheel nuts. Remove the block of wood from the upper-suspension arm and refit the rebound bump rubber.

13 Tighten the drive-shaft hub nut to a torque of 60 lb.ft and then tighten further until the split-pin holes line up. Fit a new split-pin. Refit the grease cap and hub cap.

FITTING INBOARD NEEDLE-ROLLER JOINTS

A knocking noise when the car is accelerated hard indicates that the rubber-encased joints at the inboard end of the shaft—that is away from the wheel—are worn. They should be renewed quickly, because the U-bolts can work loose from the damaged rubber and grind into the softer alloy axle casing. Check the casing to make sure it has not been worn away. If it has, a new casing will have to be fitted. This is a garage job.

To make a do-it-yourself repair easier, rubber-encased spider joints can be replaced with Hardy Spicer type joints, which have needle-roller bearings to reduce friction. The Hardy Spicer type of coupling is not affected by oil, which can damage a rubber-encased joint, but it does give a harsher feel to the transmission and tends to be noisier.

Note that if the old rubber-encased joint is sufficiently worn, it can be levered out without removing the drive-shaft, and the Hardy Spicer type fitted in its place.

Tools: A spanner to fit the U-bolt nuts; large screwdriver; jack; axle stands; round file.
Materials: A pair of universal joints of the needle-roller type; grease.

1 Jack up the front of the car and mount it firmly on axle stands placed under the body.

2 Remove the eight nuts from the U-bolts and prise out the U-bolts from the yokes on the drive-shaft and final-drive unit. Insert a

Drive-shaft yoke
Final-drive yoke

screwdriver between the two yokes and force them apart. Lever out the old spider joint.

3 Check the axle casing for damage caused by loose U-bolts. If the casing is badly scored have a new one fitted by a garage. Make sure that the yokes are free from burrs. If you find any, remove them with a round file.

4 Pull off two opposite bearing caps from the new spider, and make sure that the needle

rollers inside are correctly positioned. If necessary, hold the rollers in place with a little extra grease.

5 Fit the spider and the two caps to one of the yokes. Hold the caps firmly in place and push in two U-bolts to hold the joint in position. Tighten the U-bolt nuts.

6 Rotate the shaft and fit the two remaining caps to the bare ends of the spider. Move the

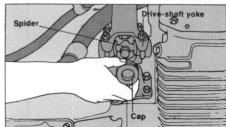

Spider
Drive-shaft yoke
Cap

shaft so that the two yokes come together.

7 Hold the caps in place and fit the two remaining U-bolts. Fit the flat and spring washer, and U-bolt nuts. Tighten the U-bolt nuts. Remove axle stands and lower the car.

Transmission /4

Replacing Variomatic drive belts

In conventional transmission systems, only a limited number of gear ratios are available—first, second, third and so on. With the Variomatic belt-driven system fitted to Daf cars, there are no such 'steps' between gears; instead, there is a smooth and continuous variation of gear ratios to suit different engine speeds and road speeds.

Drive from the engine is taken to two front pulleys. Toothed V-belts connect these to two final-drive pulleys which drive the road wheels at the rear.

At low speeds the conical flanges of each front pulley are apart; the belts ride on the pulleys' smallest diameter, giving a low gear ratio. As speed increases, centrifugal weights progressively force the front pulleys' flanges together so that the belts ride on a larger diameter. At the same time the flanges of the rear pulleys are pushed apart, so that the belts ride on a smaller diameter, to provide a higher gear ratio.

Check the condition of the belts periodically (see p. 82). If they show signs of cracking or wear, fit new ones. Never fit only one new belt; to keep the drive balanced, you must always fit new belts in pairs. Make sure that you use only belts approved by the manufacturer. Do not try to make even a temporary repair by adapting another kind of belt. It could cause damage to other parts of the transmission system.

If a drive belt breaks, you will hear it hitting the underside of the car and feel a loss of power. It should be possible to drive slowly on the remaining belt, but repair the damage as soon as possible.

Tools: Jack and axle stands; 13 mm and 19 mm ring spanners; 13 mm, 17 mm and 19 mm sockets; extension bar and ratchet; 17 mm open-ended spanner; set of metric feeler gauges; length of scaffold tube or bar (about 4 ft long) with the end covered for about 4 in. in a plastic or rubber sleeve or bound with insulating tape; two blocks of plastic or wood about 1 in. wide to hold the flanges of the rear pulleys apart.
Materials: Pair of new drive belts; clean rag; methylated spirit.

1 Release the handbrake and jack up the car. Mount all four wheels on axle stands so that the weight of the car is on the suspension (see p. 61).

2 Use a 13 mm ring spanner or socket to undo the seven bolts that secure the undertray to the bodywork. Push the exhaust pipe to one side to reach the centre bolt.

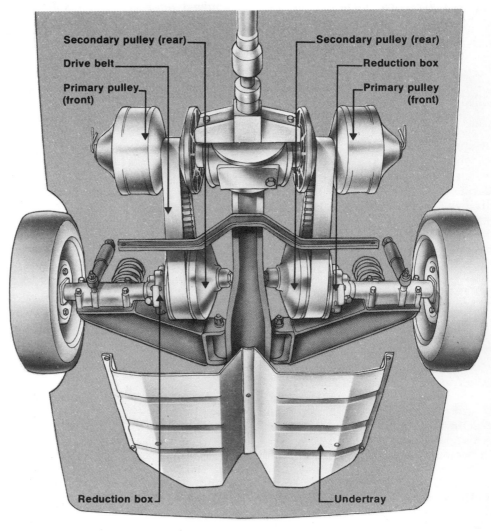

Secondary pulley (rear) — Drive belt — Primary pulley (front) — Secondary pulley (rear) — Reduction box — Primary pulley (front) — Reduction box — Undertray

3 Draw the undertray forwards, bend it down on one side and unclip

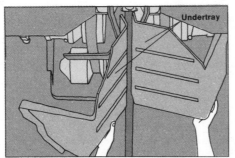

Undertray

it along its centre. Remove the two sections of the tray.

4 Use a socket on an extension arm to reach the single bolt that holds

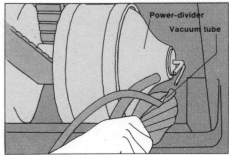

Undertray bracket — Socket

the undertray bracket to the subframe. Remove the bolt and bracket.

5 Twist the belts and look at their sides for signs of wear. If even only one belt is becoming chipped or cracked, fit a new set.

6 Wrap a piece of rag around one of the rubber vacuum tubes that are connected to the power-divider. Pull on the ends of the rag until the tube

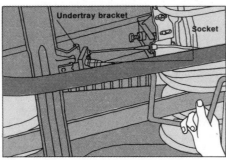

Power-divider — Vacuum tube

comes away. Do not try to hold the tube in your fingers to pull it off or you may cut your hand on the bodywork—the rag will keep you a safe distance away from sharp edges. There are four tubes, two on each side of the power-divider. Pull each of them off with the rag in the same way. Carefully examine the tubes. If they are cracked or perished, fit new vacuum tubes.

7 Use a 19 mm open-ended spanner to undo the lock-nut on the power-

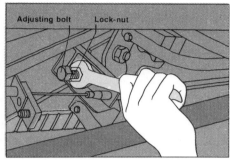

divider adjusting bolt and to undo the adjusting bolt itself.

8 Prise out the two plastic caps from the underbody with a screwdriver to

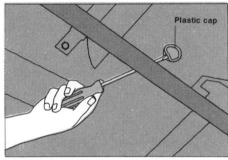

get at the two front securing bolts on the power-divider.

9 Use a 17 mm socket, extension bar and ratchet to slacken the securing bolts by four full turns. Push the

handbrake cable aside to reach the front nearside bolt; take care that the socket does not catch the cable, or it may drop into the cooling duct. Pull the belts to draw the unit forwards. The belts will slacken.

10 Make two spacing blocks from any soft material—for example,

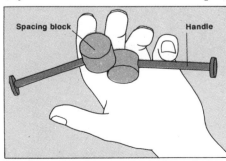

wood or plastic—so that they do not scratch the chromed surface of the

pulley flanges. Fit a handle to each so that you can put them in place without trapping your fingers.

11 Put the protected end of the length of scaffold tube between the belt at the back of the rear pulley

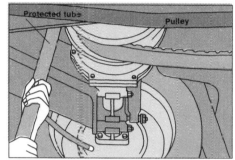

and the suspension arm. Lever the flanges of the pulleys apart; a covering of rags on the tube will protect their surfaces.

12 Insert the spacers between the pulley flanges, as near to the shaft as possible, to keep them apart.

13 Pull down on the belt to spread the front pulley flanges as far apart as possible and get the maximum amount of slack.

14 Hold the belt midway. Twist it towards the centre-line of the car.

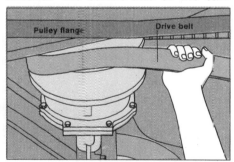

Rotate the rear wheel backwards— as if the car were in reverse—to wind the belt off the rear pulley.

15 Twist the belt and pass it over the boss of the pulley. Lift the belt clear of the rear pulley. Repeat the procedure with the belt on the other side. (Remember to keep the scaffolding tube covered when you force the rear pulley flanges apart.)

16 Use both hands to free each belt in turn from the front pulley. Discard both belts.

17 Clean the flanges of all four pulleys with a rag and methylated spirit. Make sure that there is no oil on the flange surfaces. Check the polished faces of the flanges for cracks. If they are damaged, have new pulleys fitted by a garage.

18 Slide a new belt on to the front pulley first and spread the pulley

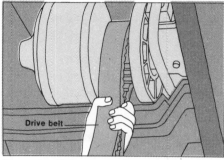

flanges. Grip the belt near the shaft to keep the pulley flanges apart.

19 Push the belt up the side of the rear pulley and twist it past the boss.

20 Twist the belt on to the rear pulley. Wind it on by turning the

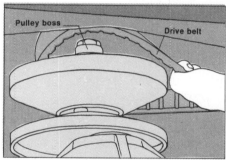

rear road wheel as if the car were moving forwards. Fit the other belt.

21 Half-tighten the power-divider adjusting bolt. Lever the rear pulley flanges apart with the covered scaffold tube and remove the spacers.

22 Turn the rear wheels until the belts ride on the outside of the rear pulleys. Then turn the wheels as if the car were travelling forwards.

23 Adjust the position of the power-divider to give correct clearance between the rear pulley flanges (see p. 83). Tighten the adjuster lock-nut.

24 Check that the power-divider unit is level by pulling the propeller shaft back against spring pressure and letting it go. If it sticks, the unit is twisted: realign it.

25 Tighten the four bolts holding the power-divider to the chassis. Refit the four vacuum pipes to the stubs on the power-divider. Make sure that the tubes are not kinked.

26 Refit the plastic caps and the undertray bracket, and bolt the undertray back in place. After 400-500 miles running, check again the clearance between the rear pulley flanges (see p. 83).

Clutch /1

Deciding whether to overhaul a clutch

When a fault in the transmission system has been traced to the clutch (see p. 211), only a motorist with a real aptitude for do-it-yourself work should consider tackling the repair and overhaul himself.

Conventional engine layout
On most front-engined, rear-wheel-drive cars, the work is straightforward—but even so it is not a job for a complete beginner.

On certain cars—for example Dafs, which have a centrifugal clutch, and Rovers, which call for specialist equipment—there is little that you can successfully undertake.

Transverse-engined cars
The gearbox on British Leyland transverse-engined cars is under the engine and it drives the front wheels. On the 1800 and 2200 models, both the engine and gearbox have to be lifted out for clutch overhaul—definitely work that should be left to a garage with heavy lifting equipment. On the Mini, 1100 and 1300 models, however, it is possible for the do-it-yourself mechanic to work on the clutch while it is still in place in the car (see p. 222).

Tools: Spanners to fit the clutch housing, manifold, pressure-plate and clutch cable nuts; clutch aligning tool; jack; axle stands or ramps; hammer; punch; strong rope.
Materials: Clutch pressure plate; thrust race or carbon thrust bearing (see p. 222); friction disc.

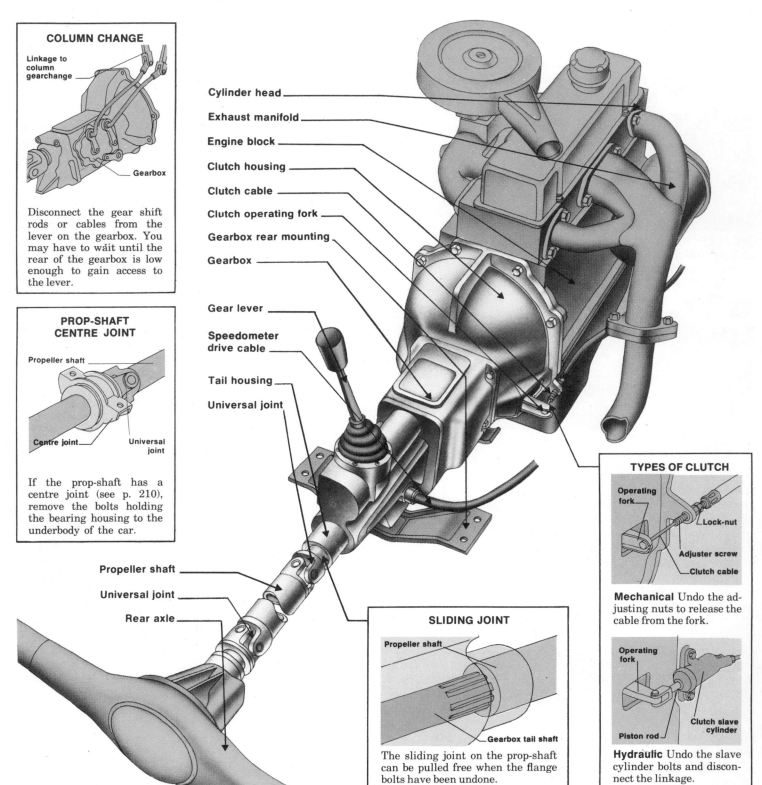

COLUMN CHANGE

Linkage to column gearchange

Gearbox

Disconnect the gear shift rods or cables from the lever on the gearbox. You may have to wait until the rear of the gearbox is low enough to gain access to the lever.

PROP-SHAFT CENTRE JOINT

Propeller shaft

Centre joint   Universal joint

If the prop-shaft has a centre joint (see p. 210), remove the bolts holding the bearing housing to the underbody of the car.

Cylinder head
Exhaust manifold
Engine block
Clutch housing
Clutch cable
Clutch operating fork
Gearbox rear mounting
Gearbox

Gear lever
Speedometer drive cable
Tail housing
Universal joint

Propeller shaft
Universal joint
Rear axle

SLIDING JOINT

Propeller shaft

Gearbox tail shaft

The sliding joint on the prop-shaft can be pulled free when the flange bolts have been undone.

TYPES OF CLUTCH

Operating fork

Lock-nut
Adjuster screw
Clutch cable

Mechanical Undo the adjusting nuts to release the cable from the fork.

Operating fork

Clutch slave cylinder
Piston rod

Hydraulic Undo the slave cylinder bolts and disconnect the linkage.

Removing the gearbox—first steps

1 Jack up the back of the car. Mount it on axle stands, or drive the rear wheels on to ramps.

2 Select neutral gear and pull the rubber boot up the gear lever shaft.

3 Press down the tabs on the washer that retains the domed gear lever cap. Unscrew the cap and remove the gear lever.

4 Release the nuts or bolts that hold the exhaust downpipe to the manifold. Let the exhaust hang down under the car.

5 Place a wooden block between the jack and the back of the sump. Jack up the block until it just touches the

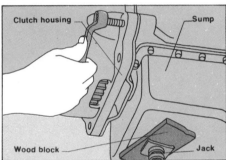

sump. If there is a steady-bracket between the sump and the gearbox, remove it. Undo the clutch bolts, but leave one loosely fitted at the top.

6 Disconnect the starter motor from the battery. Undo the bolts that hold the motor to the engine, and remove the motor (see p. 139).

7 Chalk marks on the prop-shaft and rear axle flanges to ensure they

are correctly aligned on reassembly. Remove the flange bolts. If the prop-

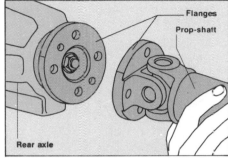

shaft has a centre joint (see p. 210) remove the bolts that hold the bearing housing to the underbody of the car.

8 Lower the prop-shaft and draw it out of the gearbox. Fasten a strong

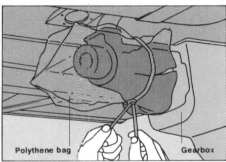

plastic or polythene bag over the tail housing—using string or an elastic band to secure it—to ensure that you do not lose the oil that could drain out of the gearbox.

9 Remove the speedometer cable from the side of the gearbox. This may be held by a single bolt or circlip, or it may have a threaded knurled cap. Remove the reversing light switch wiring, if fitted.

10 If the clutch is mechanically operated, undo the two adjusting nuts. Pull back the protective rubber boot and release the clutch cable

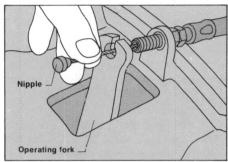

from the operating fork. Remove the boot from the cable and slide the cable from the guide bracket.

11 If the clutch is hydraulically operated (see p. 218), release the clutch slave cylinder from the side of the clutch housing. It is held either by two bolts or a circlip. This

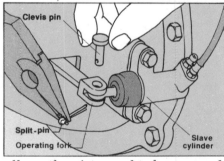

allows the piston rod to be removed. Do not press the clutch pedal after doing this, or fluid will be lost from the system.

On self-adjusting clutches, the piston must be secured by encircling the slave cylinder with string, otherwise the spring will push it out.

Taking the gearbox out of the car

1 Undo the bolts that hold the rear cross-member to the gearbox and the car body. Remove the member and lay it aside carefully.

2 Pass a rope through the gear lever hole, round the end of the gearbox,

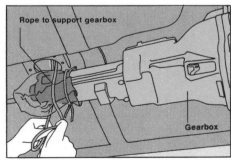

and back through the hole. Get a helper to support the weight from above the car. On heavy gearboxes always use a second jack.

3 Lower the rope and let down the jack under the back of the sump

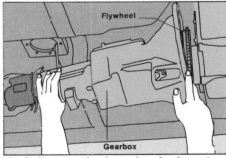

slightly until the clutch housing attached to the gearbox has cleared the engine bulkhead. Take care not to strain the engine mountings. If necessary, slacken the mounting bolts slightly. Remove the gear selector cables. Make sure the gearbox is steady and remove the remaining bolts.

4 Lie under the car and support the gearbox casing with your knees.

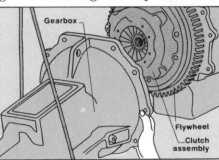

Push the gearbox straight back and support the rest of the weight with your hands beneath the clutch housing. With a heavy gearbox, make sure that the jacks take the weight.

5 Lower the gearbox gently on to your chest and pass it out to your helper from under the car.

Clutch /2

Identifying faults in the clutch mechanism

A slipping, juddering or noisy clutch is an indication of damaged or worn components. Other signs are difficulty in engaging gear or failure of the prop-shaft to turn.

The three components most subject to wear are the clutch disc, the pressure-plate assembly, and the thrust race or carbon thrust. Manufacturers recommend that if one of these components fails, all three should be renewed.

Do not buy new parts before you dismantle the clutch—it is easier to identify the correct spares if you take the old parts to a dealer.

MAKING YOUR OWN ALIGNING TOOL

1 Measure the diameter of the spigot shaft (see p. 221) with a caliper fitted inside the splines on opposite sides of the shaft.

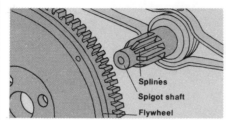

Splines
Spigot shaft
Flywheel

2 Get a piece of wood of the same diameter. Measure the smaller end of the spigot shaft which fits in the bearing in the flywheel.

3 Use a pair of compasses to draw a circle on the end of the wooden dummy shaft the same diameter as the smaller end of the spigot shaft.

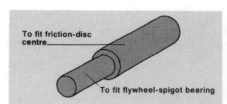

To fit friction-disc centre

To fit flywheel-spigot bearing

4 File one end of the dummy shaft to this smaller diameter so that it will fit into the spigot bearing.

THRUST RACE

Replace the thrust race if it has seized, for the pressure-plate assembly will also usually have been damaged. If the race spins freely, hold it in one hand and the bearing carrier in the other. If the race shows any in-and-out or side-to-side movement, fit a new one. If spring clips in the race hold it on the clutch fork, check that they are not broken. Fit a new race if they are.

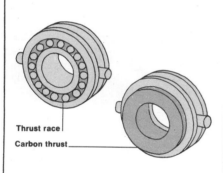

Thrust race

Carbon thrust

Carbon thrusts are fitted to spring clutches and some diaphragm clutches. On a new thrust the carbon inset stands about $\frac{3}{8}$ in. proud of the carrier. If the carbon has worn down to $\frac{1}{4}$ in., or if it turns in its housing, fit a new thrust.

DIAPHRAGM CLUTCH

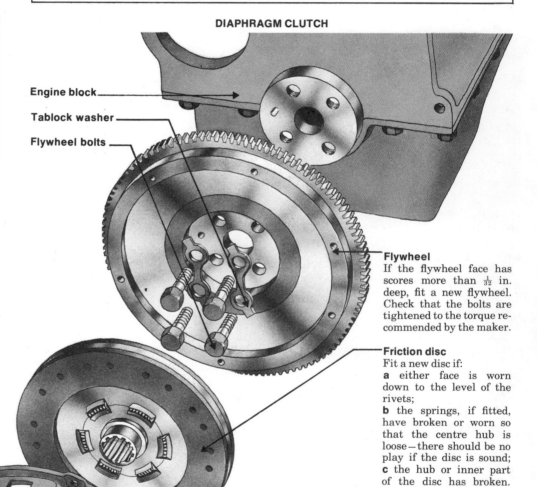

Engine block

Tablock washer

Flywheel bolts

Diaphragm

Thrust race

Pivot pin

Flywheel
If the flywheel face has scores more than $\frac{1}{32}$ in. deep, fit a new flywheel. Check that the bolts are tightened to the torque recommended by the maker.

Friction disc
Fit a new disc if:
a either face is worn down to the level of the rivets;
b the springs, if fitted, have broken or worn so that the centre hub is loose—there should be no play if the disc is sound;
c the hub or inner part of the disc has broken.

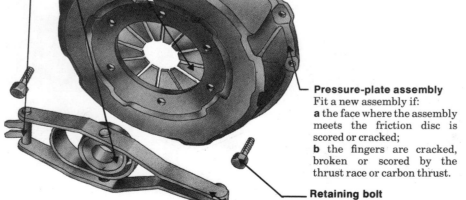

Pressure-plate assembly
Fit a new assembly if:
a the face where the assembly meets the friction disc is scored or cracked;
b the fingers are cracked, broken or scored by the thrust race or carbon thrust.

Retaining bolt

Clutch operating lever

SPRING CLUTCH

Spring

Clutch assembly

On coil-spring clutches the levers may wear because of contact with a defective carbon thrust. Fit a new pressure-plate assembly. The other components may wear in the same way as in a diaphragm clutch.

Dismantling and reassembling a clutch

1 Undo the bolts that hold the clutch pressure-plate to the flywheel half a

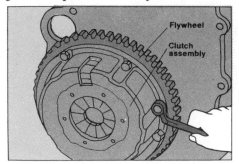

turn at a time until spring pressure is relieved. Remove the bolts.

2 Lift off the pressure-plate and the friction disc together. Clean the face

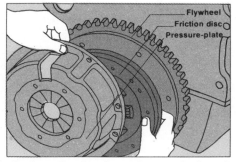

of the flywheel with methylated spirit. If the flywheel is badly scored, turn it so that the timing marks line up (see p. 164).

3 Release the locking tabs, or wire, securing the flywheel bolt heads and undo the bolts. Lift off the flywheel but do not turn the crankshaft.

Fit the new flywheel so that the timing marks line up. There are usually locating pegs to ensure that the flywheel is correctly fitted. Fit the flywheel bolts, with a new tab

lock-washer if fitted, and tighten with a torque wrench to the recom-

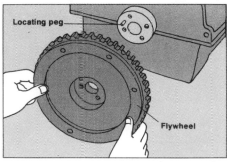

mended pressure. Bend up the tabs of the washer—or wire the bolt heads together—to secure the bolts.

4 Clean the face of the new pressure-plate with methylated spirit. Lightly grease the splines in the friction disc and the spigot shaft.

5 If the disc has 'flywheel side' marked, that side faces the flywheel. If not, the protruding centre boss should face away from the flywheel.

6 Line up the friction disc with the flywheel. Use a special aligning tool,

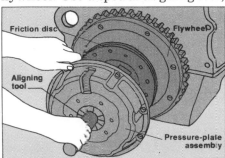

or make your own (see p. 220). Fit the pressure-plate on the flywheel pegs. Tighten the bolts, half a turn

at a time, working diagonally. When tight, remove the tool.

7 Support the weight of the gearbox. Line up the splines of the gearbox input shaft with the friction disc.

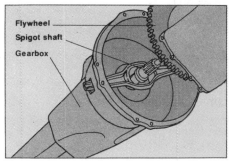

Push the gearbox home until the flange of the bell housing is tight against the engine back-plate. Fit the top clutch housing bolts.

8 Fit the cross-member to the gearbox. Jack up the gearbox until the cross-member ends are flush with the body. Fit the nuts or bolts.

9 Replace and tighten all the clutch housing bolts. Refit the speedometer cable. Fit the prop-shaft and make sure the marks on the two flanges line up (see p. 219). Connect the clutch-operating mechanism and adjust the clutch, if necessary (see p. 76).

10 Refit and connect the starter motor and reconnect the exhaust system. Lower the car. Refit the gear lever and reconnect the battery. Take the car to a quiet road and test the clutch on the road in all four gears and in reverse.

Renewing the thrust race or carbon thrust

1 Remove the clutch thrust race from the two clips in the operating lever. If a carbon thrust is fitted, pull

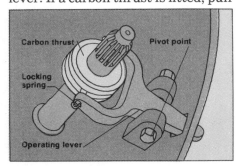

out the two locking springs from the bearing pivot stubs and lift the thrust assembly from the lever.

2 Check the operating lever for wear at the points where the thrust bearing is attached and where the lever pivots in the clutch housing.

On some models the lever pivots on a shaft. If either is worn, renew both the shaft and lever. (In some cases it may be possible to have the lever re-bushed. Ask at your local garage.)

3 On the type where the lever pivots on a fulcrum ball, check for wear at

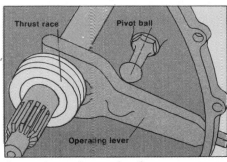

the point where the lever contacts the ball. If it is worn, renew both the lever arm and the ball. The ball is

attached to a stud that screws into the clutch housing. Unscrew it and take the parts to a dealer to make sure you get the exact replacement.

4 Fit the new thrust race to the lever. Make sure that the notches on

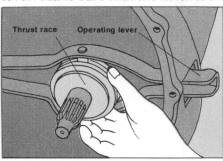

the race engage with the clips on the lever. If a carbon thrust is used, fit the two retaining springs in the end of the carbon thrust pivot shafts.

Clutch /3

Overhauling the clutch on a transverse-engined car

On transverse engines the clutch friction disc is fitted directly to the primary gear—the one that drives the other gears. The most common cause of clutch trouble is leaking oil from the primary gear oil seal. Be prepared to renew the seal whenever the clutch is dismantled. The sequence described in these pages applies to British Leyland Minis and to 1100 and 1300 ranges.

Tools: Spanners to fit the nuts and bolts on the clutch housing, starter motor and radiator bracket; socket and long bar for the flywheel nut; combined flywheel puller and clutch dismantling tool and a primary gear and seal protection tool (usually available at hire shops); ring spanners for the withdrawal tools.

Materials: Clutch friction plate; thrust race; primary gear oil seal.

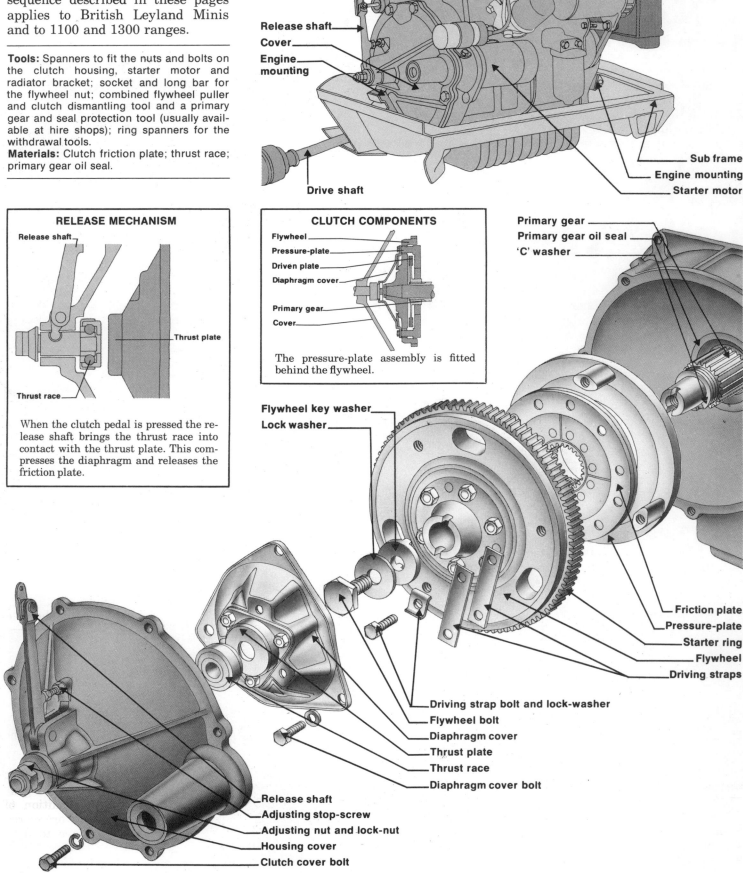

Radiator
Engine steady-bar
Clutch cylinder

Release shaft
Cover
Engine mounting

Drive shaft

Sub frame
Engine mounting
Starter motor

RELEASE MECHANISM

Release shaft

Thrust plate

Thrust race

When the clutch pedal is pressed the release shaft brings the thrust race into contact with the thrust plate. This compresses the diaphragm and releases the friction plate.

CLUTCH COMPONENTS

Flywheel
Pressure-plate
Driven plate
Diaphragm cover
Primary gear
Cover

The pressure-plate assembly is fitted behind the flywheel.

Primary gear
Primary gear oil seal
'C' washer

Flywheel key washer
Lock washer

Friction plate
Pressure-plate
Starter ring
Flywheel
Driving straps

Driving strap bolt and lock-washer
Flywheel bolt
Diaphragm cover
Thrust plate
Thrust race
Diaphragm cover bolt

Release shaft
Adjusting stop-screw
Adjusting nut and lock-nut
Housing cover
Clutch cover bolt

Removing a transverse engine clutch

1 Disconnect the battery leads. Undo the bolts that hold the battery carrier under the wing. Lift out the battery and its carrier. (This is unnecessary on the Mini, because the battery is in the boot.)

2 Undo the nuts on the thermostat housing and the bolts that hold the radiator steady-plate to the radiator cover. Lift off the steady-plate.

3 Disconnect the starter motor leads and remove the motor (see p. 139).

4 Unbolt the clutch slave cylinder from the top of the clutch housing. Draw the cylinder away but leave

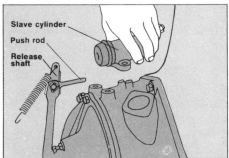

the push rod attached to the clutch release shaft. Tie the cylinder to the engine compartment bulkhead.

5 Place a jack under the engine sump at the clutch end. Use a block of wood on the jack to protect the metal. Raise the jack to the sump.

6 Undo the engine mounting bolts between the clutch housing and the front sub frame.

7 Jack up the engine until the fan blades just clear the radiator.

8 Undo the clutch cover bolts—a little at a time to avoid straining

the housing—and lift off the cover to expose the clutch. Carefully lay

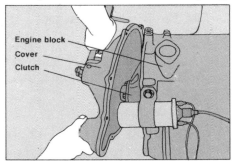

the cover aside on a clean rag or bench ready for reassembly.

9 Undo the clutch diaphragm bolts. Make sure that you undo each one

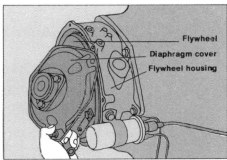

a little at a time to avoid distortion. Lift off the diaphragm cover.

10 Turn the engine flywheel so that the timing marks are at top-dead-

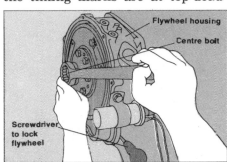

centre. Jam a stout screwdriver in the starter ring. Knock back the tab

washer on the flywheel centre bolt, and undo the bolt. Remove the bolt and the thick key-washer behind it. The key-washer has offset lugs which fit the end of the crankshaft.

11 Fit the puller to the flywheel. Screw the studs that are supplied

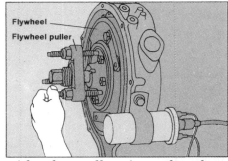

with the puller into the three threaded holes in the flywheel face. Tighten them securely.

12 Jam a screwdriver in the starter ring again, and tighten the centre bolt in the puller with a ring span-

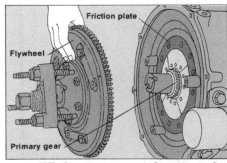

ner. While you are tightening the puller centre bolt, jar the end of the bolt with a hammer. The jolt should serve to spring the flywheel taper free. Continue pulling until the flywheel is drawn off the tapered end of the crankshaft.

13 Withdraw the friction plate and diaphragm pressure-plate.

Removing a primary gear seal

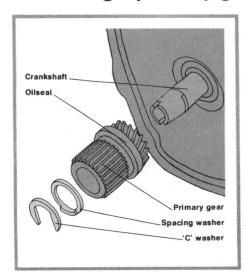

The primary gear rotates on the end of the crankshaft. Its splined end protrudes in front of the flywheel housing and its larger-diameter gear side is behind the housing. The oil seal is in the flywheel housing between the spline and the gears.

1 Slide the C-washer up from the groove in the crankshaft. Remove the bronze spacing washer.

2 Slide the special puller sideways into the groove behind the spline on the primary gear.

3 Gradually tighten the centre nut on the puller until you separate

the primary gear and its seal from the crankshaft. Discard the old

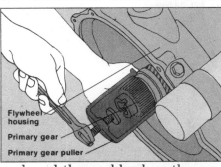

seal, and thoroughly clean the gear in petrol. Check the condition of the centre bushes. If they are scored or cracked, you will have to fit a complete new gear.

Clutch /4

Refitting a primary gear seal

1 Slide the seal protection sleeve over the splines of the primary gear to protect the lip of the new seal. Push it tight to the face of the gear.

2 Hold the new seal by its outside edge. Lubricate the centre lip with clean oil and slide the seal over the

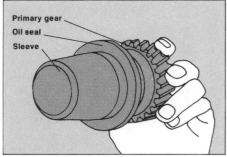

sleeve on the primary gear. Make sure that the inner lip of the seal

faces inwards. Slide the primary gear back on to the crankshaft until the outer edge of the seal just touches the flywheel housing.

3 Remove the spline protection cover and fit the seal replacement tool over the end of the crankshaft.

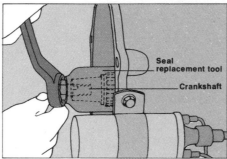

Screw the bolt into the end of the crankshaft and tighten it until the

seal is flush with the flywheel housing. Undo the bolt and remove the tool. Refit the bronze spacing washer so that the lug is at the bottom facing outwards. Fit the C-washer.

4 Check the clearance between the primary gear and the spacer. It

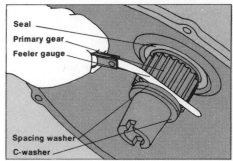

should be ·0035 in. to ·006 in. If too wide, fit a thicker spacer.

Refitting the clutch assembly

1 Dismantle the flywheel, pressure-plate and clutch friction plate. Clean them with an air pump. Clean the

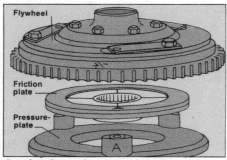

flywheel and pressure-plate faces with fine emery cloth, and wash away dust with methylated spirit.

2 When reassembling, use a new clutch friction plate. Make sure the protruding boss faces the engine.

3 Line up the 'A' mark on one of the pressure-plate lugs with the 'A' mark on the friction plate. Align both of these with the top-dead-

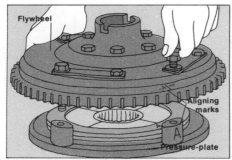

centre mark on the flywheel to ensure correct balance. Fit the three diaphragm bolts loosely to hold the clutch components to the flywheel.

4 With the friction plate still loose in the centre, slide the complete

flywheel and clutch assembly on to the crankshaft. Locate the friction

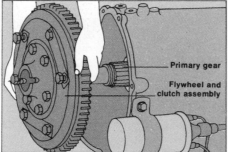

plate boss carefully on the splines of the primary gear.

5 Make sure the flywheel top-dead-centre mark is at the top. Fit the flywheel key washer. Put a new tab washer on the centre bolt and screw in the bolt.

6 Tighten the flywheel bolt to a torque figure of 110 lb.ft. (Check the figure with your dealer in case the manufacturer's recommendations have been changed.)

7 Bend the tab washer flat against the flywheel bolt head. Remove the

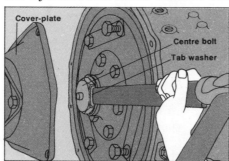

three diaphragm plate bolts. Refit the diaphragm plate and refit the bolts. Align the 'A' mark on the

diaphragm housing with the flywheel top-dead-centre mark.

8 Refit the clutch cover. Make sure that the engine earth strap is fitted

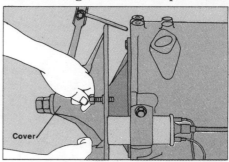

to one of the cover-bolts. Lightly tighten two opposite cover-bolts to avoid straining the metal. Lower the engine and replace the engine mounting bolts. Fully tighten each of the engine mounting and clutch cover-bolts a little at a time.

9 Refit the starter motor and radiator plate. Locate the push-rod and replace the clutch slave cylinder.

10 Check with a feeler gauge that the clearance between the clutch

lever and the adjusting-screw head is ·025 in. If necessary, adjust the screw to the correct clearance.

Windscreen wipers and washers/1

Adjusting the windscreen wiper blades

The rubber of a windscreen wiper blade should be springy and have a sharp wiping edge. If it becomes brittle or perished, change it immediately.

The blade should trail on both directions of sweep—not trail one way, and be pushed like a chisel the other. If the blade judders as it moves across the screen, remove the blade and twist the arm gently.

Refit the blade and try it again—on a wet windscreen. Keep adjusting the arm until the blade trails at the same angle when it travels in both directions.

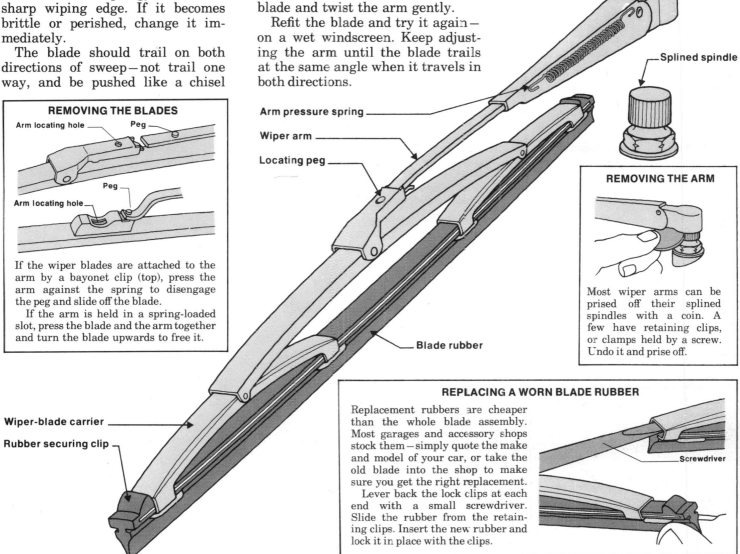

Splined spindle

Arm pressure spring

Wiper arm

Locating peg

Blade rubber

Wiper-blade carrier

Rubber securing clip

REMOVING THE BLADES

Arm locating hole — Peg

Peg

Arm locating hole

If the wiper blades are attached to the arm by a bayonet clip (top), press the arm against the spring to disengage the peg and slide off the blade.

If the arm is held in a spring-loaded slot, press the blade and the arm together and turn the blade upwards to free it.

REMOVING THE ARM

Most wiper arms can be prised off their splined spindles with a coin. A few have retaining clips, or clamps held by a screw. Undo it and prise off.

REPLACING A WORN BLADE RUBBER

Replacement rubbers are cheaper than the whole blade assembly. Most garages and accessory shops stock them—simply quote the make and model of your car, or take the old blade into the shop to make sure you get the right replacement.

Lever back the lock clips at each end with a small screwdriver. Slide the rubber from the retaining clips. Insert the new rubber and lock it in place with the clips.

Screwdriver

Checking and overhauling a windscreen washer

IF THE PIPING LEAKS

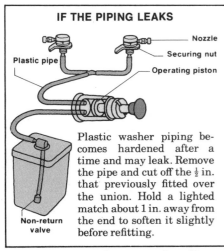

Nozzle

Securing nut

Operating piston

Plastic pipe

Non-return valve

Plastic washer piping becomes hardened after a time and may leak. Remove the pipe and cut off the ½ in. that previously fitted over the union. Hold a lighted match about 1 in. away from the end to soften it slightly before refitting.

Windscreen washers are legally required on all modern cars. Some are electric; others draw their pressure from a spare tyre; but most are hand-pumped.

The bottle must be topped up regularly (see p. 36), but do not use radiator antifreeze as it damages the paintwork. Additives, suitable for winter motoring are available from most garages and motor accessory shops.

1 Most washer blockages occur in the jet nozzles. Usually they can be cleared with a fine needle, but take care not to enlarge the jet holes.

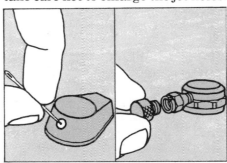

If the blockage is still not cleared, unscrew the nozzle from the bonnet and blow through it in both directions with a garage airline or foot-operated tyre pump.

2 If a blockage is stubborn, it may help to pump methylated spirit through the system.

3 Inspect the spring-loaded non-return valve at the bottom of the

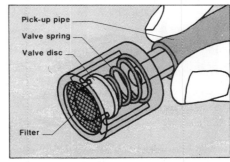

Pick-up pipe

Valve spring

Valve disc

Filter

pick-up pipe. Check that its action is free, and that the filter, if fitted, has not become clogged.

4 On electrically operated windscreen washers, check the power supply at the motor lead and at the switch terminals (see pp. 188-190).

225

Windscreen wipers /2

WHEN THE WINDSCREEN WIPERS GO WRONG			
Symptom	**Check**	**Symptom**	**Check**
Complete failure	Fuse — p. 189 Switch — pp. 190-1 Wiring and connections — pp. 188-9 Motor — p. 227 Mechanical drive — consult a garage Sheared gearbox peg — consult a garage	Complete failure (continued)	Lubrication — this page Wiring — pp. 188-9 Brushes — p. 227
		Blades park in wrong position	Adjustment — p. 225

Overhauling the rack and gearbox

Most windscreen wipers have a small electric motor which turns a connecting rod attached to a cable-rack linkage or rigid-arm linkage. Repairs to a rigid-arm mechanism are best left to a garage.

In a cable-rack drive unit, a spiral of steel wire drives the wipers on the wiper spindles. The spiral and the gears often wear at points where they touch. Turn the gears so that their unworn sides come into use.

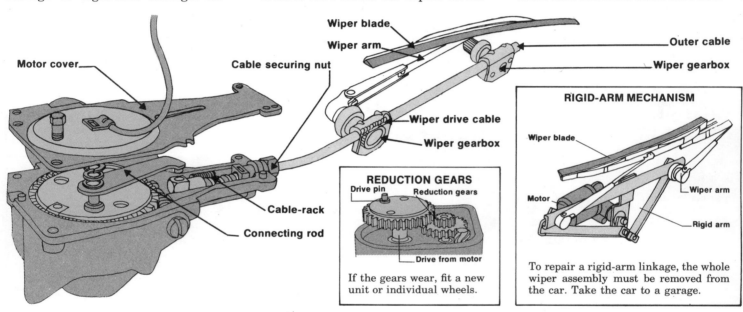

REDUCTION GEARS

If the gears wear, fit a new unit or individual wheels.

RIGID-ARM MECHANISM

To repair a rigid-arm linkage, the whole wiper assembly must be removed from the car. Take the car to a garage.

Adjusting a worn windscreen wiper cable

1 Make sure that the wiper arms are in the parked position. Disconnect the battery (see p. 36) and take off the wiper arms (see p. 225).

2 Make a mark on each wiper spindle and line it up with a mark on the bodywork so that you can find the parked position again. Undo the securing nut at the end of the cable tube nearest the wiper motor.

3 Remove the screws that secure the motor gearbox cover. Remove the

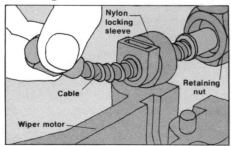

circlip and washer and free the end of the cable from the peg on the connecting rod. Draw out the cable.

4 Lubricate the gear wheel, rack and peg, with high-melting-point grease. Turn the spindles through 180 degrees so that the unworn teeth will face the cable. Mark the new position.

5 Thread the cable back in the tube with the unworn surface of the wire

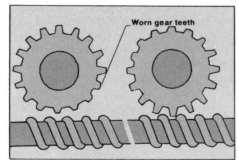

spiral facing the gear wheels. Twist the cable slightly so that it meshes with the gears.

6 Slip the cable end over the connecting rod peg. Check that the spindles are in the new parked positions. If not, take out the cable and

reset the spindles. Refit the cable and try the parking position again.

7 Replace the circlip and washer. Replace the gearbox cover and the nut on the cable tube. Reconnect the battery.

8 Refit the blades (see p. 225) and operate the wiper on a wet windscreen to check the blades' parking positions. If necessary, take off

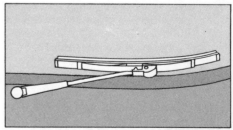

the blades and reposition them on the spindles. Make sure that you do not leave them set so that they can rest on the rubber windscreen surround. This causes perishing and increases the rate of wear.

Repairing a windscreen wiper motor

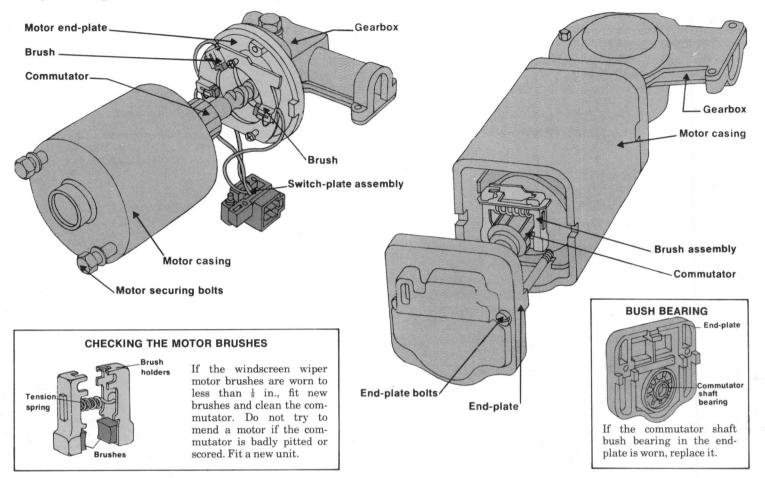

Motor end-plate
Brush
Commutator
Gearbox
Brush
Switch-plate assembly
Motor casing
Motor securing bolts
Gearbox
Motor casing
Brush assembly
Commutator
End-plate bolts
End-plate

CHECKING THE MOTOR BRUSHES

Brush holders
Tension spring
Brushes

If the windscreen wiper motor brushes are worn to less than ⅛ in., fit new brushes and clean the commutator. Do not try to mend a motor if the commutator is badly pitted or scored. Fit a new unit.

BUSH BEARING

End-plate
Commutator shaft bearing

If the commutator shaft bush bearing in the end-plate is worn, replace it.

1 If a wiper motor is not working, or if it is sluggish or erratic, disconnect the battery. Take off the wiper arms and disengage the end of the cable-rack (see p. 226).

2 Take off the electrical connections and undo the screws that hold the motor.

3 Take the motor out of the car and dismantle it on a bench. Mark the motor casing and the gearbox so that they can be correctly aligned later.

4 Undo the through-bolts that hold the motor casing to the gearbox and slide off the casing. On some motors, the plate that holds the carbon brushes is attached to the gearbox casing, and the armature comes away with the casing. Undo the brush-holder plate, which has the self-parking switch attached.

5 Other motors have brushes at the far end from the gearbox. They are mounted on a plate that is released when the through-bolts are undone. The armature remains attached to the gearbox. Remove the plate.

6 If the commutator is dirty, clean it with a cloth moistened in methy-

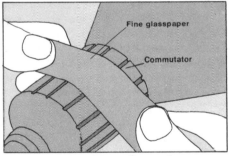

Fine glasspaper
Commutator

lated spirit. Use fine glasspaper to remove any light pitting or scoring. If the commutator is deeply scored, fit a complete new motor.

7 One-speed wiper motors have two brushes. Most two-speed motors have three brushes, but pre-1968 Lucas two-speed motors, with square

bodies, have only two. If the brushes are worn to less than ⅛ in., melt the

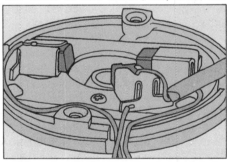

solder on their terminals and take out the brushes.

8 Obtain new brushes of the correct type. Fit them in the holders and solder the terminals if necessary.

9 Reassemble the motor and refit it in the car. Connect the cable-rack and the electrical supply, and put the wiper arms back on to their spindles. Test the wipers on a wet windscreen. Make sure the arms are parking correctly.

Replacing a bush bearing in the motor end-bracket

1 If the commutator shaft rocks when it is placed in the bush bearing in the end-bracket, the bearing is worn and must be replaced. Chip out the old bearing with a screwdriver.

2 Bathe the new bush in engine oil and squeeze it firmly between your fingers until the oil seeps through and it is thoroughly soaked. (It may help to warm the oil a little.)

3 Use a block of wood in the jaws of a vice to press the new bearing gently into place in the end-bracket. Check that the commutator shaft turns freely in the new bush.

227

Windows

Removing the trim and fittings inside the door

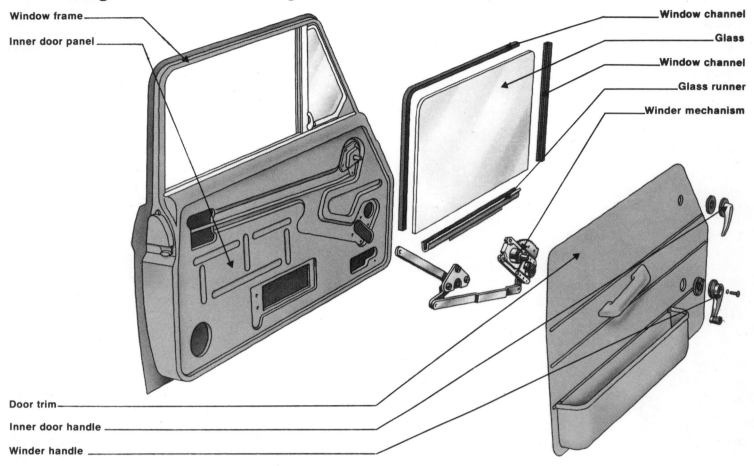

Window frame

Inner door panel

Window channel

Glass

Window channel

Glass runner

Winder mechanism

Door trim

Inner door handle

Winder handle

To get to the window-winding mechanism you have to remove the inside door panel which is usually made of plastic. First, remove the door furniture and fittings.

1 Arm rests are usually held by screws under the rest or sunk into the lower part of it. Sometimes the screws are hidden under a flap of plastic trim. If there is no sign of screws, the arm rest may be a permanent attachment to the panel. Try to remove the panel with the arm rest still attached to it.

2 On the top of some door panels there is a metal trim. Where this overlaps the plastic, it must be taken off before the panel is re-

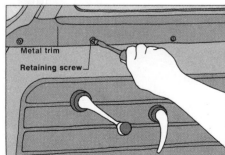

moved. Some of these trims are held by obvious screws but where there are none, the trim may be held by spring clips. Work from one end and lever off the trim with a

screwdriver. Try not to distort the metal as you remove it.

3 Handles are secured in one of three ways.
a If there is a screw in the middle of the handle, undo it and remove the handle from its remote-control spindle. There may be a shake-proof washer under the screw head and a washer between the handle and the door casing.
b Handles with a cross-pin fixing can be removed by pressing the escutcheon — the metal trim between

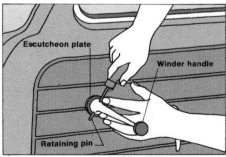

the handle and the door panel — against the door. When the retaining pin which passes through the handle shank can be seen, push it out with a bradawl. There may be a washer under the escutcheon. Refit it correctly later.
c Where a hairpin type of spring is used, push a flat piece of metal — for example a metal ruler — between

the handle and its washer. Press the spring further into the handle shank to disengage it from the groove in the spindle. Alternatively, it may be

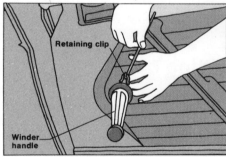

possible to pull out the clip with a piece of bent wire.

4 Flush-fitting remote controls are either fitted with obvious screws or have their fixings hidden under clip-on trimmed pads. Where there is an escutcheon, press in the door panel until the upper and lower clips of the escutcheon can be undone.

5 The door panel itself is fitted with spring clips around the edges. Lever these out gently by pushing a screwdriver or blunt chisel under the edge. Prise up one at a time and be careful: the clips may be rusty and liable to snap if too much force is used.

When the door panel is off, take off the sheet of waterproofing which may be under the panel.

Replacing a window-winder mechanism

Rain leaking down past the sealing strips may eventually rust the window-winding mechanism. It is not usually possible to service or to repair the mechanism but the whole unit can be replaced.

On most British cars the winding mechanism is a handle geared to a quadrant to which the lifting arm for the glass is attached. A spring counterbalances the mechanism. If the spring breaks or weakens, it can be replaced without renewing the whole unit.

1 To remove the winder mechanism, take off the inner door panel and unscrew the countersunk screws that hold the unit to the inner metal

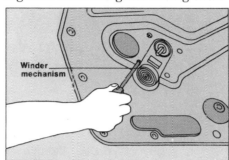

door panel. Disconnect the operating arm from the glass-lifting channel. On some cars, for example the BLMC 1100-1300 series and some Fords, there is a second bracket that holds part of the assembly to the door. Remove the three countersunk screws.

2 Lift the glass to the top of the door and tape it in place. Remove the winding mechanism through the most convenient hole. Smear the new mechanism lightly with petroleum jelly and put it in position.

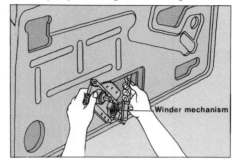

Refit the arm and secure the unit with the countersunk screws.

Adjusting cable-operated windows

Fiat The windows on many Fiats are regulated by a wire cable that runs through a pulley. If the cable becomes slack, remove the door trim and adjust the tension.

1 Inspect the wire carefully. Even a single frayed strand will cause the cable to lengthen slightly and result in faulty window operation.

2 Note that if the window regulator is to be completely removed — for example, if the cable has jammed — you should secure the cable with a clip to make sure that it cannot unwind. On most models, however, you

can adjust the cable tension, by slackening the lower pulley screws

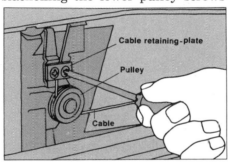

and repositioning the pulley in its slot to take up the slack. On the Fiat 850, turn the single adjusting screw in or out to take up slack.

Volkswagen A geared wheel on the window engages in the open coils of a cable. No adjustment is possible, but the unit can be replaced.

1 Remove the four screws that secure the glass-lift channel. Push the window upwards and remove the five screws that hold the window-lift mechanism, and the single screw in the ventilator frame.

2 Press the lift mechanism towards the outside skin of the door and remove it through the large hole. Lightly grease the cable before fitting the new unit.

Fitting new window channels

Window channels are in two parts — a metal runner attached to the frame and a felt or rubber insert to guide the glass. Buy replacements for the make and model of your car.

1 The rubber inserts are held by adhesive. To remove them, lower the window glass as far as possible. Gently lever out the inserts with a screwdriver. Clean out the metal

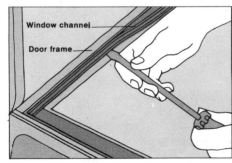

channels, apply adhesive and press the new rubber into place. Always start from the bottom of the runner to ensure that it fits correctly.

2 Felt inserts are a press fit in the metal channels and there may be a self-tapping screw or blind rivet at the upper end. Remove the rivet or screw and prise out the inserts with a screwdriver. Press in the new inserts and re-fasten.

3 Metal runners are held by screws or pop rivets. Some have tongues at the top. To disconnect the tongue,

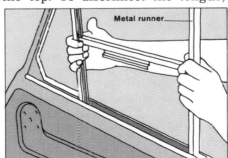

undo the screws and draw the channel downwards. Drill out rivets. Fit a new channel and secure with screws or rivets.

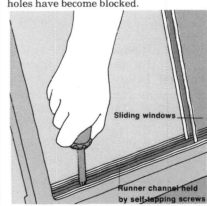

SLIDING WINDOWS

BLMC Minis have sliding windows, and the lower runner may show signs of wear — usually because the felt insert tends to hold water or because the drain holes have become blocked.

1 To renew the runner, take out the self-tapping screws or drill out the blind rivets.

2 Press the lower part of the glass inwards and remove the glass, together with the channel and the chrome retaining plate, from inside the car.

Locks and latches

Understanding how a pawl latch works

There are two main types of car door latch: the pawl type and the stirrup. In the pawl type, a latch roller slides between a striker-plate and guide bar and the latch mechanism locks into the top of the striker-plate. The latch is released by a push-button on the outer door handle and a remote-control mechanism attached to the inner handle.

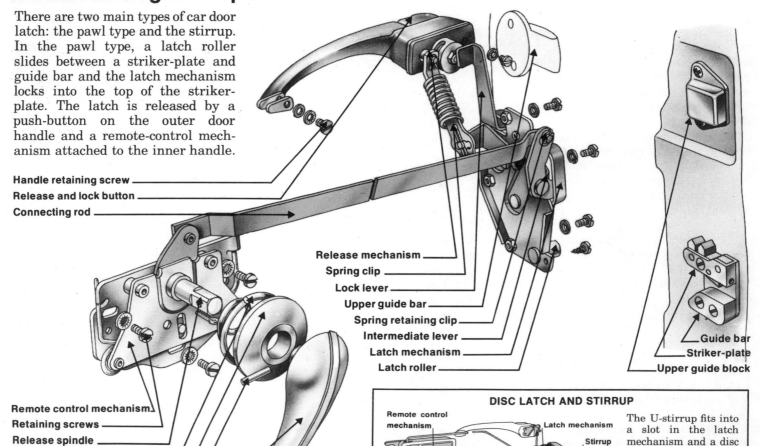

Handle retaining screw

Release and lock button

Connecting rod

Release mechanism

Spring clip

Lock lever

Upper guide bar

Spring retaining clip

Intermediate lever

Latch mechanism

Latch roller

Remote control mechanism

Retaining screws

Release spindle

Escutcheon plate tension spring

Escutcheon plate

Handle retaining pin

Inner door handle

Guide bar

Striker-plate

Upper guide block

DISC LATCH AND STIRRUP

Remote control mechanism

Latch mechanism

Stirrup

Connecting rod

The U-stirrup fits into a slot in the latch mechanism and a disc drops down to secure the door. It is released by a handle inside and a push-button outside.

Replacing a faulty door latch

Replacement parts for door latches are not readily available. If a latch fails, fit a complete new unit. There are different types of latch, but the principle of fitting the latch to the door is the same. Before unscrewing the old latch unit, make sure the internal linkages have been disconnected. The method of securing them to the latch levers will vary according to the type of mechanism.

Tools: Pliers; bladed and cross-headed screwdrivers; pin-punch.
Materials: New latch mechanism; plastic bushes; spring clips or split-pins.

1 Remove the inner door and window winding handles, arm rest and the inner door panel (see p. 228).

2 Disconnect the connecting rod between the inner door handle and the latch at the latch lever. It may be held by a spring clip, split-pin or a small nut. As the rod is pushed out, take care not to lose the plastic bush into which the rod fits.

3 Draw out the spring clip that holds the outer door handle connect-ing link to the lever on the latch mechanism. Pull the connecting link

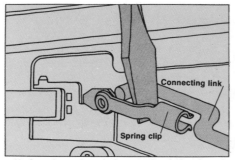

Connecting link

Spring clip

off the dowel on the end of the latch lever, and push it clear of the lever.

4 Undo the three or four screws holding the latch to the door frame.

5 On some cars the latch mechanism can be lifted off from the outside. But on others it has to be twisted slightly to clear the window-glass runners and then be removed from inside the door panel.

6 If the actual lock mechanism is damaged remove it and fit a new one.
a If the mechanism is in the press-release button on the door handle, undo the screws that hold the handle

inside the door. Lift off the handle and undo the single nut that holds

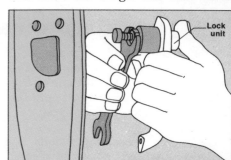

Lock unit

the lock to the handle. Fit the new lock in the same position.

b If the lock mechanism is separate from the door handle it will be connected to the handle by a lever. Remove the clip retaining the lever, release the lever. Remove the lock.

7 Secure the new latch using plastic bushes, if they are fitted, and new securing clips or split-pins.

8 Lubricate the new latch mechanism and the connecting-rod pivots. Refit the interior trim (see p. 228).

9 If necessary, realign the striker-plate (see p. 231).

Keeping the door securely closed

If a door is difficult to shut, the striker-plate may be incorrectly positioned.

The most common troubles are: the door lifts as it is closed; it closes, but engages on only the first catch; when it is fully shut the door stands proud of the body line.

If adjusting does not cure the trouble, the striker may be worn.

Tools: Cross-head and bladed screwdrivers; wax-leaded pencil.
Materials: New striker-plate.

If the door closes without lifting, but does not match the body line:

1 Mark the shape of the striker-plate in pencil on the door pillar.

2 Loosen the striker-plate screws and move it in slightly. Tighten the screws and close the door. Check the

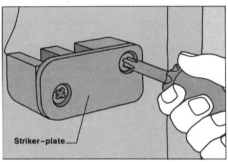

Striker-plate

body line. Repeat the operation until the door shuts flush with the body.

If you can feel the door lifting slightly when you close it:

1 Wind down the window. From outside, hold a pencil inside the door, level with the top of the striker-plate. Close the door slowly to mark a line with the pencil just above the

striker-plate. The line should be parallel to the top of the striker.

2 If the line is not parallel, reposition the striker-plate.

To fit a new striker-plate
1 Loosen the screws holding the plate to the door pillar. Remove all but one of the screws.

2 Turn the striker-plate round and replace one of the screws to secure the backing plate in the door pillar.

3 Remove the striker-plate. Fit a new striker-plate with only one screw

and remove the other screw holding the back-plate. Position the striker-

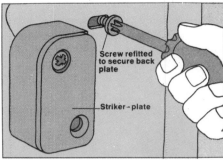

Screw refitted to secure back plate

Striker-plate

plate and fit all the screws loosely. Adjust its position and tighten.

REPAIRING DOOR HINGES

The hinge pins on which the door pivots do wear. If they are tapered bolts or serrated pins, they can be renewed.

Tools: Hammer; pin-punch; spanner.
Materials: New hinge pin; bolt.

1 Open the door and drive out the pin with a pin-punch or undo the hinge-pin nut and tap out the bolt.

2 Insert the new pin. Tap pins with serrated ends flush with the top of the hinge. Push a bolt into place. Fit the nut.

3 To adjust bolted hinges, slacken the bolts and tighten them so they support the door. Close the door.

4 Examine the gap round the door and position it by lifting or pressing on the door handle. Tighten the bolts.

Adjusting other locks on the car

Most boot catches have a U-shaped stirrup bolted to the inside lower panel of the boot. This engages a catch fitted to the boot lid. To adjust the stirrup slacken the bolts that hold it and move it about on its elongated holes. If the catch does not en-

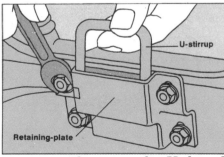

U-stirrup

Retaining-plate

gage properly, move the U-shaped stirrup upwards. If the boot lid is loose, move the stirrup down slightly. When you find the correct pattern, tighten the securing bolts.

Bonnet catches
In most cars a spring-loaded spigot, hanging down from the centre of the bonnet lid engages in a hole in the bodywork just above the grille. Just

below the hole is a spring-loaded catch that clips into a groove in the

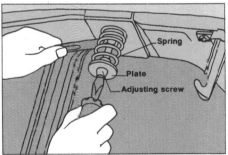

Spring

Plate

Adjusting screw

head of the spigot. There is also a safety catch at the side of the main catch to prevent the bonnet lifting if the main catch fails. The main bonnet locking catch is operated either by a knob or lever inside the car or by a catch behind the grille.

If the bonnet does not close properly slacken the lock-nut on the spigot. If the bonnet is loose, screw the spigot up. If it is tight, unscrew the spigot. Tighten the lock-nut.

Steering and ignition locks
The mechanical components of steering and ignition locks are not avail-

able as spares. If there is a mechanical failure, fit a new lock.

The lock is usually clamped in position by two bolts, whose heads—for security reasons—are broken off after assembly. These have to be drilled out before the lock can be removed—usually a garage job.

If there is an electrical fault, a new ignition switch can be fitted without disturbing the steering-

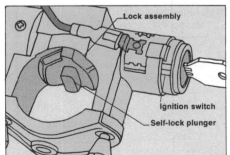

Lock assembly

Ignition switch

Self-lock plunger

lock mechanism. Disconnect the wires at the ignition switch terminals. Make a note of their positions. Undo the screws holding the ignition switch to the steering lock and remove the switch. Fit the new switch and reconnect.

Rust damage/1

When it is unsafe to repair a rusted area

Few parts of the car are unlikely to rust eventually, and there are many areas where the do-it-yourself motorist can save considerable sums of money by repairing or replacing rusted parts.

But it is important above all, before starting any work on a rusted section, to establish that the car will be structurally sound and safe to drive after the work has been carried out. If you are in doubt, seek advice at a garage.

Most popular cars today do not have their bodies fastened to a separately built chassis. Instead they are monocoque or unitary construction, where even the body panels play at least some part in strengthening the whole of the car.

If a stress-bearing section develops rust, you must have it removed and have a replacement welded in. Never try to patch it up and do not try to use any inferior replacement. If a stress-bearing part of the car is weakened either by corrosion or by a repair job, it could be disastrous in any collision. The main sections are shown below:

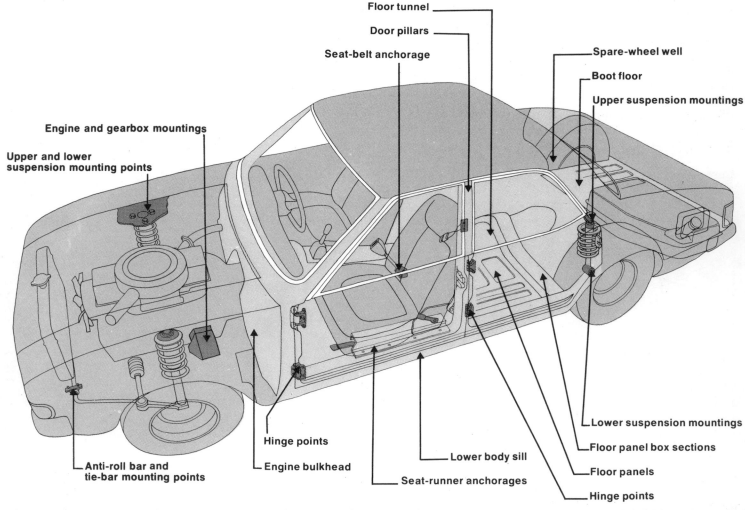

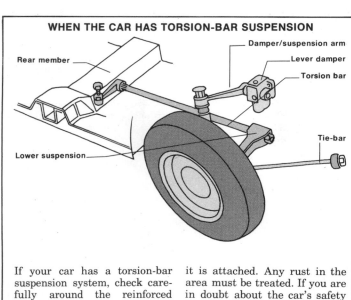

WHEN THE CAR HAS TORSION-BAR SUSPENSION

If your car has a torsion-bar suspension system, check carefully around the reinforced section of the bodywork to which it is attached. Any rust in the area must be treated. If you are in doubt about the car's safety consult a garage at once.

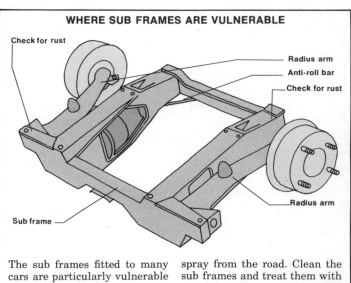

WHERE SUB FRAMES ARE VULNERABLE

The sub frames fitted to many cars are particularly vulnerable to corrosion, for they are constantly exposed to water and mud spray from the road. Clean the sub frames and treat them with an underbody compound (see p. 270). Do not treat rusted parts.

Dealing with a small rust patch

Rust forms quickly in any small chips and scratches on the paintwork. Deal with them within a fortnight, or corrosion will get a strong hold.

Tools: Screwdriver; file; fine brush.
Materials: Fine grades of wet-and-dry rubbing-down paper (grit nos. 360-400, and 400-500); white spirit; primer paint; body filler.

1 Probe the damage with a screwdriver. Rub the spot down with fine wet-and-dry paper (360-400) until the exposed metal is bright.

2 Feather the edges of the surrounding paintwork to avoid ridges after touching in. If you cannot do the painting straight away, cover

the spot with a waterproof patch which can be removed when you are ready to complete the job. But re-

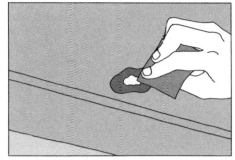

member to clean the area again, to remove any adhesive.

3 Wash and dry the treated area. Apply a thin layer of filler to the bare metal and let it harden.

4 Rub down the hardened filler to the level of the surrounding paintwork. Take care not to scratch the good paint. If you do damage the other paintwork, you will have to rub it down and repaint a much larger area than necessary. Finish off with a fine-grade wet-and-dry paper (400-500), soaked in water.

5 Wipe the area to be painted with white spirit. Use a fine brush to touch in the spot with a suitable primer and top coat.

6 Wash the new paint with clean, tepid water. Polish only when it is hard—after about six weeks—with a liquid wax polish to avoid damaging the new paintwork.

Treating rust underneath the brightwork

Corrosion attacks decorative trim and the painted metal behind it, particularly where chrome-plated steel is used. Chrome-covered plas-

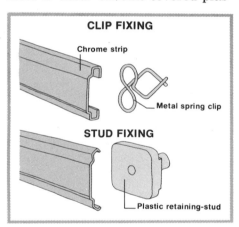

CLIP FIXING
Chrome strip
Metal spring clip
STUD FIXING
Plastic retaining-stud

tic, stainless steel or anodised aluminium are less trouble. Clean and polish chrome to prevent rust, but do not polish aluminium. Remove the trim to treat any corrosion underneath. If there are badges and

insignia, lever them gently off with a stout screwdriver.

1 Check by feeling behind the most accessible body panel which method is used to hold the decorative trim. It can be fastened by metal spring clips or plastic studs.

2 On spring clips insert a pointed piece of wood under one end of the trim. Lever gently to release the trim from the first clips. Undo all the clips in the same way.

3 If a strip is held by plastic studs, slide it lengthways off the studs. Note that these studs are often riveted to the bodywork.

4 Drill out rusted metal clips and rivet in new ones.

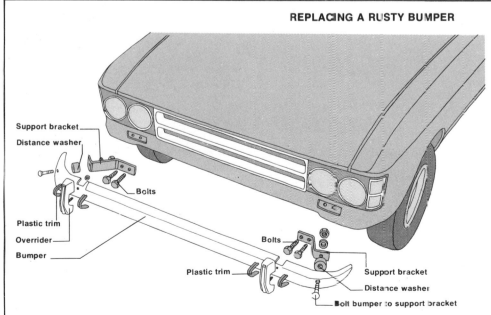

REPLACING A RUSTY BUMPER

Support bracket
Distance washer
Bolts
Plastic trim
Overrider
Bumper
Bolts
Plastic trim
Support bracket
Distance washer
Bolt bumper to support bracket

1 Undo the bolts holding the bumper to the mounting bracket. Some bumpers are also held by a centre bolt, while on others it may be necessary to remove the overriders to gain access to the bolts holding the bumper to the bracket. On some cars, the rear bumper bolts are accessible from inside the boot.

2 Undo the bolts holding the bumper support brackets to the car. If the brackets are themselves bent, damaged or badly corroded do not try to reshape them. Fit new ones.

3 Before fitting the new bumper coat the area behind the overriders with a thick layer of wax polish or a water repellent. Most overriders provide a water trap which could cause the bumper to rust.

4 Fit a replacement bumper in the reverse of the above order. If the plastic mouldings of the overriders are badly worn or damaged, try to obtain replacements—perhaps from a scrap dealer. If a distance washer is fitted, make sure its spherical face is next to the concave side of the bumper.

Bumper fastenings are often rusted, and it may be necessary to apply penetrating oil to free the nuts on the bolts between the bumper

and the support bracket. If this fails to loosen the nuts, cut them off with a hammer and chisel or a special nut-cutting tool.

Rust damage /2

Using glass fibre to mend the bodywork

Paint bubbles and rust stains are usually the first warning of spreading rust round scratched or chipped paintwork. Sand away the paint to see the extent of the damage.

Tools: Sanding disc; pliers; hammer; bradawl, paintbrush and file; scissors.
Materials: Emery paper; wet-and-dry paper (grit nos. 400-500); paint and a body-repair kit containing resin, filler powder, hardener and glass-fibre sheets.

1 Use a coarse sanding disc to remove rust-stained paintwork. Grind

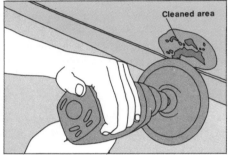

until you reach sound metal. If you have no drill, use emery paper.

2 Pull away any thin corroded metal with pliers. Hammer in the edges

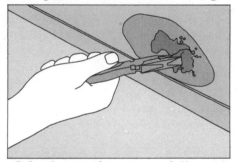

of the damaged area carefully with the ball end of a hammer to make a small, saucer-shaped depression.

Make sure that you do not distort the surrounding metal.

3 Score the edges of the bright metal with a bradawl. Cut a piece of

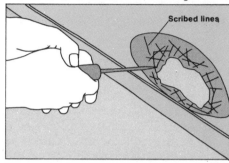

glass-fibre matting from the body-repair kit slightly larger all round than the shape of the hole.

4 Read the kit manufacturer's instructions carefully, and mix the resin and hardener in the quantities recommended. Soak the cut matting in the mixture for a few minutes, and paint some of the mixture around the edges of the hole.

5 Press the glass fibre into place against the hole and paint more of the mixture on the patch. Leave it until it has dried completely.

6 Large holes usually need several layers of glass-fibre matting. Wait until each patch has hardened before applying the next.

7 When the last layer of matting has hardened, trim the excess from around the edges with a file. Use the coarse sanding disc to feather the edges of the patch into the metal so that it does not stand proud of the

paintwork. Make sure that you do not damage the patch.

8 Mix filler powder, resin and hardener to the maker's recommended proportions. Apply the mixture gradually in layers until it is

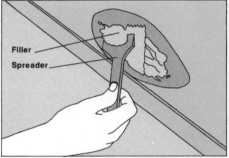

slightly higher than the surrounding body surface. Allow it to harden. At this stage it does no harm to leave the job for several days.

9 Smooth the filler with coarse paper until it is almost level with

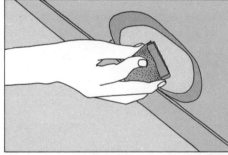

the paintwork. Shape with fine wet-and-dry (500 grit) abrasive paper. Keep it well soaked in water.

10 Fill any blemishes and sand down again if necessary. Wash the area with clean water and prepare for painting (see p. 240).

REPAIRING A RUSTED BOX SECTION

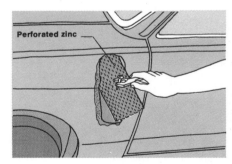

When patching closed or double-skinned sections—for example, a door panel—grind away the paint and remove any corroded metal. Spray inside the hollow with rust inhibitor. Leave it for 20 minutes, then wash down the treated surface with water. Inhibitors containing hydrochloric acid cause corrosion if left in a box section. An aerosol-type of inhibitor, containing almost pure zinc, gives good results.

To provide a key for the filler paste, roll up some chicken wire and push it into the

hole. Work plenty of paste between the wire and the inside edge of the sound metal to bond the wire into place.

Another method is to use a piece of perforated metal slightly larger than the hole. Smear paste round the inside edge of the hole and all over the metal. Push a screw into the perforation and put the metal into the hole (above right). Use the screw to position the patch against the hole. Remove the screw only when you are sure that the paste has set.

WORKING FROM BEHIND

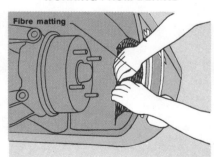

When you can reach the back of a panel put on a glass-fibre patch from the inside. The repair is stronger because the edges of the patch can be left in place instead of being sanded off. To reduce finishing time, begin by covering the front of the hole with wax-polished cardboard. Tape it to the surrounding bodywork, and apply the patch from the back. Peel off the cardboard when the repair is dry. Fill any irregularities in the glass fibre from the front.

Crash damage/1

Dealing with small dents

Slight dents on panels that do not contribute to the strength of the car can, with care, be beaten, pushed or pulled out. Avoid beating a panel out so far that it stands proud of the surrounding bodywork.

Curing a bulge can be difficult:

leave it dented and finish with filler.

Do not attempt to repair damage —however slight it may at first appear to be—if it might have affected the structural body strength; have the damage repaired professionally. Never try to beat out a

deep bodywork dent. It is likely that the metal will already have been so stretched that it will be impossible to make a satisfactory repair. Fit a replacement part (see p. 236) if possible, or take the car to a specialist body repairer.

FOUR WAYS TO REMOVE A DENT

Using a flipper
Professional panel beaters use a type of hammer called a flipper, to give the final shape to a

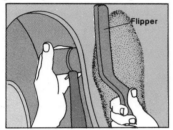

panel. Dents and marks are avoided because of the wide, slightly curved surface area.
1 Hold a piece of metal, such as a hammer head, behind the dent and tap the edges of the damaged area to draw out the metal.
2 Hold the flipper firmly and strike the dented area from above. Use short, brisk strokes to reshape the panel against the metal backing piece. Finish by filling the damaged area.

Using a jack
One way to straighten a damaged panel, when there is room to get behind it, is to press out

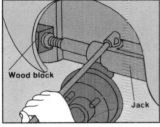

the dent gently with a jack.
1 Find a strong part of the car chassis or suspension, near the damaged area. Brace the bottom of the jack against it.
2 Hold a wood block behind the panel and gradually expand the jack until its head touches the block.
3 Gently expand the jack to press out the dent. Do not press too far. Rub down the damaged surface and fill any blemishes.

Using a drill
On some panels—for example, a door or lower body sill that is boxed in—there is no easy

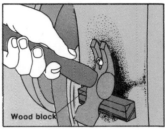

means of access to beat out a dent from behind. One way is to 'pull' out the damaged area.
1 Use an electric or hand drill to make a small hole in the centre of the dented area. Fit a self-tapping screw, leaving the screw head proud of the panel.
2 Lay a block of wood across the bottom of the dent. Fit a claw hammer under the screw head and lever gently against the wood to pull out the metal.

Curing a bulge
When a panel has been beaten out from behind, even with care, the metal may have become dis-

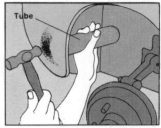

torted to form a slight bulge beyond the line of the surrounding bodywork.
1 Hold a short pipe—at least 1½ in. in diameter—with its hollow end behind the centre of the bulge.
2 From the front, strike the centre of the bulge sharply with the ball end of a hammer to make a dent in the panel. Rub down the metal and finish the repair with body-filler.

Restoring the surface finish

When a dent has been beaten out, the area must be rubbed down, cleaned and made good with body-filler.

Tools: Electric drill, rotary and orbital sanding pads; rubbing block.
Materials: Abrasive disc—80 grit; wet-and-dry abrasive paper—180, 320 and 600 grit; rust-proofing agent; cutting paste; masking tape; sheets of brown paper; resin-based filler; primer and finishing paint.

1 Fit an 80 grit rotary sanding disc in an electric drill and sand back the damaged area to bare metal.

2 Use 320 grit wet-and-dry abrasive paper and taper off the layers of

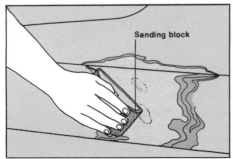

sound paintwork about 1½ in. round the damaged area.

3 Apply the rust-proofing agent to the damaged area, and leave it for

about 15 minutes. Wash the area to remove the rust-proofing agent. This is essential, because it is acid based and would cause corrosion if left. Dry the area.

4 Mix the correct proportions of the filler paste and catalyst, according to the manufacturer's recommendations. Remember that badly mixed filler may be too brittle or may take a very long time to harden.

5 Use a pliable spreader to apply the filler to the dent. Shape it to the

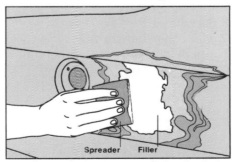

surrounding bodywork, but slightly proud, and leave it to harden.

6 Rub down the filled area, level with the bodywork, with 80 grit abrasive paper mounted on a hand

block or on an orbital sander. This gives a key for the final filler.

7 Refill any low patches, which will be clearly visible after rubbing

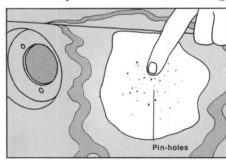

down, and check the surface for pin-holes caused by air bubbles.

8 Flatten the surface with 180 grit wet-and-dry abrasive paper, used dry. Carry on filling and rubbing until the damaged area is level with the surrounding bodywork.

9 Rub the surface, to prepare it for painting, with 320 and 600 grit abrasive paper, used wet. Use a cutting compound to clean the surrounding paint surfaces. Mask off the area and prime and paint the repaired area (see p. 239-240).

Crash damage /2

Replacing a damaged or badly rusted wing

A badly damaged or rusted wing can —on some models—be replaced by one made of glass fibre. If the original wing is bolted in position (see p. 237) the job is relatively easy. But even if the wing is spot-welded to the bodywork, it is possible to cut away the old one and rivet on a replacement glass-fibre wing.

Glass-fibre wings are available from many specialist manufacturers throughout the country. When you buy one, make sure that it is firm, with strengthening ribs, and of substantial construction. Quote the manufacturer's colour of your car, so that the replacement can be prepared in the correct colour. You then have to touch in only the seams.

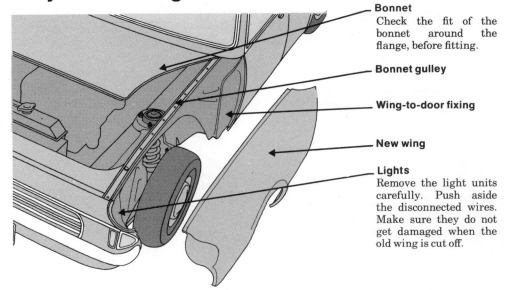

Bonnet
Check the fit of the bonnet around the flange, before fitting.

Bonnet gulley

Wing-to-door fixing

New wing

Lights
Remove the light units carefully. Push aside the disconnected wires. Make sure they do not get damaged when the old wing is cut off.

Removing an old welded wing

If the old wing is spot-welded to the bodywork, trace the line of the wing-to-body seam and mark it in chalk. The new replacement wing will give a guide to the correct shape.

Tools: Electric drill; selection of twist bits; sanding disc with coarse abrasive paper; bolster chisel; bradawl; club hammer; bladed and cross-head screwdrivers; four G-clamps; Pop-rivet kit; 2 lb. ball-pein hammer; coping saw; punch; hacksaw.
Materials: New glass-fibre wing of a matching colour; primer and paint (see p. 240).

1 Disconnect the battery leads and remove the chrome trim and badges from the damaged wing (see p. 233).

2 Disconnect the snap connector from the lamp wiring under the wing. Remove the headlamp surround and the lamp unit (see p. 192). Undo and remove the headlamp back-shell. Remove all the lamp components from the damaged wing.

3 Remove the side lamps. If the securing screws are rusted, drill

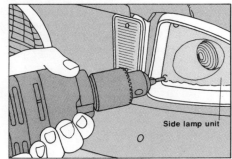

Side lamp unit

them out. Make sure that you have enough new self-tapping screws for reassembly.

4 Undo the bolts and hinges holding the bonnet to the car. On some cars it may be possible to remove only

the hinge pins: on others, unbolt the hinge plates. Lift off the bonnet.

5 On some cars it may be possible to fit a new wing without disturbing the door. On others, it may be advisable to remove the door before starting work on the damaged wing. If the door hinges have pins that can be removed, drive them out with a hammer and punch. (If necessary, unscrew the hinge bolts.)

6 Use a bolster chisel and hammer to cut along the seam between the body and the wing. Take care not to

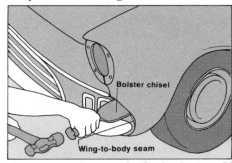

Bolster chisel

Wing-to-body seam

damage or distort the body flange. If necessary, use a hacksaw to cut round the plate where the hinge fits.

7 Use the bolster chisel to cut through the old wing where it is

Bolster chisel

Old wing

attached to the flange round the gulley. Always cut on the wing side.

8 Run a coarse grinding disc, mounted in an electric drill, round the wing-to-door flange. This will expose the spot-welds holding the wing to the door pillar.

9 Use the correct-sized bit to drill out the spot-welds along the door

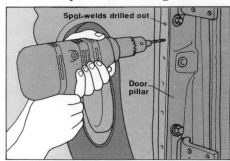

Spot-welds drilled out

Door pillar

pillar flange. Prise the wing away from the pillar.

10 Pull the old wing away from the bodywork and remove it.

11 Use a bolster chisel to trim the edges of the bodywork and remove

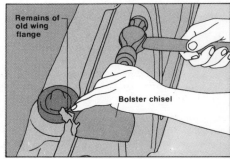

Remains of old wing flange

Bolster chisel

any pieces of the old wing flange. Check the surface of the body flanges for signs of rusting and treat them if necessary (see p. 233).

12 Make sure that you clean all the rust inhibitor off before you start to fit the new glass-fibre wing.

Fitting a pre-shaped glass-fibre wing

1 The new wing will have been shaped to fit the car, but in most

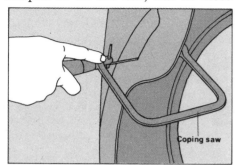

Coping saw

cases a certain amount of trimming is necessary. Trim with care, and avoid cutting the new wing flanges.

2 Clean up the edges of the body-work that match up with the wing flanges. Cut away any of the flanges that still stand proud of the body.

3 If necessary, sand down the edge of the wing flange that matches the door pillar flanges, so that the door

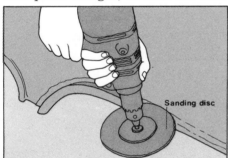

Sanding disc

fits snugly. Take care not to cut through the new wing flange. Trim the flange so that it is level with the edge of the door pillar.

4 Align the bonnet gulley and door flanges and secure the wing in this position with G-clamps.

5 Drill ⅛ in. holes at the bottom, top and centre of the flange on the

door pillar. Secure the new wing with Pop rivets.

6 Drill holes every 1 in. around the headlamp flanges. Secure them with Pop rivets to the matching flanges on the wings.

7 Drill and Pop-rivet the bonnet gulley flange to the new wing. To

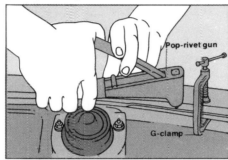

Pop-rivet gun

G-clamp

ensure complete firmness, drill the holes no more than 1½ in. apart.

8 Pop-rivet all the flanges together. Also fit rivets 1½ in. apart down the wing-to-door pillar flange. Trim the wing flange to match the door pillar.

9 Drill $\frac{5}{16}$ in. holes every 1½-2 in. round the outside edge of the head-

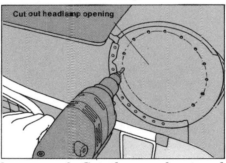

Cut out headlamp opening

lamp panel. Cut the panel out and file to a perfect circle.

10 Drill three ⅜ in. holes to take the headlamp adjusters. Replace the

back-shell. Drill the holes to take the headlamp mounting plate and

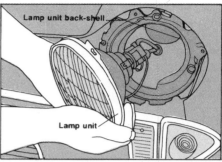

Lamp unit back-shell

Lamp unit

fix the plate with self-tapping screws. Replace the head and side-lamp units. Re-connect the wiring.

11 Use body filler (see p. 234) to fill in any areas where the fibre wing does not perfectly meet the body-

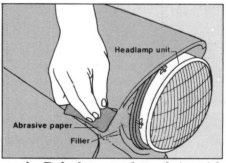

Headlamp unit

Abrasive paper

Filler

work. Rub down and touch in with primer and paint (see p. 240).

12 Refit any chrome trim and badges. Replace the door and bonnet. Make sure they both close properly. Adjust the latches if necessary (see p. 230). Replace door trim and handles.

13 If a wing mirror was fitted on the damaged section, drill a hole in a similar position in the new wing. Use penetrating oil if necessary to loosen the mirror fixing on the old wing. Lubricate the threads and transfer the mirror to the new wing.

REMOVING AND REPLACING BOLT-ON WINGS

On many cars the wings bolt on to the bodywork. Check the inside edge of the wing, at the point where it is fixed to the body, to see if you can feel any bolt heads. The bolts usually screw into captive nuts welded to the bodywork, or they have their own nuts and spring washers. Lubricate the threads with penetrating oil and wire-brush the bolt heads to remove any dirt.

Tools: Spanners to fit the wing bolts; screwdriver; axle stand and jack.
Materials: New wing; new wing bolts, if necessary; penetrating oil; sealant; paint to match the colour of the car; emery cloth.

1 Jack up the car on the side where the new wing is to be fitted. Mount the car on axle stands (see p. 61) and remove the wheel.

2 Undo the wiring to the head and side lamps from the connectors under the wing. Remove

the head and side-lamp units. Remove any trim or badges.

3 From under the wing, locate the bolt heads and undo them half-way. Do not remove them fully until you are sure all have been

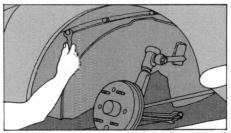

loosened and the wing is free. Remove all the bolts and lift off the old wing.

4 Clean the wing flange on the bodywork with fine emery cloth. Check that it is not

rusty. If it is, treat and paint any rusted areas (see p. 233) and allow the paint to dry.

5 Hold the new wing in position and check that it fits. Fit two or three bolts. Push the

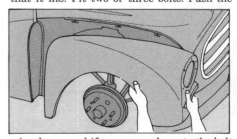

wing home and if necessary elongate the bolt holes to get the correct fit.

6 Press a sealing compound between the wing and body flanges, and tighten the bolts. Remove surplus sealant and paint the wing.

Crash damage /3

Cutting the cost of repairing a door

A badly damaged door panel can often be repaired by fitting a new outer door skin—provided that the door frame has not been damaged or buckled at any point.

Most car manufacturers supply panels that can be fitted by the do-it-yourself motorist. (Even if you think that the job is too difficult, it is advisable to buy a skin and have it fitted at a garage: this is still considerably cheaper than buying a new door.)

Remove the door by tapping out the hinge pins or unbolting it at its hinges. Remove the door handles and trim, the winder mechanism, window channels and seals and the door lock (see p. 230). Check all parts before refitting. If any have been damaged, buy and fit replacements.

Tools: Club hammer; 1 lb. ball-pein hammer; bolster chisel; wire brush; four G-clamps; electric drill; sanding disc; pincers; mallet.
Materials: New door panel; 36 and 180-grit sanding discs; epoxy resin adhesive; primer and finishing paint.

Removing and replacing a door skin

1 Fit a 36-grit sanding disc to the electric drill. Grind off the outer

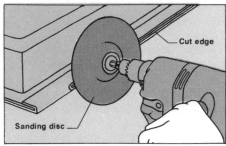

Cut edge

Sanding disc

edge of the door panel. But take care not to grind too deeply into the frame itself.

2 Lift off the lip of the panel. If it is spot-welded at any point, cut through the weld with a bolster chisel.

3 Drive the bolster chisel gently between the outer panel and the

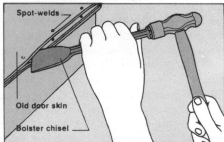

Spot-welds

Old door skin

Bolster chisel

door frame. Break any spot-welds that hold the panel.

4 Lift off the old panel. Clean the edges of the frame with a sanding disc: but make sure that you use it lightly. If the framework is rusty, treat and paint it (see p. 233).

5 Make sure the lip of the door frame has not been distorted. Use

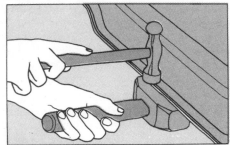

the side of the club hammer as a backing block and tap the lip level with the ball-pein hammer.

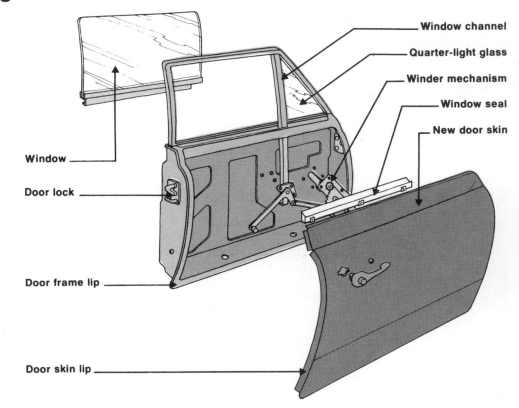

Window channel

Quarter-light glass

Winder mechanism

Window seal

New door skin

Window

Door lock

Door frame lip

Door skin lip

6 Mix a small amount of epoxy resin or metal adhesive—for example, Araldite. Apply a little at about eight points, evenly spaced, round the edge of the door frame.

7 Lay the new panel in position on the door frame and grip it firmly to the framework with G-clamps. Allow the adhesive to harden.

8 Support the door panel carefully on an even, flat surface, and strike

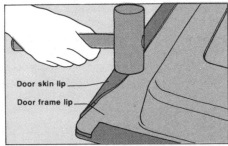

Door skin lip

Door frame lip

the lip with a wooden or hide mallet, gently bending the lip over the door frame. Tap the lip over a small area at a time until it is flat against the door frame.

9 Secure the panel at the base of the window frame with adhesive.

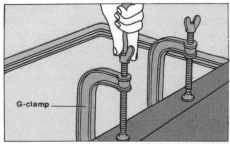

G-clamp

Clamp the two surfaces together until the adhesive has set hard.

10 Clean off any surplus adhesive when it has hardened completely with a medium-grade abrasive disc on an electric drill.

11 Make sure that all the edges of the panel are clean, and paint it with primer and top coat to match the existing finish (see p. 240). Refit the window channels and glass, window seals and winder mechanism, door lock, interior trim and handles. Refit the door to the car.

Painting / 1

The importance of repairing paintwork quickly

Damaged bodywork must be re-painted as soon as possible after it has been repaired to protect the metal from attack by rust.

Even tiny scratches in the paint-work will give rust a start from which it can spread under surrounding sound paint. They should be cleaned and touched in immediately with a brush (see p. 233). Larger areas should be sprayed with primer and paint from an aerosol can or a spray gun. Most hire shops can provide a range of equipment for car painting.

Explain exactly what you want to do, so that you can be supplied with the correct equipment and materials.

Tools: Spray gun or aerosol cans; electric drill with sanding attachment; bradawl; sharp knife.
Materials: Primer and colour paints and thinners, or aerosol cans of primer and colour; 1 in. wide masking tape; brown paper; abrasive discs and paper; paint remover; rubbing compound; cleaning solvent; metal-conditioning fluid; mutton cloths; nylon stocking; wire wool.

Masking the surrounding bodywork

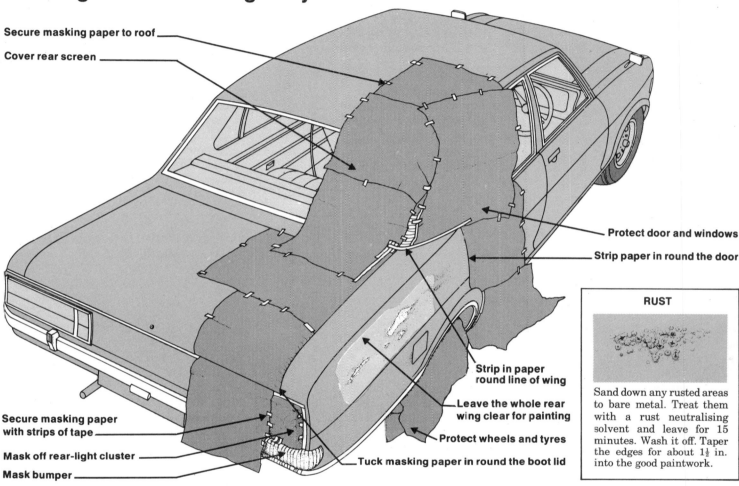

Secure masking paper to roof

Cover rear screen

Protect door and windows

Strip paper in round the door

Strip in paper round line of wing

Leave the whole rear wing clear for painting

Protect wheels and tyres

Tuck masking paper in round the boot lid

Secure masking paper with strips of tape

Mask off rear-light cluster

Mask bumper

RUST

Sand down any rusted areas to bare metal. Treat them with a rust neutralising solvent and leave for 15 minutes. Wash it off. Taper the edges for about $1\frac{1}{2}$ in. into the good paintwork.

1 Remove any badges from the area to be painted (see p. 233). If the

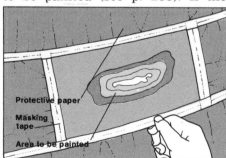

Protective paper

Masking tape

Area to be painted

damage is slight, prepare the area and mask it to leave 2 in. untouched paintwork between the damaged part and the masking tape. If the whole panel has to be painted, cover all the bright trim carefully with masking tape. The tape must pro-tect the plated parts completely, but it must not cover any of the metal to be painted. It is advisable to put on too much at first, then to cut around the trim.

2 Lay a sheet of brown paper on the car roof (or any other clean, flat surface near by) and run 1 in. wide

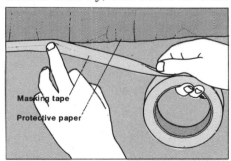

Masking tape

Protective paper

masking tape along the edge of the paper so that half the width sticks to the paper and the other half to the roof or flat surface. Leave an extra couple of inches of tape at each end of the sheet.

3 Peel the paper and tape from the roof and stick it on the edge of the area to be painted. At the edges of doors, the boot and the bonnet, stick the tape inside and fold the paper over the edge. Repeat until the area is surrounded by paper. Cover wheels that could be sprayed acci-dentally.

4 If you are spraying a door, mask the interior trim so that you can continue the paint around the edge of the door.

5 Mask all headlamps by sticking tape to the bezel right up to the edge of the area to be painted. Cut a piece of paper to cover the lamp, stick tape around it, and stick this tape to the tape on the bezel. Trim round with a sharp knife to make sure that the metal is uncovered.

Painting /2

Removing the paint and preparing the metal

Remove old paint from the area to be painted, and prepare the bare metal carefully to take the new paint. Faulty preparation will cause defects in the paintwork which can mean that the complete job has to be done again (see p. 242).

1 Use a chemical paint-remover to strip large areas. Use a bradawl or

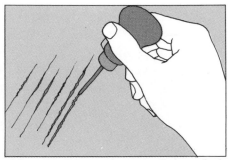

old screwdriver to score the surface so that the liquid can get under-

neath the paint. Sand off rust and any paint remaining.

2 To clear small areas use an electric drill with a coarse sanding disc. Always wear goggles for this job. Start with a coarse abrasive disc then use a medium disc. Remove the bottom layer of paint with a 120-grit disc so that the metal is not deeply scratched.

3 Scour the bare metal with wire wool and cleaning solvent, then wipe it with a clean dry cloth.

4 To provide a 'key' for new paint and inhibit corrosion, treat the surface with a metal-conditioning fluid. Neutralise the fluid according to the maker's instructions before it can dry on the metal. Do not touch the treated metal with your bare hands.

5 Clean round the whole area to be painted with a liquid cutting paste

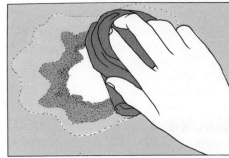

to remove all traces of silicone or wax polish, which could affect the new paint finish (see p. 242), from the surface.

6 Wash the area with clean cold water, to remove all traces of the cutting paste. Dry with a clean chamois leather. If necessary, mask the area to be painted (see p. 239).

Painting with an aerosol can

A small area of metal—a wing or a door panel, for example—can be repainted with aerosol paint. Apply primer first, then spray on colour to match the old paint on the car.

Get advice at the shop where you buy the primer and colour paints to make sure that they are suitable for each other and for the old paint on the car. If car re-spray paints and coach-builders' enamel paints are applied one on top of the other the surface may crease or craze.

Make sure that paint and propellent in the aerosol can are properly mixed—shake the can for twice as long as the maker recommends. The paint should come out in fine, even droplets.

1 Rub any adjacent old paint lightly with fine wet-and-dry abrasive paper to provide a 'key' for the new paint.

2 Hold the can upright, parallel to the metal surface and about 12 in. away from it. If the surface is horizontal—the roof, for example—do not tilt the can more than 45 degrees

or the paint may blob. Do not put on thick coats or the paint will run.

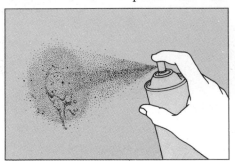

Apply the paint in light coats; two are usually enough.

3 Start spraying at one end of the bare metal and move to the other end in a straight uninterrupted sweep. Note that swinging the can in an arc is likely to make the paint patchy. Release the button at the end of the stroke—finer spray will come from the can for a moment and will blend in with any old paint left unmasked around the bare metal.

4 Move the can down slightly and spray across the panel the opposite

way, overlapping the first stroke slightly. Continue to spray back and forth until all the metal is covered.

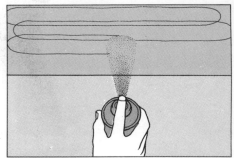

Then turn the can upside-down and give it a short squirt away from the car to clear the nozzle.

5 Let the primer dry for an hour, then rub it with 600-grit wet-and-dry abrasive paper. Soak the paper to lubricate it. Use plenty of water.

6 Dry the surface with a clean cloth and wipe it over with white spirit. If the primer is not completely even, spray another coat, let it dry and again rub down with abrasive paper and wipe with white spirit.

Putting on the colour coats

1 Buy colour paint to match the type and specification of the paint on the car. The top layer of old paint may have faded—to see its true colour rub it gently with a cloth dipped in mildly abrasive polish to remove the dull top layer of paint.

2 If the paintwork has been neglected, rub the panels adjoining the

one you are going to paint with cutting compound so that the new paint will blend with the old.

3 Rinse polished or compounded surfaces with water and dry them.

4 Spray on colour in the same way as primer, but move the can across the panel a little faster because

colour paint runs more readily than primer. Use several light coats.

5 Allow the paint to dry for an hour, then remove the masking.

6 Leave it to harden for two weeks, then rub the new paint and the adjacent old paint with fine rubbing compound to blend them together.

Painting with a spray gun

Spray guns give quicker and more uniform coverage than aerosols, so they should be used when large areas of metal are to be repainted. Guns can usually be hired. When you use a spray gun wear a mask over your mouth and nose, to pre-

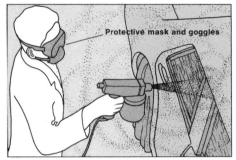

Protective mask and goggles

vent the fine spray from entering your lungs, and light goggles to protect your eyes.

1 Dilute the primer with thinner—usually 60 per cent primer to 40 per cent thinner. Always use a thinner recommended by the manufacturer of the paint.

2 Stir the mixture thoroughly and strain it into the gun through a

nylon stocking to get rid of all lumps. Test by spraying—if the

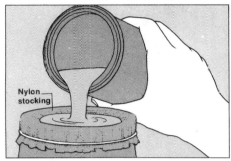

Nylon stocking

paint blobs, add a little more thinner. Shake it thoroughly.

3 Hold the spray gun parallel to the surface of the panel to be painted and about 18 in. away from it.

4 Spray on the primer one sweep at a time in the same way as for aerosol painting. To avoid runs at the beginning and end of each sweep, pull the trigger while the gun is pointing at the masking paper—where it does not matter if the paint runs at first.

5 Allow the primer to dry. If the coat is uneven, rub it down carefully

with 420-grit wet-and-dry abrasive paper to flatten it.

6 Rinse the surface with water and dry it with a clean cloth.

7 Empty the gun of paint, wipe it as clean as possible, then spray thinner through it until you are sure that the nozzle is clear of paint.

8 Wait 24 hours for the primer to harden before spraying on the colour.

9 Mix the colour with thinner: 40 per cent paint to 60 per cent thinner is the usual recommendation. Strain it through another stocking.

10 Hold the gun 18 in. away from the surface and spray on the colour coats—two are usually enough. Avoid operating the trigger jerkily.

11 Clean the gun again. Leave the paint to harden for 48 hours; then rub it over with a fine abrasive paper. Keep the paper very wet in the same way as for aerosol paint.

Giving the car a complete re-spray

For a complete re-spray, either the car must be taken off the road for some days or the job has to be done in stages, because the bare metal must not be exposed to the risks of corrosion involved in driving.

If you are able to take the car off the road, re-spray in these stages:

1 Strip the old paint off the complete car, repair any rust damage or dents and prepare the bare metal surface for the new paint (see p. 240).

2 Remove the bumpers and badges. Mask the windows and bright trim to protect them from paint. Cover the wheels with brown paper.

3 Spray on the primer, following the instructions for spray-gun painting. Start by spraying the roof and work downwards, painting the door pillars and then horizontal surfaces such as the bonnet and boot lid. Next spray diagonal or rounded surfaces such as the wings, and finally paint vertical panels. When the car is completely painted and the primer has dried it can be taken on the road.

4 Smooth down the primer coat and spray on colour (see p. 240), horizontal surfaces first. Once the colour has dried, you can take the car out.

5 Let the paint harden for about a fortnight. Then go over it with fine rubbing compound to make it shine, and wash the car.

Stage-by-stage painting
If you need to drive the car between sessions of painting, follow this panel-by-panel system:

1 Strip the old paint off one panel, repair any damage and prepare the surface for painting (see p. 240).

2 Mask the windows and any bright trim near the stripped panel and cover the wheels if necessary.

3 Paint the panel with primer. Do not drive the car until you have put primer over the bare metal.

4 Strip and paint each panel until you have sprayed the whole of the bodywork with primer.

5 Smooth down the primer and mask around one panel of the car. Paint it with colour. Continue painting each panel, masking the surrounding panels each time.

6 Leave the paint for about a fortnight, then go over it with rubbing compound and wash.

PAINTING THE WHOLE CAR STAGE BY STAGE

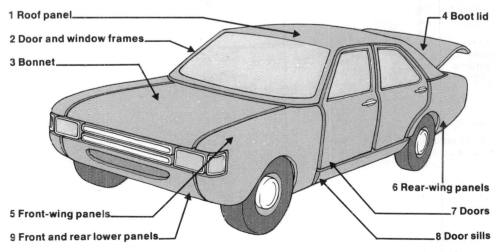

1 Roof panel
2 Door and window frames
3 Bonnet
4 Boot lid
5 Front-wing panels
9 Front and rear lower panels
6 Rear-wing panels
7 Doors
8 Door sills

Painting /3

Dealing with painting faults

The importance of careful and methodical preparation cannot be over-emphasised, for a rushed initial stage or poor spraying may cause defects to appear in the finished new paintwork.

Some of these can be dealt with by polishing to remove the defective top colour layer. Others may involve removing the colour coats completely and spraying on fresh colour over the primer.

In the worst cases, it will be necessary to strip both the colour and the primer to the bare metal. The surface must be prepared and the whole repainting job must be done again—which is not only time-consuming but expensive. Make sure, therefore, that you follow the correct stage-by-stage procedure (see p. 239) from the start of the job. Buy only good-quality paint that will match the original paintwork on the car: ask your dealer's advice if you are in doubt. Above all, keep all equipment scrupulously clean.

Unwanted paint
Check surrounding panels, particularly near the edges of the masking. If the paint is wet, wipe it off with a cloth moistened in white spirit. If it has hardened, go over it with fine rubbing compound.

Light scratches
Try polishing. If the scratches are too deep, remove the colour coat with 500-grit paper, using water as a lubricant. When the primer is exposed, mask around the area and respray colour.

Trapped dirt
Dirt trapped in the paint can often be polished away with 500 or 600-grit abrasive paper, using water or white spirit as a lubricant. Afterwards, go over the surface with fine rubbing compound. Where possible polish a complete panel to avoid a patchy appearance.

Primer showing
Thin colour-paint will allow the primer coat to show through the colour. It is caused by faulty spraying or by using too much thinner. Remove the colour coat and respray.

Teardrops
If the paint has run, try to polish away the defects with a soft cloth and a rubbing compound.

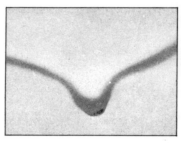

Crazing or creasing
When unsuitable paints are used together the finished coat may craze (see p. 240). Strip down to bare metal, prepare the surface and repaint with paints that are suitable for use together.

Pits
Small imperfections in the colour coat are usually caused by spraying on paint too heavily. Try to polish them out.

Ring blisters
Tiny particles trapped under the paint cause blisters. Strip to bare metal and repaint.

Boil
Bubbles are usually caused by excessively heavy coats of paint. Try to polish them away, but be prepared to have to strip off the colour coat.

Craters
These are like oversize pitting and are caused by greasy moisture which may condense in the spray gun or airline.

'Orange peel'
An uneven and mottled surface may result if the paint was not thinned enough or if the air pressure in a spray gun was too high. Polishing will often correct it, but it may be necessary to remove the colour coat and repaint.

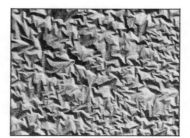

Flaking
If the old paint surface has not been properly prepared, and silicone or wax coatings have been left on the existing paintwork, the new paint will lift and flake off.

Buying and selling

Hiring a car

Deciding whether to hire or to buy

Before buying a car, study the costs of running one, and decide what the car will be used for. Your needs will be different if, for instance, it will be used mainly for shopping and local trips rather than long, high-speed journeys (see pp. 250-4).

Certain costs of owning a car—insurance, garaging, subscriptions, and depreciation—remain the same whether it is driven 50 miles a week or 500. Nor are maintenance costs necessarily less for a lower mileage. The only big difference is the cost of petrol. So if you want a car only for weekend trips and holidays, it may be cheaper to hire one.

Short-term hire

Charges are based either on the period of hire plus mileage or according to the period of hire only with no extra charge for mileage, however far the car is driven. The second arrangement is not usually available for less than three days.

Methods of charging and rates of hire vary, so compare the terms offered by several companies. You might find that a Ford Escort 1100 costs, say, £2.95 a day plus 3p a mile, but £34 a week with unlimited mileage. So if you are planning to hire for at least a week and expect to do more than 60 miles a day, the weekly rate is cheaper.

Estimate your mileage as accurately as possible, then add about 20 per cent more. On a planned 200 mile return trip, reckon on 240 miles. Remember that you usually have to pay the estimated cost of the hire in advance, and VAT has to be added.

Hiring rates give third-party insurance cover only, and the hirer is expected to pay the first part of any claim—perhaps £30 or more. You usually have to deposit this amount when you hire. If you are under 25 or over 70, you may have to pay even more.

You can have comprehensive cover for an extra payment, often called a collision-damage waiver. If you take this, no deposit is necessary. It is safer to pay for comprehensive cover. With third-party cover only, you could find yourself responsible for all repairs to the car if you have an accident—unless you can prove that the other driver was negligent.

Major hire companies operate a system under which you can rent the car at one centre and leave it at another. This can be useful in connection with rail or air trips. On an air holiday, it could save parking fees of about £1 a day at the airport.

Contract hire

Most makes of car can be hired for one, two or three years. In practice, this system—called contract hire—is used mostly by firms who run vehicles for business use. For most private motorists, it is more expensive than buying for cash. But if you drive about 10,000 miles a year, the costs might be about the same as for a new car on hire purchase.

The advantage of contract hire is

WORKING OUT THE ALTERNATIVES OPEN TO YOU

The costs shown in the table are a guide only, for small differences in cost between buying and hiring could be reversed by variations in, say, depreciation or insurance. No allowance is made for inflation. The running costs are estimated over a two-year period, and in the case of used cars it is assumed that the car is between two and four years old during the hire.

For new cars the total price includes £40-£50 for seat belts, delivery and number-plates. No discount has been included.

The hire-purchase charges are based on a deposit of 20 per cent for a new car and 25 per cent for a used car, with repayments over two years—interest rates 12 per cent a year new, 14 per cent a year used. A £2 purchase fee is added.

Standing charges include road tax, garaging, driving licence, AA subscription, interest on capital (see p. 249), and comprehensive insurance for a low rating area (60 per cent no-claim discount).

Running costs include petrol at 50p a gallon for average fuel consumption for the model.

The short-term hire charges are assessed on time plus mileage rates; weekly charges are on unlimited mileage rates. VAT and comprehensive insurance are included. Garaging is not.

For 5000 miles a year, the estimates assume 4000 miles at weekends and 1000 on holiday; for 10,000 miles a year, 7000 at weekends and 3000 on holiday.

The contract-hire charges do not include tax relief or interest on capital released (see p. 267).

Typical car	Owning a new car (bought for cash) for two years—5000 miles each year		Short-term hire—5000 miles a year for two years		Owning a used car (bought for cash) for two years—5000 miles a year	
Mini 850	Depreciation	£277.00	40 weekends (200 miles each)	£400.40	Depreciation	£188.00
	Standing charges	291.26			Standing charges	266.06
	Running costs	179.50	4 weeks unlimited mileage	117.92	Running costs	220.45
			Running costs (petrol)	120.00		
		£747.76		£638.32		£674.51
	Cost per 100 miles £7.47		**Cost per 100 miles £6.38**		**Cost per 100 miles £6.74**	
Ford Escort 1100L 2-door	Depreciation	£385.00	40 weekends (200 miles each)	£501.60	Depreciation	£240.00
	Standing charges	311.06			Standing charges	277.06
	Running costs	197.29	4 weeks unlimited mileage	136.00	Running costs	245.16
			Running costs (petrol)	147.00		
		£893.35		£784.60		£762.22
	Cost per 100 miles £8.93		**Cost per 100 miles £7.84**		**Cost per 100 miles £7.62**	
VW 1600	Depreciation	£540.00	40 weekends (200 miles each)	£616.00	Depreciation	£250.00
	Standing charges	370.36			Standing charges	315.36
	Running costs	218.27	4 weeks unlimited mileage	162.80	Running costs	267.27
			Running costs (petrol)	167.00		
		£1128.63		£945.80		£832.63
	Cost per 100 miles £11.28		**Cost per 100 miles £9.45**		**Cost per 100 miles £8.32**	
Triumph 2000 Automatic	Depreciation	£833.00	40 weekends (200 miles each)	£844.80	Depreciation	£477.00
	Standing charges	441.36			Standing charges	369.56
	Running costs	276.07	4 weeks unlimited mileage	231.00	Running costs	340.12
			Running costs (petrol)	193.00		
		£1550.43		£1268.80		£1186.68
	Cost per 100 miles £15.50		**Cost per 100 miles £12.68**		**Cost per 100 miles £11.86**	

that maintenance charges are fixed for the hire period, whereas with hire purchase the charges are likely to increase. The disadvantage is that if the 10,000 miles is exceeded, there is an extra charge of about 1½p a mile. Short-term hire could be cheaper than both, but you do not have a car continuously.

For a firm or for the motorist who is self-employed, contract hire is cheaper than buying because tax relief is allowed on renting a car. Contract hire cuts out administration costs as well as the expense of maintenance, and enables a year's operating costs to be fixed in advance. It also releases most of the motorist's available capital for investment instead of using it on a depreciating piece of equipment.

The leasing company buys the car new, maintains it and disposes of it at the end of the contract. It also provides a replacement if the hired car is off the road. The hirer usually arranges his own comprehensive insurance and pays for garaging and

petrol. He also pays a fixed rental — the first three months in advance.

The cost depends on the car required, the estimated annual mileage and what it is likely to fetch in the used-car market at the end of the contract. Cheaper contracts can be arranged under which the leasing company is not responsible for maintenance, but in that case they do not supply a replacement vehicle if the car breaks down.

Finance lease

A third way of hiring a car is finance lease. The hirer pays a fixed monthly rental, but guarantees at the beginning of the contract the residual value of the vehicle (what it will be worth at the end of the lease).

If the vehicle fetches more than the agreed value, the hirer benefits. If it fetches less, the hirer must pay the difference. A low residual value can be an advantage, because rentals are higher and bring more tax relief. In practice, finance lease is used mainly for company cars.

BUYING A SMALL CAR AND HIRING A LARGE ONE

Do not buy a large car if you need it only for an annual holiday. Consider instead owning the size of car you need most of the time and hiring a car large enough for your holiday.

Owning a Triumph 2000 Automatic

Average depreciation (1 year)	£416.50
Running costs (10,000 miles)	234.30
Standing charges (1 year)	220.68
Total	**£871.48**

Owning a Mini and hiring a Triumph 2000 Automatic for three weeks

Mini 850

Average depreciation (1 year)	£138.50
Running costs (10,000 miles)	149.80
Standing charges (1 year)	145.63

Triumph 2000

Hire 3 weeks (including insurance and VAT)	£161.70
Extra cost of petrol (2000 miles)	15.42
Total	**£611.05**

Cost of Triumph all year	£871.48
Less cost of alternative	£611.05
Total saving	**£260.43**
Saving in cost per 100 miles	**£2.60**

Contract hire — 10,000 miles a year for two years		Owning a new car bought on hire purchase — 10,000 miles a year for two years		Short-term hire — 10,000 miles a year for two years		Contract hire — 20,000 miles a year for two years		Owning a new car bought on hire purchase — 20,000 miles a year for two years	
Hire	£746.00	Depreciation	£277.00	40 weekends (350 miles each)	£532.40	Hire	£1010.00	Depreciation	£277.00
Insurance	54.40	Standing charges	305.50	4 weeks unlimited mileage	117.92	Insurance	54.40	Standing charges	305.50
Garage/Parking	104.00	Running costs	299.60	Running costs (petrol)	240.00	Garage/Parking	104.00	Running costs	507.35
Running costs (petrol)	240.00	HP charges	142.40			Running costs (petrol)	480.00	HP charges	142.40
	£1144.40		£1024.50		£890.32		£1648.40		£1232.25
Cost per 100 miles £5.72		**Cost per 100 miles £5.12**		**Cost per 100 miles £4.45**		**Cost per 100 miles £4.12**		**Cost per 100 miles £3.08**	
Hire	£838.00	Depreciation	£385.00	40 weekends (350 miles each)	£666.40	Hire	£1148.00	Depreciation	£385.00
Insurance	54.40	Standing charges	329.11	4 weeks unlimited mileage	132.00	Insurance	54.40	Standing charges	329.11
Garage/Parking	104.00	Running costs	344.41	Running costs (petrol)	294.00	Garage/Parking	104.00	Running costs	736.90
Running costs (petrol)	294.00	HP charges	180.56			Running costs (petrol)	588.00	HP charges	180.56
	£1290.40		£1239.08		£1092.40		£1894.40		£1631.57
Cost per 100 miles £6.45		**Cost per 100 miles £6.19**		**Cost per 100 miles £5.46**		**Cost per 100 miles £4.73**		**Cost per 100 miles £4.07**	
Hire	£1195.00	Depreciation	£540.00	40 weekends (350 miles each)	£814.00	Hire	£1505.00	Depreciation	£540.00
Insurance	79.20	Standing charges	395.04	4 weeks unlimited mileage	162.80	Insurance	79.20	Standing charges	395.04
Garage/Parking	104.00	Running costs	385.01	Running costs (petrol)	334.00	Garage/Parking	104.00	Running costs	823.23
Running costs (petrol)	333.50	HP charges	246.80			Running costs (petrol)	667.00	HP charges	246.80
	£1711.70		£1566.85		£1310.80		£2355.20		£2005.07
Cost per 100 miles £8.55		**Cost per 100 miles £7.83**		**Cost per 100 miles £6.55**		**Cost per 100 miles £5.88**		**Cost per 100 miles £5.01**	
Hire	£1584.00	Depreciation	£833.00	40 weekends (350 miles each)	£1108.80	Hire	£1973.00	Depreciation	£833.00
Insurance	86.40	Standing charges	478.28	4 weeks unlimited mileage	231.00	Insurance	86.40	Standing charges	478.28
Garage/Parking	104.00	Running costs	468.60	Running costs (petrol)	386.00	Garage/Parking	104.00	Running costs	993.41
Running costs (petrol)	385.00	HP charges	369.20			Running costs (petrol)	769.50	HP charges	369.20
	£2159.40		£2149.08		£1725.80		£2932.90		£2673.89
Cost per 100 miles £10.79		**Cost per 100 miles £10.74**		**Cost per 100 miles £8.62**		**Cost per 100 miles £7.33**		**Cost per 100 miles £6.68**	

A car to suit your means /1

Deciding what you can afford

Many motorists forget that the cost of a car is not only the purchase price and a few gallons of petrol a week. Depreciation, maintenance, tax and insurance must all be considered before you can be sure you can afford the car of your choice.

First establish what you can afford to spend right away—either paying for the car in full or putting down a substantial deposit. Remember the extras—delivery charges, tax and insurance and so on.

Then work out how much you can afford in weekly running costs and estimate how much you can afford to have spent overall by the time you think you will sell the car. Depreciation varies considerably from model to model.

If you are planning to buy on hire purchase, you will also have to allow the necessary amount for hire-purchase charges (see p. 266). Interest rates could add about £2 to your weekly costs for a £1000 car.

New or second-hand

For the same outlay, you can buy either a new car or an older used car. For example, there might be only a few pounds difference between a new Ford Escort 1300XL 2-door saloon and a three-year-old Triumph 2000 Mk II in good condition. But you would have to consider whether you could afford the higher running costs of the Triumph (see p. 247).

If your annual mileage is high, a new car is usually a better buy. Any faults that develop are likely to do so within the warranty period.

If your annual mileage is low, you may not benefit from the warranty to the same extent. A second-hand car might therefore be a better choice because it will not suffer the same steep drop in value.

The buying price and extras

The price of a new car will not include every essential extra.

Total price including car tax and VAT	£1200
Seat belts	16
Delivery	17
Number-plates	5
Total	£1238

The prices of these items vary widely according to the type and size of car and the manufacturer.

Usually there are optional extras which you can have fitted to the car before delivery, at extra cost. But optional extras fitted before delivery are subject to VAT and car tax. Extras fitted after delivery are not subject to car tax (which is about 10 per cent).

Money can be saved, therefore, by ordering the car without extras—such as radio, cassette player, tow bar, fog lamps and wing mirrors—and fitting them yourself or even having them fitted at a garage.

Total price including essential extras	£1238
Automatic transmission	90
Servo-assisted brakes	10
Reclining front seats	20
Metallic paint	10
Total	£1368

The price of these extras, like that of the essential extras, will vary.

Allowing for repairs

If you are buying a second-hand car, remember that you may need some of your budget for repairs. The seller should make an allowance for the cost of repairs that affect a car's handling and safety, and may be persuaded to reduce the price further to allow for other repairs.

Car costs you cannot escape

There are certain costs facing a car owner whether the car is being driven or is simply parked at the roadside. These, often known as standing costs, include licensing, insurance and—the major factor—depreciation (see pp. 9-12).

Depreciation depends partly on the car's mileage and condition and partly on the demand for it at any given time in the secondhand-car market. Depreciation is steepest from new until the car is two or three years old. For example, the trade-in price for a Ford Escort 1100 2-door saloon (just over £900 new) after two years might be £515—giving a depreciation of £390 or about £3.75 a week. After four years it might be £365—depreciation £540 or about £2.40 a week.

You can get an idea of the likely depreciation of a model by studying the prices of a similar but older model in the car-price guides. Study also used-car advertisements—these will give a guide to models in demand. If you buy a car that is likely to be a good seller, depreciation will be lower.

Smaller cars do not usually lose their price as rapidly, because the demand for large cars is limited.

Some standing costs, such as the road fund licence, are the same whichever car you drive, but insurance will normally cost more for a bigger, more powerful car. It might cost more for a foreign car (see p. 283).

You also lose money by having spent capital on buying a car when it could have been earning interest through investment. The more expensive the car, obviously the greater loss of interest.

Costs that depend on the car you choose

The most expensive single item in running a car is usually petrol. The consumption varies from car to car, but generally the amount increases with bigger and more powerful cars. The grade (star rating) needed by the car also increases the cost.

Servicing costs are similar for old and new cars, but spares and repairs are liable to be more expensive on an older car. Both servicing and repair costs tend to increase with the size of the car, but most need 15-20 hours' work every 10,000 miles. Labour charges for this work may be as high as £4 an hour depending on the area in which you live.

Construction and design also make a difference to the time involved in doing certain jobs. The cost of a particular job will be higher if other parts have to be removed first.

Some mechanical repairs—a gearbox refit, for example—tend to cost more on front-wheel-drive cars than on those with the conventional layout of a front engine driving the rear wheels.

Foreign cars may be more costly to repair because some spares are more expensive due to transport charges and import duty.

The cost of spares can vary considerably from one make to another, and it is not unusual to have to wait months for a particular part. You are more likely to get spares quickly if the car is a popular model which has been in production for two or three years.

Prices are continually increasing, but the comparative costs from one car to another are likely to remain about the same. Some cost comparisons are given in the chart opposite.

Comparing the cost of running different types of car

Small cars with engines up to 1000 cc are the cheapest to run, but their size restricts performance, space and comfort. Prices are mostly under £1000, and running costs are £7-10 a week.
Family cars with engine sizes up to 2000 cc range in price from £800 to £3500 and running costs are £10-18 a week.
Big cars with engines of more than 2000 cc range from £1500 to £16,000 and their running costs may be £15-50 a week.

Repair times

Materials not included
These are repair times recommended by the manufacturers. Operations could take longer if parts are seized or corroded

Weekly costs

Insurance for a low-rating area with 60 per cent no-claim discount

Petrol for average consumption and appropriate grade of fuel

Depreciation for two years from new

Weekly total—insurance, petrol, depreciation

Garaging, licensing, AA fee: add £1.60

Servicing costs

0-20,000 miles

0-40,000 miles
Based on the manufacturer's recommended servicing intervals and times of operation. Labour rate: £3 per hour, including VAT. Materials not included

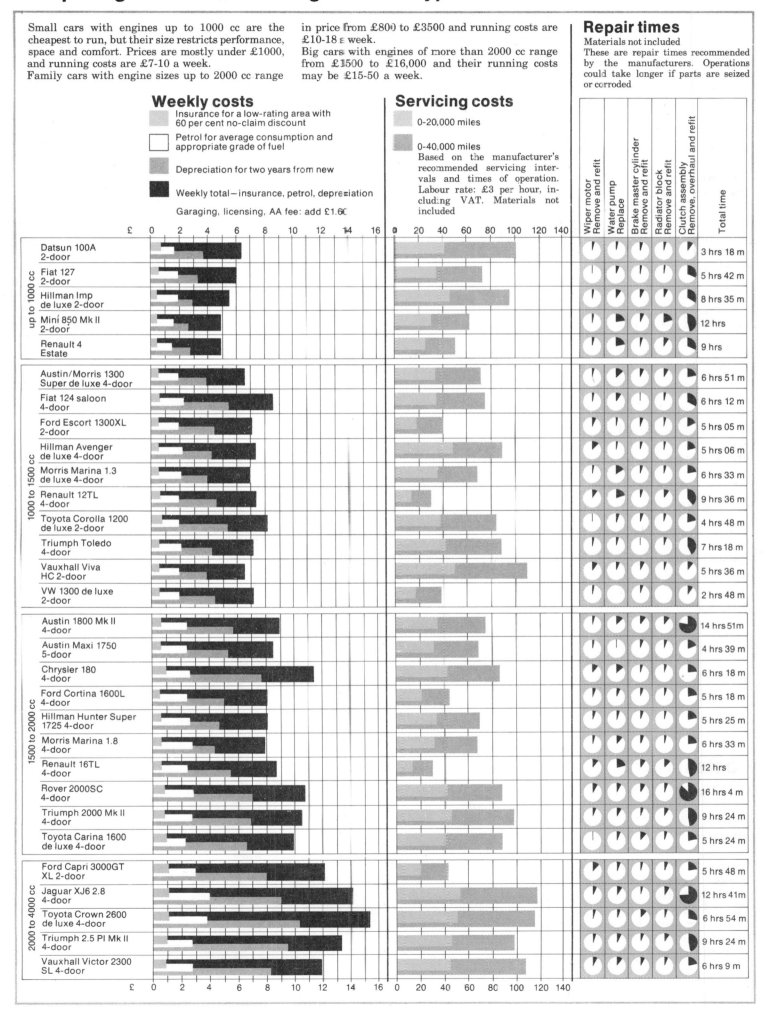

	Total time
Datsun 100A 2-door	3 hrs 18 m
Fiat 127 2-door	5 hrs 42 m
Hillman Imp de luxe 2-door	8 hrs 35 m
Mini 850 Mk II 2-door	12 hrs
Renault 4 Estate	9 hrs
Austin/Morris 1300 Super de luxe 4-door	6 hrs 51 m
Fiat 124 saloon 4-door	6 hrs 12 m
Ford Escort 1300XL 2-door	5 hrs 05 m
Hillman Avenger de luxe 4-door	5 hrs 06 m
Morris Marina 1.3 de luxe 4-door	6 hrs 33 m
Renault 12TL 4-door	9 hrs 36 m
Toyota Corolla 1200 de luxe 2-door	4 hrs 48 m
Triumph Toledo 4-door	7 hrs 18 m
Vauxhall Viva HC 2-door	5 hrs 36 m
VW 1300 de luxe 2-door	2 hrs 48 m
Austin 1800 Mk II 4-door	14 hrs 51 m
Austin Maxi 1750 5-door	4 hrs 39 m
Chrysler 180 4-door	6 hrs 18 m
Ford Cortina 1600L 4-door	5 hrs 18 m
Hillman Hunter Super 1725 4-door	5 hrs 25 m
Morris Marina 1.8 4-door	6 hrs 33 m
Renault 16TL 4-door	12 hrs
Rover 2000SC 4-door	16 hrs 4 m
Triumph 2000 Mk II 4-door	9 hrs 24 m
Toyota Carina 1600 de luxe 4-door	5 hrs 24 m
Ford Capri 3000GT XL 2-door	5 hrs 48 m
Jaguar XJ6 2.8 4-door	12 hrs 41 m
Toyota Crown 2600 de luxe 4-door	6 hrs 54 m
Triumph 2.5 PI Mk II 4-door	9 hrs 24 m
Vauxhall Victor 2300 SL 4-door	6 hrs 9 m

A car to suit your means/2

What you can get for your initial outlay

When comparing new car prices, make sure you are comparing the total prices — including car tax, VAT and essential extras. Two guides available monthly — *The Motorist's Guide to New and Used Car Prices* and *Parker's Car-Price Guide* — give current market prices including tax. For used cars they give three prices for each model, according to its condition and mileage — first class, average or good, and below average or fair. The drop in price from first-class condition to average condition is likely to be about 10 per cent. The drop between a model in average condition and the same model in below-average condition is likely to be about 20 per cent.

The price ranges shown in this table are based on the total price for new cars, and the price for used cars in average condition.

The comparisons are based on 1973 figures, and although there are fluctuations in prices from time to time the cars in each band are likely to be affected in similar ways.

Up to £300

Secondhand model	Age
Austin A40 Farini (1098 cc)	6 yrs
Ford Anglia (997 cc)	7 yrs
Hillman Super Imp (875 cc)	6 yrs
Mini 850 Mk II (848 cc)	6 yrs
Singer Gazelle Mk IV (1496 cc)	7 yrs

Up to £400

Secondhand model	Age
Citroën Dyane 6 (602 cc)	3 yrs
Ford Escort 1100 (1098 cc)	5 yrs
Humber Hawk Estate (2267 cc)	6 yrs
Morris Minor 1000 (1098 cc)	6 yrs
Renault 4 (845 cc)	5 yrs

Up to £500

Secondhand model	Age
Ford Cortina Lotus (1558 cc)	6 yrs
MG Midget Mk II (1275 cc)	5 yrs
Morris Oxford VI (1622 cc)	5 yrs
Singer Chamois Mk I (875 cc)	4 yrs
Triumph Herald 1200 (1147 cc)	4 yrs

Up to £600

Secondhand model	Age
Citroën Ami 8 (602 cc)	1 yr
Fiat 128 (1116 cc)	3 yrs
Ford Capri 1300XL 2-door (1298 cc)	4 yrs
Hillman Avenger de luxe (1248 cc)	3 yrs
Hillman Minx (1496 cc)	3 yrs

Up to £700

Secondhand model	Age
Austin 1300 Super Mk II (1275 cc)	2 yrs
Daf 44 de luxe (844 cc)	2 yrs
Datsun 100A (988 cc)	2 yrs
Fiat 127 (903 cc)	2 yrs

£700-800

New model	Engine size	Secondhand model	Age
Hillman Imp	875 cc	Ford Zephyr Four Mk IV (1996 cc)	1 yr
Mini 850	848 cc	Humber Sceptre (1725 cc)	4 yrs
Renault 4	845 cc	Morris Marina 1·8 (1798 cc)	2 yrs
		Rover 2000SC (1978 cc)	5 yrs

£800-900

New model	Engine size	Secondhand model	Age
Austin 1100 2-door	1098 cc	Austin Maxi 1750 (1748 cc)	2 yrs
Citroën Ami 8 de luxe	602 cc	BMW 2000 saloon (1990 cc)	5 yrs
Citroën Dyane 6	602 cc	Hillman Avenger GL (1498 cc)	1 yr
Daf 33	750 cc	MGB Roadster (1798 cc)	3 yrs
Mini Clubman	998 cc	Saab 99 (1709 cc)	3 yrs
Mini 1000	998 cc	Triumph 2000 Mk II (1998 cc)	4 yrs
Renault 5L	845 cc		
Simca 1000 GLS	1118 cc		

£900-1000

New model	Engine size	Secondhand model	Age
Daf 44	844 cc	Austin 1800 Mk II (1798 cc)	2 yrs
Datsun 100A	998 cc	BMW 2000 TI Lux (1990 cc)	5 yrs
Fiat 127	903 cc	Fiat 124 Sport (1438 cc)	3 yrs
Ford Escort 1100	1098 cc	Ford Zodiac Mk IV Automatic (2994 cc)	2 yrs
Hillman Avenger 2-door	1295 cc	Hillman Hunter GL (1725 cc)	1 yr
Morris Marina 1·3	1275 cc	Humber Sceptre Automatic (1725 cc)	2 yrs
Vauxhall Viva DL 2-door	1256 cc		
Volkswagen 1200	1192 cc		

£1000-1250

New model	Engine size	Secondhand model	Age
Austin Maxi 1500	1485 cc	Austin 1800 de luxe (1798 cc)	1 yr
Citroën GS Confort	1015 cc	Chrysler 180 (1812 cc)	1 yr
Daf 66	1108 cc	Daimler Sovereign (4235 cc)	4 yrs
Datsun 120Y	1171 cc	Fiat 124 Sport (1438 cc)	2 yrs
Fiat 128	1116 cc	Ford Capri 2000 GT (1996 cc)	1 yr
Ford Cortina 1600L 4-door	1599 cc	Mercedes-Benz 230 SL roadster (2306 cc)	9 yrs
Hillman Avenger GL	1498 cc	Reliant Scimitar GTE (2994 cc)	5 yrs
Morris Marina 1·8	1798 cc	Renault 16 TL (1565 cc)	1 yr
Peugeot 104	954 cc	Rover 3½ litre (3528 cc)	4 yrs
Renault 12TL	1289 cc	Saab 99 2-door (1709 cc)	2 yrs
Toyota Corolla 1200	1166 cc	Volvo 144 (1986 cc)	3 yrs
Triumph Toledo	1296 cc		
Volkswagen 1300	1285 cc		

£1250-1500

New model	Engine size	Secondhand model	Age
Austin Maxi 1750	1748 cc	Citroën DS21 (2175 cc)	2 yrs
Citroën GS Club	1220 cc	Ford Zodiac Six Mk IV Estate (2994 cc)	1 yr
Datsun 180B	1770 cc	Jaguar XJ6 2·8 litre (2791 cc)	4 yrs
Ford Consul 2000	1993 cc	NSU Ro 80 (1980 cc)	3 yrs
Ford Escort Mexico	1599 cc	Peugeot 504 Automatic (1971 cc)	2 yrs
Hillman Hunter GLS	1725 cc	Porsche 911T (2341 cc)	6 yrs
Renault 16 TL	1565 cc	Rover 2000 SC (1978 cc)	2 yrs
Toyota Carina 1600	1588 cc	Toyota Crown 2600 (2563 cc)	2 yrs
Vauxhall Magnum 2-door	2279 cc	Triumph TR6 PI (2498 cc)	1 yr
Volkswagen 1600 A	1584 cc	Vauxhall Ventora FE (3294 cc)	1 yr
Volkswagen Passat	1296 cc		

£1500-1750

New model	Engine size	Secondhand model	Age
Audi 80L 2-door	1296 cc	BMW 2000 Automatic (1990 cc)	2 yrs
Chrysler 180	1812 cc	Citroën DS 21 (2175 cc)	1 yr
Datsun 180B SSS	1770 cc	Jaguar XJ6 4·2 litre (4235 cc)	5 yrs
Ford Consul 2500L	2495 cc	Reliant Scimitar GTE (2994 cc)	2 yrs
Mazda 1800 Estate	1796 cc		
Opel Ascona 1900SR	1897 cc		
Peugeot 404	1618 cc		
Renault 17 TL	1565 cc		
Toyota Corona 2000 Mk II	1968 cc		
Triumph Dolomite	1854 cc		
Wolseley Six	2227 cc		

£1750-2000

New model	Engine size	Secondhand model	Age
Audi 80LS	1470 cc	Aston Martin DB6 (3995 cc)	6 yrs
Citroën D Super 5-21	1985 cc	Bentley S V8 (6230 cc)	11 yrs
Ford Capri 3000 GT	2994 cc	BMW 2002 (1990 cc)	1 yr
Mazda RX-2 Coupé	2292 cc	Citroën DS20 (1985 cc)	1 yr
Opel Rekord	1897 cc	Daimler Sovereign 2·8	3 yrs
Peugeot 504	1971 cc	Ford Mustang Coupé (4946 cc)	2 yrs
Toyota Corona 2000 Mk II	1968 cc	Jaguar E-type 4·2, open 2-seater	3 yrs
Triumph 2000 Mk II	1998 cc	Mercedes 2208 (2197 cc)	3 yrs
Vauxhall Ventora	3294 cc	Rolls-Royce Silver Cloud 6·3 V8	13 yrs
Volkswagen 412LE	1679 cc		
Volvo 144	1986 cc		

£2000-2500

New model	Engine size	Secondhand model	Age
Audi 100LS	1760 cc	Aston Martin DB6 (1871 cc)	5 yrs
BMW 2000	1990 cc	Bentley Continental SS (6·3 V8) (6230 cc)	13 yrs
Citroën DS23	2347 cc	Jaguar XJ6 4·2 (4235 cc)	4 yrs
Fiat 124 Coupé 1800	1756 cc	Mercedes 250 2·8 (2496 cc)	3 yrs
Renault 17TS	1565 cc	NSU Ro 80 (1980 cc)	1 yr
Rover 2200	2200 cc	Triumph Stag V8 (2997 cc)	2 yrs
Rover 3500S	3538 cc		
Saab 991 EA4	1985 cc		
Toyota Corona 2600	2563 cc		
Volvo 144S	1986 cc		

Deciding between power and comfort

Many manufacturers extend the range of models they can offer by combining a number of different engine sizes with a whole range of body sizes and styles, and differing standards of luxury or comfort.

The Ford Cortina, for example, is available in about thirty different sizes — involving three engines, three styles of bodywork, five different trim packs, plus optional automatic transmission throughout the range.

The twelve available versions of the Cortina 1600 alone show the variations in price for different body shapes and trim packages.

Trim	2-door saloon	4-door saloon	Estate car
Basic	£1056	£1092	£1214
L	£1099	£1136	£1257
XL	£1213	£1250	£1373
GT	£1268	£1305	–
GXL	–	£1468	–

What you might get in a trim pack

The trim packs or groups of accessories available vary from one manufacturer to another, but they are generally identified by code letters, which are explained in the manufacturers' advertising leaflets. There is no standard name or method of coding, but the brochures available in car showrooms usually explain

De luxe	Carpets (the basic model may have rubber mats) Reclining seats Radial-ply tyres Sun visors Reversing lamps
Super luxe	Additional outside and inside decoration Heated rear window Fully reclining seats Electric clock Anti-dazzle dipping mirror Folding armrest for rear seat
Grande luxe	Pile carpeting Vinyl roof trim Padded armrests Extra instruments Push-button radio Halogen headlamps

what you can buy. Each pack generally includes the accessories and other items available in cheaper packages within the range. Remember that you may not want all the items in one of the more expensive packs. You can save money by choosing only one or two items from a luxurious package as individual extras on a cheaper model.

	De luxe	Super luxe
Total price with essential extras	£1200	£1300
Heated rear window	£15	included
Total	£1215	£1300

The choices in one price range

The choice in any one price bracket is usually between a more powerful model with very basic fittings and one with a smaller (and therefore cheaper-to-run) engine, and more luxurious trim and accessories.

1300 4-door saloon	£1043
1300 2-door L saloon	£1049
1300 4-door L saloon	£1086
1600 2-door L saloon	£1099
1600 2-door XL saloon	£1213
2000 4-door L saloon	£1203
1300 L Estate	£1226
1600 4-door L saloon—automatic	£1226
1600 4-door GT saloon	£1305
2000 2-door GT saloon	£1320

Working out the total cost

When you have decided the approximate price range that you can afford, it is worth while trying to work out the total weekly costs you are likely to incur for any models that apparently cost about the same.

The table shows that although at least three cars are available for the capital outlay that can be afforded — in this case, £800 — the weekly cost varies considerably, partly because of the difference in depreciation between models, and partly because the running costs also differ.

Note that the figures for each do not rise together. In some cases depreciation is low, yet the cost of repairs is high. In others, increases in insurance and petrol consumption may affect the overall total.

The examples in the table are based on figures available every year in the *AA Schedule of Estimated Running Costs*. The details are not available in that schedule for each make of car, but many of the motoring magazines publish regular articles on used cars, showing the kind of expenditure you can expect on repairs and maintenance. There is certainly enough information available, from these sources combined, to allow you to work out the totals for your own particular circumstances and choice of cars.

CAPITAL AVAILABLE £800	Renault 4 748 cc New	Hillman Avenger de luxe 4-door 1248 cc 1 year old good condition	Triumph 2000 1998 cc 4 years old average condition
Buying price	£725.00	£770.00	£730.00
Extras/Repairs	40.00	20.00	30.00
Total price	£765.00	£790.00	£760.00
Trade-in after 2 years	£470.00	£500.00	£500.00
Depreciation	£295.00	£290.00	£260.00
Operating costs for 1 year (10,000 miles)			
Average depreciation	£147.50	£145.00	£170.00
Road tax	25.00	25.00	25.00
Driving licence	.25	.25	.25
AA subscription	5.50	5.50	5.50
Interest on capital	38.25	39.50	38.00
Insurance	27.20	31.60	44.00
Petrol	142.85	157.23	192.30
Oil	6.10	7.60	9.60
Tyres	11.10	12.90	15.20
Servicing	18.00	19.30	20.02
Repairs (estimate)	10.00	20.00	90.00
Total	£431.75	£463.88	£609.87
Weekly cost	**8.30**	**8.92**	**11.72**
Garaging	1.00	1.00	1.00
Total with garaging	£9.30	£9.92	£12.72

In the table, interest on capital has been calculated at a rate of 5 per cent per year, representing what you might expect to get if you decided to invest your capital.

Insurance is comprehensive for a low-rating area (see p. 282), with a 60 per cent no-claim discount (see p. 285).

Petrol costs are estimated on typical fuel consumption and recommended grades.

Oil, tyres, repairs and servicing costs are the averages given in the *AA Schedule of Estimated Running Costs* for the appropriate engine capacities.

The figure for the driving licence represents a £5 licence, which is valid for the lifetime of the driver, held over a period of 20 years.

All costs are based on late-1973 figures.

A car to fit your needs /1

Comparing the cars available in your price range

When you have decided the amount you can afford to spend, both on buying the car and on its week-to-week maintenance, consider what kind of car will best fit your needs. Choosing the right car can be your biggest single money-saver.

Remember that the larger the car you choose, the higher are likely to be the running costs and the more expensive it will be to take it abroad on holiday (see p. 24). Take account, too, of the sort of car that will keep its value.

Whether you intend to buy new or secondhand, two of the best sources of information for a potential buyer are the specifications published in manufacturers' brochures, and the details included in road test reports. Some entries are self-explanatory; others are more formidable for the motorist with little or no technical knowledge. Yet the information given can provide a useful pointer to the type of car you actually need.

Not all manufacturers and reports give the same information, but these excerpts are from a typical example.

Understanding the manufacturer's specification

ENGINE			
Front-engine rear-wheel drive			
Cylinders	4-in-line	Valve gear	Overhead; push-rod and rockers
Main bearings	5		
Cooling system	Water; pump, fan and thermostat	Carburettor	1 Ford GPD downdraught carburettor
Bore	81·0 mm. (3·19 in.)	Fuel pump	AC mechanical
Stroke	63·0 mm. (2·48 in.)	Oil filter	Full flow, renewable element
Displacement	1297 cc (79·2 cu. in.)	Maximum power	57 bhp (DIN) at 5500 rpm
Compression ratio	9·0:1 Min. octane rating 97	Maximum torque	67 lb.ft (DIN) at 3000 rpm

FRONT-ENGINE REAR-WHEEL DRIVE
The engine may be at the front or back of the car, driving either the front or rear wheels. It may be transverse (across the car, as in the BLMC Mini and 1100), with cylinders laid flat (Volkswagen Beetle), or in a front-back style (Ford Cortina). A transverse engine allows more passenger space; an engine at the rear generally means restricted luggage space at the front.

CYLINDERS
Cylinders can be positioned in a straight line, in a V formation, or horizontally opposed (in two banks with the crankshaft between them). The cylinder block is usually made of cast iron. Aluminium blocks save weight, but they have more stringent antifreeze and nut tightening requirements.

MAIN BEARINGS
An engine with a high number of main bearings—for example five in a 4-in-line engine—is likely to provide greater crankshaft rigidity, which means less vibration and wear.

COOLING SYSTEM
Some engines are cooled by water, others by air. If a water system is sealed you do not usually have to top up the radiator or put in antifreeze at intervals.

When air is the coolant, it is blown round the engine by a fan. This may be noisy in very small cars; in larger models it is quietened by metal shielding.

BORE AND STROKE
The bore is the internal diameter of each cylinder. The stroke is the distance the piston travels up and down a cylinder.

A stroke that is shorter than the bore measurement reduces piston speed and wear and allows bigger valves. But often the engine is less flexible at low speeds.

DISPLACEMENT
The engine's capacity or displacement is generally given in cubic centimetres or litres (1 litre=1000 cc). Capacity is measured by multiplying the number of cylinders by the volume of the cylinder swept by a piston. Smaller engines should use less petrol, but they tend to be driven harder. Weight and overall gearing also affect performance.

COMPRESSION RATIO
The fuel and air mixture is compressed in each cylinder to make it combustible. A ratio of 9:1 means that it is compressed into one-ninth of its original volume. In general terms, the higher the ratio, the higher the octane requirement (see pp. 7-10) and the more expensive the petrol.

VALVE GEAR
Most cars have either overhead valves (ohv) or overhead camshafts (ohc). In ohv gear, the camshaft is below the cylinder head and a push-rod opens the valves. In an ohc layout the camshaft is mounted above the valves and driven from the crankshaft by either a chain or toothed belt. The ohc gear has the fewest moving parts, so there is less noise; but when adjustment becomes necessary it is often more difficult. An overhead camshaft layout generally allows more efficient combustion, especially at high speeds.

CARBURETTOR
On most cars, a carburettor meters air and fuel to the engine. Carburettors are mainly either fixed-choke types—with the airflow passages of a fixed size—or variable jet (or choke) types. Generally, variable-jet types are less prone to troubles caused by dirty fuel. High-performance cars often have two or more carburettors. This usually results in better fuel consumption in normal use, but only if they are properly tuned. A good compromise is the double venturi design, which gives extra breathing efficiency but without such complicated adjustment. Some cars have no carburettors. They use a fuel-injection system instead. This is more accurate and should improve consumption. A lower-octane fuel can often be used, but the benefits are usually too small to offset the extra cost. If overhaul is necessary, it is more costly.

FUEL PUMP
Mechanical pumps are driven by the engine and cannot usually deliver petrol until the starter is operated. Electric pumps, operated by the battery, do not have this limitation, but are close to the fuel tank and may be less accessible for overhaul and be more affected by bad weather.

OIL FILTER
Most cars have a full-flow oil filter fitted outside the engine block to intercept any impurities circulating with the oil. Some use a throw-away cartridge, convenient but dearer than the element type which fits into a removable bowl.

MAXIMUM POWER
Brake horsepower is the amount of power the engine produces at the flywheel at the stated rpm. High bhp indicates lively performance, but note whether bhp figures are net or gross. Net bhp is a more useful figure because it is measured with all ancillaries such as fan, alternator and exhaust fitted to the engine.

If the bhp figure is accompanied by the letters DIN (Deutsche Industrie Norm) the measurement is net; if the letters are SAE (Society of Automotive Engineers of America), it is generally gross.

Sometimes a car's power-to-weight ratio is specified as bhp per ton laden. The higher the bhp per ton figure, the livelier the performance—and the more economical the car—when treated with restraint on a long run.

MAXIMUM TORQUE
Torque is the twisting force the engine exerts to turn the crankshaft; it is a measure of pulling power.

Maximum torque is usually developed at half to two-thirds of the engine's top speed. If this involves fairly high revs—say 3500—the car is capable of high speed, but may be unwilling to pull from low speed in top gear; this could impair the car's overall fuel consumption. If maximum torque comes at fairly low revs, the car is likely to be more flexible at low speeds and so be economical.

Although small engines are less flexible than larger ones, their liveliness can be increased by reducing the car's weight.

If you need a good towing car, look for generous torque at low engine revs.

TRANSMISSION

Clutch	7½ in. diaphragm spring, single dry plate, cable operated	Overall ratios	Top Third Second First Reverse	3·89 5·52 8·48 14·24 16·80
Gearbox	4-speed all synchromesh	Final drive	Hypoid bevel 3·89:1 to rear wheels	
Gear ratios	Top 1·00 Third 1·42 Second 2·18 First 3·66 Reverse 4·32	Mph per 1000 rpm	16 mph (25·8 kph)	

CLUTCH

The diameter of the driven-plate or clutch-plate is normally given in inches: the larger it is, the more power it can transmit and the longer it is likely to last.

The diaphragm-spring type is the most common; it has fewer parts and is easier and cheaper to make, as well as being lighter so that it can be operated by means of cables. Some types are hydraulically operated.

The coil-spring type uses helical springs to clamp the driven-plate between the flywheel and pressure-plate. It needs greater pedal pressure and calls for hydraulic operation, and has lost favour in recent years. But one or two highly reputable car makers still prefer it.

Virtually every modern clutch uses a dry plate rather than a fluid system, but cars with automatic transmission have a torque converter which is a form of fluid coupling.

Automatic transmission costs £100–£200 extra. Although it impairs fuel consumption, the whole power train (engine, gearbox, back axle) is less prone to cause wear and tear. It is especially useful for regular town driving. In these conditions, as well as being convenient for the driver, it offers long-term economy.

Most established clutch designs used on production cars have a reputation for reliability and longevity.

GEARBOX

Manual gearboxes usually have four or five forward gears. The more a car has, the less strain there is on the engine and the more economical it is. Gearboxes without synchromesh are cheaper, but are much less convenient for the driver.

GEAR RATIOS AND OVERALL RATIOS

Gears are stepped in sequence to adjust the torque (see p. 250) according to the load. The ratio figures show how many engine revolutions provide one turn of the propeller shaft in each gear.

Many systems have direct drive in top gear—one turn of the engine produces one turn of the propeller shaft. The ratio is given as 1·0:1. If second gear has a ratio of 2·0:1, two engine revolutions turn the shaft once.

Sometimes the gear ratios are given as an overall figure, obtained by multiplying each gear ratio by the final-drive ratio.

The best motoring is achieved by evenly spaced ratios which ensure smooth acceleration.

FINAL DRIVE

Cars with rear-wheel drive usually have a hypoid bevel rear axle. This has a crown wheel connected to the axle shafts and road wheels, and a pinion driven by the propeller shaft. The pinion is meshed below the centre of the crown wheel to reduce the height of the propeller-shaft tunnel inside the car. Helical spur gears are mainly used in many front-wheel-drive cars.

The final-drive ratio indicates how many times the pinion turns the crown wheel. A ratio of 4:1 means that the pinion turns four times and the crown wheel once; wheel and tyre size also influence overall gearing. The higher the ratio the less busy is the engine when cruising, and the more economical it may be.

MPH PER 1000 RPM

When you compare similar cars, the one with the highest road speed for each 1000 rpm (see p. 253) has the highest gearing.

Low overall gearing gives good low-speed acceleration, flexibility, and good towing ability. High gearing gives unstrained and economical cruising in the higher speed range.

CHASSIS

Steering	Rack and pinion Wheel diameter 14·75 in.	Wheels	4½ in. rims 5·50 × 12 cross-ply tyres	
Suspension front	Independent by Macpherson coil spring/ damper struts, lower links and an anti-roll bar	Brakes	Discs front, drums rear Vacuum servo	
		dimensions:	Front 8·6 in. dia. Rear 8·6 in. dia.	
rear	Leaf-sprung live axle with telescopic dampers	swept area:	Front 143 sq. in. Rear 75 sq. in. Total 218 sq. in.	

WHEELS AND TYRES

Wheel sizes are usually indicated by the rim width in inches. Sometimes this is followed by the letter J or C—the maker's code for the type of construction.

Tyre sizes are indicated in a variety of ways. For instance, 620×13 is the tyre width of 6·20 in., and wheel diameter in inches, while 165×13 is the tyre width in millimetres (16·5 mm.), and the wheel diameter in inches. Sometimes a code letter is given for the width. An example of a full tyre code is E70VR15. E is the width code, 70 the aspect ratio, V the speed rating, R means the tyres are radial, and 15 is the wheel diameter in inches.

A speed rating—the maximum safe speed for the tyre—is often given on radial plies. For example, SR means 113 mph maximum, HR 130 mph maximum, and VR safe over 130 mph.

The aspect ratio may also be given in the code. This is the distance between the rim and the tread, expressed as a percentage of the distance from one side wall to another. An average family saloon will have an aspect ratio of 82, while high-performance cars with wider, squatter tyres have an aspect ratio of 70.

Tyres of low aspect ratio are sometimes offered as an optional extra on a saloon car, particularly if it has rear-wheel drive. They cost more, but usually improve road-holding. At low speeds the ride may be harder.

If a car is fitted with cross-ply tyres as standard, radials—which give better roadholding and last longer (see p. 11)—may be offered as an optional extra. But check carefully what the reports say of their effect on ride comfort.

STEERING

Most cars use the rack-and-pinion steering system, in which a toothed rack is moved by a small pinion at the bottom of the steering shaft. As the rack travels from side to side it swivels the front wheels.

Other cars have steering boxes through which the turning effort of the steering wheel is transmitted, by means of a cam and peg or worm and nut.

There are no economy advantages in any one system.

SUSPENSION

Independent suspension lets wheels on the same axle travel up and down without affecting each other. With a live (or rigid) axle, deflection of one wheel will affect the other, influencing the car's handling and ride comfort.

A live axle is one in which the wheels are not independently suspended, but each is attached to a half-shaft. Many cars have independent suspension on the front wheels and a live axle at the rear. Independent suspension costs more, particularly on rear-wheel-drive cars.

Springing, to iron out the effect of road bumps, is provided by leaf, coil, compressed-air, gas or hydraulic springs. Leaf and coil springs are the cheapest.

Dampers stop the springs vibrating excessively, and arms or links are used to connect the axle to the chassis.

In many independent front suspension systems, strong double wishbones connect each wheel to the chassis. Another popular design is the Mac-Pherson strut layout, in which one of the wishbone linkage arms is replaced by a telescopic strut incorporating a coil spring and damper.

Many systems include an anti-roll bar connected between opposite wheels and anchored to the chassis or body. It cuts down roll on corners by restricting the height that one wheel can rise above another. A Panhard rod is often used to resist sideways distortion that could affect live-axled cars, especially those with coil springs.

BRAKES

Constant application of drum brakes may lead to overheating and possible fading (see p. 253). Disc brakes are more efficient, resisting both heat fade and water-soaking better; lining replacement is easier too. Discs are generally more expensive and may need heavier pedal pressure, so a servo is often provided to help reduce brake-pedal load.

There may be more than one hydraulic circuit in case one fails. If brake dimensions are given, assess them against the results given in the performance tables.

A car to fit your needs /2

Finding out if the acceleration is adequate

Cars are put through rigorous trials when they are tested by the AA or by major motoring magazines. The AA test, for example, includes driving at least 1000 miles on public roads in varying traffic conditions, besides performance trials at the Motor Industry Research Association's private proving ground.

Basic acceleration—the time taken to reach top speed from standstill—is shown as a graph or table in test reports. Comparing the figures for different cars of roughly the same engine size shows you which one will pull away fastest in traffic.

mph	Triumph Dolomite secs	Ford Cortina 1600 (ohc) secs	Maxi 1750 secs
0-30	4·0	4·1	4·1
0-40	6·0	6·7	6·4
0-50	8·2	10·1	9·9
0-60	11·4	15·1	14·6
0-70	15·6	21·3	21·4
0-80	21·6	32·6	32·8
0-90	31·3	—	—

The graphs are normally designed so that speed is read off vertically and time horizontally. The acceleration curve is always steep at first, as the car gathers speed in the lower gears. Then the line flattens out when top speed is reached. Small indentations appear at irregular intervals along the curve, showing loss of thrust during gear changes.

Test techniques

To make car-to-car comparison valid, testers use wheel-spinning or clutch-slipping techniques, which give maximum acceleration from standstill. These methods are too harsh for normal motoring because they cause rapid clutch wear. Consequently, the 0-30 mph times recorded by testers are better than the car will achieve in daily use, but other speed times should be attainable without damage by an accomplished driver in normal conditions, if the engine is perfectly tuned.

Testers also measure the time taken to cover ¼ mile and 1 kilometre from a standing start, using the same techniques. Typical comparisons are:

Triumph Dolomite secs	Ford Cortina 1600 (ohc) secs	Maxi 1750 secs
18·8	20·9	19·6

For most motorists, it is more important to have good acceleration for overtaking than for a standing start. Testers also therefore note how long it takes to increase speed by 20 mph in various gears. The figures show the car's ability to overtake at different speeds.

For regular fast travel on open roads, look for a car with good acceleration in the middle of its speed range—an asset for overtaking on motorways. Study the more general comments in the test reports to see if the car was noisy or vibrated at sustained high speed.

Some cars with similar times from standstill to 70 mph differ in their top-gear performance from 30 to 50 mph. For example:

0-70 mph (using all gears)
Rover 2000 SC   19·3 secs
Volvo 144 De Luxe   20·3 secs

30-50 mph (top gear only)
Rover 2000 SC   13·3 secs
Volvo 144 De Luxe   9·0 secs

If a car is capable of high speed, but is slow to pick up in top gear, a lot of gear changing will be necessary in traffic. For town driving, look for the fastest acceleration times in top gear.

Driving aids

An overdrive unit, sometimes available as an optional extra, cuts down engine noise because fewer revolutions are needed to maintain speed. It also reduces fuel consumption on long, fast journeys.

Overdrive can be useful on a lower-geared car, recommended for town use, because it improves top-gear performance on open roads.

If you drive constantly in heavy traffic, automatic transmission cuts out gear changing, but it affects acceleration. Fluid in the mechanism causes a certain amount of 'drag' when the car moves off from standstill and when it accelerates. The performance on test of the automatic Austin 1800 Mk II is typical:

mph	Automatic (using kickdown)	Manual gearbox
0-30	5·8	4·5
0-40	8·7	7·5
0-50	12·4	10·5
0-60	17·9	16·0
0-70	25·7	22·3
0-80	43·2	33·4

Manually overriding the gears gives better performance in many cases—although still not as good as a manual gearbox—but you lose the relaxation of automatic transmission.

Checking the instruments

A car's speedometer, rev-counter (tachometer) and mileage recorder (odometer) are checked against independent instruments. The true (independent) figures and the car figures are both given. If a car odometer is fast, fuel consumption will appear better than it really is.

HOW THE TEST REPORTS DESCRIBE PERFORMANCE

ACCELERATION

mph	kph	secs
0-30	0-48	4·4
0-40	0-64	7·1
0-50	0-80	10·6
0-60	0-96	16·0
0-70	0-113	22·9
0-80	0-129	36·8

Standing ¼ mile   20·5 (0–68 mph)
Standing km   38·7 (0–81 mph)

SPEED RANGE ACCELERATION TIMES IN SECONDS

mph	top	third	second
10–30	—	7·8	4·9
20–40	11·7	7·4	5·0
30–50	11·4	7·6	—
40–60	12·5	8·9	—
50–70	15·7	12·2	—
60–80	23·6	—	—

True speed – mph:	30	40	50	60	70	80
Car speedometer:	29	38	46	55	65	73
Odometer:	6% fast					
True engine speed – rpm:	1000	2000	3000	4000	5000	6000
Car tachometer:	1050	2000	3000	3950	4900	5900

The significance of 'overall gearing'

GEARING
(with 165SR13 tyres)

Top	16·3	mph per 1000 rpm
3rd	11·5	mph per 1000 rpm
2nd	8·15	mph per 1000 rpm
1st	4·9	mph per 1000 rpm

A car's gearing is affected by the size of its tyres, so manufacturers specify tyre sizes. Testers say in their report what tyres were used on the car. It would be most unusual, however, for a car undergoing trials to have tyres which did not match the specification, so you can assume that the testers' gearing figures relate to any car of the same model.

The important figure is the car's top-gear speed at 1000 rpm — the overall gearing, which can vary from 15 mph for a small car to 25 mph for a large one with overdrive.

A car with high overall gearing generally provides unstressed, quiet cruising at high speed, but it may need frequent gear changes and use more fuel in traffic.

Low overall gearing usually means that the car pulls strongly from low speed in the higher gears, but it is probably fussy and may be noisy. The car will perform better in traffic than on motorways, unless it is fitted with an overdrive.

Testers evaluate the gearing in their general comments. Look for gearing that is neither too low for quiet cruising nor too high for easy motoring in heavy town traffic.

Judging the performance of the gearbox

PERFORMANCE
MAXIMUM SPEEDS

Gear	mph	kph	rpm
Top – mean	88	142	5500
– best	91	146	
3rd	69	111	6000
2nd	45	72	6000
1st	27	43	6000

The speed achieved in each forward gear is measured at the maximum number of rpm stipulated by the manufacturer. Two figures are recorded for top gear — the highest speed achieved and the average (or mean) top speed on trial runs.

These tests show not only how powerful the car is, but also if the gear ratios provide a good rate of acceleration without straining the engine. If the top speeds in the various gears progress by fairly even jumps, the ratios are evenly spaced, which indicates that the car will be smooth and easy to drive.

Testers look for an easy synchromesh action and positive, firm movement by the gear lever. On automatic cars, the smoothness of the gearbox is judged, and comments are made on the effectiveness of the manual hold and the kickdown mechanism.

To provide an overall assessment of the gearbox, testers note its action both under trial conditions and in everyday traffic situations.

Assessing the operation of the clutch

CLUTCH
Pedal – load: 22 lb. (10 kg.)
– travel: 4¼ in. (10·8 cm)
Maximum gradient: 1 in 3 from rest

The pressure needed to push the clutch pedal to the floor may be as little as 17 lb. or as high as 45 lb. The length of pedal travel can vary from 4¼ in. to 7 in. Testers measure pressure and travel to indicate how comfortable and convenient the clutch is to use. The ideal is a clutch that requires only moderate pressure by the driver and has a pedal with short yet progressively operating travel.

Reports also state the maximum gradient on which the car will pull away from standstill. It should cope with 1 in 3. If a gradient is too steep, the clutch will slip or the engine stall because it is under too great a strain.

Measuring the efficiency of the brakes

BRAKES
RESPONSE (from 30 mph in neutral)

Load	g	Distance
20 lb.	0·40	75 ft
40 lb.	0·85	35½ ft
50 lb.	0·90	33 ft
60 lb.	0·94	32 ft
Handbrake only	0·30	100 ft

(Maximum gradient: 1 in 3)

FADE
(from 70 mph in neutral)
Pedal load for 0·5 g stops

1	25 lb.	6	35–45 lb.
2	25 lb.	7	35–45 lb.
3	25 lb.	8	35–45 lb.
4	25 lb.	9	45 lb.
5	35–45 lb.	10	45 lb.

Braking efficiency is measured according to the pressure needed on the pedal, and the distance the car covers while it is stopping from speeds of 30 mph in neutral.

In some test reports, a g measurement replaces the stopping distance. In theory, g is the ultimate stopping power — the force of gravity, which is 32 ft per second every second. So 0·5 g equals half of what is considered maximum efficiency. Testers make three other basic checks:
1 The braking performance with pedal pressure of just less than 100 lb. — the maximum effort a woman driver is expected to exert.
2 The pedal pressure needed for a stop as near as possible to 1·0 g — in effect, the fastest stop possible.

3 The progressive action and accuracy of the brake pedal.

The reports also indicate what effort is needed to stop the car with the handbrake alone, and show the holding capability of the handbrake. It must be able to keep the car stationary on a 1-in-3 hill.

Brake fade — the way brakes lose their efficiency through heavy use — is measured by checking how the pedal load has to be increased during repeated stops. Pressure of 60 lb. might produce a 0·94 g stop from 30 mph at the start of the tests, but after 15 quick stops the brakes could need 90 lb. pressure — half as much again — for the same result. A 10 lb. difference is acceptable, but 15 lb. or more is poor.

A car to fit your needs/3

How many miles to the gallon

CONSUMPTION
FUEL
Overall consumption: 31 mpg
        (9·1 litres/100 km)
Typical consumption: 26 mpg
       (10·9 litres/100 km)
Test distance: 937 miles (1508 km)

At steady speeds in top gear

	mpg	litres/100 km
30 mph	45·9	6·2
40 mph	44·4	6·4
50 mph	40·3	7·0
60 mph	35·9	7·9
70 mph	30·0	9·4
80 mph	24·0	11·8
max	20·4	13·9

Fuel (Premium 4 star 97 octane)

OIL
2810 miles per pint (7962 km/litre)

Most test reports include a table which shows a car's fuel consumption at various speeds in top gear.

An overall figure is also recorded for the car's fuel consumption throughout the whole series of road tests. Another figure, for typical consumption, is calculated over a series of runs in varying traffic conditions.

These are only guides to general economy because so much depends on how the car is driven. Small cars, in particular, show wide differences in consumption according to whether they are used in heavy traffic or for journeys on clear roads.

An overdrive unit can reduce fuel consumption at steady speeds by up to 3 miles per gallon on a 2 litre car.

Cars with automatic transmission generally use more fuel than those with manual gearboxes. On a 2 litre car the difference can be 5 mpg.

Always follow the report's advice on which grade of fuel to use. Nothing is gained by using a higher grade than necessary—it will not improve the car's performance or its economy. Using a grade that is too low can cause engine damage.

Do not forget to consider the fuel-tank capacity. A long-range tank is an asset.

Oil consumption can vary from one car to another much more than petrol consumption. Test reports base their oil-consumption figures solely on the period the car was on trial, not usually long enough for an accurate long-term estimate.

Remember that oil consumption on a new car will fall after the running-in period; engines are designed to use more oil while flush-fitting moving parts are bedding in during the first few hundred miles.

How the car handles on the move

Handling is a term used by testers to describe a car's general behaviour once it is on the move. It covers ride comfort, steering, cornering balance and road-holding ability.

A car with good road-holding keeps an impressive grip on the road up to high cornering speeds. This ability depends mainly on its suspension and tyres. But, for safety, the manner in which the grip is lost—and how predictable the loss—is even more important. It is better for the nose or tail to come out of line earlier and with a gentle, progressive action rather than later without warning.

Cars that have a predominant tendency for the front to run wide on bends are said to understeer. Cars that tighten into the turn, or even have the tail swing out, are said to oversteer. Neutral steering means that the car responds in such a way

that any deviation at one end is counterbalanced by the same degree of slip at the other.

Most car makers prefer their cars to display mild understeer in normal driving conditions, because this is most easily corrected—by applying more lock to the steering or by decelerating to re-establish front-wheel grip.

Front-wheel-drive cars usually understeer. Rear-engined cars usually show pronounced oversteer, and conventional designs (front engine driving rear wheels) can have both characteristics. It is important that handling behaviour is consistent, and that the steering gives the driver plenty of warning.

Suspension designers often find it difficult to give the best possible cornering and the most comfortable ride at the same time. Test reports

say whether the springing is absorbent or harsh at low speeds and at higher speeds. How well the suspension dampens unwanted body roll or bouncing after a bump is equally important.

Reports usually quote the car's turning circle and the number of turns of the steering wheel needed to move it from lock to lock. A car with a small turning circle is ideal for town use, as long as the steering wheel does not have to be twirled excessively or need great effort. Radial-ply tyres tend to make the steering heavy, but this is usually overcome by lower-geared steering.

Power-assisted steering is useful for heavy cars used regularly in town, but on the open road, particularly at speed, it can take away some of the 'feel' of what is happening to the front wheels.

Assessing the controls and space available

Major controls—that is, the pedals, steering wheel and gear change—should be well positioned in relation to the driving seat and one another.

Pedals should not be offset, too high or too close to one another. A steering wheel that can be adjusted for rake or reach is usually better for a family in which the drivers vary considerably in size. Instruments should be easy to read and in clear view, and all controls should be easy to find at night without using the interior light.

Testers always check on the driving visibility and note blind spots

caused by such things as thick pillars, upswept rear bodywork or windscreen wipers working at the wrong angle (a hazard on some cars converted from left-hand drive).

The list of interior dimensions should give two figures for total legroom at both back and front—one with the front seats as far forward as possible, and one with them as far back as they will go. Foot-entry space and door headroom is critical for the elderly and less agile. A prominent centre tunnel, high door sills and dangling seat belts are also best avoided.

Comments about seat comfort should be interpreted to suit your particular needs. Some people prefer firmness, especially in the lower part of the back. Smaller people may feel ill at ease in a very big, enveloping seat designed for a large, tall passenger. The more seat adjustments there are, the more likely it is that the seating will suit everybody.

When considering storage space, remember that room for oddments inside the car is as valuable as a large boot. Cars of a similar size can vary considerably in this capacity.

Choosing a new car /1

Deciding where to buy your new car

When you have decided to buy a new rather than a secondhand car, your final choice of model may to some extent be influenced by which dealers are nearest your home or work. In most cases, it is advisable to find a dealer who specialises in the make of car you are buying, and who has good maintenance and repair facilities.

It is essential, especially in the car's first year, to ensure that it is properly maintained by a skilled mechanic who is familiar with the type and model.

Finding a main dealer

Most manufacturers appoint main dealers or distributors to handle their retail sales and supply cars wholesale to other, smaller garages. (Many foreign manufacturers do this by setting up a subsidiary company or appointing a concessionaire who sells directly to the public and to other dealers.)

Main dealers, when they accept a maker's franchise to sell a particular range of cars, undertake to comply with the company's maintenance requirements and keep a good stock of models and spare parts. In most cases, they handle only one or two manufacturers' cars.

The smaller dealers who do not hold any maker's franchise are free to deal in any type of car, and they are generally able to obtain any model you want. Their advantage is often that they can offer a more personal service than the larger distributor or main dealer, but they may not be as well equipped and their staff may be untrained to deal with a whole range of cars.

The most important factor is after-sales service and maintenance, and there is little doubt that you can generally expect to get better service from a garage if you bought the car there. For that reason alone it is advisable to use a main dealer.

For example, most manufacturers guarantee that the first service—after 500-1200 miles perhaps—will be done free of charge, or at least with no labour charges. If the dealer from whom you buy a car does not hold the manufacturer's franchise he cannot take part in that scheme, and you will have the inconvenience of having to take the car for servicing to a main dealer (where you will have none of the advantages of being an already established customer).

Only franchised dealers, moreover, are kept regularly informed by the manufacturers of any changes in their servicing recommendations and of any modifications that might become necessary—especially if the car is a new, untried model. This is a factor on which your safety could depend.

If you are considering buying a foreign car, or one for which you know it is difficult to obtain parts, it is even more important to buy from a franchised dealer—who as part of his agreement with the manufacturer will have priority over unfranchised garages if there is a shortage of spares.

Ordering the car

Few dealers are likely to have the model you have chosen ready for immediate sale. You may have to wait several months for most British cars, and for luxury models the waiting period may be even longer. Dealers handling foreign cars are often able to supply cars more quickly, but always check that they are also likely to have a constant, ready supply of parts.

In most cases, even if the car can be supplied immediately, you will have to complete an order form (see p. 258). Make sure that it contains no clause that could cost you money if the deal does not go through satisfactorily within any time limit you have agreed.

For example, if the price of the car you choose rises between the time you order it and the time it becomes available, you have to pay the new price. You should also be able, however, to withdraw from the purchase and to have any deposit refunded in full. Check that the order form makes this clear.

CHECK THE WARRANTY

Most car manufacturers give a warranty with a new car. This is simply an undertaking to carry out certain repairs or provide replacement parts without charge within a specified period.

New British cars usually have such a guarantee for 12 months or 12,000 miles, whichever comes first. Some foreign car manufacturers limit them to six months, but one firm guarantees its engines for 24,000 miles.

Work done under a warranty can usually be carried out only by a garage that holds a franchise for the make concerned. If you attempt to do any repairs yourself, you will invalidate the warranty. Make sure that any faults that develop during the warranty period—such as oil leaks—are attended to before it expires.

Warranties can usually be transferred to the new owner if you sell the car.

Since the Sale of Goods (Implied Terms) Act 1973, warranties have been of greater value to the buyer, since they give him additional rights without taking anything away. Any clause in a warranty that limits a buyer's rights under the Act is void (see p. 259).

Finding out whether you can get a discount

Whether or not you can get a discount on a new car will depend on the dealer's stocks and the demand for it. You are not likely to get anything off the price of a car for which there is a long waiting list.

Dealers get commission on sales from the manufacturer, depending on their position in the selling structure. A distributor might get 20 per cent, a main dealer $17\frac{1}{2}$ per cent, a dealer with a franchise perhaps 15 per cent, and a dealer without a franchise perhaps 10 per cent.

If the dealer has a lot of cars in the pipeline or in stock he may give a discount, whether you are buying for cash or on hire purchase. In theory, distributors are able to give the biggest discount since they get the largest commission. Some may be prepared to give a bigger discount, others may not, because it would upset other franchise holders.

Dealers in small towns may have more difficulty in moving their stock, so may offer a higher discount.

Firms that advertise attractive discount savings invariably operate hire-purchase schemes and make their profits out of higher hire-purchase charges, so you may not gain anything. Some large dealers may offer you a generous discount but not be very interested in personal attention or after-sales service.

If you get a discount, it is likely to be between $7\frac{1}{2}$ and $12\frac{1}{2}$ per cent. It will be levied on the basic price of the car, not the retail price, but that has the advantage of reducing VAT slightly, since VAT is levied on the retail price. For example:

Basic price	£1002.00
Less 10% discount	100.20
	901.80
Car Tax	81.50
	983.30
VAT	98.33
Retail price	£1081.63

Any extras would have to be added to the total after Car Tax, and this would increase VAT.

Choosing a new car/2

Precautions before you buy

It is impossible to assess the performance of a car during a 'trial run' from the showroom. One of the major drawbacks is that the driver is usually preoccupied with ensuring that he does not damage the demonstration car.

To overcome this problem if you do take out a demonstration car, insist on driving at least 5 miles so that you will ultimately be able to concentrate on the car itself, not on other traffic.

Every new model is put through rigorous tests by the AA and most motoring journals, and you can use their reports to judge whether the car that attracts you in the show-

room is really suitable for your requirements. (Ask your local AA office for a Road Test Report on any car that interests you.)

Once you have made up your mind, try to hire or borrow the model of your choice for a week-end to confirm that it measures up to your expectations.

As you become used to the car's handling characteristics you will be able to pay attention to the comfort it offers: suspension and seats that appear attractive on a short run can sometimes have shortcomings that become apparent over longer distances. When you are on a quiet road, relax and make a considered

assessment of the car's design features. These are personal points that only the driver can assess.

When the new car arrives
Although every car manufacturer operates a strict quality control system, backed by pre-delivery inspections by each dealer, many new cars are found to have some defect when they are handed over to the buyer. When your own model arrives, check its condition before you accept it—first, by a thorough inspection inside and out, and then by a brief test drive. Make a note of any faults you find and ask the salesman to have them corrected.

Making sure that the instruments and driving controls work

Courtesy light Check that the interior lights go on and off when the doors are opened and closed.

Ignition warning light The red light should go out when the engine is running with only slight foot pressure on the accelerator.

Oil-pressure light Check that the amber or green light goes out within 15 seconds after the engine has been started.

Horn and trafficators Make sure that the trafficator switch returns to neutral when the steering wheel is central.

Wipers and washers Check the wiper motor at its various speeds, then test the washers.

Dashboard lights Every dial should be illuminated when the sidelights are on.

Heater and fan With the engine running, switch on the heater and check that the heater and demister fans work.

Starter and steering lock The key should be a flush fit and turn smoothly. Check that it withdraws easily when the steering is locked.

Gear lever It should be easy to engage every gear—including reverse—with the engine off. Check that the gear lever mountings are not loose.

Handbrake The lever should pass not more than 10 notches to put the brakes fully on. If there is a warning light, see that it goes out when the handbrake is released.

Brake pedal Make sure that it is not possible to press the brake pedal down to the floor.

Seat adjustment Rock the driving seat to check that it is firmly anchored. Test its forward adjustment and angle.

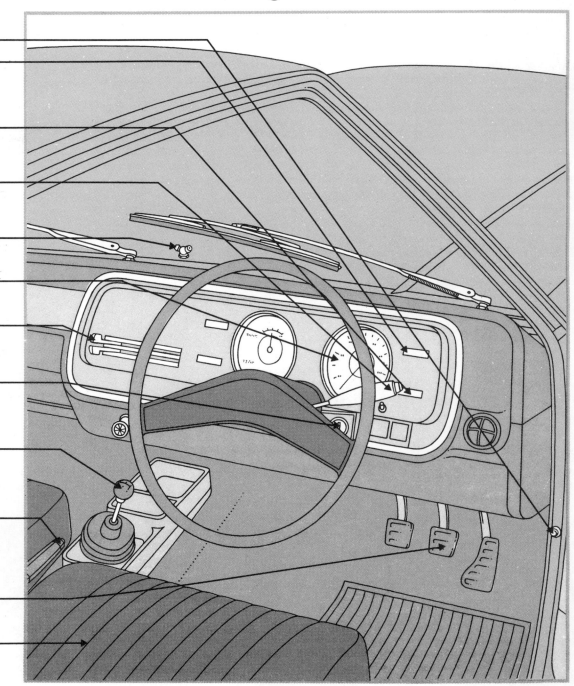

Checking for mechanical or electrical faults

Sun roof If there is a sun panel, make sure that it can open smoothly and close securely.

Seat belts Check that the seat belt anchorages are securely bolted.

Windows Winders that jerk or need more than very light effort have a faulty mechanism.

Boot lid Check the gap around the closed boot lid. It should be equal on each side to ensure that water cannot seep past the seals.

Boot lock If the boot lid has to be slammed to close it, the lock may need to be adjusted.

Trafficators Check outside the car that the rear and front trafficators work when the switch is operated. If there is a hazard warning switch, check that all four lights operate together.

Brake lights With the ignition on, the two rear brake lights should operate when the pedal is pressed.

Number-plate light Check that the number-plate light comes on with other exterior lights. It must illuminate the whole plate.

Reversing lights With the ignition on, make sure that the reversing lights come on as soon as the reverse gear is selected.

Mirror The mirror must be firm in all positions. Make sure that it does not vibrate.

Steering wheel Adjustment is needed if there is any more than minimal steering free play.

Battery Check that the terminal connections are tight and that the cells are topped-up.

Brake reservoir If the fluid level is low, ask the dealer to bleed the brakes, and top-up.

Screenwasher bottle Check that the screenwasher bottle is filled with anti-smear fluid.

Oil leaks Look for signs of oil. Ask the dealer to fit new gaskets if necessary.

Radiator Ask the dealer to check with a hydrometer to make sure that the specific gravity of the anti-freeze is up to strength.

Foglamps Check that any foglamps have been fitted more than 2 ft from the ground to comply with the law.

Number-plates Check that the front and rear plates carry the correct registration number.

Headlights and sidelights Try the various combinations of lights, including dipped head. Ask the dealer to check the beam adjustment.

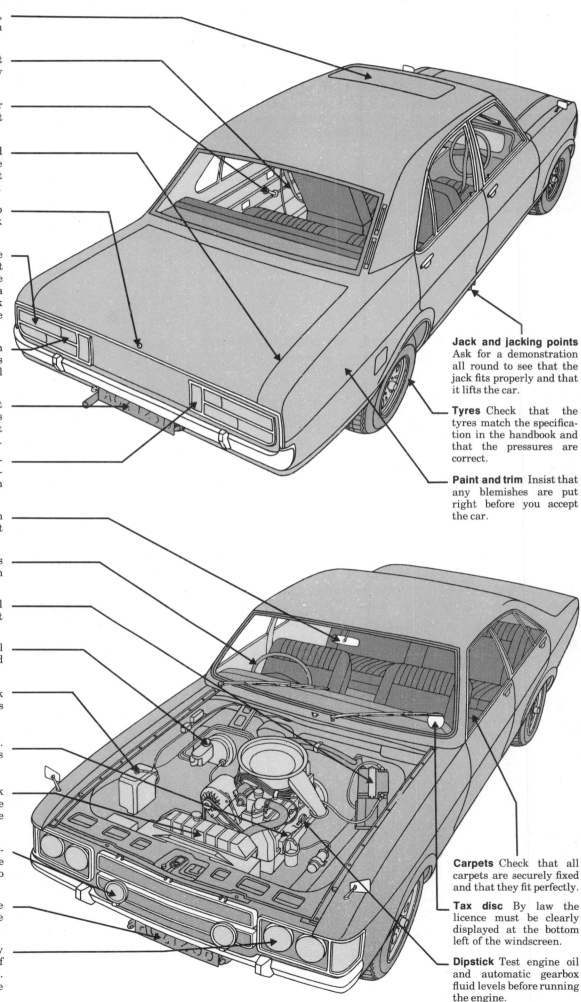

Jack and jacking points Ask for a demonstration all round to see that the jack fits properly and that it lifts the car.

Tyres Check that the tyres match the specification in the handbook and that the pressures are correct.

Paint and trim Insist that any blemishes are put right before you accept the car.

Carpets Check that all carpets are securely fixed and that they fit perfectly.

Tax disc By law the licence must be clearly displayed at the bottom left of the windscreen.

Dipstick Test engine oil and automatic gearbox fluid levels before running the engine.

Choosing a used car /1

Three ways to buy a secondhand car

There is always a risk involved in buying a used car—you can never be absolutely sure of its condition. The safest way is to buy from a reputable dealer.

Whether you are buying from a dealer or privately, always check the car's condition thoroughly and test it on the road (see pp. 260-5). Get an independent inspection by the AA or a specialist firm. This will cost about £8-£10. If a seller is unwilling to have a car inspected do not buy it. Never buy in haste.

If a car is more than three years old it should have a current DoE (MoT) certificate. This is only proof that it is roadworthy—mainly that its brakes, lights and steering are working—it is not a guarantee of the car's condition. But be wary if the certificate has expired or is just about to—or if it has been issued by the dealer himself.

Studying the market

Before you decide where to buy, find out what the car you want is likely to cost. You can get a good idea by studying car-price guides which are available monthly and car-sales columns in the Press.

Studying advertisements will also give you an idea of what sells quickly and what is advertised again and again. If you buy a car that has taken a long time to sell, you may have a similar difficulty when you come to sell it later.

The price of a car over six years old depends on its condition. If it is clean and rust free it may sell for up to £100 more than one in bad condition. Be suspicious of cars that are priced much lower than you would expect. If a price is much higher than you would expect, find out why, and whether the car is worth it.

You will probably have to pay the highest price if you buy from a dealer, since he has to make a profit, pay VAT, give a guarantee, prepare the car for sale and check its legal ownership. Buying at an auction or privately may cost less, but you take a greater risk.

Buying from a car dealer

Dealers in used cars fall generally into three types—main dealers, smaller garages and used-car traders.

Main dealers or distributors are those generally concerned with the sale of new cars, but they usually have a stock of vehicles taken in part exchange. Most of the used cars they offer are no more than two or three years old, and fairly high in price. The cars are likely to be of reasonably good standard.

Sometimes they have four-month-old cars for sale which have been demonstration models, selling about 10-15 per cent below the list price. Such cars may be bargains, but will have been driven hard. Sometimes main dealers sell off at a discount new cars that have become obsolete before being sold. These may be bargains, but remember that they will depreciate faster.

Smaller garages usually have cars available at lower prices than a main dealer. One way to check that a garage is reliable is to note whether it is AA-appointed or a member of the Motor Agents' Association.

Never buy a used car from a dealer who does not have an agreement with a workshop. He cannot do much to improve a car for re-selling or offer after-sales service.

Never assume that a car-sales area is connected with an adjacent garage—always ask at the garage first. Some garages let their fore-courts to a used-car trader, but are in no way involved in his business, and the trader does not have their backing for repairs. You may be able to buy a car from a used-car trader at a lower price than from an established local trader, but you take a greater risk.

You can sometimes get a warranty with a used car. Check what is offered; some are for parts only, not labour.

Dealers are usually reluctant to bargain with buyers, and will not often reduce the price of a car. But they may be persuaded to improve the car at no extra charge—by replacing the tyres for better ones, for example, or fitting a radio. Or they may give a better trade-in price.

But if you succeed in beating a dealer down too much, he may not offer a guarantee or be keen to put any minor faults right for you.

The dealer should agree to put right within the price asked any defects that affect the car's roadworthiness or safe handling, but if there are any other repairs or replacements to be done, they should be negotiated when you make the contract to purchase.

If you sign an order form, make sure that any agreements about repairs, and any special requirements, are noted on it. If you put a deposit on a car pending an independent inspection, you may have to sign an order form.

Make sure that it states that the deposit is returnable if the sale does not go through, and that you agree to buy only if your inspecting engineer reports to your satisfaction on the car's condition.

Buying at a car auction

Because most of the buyers at car auctions are dealers, the private buyer is in a good position to get a bargain since he will not be considering his profit on a resale. But because the dealers are in the trade, they know what they are looking for, and can quickly assess a car and its likely trouble spots. For an inexperienced private buyer it could be a hazardous purchase unless he is accompanied by someone with experience in the motor trade.

Each car offered for sale has to have a list of faults declared, but these may be in very general terms and the buyer has to interpret them in the light of experience. You can briefly inspect cars before the sale and probably listen to the engine running, but there is never a chance to road test them.

There are some safeguards. Most cars are sold 'with warranty' which means that you can take them back if anything goes drastically wrong. But the warranty may last for only one or two hours, or up to 24—per-haps until noon next day. Cars cannot be sold with warranty if they are seven years old or more (except vintage or specialist cars) or if there is no reserve price on them when they are put up for sale. These cars are sold 'as seen' and there is no redress if anything goes wrong.

If you pay by cheque, you may not be allowed to take the car until it has been cleared. Many auction companies now operate a hire-purchase scheme for buyers; you cannot take the car until the form is filled in.

Buying from a private seller

The main drawback to buying a car privately is that you have no safeguards—the seller is not bound by the Sale of Goods Act, and once you have paid you have no redress if it develops any major faults.

You must therefore take all possible steps to protect yourself. The main points to establish are that the seller is the legal owner, that the car is in a reasonable condition for the price asked, and that the terms of any contract are clear.

Try to assess a seller. Is he a householder? Is he selling from his own premises? Does he have a business address where you can contact him if necessary? A householder whom you can contact at work is most likely to be conducting an honest sale. Be careful of anyone not selling from his own home.

Do not rely on the log book as proof of ownership. Ask to see the receipted invoice of the purchase, and servicing bills. But look at the log book and check, if you can, the car's details. Note also the previous owners. If you are able to contact them you can find out something of the car's history, whether it was sold direct to the present seller and what the mileage was at the time.

Establishing that a car is not stolen can be difficult. If you have any doubts or reason to suspect that it might be, do not purchase. If you suspect there may be an outstanding hire-purchase agreement on the vehicle, try to check it—through the AA if you are a member, otherwise at a Citizens' Advice Bureau. If you have any dealings with a hire-purchase company, they may check for you for a small charge.

A private seller usually asks a higher price than he expects to get. You should be able to strike a bargain between the price he would get from a dealer and the price you would pay a dealer.

If the seller agrees to an independent inspection, he may ask for a deposit. Get a receipt. This is written evidence of an agreement. Make sure that it states that the deposit will be returned if the sale does not go through. It should also state clearly that you will buy at the price agreed only if your engineer reports favourably. If the report is not satisfactory, you must let the seller know within any time limit agreed.

The seller will not want to part with the car or log book until your cheque is cleared. But make sure when you collect the car that no parts or accessories are missing. If they are, and you can get no satisfaction from the seller, your only recourse is to sue him.

HOW THE CAR BUYER IS PROTECTED BY THE LAW

Until the Sale of Goods (Implied Terms) Act 1973 came into force, car buyers often lost many of their legal rights by signing an order form that contained an exclusion clause. Buyers of new cars often signed an agreement to accept the conditions of the seller's warranty only. Hire-purchase agreements also sometimes excluded common law rights.

Under the 1973 Act, any such exclusion clause in a document signed by a private buyer has no legal validity. But you may not be protected at an auction; this depends on the circumstances.

Under the Act, the seller is obliged to provide goods that:
1 He has the right to sell and that are not subject to claims by third parties—such as money owing on a hire-purchase agreement. Or he must say if there is any such claim.
2 Are fit for the purpose for which they are sold and are of merchantable quality.
3 Meet the description applied to them.

Thus the dealer is obliged to put right, free of charge, any defect that makes the car 'unmerchantable' or not fit for its purpose, and he must recompense you for any loss or damage arising out of the defect.

To be of 'merchantable quality' a car should be as fit as you could reasonably expect for the price paid. Thus you can expect a new car to be in perfect condition, but not a used car—its condition should be average for its make, age and usage. If you want a car for a special purpose—such as rallying—and rely on the dealer's judgment to provide it, you may be able to get your money back if the car supplied is not suitable.

The Act does not give you any protection against defects that you should have been able to see when you examined the car before buying. If you think anything is wrong with the car after you have bought it, you should go back to the seller—or to the finance company if you are buying the car on hire purchase.

Hire-Purchase Act 1965
The hire-purchase buyer has a certain amount of protection. Once you have paid more than one-third of the hire-purchase price, the finance company cannot repossess the car without legal action. But the Act applies only to transactions of less than £2000.

The three types of agreement mentioned in the Act are hire purchase, conditional sale and credit sale. Make sure that any agreement you sign is subject to the Hire-Purchase Act. You may not be protected.

A hire-purchase agreement must, by law, contain a statement of the hire-purchase price (or total price), a list of the goods to which it relates, the cash price, and the amount of each instalment and the date on which it is payable. The hire-purchase company must give you a second copy of the agreement; this is their acceptance of your contract. You are not bound by the contract until you receive it. If you have any complaints about the goods bought, take them up with the finance company, not the seller.

If you are unable to continue with hire-purchase payments, you can:
1 Get the finance company's permission to sell the car. You will have to pay the outstanding charges, but may get a rebate (see p. 272).
2 Ask the finance company if you can suspend payments for a while.
3 Give written notice of termination of the agreement and surrender the car to the company. (You cannot do this if you have a credit-sale agreement.)

You may save money by ending the agreement yourself. If you surrender the car, under the Hire-Purchase Act the most you will have to pay (apart from a successful claim for damage to the car) will be:
1 Any instalments due at the time you give notice.
2 The difference between the total amount already paid and half the hire-purchase price (or less if stated in your agreement).

If you wait for the company to repossess, the arrears will have accumulated and your liability will be greater. But if the company takes you to court, the court may order you to pay less than the amount stipulated under the Act. It cannot order you to pay more. If the company does seek repossession, if

do not surrender the car before the court proceedings; you may be allowed to keep it and pay off the debt.

If, however, the recommendations of the Crowther Report on Consumer Credit are adopted, a hire-purchase agreement will become a sale contract. The termination payment stipulated in the Act will not apply, and the buyer will be liable to repay any advance and any agreed interest.

If you buy a stolen car
If you buy a car that turns out to have been stolen, the police will impound it as evidence and later return it to its rightful owner. If you bought the car from a dealer, it was his responsibility to ensure that it was his to sell and he must stand the loss. If you bought the car privately, you will have to stand the loss—unless you can find the seller and successfully take action to recover the money. If you bought the car 'with warranty' at an auction, you can get a refund.

Undischarged hire-purchase agreements
If you buy a car for which money is still owing under a hire-purchase agreement, you should still, as a private buyer, be able to keep it, provided that you bought it without knowledge of the agreement. You can reject any claims by the finance company.

Trade Descriptions Act 1968
It is a criminal offence for a trader to give a customer a false impression of the goods he is selling. But if he does, he will be prosecuted in a criminal court. The court has the power to order compensation for the customer, but may not necessarily do so. If you are not satisfied, you will have to sue the trader in a civil court.

Settling a small claim
Suing a seller in a civil court can be costly. But it may be possible to do so at much lower cost by applying to a county court for the case to be referred to arbitration. You may be able to do this if the sum involved in the dispute is less than £75, or if it is a higher amount and the other person involved agrees.

Choosing a used car /2

Looking for dangerous and expensive defects

Always have a used car assessed professionally before you buy. But because it would be expensive to have several cars checked in this way, carry out a careful examination yourself to eliminate as many of them as possible. When you have narrowed the field, contact your nearest AA office and arrange for an engineer to check the car you have chosen. The small fee charged may save you costly repairs later.

Look especially for potentially expensive external defects: signs of rust, evidence of repainting or uneven contours caused by an accident. For example, check inside, outside and underneath the car.

List the defects in every car you see, so that later you can compare one car with another.

Inspecting underneath the car

Tyre types and possible dangerous defects

Tyre condition is a guide to a car's life, particularly the way in which it has been used and maintained. Cross-ply tyres last about 15,000 miles and radials 25,000. If the tyres look new, the car may have exceeded these mileages.

Uneven wear may be caused by steering or suspension faults (see pp. 207 and 201).

It is illegal to mix cross-ply and radial on the same axle. If there are two of each, the radials must be on the rear wheels. Make sure that the tyre walls are not in any way damaged.

Every tyre, including the spare, must have a tread depth

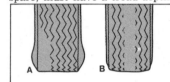

of 1 mm (see p. 36).

Tyre **A** is under-inflated, but also shows signs of wear due to bad wheel alignment. Tyre **B** has been over-inflated. Both are illegal and dangerous.

Jacking points

Always ask the owner or dealer to jack up the car at each of the jacking points. See that the sockets are clear of mud, dirt and flakes of rust, and that there

is no buckling or chipping of paint when the car is lifted. Check that the doors still open and close easily after jacking.

Wheel checks

When the car is jacked up, hold the wheels top and bottom and rock them. If there is movement, the king or swivel pins are worn.

Grip the wheel on both sides and rock it. Movement indicates worn wheel bearings. Check for steering joint wear, fluid leaks and rusty brake pipes and cables.

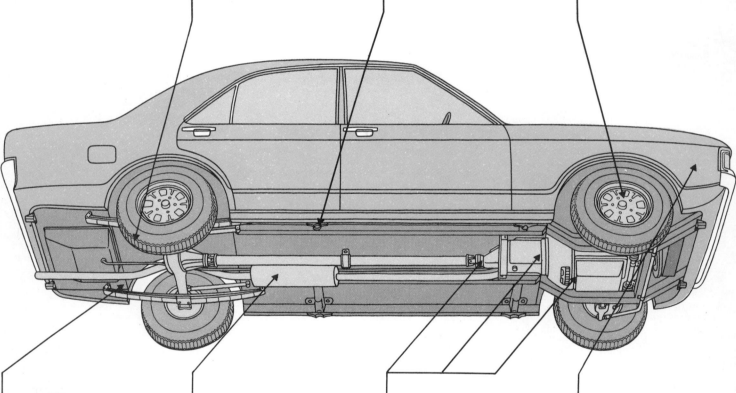

Sub-frame (where fitted)

Much of the car's strength comes from either the chassis or sub-frame, and severe faults will be costly. Check for twists and

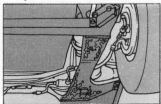

distortions—possibly due to a crash or advanced corrosion. An easy test is to jab any rust with a screwdriver. But never crawl beneath a car that is supported only by a jack.

Exhaust system

Brine working from the outside and condensation and hot gas on the inside combine to rot exhausts. Holed systems are noisy and could let dangerous

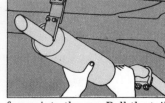

fumes into the car. Pull the tail pipe to check exhaust mountings. But beware of using brute force —you may have to pay for any damage you cause.

Oil and fluid leaks

Look for leaks before and after the test drive (see p. 265). Check the entire length of the underside, paying particular attention to the back axle and the joints between prop-shaft and gearbox, gearbox and engine, and engine block and timing cover.

If the car is in a showroom inspect the floor and the catch tray beneath the sump to see if there is any sign of oil, fluid or water leaks.

At the same time make sure that no brake fluid is seeping from joints in the brake tubing where it meets the engine compartment or the back-plate.

Wheel arches

The mud that gathers under the wings stores damp and causes rust. Scrape off the dirt and check for rust, blistering or places where the metal has been

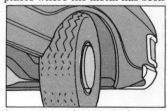

beaten out after crash damage.

If protected by underbody sealant, check for cracks or bulges. Badly applied sealant can speed corrosion (see p. 270).

Examining the bodywork and fittings

Tool kit
Ask the seller to include the kit that the manufacturer originally supplied with the car, even if it is only a jack, jack handle, wheel brace and, perhaps, one or two expanding or adjustable spanners and a plug spanner.

Spare tyre
The spare must match the other tyres. Remember that a crossply cannot go on the same axle as a radial (see p. 12). Look for damage on the walls and check the tread depth.

Crash damage
Body repairs may be visible if you stand at one end of the car and check the contours for unevenness. Look for circular marks caused by rubbing down. Patched-up damage can be betrayed by creases or beating-out marks inside the panels.

Hold a small magnet close to

any suspect bodywork. If it is not attracted to the car then the area may have been repaired with filler. If the damage is on a sill or an upright part of the frame, do not buy the car.

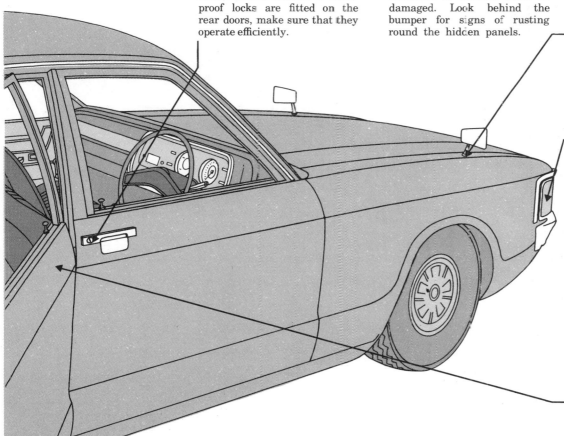

Number-plate
The registration, chassis and engine numbers should all tally with the log book and the tax disc. If they do not, ask for an explanation and check with the taxation authority. Some owners etch the registration number on a window.

Handles and locks
Look underneath all the door handles for traces of paint, which could indicate that some respraying has been done. Open and close the doors to test the action of the catches. If child-proof locks are fitted on the rear doors, make sure that they operate efficiently.

Bumpers
Check the line of the bumper against the bodywork. If it is

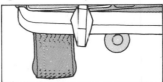

out of alignment the body structure or chassis could be damaged. Look behind the bumper for signs of rusting round the hidden panels.

Paintwork
If a car is less than three years old, any respraying is a sign that some damage has been done and repaired. On older cars, a scattering of blisters in the paint means that rust has eaten through the metal. Ignore a car with numerous patches of excess paint; this usually means that a cheap touching-up job has been done. The finish will deteriorate rapidly, and extensive corrosion will probably be revealed.

Rubber seals
Exterior fittings have rubber seals to stop water getting underneath the paintwork where it could start corrosion. Check the seals for perishing or splits. See that the trim is firmly seated on its seals.

Bodywork fittings
Any fitting which is obviously new could be the result of crash repairs. Manufacturers fit parts such as the grille and the brightwork around lights on a near-perfect shell. If any of these are

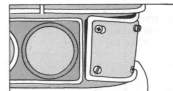

ill-fitting, possibly with screws at wrong angles, the body could be out of true. Traces of paint on fittings are a sign of a quick respray without proper masking.

Door condition
Doors should swing easily, and there should be no rattles when the car is driven. An ill-fitting door could be an indication that the car has been damaged.

Choosing a used car /3

Checking inside the car

Seat belts
Check the condition of both seat belts and make sure that they have the mark of the British Standards Institute. If the car was built before 1963, check the

anchorage points on the floor and on the door pillar. It is possible that they were fitted only after the car was made. See that they are secure and that they are not corroded.

If you intend to use a child's safety seat in the back, make sure that it can be fixed securely.

Driving seat
The condition of the driver's seat helps to show how hard the car has been used — regardless of the mileage it has

apparently done. If the seat sags badly, yet there is little wear on the passenger side, the car could have been used by a salesman who will probably have done a lot of low-gear driving in traffic. Look for other signs of hard use; for example, the rubbers on the clutch and brake pedals may be badly worn.

Roof lining and visors
The condition of the roof lining and the interior trim will give a good general guide to how well the car has been looked after. Grime on the roof, or dull patches caused by cigarette smoke, indicate that little

regular cleaning has been done, so mechanical maintenance may have been skimped too. Compare the lining with the underside of the sun visors, where the original colour can usually be seen.

Rear seats and shelf
Look for sagging in the back seats caused by weak springs, which could mean that heavy boxes have been carried by a salesman who has driven the

car hard. Remove the seat surround to see if there is rust or damp on the chassis panels.

Stains on the rear shelf usually mean that damp is penetrating the window seal. Check that no unsightly holes have been left in the shelf by the removal of a radio speaker.

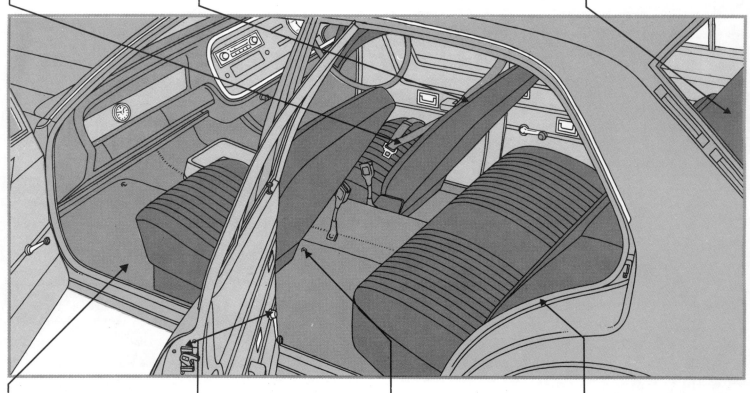

Carpets and floor
If new carpets have been fitted in a relatively new car it has obviously had hard use. Lift the carpets to look for rust in the floor panels, which would be expensive to repair. If the floor panels have rubber grommet

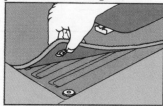

plugs, check that they are in good condition, or damp could attack the carpets from below. If there are damp patches on the carpets try to find where the moisture is coming from — the doors, side windows, rear windows or windscreen.

Winders and locks
The striker-plate on each door catch must be secure, or a jolt could throw the door open. If a door has to be lifted slightly as it is closed, the striker-plate is not properly aligned; this strains the door hinges. Check that all the door locks work, and test childproof locks. The

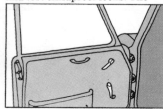

window winders should have a smooth action. If a window does not open and close fully, the winder mechanism may be worn or rusted, and could have to be renewed before long.

Weld points
Lift up the carpets just behind the front seat and inspect the floor pan carefully. Make sure the pan is held only by 'spot' welds. If you see a continuous weld joint across the floor,

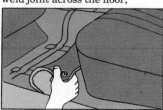

beware of buying the car — it has probably had the chassis rebuilt from two damaged models that have been joined together. A gas weld has tell-tale burn marks on each side. If you are suspicious, check with the vehicle licensing authority for your district.

Rubber door surrounds
Rubber door surrounds should not be perishing or split if they are to form an effective seal against weather and water. They must also be securely

fitted. Check the surrounds from inside the car with the doors closed. They should be flush with the door edges — not trapped. Open the doors and examine the seals where they meet the bottom front of the door frames. This is where they are most likely to come loose from the bodywork.

Wiring

Look under the dashboard if possible to examine the wiring. Even the most complex collection of wires should be neat, with no

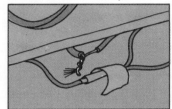

frayed insulation and no leads hanging loose. Wires should be joined by rubber or plastic snap connectors — not twisted together and bound with insulating tape.

Be suspicious of roughly repaired wiring; it could indicate an emergency job carried out after an electrical fault.

Windscreen and wipers

Scratches on the windscreen show that the wiper blades have been allowed to deteriorate

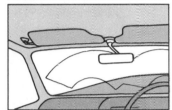

badly at some stage — a guide to general lack of care for the car. Check that the wiper arms have firm spring tension as they meet the windscreen. Blades should not be worn or torn at the edges. Switch on the wipers to test the motor and operate the windscreen washer (required by law on most cars). A broken pump will have to be renewed.

Mileage recorder

The figures on a mileage recorder should be perfectly in line. If they are not, the instrument may have been

tampered with to suggest that the car has done a lower mileage than is actually the case. This is illegal; but it is quite lawful to turn the recorder back to zero, and many reputable dealers always do this to avoid disputes. If you have doubts about the figure, check with the last owner marked in the log book.

Courtesy light

Open and close both front doors and see that the courtesy light goes on and off immediately. The

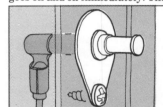

light switch may stick if it has not been properly maintained. If the switch appears to be working, but the light still fails, find out whether the bulb has blown. If there is no fault there, you could have to renew the wiring between the door switches and the light. Check that the dashboard switch for the interior light is working.

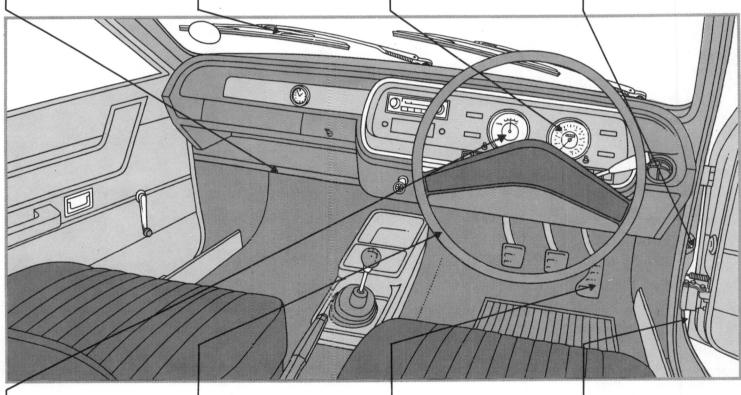

Dashboard instruments

All the dashboard dials should light when the car's sidelights are switched on. The direction indicator warning lights must flash steadily between 60 and 120 times a minute, and there should be an audible ticking.

The ignition and oil pressure warning lights should come on as soon as the ignition is switched on. If they do not, the bulbs may have blown or the wiring may be faulty.

The fuel gauge is hard to test, but the needle should move noticeably with the ignition on. If there is a radio, ask the seller whether it is to be removed before the car is sold. If so, make sure that the proper panel will be fitted to cover the hole. Try to ensure that the aerial will not be removed, leaving a bodywork hole that could speed corrosion.

Steering wheel

To test power steering, start the engine and turn the steering wheel from lock to lock. (Let the car move to protect tyres.) If there is noise at full lock, garage repairs may be needed. Check the steering wheel for

excessive play, which indicates wear in the steering mechanism (see p. 206). The wheel should be in its centre position when the front wheels are straight ahead; if the steering wheel is at a twist the car may have suffered front-end damage.

Pedal condition

The condition of the pedal rubbers is a guide to how hard the car has been used, provided that they have not obviously been replaced. If the car has done only a moderate mileage,

yet there is heavy wear on the clutch and brake pedal rubbers, most driving has probably been done in heavy traffic using low gears. Check the clutch and brake pedals for undue play which could entail expensive repairs. Test the accelerator for a smooth action.

Doors and sills

Check the door panels, particularly along the bottom, for obvious signs of rust and for blistering in the paintwork, which usually indicates that corrosion is eating through the metal. If the body sills show

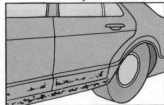

similar symptoms, repairs will be expensive. Examine the panels and sills for irregularities in the paint finish which could point to repairs after an accident — possibly with filler compound. Resprayed paint looks less hard and shiny than original paint.

Choosing a used car /4

Checking inside the engine compartment

If you are viewing the car by appointment, check that the engine is cold when you lift the bonnet. Any heat could mean that it has been run specially in advance—perhaps to disguise cold-start problems. A hot battery may have been given a fast charge to hide that it is nearly flat. If you are in doubt, ask the seller.

Look for general cleanliness in the engine compartment—usually a good indication of regular and careful maintenance. But do not be over-impressed by an engine that has been cleaned: there may still be faults.

Chassis number
The chassis number is usually engraved on a plate fixed to the bulkhead. If it does not match the log book, the car could be an insurance write-off that has been rebuilt.

Battery
Look for white crystals which show corrosion at the terminals and check that the electrolyte level is correct (see p. 36). The battery should give brisk power to the starter.

Top and bottom hoses
Look for signs of perishing or splits. Very hard or very soft hoses are suspect.

Distributor leads
Check all visible wiring for fraying and bad connections.

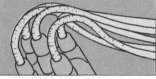

Make sure that none of the wires is contaminated with oil.

Dipstick
Drops of water or grey foam on the dipstick can mean that water is getting into the sump. Sludgy oil usually indicates poor general maintenance.

Washer bottle
Every car must by law have working windscreen washers. Check that the bottle or bag is sound, with a tightly fitting cap. Examine the supply tube for leaks. If the washer is electrically operated, check that it is in working order.

Bodywork panels
Look along the bodywork panels inside the engine compartment for traces of paint overspray.

This usually indicates that repairs have been done after a front-end collision. It may not be serious, but check.

Suspension
Give the car a firm push down at each corner. If the suspension

is correct the body should bounce once, then return to a steady position. Continued bouncing indicates faulty dampers.

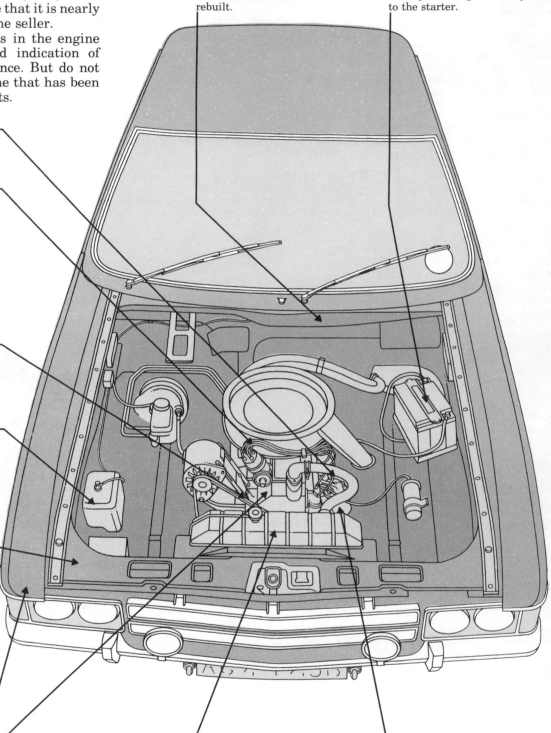

Engine number
Check the engine number with the log book. If they do not tally,

a replacement engine has been fitted. Be suspicious if this was not mentioned as a selling point.

Cooling system
Check that the metal framework of the radiator and the honeycomb are in good condition. The sealing rings and the spring in the pressure cap must be sound. Look for rust discoloration in the water or floating oil: both could involve expensive repairs. Leaks usually show as rusty or blue-green stains. If the engine is air-cooled, see that the ducts are undamaged and check that the fan is working.

Oil filter
See that the outside of the oil filter bowl is not clogged with dirt—a sure indication that the car has not been regularly

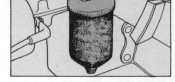

serviced. The filter should be replaced regularly (see p. 73).

Testing the car on the road

Do not buy a used car until you have tested it on the road.

If the car is more than three years old it must have a DoE test certificate before you can drive it on a public road. Check that the car is taxed and that your insurance, or the owner's, covers you.

Choose a route that includes bends which, besides testing steering and suspension, show up defective rear-wheel bearings. Listen for wheel rumble as the car leans to one side. Any unusual noises from the engine, gearbox or rear axle also call for investigation. In general, noises caused by serious defects will quickly become obtrusive.

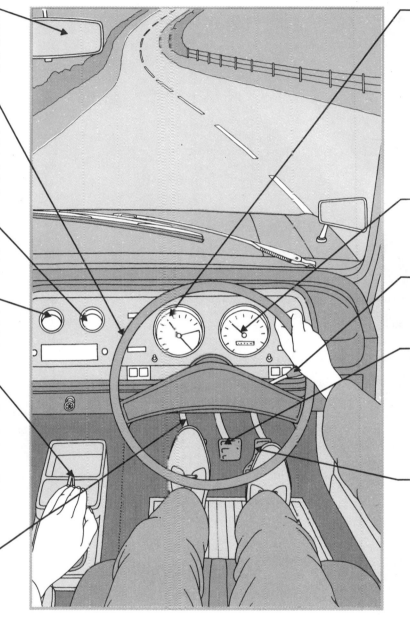

Visibility
Check that you have a good view to the rear for brake tests and check that the mirror does not vibrate at speed. Make sure none of the mirrors distorts distances.

Steering
Steering-wheel judder at low speeds can indicate worn wheel bearings. Vibration that starts at around 45-55 mph usually means the front tyres are at the wrong pressures, or that the wheels need balancing. Check for steering bias.

Oil-pressure gauge
Check the reading at 40-50 mph against the handbook. Most give a figure for that speed and for idling.

Water temperature gauge
If the temperature is abnormally high there is a cooling system fault. A consistently low temperature causes piston-ring and cylinder wear.

Gearbox
Do not double de-clutch throughout the gear range; you will not be able to detect worn synchromesh mechanisms. Accelerate hard and decelerate in each gear; if a gear disengages on its own, it is badly worn.
On a car that has automatic transmission, gear changes should be almost imperceptible. Check that the kickdown works (see p. 134).

Clutch pedal
The clutch should operate smoothly. If gears engage fiercely when the pedal is fully depressed the clutch is probably badly worn.

Rev-counter (tachometer)
Test the engine performance by accelerating in second and third gears almost in to the red 'maximum' band on the rev-counter, if one is fitted. Listen for excessive noise and vibration at high revs; these usually indicate engine wear.
If the oil pressure drops while the engine is under stress, reduce speed immediately—and do not buy the car. If the seller is not with you, warn him when you return the car.

Speedometer
Watch for any erratic movement of the speedometer needle, which indicates a damaged cable. Try to make sure that the meter is registering accurately.

Indicator switch
Check that the direction indicators cancel automatically when the steering wheel returns to normal after a turn.

Brake
Check at low speed that the brakes do not pull to one side. Drive for a couple of miles to heat up the mechanism, then test the brakes two or three times again. Use a quiet road for an emergency stop at about 25 mph, to ensure that the car pulls up in a straight line.

Accelerator
With the car stationary, press the accelerator sharply and listen for a knocking sound as engine speed increases. This warns that a big-end bearing needs replacing—an expensive job. Set the engine speed at 3000 rpm and allow it to drop to 2500 rpm. If there is a heavy rumble as power drops, the main bearings are worn.

Last-minute checks after the road test

When you return to the seller's premises do not switch off the engine immediately. Several tests can be carried out only when the engine is hot and running at tick-over.

Oil filler cap Remove the cap and watch for smoke or acrid-smelling fumes, which usually indicate wear in the bores or rings.

Engine noise A clicking from the tappets (see p. 109) at idling speed is not usually significant, but if it appears excessive and increases when you rev the engine, the valve gear is probably worn. This will involve expensive repairs.

Oil leaks Minor traces of oil on the underside of the engine or gearbox are unlikely to be serious. Significant leaks will be obvious and could indicate major faults.

Oil-pressure gauge At tick-over, with the oil thinned by driving, the reading will be low, but it should not be below 10-15 lb./sq. in.

Exhaust Rev the engine hard. Black smoke from the exhaust often indicates a relatively minor carburettor fault, but thick blue smoke indicates major engine wear.

Clutch pedal With the handbrake set, select top gear and gently let in the clutch. The engine should stall instantly. If it gradually fades, the clutch is badly worn.

If you are inspecting the car at a dealer's, he might be willing to put right any fault that you have found. Try to assess how much it would cost to do the work yourself—it may pay you to beat down the price and carry out the repairs.

Raising the money

Finding the best way to borrow money

One in three new cars, and three out of every five used cars, are bought with borrowed money. Even people who can afford to buy outright often prefer to raise a loan because:

1 Tax concessions may be available on the interest paid.
2 Repayments are made with money that is decreasing in value because of inflation.

Hire purchase
A car bought under a hire-purchase agreement remains the finance company's property until all payments have been made.

The company pays the dealer for the car and 'rents' it to you for the repayment period. When you have completed the payments, the company sells you (legally, gives you an option to buy) the car for a nominal sum—usually about £2.

While the agreement is in force you must keep the car covered by fully comprehensive insurance (see p. 287), tell the finance company of any accidents affecting the car's value and keep it in reasonable condition. You cannot sell the car without the company's permission before you have paid all the outstanding instalments.

Most finance houses require a deposit of 20-25 per cent for a new car or for one less than three years old. For a four or five-year-old car the deposit is likely to be 30 per cent, and for a car over five years old at least 40 per cent.

Repayments are normally spread over three years for newer cars and 24 or 30 months for older models.

Interest is charged at a flat rate— about $14\frac{1}{2}$ per cent a year on new cars, $16\frac{1}{2}$ per cent on those up to three years old, and $18\frac{1}{2}$ per cent on older cars.

Flat rate is interest calculated on the whole original loan. The true interest rate is much higher because your debt falls with each payment, yet you are charged interest on the money you have already repaid.

To get a rough idea of the true interest when you are quoted a flat rate, double the figure you are given and subtract 1. For example, a flat rate of 12 per cent works out at 23 per cent true rate.

Buying a new £1000 car on hire purchase over two years costs about £96 a year in interest charges after you have paid a 20 per cent deposit.

Tax relief is available under some agreements, and you may get a rebate for early settlement.

If you fall behind with your payments, and more than two-thirds of the hire-purchase price is outstanding, the finance company can repossess the car. It cannot be taken away from you without a court order if you have paid one-third of the total price, or unless you choose to end the contract.

Hire-purchase agreements on cars costing up to £2000 including interest charges must state the cash price, the hire-purchase price, the amount of each instalment and the payment dates. You must also be given a copy of the agreement.

If you do not sign it on trade premises—for example, a showroom or the finance-company offices—you have the right to cancel the deal without losing any money within four days of receiving your copy of the agreement.

Credit sale
Some finance companies offer credit-sale facilities. These are similar to hire-purchase agreements, but you become the car's owner immediately.

Tax relief can often be claimed on all but the first £35 of interest each tax year. On a £1000 car, the deposit might be about £200, with the balance repayable over three years at $13\frac{1}{2}$ per cent flat-rate interest. The total interest would be £324, of which £219 would be eligible for tax relief, provided the repayment period did not extend into a fourth tax year.

If you fall behind with the payments, the finance company can sue for the whole debt to be cleared immediately.

Dealer loans
Many dealers offer loans which have the same deposit rates, interest charges and repayment periods as ordinary hire-purchase and credit-sale agreements. The difference is that a finance company pays the money direct to the dealer, and the car becomes your property immediately.

Tax relief is available on all but the first £35 interest in each tax year. If you default on repayments the car cannot be repossessed, but you can be sued for the whole outstanding debt.

Overdrafts
Until recently, one of the cheapest ways of raising money for a car was by arranging a bank overdraft, but most bank managers prefer to give customers a personal loan instead. The major drawback with an overdraft is that the money can be recalled. Any bank will give advice on which suits your circumstances.

An overdraft is negotiable. There is no fixed rate, but it is normally set between three and five points above the minimum lending rate. With a bank rate of, say, 10 per cent the interest rate would be 13-15 per cent. But a fluctuating bank rate means that the interest rate can change at any time.

Overdraft facilities will depend on the state of your bank account, whether the bank manager is prepared to grant one, and what securities you can offer against the sum borrowed.

Personal loans
Most banks and finance companies operate personal-loan schemes. The money is paid direct to you and you pay cash for the car. The repayment period is negotiable, and interest is charged at a flat rate. No deposit is required, but a finance company will check on your credit rating and status. To get a bank loan you need a bank account. There are few formalities and you will know from the outset how much you will have to repay each month. The loan cannot be recalled.

On a £1000 loan over four years at 8 per cent you would repay

---

SAFEGUARDS YOU SHOULD TAKE

1 Make your initial deposit on a new car as low as possible. Delivery may take several months, during which you could have the use of the money or earn interest on it.

2 Check the true rate of interest before signing the agreement.

3 If you are buying on hire purchase or credit sale, make sure the agreement is worded so that tax relief is available. It should contain a clause allowing you to end the agreement without penalty within days.

4 Do not raise money through a finance broker. Many reputable finance houses do not deal with them, so you could be placed with a lending company that charges very high rates. You might also be charged a brokerage fee.

By arranging finance yourself you can select from a wide range of schemes offered by competing companies, but a broker's field is much more limited.

5 Deal only with a finance company of obvious good standing.

Most of the major lending companies are members of the Finance Houses Association, which has a code of practice and will take up legitimate complaints by the public against its members.

£1320. Tax relief would be available on interest of more than £35 each year.

Three personal-loan schemes are operated by Mercantile Credit for members of the Automobile Association. No deposit is required for any of them, and the debt is cancelled if you die before the age of 60.

Revolving loans

The attraction of a revolving loan is that after you have used it to finance car purchase, money is available later for such things as repair bills and insurance.

The finance company gives you a credit limit of up to 36 times the amount you agree to pay each month. After reducing the amount owing, you can borrow again to 'top up' the loan to the maximum.

Interest is charged at a minimum true rate of 1·60 per cent a month on the amount owed. You can increase your payments to clear the loan early, or to make your credit limit higher.

Secured loans

A second mortgage on your house is normally required for a secured loan, which allows you to borrow up to 60 times the amount of your monthly repayment figure. The minimum interest charge is a true rate of 1·50 per cent a month on the outstanding debt.

If you cannot pay

Your circumstances may alter in such a way that you have difficulty in maintaining repayments. Contact the finance house or bank immediately there is any problem, and explain the position. Terms can often be negotiated to extend the period.

Insuring the agreement

Some finance companies automatically cancel your debt if you die. If your loan is not insured in this way, some insurance companies offer policies which cover your payments in the event of unemployment, accident and sickness, as well as completing payment if you die before the loan period expires.

The premium is about £10 for each £200 in a 12 month agreement. On 24 and 36 month agreements, premiums are about £6 and £5 a year respectively.

Loans and VAT

Loans are not subject to Value Added Tax, but many hire-purchase and credit-sale deals are if the purchase price, plus interest, comes to more than £2000. VAT is then levied at 10 per cent of the yearly interest charges.

Some finance companies stipulate in the contract that you can end your hire-purchase agreement at any time within a few days, without incurring a penalty. This makes the interest charges free of VAT.

TYPES OF CREDIT — THEIR ADVANTAGES AND DRAWBACKS

	Hire purchase	Credit sale	Finance-house loan	Bank loan/overdraft	Dealer loan
Deposit	33⅓ per cent on new cars; at least 40 per cent on cars more than 5 years old	33⅓ per cent on new cars; at least 40 per cent on cars more than 5 years old	Possibly no deposit after the company has checked on your credit rating and status	Securities usually required by bank for overdrafts and secured loans, which are cheaper than unsecured loans	Difference between the price of the car and what the dealer is prepared to lend
Repayment periods	24 months	24 months	24 months	24 months. Overdrafts may be withdrawn at short notice	24 months
Tax concessions	Some agreements have a special clause allowing relief to be claimed	Relief on all but the first £35 of interest each tax year	Relief on all but the first £35 of interest each tax year	Relief on all but the first £35 of interest each tax year	Relief on all but the first £35 of interest each tax year
When you own the car	At the end of the repayment period when you have taken up the option to buy	Immediately	Immediately	Immediately	Immediately
When you can sell	At the end of the repayment period unless the hire-purchase company agrees to an earlier sale	At any time, provided you clear the outstanding debt immediately	At any time	At any time	At any time, provided you clear the outstanding debt immediately
If the car is faulty	If it cost less than £2000 the company must, in theory, pay for repairs. But the agreement may contain an escape clause	If it cost less than £2000 the company must, in theory, pay for repairs. But the agreement may contain an escape clause	The company has no responsibility. You may have a legal claim on the vendor	The bank has no responsibility. You may have a legal claim on the vendor	You may have a legal claim on the dealer as vendor of the car
If the car is stolen	You are responsible for insuring the car comprehensively so that theft is covered	You are responsible for insuring the car comprehensively so that theft is covered	You must still repay the loan. Insure the car against theft	You must still repay the loan. Insure the car against theft	You must still repay the loan. Insure the car against theft
What happens to the interest rate	No change during loan period	No change during loan period	No change during loan period	**Bank personal loan** Rate does not change **Overdraft** Interest rates can fluctuate at any time	No change during loan period

Corrosion protection / 1

Where rust can develop on a new car

Moisture, dirt, industrial fall-out, winter road salt and grit, cement dust, crop sprays and manure all help to speed corrosion in a metal car.

Rust – an all-year-round menace – quickly gains a foothold in the moisture and mud traps which are a feature of nearly all cars. Load-carrying structures are particularly vulnerable because they are built as closed, or semi-closed, box sections. These include the lower sills, the sub frames, door pillars, cross-members in the floor, and reinforcing sections of the wings, boot and the bonnet and engine compartments.

New cars are given an anti-corrosion treatment which produces a controlled etching. This offers the best protection against heavy rusting and also provides a good key for the paint.

All cars have some panels welded together and it is difficult for the initial anti-corrosion treatment to penetrate the junctions. A typical problem area is where the rear wings join the body.

The most damaging corrosion starts in the enclosed sections and rots away insidiously from the inside. Thin barrier coatings sprayed into these areas during manufacture give some protection.

The best protection against rust is to regularly wash off dirt and mud – particularly in the wheel arches and behind lamp units – and to touch in chipped paintwork. A high-pressure hose can be used on the underbody, but not on the body panels or windows.

Corrosion costs money – something like £30 to £50 every year in lost value.

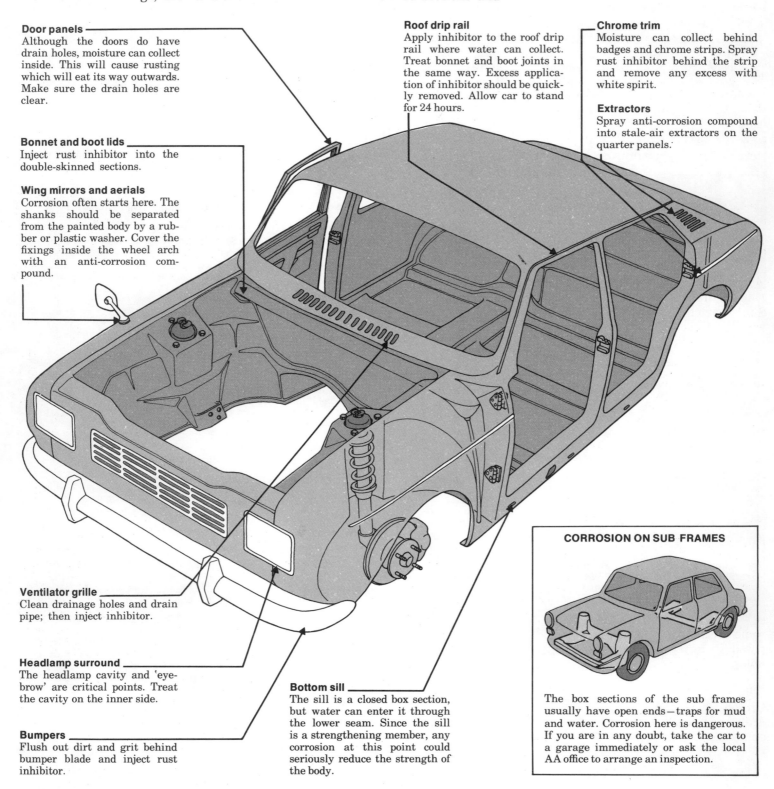

Door panels
Although the doors do have drain holes, moisture can collect inside. This will cause rusting which will eat its way outwards. Make sure the drain holes are clear.

Bonnet and boot lids
Inject rust inhibitor into the double-skinned sections.

Wing mirrors and aerials
Corrosion often starts here. The shanks should be separated from the painted body by a rubber or plastic washer. Cover the fixings inside the wheel arch with an anti-corrosion compound.

Roof drip rail
Apply inhibitor to the roof drip rail where water can collect. Treat bonnet and boot joints in the same way. Excess application of inhibitor should be quickly removed. Allow car to stand for 24 hours.

Chrome trim
Moisture can collect behind badges and chrome strips. Spray rust inhibitor behind the strip and remove any excess with white spirit.

Extractors
Spray anti-corrosion compound into stale-air extractors on the quarter panels.

Ventilator grille
Clean drainage holes and drain pipe; then inject inhibitor.

Headlamp surround
The headlamp cavity and 'eyebrow' are critical points. Treat the cavity on the inner side.

Bumpers
Flush out dirt and grit behind bumper blade and inject rust inhibitor.

Bottom sill
The sill is a closed box section, but water can enter it through the lower seam. Since the sill is a strengthening member, any corrosion at this point could seriously reduce the strength of the body.

CORROSION ON SUB FRAMES

The box sections of the sub frames usually have open ends – traps for mud and water. Corrosion here is dangerous. If you are in any doubt, take the car to a garage immediately or ask the local AA office to arrange an inspection.

Rust-proofing with a do-it-yourself kit

To give proper protection against rust and corrosion, all inner panels and box sections should be injected with a special rust inhibitor.

All rust inhibitors have common features, whether they are wax or petroleum based. They disperse moisture; they provide a barrier against moisture and oxygen by forming a pliable, unbroken film, on both metal and painted surfaces; they have great penetrating ability; and they never set hard.

When a car is professionally sealed, holes are drilled at strategic points in the body and the inhibitor is injected into the inner panels by compressed air and special rigid and flexible lances. Do-it-yourself kits are available for the motorist to rust-proof his own car. These consist of either aerosol spray cans of rust inhibitor, or a hand-operated pump with a supply canister and enough inhibitor to treat a car.

When buying one of these kits, specify the make and model of car it is to be used on. The kit will include instruction on the correct place to drill holes to gain access to inner box sections.

Apart from treating the obvious points, do not forget to treat any double-skinned sections on the boot and bonnet lids. Inject the rust-proofing material behind badges and chrome trim on the bodywork. It will dispel moisture already collecting there and seal it against future rusting. Any of the solution that gets on to the paintwork can be removed with white spirit. It takes the solution about 24 hours to solidify.

Tools: Electric drill; centre punch; hammer; file.
Materials: Do-it-yourself rust-proofing kit, including rust inhibitor and aerosol applicator with long nozzle.

Treating parts of the car that are vulnerable

Double-skin work
The area between the rear wheel-housing and the quarter panel can usually be sprayed from inside the boot. For two-door cars, also drill a

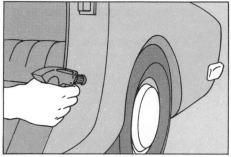

hole in the rear door pillar about 8 in. above the sill, and spray downwards. On four-door cars drill a hole in the rear pillar from the door opening.

Treating door pillars
Centre door pillars are usually welded directly on to sills, forming separate box sections. If they have drain holes, spray through them. If not, drill a hole in the pillar. On

some front door pillars, it may be possible to spray through hinge holes.

Sills
On most cars, the sills already have drainage holes. But these may be too small for the spray nozzle. Widen the holes carefully with a file, and drill one or two others as needed.

Continue spraying into each hole until the rust-proofing starts to

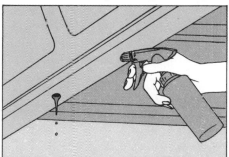

drip through the one next to it. Rusted sills seriously weaken the car's structure.

Door panels
If the doors have large drain holes, you will have to drill only one hole, just below the door latch. Point the

spray nozzle towards the bottom of the door. If the holes are small, you may have to drill a drainage hole in the door base, or you can ease off

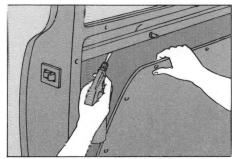

the door upholstery and spray the door in the ordinary way. Make sure that the window winding and lock mechanisms are not sprayed, or they will become difficult to operate.

Wings
Wheel arches collect dirt and dust in sheet metal folds and pockets. With road salt and water spray this dirt forms a moist paste that attacks the sheet metal. The 'eyebrows' above the headlamps are particularly exposed. Always hose wheel arches carefully when washing (see p. 38). Spray under the wings heavily

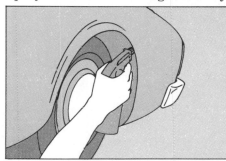

with rust inhibitor. Take particular care to clean and rust-proof between the rear of the front wing, where it joins the engine compartment panel and the front edge of the door pillar.

Sub frames
Most manufacturers provide holes in any sub frame. These can be

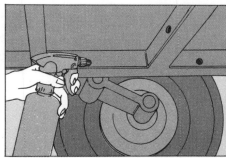

used for injecting the rust inhibitor. Severe corrosion damage in a sub frame is a source of danger, and repairs should be left to a garage.

Corrosion protection /2

Preventing corrosion on the underside

Underbody sealing protects vulnerable sections of the underbody with a thick compound that acts as a barrier to moisture and dirt. As well as preventing rust, underbody sealing helps to protect the paint from being chipped by stones and grit thrown up from the road.

A number of companies now specialise in anti-corrosion treatment.

The underbody is thoroughly cleaned first with steam or hot water jets.

Professionals will spray the solution on the underbody ensuring that it penetrates the more inaccessible areas under the car. But if you do the job yourself, you will probably have to brush it on—a dirty job. A new car should be treated as early as possible, although some anti-corrosion companies will treat cars up to four years old if the bodywork is sound.

The moving parts under the car —such as the gearbox or driveshafts and brake mechanisms—must be protected with masking tape and newspaper during the treatment, as the compound could seriously damage them.

Areas that should and should not be treated

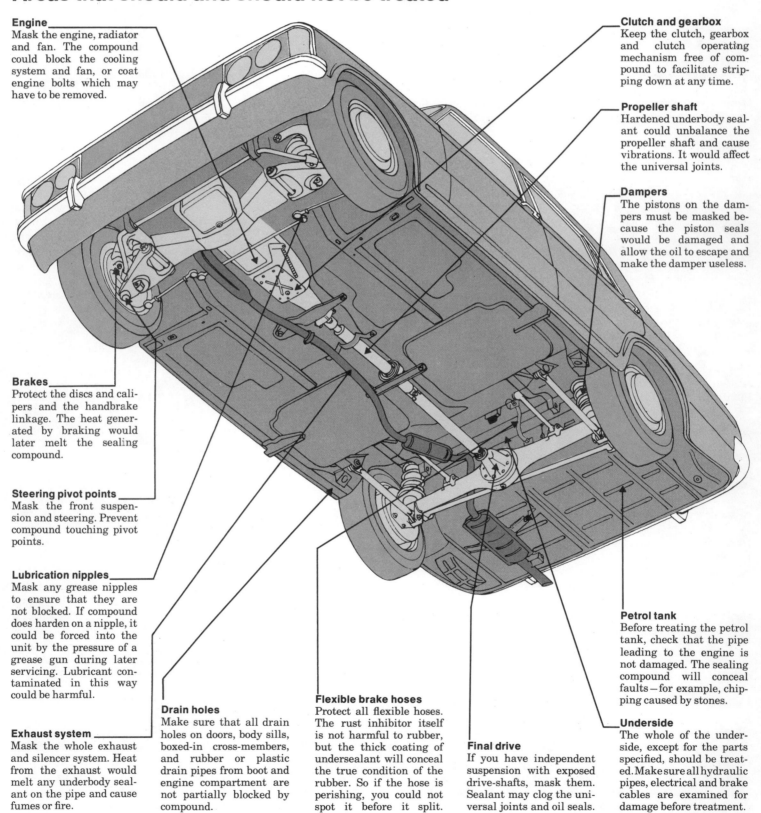

Engine
Mask the engine, radiator and fan. The compound could block the cooling system and fan, or coat engine bolts which may have to be removed.

Clutch and gearbox
Keep the clutch, gearbox and clutch operating mechanism free of compound to facilitate stripping down at any time.

Propeller shaft
Hardened underbody sealant could unbalance the propeller shaft and cause vibrations. It would affect the universal joints.

Dampers
The pistons on the dampers must be masked because the piston seals would be damaged and allow the oil to escape and make the damper useless.

Brakes
Protect the discs and calipers and the handbrake linkage. The heat generated by braking would later melt the sealing compound.

Steering pivot points
Mask the front suspension and steering. Prevent compound touching pivot points.

Lubrication nipples
Mask any grease nipples to ensure that they are not blocked. If compound does harden on a nipple, it could be forced into the unit by the pressure of a grease gun during later servicing. Lubricant contaminated in this way could be harmful.

Exhaust system
Mask the whole exhaust and silencer system. Heat from the exhaust would melt any underbody sealant on the pipe and cause fumes or fire.

Drain holes
Make sure that all drain holes on doors, body sills, boxed-in cross-members, and rubber or plastic drain pipes from boot and engine compartment are not partially blocked by compound.

Flexible brake hoses
Protect all flexible hoses. The rust inhibitor itself is not harmful to rubber, but the thick coating of undersealant will conceal the true condition of the rubber. So if the hose is perishing, you could not spot it before it split.

Final drive
If you have independent suspension with exposed drive-shafts, mask them. Sealant may clog the universal joints and oil seals.

Petrol tank
Before treating the petrol tank, check that the pipe leading to the engine is not damaged. The sealing compound will conceal faults—for example, chipping caused by stones.

Underside
The whole of the underside, except for the parts specified, should be treated. Make sure all hydraulic pipes, electrical and brake cables are examined for damage before treatment.

How to treat the underside yourself

Before starting treatment, have the underbody cleaned by steam or hot water. Use a high-pressure hose to clean any inaccessible areas — such as the tops of the wheel arches and recessed rear seat panels. Have any seriously corroded panels replaced at a garage before treatment.

Clean off all rust, and treat and respray the area before applying the sealant. If you simply cover existing rust you may curb it in that particular spot, but it will quickly reappear near by.

On older cars, a complete underbody treatment is not advisable. Corrosion will have started in enclosed sections already and will soon concentrate at the areas where the sealing is incomplete. If gaps are left on load-bearing parts, this treatment may be worse than useless as it could accelerate the process of corrosion in vital areas.

Consult the AA about the best underbody protection compound to use. Look for one that is fairly easy to apply, that has good adhesive properties and affords the best possible protection. Avoid buying cheaper substitute compounds.

Tools: Wire brush for cleaning; paint scraper; palette knife; 3 in. brush for applying underbody protection compound.
Materials: Masking tape; cardboard; newspaper and plastic covers for protection; underbody protection compound.

1 Have the car steam-cleaned at a garage or by a specialist contractor to remove oil, grease or mud. The steam-cleaning treatment will also reveal any areas that have started to rust. If you find any rusted sections, treat them yourself (see p. 232), or take the car to a garage for repair before you apply the underbody compound.

2 Jack up the car and mount it on axle stands (see p. 61). Remove the road wheels and brush off any dirt from around the wheel arches. Pay

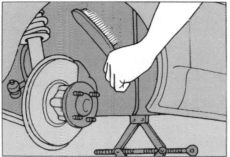

particular attention to crevices and awkward corners.

3 Apply masking tape around the edges of the wheel arches and along

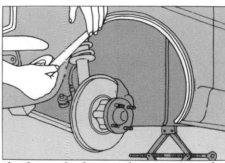

the lower body panels to protect the paintwork from the compound.

4 Use newspaper and tape to mask off the propeller shaft, the exhaust

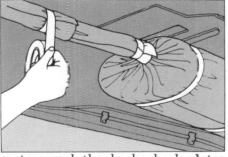

system and the brake back-plates or discs and calipers.

5 Cover the flexible rubber brake hoses with masking tape.

6 If there are any grease nipples on the suspension or steering arms, protect them with plastic caps or cover them with masking tape.

7 Cover any exposed handbrake cables with newspaper — or cardboard — secured by masking tape.

8 If you are applying the sealant by brush, paint the whole of the underside, including the steel brake pipes, up to the edge of the area you have masked. Do not forget to treat the turned-up lips inside

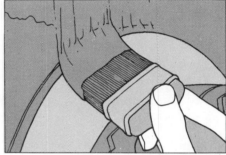

the wings which fill with grit, salt, sand and dirt. If possible, work the sealant into the areas above the headlamp back shells on the underside of the wings.

9 When the job is completed, remove all the masking from the parts

that have been protected. Use a rag moistened with white spirit to clean any of the body panels that may have inadvertently been covered with sealant during the treatment.

What the owner can do regularly to delay corrosion

The usefulness of a rust inhibitor will be reduced if you do not help to protect the car yourself during normal running and routine servicing.

1 Periodically clean the underside (see p. 38) and check the condition of the underbody protection material. If it is cracked or bulging in any place, prise off the faulty material and about 1 in. of sound material around it. Clean the surface and fill with a patching layer of the same underbody protection material.

2 It is essential to wash the car carefully. Automatic washers are not enough to combat rust because the revolving brushes cannot reach the underside or the wheel arches. Hose off caked mud as soon as possible.

3 Never put a wet car in a warm garage with all the doors and windows shut. This creates a sweatbox with ideal conditions for hastening corrosion. Let the car dry slowly in the open or in a place where there is a through draught.

4 After accident repairs, replacement panels are often not properly protected against corrosion. Use an aerosol spray kit to apply new rust inhibitor (see p. 269). Consult the AA about the brands available.

5 Check on the underside of the car also. If the underbody compound has been disturbed during the repairing process, rust could start behind it. Strip off any loose compound and clean the area behind it. Treat and paint the area and seal it with new compound.

Selling your car /1

Choosing the right time to sell

Many people sell a car every two years regardless of its age and condition. This may not necessarily be the best time to do it, certainly for the private motorist whose car is not included in his business and who is not likely to benefit from tax relief.

The two elements of motoring costs that are most altered by the car's age and condition are depreciation and repairs. Except for inflation, other costs—such as insurance, petrol, tax—are likely to remain at a similar level while you have the same car. Depreciation and repair costs should therefore govern your choice of selling time. Some makes of car are built for durability— Volkswagen and Volvo, for example. To sell one of these after two years, regardless of its mileage and condition, would mean that you would not own it long enough to benefit from its best asset.

The effect of depreciation and repair costs

The rate of depreciation varies for different models, but in general the value of any car drops most steeply in the first two years of its life.

There are of course exceptions to this rule, and it is possible—especially at the expensive end of the car market—to find cars that actually gain in value at first.

But because of the normally declining rate of depreciation, its average weekly share of your motoring bill gets smaller the longer you keep the car, up to the point when it is negligible. For example:

Ford Escort XL 1300 2-door saloon
Price new £1050

Selling price (average condition)		Average weekly cost
after 1 year	£700	£6.73
after 2 years	£600	£4.32
after 3 years	£515	£3.43
after 4 years	£430	£3.00
after 5 years	£360	£2.65
after 6 years	£300	£2.40

But depreciation depends not only on age. Several other factors, including condition, are involved. A second-hand car's trade-in value will therefore depend on how well it has been serviced and maintained, and to what extent it has been used. For every year after three years old, the bodywork condition becomes more important. A high-mileage car depreciates more quickly, so the average weekly cost of depreciation will be higher.

Ford Escort XL 1300 2-door saloon
Selling price (below average condition)

		Average weekly cost
after 1 year	£570	£9.23
after 2 years	£510	£5.19
after 3 years	£430	£4.00
after 4 years	£340	£3.41

Rising repair costs

Repair and replacement costs increase as the car gets older. For a car with an average annual mileage, costs are usually found to be highest when it is between four and six years old, that is when its mileage is 35,000-60,000 miles. Whether costs then continue to increase or flatten out depends very much on the type of car, its condition and how much it is used.

The only accurate way to assess what is likely to happen is to keep a detailed record of all your expenditure since you bought the car. But in general you can expect to have to pay for a new battery and exhaust system every two years, new sparkplugs every 10,000 miles, brake relining and new tyres every 20,000 miles, and a new clutch every 30,000 miles. There is, of course, in addition the cost of materials needed during normal servicing.

The costs combined

As depreciation steadies, the cost of repairs is still increasing, and there is a point when the combined total of these two costs begins to show an increase in the average weekly total. If you want to sell the car, it is most economical to do so just before the weekly total steadies or starts to go up, or when it reaches the limit you want your car to cost you each week. For example:

Ford Escort XL 1300 2-door saloon
10,000 miles a year

Year	Average weekly depreciation cost	Average weekly repair cost	Total
1	£6.73	21p	£6.94
2	£4.32	53p	£4.85
3	£3.43	£1.15	£4.58
4	£3.00	£1.54	£4.54
5	£2.65	£2.40	£5.05

So you would want to sell at the end of year 4.

20,000 miles a year

1	£9.23	£1.06	£10.29
2	£5.19	£2.23	£7.42
3	£4.00	£4.15	£8.15

So you would want to sell at the end of year 2.

SELLING WHEN YOU STILL OWE MONEY ON HIRE PURCHASE

If you are buying a car on hire purchase, you are not the legal owner until you have made the last payment. In law, this means that you cannot sell the car unless you have the hire-purchase company's agreement.

In most cases, the company is likely to give its permission to sell, provided that you undertake to pay off the debt in full as soon as you have completed the sale.

The hire-purchase company is legally entitled in such circumstances to ask you to pay not only the full amount outstanding, but also all the interest that would have been due if the hire-purchase loan had run its full term. In practice, many companies are prepared to allow a kind of discount on the remaining interest payments you are due to make. (And if the recommendations of the Crowther Report on consumer credit are adopted by the government, a buyer will be legally entitled to such a discount, provided that he has not seriously defaulted on his repayments and that the period of the loan was more than 20 weeks.)

The amount of any discount you might be allowed, depends on the length of the loan period and on the amount of interest that still has to be paid. Do not assume, because you are going to settle your debt halfway through the hire-purchase period, that you will be allowed a discount equal to half the interest on the loan.

Many companies calculate the amount of discount as a fraction, worked out as follows.

Step 1 Take the number of months that the loan was originally to cover—**for example 24**.

Step 2 Add the figures from 1 to 24 together: 1+2+3+4+5+6+7+8+9+10+11+12+13+14+15+16+17+18+19+20+21+22+23+24, **which equals 300**.

Step 3 Find the number of months still outstanding on the loan—**for example, 12**.

Step 4 If you are going to buy another car on hire purchase through the same company, deduct 1 from the figure you have found in Step 3—in this example, **leaving 11**.

If you are not going to use the hire-purchase company immediately, deduct 3. In this example, **that would leave 9**.

Step 5 Take the number you have found in Step 4 and add again as in Step 2. For example 1+2+3+4+5+6+7+8+9+10+11, **which equals 66**.

Step 6 To find the fraction that applies to your loan, put the figure you arrived at in Step 5 over the figure you found in Step 2—in this example, **66/300**.

Step 7 Find the full amount of interest you were due to pay on the loan—say, **£200**.

Step 8 The discount you will be allowed is
66/300 × £200 = £44
So, although you are repaying the loan halfway through, your discount is less than a quarter of the interest.

Choosing the best way to sell

There are three ways to sell a used car—to a private buyer, to a dealer or at an auction. The way you choose to sell will make a difference to the price you eventually get.

Private sale
You are likely to get the highest price from a private sale, although it will take longer and involve you in more work. You can sell either by advertising privately or through a computer car club.

Advertising can be expensive. One 20 word advertisement might cost from 80p locally to £4 in a London evening paper.

For about £3 you may be able to enrol in a computer car club which circulates lists of buyers and sellers to people living within 100 miles of each other. Registration forms are published in the motoring press. No dealers are allowed to register.

Selling to a dealer
If you sell to a dealer his offer will probably be 20-25 per cent below the current retail price, because he has to cover repairs, servicing, VAT, and any guarantee he gives on the re-sale. His offer will also depend on whether or not you are selling in part-exchange for another car.

If you are considering part-exchanging your old car for a new one, find out what discount the dealer is prepared to give if you pay cash for the new car and do not part-exchange. A dealer who has a large stock of a new model may give a discount as high as 10-12½ per cent. You might therefore save money by selling your car privately or at an auction and paying cash for the new one.

Selling by auction
Car auctions are a quick, safe and reliable way of selling, but although you can usually sell a car the day it is offered you will probably raise only the trade price—perhaps a little more if it is a clean, one-owner, low-mileage popular model. There may be an entry charge and you have to pay a fee—perhaps 5 per cent of the selling price. You have to weigh up whether the quick sale but lower price offsets the cost and risk of a private sale.

Making the car look its best for sale

Most people buying a used car are looking for something that looks as new as possible, so any work you can do to improve the car's appearance will increase your chances of making a good sale at a favourable price.

But remember that work badly done—obvious bodywork repairs or poorly touched-in paintwork—could put off a buyer. Consider first what work you are competent to do and whether the time and money you spend doing it will increase the price. As a dealer is better equipped to do most repairs and improvements, the work you do may not affect his offer sufficiently to make it worth while.

A thorough cleaning, however, will always help to improve the price. It might mean an extra 5 or even 10 per cent for an older car.

Cleaning is most important if you are selling privately. A dealer might be able to recognise a good car under a little dirt, but a private buyer might not have the experience to do so. Although he might not notice, for example, that the engine compartment was clean, he would certainly notice if it was dirty.

On the other hand, although the car's appearance is less important when selling to a dealer, a good-looking car is easier for him to sell, and he will consider any time and money he has to spend on making it saleable when making an offer.

Whichever way you are selling the car, the less reason you give the buyer to criticise it, the less opportunity he has to try to persuade you to bring down the price.

Inside the car

Windows Wash with clean water and use a chamois leather, or use a glass cleaner; leave no smears. Use methylated spirit to dissolve any film on the inside.

Dashboard Wipe with a damp cloth, then dry. Pay special attention to chrome.

Steering wheel and column Wipe with a damp cloth.

Carpets and upholstery Vacuum thoroughly and use a stiff brush if necessary. Clean with a carpet shampoo or vinyl cleaner. Wipe leather with a damp cloth, or sponge it with soapy, tepid water and dry it with a soft cloth. Do not forget door panels and head linings.

Patch torn upholstery with a piece of matching material glued under the tear.

Differences in colour can be touched in with special upholstery paint.

A fresh interior could add £10-15 to the selling price.

Pedals Wipe the rubbers with a damp cloth; replace if necessary.

Rubber mats Wash with warm water and detergent.

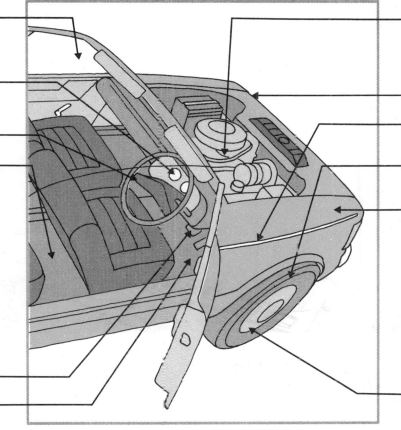

Outside the car

Engine compartment If this is clean it could add £10-15 to the selling price. Protect all the electrics then spray on a grease solvent and hose off with water. Be careful to clean round seals.

Lights Make sure that all lenses and chrome parts are clean.

Chrome work Wash and leather. If it is marked use a chrome cleaner. Do not miss corners.

Tyres Wash down the walls and paint them with tyre black. Remember the spare wheel.

Paintwork If this is good, washing and leathering are sufficient. Remove tar spots with white spirit and rinse with cold water.

Pay particular attention to areas below bumpers and doors.

Dull and faded paintwork can be improved by using a cutting compound. This does not cost much, but unless done carefully can damage the paintwork. It could, however, add £25 to the selling price. If you do not sell within a week it will dull off again and need polishing.

Wheels Remove the hub caps to clean. Polish the hub caps while off the car.

Selling your car / 2

Deciding what price to ask

No matter how good the condition of the car, always try to keep the asking price realistic. If you ask too much, you will waste money on advertising without getting offers.

To help in fixing a price, look at advertisements for similar models and at the monthly car-price guides. They usually give current retail prices. Cars are usually classified as first-class, average or below average.

Even if you intend to sell the car privately, try to find out what a dealer would offer, and what he would charge for the car when he came to sell it. A private buyer will expect to pay less than if he were to buy the same car from a dealer, since there will be no after-sales service or guarantee. You can prob-

ably strike a bargain somewhere between the current retail price asked by a dealer and his offer to you if you were trading it in.

Accessories often help to sell a car, but modifications do not. Dealers are likely to offer less for a car with altered bodywork, wide wheels, and a 'tuned' engine.

Decide whether or not to include accessories in the price. Removal may detract from the car's appearance and therefore its price — a removed aerial will leave an unsightly hole, for example. A radio can help to sell a car, so unless yours is very expensive, or unless you are selling at an auction, include it with the car. If you sell at an auction, leave the aerial but remove the radio and

cover the fascia with a blanking plate. Do not remove accessories legally necessary — such as seat belts.

If you are going to sell the Road Fund licence, include it in the overall price you ask. Otherwise, make it clear that the licence is not included. You can sell it to the new owner provided that you notify the taxation authority which issued it. If you do not sell the licence, you cannot transfer it to another car.

You can get a refund amounting to one-twelfth of the annual rate for each calendar month left on the licence. As a quick guide, allow £2 for each month left. But claim before the beginning of a month to get a refund for that month.

Precautions to take when making the sale

Once you decide to sell the car, whether privately or to a dealer, do not let the buyer know you are in a hurry. It will give him a chance to force the sale at his price.

Selling privately

Be prepared to spend time waiting for telephone calls and arranging appointments. Keep the details of all inquirers so that you can contact them again if a sale falls through.

Do not try to hurry a buyer while he is inspecting the car, or he may suspect that something is wrong. Answer any questions truthfully. Do not give a written guarantee.

If the buyer wants to try the car out on the road, this is usually a good sign that he is interested. Either drive yourself or allow him to, provided that he is a competent driver, has a licence and there is insurance cover. Never let anyone take the car alone.

If you have several prospective buyers, you will want to consider all the offers before closing the deal. So do not accept an offer (or a deposit) until you are sure about it. If a buyer is keen he may well raise his offer.

Once you have agreed to sell, arrange payment by cash or cheque. A banker's draft is the safest method, but it is not usual in car sales.

If you accept a cheque, do not part with either the car or the log book until the cheque is cleared. You can get a cheque cleared quickly by taking it to a bank and asking for it to be 'expressed'; this costs about 50p. If you go to the bank on which the cheque was drawn, you should get the answer the same day, after closing. If you go to your own bank

you should know next morning. Do not accept a cheque at the weekend from a buyer in a hurry who agrees your price without question and wants to take the car. It has been known in such a situation for the cheque to bounce.

If you agree to accept a deposit, make sure there is a time limit for the sale — say seven days — or you may lose other opportunities to sell.

Selling to a dealer

Try several dealers; you will probably find different prices offered.

You should be able to get a better price if you trade in the car in part exchange for another car. Most dealers are happy to take a car in part exchange if it is in good condition, as they can make two profits. But if your car is likely to be difficult to re-sell, the dealer may not take it in part exchange.

Dealers will usually pay more for a car they can sell quickly — a car in the showroom for a long time costs money. A dealer who has a lot of stock may not offer such a good price as one with showroom space.

If you go to a dealer who stocks the make of car you want to sell, he may make a better offer than one who does not. This is because he is more likely to be familiar with repairs and their costs, and to have spare parts and any special tools.

Assessing a car's condition and how much it will cost to make it suitable for re-sale is not easy. Some dealers may be better able to prepare for re-sale, so may offer a better price.

If you get an exceptionally high part-exchange offer from one dealer,

look for the reason behind it. Although offers will vary, there is a limit to the price a car will fetch in the used-car market, and a dealer is not likely to be over-generous without reason. If, for example, you are selling your car in part exchange for another used car, he may be adding on his excess offer to the price of the other car. Find out what price he offers for your car if you do not part exchange.

Do not accept a dealer's first offer as unalterable. He probably expects you to haggle and may be allowing for this. He might be persuaded to increase his offer by £10-£25.

Selling at an auction

To enter the car in an auction, telephone the company two or three days before the sale to reserve a lot number. Drive to the centre early on the day of the sale and give details of the car and the reserve price on the entry form — ask the auctioneer if you are not sure about the reserve price. You must give a list of major faults — if not the buyer may reject the car. Minor faults such as blown bulbs need not be declared. You can get the company's engineer to report (usually about £1.50); but this may put up the price.

Some companies will not allow a reserve price on cars more than seven years old or valued at less than £100. These cars are sold 'as seen', which means that the buyer has no comeback if he later discovers a fault.

If a reserve is not reached and the car not sold, you can remove it, usually without charge. Or you can leave it for the next sale.

Insuring your car

Comparing the terms / 1

Precautions to take before deciding to change insurers

Faced with ever-rising repair bills and steep increases in premiums year after year, many motorists are tempted to try to save money on insurance. But all too often a policy with an attractive cut-price premium can prove very expensive.

If you want to economise on your insurance premiums, take care. However varied the insurance market seems to be, all companies must operate on the same basic principle that policyholders contribute premiums to a pool, out of which claims by the minority can be met.

To make the system as fair as possible, the insurance companies generally assess the risk they are taking on any one policy by comparing the applicant's circumstances and driving history with the statistics they have gathered over the years.

More drivers and vehicles mean that the insurance pool is constantly growing, but the cost of claims is constantly rising, so more money is being paid out.

Competition within the insurance business means that premiums and discounts can vary widely, but all

Liability to third parties

> Indemnity unlimited in amount against the legal liability for death of or bodily injury to third parties including passengers and for damage to property.
>
> This indemnity also covers liability of
> (a) any permitted driver
> (b) any passenger
> (c) your employer or partner
> You are also covered while driving a private motor car or motor cycle not belonging to you nor hired under a hire-purchase agreement.

Indemnity against legal liability to third parties means that if the insured car injures or kills anyone, apart from the policyholder, or damages property, the insurance company will meet claims for compensation.

Look for a policy in which . . .
Indemnity—that is, insurance cover—is provided while you are driving other cars. (**Note:** The extension for driving other cars is always for third-party risks only— it does not cover damage to the car you are driving.)

Anyone driving your car with your permission or at your request is covered.

Legal costs are paid.

Examine carefully a policy if . . .
There is no mention of cover for damage or injury caused by passengers— called legal liability of passengers as in (b) above. Unless this is included neither you nor your passengers are covered for injury or damage caused by them, for example by opening a car door carelessly. The passenger would have to pay for the damage or for compensation for injury to the victim.

Passengers not in a properly constructed seat have no cover. For example, anyone travelling in the back of a van or in the luggage part of an estate car. (**Note:** By law, these claims would have to be paid, but the insurer might try to reclaim from you.)

Personal accident

> The policy in the name of an individual provides the following benefits for both the policyholder and his wife (or for the husband if the policyholder is a woman):
>
> 1 Death £1000 ⎤ Age limit
> or 2 Total loss of one or more limbs £1000 ⎬ 70
> or 3 Total loss of sight of one or both eyes £1000 ⎦ years

Personal accident cover means that, no matter who caused the accident, the insurance company will pay the sum stated to the policyholder and anyone else covered if they lose eyes or limbs as a result of an accident while travelling in their car. If they are killed, the sum will be paid to their estates. (Few policies cover suicides.)

Look for a policy in which . . .
A high rate of compensation is given (some policies specify as little as £500 or £250 for loss of limbs and eyes).

Cover is provided for other members of the family as well as husband and wife.

Claims are covered if made up to a year after the accident.

The age limits for compensation are the least restrictive.

The policyholder is covered while he is travelling in any other vehicle.

Payments are increased if BSI safety belts are worn at the time of the accident.

The cost of artificial limbs is covered.

Examine carefully a policy if . . .
Personal accident cover is not provided. (Because many sports cars are open, the personal accident section may be excluded, or available only at an increased premium.)

Cover is restricted to the insured—not including other members of a family living with the policyholder.

Claims must be made within three months of the accident.

The amount of a claim is reduced when, because of other claims in the same year, total claims exceed a set sum.

Age limits are unusually restrictive. Most insurance companies impose an age limit— usually 16-70 years— anyone older or younger will not qualify.

No cover is given for injury arising when a person is injured while under the influence of drugs or drink.

companies must charge their customers enough to meet any possible claims, to satisfy the law on what reserves they have available for emergencies, and make a profit.

No insurer can afford to set his premiums too high or too low without risking his business. For example, a company that is reliable with a rapid-claims service is unlikely to be able to offer very cheap premiums as well. Yet it is in your greater interest to make sure that the company is reliable, long-established (or backed by a long-established company) and able to meet any claim you might make quickly and in full.

You cannot expect to make dramatic savings on insurance without jeopardising some part of your cover. But there are useful economies that can be made.

Before you consider changing your insurance, study the specimen conditions and clauses on these and the four following pages. They are drawn from representative examples published by large and small insurance companies. Below/continued

Medical expenses

These are paid up to £50 for each occupant of the car.

If a person travelling in the insured car is injured, the company will pay medical expenses up to the limit stated.

Look for a policy in which . . .
The highest sum is offered for each person. The maximum is usually £50.

Dental treatment is included. It is not always specifically mentioned.

Examine carefully a policy if . . .
No cover is given for medical expenses.

Loss or damage

The insured is indemnified against loss or damage to the car including damage by frost and the same cover is extended to accessories (a permanently fitted wireless set being regarded as an accessory) and spare parts while in or on the car or while detached therefrom and in the insured's private garage.

If the insured car or its accessories are lost or damaged by accident, the company will pay for the damage or give compensation for the loss. If the policy contains what is known as an excess clause, however, the company will not pay the full amount. The policyholder will have to pay the amount specified by the excess clause.

Look for a policy in which . . .
Accessories are covered while on or in the car or in a private garage.

A fitted car radio and the spare tyre are specifically mentioned as accessories.

A damaged windscreen is given separate cover not subject to an excess.

Cover is provided for hotel and travelling expenses (up to a specified limit) if you have to make an unplanned overnight stop because use of the car is lost through fire, theft or accidental damage.

Examine carefully a policy if . . .
Frost damage is excluded where the car is kept in the open at night.

Damage to the car radio is excluded unless the car is also damaged.

Note: Cover is sometimes reduced to that required under the Road Traffic Acts (see p. 287) if the driver is convicted of being under the influence of drink or drugs at the time of an accident.

Emergency treatment

The policy covers indemnity against liability to pay for emergency treatment of injuries under the Road Traffic Acts. A payment under this heading does not affect the no-claim discount.

This clause must be included in all motor insurance policies, since it is a requirement under the Road Traffic Acts. A doctor giving immediate treatment or examination after an accident is entitled to a fee for each person attended, and sometimes to a mileage allowance. Hospitals are also entitled to a fee. The fees will be paid by the insurance company under this policy.

Examine carefully a policy if . . .
It is not stated that such claims do not affect the no-claim discount.

Fire and theft

Damage by fire, and loss of or damage to car up to full amount insured (including tyres, standard accessories and spare parts, whether stolen with or without the car) by burglary, housebreaking or theft is covered. If the insured owns or is liable for the structure of the garage, damage by fire up to £200 is covered provided not otherwise insured.

Look for a policy in which . . .
A car up to 12 months old is replaced with a new car if it is stolen and not returned within 28 days.

There is a payment made to compensate for loss of use each day the car is missing.

The garage is covered for the damage (up to a stated limit) while the car is in it—if it is not covered by your house policy.

Cover is provided for the unexpired portion of your Road Fund licence if it is not refundable from the authorities after the car is stolen or destroyed by fire.

Examine carefully a policy if . . .
Theft cover is excluded where the car is not kept in a locked garage overnight. (Some companies provide this cover for an additional premium.)

Accessories are not covered (unless the car is stolen) where the car is kept in the open at night.

Loss resulting from deception by a would-be buyer or his agent is excluded.

Fire or theft claims are subject to an excess clause.

Comparing the terms /2

Precautions to take before deciding to change insurers / continued

each example is a list of points for and against the policy quoted. Do not expect to find a policy with all the good points and none against. And do not rule out a whole policy just because it contains one point that is less favourable.

No one policy is best for every driver. You can only weigh one against another to see which on the whole offers the most favourable terms at the lowest price.

To reduce your premium, you can either change your insurer or get your present insurer to reduce your cover so that you pay less (see p. 288). A different insurance firm, for example, may be able to offer you a lower premium because it rates your car or the district where you live in a more favourable group (see p. 283) or because it tries to control repair costs by asking you to use an approved garage.

But, remember, there is little to be gained from moving from a good insurance firm for the sake of only a small reduction in premium. Goodwill built up by insuring with the same firm over a period of years

---

Rugs, clothing and personal effects

Up to £50 for any one occurrence will be paid for loss of or damage to rugs, clothing and personal effects in the car, whether caused by accidental means, fire or theft.

Look for a policy in which ...
There is maximum payment of at least £50 for each occurrence. (Car radios that are not securely fixed are often covered in this section. As most are worth nearly £50, there is not much left for anything else.)

Examine carefully a policy if ...
Cover is excluded. (Because many sports cars are open, this section may be excluded, or be available only at an increased premium.)

Cover for jewellery, furs, cameras and portable radios is excluded. (Most policies will not pay for loss of or damage to goods or trade samples, or for loss of or damage to money, stamps, documents or securities.)

The contents of a car parked in the open at night are not covered unless the car is stolen.

Replacement of new car

For cars not more than one year old which are damaged beyond 50 per cent of their list price or are stolen and not recovered within 28 days, a replacement car of the same make and model will be provided (subject to availability).

If a new car is stolen or damaged beyond economical repair, some companies will replace it with a similar car rather than pay compensation for the loss. Generally, if a car is a total loss, they will pay only the market value at the time of the loss. Because depreciation causes a very sharp drop in the value of a new car, your loss would be heavy without this provision.

Look for a policy in which ...
There is provision for replacement when damage is 50 per cent beyond list price rather than 60 per cent or more.

There is provision for transfer of the insurance to the new vehicle.

Examine carefully a policy if ...
Replacement of a new car is not mentioned.

Repairs and re-delivery

Repairs up to any amount covered by the insurance may be commenced at once provided that an estimate is first forwarded to your brokers or underwriters.
The underwriters will pay reasonable costs of safeguarding the disabled vehicle after an accident, of removing it to a repairer's, and of re-delivery to the insured's home address.

Look for a policy in which ...
Costs of removal to a garage are covered.

Payment for delivery after repairs is covered.

Examine carefully a policy if ...
There is no cover for the cost of towing a damaged car, or of re-delivery after repair.

A car towing or being towed is not covered.

Car laid up

If the insurance is suspended other than for fire and theft risks for four consecutive weeks or more (other than by reason of a claim), up to 75 per cent of the pro rata premium for the period of suspension will be credited, provided that the Certificate of Insurance has been returned.

Look for a policy in which ...
Between 50 and 75 per cent of the premium is refunded.

A short time limit is allowed; the minimum period is usually 30 days.

Accident damage as well as fire and theft is included.

Examine carefully a policy if ...
There is no provision for the suspension of cover.

Trailers

The policy, without extra premium, covers third-party risks while the car is drawing a trailer, including a caravan trailer. If the policy covers the car against loss or damage, the trailer (but NOT a caravan trailer) may be similarly covered on request and this extension will usually be given free of charge.

Most insurers include third-party cover for trailers while they are being towed or if they become detached while being towed. The trailer is not covered when it is parked.

Look for a policy in which ...
A luggage trailer is covered without extra cost.

Examine carefully a policy if ...
Goods or trailers under tow are not covered.

may prove valuable should you have a borderline claim or need the benefit of the doubt in some other way.

Give yourself plenty of time if you are thinking of changing your insurance—especially if you run a modified vehicle. Make sure that your new policy starts as soon as your present one runs out. It is your responsibility—not that of the insurance company—to see that you are not left without cover.

First, check that your present insurer and any others you are thinking of using are sound firms with a reputation for settling claims quickly—any saving on the premium may be wasted if when you have a claim the new insurance company does not settle promptly.

If your insurance is already arranged through a firm of brokers, discuss with them whether you could benefit by changing. If you have not previously used a broker, it may save time to find one in your area. But remember that almost anyone can describe himself as an insurance broker. To make sure that you deal with a qualified/*continued*

Car in the hands of a garage

The policy protects you while the car is in the hands of a member of the motor trade for overhaul, upkeep or repair regardless of any restriction to named drivers which may be specified in the policy; and the compulsory contributions for young and inexperienced drivers do not apply.

Look for a policy in which ...

The car is covered while being parked by a member of the staff of a hotel, restaurant or commercial undertaking.

Restrictions and excesses do not apply if the car is damaged while being parked by a member of the motor trade, or by a member of the staff of a hotel, restaurant or commercial undertaking.

Examine carefully a policy if ...

There is no mention of cover while the car is in the hands of a motor trader for repair and maintenance.

Windscreen breakage

A payment in respect of a broken car window or windscreen will be made irrespective of any excess up to the sum of £25 provided there is no further damage to the insured vehicle other than resultant scratching of the surrounding bodywork. One windscreen claim up to £25 will not prejudice the no-claim discount, but if there is any further claim during the same year of insurance, no discount will be allowed.

Look for a policy in which ...

Scratches or damage as a result of the breakage are covered.

There is no restriction on the sum paid, or it is high enough to cover the cost of your windscreen. (Some policies go up to £50.)

There is no loss of no-claim discount (see p. 280).

The claim is not subject to an excess (see p. 280).

Examine carefully a policy if ...

No separate cover is given for windscreen damage.

Scratches or damage to the paintwork caused by the breakage are not covered.

There is a low limit to the amount of the payment.

The number of claims in one year is limited.

It is stated that the claim will affect your no-claim discount, or be subject to an excess (see p. 280).

Transit

All accidental damage or loss is covered whilst in transit within the territorial limits of the insurance, including sea transit from port to port by the usual short sea routes, including risk whilst loading, unloading or being trans-shipped in transit.

Look for a policy in which ...

The car is covered while being taken or sent by sea, air or Hovercraft to and from Europe, provided the insurers are notified.

'General average', normally found in marine insurance, is included.
Note: If part of a cargo has to be thrown overboard to save the ship, all cargo owners may have to contribute to the loss.

Examine carefully a policy if ...

There is no cover between Europe and Britain.

There is no cover for loading and unloading.

Cover is limited to 65 hours' transit.

Continental use

The policy may be extended to apply while the car is in Europe, subject to the payment of an additional premium. Rates will be quoted on application.
A bail bond of £500 for Spain will be provided for an additional £1·50.

Cover is now automatically provided for EEC countries and for Austria, Sweden, Norway, Finland and Switzerland. But it is limited to the minimum legally required in the country concerned, and is not comparable with comprehensive cover or third-party only. You should notify your insurance company if you are taking your car abroad, even if you intend to rely on this limited cover. Some policies require you to do this.

Look for a policy in which ...

Cover is extended to countries outside Europe (an excess may be stipulated).

A bail bond guarantee for Spain (usually £500) is provided automatically.

Examine carefully a policy if ...

No cover is given outside the Common Market.

Cover is not mentioned or is limited to 65 hours' transit.

Cover for Customs Duty is not mentioned. If your car is taken into a country and not taken out—for example, after an accident—you will be liable for duty.

Comparing the terms /3

Precautions to take before deciding to change insurers / continued

broker, check that he is a member of one of the professional associations. If you have difficulty, write to one of the following organisations and ask for a list of their members in your work or home area.

The Association of Insurance Brokers, Craven House, 121 Kingsway, London WC2B 6PD. Telephone: 01-242 3831.

The Corporation of Insurance Brokers, 15 St Helen's Place, London EC3A 6DS. Telephone: 01-588 4387. Lloyds Insurance Brokers' Association, Lloyds Building, Lime Street, London EC3M 7DQ. Telephone: 01-623 2855.

It is, of course, possible—although more time-consuming—to find out for yourself. Ask a number of com-

panies what cover their policies provide. But remember that there is no standard form of policy; the way information is presented varies.

Compare the details you get from the companies with the examples on these pages. If any items are not covered, ask about them. If you are still in doubt, ask for a blank copy of the policy document itself.

Excess

Comprehensive policies require the policyholder to bear the first:
£50 of any Accidental Damage claim when the driver has not attained his 21st birthday.
£35 of any Accidental Damage claim when the driver is over 21 but has not attained his 25th birthday.
£25 of any Accidental Damage claim when the driver is over 25 but holds a provisional licence or has not held a triennial licence for 12 months.
The excess will be additional to any compulsory or voluntary excess applying under the policy.

Most policies include an excess for drivers under 25 and for inexperienced drivers. This excess is in addition to any other excess already in the policy. If there is a £50 excess for a person under 21 on a policy which also has a £25 accidental damage excess for another reason, the policyholder must meet the first £75 of any claim.

Look for a policy in which...

The excess is not increased for a driver under 21, or is lower than £50.

An excess is excluded while the car is being driven by a member of the motor trade.

Examine carefully a policy if...

Excess amounts are high.

An excess applies to fire, theft and windscreens.

An excess applies while the car is being driven by a member of the motor trade for repair.

Change of car

If the insured:

a) changes his private car
b) acquires an additional private car

Cover hereunder in respect thereof shall be limited to that necessary to meet the requirements of any law relating to compulsory insurance unless and until the change or addition has been notified to the Company.

This type of clause will be found in a policy only if the insurance company issues an 'open' Certificate of Insurance covering any vehicle (see p. 291).

Look for a policy in which...

A seven-day extension is automatically given to allow time to notify the insurer.

Examine carefully a policy if...

Cover is reduced to that required under the Road Traffic Acts only until the insurer has been notified.

No-claim discount

A discount in accordance with the following scale is allowed off the net renewal premium for such part of the insurance as is renewed in respect of each car which has been insured for a full year and in respect of which no claim is pending or has been made during the preceding year(s) of insurance. (Scale—see p. 285.)
In the event of a single claim occurring under a policy earning 50 per cent or 60 per cent no-claim discount, the discount will not be entirely lost at the next renewal date but will revert two steps, i.e. to 30 per cent or 40 per cent provided that the driver has not been convicted of a motoring offence arising out of the accident. Policies can be transferred from other companies without loss of bonus up to 60 per cent.
Note: The no-claim discount is not prejudiced by the operation of knock-for-knock agreements with other companies where no blame attaches to the driver of the insured car and full recovery could have been made if no such agreement had existed. The discount will not be affected by reason of a claim made solely for damage to the windscreen and/or windows of the insured vehicle subject to a limit of £25 in any one period.

Look for a policy in which...

The scale offers the best terms (see p. 285).

The discount is protected once maximum has been reached (see p. 285), so that one or more claims can be made within a specified period without the discount being affected.

The no-claim discount is not affected by: (i) claims for windscreen breakage; (ii) claims for emergency treatment.

Note: Find out also if the two points below are allowed. They are not normally stated in the policy.

The discount is not lost if the policyholder refunds the cost of a claim.

The discount is not lost if, solely because of a knock-for-knock agreement, the company pays a claim that could have been recovered in full by the policyholder.

Examine carefully a policy if...

Your position in the scale as a result of a claim is affected by a conviction for a motoring offence.

The scale offered is less favourable than other policies offer (see p. 285).

Windscreen breakage affects the discount.

A claim for emergency treatment affects the discount.

Note: All policies suspend a no-claim discount while a claim is pending (see p. 292). Most insurers apply any discount separately to a second car (see p. 289).

Right of recovery

Nothing in this policy or any endorsement thereon shall affect the right of any person insured by this policy (or of any person) to recover any amount under or by virtue of the provisions of the law of any territory in which the policy operates relating to the insurance of liability to third parties. But the policyholder shall repay to the company all sums paid by the company which the company would not have been liable to pay but for the provision of such law.

All policies include this clause. It means that the insurance company is making sure that none of the clauses or endorsements in the policy denies anyone his legal rights. But it also means that the company has the legal right to try to recover from the policyholder any costs that, but for the law requiring payment, it would not have paid.

Endorsements

The schedule forming part of the policy specifies, by indicating the number below, any endorsements to which the insurance is subject. In respect of each and every occurrence the company shall not be liable under Section X (Accidental Damage) for the amount defined by the endorsement or any amount otherwise payable in respect of loss or damage to the vehicle.
1 Excess Clause—Damage—£20
2 Excess Clause—Damage—£35

Every policy includes a schedule setting out the terms of cover—usually by indicating the numbers of the clauses that apply. If, for example, it is also endorsed 'subject to Excess Clause 1', the policyholder will have to pay the first £20 of any damage claim.

General exceptions

The policy may exclude cover:
1 For accident or injury or loss or damage occurring while the vehicle is being used for purposes not permitted by the Certificate of Insurance, or driven by any person not described in it.
2 If the vehicle is driven by anyone (including the policyholder) who is disqualified, or who has not held a licence.
3 If the vehicle is driven by anyone without the policyholder's consent.
4 For loss or damage directly or indirectly caused as a result of radio-activity, pressure waves, war, invasion, earthquake or riot.
5 For loss or damage due to wear and tear, mechanical or electrical failure, and tyre failure due to braking, cuts or bursts, or punctures.

Exclusions may be listed under general exceptions or under the clause to which they apply. Make sure you know of any exceptions that restrict the policy cover.

Legal costs

The company pays for
(a) costs and expenses arising out of a claim.
(b) legal representation at any coroner's inquest and for legal defence in any police court proceedings following an accident.
(c) defence costs up to £1000 against a charge of manslaughter or causing death by reckless or dangerous driving.

Look for a policy in which . . .

There is a high limit for legal defence costs for manslaughter or dangerous driving. (The maximum is usually £1000.)

Examine carefully a policy if . . .

No provision is made for payment of solicitors' fees.

Legal fees to defend charge of manslaughter or causing death by dangerous driving are restricted to certain groups.

No cover is provided for anyone who is under 21, or is driving a high-performance car.

No cover is provided for anyone convicted of driving under the influence of drink or drugs.

Conditions

If you break any of the conditions of the policy, the insurers can refuse to meet a claim other than as required under the Road Traffic Acts. If they are obliged to meet the claim, they may seek to recover the cost from you.

Points usually included:
1 Procedure for making a claim, with a stipulation that no admission of liability or promise of payment should be made.
2 Provision for cancelling the policy, with seven days' notice on either side.
3 Exclusion of liability except for a rateable proportion if a claim under the policy is covered by other insurance.
4 A stipulation that the vehicle is kept in roadworthy condition.
5 Exclusion of liability if the conditions are not fulfilled or if the statements in the proposal form are untrue.

Examine carefully a policy if . . .

The policyholder, in the event of an accident, has to submit to an examination under oath by anyone designated by the company.

Notice of cancellation of the policy sent to the policyholder's last known address by ordinary post is considered as served on him.

There is no provision for any return of premium to the policyholder if the policy is cancelled.

Understanding the premium/1

How the insurance company decides what to charge

One of the most important factors in insurance is the way in which the companies actually decide their premiums. Practice varies widely, particularly on details, but in most cases their first step is to establish a list of basic premiums. To do so, they are interested mainly in where the motorist lives and what type of car he drives.

They may then add an amount to cover any special risks—if they are insuring a bad driving record, for example. This gives the gross premium from which the company deducts any discounts, such as the no-claim discount, to arrive at the net premium you are charged.

Not all companies load the premium to cover a special risk. They may put a restriction on the policy instead—for example, a compulsory damage excess, which means that the driver pays the first amount of a claim for his own car. Some apply both a loading and a restriction if there is a special risk.

Not all insurance companies use the same basic premiums, the same area and car-group ratings, or apply the same discounts or loadings. Their lists of high-risk and low-risk professions may vary.

A few companies set out their basic premiums in their brochures, with examples of loadings or discounts that apply, so that you can roughly work out your net premium. But most prefer to take all the facts into account before they quote a price for a particular person. They may not give the basic premium in their quotation and, because of the different ways of arriving at the net premium, it is not always possible to compare quotations step by step.

Where do you live?

Where you live or keep your car is the first important element affecting your premium. Most companies divide Britain into areas of risk, based on traffic density and the number of claims they have had.

Because each company has had a different claims experience, the number of areas and the boundaries vary from company to company and from time to time. Many major insurance groups base their premiums on seven areas of risk, some have only three. Northern Ireland is considered separately.

HOW YOUR REGION AFFECTS THE PREMIUM

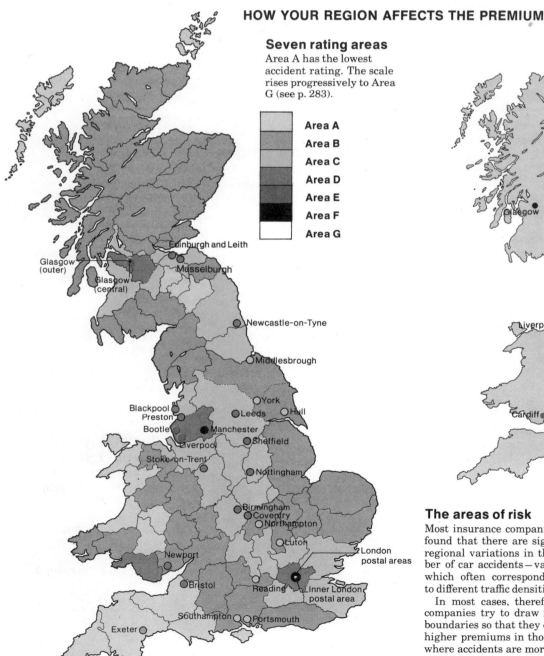

Seven rating areas
Area A has the lowest accident rating. The scale rises progressively to Area G (see p. 283).

- Area A
- Area B
- Area C
- Area D
- Area E
- Area F
- Area G

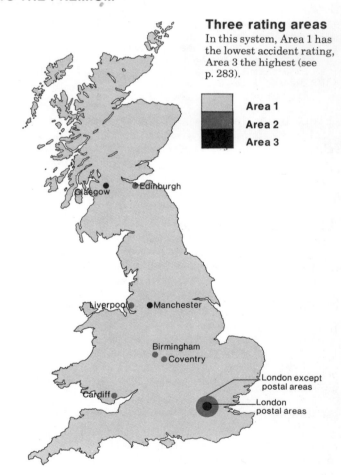

Three rating areas
In this system, Area 1 has the lowest accident rating, Area 3 the highest (see p. 283).

- Area 1
- Area 2
- Area 3

The areas of risk

Most insurance companies have found that there are significant regional variations in the number of car accidents—variations which often correspond closely to different traffic densities.

In most cases, therefore, the companies try to draw regional boundaries so that they can levy higher premiums in those areas where accidents are more likely.

Unless you live and use your car almost entirely in a densely populated city, you will generally benefit from using a company that has a high number of risk areas: the more areas, the more steps there are in the company's scale of premiums.

There is, however, a growing tendency for companies to reduce the number of area ratings—on the ground that even once-safe agricultural areas are now within daily, motorway commuting reach of major towns or cities.

Why your car influences how much you have to pay

In addition to their regional rating system, insurance companies have separate scales for groups of cars, based mainly on the cars' performance and repair costs.

The way in which the ratings vary from car to car depends on a number of factors. In some cases, certain mechanical repairs are very expensive because the parts are difficult to remove and refit. For some cars, bodywork repairs cost more because of their construction.

Foreign cars are often rated as a high risk because spare parts are sometimes more expensive or more difficult to obtain. High-powered cars are generally rated as high risks, because the companies have found that they have a high accident rate and are more expensive to repair.

How ratings vary

Every company has its own car group rating system, which reflects its own claims experience. For that reason alone, you can find differences in the premiums quoted for the same car by a number of companies.

If you believe that your car is particularly highly rated, write to the manufacturers. Many of them—especially the foreign makers and those producing high-performance sports cars—have been able to arrange special, more favourable insurance terms for their customers.

Make sure, however, that any policy you choose has all the other terms that you would want. Do not reject a company only because its basic premium is less favourable.

THE CAR RATING SYSTEM OPERATED BY INSURANCE COMPANIES

Compare the rating your existing insurance company gives your car with that of other companies. If you are in doubt, compare your findings with the lists of typical ratings below. If all other terms are equal, the company that gives your car the lowest rating is likely to charge least.

How different companies rate the same cars

Car	Company 1	Company 2	Company 3
Audi 100LS	Group 5	Group 6	Group 5
Austin 1800	2	3	3
Datsun Cherry	4	3	4
Fiat 125 Special	5	4	5
Ford Corsair V4	3	4	3
Morris Oxford	1	2	2
Toyota Crown 2600	7	6	6
Triumph 2000	3	4	4
Vauxhall Victor 2000	3	4	4
Volkswagen 411	4	3	3
Volvo 164	6	5	6

Typical examples of the seven group ratings

Group 1
Austin A40
BLMC 1100
Citroën Ami 8
Fiat 850 saloon
Ford Escort 1098 cc
Hillman Imp
Morris Minor 1000
Renault 4
Singer Chamois
Wolseley Hornet 998 cc
All pre-1960 cars not over 1100 cc
All pre-1947 cars not over 9 hp

Group 2
Austin Maxi 1500
BLMC 1300
Daf 44
Ford Cortina Mk II
Hillman Avenger
Morris Marina 1·3
Renault 8
Singer Gazelle
Triumph 1500
Triumph Toledo 1300
Vauxhall Viva 1256 cc
All pre-1960 cars between 1101 cc and 1300 cc
All pre-1947 cars between 9 hp and 12 hp

Group 3
Austin Maxi 1750
BLMC 1300 GT
Daf 55
Ford Capri
Hillman Hunter 1725 cc
Morris Marina 1·8
Renault 12
Triumph 1300 TC
Vauxhall Firenza 1600
Volkswagen Beetle 1600
All pre-1960 cars between 1301 cc and 1600 cc
All pre-1947 cars between 13 hp and 17 hp

Group 4
Austin 2200
Ford Corsair
Mini 1275 GT
Morris Marina 1·8 TC
Rover 2000
Toyota Crown 2300
Triumph Vitesse Mk I
Vauxhall Victor 2000
Volvo 144
All pre-1960 cars between 1601 cc and 2300 cc
All pre-1947 cars between 18 hp and 20 hp

Group 5
Chrysler 180
Ford Granada
Jaguar 2·4
Rover 2000 TC
Toyota Corolla 1500 Coupé
Triumph Vitesse Mk II
Vauxhall Ventora
Volkswagen K70
All pre-1960 cars between 2301 cc and 3000 cc
All pre-1947 cars between 21 hp and 26 hp

Group 6
BMW 2000
Jaguar XJ6
Triumph TR4
All pre-1960 cars between 3001 cc and 3700 cc
All pre-1947 cars between 27 hp and 33 hp

Group 7
Jaguar E type
Lancia Flavia 2000
Mazda P100 Coupé
Triumph TR6
All pre-1960 cars: 3700 cc and over
All pre-1947 cars over 33 hp

How the company arrives at the basic premium

It is the combination of two factors —where you live and what car you drive—that determines the basic premium from which the company will calculate what you should pay.

A company that operates the highest number of regional rating areas combined with a favourable group rating for your type of car, is likely to offer you the lowest terms. The more steps there are in the scale, the more chance there is that the company can fix a premium that is fair for your particular circumstances. In general this would mean that you would pay less for your insurance.

But remember that the insurance companies take other considerations into account (see pp. 284-5), and the way in which they apply discounts or restrictions after they have assessed their basic premium, may greatly affect their final quotation.

THE RANGE OF BASIC PREMIUMS AVAILABLE

Because companies group cars and define areas in different ways, the premiums for any one car vary widely. The same car might be rated in group 3, 4 or 5 by three different companies and be in area B, C or D, depending on where each company drew its boundaries. The table shows that in this example premiums could range from £91 to £153.

Area	A	B	C	D	E	F	G
Group 1	£61	£68	£74	£81	£90	£100	£106
2	£70	£79	£85	£95	£105	£116	£122
3	£81	£91	£101	£112	£126	£136	£144
4	£99	£110	£119	£133	£148	£162	£170
5	£115	£128	£137	£153	£167	£191	£200
6	£134	£142	£159	£178	£191	£221	£230
7	£160	£178	£187	£208	£211	£254	£265

How premiums vary among different companies

Even when companies agree on the car group rating and area, the premiums may be different. The table (right) shows the variations charged by three typical companies.

Cars	Company 1	Company 2	Company 3
Group 1	£101	£102	£96
2	£119	£113	£115
3	£141	£137	£129
4	£169	£162	£154
5	£197	£183	£183
6	£225	£209	£218
7	£253	£254	£260

Understanding the premium/2

Penalties the company may add to your premium

When the company has decided your basic premium (see p. 282), it may add a loading or restrict your cover (or both) for the following reasons:

Your age
If you are under 25 or over 70 the loading could be a 25 per cent increase in your premium. If you are under 21 the amount could be 75 per cent. A restriction on the policy could be a compulsory damage excess of £25-£100 (see p. 288).

People under 25 have to pay a higher premium because, as a group, they produce more claims than older drivers. Elderly drivers may have to pay higher premiums if they learn to drive late in life.

Your driving record
Insurance companies always want to know how many years you have driven without an accident, or how long you have driven without making a claim.

If you have a very bad driving record, your premium will be heavily loaded—this could be as much as 100 per cent—or you might have a high compulsory excess (perhaps £100). You could have both.

Motoring convictions are also taken into account. The more serious, such as careless driving, may attract an increased premium or an excess. Convictions for dangerous driving, or driving under the influence of drink or drugs, will mean severe restrictions in cover and a high loading.

Your lack of experience
If you are a learner driver, or have not held a full licence for 12 months, you will normally have a compulsory damage excess (see p. 288)—probably £25 if you are over 25. You may also be charged 25 per cent extra on the basic premium.

Your occupation
If your job is one that puts you in an insurance company's high-risk category, there may be a loading on your premium. It could be as much as 100 per cent. You might instead get a compulsory damage excess—perhaps £50 (see p. 288).

People generally rated as high risks include entertainers, professional boxers and wrestlers, licensees and journalists.

Your use of the car
Most companies allow for private and personal business use in their basic premiums, although some will want a higher premium for any form of business activity. If you use the car extensively for business, or it is used for business by more than one person, a 30 per cent loading is common. You might get a similar loading if you get a mileage allowance from your employer. A very high mileage, such as for commercial travelling, might attract a 60 per cent loading.

The use to which the car is put indicates what the insurance companies call the 'exposure risk'. This simply means that the more miles you drive, the more you are exposed to the risk of an accident.

Some companies ask you to state your approximate annual mileage on the proposal form; others want to know whether you regularly drive your car to work.

How you garage the car
Many companies will charge extra, or restrict the policy, if you do not normally keep the car in a locked garage—especially if you park it on the street overnight. If the car is within your fenced premises, or if you are only temporarily parked away from home, these restrictions may be reduced.

The value of your car
More expensive cars, worth more than say £2500, are likely to carry a loading. This would be at least £2.50 a year for each £500 over the price limit.

Any special risk
If there is any other reason why the insurance company considers you a special risk, your premium is likely to be loaded in some way.

Discounts you may be allowed on your premium

Before you ask for quotations, compare not only the terms of the cover but also the type and amount of the various discounts offered. You may, for example, be allowed one or more of the following discounts.

Introductory discount
If a proposer is not entitled to a no-claim discount, many companies offer an introductory discount as long as the proposer has at least 12 months' experience, is over 25, holds a full licence and has had no motoring convictions (except parking and speeding). Introductory discounts are usually 20-30 per cent.

Your car
If you drive an old car—generally one more than seven years old—you may be allowed a discount off a comprehensive policy.

A number of cars
If you insure two or more cars, many companies will give a discount (see p. 289). This could be 5-10 per cent, and might apply to both policies. You might also be able to get an introductory discount on the second policy, but you are unlikely to be allowed the same no-claim discount. You will have to start from scratch, because insurers maintain that the second car is likely to be driven by another driver most of the time.

Restricting drivers
If you restrict driving of the car to yourself, or to yourself and one other person, you can usually get a discount (see p. 286).

Voluntary damage excess
If you agree to pay the first amount of a claim for damage to your own car, you will usually be given a discount (see p. 288).

No-claim discount
Most companies offer a no-claim discount scale, whereby your premium is reduced annually (up to a certain limit) if you do not make a claim (see p. 285). This acts as an excess as well as a discount, because it is an incentive not to claim. The claim-free motorist can save up to two-thirds of the premium he would otherwise pay.

Your occupation
If your job is one that puts you in an insurance company's low-risk category, you will probably be given a discount—perhaps 10 per cent. Bank managers, policemen and teachers are among those professions generally considered as low risks.

Your age
Some companies offer 10 per cent discounts to 'mature' policyholders (between 35 and 70) provided that there is no special risk.

Your sex
Some companies consider a woman driver a lower risk than a man, and will give a 10 per cent discount.

How no-claim discounts may vary

There is no one fixed scale of no-claim discounts, but most companies offer an annual reduction in premiums, rising to a maximum of 60 per cent. In most cases, whenever a claim is made the driver has to drop back in the scale the next time the policy is renewed.

Compare the scales offered by each insurer to see which gives you the most favourable terms. They are usually set out in the company's brochure. The stages by which you benefit vary according to the scale.

Of the four typical scales given below, Scale B is probably the most widely used by the companies.

The saving shown is the percentage of your annual premium (before the no-claim discount) that you would save in five years without a claim or an increase in premium. So for the five years following a 50 per cent discount on Scale A you would save 295 per cent—on the other scales the saving would be only 290 per cent over five years. But Scale A is a seven-year scale.

Scales that offer the greatest saving usually take the longest time to achieve it, and if you make a claim your loss is greater (see p. 292).

Once you reach the maximum discount, some insurers offer concessions, such as no drop back in the scale for one claim in any two-year period. This is a protected discount—that is, a discount fixed at the maximum (or one step below).

A few insurers use what is more like the continental *bonus-malus* system. Virtually every motorist is given an introductory discount, but if a driver has an accident within the first year, his premium reverts to the basic amount.

The basic premiums tend to be higher than those for systems with a straightforward no-claim discount.

Year	Scale A		Scale B		Scale C		Scale D	
	discount	saving in next 7 years	discount	saving in next 5 years	discount	saving in next 5 years	discount	saving in next 5 years
	%	%	%	%	%	%	%	%
First	Nil	175	Nil	180	Nil	195	Nil	175
Second	30	235	30	240	40	255	25	235
Third	40	270	40	270	45	285	40	270
Fourth	50	295	50	290	50	290	50	290
Fifth	55	310	60	300	60	300	60	300
Sixth	60	320						
Seventh	65	325						

CALCULATING HOW MUCH YOU WOULD SAVE

How the discounts and loadings work

Most insurers subtract discounts, not from the total premium but progressively. This means that, except for the first deduction, the discount you get is not the stated percentage of your basic premium. The no-claim discount is usually the last deduction.

Sometimes two discounts can be combined, which makes a small extra saving.

Third-party insurance is based on a different basic premium from comprehensive, but discounts and loadings are applied in the same way.

HOW YOU MAY GAIN BY COMBINED DISCOUNTS

Separate deductions		Combined deduction	
Basic comprehensive premium	£79.00	Basic comprehensive premium	£79.00
Subtract 10% for car over 7 years old	7.90		
	£71.10		
Subtract 10% for a low-risk profession	7.11	Subtract 20% for combined old car and low-risk policyholder	15.80
	£63.99		£63.20
Subtract no-claim discount (60%)	38.39	Subtract no-claim discount (60%)	37.92
Net premium	£25.60	Net premium	£25.28

The effect of asking for extra cover

Most insurance companies are willing to provide extra cover for an additional premium charge. The way in which they levy the fee varies: some add it before deducting the no-claim discount, others operate it as a final loading. You can save by using a company that adds the extra fee before making the no-claim discount deduction.

Consider first, however, whether the extra charge is worth while. The cover is available for personal belongings in the car, for additional personal accident benefit and for extra risks to trailers. There may be better ways to get such insurance.

Additional personal accident cover provides weekly payments during a period of disablement after a motor accident—perhaps £10 a week for 26 weeks. You can usually get better terms on separate insurance covering personal accident.

Extra cover for trailers usually includes third-party risks while the trailer is detached (see Trailers, p. 278), and damage cover while the trailer is attached or detached. For horse boxes and light luggage trailers, a policy extension provides adequate and cheap cover, but for a caravan trailer there are several separate policies that give better value for money.

Additional personal effects cover means that you buy a higher limit of compensation than the policy allows. If subject to the no-claim discount, it is generally inexpensive. The alternative would be a much more expensive all-risks policy.

SAVING MONEY ON ADDITIONAL INSURANCE

Addition before no-claim discount		Addition after no-claim discount	
Premium after discounts	£63.99	Premium after discounts	£63.99
Addition for extra cover	1.50	No-claim discount (60%)	38.39
	£65.49		£25.60
No-claim discount (60%)	39.29	Addition for extra cover	1.50
Net premium	26.20	Net premium	£27.10
Net premium without extra cover would be	25.60	Net premium without extra cover would be	25.60
So extra cover costs only	60p	So extra cover costs	£1.50

Cutting your costs/1

How you can change the terms of your policy

If you want a cheaper policy, you must either find a way to reduce costs with your present insurance company, or change companies.

There are three acceptable ways to reduce the cost of a fully comprehensive policy, under which anyone is allowed to drive the insured car.

1 Restrict driving to one or two named drivers.

2 Change the cover the policy gives from fully comprehensive to third-party, fire and theft—or perhaps even to third-party only.

3 Keep the policy comprehensive, but accept a voluntary damage excess (see p. 288).

As an extreme measure, you will also be able to reduce your costs by changing to a car that has a lower insurance rating (see pp. 283, 287).

Restricting who can drive the car

Most companies will give a discount on the premium, if you agree that no one but you will drive the car—or no one but you and one other named driver.

Some companies allow the discount only if driving is restricted to husband and wife.

If cover is *compulsorily* restricted by the insurance company to one or two named drivers—this often happens with a high-performance car—a discount is seldom allowed. Drivers under 25 may not be allowed the discount, since their premiums have generally been raised or cover restricted to reflect the increased insurance risk (see p. 284).

The discount for restricting the number of drivers has one drawback—no one else can drive the car in an emergency, unless his own policy has an extension for driving other cars. If it has, the car will be covered for third-party risks only, not for any damage it suffers. If it has not, the car will not be covered by insurance at all, and the driver at the time will be liable for any damage or injury caused. He and the policyholder are also liable to be prosecuted. Both could lose their driving licences.

Although you may not be penalised in a genuine emergency, it is safer to make insurance arrangements that do not break the policy conditions or the law.

Despite any driving restrictions, most insurance companies provide the policyholder with full cover while the car is with a garage for repair or maintenance (see p. 279). But if someone at the garage takes the car for a joyride, it may not be insured, and the insurers can refuse to pay a damage claim. However, most insurers would cover the claim in some way, perhaps treating it as theft. If anyone was injured, their claim would normally be considered by the insurers of the vehicle.

HOW TERMS VARY

The discounts given in return for a restriction on the people who will be allowed to drive the car vary—and so do the conditions, as these typical examples show. Most companies favour a husband and wife, both experienced drivers, over 30 years of age.

Company 1

Policyholder and/or spouse only:	
(a) Husband over 30, wife over 25, both experienced drivers	Discount 20%
(b) Husband 25-29, wife over 25, both experienced drivers	Discount 10%

Two named drivers	
(a) Both over 30 and experienced drivers	Discount 10%
(b) Both 25-29 and experienced drivers	Discount 5%

Company 2

The policyholder (over 23) only The policyholder and spouse only, or One named person over 23	
	Discount 10%

Changing to third-party cover

You can get a significant drop in premium if you change from a comprehensive policy, to one that excludes all claims for damage to your own car and gives only third-party cover, or third-party, fire and theft (see p. 287).

About three-quarters of all the money paid out on claims is for damage to vehicles, so if the insurance company is not asked to cover this for the policyholder's car, the risk is reduced and it can offer a much lower premium. The drop is usually up to about 60 per cent of the basic comprehensive premium for third-party only, and 50 per cent for third-party, fire and theft.

Some people have so much confidence in their own driving that they think that damage to their car will always be someone else's fault, and they will be able to claim from the other driver's insurance.

This does not allow for the 'hit-and-run' driver, or damage to the car while it is parked. You cannot claim for the damage at all on a third-party policy. You can do so on a comprehensive policy, although you will lose your no-claim discount unless the driver who caused the damage can be found, and your insurance company can recover the money which it has paid out.

A third-party policy makes sense if you have an old car which, although safe and efficient, is low in value—say, worth only about £40. The cheapest net premium you can get for comprehensive cover—even with the 10 per cent discount that some companies allow for an old car—may cost as much as the value of the car itself.

Third-party cover is assessed on separate basic premiums from those used for comprehensive cover, but discounts are generally applied in the same way.

You cannot get a discount for a voluntary damage excess (see p. 288). Although excesses are common for accidental damage to the policyholder's own car, excesses for third-party claims are rare.

You can normally get a discount for restricting who drives the car.

If you do take out third-party cover, it is worth paying the small extra amount to extend cover to fire and theft also. If your car is kept in the open, there may be special conditions attached to cover for theft or extra on the premium (or both).

SECURITY AT SMALL COST

The difference between the premium for third-party-only cover and one that gives added security against fire and theft is so slight that the advantages of the extra cover outweigh the small extra cost.

Group 2 Area B	Third-party	Third-party, Fire and Theft
Basic premium	£28.00	£35.00
Subtract 10% for car over 7 years old	2.80	3.50
	£25.20	£31.50
Subtract 10% for low-risk profession	2.52	3.15
	£22.68	£28.35
Subtract no-claim discount (60%)	13.61	17.01
Net premium	£9.07	£11.34

FOUR TYPES OF INSURANCE AND THE CLAIMS THEY COVER

Comprehensive	Third-party, Fire and Theft	Third-party	Road Traffic Act Only
Emergency medical treatment fees for any person injured by your car or any car you drive on a public road or elsewhere.	Emergency medical treatment fees for any person injured by your car or any car you drive on a public road or elsewhere.	Emergency medical treatment fees for any person injured by your car or any car you drive on a public road or elsewhere.	Emergency medical treatment fees for any person injured by your car or any car you drive on a public road.
Emergency treatment for you.	Emergency treatment for you.	Emergency treatment for you.	Emergency treatment for you.
Death or injury to any person other than the driver caused by your car.	Death or injury to any person other than the driver caused by your car.	Death or injury to any person other than the driver caused by your car.	Death or injury to any person other than the driver caused by your car.
Costs incurred with the insurer's agreement for legal defence or representation after an accident resulting in a claim.	Costs incurred with the insurer's agreement for legal defence or representation after an accident resulting in a claim.	Costs incurred with the insurer's agreement for legal defence or representation after an accident resulting in a claim.	Costs incurred with the insurer's agreement for legal defence or representation after an accident resulting in a claim.
Death or injury to any person caused by you when driving someone else's car.	Death or injury to any person caused by you when driving someone else's car.	Death or injury to any person caused by you when driving someone else's car.	
Death or injury to any person caused by the negligence of passengers in your car.	Death or injury to any person caused by the negligence of passengers in your car.	Death or injury to any person caused by the negligence of passengers in your car.	
Compensation for damage to other people's property caused by your car or its towed trailer.	Compensation for damage to other people's property caused by your car or its towed trailer.	Compensation for damage to other people's property caused by your car or its towed trailer.	
Compensation for damage to other people's property caused by your driving another car.	Compensation for damage to other people's property caused by your driving another car.	Compensation for damage to other people's property caused by your driving another car.	
Costs of legal defence for charges of manslaughter or causing death by reckless or dangerous driving following an accident covered by the policy.	Costs of legal defence for charges of manslaughter or causing death by reckless or dangerous driving following an accident covered by the policy.	Costs of legal defence for charges of manslaughter or causing death by reckless or dangerous driving following an accident covered by the policy.	
Cost of loss or damage to your car by fire or theft.	Cost of loss or damage to your car by fire or theft.		
Compensation for accidental damage to your car and its accessories.			
The cost of towing your car to a repairer after accidental damage, and the reasonable cost of its re-delivery.			
Fixed benefits for death or loss of sight and/or limbs for you and your spouse.			
Medical expenses (up to a stated amount) incurred by you or your passengers as a result of an accident in your car.			
Loss of or damage to rugs, clothing and personal effects while they are in your car.			

How much cover can you buy?

Four main types of insurance cover are available, but for each type the actual terms of the policy depend on the individual company.

The policy known as Road Traffic Act Only provides only the minimum cover required by law before you can drive a car on public roads. It is generally offered only when a company is unwilling to take any greater risk with a driver—usually because of a bad claims record.

Third-party and third-party, fire and theft policies extend the cover slightly, but the widest available protection is offered by the comprehensive policy. Remember, however, that comprehensive does not mean that it covers every possible contingency.

About seventy-five per cent of all policies issued are comprehensive. All include damage to the insured car, but otherwise there are many variations in the cover offered.

Always compare the terms of several policies of similar type and price before you make up your mind (see p. 276).

The cover shown in this chart is what you could expect to find in most reasonable policies.

Changing your car to reduce insurance costs

The type of car you drive affects the premium you pay, and one way to get a cheaper policy is to choose a car that is in one of the lower-rated groups (see p. 283).

Some cars are highly rated by insurers because of the high cost of bodywork repairs, due to the method of construction. For this type of car you may be able to get better terms if you take out a policy specially arranged by the manufacturers. Ask your dealer if such a scheme is available for the make of car you have, or want to buy. Fiat, for example, operate such a scheme.

If you choose a sports car, your premium will be high (especially if you are under 25), because companies have found that the rate and cost of claims for these cars are high. But a good, claim-free record will help to lower the premium.

If you are under 25, you will get a cheaper policy if you drive an older car—something like a Morris 1000 or Austin A40. Once you have earned a reasonable no-claim discount and have more experience, you will get better terms with a newer car.

Cutting your costs /2

Agreeing to pay some of your own repair costs

The fourth way (see pp. 286-7) in which you can get a reduction in your premium, is by offering to pay the first amount of any accident repair costs to your own car.

This arrangement, known as a voluntary damage excess, applies only to comprehensive policies, since third-party cover does not include compensation for damage to

You offer to pay the first	£15	£20	£25	£50	£75	£100
Company 1 % discount	10	–	15	–	–	–
Company 2 % discount	10	–	15	20	–	–
Company 3 % discount	–	–	12	20	25	30
Company 4 % discount	–	10	15	20	–	–

the insured car. The amount you can save varies from company to com-

pany. Note, however, that not all insurance companies operate a full range of discounts. The most common is a 10 per cent reduction, if you agree to pay the first £15 of any damage to your car.

Whatever the percentage discount, the amount allowed will not be more than the amount of the damage excess. So if you accept a £15 voluntary damage excess on a premium of £160, the amount deducted from your premium will be £15 – not the full 10 per cent discount of £16.

The argument in favour of accepting a voluntary damage excess is that you would not normally make a claim if damage to your car was slight anyway, because the cost of repairs would probably be smaller than the amount you would lose on no-claim discount.

It is in these circumstances, therefore, worth getting a reduction on

your annual premium by agreeing to pay up to an agreed amount yourself.

Effect of no-claim discount

You may find that you save money only if you do not make a claim. The amount you lose if you claim may be greater than the amount you save by means of the discount.

Because the excess discount is deducted from your premium before the no-claim discount, the sum you actually save by means of the excess discount gets smaller as your no-claim discount increases.

Your reduced premium means that you stand to lose less by a drop back in the no-claim scale, but by the time you have added on the amount of the damage cost you have to pay yourself, your total loss may be greater than whatever saving you have made on your premium.

Whether, if you claim, you gain

WORKING OUT WHEN IT PAYS YOU NOT TO HAVE A VOLUNTARY DAMAGE EXCESS

If your no-claim discount is:	Your premium based on £100 before the no-claim discount is deducted amounts to:	If you accept a £15 damage excess for a 10% discount, you will save this year:	And your total pre-miums for this year and the next four years will be:	Remember, if you did not have the excess, your premiums for those five years would be:	Which means that with the damage ex-cess, you will save over five years:	But if you make a claim this year, you will drop back in the no-claim scale (see p. 285) and your premiums for this year and the next four years will total:
Nil	£100	£10	£288	£320	£32	£342
30%	70	7	234	260	26	315
40%	60	6	207	230	23	306
50%	50	5	189	210	21	243
60%	40	4	180	200	20	207

Considering a cheaper special policy

Some insurance companies offer special policies with cheaper premiums but restricted cover. They are mainly designed for low-risk drivers, and to be eligible you have to meet certain conditions. Policies often include a compulsory damage excess, and some do not give a no-claim discount.

Premiums are likely to be about £30-£60 depending on the car and area. The premium may not always be cheaper than you could get on a standard policy, but it is well worth finding out if you qualify and what it would cost you.

The types of qualification that are required are:

The driver

Must be over 25 (or 30) or under 65 (or 70).
Must have driven without a claim for three to five years.
Must have a clean driving record

for five to ten years, with no convictions apart from parking offences or one speeding offence.
Must not be in a high-risk job.

The car

Must not be a sports car or high-performance car.
May have to be a car of accepted make within Groups 1-3 (see p. 283).

Use of the car

Must be for pleasure or personal business use only.

Conditions imposed on some policies might be:

The policyholder must not allow anyone to drive who is under 25 or has had any driving convictions (apart from parking or one for speeding).
An annual mileage within a stipulated figure.

The policyholder to have no physical defect or infirmity.
The policyholder to be a total abstainer.
The policyholder to insure house contents on the same policy.
The policyholder to have worked for the same firm for five years.
Other drivers must be members of the policyholder's family and must have held a full driving licence for a year.
An excess imposed (or increased) if an inexperienced or young driver is allowed to drive.

Fleet policies

If you own a company which runs a number of vehicles for business purposes, you can get a 'fleet discount'. If the claims record of the cars is good, a discount of 30-40 per cent may be offered. The minimum number of vehicles to qualify for this is usually ten.

or lose by the excess discount, depends on the scale of your no-claim discount and your position in the scale. In general, the higher your premium and the lower your no-claim discount, the more likely you are to save.

Remember that a compulsory damage excess must be added to the voluntary excess when assessing whether you would save or lose.

Combined discounts

Discounts for restricted driving and for a voluntary damage excess can sometimes be combined. For example:

Insured only (over 30) driving	20%
£15 voluntary damage excess	10%
Combined	30%

This means a small extra saving (see p. 285), in this case 2 per cent.

THE EFFECT OF A 10% DAMAGE EXCESS IF YOU MAKE A CLAIM

The graph shows how a 10 per cent discount for a £15 voluntary damage excess will affect the amount you gain or lose if you claim with a no-claim discount on Scale B.

It shows that the lowest premium with which you would save is £89 – if you had a 40 per cent discount. If you had a nil or 30 per cent discount, you would not save unless your premium was £94, and with a 50 per cent discount unless it was £137. With a 60 per cent discount you would not save.

If your insurer uses Scale B, find the line for your percentage discount and see where it falls opposite your premium. If it is in the shaded area, you will lose if you claim.

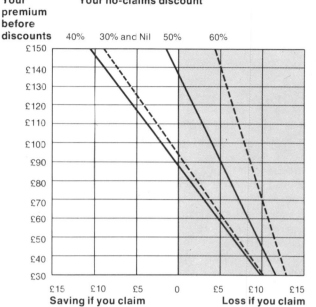

If you had not made a claim your premiums would have totalled:	So the claim costs you:	Plus the first £15 of damage, making:	If you had not taken the damage excess but made a claim this year your premiums for this year and the next four would have totalled:	If you had not made the claim your premiums for the same five years would have totalled:	So without the damage excess, a claim would cost you:	Which means that the damage excess has cost an extra:	But on this year's premium you saved:	So if you have made a claim, you have:
£288	£54	£69	£380	£320	£60	£9	£10	saved £1
234	81	96	350	260	90	6	7	saved £1
207	99	114	340	230	110	4	6	saved £2
189	54	69	270	210	60	9	5	lost £4
180	27	42	230	200	30	12	4	lost £8

Saving money when you have more than one car

If you insure two or more cars under the same policy, many insurance companies will allow you a general discount of between 5 and 10 per cent on the premium for all cars. If you also agree to restrict the number of drivers, you may get a combined discount of 20-25 per cent.

If your first-car premium was £100, it would be reduced to £90 by a 10 per cent two-car discount, and then to £45 if you had a 50 per cent no-claim discount. If you were insuring a second car for the first time, your premium for it, say £100, would be reduced to only £90 because the no-claim discount has to be earned separately for each car.

The insurers' viewpoint

There are two reasons why insurers allow a multi-car discount. First, it saves them a certain amount of expense; only one policy to issue and one renewal premium to collect.

But the main reason for the discount stems from the days when motoring was a luxury.

At that time, if someone owned two cars it was unusual for them both to be used to their full extent. One car was virtually a standby in case the first had to be taken off the road. This clearly reduced the risk compared with that of two cars under separate ownership, so a discount on both premiums was given.

The insurance companies' viewpoint today is that a second car is generally driven by someone else for most of the time. That driver cannot benefit from your no-claim discount. Of course, if you have insured the second car for some years, you are entitled to the benefit of whatever separate discount it has earned.

If you can convince your insurance company that your use of the second car will be no different from the use

of the first, it may be persuaded to give you the same no-claim discount on the second car. In the example quoted, this would make a difference of £35 to your total premium. Instead of £135 (£45+£90) it would be £100 (£50+£50). If it agrees, it is not likely to give you the two-car discount as well.

If the same discount is applied to both cars it will mean that if you claim you will lose both discounts. This will be to your disadvantage once the second car has earned more than the step back discount that will apply to the first car. For example, if both cars drop back to 40 per cent after a claim on the first car, the total premium on renewal would be £108 (£54+£54). If discounts had been earned separately and you claimed on your first car after the second car had earned a 40 per cent discount, the renewal premium would be £99 (£54+£45).

Proposal form

The importance of the proposal form

The proposal form is the basis of the contract between the insurance company and the motorist. You may be given a quotation before you complete a proposal form, but it will be subject to the acceptance of the completed form by the company. Only when the company has received the completed form, has it the full facts from which to decide what your premium should be.

It could be that after seeing the form the company will increase its original quotation, although this is not very common. You are not obliged to accept a new premium even if you have already paid the one originally asked. Find out the reason for the increase before deciding whether to accept or reject a higher premium.

Giving the company all the relevant information

When answering the questions on the form, you must not leave out any facts that might influence the insurance company in accepting the risk and deciding the premium and terms.

If you do not give truthful answers, the insurance company can refuse to deal with a claim, since you will be breaking a condition of the policy.

Answer all the questions on the form, even those which do not seem to apply to your particular circumstances. Fill in the form yourself, as you are the person responsible for the truthfulness of the answers.

Change of circumstances

You must tell your insurance company immediately there are any changes affecting the answers you gave on the proposal form—such as a new car, modifications to your car that might alter its group rating, another driver in the family, or a motoring conviction.

Some significant questions

Use
In addition to Social, Domestic and Pleasure use, will the car be used for:
(a) Commercial travelling?
(b) Business purposes by any person other than yourself?

Remember that business use by someone else would include your wife's use of the car for an evening job. If you use the car while working unpaid for a voluntary organisation, you will not normally be charged a higher premium; but practice varies, so check.

Few companies will cover you for rallies or trials unless you pay extra, although road-safety rallies are usually covered. A motor treasure hunt might be classed as a rally.

Drivers
Give details of yourself and all others who may drive the car.

or

Give details of yourself and all others who will normally drive the car.

Include all members of your immediate family who hold a driving licence, and anyone you could reasonably expect to drive.

You will usually be asked to state each person's age and occupation; how long he has been driving; whether he holds a full or provisional licence; whether he has any motoring convictions; and whether he has any physical disabilities. If all these questions are not asked outright, you may still be bound by the declaration you sign.

Do not try to hide a conviction, or the fact that a teenager may sometimes drive the car—the facts will almost certainly come to light if there is a claim, and the company can refuse to pay if it has not been told at the outset.

From your answers to this question, the insurance company may conclude that one of the additional drivers—not you—will be the main driver of the car. If so, it will ask for a premium and terms as though the additional driver, and not you, were being insured.

Claims and losses

Have there been any accidents or losses during the past three years in connection with any mechanically propelled vehicle owned or driven by you or those named? If YES give details.

Be careful to answer this question fully. Give details for all the drivers named, and for all accidents or losses —even if they were not the driver's fault and not reported.

The information required is usually the cost of damage to your car, the cost of the third-party claim, and a brief description of how the incident occurred. Most people know the costs of repairs to their own car, but an estimate is acceptable if the incident happened some time ago. The cost of a third-party claim may not be known because it was handled by the insurance company. If the insurance company thinks the amount is relevant, it will contact the previous insurers.

The insurance company is more likely to be interested in the number of incidents listed, the circumstances, and who was driving the car when each incident occurred.

Signing the declaration

'I warrant that the above statements are true, that no material facts concerning the insurance have been withheld. I agree that this proposal, whether signed by me or caused to be signed by me, shall be the basis of the contract between XYZ Co. Ltd and myself and I agree to accept the Company's standard form of policy for this class of insurance.
'If the answers to all or any of the questions have been written by others at my dictation or instruction I confirm that I have read the answers and that they are correct.'

Before agreeing to accept the standard form of policy, make sure that you understand it. If someone— such as your insurance broker— fills in the form for you, he does so as your agent, and when you sign the declaration you confirm his answers. If the answers are inaccurate, the insurance company can refuse a claim.

An alternative form of declaration

'I declare that the particulars in this proposal form are true and undertake that the motor car to be insured will not be driven by any person who to my knowledge has been refused any motor vehicle insurance or continuance thereof or suffers from any disease or physical infirmity which impairs his ability to drive. This proposal and declaration will be the basis...'

Whether or not the question was on the form, this declaration confirms that nobody who will drive has been refused insurance or has a physical disability. If someone does, your insurance is not valid.

Check the cover note

No cover attaches until the Company has accepted this proposal and has issued a Certificate of Insurance or Cover note.

You may be given a cover note as proof that you are insured, to protect you while your proposal is dealt with. Check that it provides enough cover: some notes give Road Traffic Act cover only.

Certificate of insurance

Understanding the limitations imposed by the certificate

The certificate of insurance is only proof that you are legally insured – it does not set out the terms of your contract with the insurance company. It gives the policy number, the policyholder's name, the period for which insurance is valid, the vehicle or vehicles covered, for what purposes the car or cars can be used and states who may drive.

What cars are covered

> Any private car
> (a) belonging to the policyholder or hired to him under a hire-purchase agreement or
> (b) hired to the policyholder under a hiring contract for not less than 12 months' duration.

Paragraph (b) will be included only if the policy covers a car on contract hire for more than a year.

The certificate does not usually state the vehicle's registration number, which saves the insurance company from having to issue a new certificate if you change your car.

The policyholder and the registered owner named in the car's logbook must be the same person, otherwise the certificate is invalid and there may be difficulties in licensing the car. This can be a problem when a man buys a car for his wife – it may be registered in his name and insured by her. In this case there are three possible solutions:

1 Re-register the car in the wife's name.

2 Insure the car in the husband's name.

3 Ask for a certificate that shows the registration number, and does not state that the policyholder must own the vehicle.

Insurance companies prefer you to choose **1** or **2** because of the administrative work otherwise involved.

Cover for other vehicles

> The policyholder may also drive a motor car or motor cycle not belonging to him and not hired to him under a hire-purchase agreement.

This applies to the policyholder only, and covers third-party risks only. You cannot generally get full cover without paying more under your existing policy while you are temporarily driving a hired or borrowed car.

What the car can be used for

In general there are three classes of use for private motor vehicles. The normal group A covers social, domestic and pleasure purposes, and the policyholder's personal use on business.

The next group B1 extends cover to general business use. Both A and B1 exclude hiring, racing, commercial travelling, and any purpose in connection with the motor trade.

Group B2 is like B1, but excludes only racing and carrying passengers for hire or reward.

Some companies combine B1 and B2, and other companies define groups in different ways. For example, on the certificate extracts on this page, the uses defined in paragraphs G and H, with the exclusions shown in paragraphs O and P, give the same cover – social, domestic and pleasure purposes – as defined in group A described above.

> **Limitations as to use**
> As defined in paragraphs G and H below, but subject to exclusions O and P.
> G Use for social, domestic and pleasure purposes
> H Use by the policyholder in person in connection with his business
> I Use for the policyholder's business
> J Use for the business of the policyholder's employer or partner.
>
> **Exclusions**
> N Use for hiring or for any business purposes
> O Use for hiring, commercial travelling or for any purpose in connection with the motor trade
> P Use for racing, pacemaking or speed testing
> Q Use for the carriage of passengers for hire or reward.

Exclusions are not always spelt out. On the extract shown above, N and Q are not specifically stated as exclusions; but they are not covered by the policy, because they are not among the uses permitted in paragraphs G and H.

There is no standard interpretation of the classes of use. Some insurers do not include commuting within 'social, domestic and pleasure' use, and will want a higher premium from a motorist who drives between his home and his place of work.

Giving someone a lift

Passenger insurance is compulsory and is provided in your policy; but you may not be covered if you accept money or even petrol – from people to whom you regularly give a lift to work, for example.

Cover for social, domestic and pleasure purposes – Group (A) – excludes hiring, but legal opinion differs on whether giving lifts for 'petrol money' constitutes hiring. If you are in doubt, consult your insurance company.

Who can drive the car

1 Open policy

> Person or classes of persons entitled to drive:
> The policyholder
> Any person who is driving on the policyholder's order or with his permission.

2 Restricted policy

> Persons entitled to drive:
> The policyholder
> The following named persons:

The wording on the open-policy certificate may be misleading; you must check the policy to find out who is entitled to drive. The policy may state, for example, that drivers under 25 years of age are excluded from cover. But the Road Traffic Acts do not allow an insurance certificate to specify a group of people by age, so the certificate may suggest that the policy gives wider cover than it actually does. On the policy, exclusions may be shown in the clauses or as endorsements (see p. 281).

> **CHECKING YOUR CERTIFICATE**
> Check first that a new policy gives the cover you have arranged and paid for, and then that the details given on your certificate are in agreement with the details on the policy itself.
>
> Make sure that you know of any policy endorsements. If there are any you did not expect, query them with your insurance company.
>
> Note that the following details on the certificate are correct:
>
> **1** The policy number.
>
> **2** The description of vehicles covered. It is most likely to be an open certificate (one which does not give the vehicle registration number). But if the number is given, make sure that it is the right one.
>
> **3** Your name as the policyholder. The name should be the same as the one shown for the registered owner in the car's logbook.
>
> **4** The dates of commencement and expiry. If the commencement date is different from the date shown on the policy, this may be because you were originally issued with a cover note.
>
> **5** The persons entitled to drive. Remember that the certificate will not state whether there are any endorsements on the policy. To find out who can drive, you must check your policy.
>
> **6** The definition of how the car can be used.

To claim or not to claim

Working out whether you will gain or lose

Statistics suggest that the average driver is likely to be involved in an accident—whether a minor brush with a lamp-post or something more serious—once every six or seven years. If the car is damaged, the main consideration will be who should pay the repair bill and related expenses. The two deciding factors are: who caused the accident? and what is the cost of the claim?

Who caused the accident?

If someone else is entirely to blame, and is covered for third-party risks, and his insurance company accepts liability, then you have no need to claim from your own insurance.

But as you cannot be sure at the time of the accident that the other company will pay, you must let your own insurers know what has happened in case you want to make a claim later. Make it clear that you are merely informing them, not making a claim.

If you pursue the claim against the other insurers personally, you may get involved in lengthy correspondence and cannot be sure of success. If you ask your company to deal with the claim you will not lose your no-claim discount unless they cannot recover their costs from the other company. Even then, some insurers will allow you to reimburse them and preserve your discount.

When two vehicles collide it is rare for it to be established beyond doubt that one driver is to blame. If there is a possible claim against you, your insurers should take over.

The knock-for-knock agreement

Most claims are settled under what is called the knock-for-knock agreement. This means that, if both policies are comprehensive, each company pays for the damage to its own car irrespective of who was to blame.

Each insurer then decides whether, but for the knock-for-knock arrangement, he could have recovered his costs from the other company. If he could, then you should not lose your no-claim discount. If the decision goes against you the company may listen to a protest, but its ruling is usually final and not subject to appeal.

You might consider you were not to blame even though yours was the only vehicle involved in a crash—for example, if you swerved to avoid a dog or pedestrian. But if you claim in such circumstances you will lose your no-claim discount.

It may be possible to recover your losses in a civil action, but suing either the pedestrian or dog owner is a lengthy and costly business with no guarantee of success. If the insurance company can recover their payments from the dog owner or pedestrian, they will reinstate your no-claim discount.

Cheaper not to claim

Before you claim from your insurance company, decide whether it would be cheaper to pay the repair costs yourself.

If the policy has either a voluntary or compulsory damage excess (or both), you cannot claim an amount less than the excess (or combined excesses). If the claim is greater, or you have no excess, consider whether the loss of your no-claim discount will cost more than the claim.

A claim usually drops you one step back in the discount scale and you thus incur a penalty—the difference between what you would have paid in the next five years and what you will now pay with a reduced or lost discount. The penalty varies, depending on which discount scale your company uses. (Calculations on this page have been made assuming there is no future rise in premiums.)

The heaviest penalty is when the discount is in the middle of the scale—usually 40 or 50 per cent. If you are in doubt about whether it is cheaper not to claim, ask your broker to work out what the real cost of the claim would be over the next five years.

Remember that even if you do not claim, you should inform your insurance company of the accident.

Spreading the cost

There are times, however, when it may be expedient to claim—thus spreading the penalty over a number of years—rather than find the

money all at once. Do not forget that the claim should include the cost of all damage—not just the repairs to your own car, but also third-party claims against you.

Most insurers allow drivers on the maximum no-claim discount to make one claim without dropping back to the beginning of the scale —your penalty is thus smaller than if you were in the second or third year. If you have a protected discount or your policy allows one or two claims without a fall from maximum, there is no difficulty about deciding to claim.

When the premium rises

However, the question of whether to claim is further complicated by yearly rises in premium which will increase the penalty. In the five years 1968-73 average premiums rose by more than 100 per cent.

A yearly increase of 10 per cent on a £100 premium would result in a gross premium at the end of five years of £161. A yearly increase of 20 per cent would bring it to £247. For a motorist with a 40 per cent no-claim discount on Scale B, total premiums over those next five years (one at 50 per cent discount and

	Without premium increases	With 10% premium increases	With 20% premium increases
With claim	£320	£412	£528
Without claim	£210	£277	£368
Penalty	£110	£135	£160

four at 60 per cent) would amount to £277 with 10 per cent increases, and £368 with 20 per cent increases (compared with £210 if there was no increase). But if he made a claim and dropped back to nil in the no-claim discount scale, premiums for the next five years would be £412 with 10 per cent increases, and £528 with 20 per cent increases.

IF YOU HAVE AN ACCIDENT

Following the correct procedure after an accident will help your insurers to get the car back on the road faster, and may save you money.

1 Do not admit liability even if you think you are in the wrong. An admission may be breaking the conditions of your policy. Similarly it will not help to get a written admission from the other driver. In fact this could break the conditions of his policy and his insurers might refuse cover.

2 Never make an offer to pay for any damage, no matter how slight. This could be considered an admission of liability.

3 Get the name and address of any independent witnesses.

4 Record the position in the road of your car and any other vehicles involved.

5 Note the registration numbers of other cars involved.

6 Ask to see the other driver's insurance certificate and note the name and policy number.

7 Tell your insurance company about the accident within any time limit that may be stated on the policy (generally 24 hours).

AA-Damage repairs

INDEX

Dampers-Jubilee clips

INDEX

Striker-Zenith

Typesetting, printing and binding, Purnell and Sons, Paulton
Paper, Gerald Judd Limited
Separations, Mabbut and Johnston Limited
Bookbinding material, Winter and Company London Limited

Published by Drive Publications, Berkeley Square House, Berkeley Square, London W1X 5PD